C000137504

The Criminal Appeal Reports

Volume 1 of 2006

AUSTRALIA
Law Book Co.
Sydney

CANADA AND USA
Carswell
Toronto

HONG KONG
Sweet & Maxwell Asia

NEW ZEALAND
Brookers
Wellington

SINGAPORE AND MALAYSIA
Sweet and Maxwell Asia
Singapore and Kuala Lumpur

The Criminal Appeal Reports 2006

General Editor: **Clare Barsby,**
of Gray's Inn, Barrister

Consultant Editor: **Daniel Janner Q.C.,**
M.A. (Cantab.), of the Middle and Inner
Temple, Barrister

Assistant Editors: **Eleanor Ebbatson,**
of Gray's Inn, Barrister

Matthew Brotherton,
M.A. (Cantab), of Lincoln's Inn, Barrister

Volume 1

London • Sweet & Maxwell
2006

This volume should be cited as [2006] 1 Cr.App.R.

Case Citation and Paragraph Numbering of Law Reports
From the first issue of 2001 all Sweet and Maxwell Law reports contain paragraph numbers.
Each case has been given a unique citation. This takes the form of, *e.g.* [2001] 1 Cr.App.R. 1 for
the first case reported in Volume 1 of Cr.App.R. in 2001. These case and paragraph numbers are
used as the reference point for tables of cases and legislation and for the subject index. Tables of
contents will still be referenced to page number.

ISBN-10: 0-421-96130-9
ISBN-13: 978-0-421-96130-2

Criminal Appeal Reports will continue to be the most authoritative and
accessible source in practice of full text reports (revised by the Court of
Appeal) covering all aspects of the criminal law other than sentencing
matters.

*Computerset by Hobbs the Printers Ltd, Totton, Hampshire and
printed by Antony Rowe Limited.*

No natural forests were destroyed to make this product; only farmed timber was
used and re-planted.

Appellants and Applicants

R. v A (Prosecutor's Appeal). 28

R. v Abdroikov; R. v Green; R. v Wil-
liamson 1

R. v Al-Khawaja 9

R. v Ali and Others; R. v Bhatti. 8

R. v Claydon 20

R. v Dhillon 15

R. v Dooley 21

R. v Edwards; R. v Fysh; R. v Duggan; R.
v Chohan. 3

R. v Goodwin. 22

R. v H (JR) (Childhood Amnesia) 10

R. v H (P.G.). 4

R. v Harris; R. v Rock; R. v Cherry; R. v
Faulder 5

R. v Hatton. 16

R. v Henry 6

R. v Highton; R. v Van Nguyen; R. v
Carp. 7

R. v James; R. v Karimi. 29

R. v Khela; R. v Smith (Tina) 23

R. v Lahaye 11

R. v MacPherson 30

R. v Pleydell. 12

R. v Powell. 31

R. v Renda; R. v Ball; R. v Akram; R. v
Osbourne; R. v Razaq (Ajaz) and
Razaq (Abdul). 24

R. v Robinson. 13

R. v Robinson (Dennis) 32

R. v Rogers (Philip) 14

R. v Slocombe 33

R. v Timmins 18

R. v Weir; R. v Somanathan; R. v Yaxley-
Lennon; R. v Manister; R. v Hong 19

R. v Xhabri. 26

House of Lords

R. v Becouarn.........................2
R. v Rimmington; R. v Goldstein 17

Divisional Court

R. (Hasani) v Blackfriars Crown Court 27
R. (TP) v West London Youth Court 25

Table of Cases

AB (Child Abuse: Expert Witnesses), Re (1995) . . . . .5[H4], 5[272]
Anderton v Ryan (1985) . . . . .29[18]
Asch v Austria (1991) . . . . .26[H6]
Attorney General v PYA Quarries Ltd (No.1) (1957) . . . . .17[18], 17[26], 17[44], 17[47]
Attorney General for Jersey v Holley (2005) . . . . . . 29[H2], 29[H3], 29[H7], 29[1], 29[5], 29[19],
    29[20], 29[23], 29[27], 29[28], 29[29], 29[30], 29[31], 29[32], 29[33], 29[36], 29[37], 29[38],
    29[39], 29[43], 29[45], 29[51], 29[64], 29[65]
Attorney General's Reference (No.1 of 1990) (1992). . . . . .25[14]
Attorney General's Reference (No.4 of 2004) (2005). . . . . 14[H4], 14[10], 14[14], 14[18], 14[20],
    14[21], 14[23]

Barnes v Akroyd (1871). . . . . .17[16]
Beckford v R. . . . . 16[21], 16[22]
Black-Clawson International Ltd v Papierwerke Waldhof-Aschaffenberg AG (1975). . . . . . .17[33]
Brumarescu v Romania (2001) . . . . .17[33]

Clark (Inspector of Taxes) v Clark (2001). . . . . 22[H3]
Crummock (Scotland) Ltd v HM Advocate (2000). . . . . .1[22]
Curtis v Wild (1991) . . . . .22[31]

Davis v Johnson (1979) . . . . .29[34]
De Lasala v de Lasala (1980) . . . . .29[20]
Deacon v Evans (1911) . . . . .22[43]
DPP v Armstrong (Andrew) (1999). . . . . .20[25], 20[26], 20[30], 20[31]
DPP v Humphrys (1997) . . . . .25[14]
DPP v M (A Minor) (2004) . . . . 14[H5], 14[6], 14[10], 14[17], 14[19], 14[20], 14[21], 14[23]
DPP v Majewski (1997). . . . . 16[14], 16[16]
DPP v P (1991) . . . . 19[34], 19[36]
DPP v Smith (2002). . . . . .23[24]
DPP v Withers (1975) . . . . .17[24]
Dial and another v State of Trinidad and Tobago (2005) . . . . .5[101]
Doorson v The Netherlands (1996) . . . . 9[23], 9[26]

E v DPP (2002) . . . . .15[16]
European and Australian Royal Mail Co v P & O Steam Navigation Co (1864) . . . . .22[12]

Fothergill v Monarch Airlines Ltd (1981). . . . . .17[33]

G v Federal Republic of Germany. . . . . .17[35]
Grayned v City of Rockford (1972). . . . . .17[33]

H v DPP (2003) . . . . .15[19]
Hargreaves v Diddams (1874). . . . . .17[16]
Hashman and Harrup v United Kingdom (1999). . . . . .17[36]
Herczegfalvy v Austria (1993) . . . . .25[23]
Hunter v Canary Wharf Ltd (1997) . . . . .17[5]

Inco Europe Ltd v First Choice Distribution (2000) . . . . .28[15]

Jones v Wrotham Park Settled Estates (1980). . . . . .28[14]

Kadhim v Brent LBC Housing Benefit Board (2001). . . . . 29[H9]
Kammins Ballrooms Co Ltd v Zenith Investments (Torquay) Ltd (1971) . . . . .28[14]
Kokkinakis v Greece (1993) . . . . 17[33], 17[35], 17[36]
Kostovski v The Netherlands (1990). . . . . .9[18], 26[H6]

Lawal v Northern Spirit Ltd (2003). . . . . 1[15], 1[16]

Lee v Simpson (2001) . . . . .17[16]
Lowery v R (1974). . . . . .6[15]
Luc Thiet Thuan v R. (1996). . . . . 29[10], 29[11], 29[14], 29[24], 29[35]
Luca v Italy (2003) . . . . .9[19]

Mayor of Southport v Morriss (1893) . . . . 22[28], 22[31]
Medicaments and Related Classes of Goods (No.2), Re (2001) . . . . .1[15]
Miliangos v George Frank (Textiles) Ltd (1976). . . . . 29[22], 29[33]
Morden v Porter. . . . . .17[16]

National Justice Cia Naviera SA v Prudential Assurance Co Ltd (Ikarian Reefer) (1993) . . . .5[H4],
                                                                                          5[271]

O'Brien v Chief Constable of South Wales Police (2005) . . . . 3[54], 19[H9], 19[34], 19[35]
Overseas Tankship (UK) Ltd v Morts Dock & Engineering Co Ltd (The Wagon Mound)
       (1961) . . . . .29[34]

Palmer v R. (1971). . . . . .16[19]
Perks v Clark (2001) . . . . .22[25]
Polemis, Re (1921). . . . . .29[34]
Porter v Magill (2002) . . . . 1[15], 25[21]
Practice Statement (Judicial Precedent) (1966). . . . . 29[18], 29[21], 29[33]
Pullar v United Kingdom (1996). . . . . 1[16], 1[22]

R. v A (No.2) (2001) . . . . 26[H6]
R. v AS (2004). . . . . .31[21]
R v Abdrokov (2004). . . . . .1[H8]
R. v Adler (1964). . . . . .17[59]
R. v Anderson (1985). . . . . 8[119], 8[125]
R. v B (2005) . . . . .33[17]
R. v B (C) (2004). . . . . 32[62], 32[78]
R. v Bathurst (1968). . . . . .2[10]
R. v Beckford (1996). . . . . .25[14]
R. v Bonython (1984) . . . . .5[270]
R. v Bovell and Dowds (2005) . . . . 3[1], 3[32], 3[50], 7[1]
R. v Boyson (1991) . . . . .8[55]
R. v Bradley (2005) . . . . 4[2], 4[3], 4[5], 4[7], 4[8]
R. v Browning (1998) . . . . .8[129]
R. v Butterwasser (1948). . . . . 2[10], 2[11]
R. v Caldwell (1981) . . . . .8[128]
R. v Campbell (1997). . . . . 29[11], 29[35]
R. v Camplin (1978) . . . . 29[8], 29[10], 29[14], 29[17], 29[24], 29[49]
R. v Cannings (2004). . . . . 5[4], 5[102], 5[135]
R. v Churchill (No.2) (1967) . . . . .8[125]
R. v Clark (Mark) (2003). . . . . .17[33]
R. v Clark (No.2) (1964) . . . . .17[59]
R. v Clarke (1995) . . . . .5[270]
R. v Coles (1995). . . . . 6[13], 6[14]
R. v Cowan (1996). . . . . 2[H4], 2[12], 2[16], 2[23], 2[26]
R. v Crawley (1862). . . . . .17[14]
R. v Curr (1967). . . . . .20[H4], 20[20], 20[23], 20[25], 20[28], 20[29]
R. v D (2002) . . . . .31[21]
R. v Derby Crown Court, Ex p. Brooks (1984). . . . . .18[22]
R. v Dossi (1992). . . . . .28[22]
R. v Duffy (1966). . . . . .24[83]
R. v Easton (1995). . . . . .19[101]
R. v Edwards (2005) . . . . 19[34], 19[36]
R. v Edwards, Fysh, Duggaen and Chohan (2005) . . . . 7[1], 7[11]
R. v El Kurd (2001). . . . . 8[103], 8[113]
R. v Eskdale (2001) . . . . .17[27]
R. v Fairbanks (1986) . . . . .11[15]

R. v Faqir Mohammed (2005) . . . . .29[29]
R. v Field (1993) . . . . .11[16]
R. v Figg (2004). . . . . .18[6]
R. v Fisher (1969) . . . . .18[27]
R. v Ford (1989). . . . . .1[20]
R. v G (2004). . . . . 8[128], 17[56]
R. v Gough (1993) . . . . .1[15]
R v Graham (1997) . . . . .23[29]
R. v Green (2004) . . . . 1[H10]
R. v Griffiths (1998) . . . . .23[22]
R. v H (1995). . . . . 19[47], 19[48]
R. v Hakala (2002). . . . . .5[101]
R. v Hanratty, decd (2002). . . . . 5[101], 5[217]
R v Hanson and others (2005) . . . . . . 3[1], 3[2], 3[3], 3[35], 3[58], 3[77], 7[1], 7[11], 7[55], 7[56],
                                                                            7[59], 32[83], 32[86]
R. v Harley (2002). . . . . .17[27]
R. v Harmer (2005) . . . 8[H4], 8[H6], 8[H7], 8[99], 8[100], 8[110], 8[113], 8[115], 8[139], 8[140],
                                                                            8[141], 8[148]
R. v Henson (1852) . . . . 17[13], 17[19]
R. v Highton (2005). . . . . 19[44], 19[45]
R. v Hinton (1995). . . . . .18[6]
R. v Hodgson (1973) . . . . 18[4], 18[27]
R. v Holliday and Leboutillier (2004) . . . . .17[27]
R. v Horseferry Road Magistrates' Court Ex p. Bennett (1994) . . . . .18[22]
R. v Hussain (2002) . . . . .8[103], 8[113], 8[125], 8[146]
R. v Iles (1998) . . . . .18[6]
R. v Ishtiaq Ahmed (2002). . . . . .5[101]
R. v J (2005). . . . . 17[53], 18[H5], 18[7], 18[8], 18[9], 18[10], 18[11], 18[12], 18[25], 18[26],
                                                                            18[29], 19[87], 19[88]
R. v Jackson (1953) . . . . 2[H10]
R. v Jarvis (1862). . . . . .17[14]
R. v Johnson (Anthony) (1996) . . . . 17[H7], 17[26], 17[37], 17[38], 17[48]
R. v Jones (2003). . . . . .18[6]
R. v K (2002). . . . . 18[22], 18[25]
R. v Kai-Whitewind (2005). . . . . 5[102], 5[135]
R. v Latif (1996) . . . . .18[22]
R. v Lowrie (2004). . . . . .17[27]
R. v Lucas (1981). . . . . 2[6], 32[85]
R. v M; R. v Kerr; R. v H (2001). . . . . .25[15]
R. v McBride (1961) . . . . 12[21], 12[26]
R. v McCoy (1999) . . . . 9[29], 19[52], 19[53]
R. v McCready (1978). . . . . .11[16]
R. v MacPherson (2006) . . . . .31[33]
R. v Madden (1975). . . . . 17[19], 17[20]
R. v Mahmood and Manzur (1997) . . . . .8[37]
R. v Mandair (1994). . . . . .11[16]
R. v Martinez-Tobon (1994) . . . . 2[H10]
R. v Masih (1986) . . . . 6[H4], 6[10], 6[12], 6[14]
R. v Maxwell (1990) . . . . .11[15]
R. v Medley (1834) . . . . 17[13], 17[16], 17[30]
R. v Mertens (Jan Paul) (2004) . . . . . 32[H5], 32[61], 32[63], 32[70], 32[79], 32[80], 32[81], 32[82]
R. v Millward (1986). . . . . .17[25]
R. v Mir and Beg (1994) . . . . .8[125], 8[126], 8[128], 8[129]
R. v Mirza (2004). . . . . .1[22]
R. v Misra (2004). . . . . 17[H5], 17[33], 17[49]
R. v Mochan (1969). . . . . .18[27]
R. v Montila (2005) . . . . . . 8[H4], 8[H6], 8[H7], 8[70], 8[83], 8[96], 8[102], 8[103], 8[104], 8[106],
                                                          8[112], 8[113], 8[131], 8[132], 8[139], 8[147], 8[148]
R. v Moore (1832) . . . . .17[13]
R. v Morhall (1995). . . . . 29[10], 29[24], 29[60]
R. v Moule (1964) . . . . .17[59]

R. v Mullen (2000). . . . . .23[29]
R. v Murrell (John David) (2005) . . . . .32[H5], 32[61], 32[73], 32[80], 32[81], 32[82]
R. v Mutch (1973) . . . . 2[H10]
R. v Napper (1995) . . . . 2[23], 2[26]
R. v Newbon (2005). . . . . 28[10], 28[11]
R. v Newton (1983) . . . . .4[2]
R. v Nicholson (1947) . . . . .19[7]
R. v Norbury (1978). . . . . 17[24], 17[37], 17[46], 17[48], 17[59]
R. v O'Connor (1991) . . . . 16[15], 16[17], 16[25]
R. v O'Grady (1987) . . . . . . 16[H4], 16[7], 16[10], 16[15], 16[16], 16[17], 16[18], 16[19], 16[23],
                                                                                      16[24], 16[25], 16[28]
R. v O'Neil (2005). . . . . .19[7]
R. v Ong (2001). . . . . .17[22]
R. v Parker (1993) . . . . .8[129]
R. v Parker (1997) . . . . .29[11]
R. v Pendleton (2001) . . . . 5[101], 5[141]
R. v Pickford (1995) . . . . 20[13], 20[16], 20[17]
R. v Poulton and Celaire (2003) . . . . .3[17]
R. v Price (Richard Lyn) (2004) . . . . .32[H5], 32[60], 32[61], 32[62], 32[72], 32[78], 32[80],
                                                                                              32[81], 32[82]
R. v Pritchard, Re (2004). . . . . .27[3]
R. v Randall (2003) . . . . 6[15], 32[H4], 32[58], 32[65], 32[66], 32[67], 32[69], 32[75], 32[76],
                                                                                              32[78], 32[81]
R. v Rhodes (1899) . . . . 2[H10]
R. v Rizvi and Chisti (2003) . . . . 8[H4], 8[H7], 8[91], 8[115], 8[116], 8[125], 8[131], 8[132],
                                                                                              8[133], 8[134]
R. v Robertson (1987) . . . . .8[34]
R. v Rowland (Philip) (2003). . . . . 29[H9]
R. v Ruffell (1991). . . . . .17[21]
R. v Rumble (2003) . . . . .15[18]
R. v Ryan (1999) . . . . .8[129]
R. v Sakavickas (2005) . . . . . . .8[H4], 8[H7], 8[94], 8[115], 8[126], 8[129], 8[134], 8[135], 8[136],
                                                                                                       8[138]
R. v Sangha (1988) . . . . .8[128]
R. v Saunders (1987) . . . . .11[14]
R. v Secretary of State for the Home Department Ex p. Quinn (2000). . . . . .25[19]
R. v Sellick (2005). . . . . 9[H4], 9[21], 9[24], 9[26], 9[29]
R. v Shaw (1994). . . . . .20[29]
R. v Shivpuri (1986) . . . . 29[18], 29[19]
R. v Shorrock (1994) . . . . 17[21], 17[39], 17[56]
R. v Silcot and others (1991). . . . . .6[13]
R. v Simpson (2003) . . . . .29[37]
R. v Singh (2003). . . . . 8[H7], 8[113], 8[125], 8[141], 8[146], 8[147], 8[151]
R. v Siracusa (1990). . . . . .8[119]
R. v Smith (Josephine) (2002) . . . . 29[H9]
R. v Smith (Morgan James) (2001) . . 29[H2], 29[H3], 29[H5], 29[H7], 29[1], 29[4], 29[5], 29[12],
      29[17], 29[19], 29[20], 29[23], 29[24], 29[27], 29[28], 29[29], 29[30], 29[31], 29[32], 29[35],
              29[36], 29[39], 29[43], 29[45], 29[50], 29[51], 29[62], 29[63], 29[64], 29[65]
R. v Soul (1980). . . . . 17[20], 17[36], 17[59]
R. v Springfield (1969) . . . . .11[16]
R. v Stacey (2001) . . . . .5[182]
R. v Stephens (1866) . . . . .17[15], 17[16], 17[30], 17[39]
R. v Stevenson (1862) . . . . .17[14]
R. v Taylor (1999) . . . . .2[16]
R. v Thorpe (1972). . . . . 12[21], 12[26]
R. v Timmis (1976) . . . . .15[11]
R. v Turner (1974). . . . . 6[10], 6[15], 10[H4], 10[48]
R. v Toner (1991). . . . . 6[H4], 6[12]
R. v Van Dongen (2005) . . . . 29[28], 29[31]
R. v Vantandillo (1815) . . . . 17[13], 17[19]
R. v WR (2005) . . . . 18[9], 19[87], 19[88]

R. v Waite (1892)..20[12]
R. v Weller (David Allen) (2003) ....29[H9]
R. v White (Anthony) (2001)...............................14[H6], 14[9], 14[17], 14[21]
R. v White and Ward (1757) ....17[13]
R. v Whitehouse (1977)..........................20[H3], 20[15], 20[16], 20[19], 20[38]
R. v Williams (1893) ....20[12]
R. v Williams (Gladstone) (1984) ....16[13], 16[20], 16[22]
R. v Williamson (2005) ....1[H12]
R. v Wilson (1983)...11[16]
R. v Winfield (1939) ....19[43]
R. v Withers (1975) ....17[20]
R. v Woodward (1995)...........................12[H4], 12[19], 12[21], 12[26], 12[27]
R.(L and another) v Secretary of State for the Home Department (2003) ....17[33]
R. (on the application of DJ) v Mental Health Review Tribunal (2005).................25[23]
R. (on the application of Ebrahim) v Feltham Magistrates Court (2001) ....25[14]
R. (on the application of Haw) v Secretary of State for the Home Department (2005) ......28[18]
R. (on the application of S) v Waltham Forest Youth Court (2004) ....25[24]
Reed and Lillee v Newcastle City Council (2002) ....5[220], 5[251]
Ross v Weeks (1913)..22[31]

S and G v United Kingdom (1991) ....17[36]
SC v United Kingdom (2004) .... 25[H3], 25[5], 25[10], 25[22], 25[25], 25[27], 25[29]
S.W. v United Kingdom; C.R. v United Kingdom (1995).....................17[33], 17[35]
Sedleigh-Denfield v O'Callaghan (1940) ....17[17], 17[21]
Selvey v Director of Public Prosecutions (1968)..................................2[10]
Sherras v De Rutzen (1895)...17[16]
Soltau v De Held (1851) ....17[13]
Spectrum Plus Ltd (In Liquidation), Re (2005)...................................29[H9]
Steedman v Scofield (1992).............22[H3], 22[5], 22[15], 22[19], 22[20], 22[21], 22[23]
Sunday Times v United Kingdom (No.2) (1991) ....25[23]
Sunday Times v United KingdomWaddington v Miah (1974) ....17[33]

Tai Hing Cotton Mill Ltd v Liu Chong Hing Bank Ltd (1986).......................29[21]

V v United Kingdom (2000) ....25[9]
Von Rocks (1998)..22[21], 22[24], 22[26]

Warner v Metropolitan Police Commissioner (1968) ....17[33]
Wells v Owners of the Gas Float Whitton (No.2) (1897) ....22[29]
Wingrove v United Kingdom (1996)...17[36]

X Ltd and Y v United Kingdom (1982)...17[35]

Young v Bristol Aeroplane Co Ltd (1944)...............................29[H9], 29[33]

Table of Statutes

1854   Merchant Shipping Act....... 22[28]
1861   Offences Against the Person Act (24 &
      25 Vict. c.100)
      s.18 ...... 11[H1], 11[H2], 11[H3],
         11[H4], 11[H6], 11[1], 11[7],
         11[8], 11[9], 11[11], 11[16],
         11[18], 11[20], 11[21], 27[3]
      s.20 ...... 11[H1], 11[H2], 11[H3],
         11[H4], 11[H6], 11[1], 11[7],
         11[8], 11[9], 11[10], 11[12],
         11[16], 11[18], 11[20], 11[21]
      s.21 .... 1[40]
      s.35 .... 22[4]
      s.47 .... 27[3]
1885   Criminal Law Amendment Act (48 & 49
      Vict. c.69)
      s.5 .... 18[19]
1894   Merchant Shipping Act.. 22[5], 22[32]
      s.220 ...... 22[42], 22[43], 22[44]
      s.742 .... 22[15]
1898   Criminal Evidence Act (61 & 62 Vict.
      c.36)
      s.1 .... 2[H3], 2[H9], 2[20]
      s.1(3)............... 2[H1], 2[H2]
      s.1(3)(ii) .... 24[19]
      s.1(b)................... 2[10]
      s.1(e)................... 2[9]
1911   Maritime Conventions Act
      s.8 .... 22[15], 22[31]
      s.10 .... 22[15]
1915   Indictments Act
      s.2 .... 8[152]
1945   Family Allowance Act .... 20[23]
1956   Sexual Offences Act (4 & 5 Eliz. 2
      c.69) .... 18[3], 28[H3]
      s.5 .... 18[15]
      s.6 ... 18[H5], 18[6], 18[7], 18[15],
         18[25], 18[27]
      s.6(1)...... 18[H1], 18[H2], 18[5],
         18[6], 18[25], 19[88]
      s.10 .... 18[15]
      s.14 ...... 18[H1], 18[H2], 18[H5],
         18[6], 18[7], 18[22], 18[27],
         28[H1], 28[H5], 28[20]
      s.14(1).. 9[H6], 9[1], 18[4], 18[25],
         19[H22], 19[76], 28[H6], 28[5]
      s.14(2)................... 18[4]
      s.37 .... 18[5]
      s.37(2).................. 19[88]
      Sch.2, para.10(a).. 18[H1], 18[H2],
         18[5], 18[7], 19[88]
      Sch.2, para.14(a).......... 18[15]
      Sch.10 .... 18[27], 18[29]
1957   Homicide Act
      s.3 .... 29[1], 29[7], 29[8], 29[10],
         29[13], 29[14], 29[17], 29[27]

1960   Indecency with Children Act
      (c.33)................... 28[5]
      Administration of Justice Act
      s.1 .... 25[H5]
1964   Obscene Publications Act...... 21[5]
      Criminal Procedure (Insanity) Act
      s.4 .... 25[15], 27[H1], 27[H2],
         27[H3], 27[2], 27[3], 27[7],
         27[14], 27[15]
      s.4(6)................... 27[14]
      s.4A...... 27[H1], 27[H2], 27[H3],
         27[2], 27[8], 27[14]
      s.4A(2) .... 27[12]
      s.5 .. 27[H3], 27[2], 27[11], 27[14],
         27[15]
      s.5(1)................... 27[9]
      s.5(2)..... 27[H1], 27[H2], 27[H3],
         27[5], 27[9], 27[12], 27[15]
      s.5A(4) .... 27[5], 27[10]
      s.5A(6) .... 27[11]
1967   Criminal Law Act (c.58)...... 18[H3]
      s.3(1)................... 24[83]
      s.6 .... 18[24], 23[23]
      s.6(2)................... 11[14]
      s.6(3)..... 11[H3], 11[H4], 11[H5],
         11[13], 11[14], 11[16], 11[17],
         11[21], 18[H1], 18[H2], 18[11],
         18[27]
1968   Criminal Appeal Act (c.19)
      s.3 .... 18[23]
      s.3(a)................... 18[23]
      s.23 .... 10[H2], 10[H3], 10[5],
         10[28], 10[38]
      s.23(2)(c).................. 6[7]
      s.33(2)..... 8[152], 14[25], 29[65],
         32[87]
      s.44A............ 10[H6], 10[5]
      Theft Act (c.60)
      s.1(2)................... 21[3]
      s.21 .... 21[14]
1969   Post Office Act (c.48)
      s.78 .... 17[24]
1971   Misuse of Drugs Act (c.38)
      s.28(3).................. 7[39]
      Criminal Damage Act (c.48)
      s.1(1)................... 17[56]
      s.1(2)................... 17[56]
1974   Juries Act (c.23)
      s.1 ..... 1[H1], 1[H2], 1[H7], 1[7],
         1[10]
      s.9 .... 1[19]
      s.9A.................... 1[19]
      s.9A(2) .... 1[11]
      s.12 .... 1[20]
      s.12(1)................. 1[20]

1977 Criminal Law Act (c.45)
    s.1 .... 8[H2], 8[H4], 8[H8], 8[14],
        8[66], 8[103], 8[142]
    s.1(1) .... 8[H2], 8[H3], 8[H9],
        8[H10], 8[2], 8[8], 8[67], 8[81],
        8[83], 8[116], 8[127]
    s.1(1)(a) ...... 8[H1], 8[H4], 8[H5],
        8[96], 8[103], 8[105], 8[111]
    s.1(1)(b) .... 8[103]
    s.1(2) .. 8[H1], 8[H4], 8[H6], 8[82],
        8[83], 8[96], 8[109], 8[112],
        8[113], 8[115], 8[118], 8[119],
        8[124], 8[125], 8[128], 8[131],
        8[137], 8[138], 8[139], 8[144],
        8[152]
    s.1(2)(b) .... 8[127]
    s.51 .... 17[29]
1978 Interpretation Act (c.30)
    s.17 .... 28[12]
    s.17(1) .... 28[12]
    s.17(2)(a) .... 22[8]
    s.17(2)(b) .... 22[8]
    Protection of Children Act (c.37)
    s.1 .... 19[5], 19[9], 21[H3]
    s.1(1)(c) ... 21[H1], 21[H2], 21[H4],
        21[1]
1980 Highways Act (c.66)
    s.137 .... 17[29]
1981 Criminal Attempts Act (c.47)
    s.5 .... 8[H1]
1984 Police and Criminal Evidence Act (c.60)
    s.24 .... 8[84]
    s.74 .... 8[27], 8[28], 8[37]
    s.75 .... 8[27], 8[39]
    s.78 .... 3[44], 3[71], 6[16], 7[H7],
        7[13], 7[14], 8[28], 8[42], 13[H4],
        13[18], 13[21], 19[14], 19[15],
        19[19], 19[44], 19[46], 19[95],
        26[15], 31[16], 31[27]
1986 Public Order Act (c.64). ...... 17[59]
    s.2(1) .... 19[H24], 19[106]
    s.4 .... 14[2], 23[H3], 23[H8]
    s.5 .... 3[43], 3[48]
1987 Criminal Justice Act (c.38)
    Pt 1 .... 4[H2], 4[1], 4[6]
    s.7 .... 4[H6], 4[1]
    s.8 .... 4[H1], 4[H2], 4[H3], 4[H5],
        4[3], 4[6], 4[8]
    s.9 .... 4[H5], 4[1]
1988 Income and Corporation Taxes Act
    (c.1) .... 22[25]
    Malicious Communications Act (c.27)
    s.1 .... 17[29], 17[50]
    Criminal Justice Act (c.33)
    Pt IV .... 8[141], 8[144]
    Pt VI .... 8[117]
    s.23 ..... 9[H2], 9[H5], 9[3], 9[13],
        9[16], 19[15]
    ss.23-26 .... 9[20], 19[19]
    ss.23-28 .... 9[12]
    s.25 ..... 9[H2], 9[3], 9[H5], 9[14]

1988 Criminal Justice Act (c.33)—cont.
    s.26 ..... 9[H2], 9[H5], 9[3], 9[12],
        9[14], 19[15], 19[50]
    s.71(9)(c) .... 8[78]
    s.93 .... 8[77]
    s.93A. 8[77], 8[80], 8[120], 8[125],
        8[135], 8[136], 8[137], 8[138]
    s.93A(7) .... 8[77]
    s.93B .... 8[77]
    s.93C .. 8[H3], 8[77], 8[79], 8[102],
        8[131]
    s.93C(2) ...... 8[H1], 8[H3], 8[H4],
        8[H6], 8[H8], 8[H10], 8[8], 8[83],
        8[86], 8[96], 8[97], 8[98], 8[113],
        8[139], 8[152]
    s.93C(2)(b) .... 8[117], 8[142]
    s.93D .... 8[77]
    Road Traffic Act (c.52)
    s.3A .. 23[H2], 23[4], 23[10], 23[11]
    s.3A(1)(b) .... 23[H6]
    s.4 .... 23[11]
    s.4(1) .... 23[H6], 23[10]
    Road Traffic Offenders Act (c.53)
    s.24 ...... 23[H1], 23[H4], 23[H5],
        23[10], 23[11], 23[19], 23[21]
    s.24(1) .... 23[18]
    s.36 .... 23[19]
1989 Irish Jurisdiction of Courts (Maritime
    Convention) Act .... 22[21]
1990 Criminal Justice (International Co-
    operation) Act (c.5)
    s.14(1) .... 8[70]
    s.14(2) .... 8[70]
    Environmental Protection Act (c.43)
    s.33 .... 17[29]
    s.79(1) .... 17[29]
1991 Criminal Procedure (Insanity and Unfit-
    ness to Plead) Act (c.25)
    s.2 .... 27[H1]
    Road Traffic Act (c.40)
    s.24 .... 23[H1], 23[H4]
    Water Resources Act (c.57)
    s.85 .... 17[29]
1993 Criminal Justice Act (c.36)..... 8[77]
    s.31 .... 8[H1], 8[H3]
1994 Trade Markes Act (c.26)
    s.92 .... 21[3]
    Criminal Justice and Public Order Act
    (c.33)
    s.1(1) .... 33[8]
    s.35 ... 2[H1], 2[H2], 2[H3], 2[H9],
        2[5], 2[6], 2[8], 2[11], 2[12], 2[13],
        2[16], 2[17], 2[20]
    s.63 .... 17[29]
    s.84(2) .... 21[H1]
    s.168(3) .... 21[H1]
    Sch.11 .... 21[H1]
    Drug Trafficking Act (c.37)
    Pt II .... 8[67]
    s.49 .... 8[H2], 8[69], 8[70], 8[77],
        8[102]

1994	Drug Trafficking Act (c.37)—cont.	
	s.49(1)	8[94]
	s.49(2)	8[H1], 8[H2], 8[H3], 8[H4], 8[H5], 8[H6], 8[H8], 8[H9], 8[H10], 8[2], 8[8], 8[67], 8[86], 8[88], 8[92], 8[94], 8[96], 8[97], 8[98], 8[113], 8[131], 8[139], 8[152]
	s.49(2)(b)	8[117], 8[142]
	s.50	8[77]
	s.50(1)	8[71]
	s.50(4)	8[72]
	s.51	8[77]
	s.51(1)	8[73]
	s.52(1)	8[75]
	s.53	8[75], 8[77]
1995	Merchant Shipping Act (c.21)	22[27]
	Pt I	22[11], 22[12]
	Pt III	22[18], 22[36], 22[40]
	s.24	22[18], 22[36]
	s.42	22[38]
	s.47	22[37]
	s.48	22[37]
	s.49	22[37]
	s.58	22[H2], 22[H3], 22[H4], 22[2], 22[3], 22[4], 22[7], 22[8], 22[9], 22[10], 22[18], 22[35], 22[36], 22[40], 22[41], 22[42], 22[45], 22[46]
	s.58(1)	22[5]
	s.58(2)	22[H1], 22[44]
	s.58(2)(a)	22[H2], 22[H5], 22[1]
	s.58(4)	22[44]
	s.313	22[H2], 22[H3], 22[6], 22[14], 22[17]
	s.313(1)	22[H2], 22[5]
	s.313(3)	22[H1]
	Criminal Appeal Act (c.35)	
	s.9	29[H5]
	s.9(1)	10[H6], 10[5]
1996	Criminal Procedure and Investifations Act	
	s.29	17[2]
	s.37	17[3]
	s.37(5)	17[3]
	s.37(9)	17[3]
1997	Protection from Harassment Act (c.40)	
	s.1	17[29]
	Sex Offenders Act (c.51)	33[H2]
	s.1(4)	33[16]
	s.4(1)(a)	33[7], 33[9]
1998	Crime and Disorder Act (c.37)	
	s.28	14[H2], 14[H7], 14[H8], 14[5], 14[6], 14[9], 14[10], 14[13], 14[16], 14[24]
	s.28(1)(a)	14[9], 14[17], 14[21]
	s.28(4)	14[H1], 14[H2], 14[H3], 14[H7], 14[6], 14[8], 14[9], 14[13], 14[14], 14[15], 14[17], 14[18], 14[19], 14[20], 14[23], 14[24], 14[25]
1998	Crime and Disorder Act (c.37)—cont.	
	s.30	14[9]
	s.31	14[H8], 14[5], 23[15]
	s.31(1)(a)	14[H1], 14[H2], 14[H9], 14[1], 23[H3], 23[H8]
	s.31(6)	23[H1], 23[H3], 23[H4], 23[18]
	s.32	17[29]
	ss.73-79	33[8], 33[11]
	s.73(3)	33[10], 33[11]
	s.75(1)	33[10]
	s.75(2)	33[10]
	s.75(4)	33[16]
	s.76(1)	33[10]
	Sch.8, para.144	33[9]
	Human Rights Act (c.42)	26[33]
	s.1(5)	21[4]
	s.3	1[11], 7[14]
	s.6	1[22]
	s.6(1)	1[H1]
	s.6(2)	1[14]
	s.6(3)	1[13]
	Sch.1	17[H1], 9[H1], 26[H1]
1999	Youth Justice and Criminal Evidence Act (c.23)	
	s.27(1)	31[11], 31[23]
	s.27(2)	31[16], 31[23], 31[26], 31[27]
	s.41	24[37]
	s.53	30[H2], 30[17], 30[19], 31[H1], 31[H3], 31[H5], 31[18]
	s.53(1)	30[H1], 30[H2], 31[17]
	s.53(1)(a)	30[25], 30[26]
	s.53(1)(b)	30[25], 30[26]
	s.53(2)	30[H1], 30[H2]
	s.53(3)	31[H3], 31[17], 31[18], 31[40]
	s.53(3)(a)	30[H1], 30[H2], 30[H3]
	s.53(3)(b)	30[H1], 30[H2], 30[H3]
	s.54	30[H1], 30[H2], 30[17]
	s.54(2)	31[17]
	s.63	30[H1], 30[H2], 30[17]
	s.67(1)	2[H1]
	Sch.4, para.1(1)(7)	2[H1]
2000	Powers of Criminal Courts (Sentencing) Act (c.6)	
	Pt V	33[11]
	s.2(1)	27[11]
	s.90	33[18]
	s.91	33[18]
	ss.100-107	33[11]
	s.100(3)	33[11]
	s.101(1)	33[11]
	s.102	33[11]
	s.102(4)	33[16]
	s.103	33[11]
	s.143	3[H5], 3[4]
	Postal Services Act (c.26)	
	s.85	17[29]
	s.85(1)	17[50]
	s.85(4)	17[50]

2001 Anti-Terrorism, Crime and Security Act (c.24)
s.114 . . . . 17[29]
2002 Proceeds of Crime Act (c.29) . . . 8[76]
Pt 7 . . . . 8[77]
2003 Communications Act (c.21)
s.127 . . . . 17[29]
Courts Act (c.39)
s.109(1) . . . . 8[152]
Sch.8, para.67 . . . . 8[152]
Sexual Offences Act (c.42) . . . . 18[3], 28[H2], 28[2]
s.1 . . . . 20[1]
s.2(2) . . . . 20[1]
s.2(3) . . . . 20[1]
s.7 . . 19[H2], 19[H16], 19[3], 19[6], 19[9]
s.8 . . . . 28[5]
s.9 . . . . 18[6], 28[H5]
s.9(1) . . . . 18[5], 28[H1], 28[20]
s.9(2)(a) . . . . 18[5]
s.11 . . . . 20[19]
s.81 . . . . 33[12]
s.82 . 33[H1], 33[H4], 33[7], 33[14]
s.82(1) . . . . 33[H2], 33[H3], 33[12], 33[19]
s.82(2) . . . . . 33[H2], 33[13], 33[15]
s.82(6) . . . . 33[12]
s.83 . . . . 33[1]
s.84 . . . . 33[1]
s.91(1)(a) . . . . 33[H2], 33[H5], 33[1]
s.91(2) . . . . . 33[H2], 33[H5], 33[1]
s.131 . . . . 33[14], 33[19]
s.131(a) . . . 33[H1], 33[H2], 33[14], 33[17], 33[19]
s.131(a)-(e) . . . . 33[17]
s.131(f) . . . . 33[18]
s.131(f)-(j) . . . . 33[17], 33[18]
s.140 . . . . 28[10], 28[17]
s.141 . . . . 28[9], 28[17]
s.141(2) . . . . 28[10]
s.141(2)(b) . . . . 28[9]
Sch.7 . . . . 28[2], 28[10], 28[17]
Criminal Justice Act (c.44) . . . . . 1[7], 4[H6], 19[1]
Pt II . . 4[H2], 9[12], 19[13], 24[H2], 24[H3], 24[1], 24[24], 32[83]
Pt XI . . . . 7[1]
s.58 . . . . 28[H6], 28[3]
s.98 . . 3[43], 7[4], 19[H1], 19[H13], 19[90], 19[94]
s.98(b) . . . . 3[43]
ss.98-110 . . . . 19[6]
ss.98-113 . . . . 3[1], 7[1]
s.99(1) . . . 19[H14], 19[19], 19[35], 19[36], 19[90], 19[95], 19[120]

2003 Criminal Justice Act (c.44)—cont.
s.100 . . 7[H4], 7[48], 7[51], 19[H1], 19[H4], 19[2], 19[36], 19[74], 24[H1], 24[H7], 24[H8], 24[H9], 24[H10], 24[H11], 24[44], 24[47], 24[55], 24[57], 24[58], 24[59], 24[60], 24[71]
s.100(1) . . 19[H4], 19[H10], 19[70], 19[73], 24[76]
s.100(1)(a) . . . . 19[64]
s.100(1)(b) . . 19[63], 19[64], 24[73]
s.101 . . 2[27], 3[H2], 7[H1], 7[H5], 7[2], 7[14], 7[33], 7[40], 19[H1], 19[H2], 19[H13], 19[2], 19[94]
ss.101-106 . . . . 19[35], 19[36]
s.101(1) . . 3[H1], 3[H2], 3[3], 3[69], 7[3], 7[11], 19[H1], 19[2], 19[35], 19[90], 19[91]
s.101(1)(a) . . . . 7[9]
s.101(1)(b) . . . . 7[9]
s.101(1)(c) . . . . 7[5]
s.101(1)(c)-(g) . . . . 24[H1], 24[H4], 24[27]
s.101(1)(d) . . . . . 3[8], 7[H3], 7[H6], 7[6], 7[8], 7[9], 7[13], 7[20], 7[31], 7[39], 7[40], 19[H3], 19[H5], 19[H8], 19[2], 19[5], 19[19], 19[32], 19[33], 19[36], 19[37], 19[42], 19[43], 19[45]
s.101(1)(e) . . 7[7], 19[117], 19[118]
s.101(1)(f) . . . . 7[7], 19[H3], 19[2], 19[14], 19[15], 19[19], 19[32], 19[43], 19[44], 24[H4], 24[19]
s.101(1)(g) . . . . 7[H2], 7[H4], 7[H5], 7[1], 7[7], 7[13], 7[19], 7[20], 7[22], 7[48], 7[50], 7[51], 7[53], 7[54], 19[H3], 19[9], 19[14], 19[15], 19[19], 19[32], 19[45], 24[H5], 24[35]
s.101(3) . . 3[9], 3[46], 3[71], 7[H5], 7[H8], 7[12], 7[20], 7[23], 7[40], 7[53], 7[58], 19[2], 19[14], 19[19], 19[38], 19[40], 19[42], 19[44], 19[45], 19[46], 19[90]
s.101(4) . . . . . 3[46], 19[90], 19[91]
s.102 . . . . . . 7[5], 19[H13], 19[90], 19[94]
s.103 . . 7[6], 7[14], 19[H1], 19[H2], 19[H13], 19[94]
s.103(1) . . 7[8], 7[9], 19[33], 19[90]
s.103(1)(a) . . . . 19[5], 19[19]
s.103(1)(b) . . 3[33], 19[H8], 19[19], 19[37]
s.103(2) . . . . . 3[46], 7[12], 19[H7], 19[7]
s.103(2)(a) . . . . 19[7]
s.103(2)(b) . . . 19[H2], 19[5], 19[7], 19[9]
s.103(3) . . . . 3[72], 7[12]
s.103(4) . . . . 3[46]
s.103(4)(b) . . . . 19[5], 19[6]

2003   Criminal Justice Act (c.44)—*cont.*
        s.104 . . . . 7[7]
        s.105 . . . . 7[7]
        s.105(1) . . . . 24[H1]
        s.105(1)(a) . . . . 24[H4], 24[19]
        s.105(1)(b) . . . . 24[H4], 24[19]
        s.105(3) . . . 24[H1], 24[H3], 24[H4],
                                              24[21]
        s.105(6) . . . . 19[19], 19[43], 19[45]
        s.106 . . . . 7[7], 24[35]
        s.106(1)(c) . . . . 24[H1], 24[H6],
                               24[35], 24[37], 24[38]
        s.107 . . . . . . 19[2], 24[H1], 24[H4],
                               24[26], 24[27]
        s.107(5) . . . . 24[H4], 24[27]
        s.110 . . . . 7[40], 19[19]
        s.110(1) . . . . 24[H1], 24[60]
        s.112 . . . . 7[4]
        s.112(1) . . 19[H1], 19[H6], 19[H13],
                   19[90], 19[94], 19[118], 24[H1]
        s.114 . . . . . 26[H1], 26[H3], 26[H4],
                   26[12], 26[29], 26[30], 26[38],
                                              26[42]
        s.114(d) . . . 26[H2], 26[H3], 26[32],
                                              26[36]
        s.117 . . . . 26[14]
        s.118 . . . . 26[12]

2003   Criminal Justice Act (c.44)—*cont.*
        s.118(1) . . . . 7[4]
        s.119 . . . . 26[14]
        s.120 . . . . . 26[H1], 26[H2], 26[H3],
                   26[H4], 26[13], 26[14], 26[29],
                               26[30], 26[36]
        s.120(4) . . . . 26[32], 26[39]
        s.120(5) . . . . 26[35]
        s.120(6) . . . . 26[35]
        s.120(7) . . . . 26[H3], 26[35]
        s.121 . . . . . 26[H1], 26[H2], 26[14],
                               26[29], 26[39]
        s.121(1)(a) . . 26[H3], 26[31], 26[39]
        s.121(1)(c) . . . . 26[H3], 26[31],
                               26[37], 26[39]
        s.126 . . . . . 26[H1], 26[H3], 26[H4],
                   26[15], 26[29], 26[32], 26[42]
        s.140 . . . . 4[H1], 4[H3], 4[4], 28[2]
        s.141 . . . . . 4[H1], 4[H3], 4[4], 4[5],
                                              4[7]
        s.141(2)(b) . . . . 28[2]
        s.321 . . . 1[H1], 1[H2], 1[H7], 1[10]
        Sch.33 . . . . 1[H1], 1[H2], 1[10]

2004   Domestic Violence, Crime and Victims
        Act (c.28) . . . . 8[152]
        s.22 . . . . 27[H1], 27[3]

Table of Statutory Instruments

1971   Indictment Rules (SI 1971/1253)
     r.4(2) . . . . 8[150], 8[152]
1991   Merchant Shipping Act 1970 (Unregis-
     tered Ships) Regulations (SI 1991/
     1366)
     reg.4 . . . . 22[8], 22[40]
1996   Merchant Shipping (Distress Signals
     and Prevention of Collisions) Regu-
     lations (SI 1996/75)   22[H4], 22[45]
2004   Sexual Offences Act 2003 (Commence-
     ment) Order (SI 2004/874) . 28[H1],
         28[H2], 28[2], 28[9], 28[13]
2005   Criminal Justice Act (Commencement
     No.8 and Transitional and Saving
     Provisions Order) (SI 2005/950) 4[2]

Table of European Legislation

European Convention of Human Rights
  Art.6 . . . 1[H6], 1[16], 7[14], 9[H3],
    9[1], 9[17], 9[20], 9[22], 9[28],
    9[31], 19[38], 25[H1], 25[H2],
    25[H3], 25[H5], 25[2], 25[4],
    25[13], 25[17], 25[23], 25[27],
    25[29], 26[H3], 26[42]
  Art.6(1) . . . . 9[17], 9[19], 9[22],
    9[23], 25[10], 25[11], 25[16],
    25[22]
  Art.6(3) . . . . 9[23]
  Art.6(3)(c) . . . . 25[11]

1950 European Convention of Human
  Rights—*cont.*
  Art.6(3)(d) . . . . 9[H1], 9[H2], 9[H3],
    9[H5], 9[17], 9[18], 9[19], 9[22],
    9[23], 26[H1], 26[H3], 26[43],
    26[44]
  Art.7 . . . . 17[H2], 17[H4], 17[H10],
    17[2], 17[45], 17[46]
  Art.7(1) . . . . 17[H1]
  Art.8 . . . . . 17[H2], 17[H10], 17[2]
  Art.10 . . . . 17[H2], 17[H10], 17[2]
  Art.10(2) . . . . 25[23]

Key Word Index

References in this index are to case number.

ABUSE OF PROCESS
Trial in youth court
*Claimant having low IQ—Judge determining on balance of probabilities
fair trial possible—Whether youth or limited intellectual capacity leading
to breach of Convention right to a fair trial—Proper test to be applied—
Whether youth court able to adapt procedures to enable proper partici-
pation by young defendant with incapacity—European Convention on
Human Rights Art.6*

R. (TP) v West London Youth Court
QB [2006] 1 Cr.App.R. 25

ALTERNATIVE VERDICTS
Jurisdiction to return verdicts of guilt on lesser offences
*Trial judge ordering stay of proceedings against one appellant in respect of
offences charged but allowing jury to consider returning alternative verdict
in relation to same events—At trial of second appellant jury unable to reach
verdict on offence charged and discharged by judge from returning verdict
on that charge but invited to consider alternative charge—Whether jurisdiction to return verdicts on lesser alternative charges—Road Traffic Act
1988 (c.52), ss.3A (as inserted by Road Traffic Act 1991 (c.40), s.3),
4(1)—Road Traffic Offenders Act 1988 (c.53), s.24 (as substituted by the
Road Traffic Act 1991 (c.40), s.24)—Crime and Disorder Act 1998 (c.37),
ss.31(1)(a), 31(6)*

R.v Khela
R. v Smith (Tina)
CA [2006] 1 Cr.App.R. 23

ASSAULT
Alternative verdict
*Defendant charged on indictment with single count of wounding with
intent—Jury directed on availability of verdict on lesser offence of wounding—Jury acquitting defendant of count on indictment but finding defendant
guilty of wounding—Whether judge correct to leave lesser offence for con-*

sideration by jury—Whether better practice to include count on indictment alleging lesser offence—Offences against the Person Act 1861 (24 & 25 Vict. c.100), ss.18, 20—Criminal Law Act 1967 (c.58), s.6(3)

R. v Lahaye
CA [2006] 1 Cr.App.R. 11

CHILD, INDECENT PHOTOGRAPH OF
Data on computer
Indecent images of children downloaded from internet file-sharing network—Held in folder accessible by other network members—Whether images possessed "with a view to" their being distributed or shown—Whether offence committed where sole intention was to transfer images to part of computer not accessible by others—Protection of Children Act 1978 (c.37), s.1(1)(c) (as amended by the Criminal Justice and Public Order Act 1994 (c.33), ss.84(2), 168(3) and Sch.11)

R. v Dooley
CA [2006] 1 Cr.App.R. 21

CONSPIRACY
Concealing the proceeds of crime
Defendants charged with conspiracy to conceal, disguise or remove from the jurisdiction bank notes, knowing or having reasonable grounds to suspect the money to be the proceeds of drug trafficking or criminal conduct—Whether suspicion as to the character of the money sufficient for offence of conspiracy—Criminal Law Act 1977 (c.45), s.1(1)(a),(2) (as substituted by Criminal Attempts Act 1981 (c.47), s.5)—Criminal Justice Act 1988 (c.33), s.93C(2) (as inserted by Criminal Justice Act 1993 (c.36), s.31)—Drug Trafficking Act 1994 (c.37), s.49(2)

R. v Ali
R. v Bhatti
CA [2006] 1 Cr.App.R. 8

ESCAPE FROM LAWFUL CUSTODY
Elements of offence
Judge's direction to the jury—Whether direction articulated elements—Whether sufficiently coherent—Significance of passage of time and difficult factual issues in summary for jury—Importance of care in making directions as to law

R. v Dhillon
CA [2006] 1 Cr.App.R. 15

EVIDENCE
Bad character

Admission of defendant's bad character to establish propensity to commit type of offence—Previous offence not in same category as offence charged—Whether evidence of previous offence admissible—Criminal Justice Act 2003 (c.44), ss.101, 103

Evidence of bad character relevant to important issue between prosecution and defence—Prosecution applying pursuant to statutory provisions to adduce evidence of defendant's bad character—Whether common law rules on similar fact evidence relevant—Criminal Justice Act 2003, s.101(1)

Defence witness cross-examined as to caution for drug-related offence—Whether caution relevant to witness's—Credibility—Criminal Justice Act 2003, s.100

Defendant 39-year-old man charged with sexual offences against 13-year-old girl—Defendant when aged 34 involved in sexual relationship with 16-year-old girl—Prosecution applying to adduce evidence of relationship to show "misconduct"—Whether lawful behaviour capable of constituting "misconduct"—Whether evidence admissible at common law—Criminal Justice Act 2003, ss.98, 101, 103, 112(1)

Appellants charged with violent disorder—Co-defendant claiming to have acted in self-defence in response to threat from appellants—Co-defendant applying to adduce evidence that appellants had propensity to violent conduct—Whether evidence admissible at common law

R. v Weir
R. v Somanathan
R. v Yaxley-Lennon
R. v Manister
R. v Hong and De
CA [2006] 1 Cr.App.R. 19

EVIDENCE
Bad character

Defendant creating but subsequently withdrawing false impression as to character—Reprehensible behaviour other than the commission of an offence—Evidence "given" of an imputation made during questioning under caution—Bad character of complainant and defendant's witness—Criminal Justice Act 2003 (c.44), ss.100, 101(1)(c)—(g), 105(1), 105(3), 106(1)(c), 107, 110(1), 112(1)

R. v Renda
R. v Ball
R. v Akram
R. v Osbourne
R. v Razaq (Ajaz) and Razaq (Abdul)
CA [2006] 1 Cr.App.R. 24

EVIDENCE
  Bad character
  Evidence of defendant's bad character admitted following attack on another's character—Whether capable of showing propensity to commit offences of kind charged or solely relevant to credibility—Criminal Justice Act 2003 (c.44), s.101

R. v Highton
R. v Van Nguyen
R. v Carp
CA [2006] 1 Cr.App.R. 7

EVIDENCE
  Bad character
  Judge's directions to jury to contain clear warning to jury against placing undue reliance on previous convictions—Criminal Justice Act 2003 (c.44), s.101(1)

R. v Edwards
R. v Fysh
R. v Duggan
R. v Chohan
CA [2006] 1 Cr.App.R. 3

EVIDENCE
  Character
  Defendants tried jointly—Cut-throat defence—Second defendant adducing evidence of first defendant's bad character to support defence of duress— Evidence not admissible at behest of Crown—Judge directing jury to take account of all evidence when considering cases against each defendant— Whether bad character evidence relevant only to second defendant's case—Whether misdirection

R. v Robinson (Dennis)
CA [2006] 1 Cr.App.R. 32

EVIDENCE
  Competence of witness
  Indecent assault—Child complainant—Interview and trial taking place some time after alleged incident—Whether prosecution discharging onus of demonstrating competence—Youth Justice and Criminal Evidence Act 1999 (c.23) s.53

R. v Powell
CA [2006] 1 Cr.App.R. 31

EVIDENCE
Competence of witness
Indecent assault—Child complainant—Whether such complainant competent witness—Proper approach to issue in common law and statute—Youth Justice and Criminal Evidence Act 1999 (c.23), ss.53(1), (2), (3)(a)(b), 54, 63

R. v MacPherson
CA [2006] 1 Cr.App.R. 30

EVIDENCE
Expert medical evidence
Admissibility—Defendant having IQ of 75—Whether expert evidence admissible as to defendant's ability to form mens rea

R. v Henry
CA [2006] 1 Cr.App.R. 6

EVIDENCE
Expert medical evidence
Shaken baby syndrome—Triad of intercranial injuries strong pointer to syndrome but not diagnostic—Unified hypothesis not credible alternative cause of triad—Guidance as to expert witnesses

R. v Harris
R. v Rock
R. v Cherry
R. v Faulder
CA [2006] 1 Cr.App.R. 5

EVIDENCE
Expert psychological evidence
Convictions for offences of sexual abuse dependent upon childhood memory—Doubt cast on reliability of memory in expert psychological report—Whether evidence relevant and admissible—Whether evidence furnished information likely to be outside knowledge and experience of jury—Warning appropriate to be given to jury if evidence admitted

R. v X (Childhood Amnesia)
CA [2006] 1 Cr.App.R. 10

EVIDENCE
  Hearsay

  Defendant charged with fraud—Preparatory hearing held—Hearsay pro-
  visions coming into force between preparatory hearing and empanelment
  of jury—Whether trial commencing with preparatory hearing for purpose
  of provisions—Whether provisions applicable—Criminal Justice Act
  1987 (c.38), s.8—Criminal Justice Act 2003 (c.44), ss.140, 141

                                                         R. v H
                                        CA [2006] 1 Cr.App.R. 4

EVIDENCE
  Hearsay

  Previous statement of complainant—Appellant allegedly kidnapping, rap-
  ing and forcing complainant to work as prostitute—Complainant directly
  or indirectly communicating with third parties during alleged ordeal—
  Whether third parties able to give evidence as to communications—Whether
  statutory provisions allowing hearsay evidence infringing right to fair
  trial—Human Rights Act 1998 (c.42), Sch.1, Pt I, Art.6(3)(d)—Criminal
  Justice Act 2003 (c.44), ss.114, 120, 121

                                                       R. v Xhabri
                                        CA [2006] 1 Cr.App.R. 26

EVIDENCE
  Voice identification

  Widow of deceased having received telephone call with threats at time of her
  husband's disappearance—Such person upon hearing a defendant speaking
  at trial purportedly recognising his voice as that of the caller—Some of co-
  defendants, but not Crown, applying for evidence to be adduced—Whether
  evidence of such voice recognition admissible—Appropriate test as to
  admissibility

                                                      R. v Robinson
                                        CA [2006] 1 Cr.App.R. 13

EVIDENCE
  Witness

  Prosecution witness dying before trial—Judge allowing witness statement
  to be read to jury—Whether defendant's Convention right to fair trial
  breached—Human Rights Act 1998, Sch.1, Pt.I, Art.6(3)(d)

                                                     R. v Al-Khawaja
                                        CA [2006] 1 Cr.App.R. 9

FITNESS TO PLEAD
Arraignment
Claimant initially found unfit to plead—Jury finding claimant having done act—Medical evidence indicating claimant fit to plead at disposal hearing—Whether judge having to decide again whether claimant fit to plead—Whether jury required again to find claimant having done act—Whether judge required to order absolute discharge of claimant—Criminal Procedure (Insanity) Act 1964 (c.84), ss.4, 4A, 5(2) (as amended by Criminal Procedure (Insanity and Unfitness to Plead) Act 1991 (c.25), s.2 and Domestic Violence, Crime and Victims Act 2004 (c.28), s.22)

R. (Hasani) v Blackfriars Crown Court
QB [2006] 1 Cr.App.R. 27

HOMICIDE
Provocation
Proper direction to jury in relation to defence of provocation—Conflict of authority—Judicial Committee of Privy Council, composed of nine members, not applying earlier House of Lords' decision—Whether Privy Council's decision to be preferred

R. v James
R. v Karimi
CA [2006] 1 Cr.App.R. 29

HOMICIDE
Self-defence
Mistaken belief induced by voluntary intoxication—Defendant charged with murder—Self-defence claimed on basis of drunken mistake—Whether entitled to rely on mistake induced by drunkenness

R. v Hatton
CA [2006] 1 Cr.App.R. 16

INCITEMENT
Incitement to commit buggery
Defendant convicted of inciting boy under 14 to commit buggery—Incitement occurring prior to abrogation of irrebuttable presumption that boy under 14 incapable of sexual intercourse—Whether offence committed—Whether mens rea of incitee relevant

R. v Claydon
CA [2006] 1 Cr.App.R. 20

JURY
  Panel
  *Police officer or prosecuting solicitor serving as juro—Whether breaching
  defendant's right to fair trial—Whether leading to perception of bias—
  Juries Act 1974 (c. 23), s.1 (as substituted by Criminal Justice Act 2003
  (c.44), s. 321, Sch.33)—Human Rights Act 1998, Sch.I, Pt.1, Art.6(1)*
                                                                R. v Abdroikov
                                                                    R. v Green
                                                               R. v Williamson
                                                      CA [2006] 1 Cr.App.R. 1

NUISANCE
  Public nuisance
  *Common law offence—Whether offence still existing—Whether definition
  complying with requirements of certainty—Whether separate acts against
  different individuals capable of constituting public nuisance—Whether
  foreseeability of actual nuisance necessary—Human Rights Act 1998
  (c.42) Sch.I, Pt 1, Art.7(1)*
                                                              R. v Rimmington
                                                                R. v Goldstein
                                                     CA [2006] 1 Cr.App.R. 17

PUBLIC ORDER
  Racially aggravated offence
  *Appellant acting aggressively and calling Spanish women "bloody
  foreigners"—Appellant charged with racially aggravated abusive or insulting words or behaviour—Whether "foreigners" describing racial group—
  Whether words used capable of demonstrating hostility towards victims
  based on membership of racial group—Crime and Disorder Act 1998
  (c.37), ss.28(4), 31(1)(a)*
                                                           R. v Rogers (Philip)
                                                     CA [2006] 1 Cr.App.R. 14

RIGHT TO REMAIN SILENT AT TRIAL
  Direction to jury as to inferences
  *Judge ruling that defendant's imputations on character of prosecution wit-
  nesses entitled prosecution, should the defendant give evidence, to cross-
  examine him as to previous convictions—Defendant electing not to give evidence—Judge directing jury that they could if they thought it proper draw
  the inference that the only sensible reason for silence at trial was that the*

defendant could not give an answer to, or explanation of, the prosecution evidence, or none that would withstand cross-examination—Whether judge entitled to give such direction—Whether judge ought to direct jury that the defendant could have been motivated by reasons other than inability to explain or answer the prosecution case—Criminal Evidence Act 1898 (61 & 62 Vict c.36), s.1(3) (as amended by Youth Justice and Criminal Evidence Act 1999 (c.23), s.67(1), Sch.4, para.1(1)(7))—Criminal Justice and Public Order Act 1994 (c.33), s.35

R. v Becouarn
HL [2006] 1 Cr.App.R. 2

ROAD TRAFFIC
Dangerous driving
Causing death by—Evidence of drug consumption—Whether admissible—Whether quantitative evidence necessary—Whether necessary to establish likely or actual adverse effect on driver

R. v Pleydell
CA [2006] 1 Cr.App.R. 12

SEXUAL OFFENCES
Indecent assault
Appellant charged with rape of 14-year-old girl—Consensual sexual intercourse admitted—Prosecution for unlawful sexual intercourse time-barred—Alternative verdict of indecent assault based on admitted conduct left to jury—Whether lawful—Sexual Offences Act 1956 (4 & 5 Eliz. 2, c. 69), ss.6(1), 14, Sch.2, para.10(a)—Criminal Law Act 1967 (c.58), s.6(3)

R. v Timmins
CA [2006] 1 Cr.App.R. 18

SEXUAL OFFENCES
Indecent assault
Conduct offence under old and new statutes—Uncertain whether occurring before or after new statute coming into force—Practice to be followed in framing indictment—Sexual Offences Act 1956 (4 & 5 Eliz. 2, (c.69)), s.14—Sexual Offences Act 2003 (c.42), s.9(1)—Sexual Offences Act 2003 (Commencement) Order 2004 (SI 2004/874)

R. v A (Prosecutor's Appeal)
CA [2006] 1 Cr.App.R. 28

SEXUAL OFFENCES

Notification requirements

Defendant as young person convicted of sexual offence and sentenced to detention and training order—Defendant subject to notification require-ments—Relevant notification period—Whether whole term of detention and training order "equivalent" to sentence of imprisonment—Whether defendant failing to register within period—Sexual Offences Act 2003 (c.42), ss.82, 131(a)

R. v Slocombe
CA [2006] 1 Cr.App.R. 33

SHIPPING

Injury to another

Liability for—Defendant's jet ski colliding with another causing serious injury—Whether jet ski "vessel"—Whether "used in navigation"—Whether defendant "master of ship"—Whether guilty of offence under ship-ping Act—Merchant Shipping Act 1995 (c.21), ss.58(2), 313(3)

R. v Goodwin
CA [2006] 1 Cr.App.R. 22

R. v ABDROIKOV
R. v GREEN
R. v WILLIAMSON

COURT OF APPEAL (Lord Chief Justice (Lord Woolf), Mr Justice
Richards and Mr Justice Henriques): June 30; July 28, 2005

[2005] EWCA Crim 1986; [2006] 1 Cr.App.R. 1

(LT) Crown Prosecution Service; Exclusion; Impartiality; Juries; Police officers;
Right to fair and public hearings

H1   JURY
      Panel
      *Police officer or prosecuting solicitor serving as juror—Whether breaching
      defendant's right to fair trial—Whether leading to perception of bias—Juries
      Act 1974 (c.23), s.1 (as substituted by Criminal Justice Act 2003 (c.44), s.321,
      Sch.33)—Human Rights Act 1998 (c.42), Sch.I, Pt.1, Art.6(1)*

H2   In the first case, the appellant was charged with attempted murder. At the trial,
      while the jury were in retirement and immediately before they were sent home
      over a bank holiday weekend, the foreman of the jury sent the judge a note in
      which he explained that he was a serving police officer who was due to report
      for duty on the bank holiday Monday, when he might come into contact with
      police officers in the case. As a result of the amendment made to s.1 of the Juries
      Act 1974 by s.321 of, and Sch.33 to, the Criminal Justice Act 2003 police officers
      and other individuals concerned with the administration of justice were eligible
      for jury service. The judge directed the police officer not to report for duty on the
      Monday and he drew the matter to the attention of counsel, although no objection
      was raised concerning the officer's presence on the jury. The appellant was con-
      victed and he appealed on the ground that the presence of a serving police officer
      on the jury had deprived him of a fair trial.

H3   In the second case, the appellant was charged with, and convicted of, assault
      occasioning actual bodily harm and of having an article with a blade or sharp
      point in a public place. Subsequently, his solicitor discovered that on the jury
      which had convicted him had been a police officer who served in the same bor-
      ough as one of the police officers in the case, although the two officers did not
      know each other. The appellant appealed on the ground that the convictions
      were unsafe by reason of the fact that the first police officer had served on the
      jury.

H4   In the third case, the appellant was charged with two counts of rape. At the start
      of the trial, the judge showed counsel a letter from one of the jurors, which
      explained that the juror was a solicitor employed by the Crown Prosecution Ser-

vice. The appellant's counsel objected to the presence of that juror on the jury because he was an employee of the agency which was bringing the prosecution. The judge, having established that the juror did not know any particular member of the Crown Prosecution Service connected with the case, ruled against the objection. The appellant was convicted and he appealed on the ground that the judge's ruling was wrong.

H5   **Held,** dismissing the appeals, that it was necessary to draw a distinction between the eligibility of a person to serve on a jury and the issue of whether a particular eligible person should be prevented from sitting on a particular jury at a particular place. As to eligibility, police officers, members of the prosecution service or other persons involved in the administration of justice should not, because that was their occupation, be automatically regarded as being disqualified from a jury. When they became members of the jury, they served on the jury in the same way as any other member of the public in their capacity as citizens eligible for jury service, and they took the jury oath which made it clear that it was their solemn duty to determine the case on the evidence. If they had no personal knowledge of the defendant or others involved in the trial process, above that of their fellow jurors, they could be expected to comply with the terms of their oath and the directions which the judge would give them. Accordingly, a fair minded and informed observer would not conclude that there was a real possibility that a juror was biased merely because his occupation was one which meant that he was involved in some capacity or other in the administration of justice. The position was, however, different if the juror had a special knowledge either of individuals involved in the case or as to the facts of the case apart from that provided by the evidence. If that was the situation, the juror must draw the matter to the attention of the judge, who should then exercise his discretion to decide whether that juror should become or remain part of the jury. If an issue arose as to whether a juror had knowledge which made him unsuitable to sit on that jury, it was necessary to determine whether, in all the circumstances, the requirements of fairness had been met. However, there was nothing in the particular circumstances of the appellants' cases to give rise to any cause for concern with regard to the presence of a police officer or a solicitor employed by the prosecuting body on the jury and, accordingly, the principle of fairness had not been offended in any of the three cases (post, paras [25]–[37], [47], [66], [73]).

H6   *Per curiam.* In determining whether, in all the circumstances, the requirements of fairness had been met there was no need to distinguish between the position under Art.6 of the Convention for the Protection of Human Rights and Fundamental Freedoms and the position at common law since the approach was now the same in both, at least in the great majority of cases (post, para.[37]).

H7   (For s.1 of the Juries Act 1974, as substituted by s.321 of the Criminal Justice Act 2003, see *Archbold* 2005, para.4–200).

Appeals against conviction

H8 *R. v Abdroikov*

On August 31, 2004 at the Central Criminal Court (Judge Beaumont Q.C., the Common Sergeant of London) the appellant, Nurlon Abdroikov, was convicted of attempted murder (count 1). Verdicts of not guilty were entered on the alternative counts of attempting to choke (count 2) and making a threat to kill (count 3). He then pleaded guilty to a further offence of attempting to choke a different victim (count 5). On November 19, 2004 the appellant was sentenced to 11 years' imprisonment on count 1 and a consecutive term of five years' imprisonment on count 5, making a total term of 16 years' imprisonment. He was recommended for deportation. At the hearing he was granted leave to appeal against conviction on the ground that the presence of a serving police officer on the jury deprived him of a fair trial.

H9 The facts appear in the judgment of the court.

H10 *R. v Green*

On October 5, 2004, in the Crown Court at Woolwich (Judge Statman) the appellant, Richard John Green, was convicted of assault occasioning actual bodily harm and of having a bladed or pointed article. He was sentenced to concurrent sentences of seven weeks' imprisonment for those offences. At the outset of the hearing he was granted leave on the same ground as Abdroikov.

H11 The facts appear in the judgment of the court.

H12 *R. v Williamson*

On February 3, 2005 in the Crown Court at Warrington (Judge Hale) the appellant, Kenneth Joseph Williamson, was convicted of two counts of rape and sentenced to 10 years' detention in a Young Offender Institution. Leave to appeal against conviction was granted by the full court.

H13 The facts appear in the judgment of the court.

H14 *Richard Carey-Hughes Q.C.* and *Michael Maher* (assigned by the Registrar of Criminal Appeals) for Abdroikov.
Richard Carey-Hughes Q.C. and *Richard Hutchings* (assigned by the Registrar of Criminal Appeals) for Green.
Richard Carey-Hughes Q.C. and *Simon Berkson* (assigned by the Registrar of Criminal Appeals) for Williamson.
Mark Heywood and *Bobbie Cheema* (instructed by the Crown Prosecution Service, Headquarters) for the Crown.

Cur. adv. vult.

July 28. Lord Woolf C.J. handed down the judgment of the court.

Introduction

1 This is a judgment of the court to which all members of the court have contributed.

2   The three appellants, Mr Abdroikov, Mr Green and Mr Williamson appeal to this court against their convictions. There is no factual connection between the circumstances of the offences of which they were convicted. The only link between the appeals is the fact that in the case of each appellant there is a complaint as to the composition of the jury at their respective trials. The jurors to whom objection is taken in the cases of Green and Abdroikov were serving police officers. In the case of Williamson, the objection is taken to a juror who is employed as a prosecuting solicitor by the Crown Prosecution Service (the "CPS").

3   In the case of Abdroikov, the presence of the police officer on the jury was only revealed by a note from the jury which referred to the fact of the presence of the police officer. The note was handed to the judge during the jury's retirement.

4   In the case of Green, the presence of a police officer on the jury was discovered inadvertently by a solicitor acting for the defendant sometime after the trial was over.

5   In the case of Williamson, the solicitor sent a letter to the court setting out his position. The letter was drawn to the attention of counsel appearing on behalf of Williamson. The counsel objected to the presence of that juror on the jury for cause because he was an employee of an agency which was bringing the prosecution. The trial judge ruled against the objection. Williamson contends that the ruling was wrong.

6   Before considering the merits of the individual appeals further, we will consider the issue of when those whose occupation is within the criminal justice system should be empanelled as members of juries.

The statutory provisions

7   Prior to the coming into force of the relevant provisions of the Criminal Justice Act 2003 ("the 2003 Act"), the presence of the two police officers and the employee of the CPS would have been unlawful under s.1 of the Juries Act 1974 ("the 1974 Act") which provides:

> "Subject to the provisions of this Act, every person shall be qualified to serve as a juror in the Crown Court, the High Court and county courts and be liable accordingly to attend for jury service when summoned under this Act, if—
>> (a) he is for the time being registered as a parliamentary or local government elector and is not less than eighteen nor more than [seventy] years of age; and
>> (b) he has been ordinarily resident in the United Kingdom, the Channel Islands or the Isle of Man for any period of at least five years since attaining the age of thirteen,
> but not if he is for the time being ineligible or disqualified for jury service; and the persons who are ineligible, and those who are disqualified, are those respectively listed in Parts I and II of Schedule 1 to this Act."

8   Parts I and II of Sch.1 contain 4 groups, (Groups A, B, C and D). Group A identified different members of the judiciary who are or had at any time been such a
member of the judiciary as ineligible. Group B identified others concerned with
the administration of justice including barristers and solicitors and "a member of
any police force" and any person who at any time within the last 10 years has
been a person falling within any description specified in this Group. Group C
dealt with persons in holy orders and Group D dealt with the ineligibility of mentally disordered persons.

9   Part II sets out the persons who are disqualified, including those who had been
sentenced to specified custodial sentences.

10   Section 321 and Sch.33 of the 2003 Act substituted a new Pt I to Sch.1 of the
1974 Act. This omitted all reference to those who were ineligible for jury service
who fell within Groups A, B and C. Mentally disordered persons are, however,
now not qualified to attend for jury service in consequence of an amendment
to s.1 the 1974 Act. Part II of the new Schedule still disqualifies those who
have received custodial sentences and in addition those on bail in criminal proceedings.

11   The parliamentary intention behind the legislative changes as to eligibility and
liability to attend for jury service is clear. It is to widen significantly the range of
those who are eligible and liable for jury service. This intention is supported by
the limitations which are placed on the discretion of the appropriate officer to
defer jury service. These are now contained in s.9A(2) of the 1974 Act and
apply in particular where a deferral of the attendance of the person summoned
has previously been made or refused under subs. (1) or subs.(1A) of the 1974 Act.

The appellants' general submissions

12   Mr Richard Carey-Hughes Q.C. on behalf of the appellants, contends that it is
axiomatic that a trial must be fair and be seen to be fair and for this to be the situation, the tribunal conducting the trial must be free from actual or apparent bias.
Furthermore, he relies upon Art.6 of the European Convention for the Protection
of Human Rights and Fundamental Freedoms ("the Convention") which provides;

> "In the determination of . . . any criminal charges against him, everyone is
> entitled to a fair and public hearing within a reasonable time by an indepen-
> dent and impartial tribunal established by law."

13   Mr Carey-Hughes relies on s.6(1) and (3) of the Human Rights Act 1998.
Those provisions of the Act provide:

> "(1) It is unlawful for a public authority to act in a way which is incompat-
>   ible with a Convention right.
> (3) In this section 'public authority' includes—
>   a) 'A court or tribunal, and . . .'"

14   These provisions have, however, to be read subject to s.6(2) which provides:

"Sub-section (1) does not apply to an act if—

    a) as the result of one or more provisions of primary legislation, the authority could not have acted differently or

    b) in the case of one or more provisions of, or made under, primary legislation which cannot be read or given effect in a way in which is compatible with the Convention rights, the authority was acting so as to give effect to or enforce those provisions."

15   There is no doubt as to the obligation for a trial to not only be fair but appear to be fair and the need for an independent tribunal to conduct the trials. In addition, the test which is now to be applied is clearly established as being whether the fair minded and informed observer having considered the facts would conclude that there is a real possibility that the tribunal was biased. (See *R. v Gough* (1993) 97 Cr.App.R. 188; [1993] A.C. 646, *Re Medicaments and Related Classes of Goods (No.2)* [2001] 1 W.L.R. 700 at 727 and finally, the speech of Lord Hope of Craighead in *Porter v Magill*, [2002] 2 A.C. 357 at [103].

16   Reliance is also placed upon *Pullar v United Kingdom* (1996) 22 E.H.R.R. 391, in which it was observed that in situations in which juries do not give reasons for their verdicts and where there is a prohibition on investigating what transpired in the jury room "additional emphasis should be placed in the existence of objective guarantees [of impartiality]". Mr Carey-Hughes' concern was not with individuals being "closely connected" with the legal system but with their being "closely connected" with the prosecution. Here, he prays in aid the decision of the House of Lords in *Lawal v Northern Spirit Ltd* [2003] UKHL 35; [2003] I.C.R. 856. In that case, the Appellate Committee of the House of Lords considered the position of a Queen's Counsel appearing on an appeal before the Employment Appeal Tribunal ("EAT"), who had sat as a part-time judge in the EAT with one or both of the lay members hearing that appeal. In giving its considered opinion, the Committee made it clear that "there is now no difference between the common law test of bias and the requirements under Art.6 of the Convention of an independent and impartial tribunal" (para.14). The Committee added that the "public perception of the possibility of unconscious bias is the key" (para.14). The Committee concluded that the practice in the EAT of part-time judges appearing as counsel before a panel of the EAT consisting of one or two lay members with whom they had previously sat should be discontinued. The basis for the Committee's conclusion was that a legally qualified judge when sitting judicially is likely to have particular influence upon lay members because of the role of the EAT, which is to determine questions of law.

17   This is an area where there has been no shortage of reports and reviews. In relation to the position as it existed before the 1974 Act we were referred to the report of the Departmental Committee on jury service, the *Morris Report*, Cmnd.2627 (1965), and the report of the Royal Commission on Criminal Justice 1993 (the Runciman Commission). In addition we have considered the Review of the Criminal Courts of England and Wales (2001) by Auld L.J. and the response of the Criminal Bar Association to that Review. The Auld Review was almost certainly the catalyst for the change in the law. Auld L.J. deals with ineligibility in his

Review at para.27 of c.5. The whole of his remarks on the subject is highly relevant but we draw particular attention to paras 30 and 31 of c.5 which are in these
terms:

> 30. "There is also the anxiety voiced by some that those closely connected
> with the criminal justice system, for example, a policeman or a prosecutor,
> would not approach the case with the same openness of mind as someone
> unconnected with the legal system. I do not know why the undoubted risk
> of prejudice of that sort should be any greater than in the case of many others
> who are not excluded from juries and who are trusted to put aside any pre-
> judices they may have. Take, for example shopkeepers or house-owners
> who may have been burgled, or car owners whose cars may have been van-
> dalised, many government and other employees concerned in one way or
> another with public welfare and people with strong views on various contro-
> versial issues, such as legalisation of drugs or euthanasia. I acknowledge
> that there may be Article 6 considerations in this. But it would be for the
> judge in each case to satisfy himself that the potential juror in question
> was not likely to engender any reasonable suspicion or apprehension of
> bias so as to distinguish him from other members of the public who
> would normally be expected to have an interest in upholding the law. Pro-
> vided that the judge was so satisfied, the over-all fairness of the tribunal
> and of the trial should not be at risk.
>
> 31. As I have said, I consider that there is a strong case for removal of all the
> categories of ineligibility based on occupation. My one reservation has been
> as to judges. I say that, not because I consider that they are too grand for the
> task or that their work is so important that they could not be spared for it. On
> the contrary, I consider that it would be good for them and the system of jury
> trial if they could experience at first hand what jurors have to put up with. In
> particular, it would surely help them see how well or badly they and all those
> concerned in the process assist jurors in their task. And I have been hear-
> tened by the knowledge that judges have sat on juries or been potential
> jurors in the USA. A number have spoken warmly of the experience.
> They include Judith S Kaye, the Chief Judge of the State of New York,
> Shirley Abrahamson, Chief Justice of the Wisconsin Supreme Court and
> Justice Breyer, of the Supreme Court of the USA who gave an account at
> the American Bar Association Meeting in London in July 2000 of his jury
> service."

The case for the Crown

18   In his submission on behalf of the Crown, not surprisingly, Mr Heywood relied
on the clear language of the amendments made by the 2003 Act. He submits that
these were changes made by the democratically elected legislature for the legitimate purpose of maximising the pool of responsible and professional people
available to perform the important civic function of serving on a jury. He submits
that a fair trial is best achieved by random selection, provided that safeguards
exist to guarantee objective impartiality. It is his contention that there is no objec-

tion in principle to either a police officer or a crown prosecution service employee serving on a jury in a criminal trial. Furthermore, there is no actual partiality established in the case of any of the three jurors, who are the subject of these appeals. Their impartiality should therefore be assumed.

19   Mr Heywood also points to the power of the Lord Chancellor to issue guidance as to the manner in which the functions of the appropriate officer (summoning officer) under s.9 and 9A of the 1974 Act as amended are to be exercised. Mr Heywood relies in particular on para.4 and para.18 of the guidance ("Guidance for summoning officers when considering deferral and excusal applications" *www.hmcourts-service.gov.uk/courtfinder/forms/jury_summoning_guidance.pdf*) which was issued. The guidance is in these terms:

> "4. The normal expectation is that *everyone* summoned for jury service will serve at the time for which they are summoned. It is recognised that there will be occasions where it is not reasonable for a person summoned to serve at the time for which they are summoned, in such circumstances, the summoning officer should use his or her discretion to defer the individual to a time more appropriate. Only in extreme circumstances, should a person be excused from jury service.
> *The summoning officer exercising his discretion should observe the following principles . . .*
> 18. Members of the judiciary or those involved in the administration of justice who apply for excusal or deferral on grounds that they may be known to a party or parties involved in the trial should normally be deferred or moved to an alternative court where the excusal grounds may not exist. If this is not possible, then they should be excused. Paragraph 4 (above) applies"

20   Mr Heywood relies on s.12 of the 1974 Act. Section 12(1) gives the judge the right to determine any challenge for cause of a juror. He also refers to the residual discretion of the judge at common law which was explained by Lord Lane C.J. in *R. v Ford* (1989) 89 Cr.App.R. 278 at 280:

> "At common law a judge has a residual discretion to discharge a particular juror who ought not to be serving on the jury. This is part of the judge's duty to ensure that there is a fair trial. It is based on the duty of the judge expressed by Lord Campbell C.J., in *Mansell* (1857) 8 E. & B. 54."

21   As Mr Heywood points out, the common law power to challenge is clearly restricted. However, it is to be remembered that Lord Lane's judgment was given in a case decided before the Human Rights Act 1998 came into force.

22   Having referred to ss.3 and 6 of the Human Rights Act 1998 and Art.6 of the Convention, Mr Heywood contends that the case law of the the European Court of Human Rights does not provide grounds for the conclusion that in the absence of evidence of subjective partiality and an established connection between a juror and a party an involvement in the administration of justice will, of itself, give rise to a finding of objective impartiality, still less that the holding of an office or occupation connected to the administration of justice will do so. In this connection, he refers to *Crummock (Scotland) Ltd v HM Advocate* The Times,

May 9, 2000 and *Pullar v United Kingdom* (1996) 22 E.H.R.R. 391. He also refers to Lord Rodger of Earlsferry's speech in *R..v Mirza* [2004] UKHL 2; [2004] 2 Cr.App.R. 8 (p.112); [2004] 1 A.C. 1118 at [152] where he said:

> "The risk that those chosen as jurors may be prejudiced in various ways is, and always has been, inherent in trial by jury. Indeed, only the most foolish would deny that judges too may be prejudiced, whether, for example, in favour of a pretty woman or a handsome man, or against one whose dress, general demeanour or lifestyle offends. The legal system does not ignore these risks: indeed it constantly guards against them. It works, however, on the basis that, in general, the training of professional judges and the judicial oath that they take mean that they can and do set their prejudices on one side when judging a case. Similarly, the law supposes that, when called upon to exercise judgment in the special circumstances of a trial, in general, jurors can and do set their prejudices aside and act impartially. The recognised starting-point is, therefore, that all the individual members of a jury are presumed to be impartial until there is proof to the contrary."

23   The safeguards that Mr Heywood relies on also include:

a) The random selection process to which we have already referred;
b) The guidance given to prospective jurors from a number of sources making clear the juror's responsibility to draw to the attention of a judge where, during a trial, a juror recognises the defendant or witness or the judge, an advocate or solicitor.

In addition Mr Heywood refers to the guidance contained in a video recording shown to jurors on the first day of their service and the guidance which was issued by the Metropolitan Police's Assistant Commissioner on May 10, 2004 the effect of which is that, where possible, police officers should not "attend a court where their operational command unit is situated".

Our general conclusions

24   No complaint can be made as to the manner of selecting the members of the jury thought to be eligible based on the literal meaning of the legislation. The panel was selected to be summoned randomly by a computer system installed at the Jury Central Summoning Bureau. This was about the most random method of selection that could be devised. The original summoning is then followed by ballot from among those summoned to attend the court.

25   We emphasise that it is necessary to draw a distinction between the eligibility of a person to serve on a jury and the issue of whether a particular eligible person should be prevented from sitting on a particular jury at a particular place. As to eligibility, we reject a suggestion that police officers, members of the prosecution service or other persons involved in the administration of justice, including judges, should, because this is their occupation, be automatically regarded as being disqualified from a jury. Our initial view that their service on the jury could be undesirable is conditioned by the fact that traditionally, the holders of these occu-

pations have not been eligible for jury service. But approaching the question of their eligibility from first principle, there appear to be few reasons why, in general, they should be excluded from the obligation of the public generally to shoulder the important responsibility of sitting on a jury.

26   The first reason for exclusion is that the juror's involvement in the justice system means the juror would know more about the workings of the court systems than would a normal citizen. In particular, they might be in a position to draw inferences that other members of the jury who did not share the same occupation would not be able to draw. For example, they might be able to infer that a defendant had previous convictions when a less well informed member of the jury would not be able to draw that inference. The other reason is that, because of their occupation, they may be able to play an unduly dominant role in the jury's deliberations. The third reason is that, because of their close connection with the criminal justice system, they might not approach the case with the same open-mindedness of someone unconnected with the legal system.

27   As to these reasons, we share the same view as Auld L.J. in his report. They do not in themselves justify concluding that individuals should be disqualified from being among the members of the jury by reason of their occupation alone. The starting point for our conclusion is that, when they become members of the jury, they are not becoming members of the jury in their capacity as policeman or a prosecuting solicitor. Having been randomly selected, they serve on the jury in the same way as any other member of the public in their capacity as a citizen eligible for jury service. They then take the jury oath which makes it clear that it is their solemn duty to determine the case on the evidence. Furthermore, like other juries, they will hear the judge direct them clearly as to what is their role and that they must decide the case only on the evidence. If they have no personal knowledge of the defendant or others involved in the trial process, above that of their fellow jurors, they can be expected to comply with the terms of their oath and the directions which the judge will give them. They will have to disregard matters which are irrelevant, but that is the requirement for any juror.

28   Their special knowledge of the criminal justice system could mean that they could draw inferences, but the guidance which they receive both before they become members of the jury and after they have become members of the jury should avoid their using their knowledge of the system in a way which is unfair to the defendant.

29   We, of course, accept the danger of a juror being unconsciously prejudiced. However, with any juror, there is a danger of having prejudices. The variety of prejudices that jurors can have are almost unlimited

30   The fact that there are 12 members of the jury of which at least 10 must be agreed is a real protection against the prejudices of an individual juror resulting in unfairness to a defendant. In addition, it is to be hoped and expected, that those who are employed in the administration of justice will be particularly careful not to act in a manner which is inconsistent with their duty as members of the jury and in particular, to exercise the independence of mind which is required of all jurors and to be on their guard to reach their verdict only on the evidence in accordance with the directions from the trial judge. It is our view that a fair minded and

informed observer would not conclude that there was a real possibility that a juror was biased merely because his occupation was one which meant that he was involved in some capacity or other in the administration of justice.

31   As to an individual because of his occupation unduly dominating a jury, again our view is the same as that of Auld L.J. for the reasons he gives. We do not believe that today, a juror would or might have an unacceptable influence on his fellow jurors because of his occupation. In some cases were the jury to become aware of the occupation of a juror as a policeman or some other occupation involved in the administration of justice, it could reduce rather than increase his influence on his fellow jurors. It is to be remembered that a trial judge usually appreciates that there is at least a risk that the jury might draw an inference as to the judge's view on the innocence or guilt of the accused and for that reason, he warns the jury that if they draw any such inference, they should put it out of their mind if they disagree with it because their decision on the facts is the critical decision.

32   Of course, there will always be risks that any juror will depart from his or her solemn duty, but the system cannot work on the basis that this risk can be excluded. Justice systems can only strive for perfect fairness but it would be foolish not to recognise there will be occasions when it is actually not achieved. Despite this shortcoming, which is inherent in any system dependent upon individuals' decision, in this jurisdiction, the view of the public generally is that normally, the jury trial is the fairest form of trial available. We have great faith in the ability of 12 persons randomly selected, and properly directed, to provide justice in the generality of cases.

33   The position is, however, different if the juror has a special knowledge either of individuals involved in the case or as to the facts of the case apart from that provided by the evidence. If this is the situation, it is now clearly recognised that the juror must draw the matter to the attention of the judge. Here, we commend the fact that the recorded video shown to jurors immediately before their service commences contains under the sub-title "The Trial", the following words:

> "Once the jury has been selected the court clerk will read out the charges made against the defendant. If you realise that you know anyone or have any other connection with the trial on which you are serving, please tell the usher immediately."

This is followed by the presenter stating:

> "It is vital that your opinion is based purely on what you see and hear both within the courtroom and you are not influenced by any outside factors. Please don't discuss any details of the trial with anyone other than your fellow jurors, not even members of your family and please don't remove any items of evidence or notes from the courtroom. It is very important that if anyone approaches you about the trial or tries to influence you in any way, you do not discuss it with any member of your jury and tell the jury officer or usher immediately."

34   This recording was introduced in June 2005 and would not have been used at the time of the trials which are the subject of these appeals. The earlier form of video which would have been in use at the time of the trial was not significantly different. In particular, it concluded by saying "Remember, if you know anyone involved in the case, tell a court official immediately".

35   It is our view that the general advice provided to jurors should be adequate to draw to their attention the need to alert the court if they have any special knowledge. Further guidance is, however, desirable and has been provided for those involved in the administration of justice to avoid them being summoned to appear at courts where the likelihood of their being well known to those connected with the trial is undesirably high.

36   It is obviously good sense to try and avoid situations where the suitability of a juror to sit on a particular trial will be likely to be questioned. If despite this a situation does arise where a juror knows those taking part in the proceedings, then the judge in the normal way should exercise the discretion he has to decide whether that juror should become or remain part of the jury.

37   If an issue arises as to whether, despite the precautions that are taken, a member of the jury has knowledge which makes him or her unsuitable to sit on that jury, the usual test as indicated by Lord Hope in the *Porter* case has to be applied in all the circumstances to determine whether the requirements of fairness have been met or not. In making that determination, there is no need to distinguish between the position under Art.6 and the position at common law. In our understanding, the approach is now the same in both, at least in the great majority of cases.

38   We turn now first to the case of Abdroikov and then to the appeals of Green and Williamson.

Nurlon Abdroikov

39   The indictment against the appellant Nurlon Abdroikov charged him with offences against two separate victims. Counts 1 to 4 related to an incident on April 14, 2002 when a man called Nicholas Faulkner met him and invited him back home. The appellant attacked Mr Faulkner in the bedroom and tied him up on the bed. Mr Faulkner fell to the floor while attempting to escape. The appellant then pushed a duvet into his face and smothered him, at the same saying "I am going to kill you". Mr Faulkner lost consciousness. When he woke up, the appellant punched him about the head and body, repeating the threat "I am going to kill you". He took Mr Faulkner's belt and used this to strangle him, while asking him to hand over his credit cards and threatening to kill him. He stood on Mr Faulkner's shoulders to tighten the belt. Mr Faulkner lost consciousness again. Upon regaining consciousness he discovered that personal property from his flat had been stolen. The attack on Mr Faulkner was charged as attempted murder (count 1), with alternative counts of attempting to choke (count 2) and making a threat to kill (count 3). There was a separate count of theft in relation to the personal property (count 4).

40   Counts 5 to 7 related to an incident on August 31, 2002 when a woman called P was walking home at about 5am. The appellant grabbed her from behind, took

hold of her neck and punched her about the face, while threatening her by saying "I will kill you, I want to rape you". He dragged her into the next road. Although still forcibly holding her, he then entered into a conversation with her and offered her a cigarette. He said that if she allowed him to have sex with her he would let her go. When she refused, he continued to talk to her. She attempted to escape but was punched again around the neck. A passer-by then walked up to them and the appellant left the scene. The attack on Mrs P was charged as an offence contrary to s.21 of the Offences against the Person Act 1861, namely an attempt to choke, suffocate or strangle with intent to enable an indecent assault (count 5), with alternative counts of indecent assault (count 6) and making a threat to kill (count 7).

41   The proceedings took a somewhat complex course. First, in February 2003, the appellant pleaded guilty to the count of theft (count 4). Then, in February 2004, he pleaded guilty to making a threat to kill Mr Faulkner (count 3) and attempted choking of Mrs P (count 5). The Crown decided to accept those pleas and not to pursue the other matters to trial. When the appellant was seen by a probation officer for the purpose of preparing a pre-sentence report, however, the account he gave to her made it clear that his pleas to counts 3 and 5 were equivocal. He was subsequently allowed to change those pleas and the case was listed for trial. It was ordered that counts 1 to 3 be tried first.

42   Following a trial at the Central Criminal Court before the Common Sergeant of London (Judge Beaumont) and a jury, on August 31, 2004 the appellant was convicted on count 1. Verdicts of not guilty were returned on the alternative counts 2 and 3. The appellant then entered a plea of guilty to count 5, making a further trial unnecessary. Counts 6 and 7 were ordered to lie on the file.

43   On November 19, 2004 the appellant was sentenced to a term of 11 years' imprisonment on count 1 and a consecutive term of five years' imprisonment on count 5, making a total term of 16 years. No separate penalty was imposed on count 4. He was also recommended for deportation.

44   The matter came before this court by way of a renewed application for leave to appeal against conviction, following refusal of leave by the single judge, and an appeal against sentence by leave of the single judge. At the hearing we granted leave to appeal against conviction on the one ground that the presence of a serving police officer on the jury deprived the appellant of a fair trial. We refused leave on the remaining grounds.

45   The fact that there was a police officer on the jury came to light because, while the jury were in retirement and immediately before they were sent home over a bank holiday weekend, the foreman sent the judge a note in which he explained that he was a serving police officer and was due to report for duty on the bank holiday Monday, during the course of which he might come into contact with officers in the case. He sought guidance. The judge directed him not to report for duty on that day. The matter was drawn to the attention of counsel at the time and no objection was raised concerning the police officer's presence on the jury.

46   In contending before us that the presence of the police officer on the jury made the trial unfair, Mr Carey-Hughes relied on the general arguments that we have already considered. He accepted that the officer concerned had behaved respon-

sibly in sending the note he did to the judge. He also accepted that the case did not involve any major issue between the appellant and the police. He drew our attention, however, to one matter of dispute. The appellant admitted having tied up Mr Faulkner by the hands, but denied having also tied him by the feet. A woman police officer gave evidence that she had seen indentations around Mr Faulkner's lower legs as if he had been bound there. The defence case was that those markings were not visible in the photographs and the officer had exaggerated her account.

47   In our judgment there was nothing in the particular circumstances of the case to give rise to any cause for concern with regard to the presence of a police officer on the jury. The case falls squarely within the general issues of principle discussed above. Accordingly, our conclusion that the presence of a police officer on a jury does not in itself offend the principles of fairness leads us to dismiss Mr Abdroikov's appeal against conviction.

48   We should also mention briefly the grounds of appeal in respect of which we refused the renewed application for leave.

49   First, the probation officer who saw the appellant for the purpose of preparing a pre-sentence report following the original (subsequently vacated) pleas of guilty was called as a prosecution witness at trial to give evidence that the appellant had given her an account that was inconsistent with his case at trial. There was no dispute about the admissibility of her evidence. But as a result of her cross-examination and of evidence then given by the appellant, the jury came to learn of the appellant's previous pleas of guilty. The appellant himself told the jury that he had pleaded guilty to making threats to kill Mr Faulkner, seeking to explain it away as part of a "deal" with the prosecution whereby the more serious allegations in counts 1 and 2 were not proceeded with.

50   The judge ruled that it would be unfair to Mr Faulkner to leave matters as they were, owing to the risk that the jury might think that in agreeing to a deal at the time of the appellant's original pleas the prosecution had been making a judgment about the credibility of Mr Faulkner. The judge dealt with this by explaining to the jury, both at the time when the matter arose and in his summing up, that in February 2004 the appellant had been facing two sets of charges, one in relation to Mr Faulkner and one in relation to another person; he had pleaded guilty to one charge in relation to each; the prosecution had to decide whether it was in the public interest in those circumstances to proceed with jury trials; it had then become clear in the probation officer's interview of the appellant that he was saying to her that he was not guilty of either offence; and the judge had therefore allowed the pleas to be withdrawn, so that the charges in relation to Mr Faulkner were now before this jury and the charges in relation to the other person would have to be considered by another jury at another time. The judge emphasised to the jury that they should regard the appellant as innocent of those other charges and should not speculate about them.

51   Mr Carey-Hughes submitted that the way in which the judge dealt with the matter was unfair and prejudicial to the appellant and rendered his conviction on count 1 unsafe. The jury should not have been told that the prosecution had decided on the earlier occasion not to proceed with counts 1 and 2 only because the appellant

had pleaded guilty to something else. The jury should either have been directed to ignore the evidence about the deal or should have been discharged.

52   We reject those submissions. We are satisfied that the situation that arose, unfortunate and difficult though it was, did not call for the discharge of the jury. In dealing with it by the directions he gave the jury, the judge struck a fair balance between the interests of the prosecution and the interests of the defence. He ensured that the jury were not misled, but equally ensured that they did not speculate about the other charges or hold them against the appellant.

53   The other ground of appeal against conviction was that the judge was wrong to reject a submission of no case to answer on count 1. It was submitted that there was no evidence upon which the jury could find an intention to kill, as opposed to an intention to frighten the victim. We disagree. In our judgment there was plainly sufficient evidence for the issue to be left to the jury.

54   That brings us to the appeal against sentence. Although points were made about the individual components of the sentence, the main thrust of the submissions on the appellant's behalf was that an overall term of 16 years' imprisonment did not properly reflect the principle of totality.

55   On that one issue we find ourselves in agreement with the case advanced for the appellant. This was not an easy matter for the judge, given the seriousness of each of the separate offences for which the appellant fell to be sentenced. If either sentence had stood alone, we do not think that there would be any basis for interfering with it. We have reached the conclusion, however, that an overall term of 16 years for the two offences together was somewhat too long. In our judgment an appropriate overall term would have been 14 years. In order to produce that outcome, we allow the appeal against sentence to the extent of substituting a sentence of nine years' imprisonment for the sentence of 11 years on count 1, leaving in place the consecutive sentence of five years' imprisonment on count 5.

Richard John Green

56   Richard Green was convicted on two Counts at the Woolwich Crown Court on October 5, 2004. He was sentenced to concurrent sentences of seven weeks' imprisonment for offences of assault occasioning actual bodily harm and having a bladed or pointed article. We granted leave to appeal at the outset of the hearing. The appeal raises the same point as that in Abdroikov, namely whether the presence of a police officer on the jury made the trial fair.

57   The two counts arose from the same incident, which took place on March 18, 2004. Richard Green was seen in a public area by two police officers one of whom was Police Sergeant Burgess who suspected that Mr Green might be intending to steal a wheel from a wrecked car. He informed Mr Green that he was to be searched for articles for use in committing theft.

58   Police Sergeant Burgess then asked Mr Green if he had anything he should not have on his person. Mr Green handed over a plastic bag full of sterilized needles. Police Sergeant Burgess again asked if Mr Green had anything "he should know about" to which Mr Green replied "no". When Police Sergeant Burgess went to

put his hand into one of Mr Green's pockets the Sergeant pricked himself on a needle causing him to bleed.

59   Mr Green's defence to having a pointed article was that he did so "for good reason". He was a drug addict and had obtained all the needles, including the one in his pocket, for a project run by an NHS Trust. He had used the needle in his pocket to inject himself with heroin—something he would normally do in private as he had felt ill.

60   As regards the assault occasioning actual bodily harm, Mr Green's case was that he had completely forgotten the needle was in his pocket. When he had been asked by the Sergeant whether there was anything further he had on him that the Sergeant should know about he had replied "No". Sergeant Burgess then immediately went towards Mr Green to search him denying Mr Green the opportunity to search himself as he would have done, which would have obviated the danger of Sergeant Burgess pricking himself.

61   There was thus a factual issue to be determined as between the Police Sergeant and the appellant Richard Green. Unbeknown to the appellant and his legal advisors there was serving upon the jury a police officer, one PC Mason. This fact only came to the notice of the appellant's solicitors several weeks after the conviction when by accident his solicitor learned of the fact whilst visiting a police station.

62   The sole ground of appeal was that the convictions were unsafe by reason of the fact that a police officer was serving on the jury, that he was a serving police officer in the same borough as Sergeant Burgess and that there was a real danger of bias. Mr Carey-Hughes submitted that there was a significant issue between Mr Green and Sergeant Burgess crucial to the element of recklessness and foresight, which lay at the heart of the appellant's case. The crux of the case as it impacted upon the subjective element of recklessness was whether Mr Green was aware that he had the needle in his pocket. Evidence was received from the officer as to what Mr Green said, which was contradicted by Mr Green's own account. The credibility of Sergeant Burgess was therefore of the utmost importance, as was the credibility of Mr Green. Mr Heywood for his part, whilst acknowledging the existence of such an issue, chose to describe it as a narrow issue.

63   The following are agreed facts:

(i) Sergeant Burgess served at Thamesmead Police Station in the Royal Borough of Greenwich from February 2000 until his transfer to the Borough of Sutton in April 2004. PC Mason completed his initial training at Hendon in 2003. He was transferred to the Royal Borough of Greenwich and undertook his Street Duties Course, which entailed his spending some time at each of the Police Stations in the Borough. In June 2003, after completing his course, PC Mason was posted to Eltham Police Station and has worked there since.

(ii) We have read a statement from Sergeant Burgess indicating that he did not recognise any juror as being a police officer and a further statement indicating that he did not know a police officer by the name of James Mason and had never met anyone by that name in the police service.

64   In contending before us that the presence of the police officer on the jury made
the trial unfair, Mr Carey-Hughes stressed the issue between the appellant and
Sergeant Burgess and pointed to the fact that both PC Mason and Sergeant Burgess had served in the same Borough at the same time. He submitted that a fair
minded and informed observer would conclude that there was a real possibility
or real danger that the jury were or would be biased.

65   Mr Heywood was not able to tell us how it came about that PC Mason served in
a jury hearing such a case having regard to the written guidance issued to the
Metropolitan Police Service by the Assistant Commissioner (Human Resources)
indicating that "where possible, police officers should not attend the Court where
their Operational Command Unit commits its work". However, Mr Heywood
invited us to conclude that since neither had met or knew one another there
was no evidence whatsoever of any personal partiality and thus the impartiality
of PC Mason was therefore to be presumed. There was no evidence that the juror
ignored instructions or improperly failed to alert the court to any relevant matter.
The jury was directed to decide the case only according to the evidence they had
heard, to put aside sympathies and to treat the Defendant's evidence in no different way. Mr Heywood submitted there was no sufficient basis upon which to
conclude that the applicant's fears as to impartiality were objectively justified.

66   In our judgment there was nothing in the particular circumstances of this case
to give any continuing cause for concern with regard to the presence of PC Mason
on the jury. Having satisfied ourselves that the two police officers were not
known to one another, we fall back on the conclusion discussed above, namely
that the presence of a police officer on a jury does not in itself offend the principles of fairness and thus we dismiss Mr Green's appeal against conviction.

Kenneth Joseph Williamson

67   The facts can be stated quite briefly. We granted leave to appeal against conviction. On February 3, 2005 in the Crown Court of Warrington the appellant was
convicted of 2 counts of rape and sentenced to 10 years' detention in a Young
Offender Institution.

68   The allegation was that the appellant, having obtained a key to the complainant's home, lay in wait and entered her home late at night shortly after the
complainant had returned. He entered her bedroom, threatened her with a
knife and raped her vaginally and anally. When interviewed the appellant denied
having intercourse with the complainant and denied going to the house that night.
Subsequently a full DNA profile obtained from semen from the complainant's
underwear matched the appellant's. At trial he admitted lying in interview, saying
it was attributable to shock at being arrested, and alleged consent.

69   Summonsed for jury service was a solicitor serving in the Crown Prosecution
Service by the name of Martin McKay-Smith. He wrote a letter addressed to
H.H.the Judge sitting at Warrington Crown Court. It reads:

> "Your Honour,
> I have been summonsed as a member of the jury to serve at Warrington from
> 31st January. I am eligible to do so following the changes brought about by
> the Criminal Justice Act 2003.

I work for the Crown Prosecution Service and have done so since its incep-
tion in 1986. Prior to that I worked for the Greater Manchester Council as a
prosecuting solicitor, having been in private practice as a solicitor for five
years in Nottingham and Chester before that.

I am a Higher Court Advocate and have practised as such in many local
courts including this one since 1998, on behalf of the Crown. I have not however conducted a trial in the Crown Court, despite preparation for two,
which were not able to proceed.

At present I work for the arm of the service, which advises police on charging out of office hours. On 30th of January I was so engaged and will be
doing so again from 1700 on the 31st January.

As a matter of policy, the CPS has asked those summoned to ensure the
Judge has all the necessary information to hand in order to exercise discretion as to the feasibility of the individual serving.

Hence this letter, which can be amplified if your Honour requires it.

Yours faithfully

Martin McKay-Smith, Solicitor, Crown Prosecution Service"

70   When Mr McKay-Smith was called to sit on the jury the trial judge handed the
letter to defence counsel who took instructions from his lay client and thereafter
upon instructions he sought to challenge the juror for cause asserting that there
would be some presumed or actual partiality in the juror by reason of his employment. The challenge was rejected by the judge on the basis that there was nothing
to prevent the juror from sitting by law. He did not know any particular member of
the CPS connected with the case. If this juror was not allowed to sit then no member of the CPS could sit on any jury and that was not what Parliament had clearly
intended. Apart from Mr McKay-Smith's sitting on the jury no other complaint is
made.

71   Mr Carey-Hughes submitted that in the case of a prosecution brought by the
Crown Prosecution Service the presence on a jury of a person employed by the
Service itself evidently causes the case to fail the test in relation to bias.

72   Mr Heywood submitted that there was no basis at all for a claim of personal
partiality (as was conceded). The issue in the case was a stark dispute of fact
between complainant and defendant. The juror properly raised the matter according to the issued guidance thereby permitting the defendant to make submissions
and the trial judge to rule on all of the facts then known.

73   In the circumstances there was no basis upon which to allege objective impartiality and no basis upon which to contend that fears as to impartiality could be
objectively justified. Having concluded that the presence of a CPS employee
on a jury does not itself offend the principle of fairness we dismiss
Mr Williamson's appeal against conviction.

Appeals against conviction dismissed.
Abdroikov's appeal against sentence allowed.

R. v BECOUARN

House of Lords (Lord Steyn, Lord Hoffmann, Lord Hope of
Craighead, Lord Scott of Foscote and Lord Carswell):
June 16; July 28, 2005

[2005] UKHL 55; [2006] 1 Cr.App.R. 2

(LT) Adverse inferences; Character; JSB specimen directions; Lucas directions;
Previous Convictions; Right to Silence

H1 RIGHT TO REMAIN SILENT AT TRIAL
   Direction to jury as to inferences
   Judge ruling that defendant's imputations on character of prosecution witnesses entitled prosecution, should the defendant give evidence, to cross-examine him as to previous convictions—Defendant electing not to give evidence— Judge directing jury that they could if they thought it proper draw the inference that the only sensible reason for silence at trial was that the defendant could not give an answer to, or explanation of, the prosecution evidence, or none that would withstand cross-examination—Whether judge entitled to give such direction— Whether judge ought to direct jury that the defendant could have been motivated by reasons other than inability to explain or answer the prosecution case—Criminal Evidence Act 1898 (61 & 62 Vict c.36), s.1(3) (as amended by Youth Justice and Criminal Evidence Act 1999 (c.23), s.67(1), Sch.4, para.1(1) (7))—Criminal Justice and Public Order Act 1994 (c.33), s.35.

H2   The appellant was selected at an identification parade as having been the gunman in the shooting of two men and he was charged with their murder. The appellant presented a prepared statement in which he denied that he had been present at the scene of the murder, and he also stated that witnesses had deliberately made false identifications for their own improper purposes. The judge at what became the first of two trials ruled under s.1(3) of the Criminal Evidence Act 1898, as amended, that the appellant's previous convictions could be put to him if he chose to give evidence. The appellant elected not to give evidence at that trial. The jury failed to agree upon a verdict and were discharged. At the retrial, counsel did not seek to challenge or vary the ruling as to cross-examination as to previous convictions. The appellant again decided not to give evidence. The judge gave the jury a direction under s.35 of the Criminal Justice and Public Order Act 1994, that they could, if they thought it proper to do so, draw the inference that the only sensible reason for the appellant's failure to give evidence was that he could not give an answer to, or explanation of, the prosecution evidence, or none that would have stood up to cross-examination. The appellant was convicted. He appealed against conviction, submitting that it was unfair to him that a s.35 direction was given, because at least one of the reasons for his not giving evidence was, or might have been, that he feared the prejudicial effect which could have followed if the jury learned of his previous convictions; and, alternatively, that the judge should have directed the jury that there could have been reasons for the appellant's failure to give evidence other than inability to give an explanation or answer. The Court of Appeal dismissed the appellant's appeal. The appellant appealed to the House of Lords.

H3   **Held,** dismissing the appeal, that where the defendant in a trial had previous convictions and knew that, as a result of the application of s.1 of the Criminal Evidence Act 1898 he was liable, if he chose to give evidence, to be cross-examined so as to elicit those convictions, and where he then chose not to give evidence, a judge was entitled to give the jury a direction under s.35 of the Criminal Justice and Public Order Act 1994 that an adverse inference might be drawn against the defendant. Furthermore, the jury did not have to be directed that there might have been reasons for not giving evidence other than the inability to give an explanation or answer to the prosecution case. However, the judge had an overriding discretion to decline to allow convictions to be put or inferences to be drawn where he thought it unfair in the circumstances of the particular case. Accordingly, since there was no error in the ruling as to cross-examination as to previous convictions and the judge had been entitled to make a s.35 direction, the conviction on two counts of murder was safe (post, paras [1–4], [23]–[26]).

H4   *R. v Cowan* [1996] 1 Cr.App.R. 1; [1996] Q.B. 373, CA, approved.

H5   Decision of the Court of Appeal (Criminal Division) [2003] EWCA Crim 1154 affirmed.

H6   *Per curiam.* The Judicial Studies Board direction was to be regarded as sufficiently fair, emphasising as it did that the only sensible explanation of the defendant's failure to give evidence was that he had no answer to the case against him, or none that could have stood up to cross-examination. However, trial judges had full discretion to adapt even a tried and tested direction if they considered that to do so gave the best guidance to a jury and fairest representation of the issues (post, para.[25].)

H7   (For the right to remain silent at trial and proper inferences, see Archbold 2005, paras 4–305 and following).

Appeal from the Court of Appeal, Criminal Division

H8   The appellant, Darren Becouarn, was granted leave by the House of Lords (Lord Bingham of Cornhill, Lord Rodger of Earlsferry and Lord Carswell) to appeal from the judgment on April 4, 2003 of the Court of Appeal, Criminal Division (Tuckey L.J., Keith J. and Sir Brian Smedley) dismissing his appeal against his conviction in the Crown Court at Liverpool on May 26, 2000 of two offences of murder.

H9   The Court of Appeal certified that a point of law of general public importance was involved in its decision, namely: "(1) Where an accused has previous convictions and knows that as a result of the application of section 1 of the Criminal Evidence Act 1898 (as amended) he is liable to be cross-examined so as to elicit those convictions, is it always appropriate to give the jury a direction under section 35 of the Criminal Justice and Public Order Act 1994 that an adverse inference may be drawn against him if he decides not to give evidence; and if so: (2) What should be the terms of such direction?"

H10   At the hearing of the appeal on June 16, 2005 the following additional cases were cited in argument: *R. v Jackson* (1953) 37 Cr.App.R. 43; [1953] 1 W.L.R. 591, CCA; *R. v Martinez-Tobon* (1994) 98 Cr.App.R. 375, CA; [1994] 1 W.L.R. 388, CA; *R. v Mutch* (1973) 57 Cr.App.R. 196, CA; *R. v Rhodes* [1899] 1 Q.B. 77; *Waugh v R.* [1950] A.C. 203, PC.

H11   The facts appear in the opinion of Lord Carswell.

H12   *Andrew Edis Q.C.* and *Stuart Driver* (instructed by Sharpe Pritchard for Roberts Moore Nicholas Jones, Birkenhead) for the appellant.
David Perry and *Sarah Whitehouse* (instructed by the Crown Prosecution Service) for the Crown.

    Their Lordships took time for consideration.

Lord Steyn
My Lords,

1   I have had the advantage of reading in draft the opinion of my noble and learned friend Lord Carswell. I agree with it. I would also make the order which he proposes.

Lord Hoffmann
My Lords,

2   I have had the advantage of reading in draft the speech of my noble and learned friend Lord Carswell. For the reasons he gives, with which I agree, I would dismiss this appeal.

Lord Hope of Craighead
My Lords,

3   I have had the advantage of reading in draft the speech of my noble and learned friend Lord Carswell. I agree with it, and for the reasons he gives I too would dismiss the appeal.

Lord Scott of Foscote
My Lords,

4   For the reasons given by my noble and learned friend Lord Carswell, with which I agree, I too would dismiss this appeal and make the order which he proposes.

Lord Carswell

My Lords,

5   The appellant Darren Becouarn was on May 26, 2000 convicted in the Crown Court at Liverpool after a retrial before Gray J. and a jury on two counts of murder and sentenced to imprisonment for life. His defence involved imputations on the character of the main prosecution witnesses, and accordingly by the nature of the questions asked on his behalf in their cross-examination he put his character in issue. The judge at the previous trial Owen J. ruled that his previous convictions could be put to him if he gave evidence. The appellant did not give evidence either at that trial or on the retrial. On the retrial Gray J. directed the jury, in accordance with s.35 of the Criminal Justice and Public Order Act 1994 ("the 1994 Act"), that they could, if they thought proper to do so, draw the inference that the only sensible reason for his failure to give evidence was because he could not give an answer to or explanation of the Crown evidence, or none that would have stood up to cross-examination.

6   The appellant claimed in the Court of Appeal and before your Lordships' House that the direction was unfair to him, because at least one of the reasons for his not giving evidence was, or might have been, because he feared the prejudicial effect which could have followed if the jury learned of his previous convictions. It was submitted on his behalf that the judge should have decided either that his convictions should not be put in evidence or that in the circumstances a s.35 direction should not be given. Failing that, it was suggested that he should have given a *Lucas* type direction (*R. v Lucas* (1981) 73 Cr.App.R. 159; [1981] Q.B. 720), indicating that there may have been reasons for the appellant's failure to give evidence other than inability to give an explanation or answer.

7   The facts proved by the prosecution at the appellant's trial have been succinctly set out in the judgment of the Court of Appeal and I can summarise them briefly. On October 1, 1998 two men, Kevin McGuire and Nathan Jones, were shot dead in a gymnasium by a gunman who escaped after the shooting on the back of a motor cycle. The appellant, who was arrested some four months later, was identified at an identification parade as the gunman by three witnesses who were in the gymnasium at the time. The appellant's case was that they deliberately made false identifications for their own improper purposes.

8   In addition there was an amount of circumstantial evidence which tended to connect the appellant with the acquisition and disguise of the getaway motor cycle. The Crown also relied on evidence concerning a call made from a mobile telephone traced to the appellant or his family very close to the time of the shooting. The Court of Appeal concluded that the prosecution evidence was such that the jury were quite entitled to convict on it and, since they considered that the jury were properly directed, the prosecution was safe. In my opinion the Court of Appeal was quite correct in this conclusion, subject to the issue about s.35 of the 1994 Act, and I do not regard it as necessary to examine this issue further. I shall instead focus on the main issue argued before the House, the effect of permitting the jury to draw an inference under s.35 in the circumstances of the case.

9   The position of a defendant in a criminal trial and the options open to him in relation to giving evidence have changed in very material respects since the end of the 19th century. Until the passage of the Criminal Evidence Act 1898 ("the 1898 Act") the law did not permit him to give evidence on oath on his own behalf, restricting him to giving an unsworn statement from the dock. That Act made him generally a competent witness in his own defence, but did not make him compellable. From that time the defendant was quite entitled to decline to give evidence—the privilege generally termed the right of silence—but if he did testify, he was liable under s.1(e) of the Act to be asked any question in cross-examination, notwithstanding that it would tend to criminate him as to any offence with which he was charged in the proceedings.

10   Several consequences followed from other provisions in the 1898 Act. First, the prosecution was not permitted to comment adversely on the defendant's failure to give evidence (s.1(b)) and the trial judge's ability to comment on that was fairly closely circumscribed. The judge was in most cases bound to direct the jury that the defendant was fully entitled to sit back and see if the prosecution had proved its case, and that they must not make any assumption of guilt from the fact that he had not gone into the witness box (see, e.g. *R. v Bathurst* (1968) 52 Cr.App.R. 251 at 257; [1968] 2 Q.B. 99, 107–8, per Lord Parker C.J.). The second consequence was that the defendant could not be asked about any previous convictions, unless he had "lost his shield" and incurred liability to such cross-examination by reason of, inter alia, putting his character in issue. This could occur if questions were asked or evidence was given with a view to establish his good character or, most commonly, if he attacked the character of the prosecution witnesses: s.1(f), and see the decision of the House in *Selvey v Director of Public Prosecutions* (1968) 52 Cr.App.R. 443; [1970] A.C. 304 on the operation of this provision. Thirdly, if the defendant put his character in issue by attacking the character of the prosecution witnesses, but did not himself give evidence, he escaped the consequences of having his convictions put in evidence (*R. v Butterwasser* (1948) 32 Cr.App.R. 81; [1948] 1 K.B. 4).

11   Although practitioners reckoned that the ability to give evidence conferred by the 1898 Act was a not unmixed blessing, it enabled those defendants who wished to put forward their own evidence in support of their case to do so, while those who wished to stay silent and challenge the sufficiency of the prosecution case were able to follow that course. Criticism of the state of the law, not least of the effect of the ruling in *Butterwasser*, and the degree of advantage which it conferred on defendants in criminal trials, mounted—in the Eleventh Report of the *Criminal Law Revision Committee*, Cmnd 4991 (1972), p.83 at [131], it is stated that "To many it is highly objectionable that the accused should be able to do this with impunity." Eventually Parliament enacted the provisions contained in s.35 of the Criminal Justice and Public Order Act 1994, with the objective of redressing the perceived imbalance:

Effect of accused's silence at trial

"35 (1) At the trial of any person . . . for an offence, subsections (2)
and (3) below apply unless—
  (a) the accused's guilt is not in issue; or
  (b) it appears to the court that the physical or mental condition
     of the accused makes it undesirable for him to give evi-
     dence;
  but subsection (2) below does not apply if, at the conclusion of
  the evidence for the prosecution, his legal representative
  informs the court that the accused will give evidence or,
  where he is unrepresented, the court ascertains from him that
  he will give evidence.
(2) Where this subsection applies, the court shall, at the con-
    clusion of the evidence for the prosecution, satisfy itself (in
    the case of proceedings on indictment, in the presence of the
    jury) that the accused is aware that the stage has been reached
    at which evidence can be given for the defence and that he can,
    if he wishes, give evidence and that, if he chooses not to give
    evidence, or having been sworn, without good cause refuses to
    answer any question, it will be permissible for the court or jury
    to draw such inferences as appear proper from his failure to
    give evidence or his refusal, without good cause, to answer
    any question.
(3) Where this subsection applies, the court or jury, in determining
    whether the accused is guilty of the offence charged, may draw
    such inferences as appear proper from the failure of the
    accused to give evidence or his refusal, without good cause,
    to answer any question.
(4) This section does not render the accused compellable to give
    evidence on his own behalf, and he shall accordingly not be
    guilty of contempt of court by reason of a failure to do so.
(5) For the purposes of this section a person who, having been
    sworn, refuses to answer any question shall be taken to do so
    without good cause unless—
  (a) he is entitled to refuse to answer the question by virtue of
     any enactment, whenever passed or made, or on the
     ground of privilege; or
  (b) the court in the exercise of its general discretion excuses
     him from answering it.
(6) . . .
(7) This section applies—
  (a) in relation to proceedings on indictment for an offence,
     only if the person charged with the offence is arraigned
     on or after the commencement of this section;
  (b) in relation to proceedings in a magistrates' court, only if
     the time when the court begins to receive evidence in

the proceedings falls after the commencement of this section."

12   Very shortly after the 1994 Act came into operation a challenge was mounted to the validity of directions given in pursuance of s.35. In *R. v Cowan* [1996] 1 Cr.App.R. 1; [1996] Q.B. 373 the Court of Appeal considered the effect of the section and the specimen direction published by the Judicial Studies Board ("JSB") as a suggested model for use by judges when s.35 applied. The specimen direction, set out at pp.6–7 and 380–381, was in the following terms:

> "'The defendant has not given evidence. That is his right. But, as he has been told, the law is that you may draw such inferences as appear proper from his failure to do so. Failure to give evidence on its own cannot prove guilt but depending on the circumstances, you may hold his failure against him when deciding whether he is guilty. [There is evidence before you on the basis of which the defendant's advocate invites you not to hold it against the defendant that he has not given evidence before you namely . . . If you think that because of this evidence you should not hold it against the defendant that he has not given evidence, do not do so.] But if the evidence he relies on presents no adequate explanation for his absence from the witness box then you may hold his failure to give evidence against him. You do not have to do so. What proper inferences can you draw from the defendant's decision not to give evidence before you? If you conclude that there is a case for him to answer, you may think that the defendant would have gone into the witness box to give you an explanation for or an answer to the case against him. If the only sensible explanation for his decision not to give evidence is that he has no answer to the case against him, or none that could have stood up to cross-examination, then it would be open to you to hold against him his failure to give evidence. It is for you to decide whether it is fair to do so.' (The words in square brackets are to be used only where there is evidence.)"

13   The three appellants in *Cowan* were convicted of different crimes in different trials. None of them gave evidence at their trials. In the case of two it was stated to the Court of Appeal that it was because they wished to avoid cross-examination about their previous convictions, and in the case of the third, who had no convictions, it was alleged that he had a strong but sensitive reason which was not disclosed either to the court of trial or the Court of Appeal. The judge in each case gave the jury a direction that they could draw inferences from the defendant's failure to give evidence. In one case the direction was modelled on the JSB specimen and in the other two the judges used their own wording. It was submitted on behalf of each appellant that the operation of s.35 in those circumstances was unfair and contrary to established principles of the criminal law and that the convictions should be set aside. The content of the individual directions was also attacked. The Court of Appeal rejected the general argument based on unfairness. It upheld two of the convictions, but allowed the appeal in the third case on grounds related to the content of the direction.

14   Counsel for the appellants suggested in argument a number of reasons for silence at trial which might be consistent with innocence, including the existence of previous convictions on which the defendant might be cross-examined. Lord Taylor of Gosforth C.J., giving the judgment of the court, regarded this reason as an insufficient ground for claiming that the jury should not be told that it might draw an adverse inference from the defendant's failure to give evidence, stating at pp.6 and 380:

> "In particular, we should deal specifically with two of the suggested 'good reasons.' First, the general proposition that a previous criminal record upon which a defendant could be cross-examined(if he has attacked prosecution witnesses) is a good reason for directing a jury that they should not hold his silence against him, would lead to a bizarre result. A defendant with convictions would be in a more privileged position than one with a clean record. The former could avoid submitting himself to cross-examination with impunity; the latter could not. We reject that proposition."

15   Lord Taylor expressed approval of the JSB specimen direction and went on, at pp.7 and 381, to set out certain essentials for a sound direction on this issue:

> "We consider that the specimen direction is in general terms a sound guide. It may be necessary to adapt or add to it in the particular circumstances of an individual case. But there are certain essentials which we would highlight. (1) The judge will have told the jury that the burden of proof remains upon the prosecution throughout and what the required standard is. (2) It is necessary for the judge to make clear to the jury that the defendant is entitled to remain silent. That is his right and his choice. The right of silence remains. (3) An inference from failure to give evidence cannot on its own prove guilt. That is expressly stated in section 38(3) of the Act. (4) Therefore, the jury must be satisfied that the prosecution have established a case to answer before drawing any inferences from silence. Of course, the judge must have thought so or the question whether the defendant was to give evidence would not have arisen. But the jury may not believe the witnesses whose evidence the judge considered sufficient to raise a prima facie case. It must therefore be made clear to them that they must find there to be a case to answer on the prosecution evidence before drawing an adverse inference from the defendant's silence. (5) If, despite any evidence relied upon to explain his silence or in the absence of any such evidence, the jury conclude the silence can only sensibly be attributed to the defendant's having no answer or none that would stand up to cross-examination, they may draw an adverse inference."

He then added, at pp.7 and 383:

> "Finally, we wish to make it clear that the rule against advocates giving evidence dressed up as a submission applies in this context. It cannot be proper for a defence advocate to give to the jury reasons for his client's silence at trial in the absence of evidence to support such reasons."

16   The decision in *Cowan* was followed in *R. v Taylor* [1999] Crim. L.R. 77. The appellant, who had previous convictions, did not give evidence, and the trial judge gave a direction in accordance with s.35. The Court of Appeal rejected a submission by the appellant's counsel that the judge should have not have told the jury that they could draw inferences from the defendant's failure to give evidence. Buxton L.J., giving the judgment of the court, referred to Cowan and said that even if they were not bound by that decision they would follow it without hesitation.

17   At the first trial of the appellant in December 1999 an application was made on his behalf to the trial judge Owen J. to exercise his discretion not to allow cross-examination of him in relation to his previous convictions. The judge gave a considered ruling, in which he took into account the impact of s.35 of the 1994 Act. He ruled that the convictions could be put in, with the exception of a recent one which included two counts of possession of a firearm with intent to commit an indictable offence, on the ground that if that conviction were revealed to the jury they might well, despite warning, consider propensity rather than credibility. The jury at that trial failed to agree and when his retrial took place before Gray J. the appellant's counsel did not seek to challenge or vary the ruling made by Owen J.

18   When summing up to the jury Gray J. gave them the following direction concerning the appellant's failure to give evidence:

> "I now turn to the defence case. I cannot summarise the defence evidence because, as you know, the defence has not called Darren Becouarn to give evidence, nor have witnesses been called on his behalf. Nor, you have been told, did Darren Becouarn answer the questions that were asked of him during several police interviews. That, members of the jury, is [his] right. It is his right not to answer questions asked of him in interview and it is his right to remain silent at the trial and to require the prosecution to prove the case against him if they can.
>
> You must not assume, members of the jury, that he is guilty just because he has not given evidence because a failure to give evidence cannot on its own prove guilt. However, as the defendant has been told, depending on the circumstances you may take into account his failure to give evidence when deciding on your verdict.
>
> In the first place when considering the evidence that you have heard from the prosecution side you may bear in mind that there is no evidence from the defendant himself which in any way undermines or contradicts or explains the evidence that has been laid before you by the prosecution.
>
> In the second place if, and I stress the word, if, if you think in all the circumstances it is right and fair to do so you are entitled, when deciding whether the defendant is guilty of the offences with which he is charged, to draw such inferences from his failure to give evidence as you think proper. In simple terms that means that you may hold his failure to give evidence against him. You will want to know what inferences you can properly draw from the defendant's decision not to give evidence. You should not start to consider whether to draw an adverse inference from the defendant's failure to give evidence until you have concluded that the prosecution case against him

is sufficiently compelling to call for an answer from him. So if you do not think the prosecution case is sufficiently compelling to call for an answer, then you should not consider drawing any adverse inference against him from his failure to give evidence.

If, and only if, you conclude that there is a sufficiently compelling case to call for an answer by him then you may think that if he had an answer to it he would have gone into the witness box and told you what that answer is. If, in your judgment, the only sensible reason for his decision not to give evidence is that he has no explanation or answer to give, or none that would stand up to cross-examination, then it would be open to you to hold against him his failure to give evidence. That is to take it into account as some additional support for the prosecution case. You are not bound to do so, it is a matter for you to decide whether you should do so."

Counsel acknowledged before the House that that was a proper direction, given the existence of the decision in Cowan, which was binding upon the judge.

19   Before the Court of Appeal (Tuckey L.J., Keith J. and Sir Brian Smedley) counsel for the appellant invited the court to re-examine the decision in *Cowan*, which he submitted was wrong. He argued that the direction was misleading: the judge may believe from the course taken that the defendant has not given evidence because of his previous convictions, accordingly to direct the jury that they may infer that the only sensible reason is that he has no answer to the prosecution case will mislead them and is unfair. He submitted in the alternative that the judge should have given a direction akin to a Lucas direction on the reasons for lying, on the lines that there may be various possible other reasons why the defendant did not give evidence, as to which they cannot speculate. The court rejected both these arguments, holding that the direction was sound and in accordance with authority, and dismissed the appeal.

20   The Court of Appeal certified that two points of law of general public importance were involved in its decision, but refused leave to appeal. The certified questions were as follows:

"1. Where an accused has previous convictions and knows that as a result of the application of section 1 of the Criminal Evidence Act 1898 (as amended) he is liable to be cross-examined so as to elicit those convictions, is it always appropriate to give the jury a direction under section 35 of the Criminal Justice and Public Order Act 1994 that an adverse inference may be drawn against him if he decides not to give evidence; and if so
2. What should be the terms of such direction?"

21   Mr Edis Q.C. for the appellant argued that unfairness resulted from the appellant's being faced with an impossible dilemma, which required him to make an invidious choice. If he did not give evidence, his convictions would not be mentioned, but the judge would direct the jury that they could draw an inference that the only sensible reason for his failure to give evidence was that he could not face cross-examination on his case. This might only be one of several reasons, and possibly a minor one, but his counsel could not put forward possible reasons,

while prosecuting counsel could make very damaging comments about the defendant's silence. If, on the other hand, he did give evidence, so avoiding the damaging inference, he could be cross-examined about his previous convictions. That should in theory be done only for the purpose of damaging his credit, the principle being that since he has sought to undermine the credit of the prosecution witnesses it would be inequitable if the jury were allowed to entertain the impression that he was a person of good character deserving of credit. It is, however, a matter of notoriety that juries in practice are likely to regard them as indicators of propensity and so supportive of guilt. That piece of folk knowledge received some verification from a study commissioned by the Home Office and based on research carried out on the effect of bad character evidence on mock jurors (Sally Lloyd-Bostock, *The Effects on Juries of Hearing about the Defendant's Previous Criminal Record: a Simulation Study* [2000] Crim.L.R. 734).

22   Mr Edis accordingly submitted that the judge in a case such as the present should either refuse to allow the defendant's convictions to be put to him or decline to make or permit adverse comment on his failure to give evidence. In the alternative, he repeated the suggestion which he had advanced in the Court of Appeal that the judge should give the jury a *Lucas*-type direction about possible reasons why the defendant may have wished to avoid giving evidence.

23   I am unable to accept that the operation of the law as contained in the decision in Cowan is unfair, certainly not to a degree which would require that law to be changed. It has to be remembered that the defendant's convictions can be put to him only in the defined circumstances set out in s.1(f) of the 1898 Act, the material one for present purposes being when he has attacked the character of the prosecution witnesses. In those circumstances it would in my view be altogether wrong if he could avoid having his own credibility undermined by the omission of reference to his previous convictions when he gives evidence. That would be misleading to the jury in a case where their decision may depend to a material extent on assessing the credibility of the prosecution witnesses and that of the defendant. It would be equally wrong if he could stay out of the witness box but still avoid having legitimate comment made about his failure to give evidence. It would also create the quite unjustifiable distinction between defendants with previous convictions and those with none to which Lord Taylor of Gosforth C.J. referred in *R. v Cowan* [1996] 1 Cr.App.R. 1; [1996] Q.B. 373. I would affirmatively agree with his remark at pp.6 and 380 of that case, which he repeated in *R.. v Napper* (1995) 161 J.P. 16, 22, that the operation of s.35 is not to be reduced or marginalised.

24   I do not find the suggestion made on behalf of the appellant of a *Lucas* type of direction helpful. Allusive hints of the nature contained in the suggested draft direction put forward in the appellant's printed case would be likely either to signal to jurors that the defendant has previous convictions or to set them off on a trail of unfounded speculation about the existence of other imaginary reasons. Secondly, fear of allowing in his convictions may be one element in his decision not to give evidence, but reluctance to face cross-examination may be another and much more predominant element. There does not appear to be any good reason why a defendant should shelter behind the suggestion that there may be

some compelling reason for his failure to give evidence other than fear of cross-examination, when that may be quite misleading. I entirely agree with the observations of Tuckey L.J. at [26] and [27] of his judgment in the Court of Appeal:

> "26. The problem about this is that it does not cure the ill from which the current directions are said to suffer. It is misleading because in a case such as the present it does not and cannot suggest the reason why the defendant had not given evidence. We are not, therefore, persuaded that a modified direction of the kind suggested should be given in a case of this kind or should have been given in this case.
>
> 27. So what of this case? If ever there was a case for allowing cross-examination of the appellant on his previous convictions, this was it. It would have been quite unfair for him to have been allowed to attack the character of the prosecution witnesses in the way he did without the jury knowing about his character if he chose to give evidence. He did not, however, have to give evidence. The Act preserved his right of silence. No one knows why in fact the appellant decided not to give evidence. When he made this decision, for whatever reason, he knew what the consequences would be as a result of Owen J's ruling and the statutory warnings which the judges at his trials were required to and did give him."

25   I would regard the specimen JSB direction on drawing inferences as sufficiently fair to defendants, emphasising as it does that the jury must conclude that the only sensible explanation of his failure to give evidence is that he has no answer to the case against him, or none that could have stood up to cross-examination. This direction has been used for some years and appears to have stood the test of time. It goes without saying, however, that trial judges have full discretion to adapt even a tried and tested direction if they consider that to do so gives the best guidance to a jury and fairest representation of the issues.

26   I accordingly consider that the decision in Cowan was correct and that the Court of Appeal correctly decided the present case. I would dismiss the appeal. I would answer the first certified question in the affirmative, qualifying it by deleting the word "always", since there is an overriding discretion in the trial judge to decline to allow convictions to be put or inferences to be drawn where he thinks it unfair in the circumstances of the particular case: see *R.v Cowan* [1996] 1 Cr.App.R. 1,[1996] Q.B. 373, 380, 381–382 and cf *R. v Napper* (1995) 161 J.P. 16, 22, *per* Lord Taylor of Gosforth C.J. The second question then does not arise.

27   It only remains to add that s.101 of the Criminal Justice Act 2003, which came into force on December 15, 2004 has effected a material change in the law which will generally make the problems considered in this appeal no longer material. It is not necessary in this appeal, however, to explore that development and I would reserve further comment on the effect of the 2003 Act until the matter arises for determination.

Appeal dismissed.

R. v EDWARDS
R. v FYSH
R. v DUGGAN
R. v CHOHAN

COURT OF APPEAL (The Vice President (Lord Justice Rose),
Mr Justice Holland and Mr Justice Richards): June 29, 2005

[2005] EWCA Crim 1813; [2006] 1 Cr.App.R. 3

(LT) Bad character; Previous convictions; Propensity; Summing up; undue reliance

H1   EVIDENCE
     Bad character
     Judge's directions to jury to contain clear warning to jury against placing undue reliance on previous convictions—Criminal Justice Act 2003 (c.44), s.101(1).

H2   The judge's summing up must contain a clear warning to the jury against placing undue reliance on previous convictions, which could not, by themselves, prove guilt. The jury should be told why they had heard the evidence and the ways in which it was relevant to and might help their decision, bearing in mind that relevance would depend primarily, though not always exclusively, on the gateway in s.101(1) of the Criminal Justice Act 2003[1] through which the evidence had been admitted. Provided the judge gave such a clear warning, explanation and guidance as to use, the terms in which he or she did so could properly differ (post, para.[3]).

H3   *Per curiam* The summing up by Judge Mort in the case of Chohan could serve as a model in many cases where evidence of bad character is admitted (post, para.[77]).

H4   (For evidence of bad character, see *Archbold* 2005, paras 13–55 and following).

---

[1]   Criminal Justice Act 2003, s.101 provides: "(1) In criminal proceedings evidence of the defendant's bad character is admissible if, but only if— (a) all parties to the proceedings agree to the evidence being admissible, (b) the evidence is adduced by the defendant himself or is given in answer to a question asked by him in cross-examination and intended to elicit it, (c) it is important explanatory evidence, (d) it is relevant to an important matter in issue between the defendant and the prosecution, (e) it has substantial probative value in relation to an important matter in issue between the defendant and a co-defendant, (f) it is evidence to correct a false impression given by the defendant, or (g) the defendant has made an attack on another person's character.

Applications for leave to appeal and Appeals against conviction

H5 *R. v Edwards*

On February 24, 2005 in the Crown Court at Manchester (Mr Recorder Fines-tein) the defendant, Karl Adrian Edwards, was convicted on two counts of common assault (counts 1 and 2), and of having a bladed article in a public place (count 4). He was acquitted on count 3, of having an offensive weapon. He was sentenced to consecutive terms of two months' imprisonment on each of the counts of common assault and to a further eight months consecutively for possession of a bladed article, making a total sentence of 12 months' imprisonment, and an order was made under s.143 of the Powers of Criminal Courts (Sentencing) Act 2000 for forfeiture of the knife. His applications for leave to appeal against conviction and sentence were referred to the Full Court by the Registrar.

The facts and grounds of appeal appear in the judgment of the court.

H6 *R. v Fysh*

On February 9, 2005 in the Crown Court at Norwich (Judge Worsley) the defendant, Stephen John Fysh, was convicted of having an offensive weapon (count 2), and common assault (count 3). On March 23 he was sentenced to concurrent terms of nine months' imprisonment on count 2 and five months' imprisonment on count 3, making a total sentence of nine months' imprisonment. He appealed against conviction by leave of the single judge.

The facts and grounds of appeal appear in the judgment of the court.

H7 *R. v Duggan*

On March 4, 2005, in the Crown Court at Snaresbrook (Mr Recorder Marshall) the defendant, James Edward Duggan, was convicted of wounding with intent to cause grievous bodily harm and sentenced to five years' imprisonment. His application for leave to appeal against conviction and sentence was referred to the Full Court by the Registrar

The facts and grounds of appeal appear in the judgment of the court.

H8 *R. v Chohan*

On February 8, 2005 in the Crown Court at Manchester (Judge Mort) the defendant, Naveed Nasir Chohan, was convicted of robbery (count 1), possession of an imitation firearm while committing a Schedule 1 offence (count 2) and possession of an imitation firearm with intent to cause fear of violence (count 3). He was sentenced to 10 years' imprisonment on count 1 and to three years' imprisonment concurrently on each of counts 2 and 3, making a total sentence of 10 years' imprisonment. His application for leave to appeal against conviction was referred to the Full Court by the Registrar.

H9 *Farrhat Arshad* (assigned by the Registrar of Criminal Appeals) for Edwards.
Jeremy Lynn (assigned by the Registrar of Criminal Appeals) for Fysh.
James McCrindell (assigned by the Registrar of Criminal Appeals) for Duggan.
John Samuels (assigned by the Registrar of Criminal Appeals) for Chohan.
Bruce Houlder Q.C. and *Alaric Bassano* (instructed by the Crown Prosecution Service) for the Crown.

Rose L.J. (Vice President) gave the judgment of the court.

1   These four cases have been listed and heard together because they provide further examples to add to those previously considered by this Court in *R. v Hanson and others* [2005] EWCA Crim 824; [2005] 2 Cr.App.R. 21 (p.299) and *R. v Bovell and Dowds* [2005] EWCA Crim 1091; [2005] 2 Cr.App.R. 27 (p.400) of the admissibility of bad character under ss.98 to 113 of the Criminal Justice Act 2003.

2   Because of grounds which have been advanced in the cases of Fysh and Duggan in particular, in relation to alleged noncompliance in the respective summings-up with observations made by this court in para.18 of *Hanson*, it is convenient, before turning to the individual cases, to make some general observations in relation to that part of that judgment.

3   The guidance proffered in para.[18] of *Hanson* as to what a summing-up should contain was, as is apparent from the last sentence of the paragraph, not intended to provide a blueprint, departure from which will result in the quashing of a conviction. What the summing-up must contain is a clear warning to the jury against placing undue reliance on previous convictions, which cannot, by themselves, prove guilt. It should be explained why the jury has heard the evidence and the ways in which it is relevant to and may help their decision, bearing in mind that relevance will depend primarily, though not always exclusively, on the gateway in s.101(1) of the Criminal Justice Act 2003, through which the evidence has been admitted. For example, some evidence admitted through gateway (g), because of an attack on another person's character, may be relevant or irrelevant to propensity, so as to require a direction on this aspect. Provided the judge gives such a clear warning, explanation and guidance as to use, the terms in which he or she does so can properly differ. There is no rigid formula to be adhered to. That said, there is, in the case of Chohan, a summing-up by Judge Mort which seems to us to be almost impeccable and which could serve as a model in many cases where evidence of bad character is admitted. We shall rehearse the relevant passage in that summing-up when dealing with Chohan's application.

4   We turn, first, to the case of Edwards. On February 24, 2005 at Manchester Crown Court, following a trial before Mr Recorder Finestein, this defendant was convicted on two counts of common assault, on counts 1 and 2, and of having a bladed article in a public place on count 4. He was acquitted on count 3, of having an offensive weapon. He was sentenced to two months' imprisonment on each of the counts of common assault consecutively to each other, and to a further eight months consecutively for possession of a bladed article. His total sentence was therefore 12 months' imprisonment, and an order was made under s.143 of the Powers of Criminal Courts (Sentencing) Act 2000 for forfeiture of the knife. His applications for leave to appeal against conviction and sentence were referred to the Full Court by the Registrar.

5   The facts were these. On April 30, 2004 two police officers stopped the defendant, who was driving a motor vehicle along Queen's Road, Manchester. They asked to see his licence and searched his car. They discovered a bottle of ammonia, which gave rise to count 3, in relation to which, as we have said, he was acquitted. The officers sought to arrest the defendant. A scuffle ensued.

The officers and the defendant sustained minor injuries. The defendant was taken to a police station where he voluntarily handed over a lock-knife, which gave rise to count 4. It was the prosecution case that the defendant had assaulted the officers while they were lawfully seeking to arrest him and that he had no good reason for being in possession of the lock- knife. It was the defence case that the police officers had carried out an unprovoked assault on the defendant. He claimed to have a good reason for being in possession of the lock-knife, namely, he had used it on a fishing trip a couple of days previously, and had then completely forgotten about it.

6   The first of the officers to give evidence, PC Smithwaite, described the defendant swearing at him and being generally obstructive when he, the officer, reached his car. There was a struggle inside the car as the other officer, Constable Bryson, went to get the keys. Then there was a struggle outside the car, during which the officers restrained the defendant by getting him onto the floor. The officer admitted in cross-examination that, during this altercation, he had himself sworn at a passerby. Constable Bryson gave a similar account of the aggressive and uncooperative nature of the defendant's behaviour. A further officer described the knife as being located, not as the defendant claimed on his belt, but down the front of his trousers inside his jeans.

7   In interview, the defendant essentially said nothing in response to questions; he read a prepared statement, denying the offences and saying he had been mistreated by the police.

8   At the outset of the trial, the prosecution sought to adduce evidence of the defendant's previous convictions for robbery and dwelling-house burglary in 1992 in relation to the issue of credibility pursuant to s.101(1)(d). The Recorder ruled, at that stage, that, due to the age of the offences, it would not be right to allow that material to go before the jury. However, during the course of the prosecution case, the defence mounted a severe attack on the prosecution witnesses. Accordingly, the prosecution case made a further application to introduce evidence of bad character, under gateway (g) because of that attack.

9   On behalf of the defence, Miss Arshad accepted that the defendant had attacked the character of the two prosecution witnesses. But she invited the Recorder to exclude the evidence under s.101(3) on the basis that, by reason of the length of time, it would be unjust for the evidence to be admitted, bearing in mind that the offences were 13 years old; and their prejudicial effect, it was said, would outweigh their probative value. The Recorder ruled that, in view of the sustained attack on the character of the police, the jury was entitled to know about the 1992 conviction and he would direct the jury to give such weight to them as they saw fit.

10   The defendant gave evidence. He said that he was gratuitously and offensively treated by the police, whereas he had not been guilty of any bad conduct towards them. They had assaulted him and had caused him pain in the manner they applied and pulled down the handcuffs. Constable Smithwaite had told a passerby to "fuck off". He said the lock-knife was not his. Two days earlier it had been handed to him by a friend, on a fishing expedition to cut the lines. He had hooked the knife onto his jeans (the ones which he was wearing at the time of

his arrest). It had been there for two days, and he had simply forgotten about it. He called his friend to confirm that he was the source of the knife. A young woman also gave evidence of the manner of application of the handcuffs by the police officers.

11   In passing sentence, the Recorder said that the defendant had behaved in a wholly aggressive way in assaulting the police, acting in their duty. Fortunately, the injuries were not serious, but the offences were so serious that only a custodial sentence was appropriate.

12   The defendant, who is 34 years of age, has a large number of previous convictions since 1991, mainly for driving and theft related offences. But, in 1992, as we have indicated, he was convicted of robbery and burglary from a dwelling and also assault occasioning actual bodily harm.

13   The submission which is made to this court by Miss Arshad, on behalf of the defendant, is confined to a single ground of appeal, namely, that the previous 1992 convictions ought not to have gone before the jury. She submits that, when he ruled against the first application to admit that evidence under gateway (d), the Recorder had expressed the view that to admit that evidence would have so adverse an effect on the fairness of the proceedings that it ought not to be admitted at that stage. It is apparent from the transcript of the first ruling on February 21, that the Recorder, having referred to the offences being committed 13 years ago, said:

> ". . . to allow that in at this stage would seem to be on balance to have such an adverse effect on the fairness of the proceedings that the court ought not to admit it . . ."

He went on to say:

> ". . . I have to balance the type of conviction that would go before the jury as against the allegation that the defendant faces, and in the context of this case, there are offensive weapons, be it CS gas or a knife and incidents of effectively common assault on police officers, and to allow that in for these offences it seems to me would have an adverse effect on the fairness of the proceedings, but more fundamental as I have indicated, I think it is the age of the conviction which plainly must be taken into account, and, having regard to the balancing act that I have to do, . . . I think it is perfectly clear on the authorities that these should not be allowed in, and so I do not allow them in."

That conclusion as to the impact of the 1992 matters on the fairness of the proceedings, Miss Arshad submits, was a finding which bound the Recorder when the later application was made, following the attack upon the prosecution witnesses.

14   As it seems to us, the difficulty with that submission is that the fairness of the proceedings and the impact on it of admitting the evidence, has to be gauged at the time at which the application is made and by reference to the gateway under which admissibility is sought. At the initial stage there had been no attack on the character of the prosecution witnesses. In that regard, when dealing with the mat-

ter at the time of the second application, the Recorder, as appears from the transcript, said this:

> "I have come to the conclusion that there is a difference now between the prosecution arguments, the difference being a sustained attack upon the character of the police, and it seems to me that, even though these convictions are of a serious nature and of some age, the jury are entitled to know about this conviction, that I think they would be misled seriously if they did not know of this matter."

In our judgment, that was a conclusion which was not only open to the Recorder, it is one which he was, in the circumstances as we have described them, right to reach.

15   The second submission made by Miss Arshad is that, in admitting the evidence under gateway (g) because of its relevance to credibility and permitting the jury to know of a conviction in relation to the defendant's capacity to tell the truth, the learned Recorder adopted the wrong approach. He ought, Miss Arshad submits, to have admitted, rather than this conviction for a very serious offence of dishonesty, different convictions to be found in the defendant's record in more recent years.

16   The difficulty with that submission, as it seems to us, is that the convictions in more recent years included four convictions for offences of violence. Had the Recorder admitted those, it might well have been said that they had a significantly prejudicial effect against the defendant when he was facing charges of using violence: an impact which far outweighed the probative value of those offences. It is therefore, in our view, an impossible contention that the learned Recorder was wrong to admit an offence of dishonesty, but not to admit offences of violence. In those circumstances, there is, as it seems to us, no arguable ground of appeal in relation to conviction so far as Edward's is concerned. That application is refused.

17   In relation to sentence, Miss Arshad submits, first, that, bearing in mind the improvement in recent years in the defendant's behaviour, compared with more distant features of his criminal past, it was particularly incumbent upon the Recorder, before sentencing, to obtain a pre-sentence report. This he declined to do. Secondly, Miss Arshad submits, by reference to the guideline case of *R.v Poulton and Celaire* [2003] 1 Cr.App.R.(S.) 116 (p.610), a sentence of eight months' imprisonment, in relation to the bladed article, was significantly too long. Thirdly, she submits that it was wrong in principle to impose consecutive sentences for the assaults on the two police officers which essentially arose out of the same incident.

18   Each of those three points, in our judgment, is well made. Having regard to their combined impact, we indicated that leave to appeal against sentence would be granted, and we now quash the total sentence of 12 months imposed by the learned Recorder, and substitute for it a total sentence of nine months, made up as follows: for each of the offences of common assault, the sentence will be three months, but those sentences will run concurrently with each other. For the offence in relation to the bladed article, the sentence will be six

months consecutively to the three months on the other two counts. The appeal
against sentence is therefore allowed as we have indicated.

19   We turn to the case of Fysh. On February 9, 2005 at Norwich Crown Court, following a trial before Judge Worsley, this defendant was convicted of having an
offensive weapon, on count 2, and common assault on count 3. On March 23,
he was sentenced to nine months on count 2 and five months'concurrently on
count 3. The total sentence was therefore nine months' imprisonment. He appeals
against conviction by leave of the single judge.

20   The facts were these. On September 18, 2004 the defendant went to the home
in South Lynn of a man called Nicholas Moore. The defendant's friend drove him
there in a Rover car, but remained in the car throughout. The defendant knocked
on Mr Moore's door. He answered. The defendant accused Mr Moore of assaulting his son. Voices were raised. Mr Moore and his wife said that the defendant
struck Mr Moore with some form of cosh, made from a sock containing something hard. Two 999 calls were made during the incident. The first by Mrs
Moore, in which she at first described the weapon as a baseball bat, but, later
in the conversation, said it was a sock containing, possibly, coins. There was a
similar confusion in a second similar call.

21   The woman police constable called to the incident described Mr Moore as
having an injury to the right side of his face, by his eye. There was redness, swelling and a small cut but she conceded that she had got the location wrong when
she was cross-examined.

22   The defendant was known to the Moore family as, twenty years earlier, he had
been engaged to Mr Moore's sister.

23   When the defendant was arrested and interviewed he said nothing. He was,
however, picked out on identity parades by four witnesses. It was the prosecution
case that the defendant had a cosh of the character which we have described and,
when he confronted Mr Moore at his house, he deliberately struck out at him
twice, and one of those blows struck Mr Moore's eye causing injury. It was the
defence case that the defendant had been at Mr Moore's home on this day, but
he had not touched Mr Moore with a weapon or anything else.

24   The judge indicated that, whether the defendant gave evidence or not, he
would have to consider whether bad character was admissible, and he contemplated that it might be, under gateways (g) and/or (d) of s.101. He also
indicated that he would not go back beyond 1986, in relation to the defendant's
record, in the event that he allowed evidence to be admitted of previous convictions.

25   The evidence for the prosecution came from Mr Moore and Mrs Moore and
from Stephen Coe and Spencer Canon who had been sitting in the kitchen of
the Moores' house. Mr and Mr Moore and Stephen Coe all described the defendant as using a weapon of the kind which we have described or, so far as Stephen
Coe is concerned, he said he saw it raised above the defendant's head, though he
did not actually see him strike Mr Moore. Spencer Canon also referred to the
defendant holding what he described, initially, as a rounders bat, but later,
after discussion with others, he realised was an old sock.

26   The Crown applied to adduce previous convictions of the defendant, not by any means all of them, but those starting with a conviction for common assault in 1999. The application also related to an offence of theft by shoplifting, in May 2002, making a false statement in order to obtain benefit or payment, including three offences taken into consideration, in August 2002, battery, in March 2002 and a further offence of theft by shoplifting in August 2002.

27   The learned judge ruled that these convictions were evidence of bad character, admissible under one of the gateways, in particular, gateways (d) and (g) and he concluded that there was no basis for excluding those convictions from being admitted.

28   The learned judge concluded that propensity to untruthfulness was an issue under gateway (d).

29   The submission which is made by Mr Lynn, on behalf of the defendant is that the judge was wrong to permit this evidence to be adduced. Mr Lynn points out that there was some confusion at the time of trial in February as to the rules applicable. The new Criminal Procedure Rules had not come into force and the old Crown Court rules, in particular r.23E(3) of the Crown Court (Amendment No.3) Rules 2004 (SI 2004/2991), appeared to govern the position. Those rules have now been replaced since April 2005 by the new Criminal Procedure Rules.

30   In the light of the applicable rules Mr Lynn submits, first, that no notice was given by the prosecution of their intention to rely upon these convictions and there was no reason why appropriate notice could not have been given. By reason of the absence of notice, Mr Lynn submits that there was prejudice to the defence in two respects. First, there was a lack of time for him to prepare an argument against admissibility under the new statutory provisions. He accepts that he did not seek from the judge an adjournment, and that the judge said that, if he needed time further to consider the matter, he could have it. As it seems to us, there can have been no prejudice on this basis.

31   The second basis for prejudice, Mr Lynn submits, is that the facts were not agreed because no notice had been given and no adequate pre-trial enquiries had, in consequence, been made. The defendant was cross-examined about the facts of one of these offences. Mr Lynn submits the defendant was embarrassed in consequence, because the explanation which he had to give in relation to one of the offences was that it did not involve entry into someone else's home, and the victim of the offence was his girlfriend. Clearly, it is unfortunate that there was cross-examination in those circumstances.

32   As this court has previously pointed out, (see *Bovell and Dowds* para.2) it is important that provisions in relation to notice are observed so that adequate enquiries can be made on both sides as to the circumstances of offences, in so far as those circumstances may be relevant when the question of the admissibility of previous convictions arises. But, in the circumstances of this case, we are unpersuaded that the unfortunate cross-examination to which we have referred was such as, even arguably, to render the defendant's conviction unsafe. We say this in view of the limitation placed by the learned judge on the number of the defendant's abundant previous convictions which could be placed before

the jury and having regard to the nature of the evidence against the defendant which, on any view, was substantial and came from a number of sources.

33   The second ground which was advanced in oral submissions by Mr Lynn was that the learned judge, in admitting previous convictions for offences of dishonesty, failed to consider the question of whether such offences gave rise, in the terms of the statute, to a propensity to be untruthful (see s.103(1)(b)). As this court has previously pointed out, dishonesty does not necessarily equate with a propensity to be untruthful. It may be that the offences of theft by shoplifting, had the appeal centred on that aspect of the matter alone, could properly be regarded as not showing a propensity to be untruthful, rather than merely dishonesty. That cannot, however, be said in relation to the offences of benefit fraud, committed on four occasions.

34   Mr Lynn accepted that, in any event, if the evidence was properly admissible under gateway (g), as well as under gateway (d), there could not be the same objection to the admissibility of the offences of dishonesty. Mr Lynn submitted that the judge's basic consideration, as he put it, in relation to admissibility was under gateway (d). He submits that if the convictions had not been admitted, there was a real likelihood that the defendant would have been acquitted. It is, at that point, convenient to refer to the observation made by the judge in the course of his ruling as to bad character, which is in the transcript. He said this:

> "So far as gateway (g) is concerned, yes, it is an inevitable consequence of the defendant's case that the prosecution witnesses have to be attacked by counsel as having made this up and put their heads together, as was put squarely to them, and rightly to them, by Mr Lynn, cooked up a story, invented a malicious and unpleasant story, a fraud."

As it seems to us, once it is accepted, as it was in the court below and is here, that the attack on the prosecution witnesses amounted to an allegation of conspiracy to put their heads together, in order falsely to implicate the defendant, the judge's ruling under gateway (g) was, as he described it himself "inevitable". In our judgment, there is no substance in the grounds of appeal so far as Fysh is concerned.

35   We add this, by reference to one of the written grounds not supported in oral submission before us today by Mr Lynn, that there is no sustainable criticism to be made of the terms in which the learned judge summed up this matter to the jury. It is correct that he did not have the advantage, if such it be, of this court's judgment in *Hanson*, in relation to the distinction between a propensity to untruthfulness and dishonesty. In the course of his summing-up he equated the two. But the judge's summing-up followed, closely, the specimen direction given by the Judicial Studies Board, in December 2004, in relation to the admissibility of evidence of bad character and the blemish upon it which we have identified it does not give rise to any reason for regarding the defendant's conviction as unsafe. Fysh's application is therefore dismissed.

36   We turn to the case of Duggan. On March 4, 2005, at Snaresbrook Crown Court, following a trial before Mr Recorder Marshall, this defendant was convicted of wounding with intent to cause grievous bodily harm and sentenced to

five years' imprisonment. His application for leave to appeal against conviction and sentence was referred to the Full Court by the Registrar. The incident giving rise to the charge occurred on the evening of April 25, 2004 in the Walkabout public house on Upper Street, Islington. There was an altercation between the defendant and a woman called Susan Green. She sustained an injury from glass to the outside of her right hand, a deep laceration of her right middle finger, a black eye and a bruised jaw.

37   It was the prosecution case that the defendant had deliberately punched the complainant in the face, whereupon she had raised her hands in protection and the defendant then thrust a glassed object towards her, injuring her hand. The defendant's case was that the complainant had thrust a pint glass towards his face and, as he raised his hand to protect himself, the bottle he was holding had collided with the glass, so that injuries were caused to the complainant's hand. He said that his arm must have inadvertently connected with the complainant's face, causing the bruising. The central issue was self-defence in the context of which of the two was the aggressor.

38   The evidence from Susan Green was that, on her way back from buying a round of drinks, she was bumped into from behind so her drink spilled. She tapped the defendant on the shoulder and spoke to him, but he was offhand. She asked whether he was going to apologise and he effectively spat out the word "no" and threw his drink in her face. She thereupon threw her drink on him. At that stage, he punched her in the face with a clenched fist, straight to the eye. She was shocked. She held up her hands to protect herself; her glass by this stage had gone out of her hands. She could not say what the man had in his hands and she was not able to say precisely what happened after that. She denied in cross-examination that her hand injury was sustained when she was punched in the face. The two incidents were separate and her hand had been injured after she had been punched. She had done nothing violent. Evidence confirmatory of her account was given by Beth Howells, who said that it might have been 10 to 12 seconds after the punch that she saw the attack with the glass.

39   A Policewoman Constable came to the scene. When she arrived, the defendant was being aggressive and shouting at the door staff: "You're a fucking cunt". She warned him about his behaviour and he shouted: "Your mother blows fucking Pakis". She arrested him for a public order offence. Details were taken by another officer, in relation to the assault on Susan Green and the defendant was arrested for that. He continued to be racially abusive. When he was told he was being arrested for a racially aggravated public order offence, he claimed, falsely as he later said, to be a member of the British National Party and proud of it. He continued with similar insults and refused to give his name. He declined the services of a solicitor and did not answer any questions in interview.

40   He gave evidence that he had been drinking and watching football during the day. He had eight beers over three or four hours but was not drunk. The atmosphere in the pub had been "lovely". The complainant had bumped into him rather than the other way round. She had moved her glass to his face and he was afraid she was going to glass him, so he brought up his arm to protect himself. He had a bottle of beer in his hand, which must have broken the complainant's

glass. He assumed, although he had not felt it, that his arm must have carried on and must have hit her on the face. He had been asked to leave by a bouncer.

41   He said in relation to his previous convictions, as to the rulings about which we shall in a moment come, that he always pleaded guilty. He was not in fact a member of the BNP but he did not dispute what the police officer said he had said. He claimed that he was upset because he was being arrested for nothing at all. He described himself as a gentleman. Both of the witnesses against him were lying.

42   The judge ruled, in relation to the admission of evidence of bad character, that although the Crown's application was out of time, and that no notice in accordance with the rules had been given, it was in the interests of justice that the application should succeed because no prejudice had resulted to the defence from the lack of notice.

43   The Recorder said that the defendant's convictions for assault and theft, in 1998, and for an offence contrary to s.5 of the Public Order Act 1986 committed in 2003 , were clearly bad character within the meaning of s.98. In addition the defendant had pleaded guilty to a racially aggravated s.5 Public Order Act 1986 offence, which arose from the events following his arrest for the wounding of Miss Green. That offence also, in the Recorder's judgment, came within the definition of bad character. He rejected a defence submission that that evidence came within the exception in s.98(b) as being "misconduct in connection with the investigation . . . of that offence."

44   The Recorder ruled that the defendant's behaviour, after the offence, was admissible as being relevant to his demeanour and state of mind at the time of the offence. It was clearly capable of informing the jury of what was happening so soon after the crucial events. There was no prejudice in admitting the evidence, such as to lead to exclusion under s.78 of the Police and Criminal Evidence Act 1984 and therefore the evidence was admissible.

45   The Crown sought to admit the previous convictions under gateway (d), on the basis that the matters in issue between the parties were who attacked whom and whether the defendant was telling the truth in relation to self-defence. The Recorder ruled that the convictions for violence or disorder were relevant to the issue of self-defence. They showed a clear pattern of attacking people, so that the Crown could properly adduce the evidence to establish propensity. The Recorder said he was not satisfied that the defendant's honesty was a substantial issue, so that his conviction for theft ought to be admitted.

46   Having referred to s.101(3) and (4) the Recorder said he was satisfied that the evidence would not have such an adverse effect on the fairness of the proceedings that it ought to be excluded: on the contrary, it was capable of informing the jury of precisely what they needed to know. Although the first assault was committed when the defendant was 16, it could not be said to be one-off in view of his more recent offending in November 2002. Although the offences were not of the same description or category, for the purposes of s.103(2) and (4), that did not preclude admissibility.

47   There was an issue about whether the earlier conviction was for assaulting occasioning actual bodily harm or, as the defendant maintained, for common assault. That is one of the aspects which give rise to this application for leave

to appeal. We shall return to it a little later. The learned Recorder ruled that the underlying facts in relation to the conviction in 1998, for which no memorandum of conviction was then available, should not be admitted.

48   In passing sentence, the Recorder described the attack as unprovoked and vicious, on a slightly built young woman who presented absolutely no threat. She had been fun loving and carefree, but was now concerned about going out into rowdy places. The Recorder commented that there was little mitigation. The defendant was young (he is 22) and the Recorder commented that his record could have been worse but it was hardly a commendation. It was, the Recorder said, clear that he had not learned his lesson from previous offending, and it was to be pointed out that he had committed this offence during the period of a conditional discharge, imposed in December 2003, for 12 months, for an offence contrary to s.5 of the Public Order Act 1986.

49   The learned Recorder also referred to the illness of the defendant's mother, who, sadly, has multiple sclerosis and, until his incarceration, the defendant was her main carer. It is apparent from material before this court that she is finding it difficult to manage without him.

50   On behalf of the defendant, Mr McCrindell advances a number of grounds of appeal in seeking to challenge the defendant's conviction. First, he says, rightly, that it was not until the morning of the trial that antecedents were obtained and there had been no previous notice of an intention to rely on the defendant's previous convictions. Mr McCrindell refers to para.[2] in the judgment of this court in *Bovell and Dowds*, which stressed the importance of the rules being adhered to, so that, in particular, the defence are in a position to deal with the matters on which the prosecution rely, and both sides can make such enquiries as may be necessary with regard to the circumstances of convictions sought to be relied on. Mr McCrindell points out, rightly, that, if the rules had been complied with, everyone would have been clear as to exactly what evidence was to go before the jury.

51   So far as the admissibility of the convictions is concerned, Mr McCrindell stresses the difficulties arising from the want of notice in investigating the nature of what was said to be an assault occasioning actual bodily harm. It is apparent from the memorandum of conviction, which has been obtained since trial, that the offence of which the defendant was previously convicted, which was the subject of dispute (it is to be noted the only subject of dispute) was common assault, not assault occasioning actual bodily harm. So far as that is concerned, however, the learned judge, directed the jury that it was probably best to assume for safety "that it was a conviction of common assault".

52   So far as the defendant's aggressive behaviour after the incident and following the arrival of the police officers is concerned, Mr McCrindell makes no complaint about want of notice in relation to that because statements from prosecution witnesses served on the defence described that conduct on which the prosecution wished to rely. The want of notice in relation to the convictions, as it seems to us, did not give rise to any prejudice so far as the defence were concerned. Clearly, it may well have been prejudicial had the matter proceeded wrongly on the basis that the offence was assault occasioning actual bodily harm, rather

than merely common assault. But, by virtue of the direction given by the Recorder in his summing-up, it is apparent that the case did not proceed on that basis.

53　　The second ground advanced by Mr McCrindell is that the material before the court, on the basis of which the bad character evidence was admitted, was of poor quality, in that it was derived from the police national computer. The difficulty with that submission, as it seems to us, is that there was nothing in dispute by the defence, in relation to the material from the police national computer, apart from the nature of the assault to which we have already referred. There is, in consequence, no substance in that ground.

54　　The third ground advanced by Mr McCrindell is that the bad character evidence should not have been admitted. In particular, in that regard, he refers to the speech of Lord Phillips of Worth Matravers in the civil, similar fact, case of *O'Brien v Chief Constable of South Wales Police* [2005] UKHL 26; [2005] 2 W.L.R. 1038. At paras [12] and [52] Lord Phillips of Worth Matravers, observed that the statutory provisions with which this court is presently concerned "require an enhanced relevance in order to ensure that the ambit of the trial remains manageable." As it seems to us, there was an enhanced relevance in relation to the earlier convictions and the events after these offences, so far as the defendant's behaviour is concerned. In our judgment, such matters were capable of establishing propensity to violence relevant to the crucial issue as to who was the aggressor.

55　　There are further grounds, 4, 5 and 6, in relation to the use of unchallenged racist language. But for the reasons which we have already indicated, the learned Recorder was entitled to conclude that they showed a high level of aggression on the defendant's part, immediately following the incident giving rise to the s.18 offence.

56　　Ground 7 is a further complaint about reliance on the police national computer with which we have sufficiently dealt.

57　　Grounds 8 to 12 are critical in various respects of the summing-up. It is said that, in Mr McCrindell's words, "this went a little bit too far", when the learned Recorder said that the prosecution case was that the defendant was an aggressive man who had been aggressive on this night. Something which goes a little bit too far, even if it does—and we are not persuaded that it does—is an insubstantial basis on which to suggest that a summing-up is so defective as to render a conviction arguably unsafe.

58　　Mr McCrindell relies on the observations made in para.[18] of this court's judgment in *R. v Hanson* [2005] 2 Cr.App.R. 21 (p.299), and submits that further directions in accordance with that judgment ought to have been given. Of course, that judgment was not available at the time of the Recorder's summing-up, and we have already, at the beginning of this judgment, referred to the way in which para.[18] in *Hanson* should be understood.

59　　The further criticism is made that, the Recorder's use of the phrase "you have been permitted to hear of these convictions . . . .", in the context of an explanation by the Recorder as to why those convictions were before the jury was terminology which might induce in the jury's mind a belief that the Recorder himself had already decided that the convictions were determinative of issues which the jury had to decide. We are wholly unpersuaded that that is a possible interpretation of that passage in the summing-up. In our judgment, without descending into further detail, there is no substance in any of the criticisms of the summing-up. Accordingly, leave to appeal against conviction is refused.

60   So far as sentence is concerned, the submission which is made in the written grounds of appeal and to which the court indicated it was sympathetic, is that five years is somewhat longer than is necessary in this case, having regard, in particular, to the degree of injuries sustained by the victim. The significant injury, as we have indicated, was to the hand rather than to the face. That is a matter to which, in reaching the appropriate sentence, attention should be paid. The court indicated that it was minded to reduce the sentence to one of four years' imprisonment. In a late submission, Mr McCrindell suggested that a figure below that might, in all the circumstances, having regard to the defendant's possible release dates, might be possible. In our judgment, five years was somewhat longer than necessary, even following a trial. Accordingly that sentence is quashed. We substitute for it a sentence of four years' imprisonment. We see no justification for going below that figure, in the light of all the circumstances in this case. Albeit that the physical injuries were not serious, the offence has had a serious impact upon the victim.

61   The appeal against sentence is therefore allowed in the way and to the extent which we have indicated.

62   We come, finally, to the application of Chohan. On February 8, 2005 at Manchester Crown Court, following a trial before Judge Mort, this defendant was convicted on count 1 of robbery, on count 2 of possession of an imitation firearm while committing a Sch.1 offence and on count 3 of possession of an imitation firearm with intent to cause fear of violence. He was sentenced to 10 years' imprisonment on count 1 and to three years' imprisonment concurrently on each of counts 2 and 3. The total sentence was therefore 10 years' imprisonment. His application for leave to appeal against conviction has been referred to this court by the Registrar.

63   The facts were these. A couple of days prior to the incident which formed the basis of the three counts, an 89 year old man called Sidney Marsh was visited at home by the defendant, who claimed that his mother had been robbed and he was looking for the culprits. He said he had written their descriptions on a piece of paper which he gave to Mr Marsh.

64   On May 19, 2003 Mr Marsh was again at home, in Solway Close, Oldham. The defendant arrived and shouted through the window: "I've found those lads." He walked into the kitchen, shook the complainant by the shoulders, produced what appeared to be a gun, pointed it at Mr Marsh's chest and said: "I want a fiver". Mr Marsh went to get a £5 note and the man took his wallet from him. That gave rise to counts 1 and 2. Astonishingly, when his robber had left his home, this 89 year old victim gave chase. He told a neighbour he had been robbed. Two women neighbours gave chase for a short while and confronted the man, who pointed a gun at them, giving rise to count 3. They backed off. He made good his escape.

65   The identification of the robber as the defendant rested upon a prosecution witness called Donna Marsh. She happened to be nearby, in Lee Street, when, she
said, the defendant, whom she knew as "Tony", ran past her. The issue, essentially, was whether she was right. The two women neighbours who had given
chase, although they gave descriptions of the man they chased, were unable to
pick him out on an identification parade.

66   Donna Marsh described seeing the man running away. She had a clear view of
him. She turned and said "Hello". He replied. She knew him as Tony. He was an
Asian man, about 30, five feet eight or nine, stocky and wearing a hat. She had his
face in sight for a minute or so. He had a gun in his hand. At this time, that is May
2003, she had known him for about a year. Her evidence (and to the circumstances in which it was admitted in this form we shall come in a moment), was
that she had seen him a lot, indeed every other day for a year or so, because
she bought heroin from him. She was taking heroin three or four times a day.
She used to meet him at the bottom of Lee Street, the street in which he was
when she saw Mr Marsh's assailant running away. She also met him at The Junction pub.

67   On August 25, 2004 she picked out the defendant on a VIPER parade as being
the man she had seen the previous May. The reason why there had been so long a
lapse of time between the offence of robbery and the VIPER parade was because,
for most of that period, from a time starting two days after the commission of this
offence, the defendant had been out of this country.

68   She said that she had not wanted to say that she was a heroin user. That was
why, in the first statement which she made to the police, she only referred to
knowing the defendant from seeing him around and in a pub. She thought she
had mentioned the gun in her first statement, but it was not there. She said she
had no reason to invent her evidence.

69   There were submissions made to the judge in relation to two different categories of evidence namely Donna Marsh and the defendant's previous
convictions. In relation to Donna Marsh she made a second statement on January
8, 2005 describing the basis on which she was able to recognise the defendant,
namely the frequency of their encounters during heroin dealings. The prosecution sought to adduce it, under gateway (c) of s.101(1), that is to say, that it
was "important explanatory evidence". explanatory, of course, in relation to
the basis of her identification.

70   The judge ruled that, in such a case, it was inevitable that the jury, who would
have to be directed as to the caution necessary in identification by reference to
Turnbull would have to consider the circumstances in which the witness claimed
to be able to identify the defendant. It would, the judge concluded, be difficult
properly to understand other evidence in the case without knowing the background of the heroin dealings which, he concluded, went to the heart of matters.

71   The wording of s.101(3) of the Act, whereby the court must not admit evidence
under gateways (d) or (g) if it appears that it would have such an adverse effect on
the fairness of the proceedings that the court ought not to admit it, suggested, the
judge said, that s.78 of the Police and Criminal Evidence Act 1984 was not applicable in relation to gateways (d) and (g). But, he concluded, even if he was wrong,

he would not exercise his discretion in this case to exclude the evidence, bearing in mind the vital importance to the identification by Donna Marsh of the explanatory evidence.

72   Submissions were also made in relation to the defendant's previous convictions, of which there are a considerable number. The application related to a robbery/assault with intent to rob, in 1992, and three burglaries in 2000. The Crown sought to adduce that evidence as to those convictionsunder gateway (d) on the basis that they were relevant to an important matter in issue, namely, a propensity to commit the type of offence with which the defendant was charged. They fell under subs.(1)(a), in that they were of the same description or category as the offence charged and, therefore, were admissible, subject to s.103(3), in relation to the length of time since the conviction, or any other matter, which rendered them inadmissible. The judge concluded that, despite the lapse of time, it was not unjust to admit the robbery conviction in 1992, bearing in mind the defendant's continuing criminality thereafter and the fact that it was a serious robbery at knife-point, which was material in the present case. Furthermore, the three burglaries in 2000 were relevant because they involved very similar methods of operation, namely gaining entry, by falsity, into the homes of the elderly. The judge concluded that it would not have such an adverse effect on the fairness of the proceedings that they ought not to be admitted. Furthermore, so far as the robbery in 1992, was concerned, although that offence was old, it demonstrated a propensity to commit offences involving the use of a weapon against a householder.

73   The defendant in evidence said that he had not been at Mr Marshall's house on May 19, nor had he had a gun. He had never been a drug dealer. He had gone to Pakistan soon after the offence because his wife's mother was there and she had been taken ill. He said that, in interview, he had not known what was meant by the name Donna Marsh: he only knew her by her first name. He claimed to have recognised her when he came to court. He had known her for several years, as they were both heroin users. He claimed, and it is to be emphasised that this was denied by Donna Marsh, that he had had a sexual relationship with her. He suggested that she must have lied about seeing him running away from the robbery because he had not told her that he had remarried.

74   On behalf of the defendant, Mr Samuels submits that the judge was wrong to admit Donna Marsh's second statement describing the heroin dealing with the defendant. Mr Samuels accepted, rightly, that only a fraction of the defendant's record went before the jury by reason of the judge's ruling. He submits that it would have been possible to edit the statement in relation to the heroin dealing, in order to disclose a frequency of encounters, without disclosing the reason for those encounters. The prejudice arising from the allegation of heroin dealing was such that the judge ought not to have admitted the statement in the form which he did. It is to be noted that whereas initially, the defence based upon a challenge to the frequency of the association between the defendant and Donna Marsh it later changed to a claim of deliberate dishonesty by her, promoted by malice.

75   In our judgment, the circumstances of this case, in relation to identification, were such that no sustainable criticism can be made of the judge's decision to

admit in evidence the witness Donna Marsh's second statement. Only if that was done, as it seems to us, would it be possible for her sensibly to explain, not least, in the face of the different defences emanating from the defendant, the basis of her ability to identify him in the circumstances which she did.

76   So far as the admission of the 1992 robbery and the three dwelling-house burglaries in 2000 are concerned, Mr Samuels was frank enough to concede that the circumstances of the three burglaries were, as he put it, "uncomfortably close" to the offence charged. As it seems to us, that was a reason not for excluding the evidence of those convictions but for admitting it. The judge's exercise of discretion, in relation to the admission of these convictions was, as it seems to us, impeccably performed. No suggestion is made that he took into account inappropriate considerations or failed to take into account appropriate considerations. Accordingly, the application for leave to appeal against conviction on behalf of Chohan fails.

77   Before leaving the case of Chohan, it is, as we foreshadowed at the beginning of this judgment, perhaps helpful to refer to the summing-up of Judge Mort in Chohan's case:

> "In this case you have heard evidence that Mr Chohan has a bad character, in the sense that he has got criminal convictions and you have heard, it is alleged, that he otherwise misconducted himself by supplying heroin to Donna Marsh. It is important that you understand why you have heard this evidence and how you can use it. As I will explain in more detail later, you must not convict Mr Chohan only because he has got a bad character. You have heard of this bad character because, first of all, in relation to the allegation that he was supplying drugs to Donna (and bear in mind it is her allegation that that is the position) it may help you to understand other evidence in the case, namely how is it that Donna Marsh was so confident that the man running past her on Lee Street, running away from Mr Marsh and from the two women, was the defendant. The reason being because she was seeing him several times a day when acquiring drugs from him. So it may help you to consider the accuracy and reliability of her identification and it may help you to understand the case as a whole. You have heard, in relation to the previous convictions, of his bad character and it may help you to resolve an issue that has arisen between the defence and the prosecution, namely the question whether he has a propensity or a tendency or an inclination to commit offences of the kind with which he is charged. If you think it is right, you may take the previous convictions into account, in deciding whether or not Mr Chohan committed the offences with which he is now charged. The prosecution rely on the robberies in 1992 because they show that he has a tendency to use weapons to threaten violence to steal and two instances have been given to you where a sheath knife was used, one in order to steal and one whereby theft actually took place and it is said, ten years on, now he is using a handgun. The prosecution rely on the burglaries in 2000 because they say that they show that the defendant has a tendency to use bogus explanations to trick his way into

older people's homes in order to steal from them . . . So the prosecution's case there is that it is, on this occasion, a combination of pretending to be looking for people who have robbed his mother, asking for a pen and paper to write down the description of the alleged robberies and then using the pretext, coming back and saying: 'We have found them' going in, producing the gun and stealing wallet. So the Crown are saying here there is a tendency to commit robberies with a weapon and to target the elderly with bogus explanations and, therefore, they say it makes it more likely that he is guilty of the offence. The defence, on the other hand, say, first of all, these robberies were ten years ago, he described himself, 'I was about 16 or 17 at the time, the burglaries were three years old, I always pleaded guilty to offences that I had been arrested for' and it is, in fairness to the defence, a matter which you can take into account, deciding what impact the convictions had on his truthfulness. Mr Samuels put it in a well known phrase from Casablanca of 'rounding up the usual suspects' and that is what obviously you must be very careful about . . .

If you do conclude that, at the time of these offences in May, 2003, Mr Chohan did have a propensity to commit offences of that type, namely robberies with weapons or targeting the elderly with bogus explanations to get entry into the property, then you can consider whether it makes it more likely that he committed the offences in May, 2003. You have to decide to what extent, if at all, his character helps you when you are considering whether or not he is guilty. You must not convict simply because of his convictions, nor mainly because of them. The propensity or tendency amounts to some additional evidence pointing to guilt, but please bear in mind, even if he did have such a tendency, it does not necessarily prove that he would commit further offences or that he has committed these offences.

You are also entitled to consider the evidence of Mr Chohan's previous convictions in the following way. If you think it right, you may take into account, when deciding whether or not his evidence to you was truthful, because a person with convictions for dishonesty may be less likely to tell the truth, but it does not follow that he is not capable of telling the truth. Indeed, Mr Chohan says, 'The fact that on the previous occasions I have been arrested and I have always held my hands up means that, when I plead not guilty, I am likely to be telling the truth' and you decide to what extent his character helps you when judging his evidence. So that is the extent to which the evidence of his previous convictions may be used for the particular purposes I have just indicated, if you find it helpful."

That approach is not only, rightly not criticised by Mr Samuels in this case, but, subject to one refinement in relation to the distinction drawn between propensity to dishonesty and propensity to untruthfulness in para.[13] of *Hanson*, it provides an impeccable summing-up which may well afford useful guidance in other cases where summing up the significance of previous convictions.

78   For the reasons which we have given, Chohan's application for leave to appeal against conviction is refused.

79   Although we have not, in the course of this judgment, referred expressly to the written submissions provided for the court's benefit by Mr Houlder Q.C., on behalf of the Crown, we are greatly indebted to him for the submissions which he made in relation to each of these cases.

Edwards' application for leave to appeal against conviction refused; appeal against sentence allowed.
Fysh's appeal against conviction dismissed.
Duggan's application for leave to appeal against conviction refused; appeal against sentence allowed.
Chohan's application for leave to appeal against conviction refused.

R. v H (P.G.)

COURT OF APPEAL (Lord Justice Maurice Kay, Mr Justice Field, Judge Moss Q.C.): July 1; 21, 2005

[2005] EWCA Crim 2083; [2006] 1 Cr.App.R. 4

⟨LT⟩ Commencement; Criminal Evidence, Hearsay Evidence, Institution of proceedings; Legislation; Preparatory Hearings, Statutory provisions

H1   EVIDENCE
         Hearsay
         Defendant charged with fraud—Preparatory hearing held—Hearsay provisions coming into force between preparatory hearing and empanelment of jury—Whether trial commencing with preparatory hearing for purpose of provisions—Whether provisions applicable—Criminal Justice Act 1987 (c.38), s.8—Criminal Justice Act 2003 (c.44), ss.140, 141.

H2   H was charged with conspiracy to defraud. The case against him proceeded under Pt. 1 of the Criminal Justice Act 1987 which, by s.8[1], provided that if the judge ordered a preparatory hearing the trial began with that hearing. On February 9, 2005 a preparatory hearing was held at which H was arraigned and various other matters considered but no evidence was heard. On April 4, 2005 the hearsay provisions in Ch.1 of Pt 11 of the Criminal Justice Act 2003 came into force. By s.141 of that Act no provision in Pt 11 had effect in relation to criminal proceedings begun before the commencement of that provision. On April 22, the judge acceded to an application made by the Crown pursuant to Pt 11 for the admission of hearsay evidence. H brought an interlocutory appeal on the ground that by s.8 of the 1987 Act the trial had begun for all purposes with the preparatory hearing on February 9, and accordingly, since the hearsay provisions had not come into force until April 4, the Crown could not rely on them.

H3   **Held,** dismissing the appeal, that s.8 of the 1987 Act fixed the point of the commencement of the trial for purposes connected with that Act including the need to identify and tie in the trial judge from an early stage and for rulings made at such a stage to remain binding on all the parties. The purpose of s.141 of the 2003 Act was different. The reference to proceedings "in which the strict rules of evidence apply" in s.140 meant primarily trials in which a jury or judge was determining factual issues between the prosecution and the defence. Accordingly, the proceedings did not begin for the purposes of the hearsay provisions until the jury was empanelled or the judge embarked on his task. In those circumstances, the new hearsay provisions applied in the instant case (post, paras [7, 9]).

---

[1]   Criminal Justice Act 1987, s.8: post, para.3

H4   *Per curiam.* Even if evidence has been heard at a preparatory hearing held before April 4, 2005, since the trial before a jury involves a different fact-finding exercise, the new hearsay provisions are applicable to a trial heard after that date (post, para.[8]).

H5   (For s.8 of the Criminal Justice Act 1987, see *Archbold* 2005, para.[2–112]; for s.140 of the Criminal Justice Act 2003, see *ibid.* para.8–67d)

Interlocutory appeal under s.9 of the Criminal Justice Act 1987

H6   The appellant, H, was due to stand trial with seven other defendants, in the Crown Court at Cardiff (Judge Bidder Q.C.) on charges of conspiracy to defraud. On February 9, 2005 a preparatory hearing was held, pursuant to s.7 of the Criminal Justice Act 1987, at which the defendants were arraigned and entered pleas of not guilty. On April 22, 2005 the prosecution applied for the admission of hearsay evidence pursuant to the provisions of the Criminal Justice Act 2003 which had come into force on April 4, 2005. On June 13, 2005, the trial judge ruled that the new hearsay provisions would apply to the trial. He gave leave to H to appeal against that ruling.

H7   The facts and grounds of appeal appear in the judgment of the court.

H8   *Richard Sutton Q.C.* and *Adam Kane* (instructed by Hallinan, Blackburn, Gittings & Nott) for the appellant.
Peter Davies (instructed by the Crown Prosecution Service, Newport) for the Crown.

Cur. adv. vult.

July 1.   Maurice Kay L.J. gave the judgment of the court.

1   This is an interlocutory appeal under s.9 of the Criminal Justice Act 1987. We shall refer to the appellant as H. Together with seven other defendants he is now standing trial in the Crown Court at Cardiff in relation to allegations of conspiracy to defraud. It is anticipated that, following that trial, further trials will take place involving the same and additional defendants. The case is proceeding pursuant to the provisions of Pt 1 of the Criminal Justice Act 1987. On February 9, 2005 a preparatory hearing was held pursuant to s.7 of the 1987 Act. The defendants were arraigned and entered pleas of not guilty. Various matters were considered. The preparatory hearing was then adjourned. On April 4, 2005 a number of the provisions of the Criminal Justice Act 2003 came into force. They include the provisions on hearsay evidence. Although counsel for the prosecution had first thought that the new hearsay provisions would not apply to the forthcoming trial, he later had a change of heart and on April 22, 2005 the prosecution applied for the admission of hearsay evidence pursuant to the provisions of the 2003 Act. In due course there was a hearing before the trial judge and on June 13, 2005 he ruled that the new hearsay evidence provisions will apply to the

trial. The present appeal, for which leave was given by the trial judge, is against that ruling.

2   It is well-known that the sequential coming into force of parts of the 2003 Act has already caused difficulty in the context of pending trials. In *R. v Bradley* [2005] EWCA Crim 20; [2005] 1 Cr.App.R. 24 (p.397) this court held that the new provisions in relation to bad character which came into force on December 15, 2004 applied to all trials and *Newton* (*R. v Newton* (1983) 77 Cr.App.R. 13) hearings begun after that date, regardless of when the defendant had been charged or arraigned. Rose L.J. trenchantly criticised the lack of clarity in statutory provisions relating to commencement. That criticism does not appear to have been heeded because the statutory instrument by which the hearsay provisions were subsequently brought into force, namely the Criminal Justice Act 2003 (Commencement No.8 and Transitional and Saving Provisions) Order 2005 (SI 2005/950) has given rise to precisely the same kind of difficulty in the present case.

3   We apprehend that in relation to the generality of prosecutions the position regarding the new hearsay provisions is resolved by analogy with *Bradley*. In other words, they apply to trials and other hearings such as *Newton* hearings beginning on or after April 4, where findings of fact are made and to which the strict rules of evidence apply. The present problem arises because this case is proceeding under the provisions of the Criminal Justice Act 1987. The preparatory hearing did not involve the hearing of evidence. Nevertheless, the difficulty is that by s.8 of the 1987 Act:

"(1) If a judge orders a preparatory hearing, the trial shall begin with that hearing.

(2) Arraignment shall accordingly take place at the start of the preparatory hearing."

The submission is therefore made on behalf of the appellant that the present trial began for all purposes on February 9, two months before the new hearsay provisions came into force. If that is right, the prosecution will not be able to rely on the new provisions in the current trial.

4   The hearsay provisions are to be found in Pt 11of the 2003 Act. Section 141 provides:

"No provision of this Part has effect in relation to criminal proceedings begun before the commencement of that provision."

By s.140, "criminal proceedings" means "criminal proceedings in relation to which the strict rules of evidence apply".

5   These are the words that led the court in *Bradley* to conclude that the criminal proceedings referred to in s.141 are trials and *Newton* hearings. However *Bradley* was not concerned with any complication arising under the 1987 Act.

6   The position for which the appellant contends would have the effect that, at the moment, the new hearsay provisions would apply to most criminal trials commenced on or after April 4, but not to trials under Pt 1 of the 1987 Act in relation to which a preparatory hearing has taken place before that date but a

jury is not empanelled until a later date. We would find such a dichotomy to be very surprising indeed. If the intention had been to have two different regimes operating at the same time, depending on whether or not the case came under the 1987 Act, we would have expected express provision to that effect, in the form of express reference to the 1987 Act. However, there would be no obvious reason for such a distinction and we would be anxious not to sanction one unless the wording of the statute compelled us to do so. The new hearsay provisions may accrue for the benefit of the defence as much as for the prosecution. It would be strange indeed if a defendant in a serious fraud trial proceeding under the 1987 Act were to be denied resort to provisions which apply generally to other prosecutions.

7   The issue in *Bradley* was resolved by means of a purposive approach. We propose to adopt the same approach here. In our judgment, s.8 of the 1987 Act fixes the point of the commencement of "the trial" for purposes connected with the 1987 Act. These include the need to identify and tie in the trial judge from an early stage and for rulings made at such a stage to remain binding on the parties, subject to any appeal. The purpose of s.141 of the 2003 Act is totally different. It was identified by this court in *Bradley*. We are confident that the reference to proceedings "in which the strict rules of evidence apply" means, primarily, trials in which a jury (or the judge) is determining factual issues between the prosecution and the defence. In relation to such circumstances, the proceedings in question do not begin until the jury is empanelled (or the judge embarks on his task). This conclusion is consistent with *Bradley* and produces uniformity as between prosecutions of different types.

8   In the present case no evidence was heard at the preparatory hearing. If it had been, the new hearsay provisions would not have applied. It is suggested on behalf of the appellant that, if that had been the case, it would have determined for all time in the present case that the new provisions would remain inapplicable. We do not consider that to be correct. In our judgment the new provisions would still have been applicable to the trial which has recently commenced. The trial before the jury involves a separate fact-finding exercise with the different consequences envisaged by *Bradley*. We are fortified in this conclusion by consideration of the case of another defendant in the present case. A defendant to whom we shall refer as C was permissibly absent from the preparatory hearing on February 9. He was only arraigned at a later date, albeit still before April 4. However, consider the position which would arise if he had been arraigned on or after April 4. In his case, s.8 of the 1987 Act would have the effect that his preparatory hearing began on the date of arraignment and his trial began at that point. If the position were that contended for by Mr Sutton Q.C. on behalf of the appellant, during the trial before the jury the new hearsay provisions would apply to that defendant (both to his detriment and to his benefit) but would not apply to the other defendants who had been arraigned in February. In our judgment, that is just the kind of situation that *Bradley* was anxious to avoid.

9   It follows from what we have said that the hearsay provisions of the 2003 Act
are applicable to the trial before the jury in this case. Accordingly this appeal is
dismissed.

Appeal dismissed.

R. v HARRIS
R. v ROCK
R. v CHERRY
R. v FAULDER

COURT OF APPEAL (Lord Justice Gage, Mr Justice Gross and
Mr Justice McFarlane): June 16, 2005; July 21, 2005

[2005] EWCA Crim 1980; [2006] 1 Cr.App.R. 5

(LT) Fresh evidence; Grievous bodily harm; Manslaughter; Medical evidence;
Murder; Non accidental injury; shaken baby syndrome

H1   EVIDENCE
   Expert medical evidence
   Shaken baby syndrome—Triad of intercranial injuries strong pointer to syn-
   drome but not diagnostic—Unified hypothesis not credible alternative cause of
   triad—Guidance as to expert witnesses

H2   The accepted hypothesis was that shaken baby syndrome ("SBS"), more properly called non-accidental head injury ("NAHI"), depended on findings of a triad
   of intercranial injuries consisting of encephalopathy, subdural haemorrhages and
   retinal haemorrhages. For many years the coincidence of those injuries in infants
   had been considered to be the hallmark of NAHI but the supposed infallibility of
   the triad had subsequently been challenged by a hypothesis known as the unified
   hypothesis. It was so called because it relied on the proposal that there was one
   unified cause of the three intracranial injuries constituting the triad which was
   not necessarily trauma.

H3   As a result of critical medical papers published in the medical journals the unified hypothesis could no longer be regarded as a credible or alternative cause of
   the triad of injuries. However, although the triad had not been undermined in the
   manner envisaged by the authors of the unified hypothesis and it remained a
   strong pointer to NAHI, on its own it was not possible to find that the triad automatically and necessarily led to a diagnosis of NAHI. Cases of alleged NAHI
   were fact-specific and had to be determined on their individual facts. It was for
   the jury to resolve differences between medical opinions, taking into account
   all the circumstances, including the clinical picture (post, paras [56]–[57],
   [68]–[70]).

H4   *Per curiam* It might be helpful for judges, practitioners and experts to be
   reminded of the guidance concerning expert witnesses provided by Cresswell
   J. in *National Justice Cia Naviera SA v Prudential Assurance Co Ltd (Ikarian
   Reefer)* [1993] 2 Lloyd's Rep 68 at 81 and Wall J. in *In re AB (Child Abuse: Expert
   Witnesses)* [1995] 1 F.L.R. 181 which was very relevant in criminal proceedings.

The new Criminal Procedure Rules provided wide powers of case management to the court. Rule 24 and para.15 of the Plea and Case Management form made provision for experts to consult together and, if possible, agree points of agreement or disagreement with a summary of reasons. In cases involving allegations of child abuse the judge should be prepared to give directions in respect of expert evidence taking into account the guidance given by Cresswell and Wall JJ. If that guidance was borne in mind and the directions made were clear and adhered to, it ought to be possible to narrow the areas of dispute before trial and limit the volume of expert evidence which the jury would have to consider (post, paras 270–273).

H5   (For expert evidence, see *Archbold* 2005, para.10–64 and following)

Appeals against conviction

H6   *R. v Harris*

On September 7, 2000 in the Crown Court at Nottingham (Butterfield J.) the appellant, Lorraine Harris, was convicted of the manslaughter of her infant son, Patrick, aged four months. She was sentenced to three years' imprisonment. The facts and grounds of appeal appear in the judgment of the court.

H7   *R. v Rock*

On September 21, 1999 in the Crown Court at Chelmsford (McKinnon J.) the appellant, Raymond Charles Rock, was convicted of the murder of Heidi Smith, aged 13 months. He was sentenced to imprisonment for life. The facts and grounds of appeal appear in the judgment of the court.

H8   *R. v Cherry*

On October 9, 1995 in the Crown Court at Birmingham (Judge Crawford) the appellant, Alan Barry Joseph Cherry, was convicted of the manslaughter of Sarah Eburne-Day, aged 21 months. He was sentenced to two years' imprisonment. The facts and grounds of appeal appear in the judgment of the court.

H9   *R. v Faulder*

On April 28, 1999 in the Crown Court at Teesside Crown Court (Judge Whitburn) the appellant, Michael Ian Faulder, was convicted of inflicting grievous bodily harm, contrary to s.20 of the Offences against the Person Act 1861, on his infant son, N, aged seven weeks. He was sentenced to 30 months' imprisonment. The facts and grounds of appeal appear in the judgment of the court.

H10   *Michael Mansfield Q.C.* and *Peter Wilcock* (instructed by Stephensons, Wigan) for Harris and Cherry.

Michael Mansfield Q.C. and *James Gregory* (instructed by Stephensons, Wigan) for Rock.

Michael Mansfield Q.C. and *Robert Woodcock* (instructed by Brennans, Wallsend, Tyne & Wear) for Faulder.

Richard Horwell and *Zoe Johnson* (instructed by the Crown Prosecution Service), for the Crown.

Cur. adv. vult.

July 21.   Gage L.J. handed down the judgment of the court.

1   In these four appeals, which have been heard together, four carers, as they have been described, appeal against convictions for manslaughter, Lorraine Harris; murder, Raymond Charles Rock; manslaughter, Alan Barry Joseph Cherry; and s.20 inflicting grievous bodily harm, Michael Ian Faulder. The victims were Patrick McGuire, aged four months, in the case of Harris; Heidi Smith, aged 13 months, in the case of Rock; Sarah Eburne-Day, aged 21 months, in the case of Cherry; and N, aged seven weeks, in the case of Faulder. Throughout this judgment we shall refer to the victims by their christian names and to the appellants by their surnames. Patrick was the son of Harris; Heidi was the daughter of Rock's partner; Sarah was the daughter of Cherry's partner; and N was Faulder's son. At the time immediately before each of the victims became seriously ill each was in the sole care respectively of Harris, Rock, Cherry and Faulder.

2   All of the appellants were convicted following trials. On September 7, 2000 at Nottingham Crown Court Harris was convicted of manslaughter and sentenced to three years' imprisonment. On September 21, 1999 at Chelmsford Crown Court Rock was convicted of murder and sentenced to imprisonment for life. On October 9, 1995 at Birmingham Crown Court Cherry was convicted of manslaughter and sentenced to two years' imprisonment. On April 28, 1999 at Teesside Crown Court Faulder was convicted of s.20 inflicting grievous bodily harm and sentenced to 30 months' imprisonment.

3   The common thread running through each of these four appeals is a submission that since these convictions medical research has developed to the extent that there is now "fresh evidence" which throws doubt on the safety of each conviction.

4   Following the judgment of this Court in *R. v Cannings* [2004] EWCA Crim 1; [2004] 2 Cr.App.R. 7 (p.63); [2004] 1 W.L.R. 2607 the Law Officers set up an Interdepartmental Group to review convictions of defendants in alleged "battered babies" cases. As a result of that review letters were sent to Harris and Cherry advising that each might feel it appropriate for the safety of her or his conviction to be considered further by the Court of Appeal. Each lodged notices of appeal and sought extensions of time in which to apply for leave. Each has been granted an extension of time and leave to appeal. Rock had already lodged a notice of appeal. He appeals with the leave of the Court. In the case of Faulder his appeal comes to this Court by way of a reference from the Criminal Cases Review Commission. Mr Michael Mansfield Q.C. is leading counsel for all four appellants. Mr Richard Horwell leads for the Crown in each appeal.

5   These appeals have involved the court receiving (by agreement of the parties) evidence from 10 medical expert witnesses called on behalf of the appellants and eleven called on behalf the Crown. We also received the written evidence of four further witnesses. In general terms the issues between the two sets of medical expert witnesses are as follows. First, the evidence called on behalf of the appellants relied on recent research which it is said demonstrated that long held medical opinion of the conventional signs giving rise to inferences of unlawful assaults on infants and very young children is unreliable. The basis of this chal-

lenge was a hypothesis based on recent research. However there were also other associated medical issues. The Crown's medical witnesses do not accept that the hypothesis is correct or that it is supported by the new research.

6   Secondly the Crown do not accept that the fresh evidence in relation to other specific issues in any way renders the convictions of these appellants unsafe.

The trials

Harris

7   Harris faced a single count of manslaughter. In summary the evidence was as follows. Patrick was born on August 13, 1998. He was the son of Lorraine Harris and Sean Maguire all of whom lived in the same house with two daughters of Harris from a previous relationship. The evidence showed that, although the pregnancy was not planned, both Harris and Maguire were happy about the impending birth. After his birth, Patrick gave every indication of being a thriving and much loved baby. Maguire described Harris as being as happy as he had ever known her. Harris received support from Maguire's mother and her own mother. There were no financial difficulties and health professionals said that the family gave the impression of perfection.

8   On December 4, 1999 Harris took Patrick for his third immunisation. The rest of the day passed without any significant event. Maguire was on night shift and Harris remained in the house with Patrick. Shortly before 1.00am on December 5, 9 Harris noticed that Patrick was having difficulty breathing and called Dr Barber, the GP. Whether or not this was in evidence at the trial, it is agreed that in the telephone call Harris said to Dr Barber:

> "I woke up to give him his feed and he wasn't breathing. Not until I picked him up and sort of shook him. He seems as right as rain now."

9   Dr Barber stated that on arrival Harris appeared calm and controlled. Dr Barber had formed the opinion that Harris was an experienced and sensible mother. He examined Patrick. Patrick's eyes were normal and he had all the appropriate reflexes. He recorded Patrick's temperature as 38.2, mildly raised. There were no signs of abuse or bruising. Patrick's chest was clear and although he was a little "snuffly" Dr Barber concluded that there was nothing wrong with him. He left the house at 1.30am.

10   At 2.34am Harris made a 999 call to the emergency services and reported that Patrick would not wake up. An ambulance arrived seven minutes later. The crew endeavoured to resuscitate Patrick. They recorded that Patrick did not have a pulse and was making no respiratory effort although he was still warm. Patrick and Harris were taken to Derby Children's Hospital arriving at 3.15am Patrick was put on a life support machine. The evidence was that Harris was "plainly in considerable stress and crying." Patrick was noted as having fixed and dilated pupils and retinal haemorrhages.

11   Patrick was seen by Dr Dodd a consultant paediatrician, who examined him at approximately 4.30am. He described Patrick as having widely dilated pupils enabling him to make a clear examination of the retina. He found gross preretinal

haemorrhages which were so extensive that he could not recall seeing any that were worse. There were no external injuries. He was so concerned about Patrick's condition that he arranged for him to be transferred to the specialist unit at Nottingham. In Nottingham a blood sample test was taken. The test showed that there was marked hypofibronogenemia. Despite the best efforts of the medical team caring for him Patrick died on December 6, 1999.

12   In late March 2000 Harris was arrested and interviewed about these events. In the summing-up the judge described Harris' answers at interview as entirely consistent with the evidence which she gave at her trial.

13   The prosecution called a number of expert medical witnesses both as to fact and also opinion evidence. Those witnesses were Dr Bouch, a Pathologist, who had conducted a post mortem on Patrick. He concluded that Patrick had died as a result of a shake which caused bleeding into the skull around the brain. He described what he meant by a "shake" as much more than rough handling. Prof. Green, a paediatric pathologist, with a special interest in ophthalmic pathology gave evidence that there was extensive bleeding in the vitreous of the left eye and extensive haemorrhaging of the retina. The bleeding in the right eye was less extensive. His conclusion was that his findings were those typically seen when shaking or, shaking and an impact had occurred. A consultant haematologist, Dr Giangrande, who specialised in blood diseases, gave evidence to the effect that the low level of fibrinogen in the Patrick's blood system, in his opinion, was the result of an injury sustained by Patrick and not a pre-existing condition. However he was unable to rule out the possibility that that condition was present before the brain injury was caused. Finally, the prosecution called Mr Punt, a consultant paediatric brain surgeon. His evidence was that the amount of blood over the surface of the brain shown on the scan and the description of the amount of blood over the surface of the brain at post mortem was not sufficient to cause Patrick's death. In his opinion it was injury to the brain itself which caused death; and that the brain injury was caused either by shaking or an impact or a combination of both. In his opinion whatever caused the injury to the brain was likely to have been in consequence of an incident after Dr Barber had left the home at 1.30am. In his view it was extremely improbable that the injuries were the result of a bleeding disorder.

14   Harris, a woman of good character, gave evidence in her own defence. Her evidence was that on the evening of December 4, 1998 Patrick became "chesty and grunty". Because he had difficulty in breathing she called out Dr Barber. After his visit she put Patrick in his cot. He seemed to have settled a bit. When she awoke approximately an hour later she checked him. His arms were on the top of the covers; he was a bit pale and cold. When she picked him up he was floppy. She said that she panicked and put him down in the cot. She telephoned her mother and then the ambulance. She vaguely remembered bouncing him on her knee whilst she was on the telephone. At interview she had said that she had Patrick on her knee when she telephoned the ambulance and that she remembered her knees "were going ten to the dozen." In evidence she said that she found it difficult to remember the sequence of events because she had tried to put it out of her mind. She accepted that she had told the doctor on the telephone

that Patrick had stopped breathing in order to make him hurry. She said she was unable to offer any explanation for his injuries.

15   On her behalf three expert medical witnesses gave evidence. They were Dr Batman, a consultant histopathologist; Dr Jones, a consultant paediatrician; and Dr Macdonald, a consultant neuropathologist. Dr Batman thought that there were three possible causes of Patrick's death. They were (a) natural causes such as bleeding from a blood disorder; (b) shaking with or without impact; and (c) re-bleeding of an old blood clot. He regarded the latter as the least likely of three. In evidence, Dr Jones stated that his conclusion was that the findings were entirely consistent with a bleeding disorder. However he conceded that one would have expected more blood than was present if there was a blood disorder. He accepted that the findings were consistent with Patrick having been shaken and he agreed that he had never seen a child with fibrinogen deficiency which had died. Dr Macdonald concluded that Patrick's injuries were not the result of a severe non-accidental injury although he conceded that the extent of the haemorrhages inside the vitreous jelly of his eye equated to a quite severe shaking. But the fact that there was no bleeding on the optic nerve of the right eye was a contra-indication.

16   In a summing-up, about which there is and can be no criticism, the judge described the issue for the jury as follows:

> "The prosecution assert that she killed Patrick by deliberately shaking him violently or by shaking him violently and then throwing him down in his cot so as to cause bleeding inside his skull, thus leading to his collapse and death. The defendant denies that she did any such thing. She cannot explain her son's collapse and death, but maintains that she did nothing which might have brought about that death. If you are not sure that the defendant killed Patrick, then you find her not guilty".

After deliberating for just short of three hours the jury returned a verdict of guilty of manslaughter.

Rock

17   Rock faced an indictment charging him with the murder of Heidi Smith. Heidi Jane Smith was born on May 10, 1997 and was the daughter of Lisa Hudson and James Smith. Lisa Hudson's relationship with James Smith did not last long and by March 1998 she was living at the home of Rock. Rock was aged 26 and had previously been married with two children of his own. His children lived with their mother.

18   The evidence was that Heidi was a happy, healthy baby and hardly ever cried. In general Rock was very good with and doted on Heidi. There was evidence that he was concerned about her well-being and showed no hostility towards her. However, Lisa Hudson said in evidence that Rock had a temper. She spoke of an incident about two weeks before Heidi's death when Heidi was grizzly and would not settle. She said that on that occasion Rock held Heidi to his face and

said "shut up" in what she thought was a nasty fashion. On another occasion Rock complained that "Its Heidi this and Heidi that".

19   On June 2, 1998 Lisa's mother, Thelma Hudson, was looking after Heidi. At 6.30pm Thelma took Heidi back to Rock's home after he had returned from work. Lisa Hudson was still at work. Thelma Hudson placed Heidi in her cot at 6.35pm. She said that when she left Heidi was asleep and breathing normally. At 7.08pm Thelma Hudson telephoned Rock and spoke to him. From approximately 7.00pm Lisa Hudson could not get a response from the telephone at Rock's home. A next door neighbour, Gail Banham, said that some time between 7.05pm and 7.10pm, from her kitchen, she could hear screaming coming from one of the homes at the back of her house. She said that the screaming sounded like a very sustained temper tantrum of a child aged between nine months to eighteen months. She also heard someone shouting at the child. It was a male and youngish. He was swearing and told the child to "fucking shut up". The screaming did not stop. She went to the front of her house where she could hear nothing but then returned to her back kitchen. The screaming continued and she heard the same voice telling the child to shut up. The screaming continued but as she finished dishing up a meal it stopped and went completely silent. Her evidence was that this occurred at 7.20pm. In the unused material there were statements from police officers concerning an experiment conducted by them to see if shouting in one house could be heard in the other. The result of this experiment was inconclusive.

20   However, Rock, in evidence, agreed that he had told Heidi to shut up but it was in the context of a longer sentence in which he said "you heard your mum, you've got to shut up". He said that after Thelma Hudson had telephoned him he checked that Heidi was asleep and went downstairs to watch a video. During this time he heard loud crying. He went upstairs and found Heidi sitting up in her cot, red-faced and very upset. He said that he picked her up by her armpits and placed her in the crook of his right arm with his left hand under her bottom. He then rocked her from side to side at the same time trying to wind up the mobile on the top of the wardrobe. Heidi slipped through his arms onto the floor. He said that he saw Heidi hit the floor; she did not bang her head but did not stop crying. He immediately picked her up. She was completely still and not breathing. He patted her on the back saying "come on Heidi sweetheart". He then held her in front of him but did not violently shake her. He shook her lightly by placing her on the floor where she was having the occasional spasm. He tried to give her mouth to mouth resuscitation but on the fourth occasion she began to vomit. He took her to the bathroom, held her face down over the sink and banged her back to allow the sick to come out. His evidence was that she began vomiting again. Seeing this he ran downstairs with Heidi and dialled 999. His telephone call was timed at 7.27pm. The paramedics arrived at 7.37pm. They found Heidi lying on the floor in a dimly lit room. Rock told them that he had dropped Heidi onto her bottom whilst he had been trying to wind up a clockwork toy. He told them that Heidi had not hit her head on the floor as he had been able to catch and support her head before it hit the floor. He then picked her up and she had gone limp and stopped breathing. He told them that he had tried mouth-to-

mouth resuscitation and Heidi had vomited. One of the paramedics saw signs of vomit around Heidi's mouth. He said that on the way to the hospital in the ambulance Rock had asked questions such as "has she got brain damage?" "Has she got lung damage?" On arrival at the hospital Heidi was taken straight to the resuscitation room. She was subsequently transferred to the Intensive Treatment Unit as she was having spasmodic fits; both her eyes were rolling to the left; she was pale but breathing and unconscious.

21   At the hospital, Rock gave an account of events to both Lisa and Thelma Hudson and all of the medical staff. His explanation of the incident was much the same as that which he gave in evidence. He maintained that Heidi did not bang her head when she fell and he told no one that he had shaken her. To Lisa Hudson he said "I am so sorry, I dropped her on her bum". And later in the hospital chapel, "I killed her, I killed her. Please God let her live, save her."

22   The prosecution called a number of medical witnesses including expert witnesses. A consultant ophthalmic surgeon said that he examined Heidi's eyes when she was comatose and on a ventilator. He found massive retinal haemorrhaging at all layers on both retinas. There was also tenting/pulling forward of the major retinal vessels or folds. He concluded that in the absence of any specific medical condition the haemorrhages and tenting were the result of severe acceleration and deceleration forces. He said that he had never seen such severe damage to a person's retina. Dr Jaspan, a consultant neuroradiologist (one of the expert witnesses called by the Crown in these appeals) examined a CT scan taken at 10.25pm on June 2, 1997. He found a thin layer of blood lying along the falx and within the brain at the back of the head. In his opinion these findings were consistent with trauma. In his view the disrupted delicate blood vessels in the brain had been damaged and the damage was profound and irreversible. He concluded that the trauma was so severe as to render Heidi immediately unconscious and that the injuries were highly characteristic of violent shaking. In his opinion dropping a child on its bottom was inconsistent with Heidi's injuries.

23   Mr Jonathan Punt, a consultant paediatric neurosurgeon, also examined the first CT scan of June 2, and agreed with Dr Jaspan's conclusions. He concluded that the degree of violence required to cause the injuries to Heidi was "extreme; grossly in excess of any vigorous handling, even rough handling."

24   Dr Cary, a pathologist, conducted the post mortem on the same day as the life support machine had been discontinued. He found a number of superficial bruises over Heidi's body. In addition there was bruising within the scalp over the back of head and bleeding around the optic nerve. The brain was swollen and there was bleeding on the surface of the brain. There was no skull fracture. He said that in his opinion the head injuries in conjunction with the retinal detachment in both eyes were consistent with shaken baby syndrome (SBS). In his view the cause was shaking or shaking plus an impact which caused injuries to the brain. He said that the force required was "shaking as hard as you can". Further, he concluded that the changes which had occurred to Heidi's eyes meant that there must have been several shakes back and forth with acceleration and deceleration.

25   A professor of forensic pathology, Prof. Michael Green, gave evidence that there were haemorrhages around both optic nerve roots and that the retina had

started to pull away. There was a detachment between the sclera and the retina and extensive bleeding around the optic nerve. In his view the injuries were typical of a serious shaking plus impact.

26   Finally, Dr Christine Smith, a consultant neuropathologist, called by the prosecution, described the brain as swollen and said that she had found on the inner surface of the dura remnants of blood. There was also widespread damage to nerve cells. She concluded that the injuries to the brain were consistent with trauma which had caused the brain to move in relation to the skull. She said that the most likely cause of the haemorrhaging to the eyes was shaking. She said there was no evidence of natural diseases present which could have lead to Heidi's death.

27   Rock gave evidence in his own defence. We have already referred to his version as to how he came to drop Heidi on the floor. He denied shaking Heidi but accepted that as a father he knew the consequences of shaking a baby could be fatal. He accepted in cross-examination that he had not told the doctors or the police that Heidi had become floppy after he had shaken her. He said that feelings of guilt were the reason for him not telling the police. He confessed that at the hospital it was obvious to him that Heidi was suffering from brain damage but he did not tell the doctors about shaking Heidi.

28   No expert witnesses were called on Rock's behalf.

29   In his summing-up the judge told the jury that Rock admitted shaking Heidi. He said:

> "It is for you to say, but you may think that, in the end, the defendant was bound to admit that he had shaken Heidi, and shaken her before she became floppy, because the evidence that she was shaken is so strong, so overwhelming. How else were those injuries caused to Heidi, if it were not by the defendant shaking her, and shaking her with considerably excessive force? That is a question you are entitled to ask yourself, obviously. There is no question of accident here. It is not suggested that what the defendant did was done otherwise than deliberately."

30   The judge went on to direct the jury that the difference between murder and manslaughter was one of intention. Further, he told them that there was a third possible verdict and that was not guilty of anything. He continued:

> "So, I must leave it open for you to say whether the defendant is not guilty of anything. I am allowed, however, to suggest to you that not guilty of anything is not a realistic verdict in this case. As I say, you decide this case. If you think that the defendant's account that he did not shake Heidi violently so as to cause those injuries to Heidi from which she died, that his account is true or may be true, then he is entitled to be acquitted both of murder and manslaughter."

After deliberating for a period of forty minutes the jury returned a verdict of guilty of murder.

Cherry

31   Cherry faced an indictment charging him with the manslaughter of his partner's daughter Sarah. Sarah's mother, Mrs Shirley Eburne-Day, and her
children including Sarah and Cherry, at the time of the incident giving rise to
the charge, were all living together at Mrs Eburne-Day's home. Sarah was the
youngest of Mrs Eburne-Day's three children. Mrs Eburne-Day and Cherry
had lived together for some months. The evidence suggested that he was a
good step-father to the children. On Thursday February 3, 1994, in the morning,
Sarah was left in the sole care of Cherry. Earlier in the week she had developed a
thumb infection for which a doctor had prescribed antibiotics. After taking some
medicine on February 2, Sarah was sick so different antibiotics were prescribed.

32   On the morning of February 3, 1994, at about 8.30am, Mrs Eburne-Day left
Sarah at home with Cherry whilst she drove her two older children and a neigh-
bour's daughter to school. The plan was that Cherry would take Sarah to Mrs
Eburne-Day's father's home where, in the course of the morning, Cherry and ·
Mrs Eburne-Day would meet before both went to Birmingham for Cherry to
attend a job interview.

33   That morning Sarah was a little better than on the previous day and appeared to
be behaving perfectly ordinarily. Mrs Eburne-Day said that she had no concerns
about leaving her. She said that she and Cherry had discussed Sarah's health and
decided that she was fit enough to be left with her grandparents. In evidence,
Cherry said that he disagreed. He said that Sarah was not very well on Thursday
morning. She was not in a bright condition and wanted to sleep and be cuddled by
her mother. He denied that he had any conversation with Mrs Eburne-Day about
Sarah's health that morning.

34   Lianne Osbourne, a next door neighbour, called that morning for a lift to
school. Before leaving with Mrs Eburne-Day she said that she saw Cherry briefly.
He was wearing dark trousers, a white striped shirt and a red brown paisley pat-
terned tie. Apart from his jacket he appeared almost ready to go out. In evidence
Cherry denied that when seen by Lianne Osbourne he had been fully dressed for
work.

35   There was evidence that Cherry was next seen in the street in a distressed state
seeking assistance from various neighbours. Sarah's grandfather, Mr Eburne-
Day, received a telephone call from Cherry at precisely 8.55am asking him to
call an ambulance, which he did. Mrs Redding, a neighbour and trained nurse,
saw Sarah just before the ambulance arrived. She said that Sarah appeared to
be dead or on the verge of death. She applied resuscitation techniques until the
ambulance arrived at approximately 9.20am. Sarah was taken first to George
Eliot Hospital in Nuneaton but was later transferred to the Intensive Therapy
Unit at Birmingham Children's Hospital. In spite of all medical efforts Sarah
died about 48 hours later.

36   On February 4, 1994 Cherry was arrested on suspicion of causing grievous
bodily harm with intent. This was before Sarah had been pronounced dead. He
was interviewed by police and explained that he had left Sarah standing on a
small yellow chair whilst he went upstairs briefly to put on a shirt and tie. Appar-

ently, it had been Sarah's habit to stand on the yellow chair in order to look out of the window at the front of the house. He explained that when he returned he found Sarah lying on the floor motionless and making gurgling noises. He said that he picked her up and described her body feeling like a rag doll. She did not respond and therefore he telephoned her grandfather to ask him to telephone for an ambulance. He explained that she must have become suddenly ill and fallen from the chair. He denied shaking her or throwing her around but said that she had fallen out of her sister's bed at the weekend. On February 6, 1994 he was charged with the murder of Sarah and after caution replied "I'm not guilty. I've committed no offence". In the event, the Crown proceeded with a charge of manslaughter rather than murder.

37   At trial, giving evidence in his own defence, Cherry repeated what he had said at interview. He said that after going upstairs to finish off dressing for "only a few minutes" he returned to find Sarah "lying on the floor, obviously badly injured." He said that when he picked Sarah up and tried to pat her back he removed "some yellow stuff from her mouth".

38   At trial the prosecution called a number of medical witnesses. Doctor (now Professor) Whitwell conducted the post mortem upon Sarah. Her finding was that death had been caused by "cerebral swelling and subdural haematoma". In addition, she found two bruises at the back of the head (3.5cms and 1.5cms in diameter and on opposite sides) and five small areas of bruising higher up. In her opinion the five smaller bruises were consistent with pressure from fingers. In cross-examination she did not accept that the injuries could have been caused by falling from the yellow chair. She said that the injuries were more consistent with Sarah's head being forcibly put against something. In her opinion it was highly unlikely that Sarah could have injured herself by banging her head against the floor although that was not impossible. She said it was unlikely the injuries could have been caused by a single fall because there were two separate areas of impact and two separate bruises, although she could not exclude this absolutely.

39   A radiologist, Dr Chapman, stated that it was very rare for a child to have this kind of bleeding from a domestic fall. In his opinion a fall from the yellow chair had not caused Sarah's injuries. Dr Akuba, a neurological registrar, in a witness statement, said that she had inserted a tube into Sarah's skull as part of her treatment and recorded that "Cerebral spinal fluid emerged under moderate pressure. It was yellow and looked like old blood. Query, query".

40   Dr Rylance, a consultant paediatrician, having seen Sarah at Birmingham Children's Hospital, took the view that her injuries were non-accidental. He was asked about a previous statement which he had made and in which he stated that the injury giving rise to blood inside the skull occurred almost certainly more than 12 hours previously and probably more than 36 hours previously. He said in evidence that he had since changed his opinion and in fact it could have been $10\frac{1}{2}$ or 11 hours previously. He said that Sarah's vomiting the day before was more likely to have been caused by the medicine than a previous brain injury because when she stopped taking the medicine she stopped vomiting.

41   Finally, the prosecution called Mr Flint, a surgeon, who described the five small bruises on Sarah's head which were, in his opinion, indicative of her having been held. The two bruises on the back of her head suggested at least two blows. In his opinion it was very unlikely that the bruises were caused by her slipping backwards from the chair and hitting her head on the floor. In his opinion a healthy child could not sustain such injuries revealed by the post mortem by falling the short distance from the chair onto the carpeted floor.

42   In addition to his own evidence, there was called on Cherry's behalf a neurologist Dr West and a consultant pathologist, Dr Ackland. Dr West had viewed films taken by Dr Whitwell. He said that what he saw was consistent with a child having aspirated liquid which was a frequent complication of head injuries. Dr Ackland did not rule out the possibility of abuse causing the injuries but was of the opinion that an accidental fall from the chair was a significant possibility. In his opinion there was a small possibility that Sarah had some earlier injury that was aggravated by the fall but he did not regard that as a high possibility. He said that the five marks on Sarah's head may have been caused by a firm grip during the medical treatment.

43   In his summing-up the judge described the issue for the jury to decide in the following terms:

> "The cause of her death was a swelling of the brain caused by an impact of one sort or another. It is the prosecution case that the impact was in consequence of an unlawful blow delivered by this defendant. Your task will be to decide whether that case is proved or not."

After deliberating for just over two and a half hours the jury returned a unanimous verdict of guilty of manslaughter.

Faulder

44   At trial Faulder faced an indictment containing 2 counts. They were count 1, a s.18 offence of causing grievous bodily harm with intent; and count 2 an alternative s.20 offence. He was convicted of the latter offence. The evidence showed that at 10.30pm on Friday February 13, 1998 N then aged seven weeks (but born two weeks premature) was admitted to the Dryburn Hospital with severe injuries. On the following day N was transferred to a specialist unit at the Newcastle General Hospital where his condition deteriorated over the following week. Although there was concern that he might not survive he recovered and was transferred back to Dryburn Hospital on March 5, 1998. On March 16, 1998 he was discharged from hospital.

45   The event which led to N's admission to hospital occurred at the home occupied by Faulder and his partner. It was common ground that at the time Faulder was the sole carer of N. His case was that N's injuries were caused entirely accidentally. He said that he had dropped N and that in falling N struck and injured his head. The case for the prosecution was that Faulder had caused the injuries by a deliberate act or actions.

46   The prosecution case was based on the assertion that the extensive brain injuries sustained by N and revealed on x-ray and brain scans could not have been occasioned in the manner described by Faulder. The prosecution relied on the evidence of three expert witnesses for the proposition that Faulder must have shaken N and thrown him onto the floor.

47   Dr Camille de San Lazaro at the time a consultant paediatrician at the Royal Victoria Infirmary gave evidence that the injuries sustained by N were consistent with shaking and were not consistent with Faulder's account. She said that his version of the events could not account for the subdural haemorrhages. She further stated that in relation to Faulder's account of N making a sudden arching movement which caused him to drop N that at that age the child would have had insufficient muscle tone to achieve the movement described by Faulder. Further Faulder's description of N falling onto a pushchair and then a highchair before hitting the floor would have had the effect of breaking N's fall rather than exacerbating it.

48   Dr Alexander, a consultant paediatrician at the Newcastle General Hospital, gave evidence that on examination of N on February 14, 1998 he found a triangular bruise on the top of N's head and two bruises on the forehead over the right eye. He said that the child's fontanelle was unusually tense, symptomatic of swelling of the brain due to brain damage. In his opinion the CT scan showed bilateral subdural haemorrhages. He conceded that the superficial marks on N's face and head were consistent with Faulder's account but asserted that this account did not provide an explanation for the bruise on the right side of the forehead or the severity of the brain injuries. In his opinion the brain injuries were such as were commonly caused by repeated shaking with considerable force, and the clinical findings were more consistent with non-accidental injury than with an accident.

49   Mr Gholkar, a consultant neuroradiologist, having examined the brain scans concluded that the evident changes in the appearance of the brain were due to severe brain damage unlikely to have been occasioned in the manner described by Faulder and were characteristic of shaking injuries.

50   There was no evidence of retinal haemorrhages and there was some dispute as to the extent to which retinal haemorrhages were to be found in babies with "shaking" injuries. Dr de San Lazaro stated that her study showed that 53 per cent of children believed to have been shaken, had retinal haemorrhages.

51   Faulder gave evidence in his own defence. He said that he did not deliberately cause the injuries. He explained how he had dropped N by accident when attempting to place him into his pushchair. He said that he had been holding him along his arm with his hand supporting the baby's head. The baby moved suddenly and fell on to the edge of the pushchair. This caused him to bounce off the pushchair and on to the concrete floor bouncing his head on the adjacent highchair as he fell. Faulder conceded that the baby had been crying for twenty minutes but said that he had not lost his temper. He maintained that he did not shake nor forcibly place N into his pushchair. His answers at interview were consistent with his evidence at trial.

52   Dr Rushton a paediatric pathologist gave evidence for Faulder. He put forward the possibility that N's contact with the pushchair and highchair might have lead to the production of rotary forces that accelerated the head and increased the force of contact with the floor. He noted that the three external injuries (bruises) found on the baby's head were consistent with Faulder's explanation but were difficult to explain if the injuries were due to shaking or a single impact injury. He also referred to the lack of retinal haemorrhages saying that in his opinion the cause of retinal haemorrhages was not fully understood. In his view subdural hae-morrhages could be caused by shaking or impact but they might also be consistent with injury caused in the manner described by Faulder.

53   The judge directed the jury in his summing-up that the first question for it to decide was:

> "Was this or may it have been accident or design? If you come to the con-clusion that this is or may have been a tragic accident it follows that the defendant cannot be guilty of count 1 or count 2 and must be acquitted by you. That is the simple issue for you to decide."

54   After deliberating for just less than two hours the jury returned a verdict of guilty of count 2.

55   On conviction Faulder applied for leave to appeal against conviction and sen-tence and for an extension of time. His applications were refused by the single judge.

The triad and the unified hypothesis

56   At the heart of these appeals, as they were advanced in the notices of appeal and the appellants' skeleton arguments, was a challenge to the accepted hypothesis concerning "shaken baby syndrome" (SBS); or, as we believe it should be more properly called, non-accidental head injury (NAHI). The accepted hypoth-esis depends on findings of a triad of intracranial injuries consisting of encephalopathy (defined as disease of the brain affecting the brain's function); subdural haemorrhages (SDH); and retinal haemorrhages (RH). For many years the coincidence of these injuries in infants (babies aged between one month and two years) has been considered to be the hallmark of NAHI. Not all three of the triad of injuries are necessary for NAHI to be diagnosed, but most doctors who gave evidence to us in support of the triad stated that no diagnosis of pure SBS (as contrasted with impact injuries or impact and shaking) could be made without both encephalopathy and subdural haemmorhages. Professor Carol Jenny, a paediatrician and consultant neuro-trauma specialist called by the Crown, went further and said that she would be very cautious about diagnos-ing SBS in the absence of retinal haemmorhages. In addition, the Crown points to two further factors of circumstantial evidence, namely that the injuries are invari-ably inflicted by a sole carer in the absence of any witness; and that they are followed by an inadequate history, incompatible with the severity of the injuries.

57   Between 2000 and 2004 a team of distinguished doctors led by Dr Jennian Geddes, a neuropathologist with a speciality in work with children, produced

three papers setting out the results of their research into the triad. In the third paper "Geddes III", the team put forward a new hypothesis, "the unified hypothesis", which challenged the supposed infallibility of the triad. It was called the unified hypothesis because it relied on the proposal that there was one unified cause of the three intracranial injuries constituting the triad; that cause was not necessarily trauma. It is important to note that the new hypothesis did not seek to show that the triad was inconsistent with NAHI. It did, however, seek to show that it was not diagnostic.

58   When Geddes III was published it was, and still is, very controversial. It is not overstating the position to say that this paper generated a fierce debate in the medical profession, both nationally and internationally. In the course of the hearing of these appeals we have heard evidence from a number of very distinguished medical experts with a range of different specialities most of whom had in witness statements expressed views on one side or other of the debate. However, early on in the hearing it became apparent that substantial parts of the basis of the unified hypothesis could no longer stand. Dr Geddes, at the beginning of her cross-examination, accepted that the unified hypothesis was never advanced with a view to being proved in court. She said that it was meant to stimulate debate. Further, she accepted that the hypothesis might not be quite correct; or as she put it:

"I think we might not have the theory quite right. I think possibly the emphasis on hypoxia—no, I think possibly we are looking more at raised pressure being the critical event."

And later in her evidence:

"Q. Dr Geddes, cases up and down the country are taking place where Geddes III is cited by the defence time and time again as the reason why the established theory is wrong.
A. That I am very sorry about. It is not fact; it is hypothesis but, as I have already said, so is the traditional explanation. . . . I would be very unhappy to think that cases were being thrown out on the basis that my theory was fact. We asked the editor if we could have "Hypothesis Paper" put at the top and he did not, but we do use the word "hypothesis" throughout."

59   Despite these frank admissions the triad and Geddes III have been a focus of much of the medical issues in these appeals. We propose to set out the salient features of each in a little more detail. We do so not only as a backdrop to these appeals but in an effort to inform those involved in future trials as to the current accepted state of medical science, as we understand it from the evidence before us, on some of the very difficult issues which are raised in criminal and civil trials involving allegations of NAHI.

The anatomy

60   In order to explain the two hypotheses it is necessary to set out some of the anatomy involved in terms which can be understood by laymen and which

from a medical viewpoint may seem somewhat simplistic. At the outset, in order to assist the reader, we attach as annexes to this judgment a glossary of medical terms (app.A), and diagrams of the head (app.B).

61   The brain is encased in three membranes. The one immediately surrounding the brain is the pia mater. The next one is the arachnoid. Between the pia and the arachnoid is an area known as the subarachnoid space. The third membrane, which surrounds the brain and continues down the body surrounding and protecting the spinal cord, is the dura. Between the dura and the arachnoid is the subdural space. Between the dura and the arachnoid there are veins running between the two membranes which are called bridging veins.

62   The brain is divided into two halves or cerebral hemispheres. The two hemispheres are separated by the falx which itself is part of the dura. Below the cerebral hemispheres the brain is joined to the spinal cord at the craniocervical junction, which, as its name implies, is situated in the neck. The spinal cord extends down from the brain, through the foramen magnum and into the spine.

The triad

63   As already stated when the three elements of the triad coincide for some years conventional medical opinion has been that this is diagnostic of NAHI. Typically the brain is found to be encephalopathic; bleeding is found in the subdural space between the dura and the arachnoid subdural haemmorhages; and there are retinal haemorrhages. There may also be other pathological signs such as subarachnoid bleeding and injuries at the cranio-cervical junction. Further, there may be injuries to nerve tissue (axonal injuries) and external signs of broken bones, bruising and other obvious injuries such as extradural oedema (bruising). Determining these findings requires medical experts from a number of different disciplines interpreting often very small signs within the complex structures of an infant's brain and surrounding tissue.

64   The mechanism for these injuries is said to be the shaking of the infant, with or without impact on a solid surface, which moves the brain within the skull damaging the brain and shearing the bridging veins between the dura and the arachnoid. The shaking may also cause retinal haemorrhages. In the sense that the explanation for the triad is said to be caused by shaking and/or impact it also is a unified hypothesis, albeit that each element is said to be caused individually by trauma.

65   The triad of injuries becomes central to a diagnosis of NAHI when there are no other signs or symptoms of trauma such as bruises or fractures.

The unified hypothesis ("Geddes III")

66   Dr Geddes and her colleagues, following research into almost fifty paediatric cases without head injury, proposed that the same triad of injuries could be caused by severe hypoxia (lack of oxygen in the tissues) which in turn led to brain swelling. The hypothesis was that brain swelling combined with raised intracranial pressure (ICP) could cause both subdural haemorrhages and retinal haemmorhages. Thus, it was argued that any incidents of apnoea (cessation of breathing)

could set in motion a cascade of events which could cause the same injuries as seen in the triad. It will be appreciated that there are many events which could accidentally cause an episode of apnoea.

67   In Geddes III the unfied hypothesis was summarised as follows:

"Our observations in the present series indicate that, in the immature brain, hypoxia both alone and in combination with infection is sufficient to activate the pathophysiological cascade which culminates in altered vascular permeability and extravasation of blood within and under the dura. In the presence of brain swelling and raised intracranial pressure, vascular fragility and bleeding would be exacerbated by additional hemodynamic forces such as venous hypertension, and the effects of both sustained systemic arterial hypertension and episodic surges in blood pressure."

Thus, it was suggested that all the injuries constituting the triad could be attributed to a cause other than NAHI. We understand that this paper has been much cited in both criminal and civil trials since its publication.

68   The criticism of Geddes III is that it is not hypoxia and/or brain swelling which causes subdural haemorrhages and retinal haemorrhages but trauma. As an example of why the hypothesis is not correct Dr Jaspan, giving evidence in the appeal of Rock, demonstrated that CT scans taken of Heidi's brain showed that there was little or no brain swelling at a time when subdural haemorrhages and retinal haemorrhages were shown to be present. As a result of critical papers published in the medical journals, as we have already stated, Dr Geddes when cross-examined frankly admitted that the unified hypothesis could no longer credibly be put forward. In cross-examination she accepted that she could no longer support the hypothesis that brain swelling was the cause of subdural haemorrhages and retinal haemmorhages. She did, however, state that she believed that raised intracranial pressure ("ICP") might prove to be an independent cause of both lesions. When asked by Mr Horwell if she had published a paper on this hypothesis she said that she had not and that her research was still incomplete. It was clear from subsequent questions in cross-examination that this work was still in its early stages and that many questions remain, as yet, unresolved.

69   In our judgment, it follows that the unified hypothesis can no longer be regarded as a credible or alternative cause of the triad of injuries. This conclusion, however, is not determinative of the four appeals before us. There are many other medical issues involved in cases of alleged NAHI. Further, there remains a body of medical opinion which does not accept that the triad is an infallible tool for diagnosis. This body of opinion, whilst recognising that the triad is consistent with NAHI, cautions against its use as a certain diagnosis in the absence of other evidence. These four appeals raise different medical issues and do not necessarily fail because the unified hypothesis has not been validated. But it does mean that the triad, itself a hypothesis, has not been undermined in the way envisaged by the authors of Geddes III.

70   Mr Horwell, in his final submissions invited the Court to find that the triad was proved as a fact and not just a hypothesis. On the evidence before us we do not think it possible for us to do so. Whilst a strong pointer to NAHI on its own we

do not think it possible to find that it must automatically and necessarily lead to a diagnosis of NAHI. All the circumstances, including the clinical picture, must be taken into account. In any event, on general issues of this nature, where there is a genuine difference between two reputable medical opinions, in our judgment, the Court of Criminal Appeal will not usually be the appropriate forum for these issues to be resolved. The focus of this Court will be (as ours has been) to decide the safety of the conviction bearing in mind the test in fresh evidence appeals which we set out below. That is not to say that such differences cannot be resolved at trial. At trial, when such issues arise, it will be for the jury (in a criminal trial) and the judge (in a civil trial) to resolve them as issues of fact on all the available evidence in the case (see *R v Kai-Whitewind* [2005] EWCA 1092; [2005] 2 Cr.App.R. 31 (p.456)).

71 Before we leave Geddes III we must mention some evidence given by the first witness we heard, Dr Waney Squier, a consultant neuropathologist, which was the subject of some further investigation by the Crown's witnesses and further oral evidence. Dr Squier produced a slide taken from the brain of a four week old baby which she said demonstrated blood oozing from the dura into the sub-dural space. In her opinion this showed that intradural haemorrhages could leak into the subdural space and could be mistaken for subdural haemorrhages caused by shearing of the bridging veins. In that respect it challenged the diagnostic value placed on subdural haemmorhages by the triad. Mr Horwell asked for the slide and other slides made in respect of the same brain to be released for examination by the Crown's experts. We heard evidence in respect of this discrete issue on the last day of evidence.

72 In summary, two paediatric neuropathologists, Dr Rorke-Adams and Dr Hard-ing, said that the slide did not show intradural bleeding but was an example of the process of organisation of an earlier subdural haemorrhage.

73 It is unnecessary for us to go into the detail of this dispute. It is sufficient to say that having heard both sides forcefully express their views we are unable to resolve this issue and find, as Mr Horwell invited us to, that Dr Squier's evidence on it cannot be accepted. We content ourselves with the observation that even on the interpretation of objective evidence there can be two views expressed by highly experienced and distinguished medical experts.

Geddes I and II

74 Although, for the reasons already explained, the unified hypothesis can no longer stand as a credible alternative to the triad, a number of issues of general importance in respect of the triad remain. So far we have made no mention of the first two papers produced by Dr Geddes and her co-authors, which we will refer to as Geddes I and Geddes II. These papers represent conclusions reached in respect of research into a cohort of infants all of whom died from inflicted head injuries. Using a technique pioneered by Dr Geddes, the authors sought to ident-ify axonal damage (damage to the nerve tissues) in the brains of these infants. The technique involved detecting the presence of beta-amyloid precursor protein (β-APP) (a protein that builds up where axons have been damaged). The research

showed that widespread axonal damage, interpreted as vascular rather than traumatic, was present in 13 of the 37 cases. Conversely, widespread traumatic
axonal damage was found in only two cases and in both cases there were other
very clear signs of trauma (for example bilateral skull fractures). The authors
concluded that their findings strongly suggested that severe traumatic axonal
damage is a rarity in infant NAHI unless there is considerable impact, and that
the diffuse brain damage which was responsible for loss of consciousness in
the majority of cases was caused by starvation of oxygen (hypoxic) rather than
direct trauma to the brain.

75   The principle conclusion of Geddes II was that shaking an infant might cause a
stretching injury at the cranio-cervical junction to nerves which control the
child's cardio-respiratory system. In all the cases analysed the stretch injury itself
was survivable, what was life-threatening was the consequent hypoxic injury and
brain swelling that followed as a result of the damaged cardio-respiratory nerves
failing to function. The minimum degree of shaking force required to produce
such a stretch injury is unknown and a death may be caused in the manner
suggested by much less force than hitherto supposed. Although the results of
this research, as we understand it, are not challenged by those who criticise the
unified hypothesis, Mr Horwell submitted that its effect was limited. For instance
he submitted that it had no application to, and could not explain, cases involving
subdural bleeding and/or retinal haemmorhages.

Degree of force

76   This leads on to a very important issue which arises in these appeals and will no
doubt arise in many cases where the triad of injuries are present. It is the question
of how much force is necessary to cause those injuries. There is a measure of
common ground between the doctors on this issue. Generally it is agreed that
there is no scientific method of correlating the amount of force used and the
severity of the damage caused. To state the obvious, it is not possible to carry
out experiments on living children. Further, experience shows that the human
frame reacts differently in different infants to the same degree of force. However
the medical opinion on this issue appears to be divided into those who maintain
that severe injuries can confidently be ascribed to a traumatic cause, for example
(but not only) Dr Rorke-Adams, a very experienced paediatric neuropathologist,
and those who maintain that very little force may cause very serious injuries, for
example Dr John Plunkett, a distinguished anatomical, clinical and forensic
pathologist.

77   It is quite impossible for this court to make any finding on this issue beyond
referring to some general propositions with which both counsel agreed. First,
common sense suggests that the more severe the injuries the more probable
they will have been caused by greater force than mere "rough handling". We
note that the most recent *Update from the Ophthalmology Child Abuse Working
Party; Royal College of Ophthalmologists (2004)* concludes:

"It is highly unlikely that the forces required to produce retinal haemor-rhage in a child less than 2 years of age would be generated by a reasonable person during the course of (even rough) play or an attempt to arouse a sleeping or apparently unconscious child."

78   Secondly, as Mr Peter Richards, a very experienced neurosurgeon with a speciality in paediatrics, pointed out, if rough handling of an infant or something less than rough handling, commonly caused the sort of injuries which resulted in death, the hospitals would be full of such cases. In our view this points to the fact that cases of serious injuries caused by very minor force such as might occur in normal handling or rough handling of an infant, are likely to be rare or even extremely rare.

79   But, thirdly, as Dr Plunkett demonstrated by his research and in particular by reference to an amateur video of a child falling from a three foot high railing, described as part of a play tree-house, which resulted in catastrophic injuries, there will be cases where a small degree of force or a minor fall will cause very severe injuries. We shall have more to say about Dr Plunkett's research later in this judgment, but at this stage we repeat that the evidence suggests that cases where this occurs are likely to be very rare.

80   Fourthly, although the younger the infant or child, the more vulnerable it is likely to be, it is not possible to conclude that age is necessarily a factor in decid-ing whether injuries are caused by strong force or a minimal degree of force or impact. The balance of the evidence is that, although an infant's skull is more pli-able than that of an older child, the internal organs and vessels are as robust as those of an older child. The vulnerability of an infant arises from the fact that its head is generally larger in proportion to its body than in an older child and its neck muscles are weaker and not as well developed as in older children, hence the significance of injuries at the site of the craniocervical junction.

Biomechanics

81   In simple terms "biomechanics" is the application of traditional engineering principles to living organisms.

82   Many of the experts who gave evidence before us made reference to research in the field of biomechanics. The following extracts from the evidence demonstrate how the "biomechanics" argument was deployed by both sides.

83   Dr Squier referred to the "huge amount of evidence about the biomechanics" of shaking which had caused her to revise her views on the diagnosis of shaking.

84   Dr Geddes stated that belief that thin film subdural haemorrhages were caused by the rupture of bridging veins was "biomechanically exceptionally unlikely". She relied upon biomechanical research to support the view that shaking on its own cannot cause subdural haemorrhages and retinal haemorrhages without also significant structural damage to the neck and probably also a degree of axo-nal injury.

85   Dr Plunkett stressed the importance of understanding the mechanics of injury.

86   Dr Adams, referring to biomechanical research by Ommaya, considered that shaking was an improbable direct cause of retinal haemorrhage.

87   Mr Richards warned that, however good the biomechanical calculations may be, they do not always appear to give an answer that is common sense. He went on to stress the limits of current knowledge and understanding:

"Nobody really knows whether, when you shake a child, it is just back and forth or there is rotation as well. What does the head do? Does it decelerate against the back? Does it decelerate against the chin? When you put the child down, there must be an element of deceleration. It is a complex problem."

88   Of course none of the witnesses who gave evidence in the appeal was themselves an expert in biomechanics. Such were the number of references to biomechanics during the early days of the hearing that it became inevitable that some direct expert evidence on the subject was required. To that end the appellants filed a report by Dr Thibault and the Crown filed a report by Dr Gina Bertocci (dealing specifically with the case of Cherry). Because of the logistics involved, not least the constraints of time, it was not possible for either of these witnesses to give oral evidence. Consequently we are left to evaluate this important area by comparing and contrasting the views expressed on paper by Dr Thibault and Dr Bertocci.

89   Dr Thibault is a biomechanical engineer whose work has a particular emphasis on "Paediatric Head Injury Mechanics". Dr Thibault is not a doctor of medicine and holds a PhD in mechanical engineering. He has apparently performed experiments that have sought to mirror the age-dependant mechanical behaviour of the infant skull, sutures and brain. Part of the work in this field is to determine the amount of physical force that a living system can tolerate and thereby identify the "injury threshold" or "injury tolerance criteria". When the relevant threshold or criteria is exceeded the system or tissue will fail; for example stress on a bone will cause the bone to fracture if the stress exceeds the injury threshold.

90   Dr Thibault explained that whereas there is a substantial body of research into the mechanics of adult head injury, until recently there has been relatively little similar work in relation to paediatric head injury. He reported:

"It has been demonstrated experimentally and validated through real-world accident analysis that various intracranial pathologies result from excessive angular acceleration of the head. In general, angular acceleration of the head creates relative motion between the brain and the skull, causing potentially injurious strain within the intracranial neural and vascular tissues (bridging vessels, deep central white matter). The nature, distribution and severity of the resulting pathology depend not only on the angular acceleration magnitude, but also on its direction, onset rate and duration."

91   Like Dr Plunkett, Dr Thibault (relying on the research of Prange and others) drew attention to the ability of the skull of an infant to react to force by deforming itself and thereby causing internal injury to the brain substance and/or cranial vascular system.

92   In general terms, Dr Thibault joined issue with the conventional view that short falls are a frequent occurrence for young children and serious or fatal injuries

from such falls are rare. Recourse is also typically made to information about high speed traffic accidents or falls from two storey buildings. Dr Thibault considered such an approach to be simply "arbitrary, unscientific and meaningless" in that there is no attempt to evaluate the actual loads and forces at play in each individual case, which would need to include data regarding the child's orientation at impact, kinematics (motion) of the body, impact surface and anatomical impact locations. Dr Thibault is clear that impacts arising from falls can result in serious and fatal brain injuries.

93   The appellants rely upon the report of Dr Thibault for the following submissions:

   a) Shaking only could not produce the documented pathologies seen in these children;
   b) If "violent shaking" of the sort required to produce the documented injuries had taken place one would have expected cervico-medullary injury, cervical spine and spinal cord injury.

94   The Crown's expert, Dr Bertocci, is also a mechanical engineer by training and is Associate Professor of Biomechanics and Director of the Injury Risk Assessment and Prevention Laboratory in the University of Louisville, Kentucky, USA. Her primary area of research is injury biomechanics in cases of child abuse and paediatric falls. Dr Bertocci's report is very largely focussed upon the Cherry case and is not intended to be a comprehensive analysis of the biomechanical factors in play in each of these cases.

95   One general observation that Dr Bertocci, however, made is based upon her research into falls either from ground level or from nine inches above ground. Her conclusion in this regard is that the forces involved in such falls are well below the threshold said to be required to produce diffuse axonal injury in an infant, suggesting that there is a very low risk of DAI in such falls.

96   In this section of our judgment we have done no more than summarise this evidence. Where such evidence is called by one or other party or both in future litigation it will be for the jury (in a criminal trial) or the judge (in a civil trial) to evaluate it in the light of the cross-examination and all the other evidence.

Retinal haemorrhages

97   Retinal haemorrhage is the third limb of the triad. It will be recalled that Prof. Carol Jenny told us that in her view in a case of pure shaking extreme caution should be exercised before a diagnosis of NAHI is made in the absence of retinal haemorrhage. We see the force of this evidence. In cases of injuries alleged to have been caused by an impact or impacts, the evidence suggests that it is not a prerequisite for retinal haemorrhages to be found. Again, we understand the logic of this proposition.

98   It is agreed between the expert ophthalmologists and ophthalmic surgeons that a rapid rise in intracranial pressure can cause retinal haemorrhages although the amount and type of pressure required to cause such haemorrhages is a matter of debate. The appellants' expert ophthalmic surgeon, Dr Gillian Adams, said that

retinal haemorrhages could be caused by a spike or surge of venous pressure. Mr Peter Richards said that in his experience of carrying out brain surgery artificially induced very high venous pressure did not cause retinal haemorrhages.

99   Some of the ophthalmic experts stated that retinal haemorrhages caused by shaking or impact demonstrate entirely different characteristics from retinal haemorrhages arising from other causes. Others said that no distinction can be made between retinal haemorrhages arising from different causes.

100   Again, in the context of these appeals, we make no findings in respect of these differences of opinion. In future cases before a criminal or civil court, the type and extent of retinal haemorrhage and its place in the constellations of symptoms will be a matter for the court to evaluate in each individual case. We bear them in mind when reaching our conclusions in these four appeals. We also bear in mind Mr Horwell's submission that the real question in these appeals is how much force is necessary to cause not just one element of the triad but all three.

The Law

101   The principles on which this Court should act in appeals involving fresh evidence are not in dispute. They were clearly set out in *R. v Pendleton* [2001] UKHL 66; [2002] 1 Cr.App.R. 34 (p.441); [2002] 1 W.L.R. 72 by Lord Bingham of Cornhill (see in particular paras [18] and [19]). They were repeated by Lord Brown of Heaton-under-Heywood in a recent case in the Privy Council: *Dial and another v State of Trinidad and Tobago* [2005] UKPC 4; [2005] 1 W.L.R. 1660. Lord Brown said (see paras [31] and [32]):

> "31 In the board's view the law is now clearly established and can be simply stated as follows. Where fresh evidence is adduced on a criminal appeal it is for the Court of Appeal, assuming always that it accepts it, to evaluate its importance in the context of the remainder of the evidence in the case. If the court concludes that the fresh evidence raises no reasonable doubt as to the guilt of the accused it will dismiss the appeal. The primary question is for the court itself and is not what effect the fresh evidence would have had on the mind of the jury. That said, if the court regards the case as a difficult one, it may find it helpful to test its view "by asking whether the evidence, if given at the trial, might reasonably have affected the decision of the trial jury to convict": *R. v Pendleton* [2002] 1 W.L.R. 72, 83, para 19. The guiding principle nevertheless remains that stated by Viscount Dilhorne in *Stafford's* case [1974] AC 878, 906, and affirmed by the House in *R v Pendleton*:
>
> > 'While . . . the Court of Appeal and this House may find it a convenient approach to consider what a jury might have done if they had heard the fresh evidence, the ultimate responsibility rests with them and them alone for deciding the question [whether or not the verdict is unsafe]'
>
> 32 That is the principle correctly and consistently applied nowadays by the criminal division of the Court of Appeal in England — see, for example, *R v Hakala* [2002] EWCA Crim 730, *R v Hanratty, decd* [2002] 3 All ER 534 and *R v Ishtiaq Ahmed* [2002] EWCA Crim 2781. It was neatly expressed by Judge LJ in *R v Hakala*, at para 11, thus:

'However the safety of the appellant's conviction is examined, the essential question, and ultimately the only question for this court, is whether, in the light of the fresh evidence, the convictions are unsafe.'"

102 Mr Mansfield Q.C. also drew our attention to passages in the judgments of this court in *R. v Cannings* [2004] 2 Cr.App.R. 7 (p.63) and *R. v Kai-Whitewind* [2005] 2 Cr.App.R. 31 (p.456). In particular in opening he referred to [22] of *Cannings*:

> "These observations serve to highlight the second problem which can arise in this case, and cases like Sally Clark and Trupti Patel. We have read bundles of reports from numerous experts of great distinction in this field, together with transcripts of their evidence. If we have derived an overwhelming and abiding impression from studying this material, it is that a great deal about death in infancy, and its causes, remains as yet unknown and undiscovered. That impression is confirmed by counsel on both sides. Much work by dedicated men and women is devoted to this problem. No doubt one urgent objective is to reduce to an irreducible minimum the tragic waste of life and consequent life-scarring grief suffered by parents. In the process however much will also be learned about those deaths which are not natural, and are indeed the consequence of harmful parental activity. We cannot avoid the thought that some of the honest views expressed with reasonable confidence in the present case (on both sides of the argument) will have to be revised in years to come, when the fruits of continuing medical research, both here and internationally, become available. What may be unexplained today may be perfectly well understood tomorrow. Until then, any tendency to dogmatise should be met with an answering challenge".

But as the court was careful to point out later in the judgment at [178] this does not mean that fanciful doubts are a basis for rejecting expert evidence. With the general observations, referred to above and the legal principles in mind, we turn to the individual appeals. Furthermore, the limits of *Cannings* and its proper use were carefully explored in *Kai-Whitewind*, at [73]–[92], in observations with which we wholeheartedly agree.

Harris

103 Mr Mansfield Q.C. submits that there is a body of fresh evidence which is sufficient to cause this court on a review to quash the conviction. Mr Horwell submits that the fresh evidence has not in any way undermined the safety of the conviction.

104 Before we outline and discuss the fresh evidence we must refer in a little more detail to the evidence given at trial. Although Harris said that Patrick had been showing signs of some infection before December 4, 1998 on that day he was seen by a health visitor, Margaret Savill, and a doctor, Dr Michael Tory, at Boulton Clinic in Alvaston both of whom pronounced him fit to be given his third immunisation against diphtheria, tetanus, whooping cough, polio and HIB. State-

ments of their evidence to that effect were read at trial. In his statement, Dr Tory said that a child would not be given this injection unless he was satisfied that it was not suffering from a raised temperature, vomiting or diarrhoea. A mild cold or snuffle would not have prevented the injection being given.

105   On arrival at Harris' home at 2.41am the paramedic crew noted that Patrick was unconscious, cold, not moving, pulseless and not breathing. At 2.55am the crew diagnosed that he was suffering from cardio-respiratory arrest. Dr Adams, an ophthalmic surgeon called on behalf of Harris, interpreted diagrams of the eyes made by the crew as showing that the pupils were fixed and dilated. In any event this finding was made by Dr Bertenshaw who examined Patrick at 03.15am at the Derby Children' Hospital.

106   After being transferred from Derby to the Queens Medical Centre in Nottingham a CT scan was carried out at 11.50am. The findings were recorded by the radiologist and his conclusion was:

"Diffuse cerebral swelling and oedema secondary to hypoxia/ischaemia. Thin subdural haematoma in the para-falsine region. The appearances are suspicious of shaking or shaking—impact injury"

107   Following Patrick's death a post-mortem was carried out by Dr Bouch with Dr McKeever, a paediatric pathologist, in attendance. The findings relevant to this appeal are set out in Dr Bouch's witness statement of March 22, 1999. Paragraph 5 reads:

"The post-mortem examination confirmed a markedly swollen and softened brain and softened spinal cord with small amounts of subdural haemorrhage around the tentorium cerebelli at the foramen magnum and in the subdural space along the length of the spinal cord. Detailed examination by Professor Lowe confirmed widespread hypoxic (anoxic or ischaemic) changes within the brain resulting in marked swelling, necrosis of the cerebellum, haemorrhage into the left lateral ventricle and subarachnoid haemorrhage over the surface of the spinal chord and medulla. Professor Green confirmed extensive haemorrhages through the retina and the vitreous of both eyes with some retinal detachment"

Dr Bouch recorded the cause of death as cerebral hypoxia/ischaemia; intracranial haemorrhage; shaken baby syndrome. In his witness statement Dr Bouch said he had been advised that Patrick may have been shaken as part of an attempt to revive him. He said that he could not exclude such a shake as having caused the injuries but commented "accepted medical opinion is that the force required to produce injuries from shaking is greater than that resulting from rough handling of an infant". As already noted, Dr Punt said that the blood on the surface of the brain was not sufficient to cause Patrick's death. In his opinion it was the injury to the brain, caused by shaking, which caused his death.

The new evidence on the appeal

108   In this appeal we have heard evidence from the following witnesses called on behalf of Harris: Dr Waney Squier, a consultant neuropathologist, with a speciality in examining children's brains; Dr Jennian Geddes, although her evidence was primarily confined to general matters; Prof. Philip Luthert, a consultant ophthalmic pathologist and neuropathologist; Dr Gillian Adams, a consultant ophthalmic surgeon; Prof. James Morris, a consultant pathologist; Dr Robert Sunderland, a consultant paediatrician; and Dr Philip Anslow, a consultant neuroradiologist.

109   The Crown called the following witnesses: Dr Lucy Rorke-Adams, a consultant paediatric neuropathologist; Mr Peter Richards, a consultant neurosurgeon; Dr Richard Bonshek, a consultant ophthalmic pathologist; Mr R Gregson, a consultant ophthalmic surgeon; Dr William Lawler, a forensic pathologist; Dr Carole Jenny, a consultant paediatrician and consultant neuro trauma specialist; Prof. Klein, a consultant physician; Dr Timothy Jaspan, a consultant radiologist; Dr Paul Giangrande, a consultant haematologist; and Dr Mark Peters, a consultant paediatric intensivist. We have also read statements submitted from the following experts on behalf of the Crown: Dr Harish Vyas, a consultant in paediatric intensive care and respiratory medicine; and Dr Angie Wade a senior lecturer in medical statistics.

110   All these witnesses are clearly very experienced doctors in their own field. We shall summarise the evidence which they gave according to their respective specialities and only so far as is necessary to explain the important issues in this appeal.

The neuropathologists

111   The reports provided by Dr Waney Squier and Dr Rorke-Adams disclosed a head-on collision between these two experts on the pathological findings and on the cause of death. In our judgment they are the two of the most important witnesses in this appeal. Much of the debate has been focussed on the pathological findings and their interpretation.

112   Dr Waney Squier is a consultant and clinical lecturer at the Department of Neuropathology at the Radcliffe Infirmary, Oxford. Dr Rorke-Adams is the clinical professor of paediatrics at the University of Pennsylvania. She is clearly a very experienced and well respected member of her profession.

113   Dr Waney Squier started with the forensic disadvantage of having provided a report dated February 10, 2000 for Harris's trial solicitors in which she concluded that Patrick's injuries were non-accidental and consistent with shaking. Unsurprisingly, she was not called at trial to give evidence on Harris' behalf. She explained that, influenced by the research carried out by Dr Geddes since the trial, she had re-examined her own work in the light of the Geddes research. As a result in this case she had changed her mind and now concluded that the brain findings were of severe swelling and hypoxic/ischaemic injury; and that there was no incontrovertible evidence of trauma. She relied upon the history given by Harris and the clinical evidence as support for her conclusions.

114   Dr Rorke-Adams, having examined all the pathological evidence, the history
and the clinical history concluded that the injuries to the brain, the subdural haemorrhages and retinal haemorrhages, were all clear evidence of traumatic
injuries caused by strong force.

115   In the course of their evidence each of these witnesses commented on brain slices and photographs taken at the post mortem. Their evidence in respect of the
findings demonstrated by the photographs and slices was in sharp conflict in a
number of instances.

116   Photographs, G-H 1, 2 and 3, were said by Dr Rorke-Adams to show clear evidence of brain injury caused by trauma. She said that there could be no other
cause. Dr Squier was of the opinion that the injuries shown in the photographs
1 and 3 and damage to nerve tissue at the cervicocranial junction were probably
not caused by trauma and were consistent with herniation of the brain at the foramen magnum. She said herniation was caused by the pressure of the swelling
brain when it impacted with the narrowing channel of the foramen magnum.
As to the blood shown in photograph two Dr Squier said this was intrafalcine
bleeding (bruising) within the membrane, seen at post mortem which was an
extremely common finding in babies who have suffered from failure from
blood or oxygen supply.

117   There was no dispute that photographs G-H 4 and 5 showed subdural haemorrhages in the areas of the spinal cord. However, Dr Rorke-Adams gave as the
explanation for these that the vertebral arteries must have been ruptured causing
massive subarachnoid bleeding and subdural haemorrhages. She accepted that
the post mortem revealed no soft tissue injuries to the neck but pointed out this
explanation fitted with the combination of findings.

118   Dr Squier described the subdural haemorrhages of the spine as probably
caused by blood seeping down from the haemorrhage at the craniocervical junction. She said it was a common finding. Further, she did not accept that such
subdural haemorrhages as were found at post mortem were caused by trauma.
She said that it was local tissue necrosis causing bleeding exacerbated by a clot-
ting disorder (DIC). In addition she said that she had seen cases where bleeding
had seeped from the dura into the subdural space. As an example of this she provided her findings in the case to which we have referred in paras 71 to 73.

119   In our judgment there are difficulties with the evidence of both these doctors in
respect of their findings. The problem so far as Dr Squier is concerned is threefold. First her explanation of herniation as the cause of haemorrhages in the area
of the foramen magnum is, on the evidence we have heard, to say the least controversial. Dr Rorke-Adams dismissed this explanation as impossible. Mr Peter
Richards said that in his 20 years experience as a surgeon he had never seen a case
of herniation of the brain causing haemorrhaging at this site. He described
Dr Squier's evidence on this point as astonishing. Secondly, Dr Squier can provide no explanation for the mechanism that triggered these injuries. All she can
say is that the primary source of the injuries was some form of brain swelling, but
she was unable to give any precise cause for the swelling. In her view the most
likely explanation was sepsis or infection; and the least likely was trauma.
Beyond that she frankly admitted she did not know. Thirdly, Dr Giangrande,

whose evidence was not challenged, said that there was no question of DIC playing any part in any of these injuries.

120   So far as Dr Rorke-Adams is concerned, in our judgment, there are also difficulties in respect of her evidence. First, the injury to the brain which she described by reference to photographs G-H 1, 2 and 3 are not referred to in the post mortem report of Dr Bouch. Secondly, her explanation of a rupture of the vertebral artery may not be entirely consistent with there being no evidence of a soft tissue injury to the neck. But, as she pointed out, at post mortem the vertebral arteries were not dissected. Thirdly, subdural haemorrhages of the spine would appear to be very rare. Fourthly, the subdural haemorrhages described by her are neither thin-film nor situated in the classic position for SBS namely at the top of the head.

121   Before leaving the evidence of the two neuropathologists it is convenient to refer to the evidence given in this appeal by the neuroradiologists, Dr Anslow and Dr Jaspan. And we should also refer to the evidence of Mr Peter Richards. Dr Anslow and Dr Jaspan agreed that the CT scan taken at 11.50am on December 5, at the Queens Medical Centre showed a swollen brain. The sole issue between them was whether the scan showed subdural haemorrhages in the area of the posterior falx (photograph G-H 2). Dr Jaspan concluded that it was subdural; Dr Anslow that it was intradural. In the end this dispute was resolved by Dr Rorke-Adams stating that the photograph taken at post mortem, rather than the scan, showed interdural bleeding or interfalcine bleeding that is bleeding between the two dural layers in and either side of the falx.

122   Mr Richards, an obviously very experienced neurosurgeon, had no doubt that a finding that the triad of injuries was present was correct. He was equally not in doubt that the force used to cause these injuries must have been more than rough handling. In cross-examination he agreed that he was unable to say what was the minimum force which could give rise to similar injuries.

The ophthalmic witnesses

123   The measure of agreement between the witnesses in this area of expertise was a little greater than that between Dr Squier and Dr Rorke-Adams. There was no dispute that the retinal haemorrhages were quite severe injuries and that they could have been caused by shaking. Dr Rorke-Adams had described the retinal haemorrhages as severe and towards the top end of the scale. This description was similar to descriptions given by other witnesses. There was also no dispute that on their own retinal haemorrhages findings were not diagnostic of SBS. Next, it was agreed that a sharp surge in ICP could cause retinal haemorrhages although the degree of raised ICP necessary to cause such injuries was not agreed. We have already referred to Mr Richards' experience of carrying out brain surgery procedures designed to increase venous pressure substantially, but which had not caused retinal haemorrhages (see para.99).

124   On the question of the force required to produce retinal haemorrhages by shaking we have referred to the 2004 paper produced by the working party of the Royal College of Ophthalmologists. No witness was able to provide a measure of the force required. Mr Mansfield Q.C. asked each witness what was the mini-

mum force required. For obvious reasons no witness was able to provide an answer to this question.

125   Dr Adams expressed the opinion that the fact that the ambulance crew noted Patrick's pupils to be fixed and dilated at 2.41am on December 5, was a sign that the brain was swollen at that stage. She said fixed and dilated pupils were a clinical sign of brain swelling. Brain swelling caused stretching of the third nerve which in turn affected the pupils of the eyes. In her opinion the retinal haemorrhages were caused by raised intercranial pressure, a more probable cause than shaking. However, she said that in the absence of evidence of brain swelling the cause of retinal haemorrhages may well be shaking. On the question of the force necessary to cause retinal haemorrhages she said that the fact that the injuries were at the top end of the scale did not provide any information as to their aetiology and "You have to look at the whole picture."

126   Dr Jaspan and Mr Richards did not accept that there could have been brain swelling at 2.41am. Dr Jaspan, in his report, said that if a CT scan had been carried out at the time when retinal haemorrhages was first seen at Derby Children's Hospital little brain swelling would have been evident. In evidence, Dr Jaspan said one to two hours after an apnoeic incident one can start to see mild and subtle signs of swelling. The swelling may then progress swiftly in relatively few hours; or in other cases it could take twenty-four to forty-eight hours. Mr Richards said that ICP is normal for some hours after an apnoeic incident, possibly four to five hours before it starts to rise slowly. Mr Gregson also disagreed with Dr Adams on this point. He said that the more likely explanation was at that time, in a period of cardio-arrest, the part of the brain which controls the pupils had become hypoxic (Patrick was noted as pulseless). This would have caused the pupils to become fixed and dilated. This explanation was put to Dr Adams, she said explanation was more probable and that the explanation given by Mr Gregson was one which only occurred when the infant was near death.

127   The impact of this issue is that, if Dr Adams may be correct, brain swelling may have taken place sooner than supposed by the Crown's witnesses making it possible that there was a cause for the retinal haemorrhage findings other than shaking.

128   Professor Luthert described the critical issue of the retinal haemorrhage findings in this appeal as whether it was feasible that there had been a significant and rapid increase in intracranial pressure so as to cause them. When asked whether subdural haemorrhages and retinal haemorrhages were associated with cardiac arrest, he said it was not in the context of events in hospital but the possibility of low brainstem damage might be important and might well produce a pattern of cardio-respiratory arrest which is rather different from that seen in other contexts. Although he described the retinal haemorrhages findings in Patrick's case as typical of those found in cases of alleged NAHI, Prof. Luthert was one of those doctors who was concerned that the triad was a hypothesis and that the full aetiology of the injuries comprising the triad was not "necessarily known."

129   Mr Gregson described the retinal haemorrhages findings as very severe and was of the opinion that they could only have been caused by a severe degree of

trauma. Dr Bonshek agreed with this opinion. In his report he described the injuries as highly suggestive of non-accidental injury. Both Mr Gregson and Dr Bonshek agreed that the degree of injury was not necessarily commensurate with the degree of force used to create it.

Evidence of a possible infection

130   One of the difficulties faced by Harris at trial and in this appeal is to suggest what was the cause of Patrick's collapse, if it was not shaking. Of course, as Mr Mansfield Q.C. properly pointed out, a defendant faced with an allegation of unlawfully shaking an infant so as to cause injury or death, does not have to provide evidence of, let alone prove, an alternative cause. Nevertheless in cases such as this both prosecution and defence will seek to prove respectively either that there was no alternative cause or that there was one. Not surprisingly we have heard a good deal of evidence on the issue of whether or not Patrick's condition might have been caused by some form of infection. We have already noted Dr Squier's opinion that the primary cause of brain swelling in this case was or may have been infection. To deal with this issue we heard evidence principally, but not exclusively, from Prof. Morris and Dr Sunderland called on behalf of Harris; and Dr Carole Jenny, Prof. Klein and Dr Mark Peters called on behalf of the Crown.

131   We shall deal with this issue comparatively shortly for the reason that in his final submissions Mr Mansfield Q.C. accepted that every possible infection suggested by Prof. Morris and Dr Sunderland as a possible cause of Patrick's collapse was effectively disproved by the evidence called on behalf of the Crown.

132   Apart from the fact that there is some evidence that Patrick had, at worst, an upper respiratory chest infection, probably a cold, for a day or two before December 4, 1998 there was no evidence at all to suggest that he had any other infection, let alone one which might have been sufficiently severe as to cause his death. In the end Prof. Morris was driven to suggest that there was a possibility that the ambulance crew arrived at the precise moment when Patrick was suffering an unexplained episode from which he would not have recovered. Professor Morris suggested that it was the resuscitative procedures which had kept him alive thereby giving his brain time to swell. We regard this suggestion as speculative and fanciful.

133   Dr Sunderland suggested that the history given by Harris of Patrick grunting and having difficulty breathing might have been bronchilitis caused by respiratory syncital virus (RSV). In our judgment this suggestion was effectively demolished by the evidence of Dr Mark Peters.

134   There is however one matter which cannot be disposed of so summarily. Professor Morris advanced the theory that although Patrick's death could not be categorised as a SIDS (sudden infant death syndrome), it could be akin to SUDI: that is a sudden unexplained death from a natural cause or natural disease. His report prepared for this appeal sets out statistics relating to SIDS and SUDIs. These statistics have been comprehensively criticised in a statement made by

Dr Angie Wade. Further, she points out that Prof. Morris is a pathologist not a statistician.

135   In our judgment, leaving aside Prof. Morris' statistics, the general point being made by him is the obvious point that the science relating to infant deaths remains incomplete. As Mr Richards said when asked a question in the context of the amount of force necessary to cause injuries, he agreed that the assessment of injuries is open to a great deal of further experimentation and information. He assented to the proposition "We don't know all we should". Similarly, Prof. Luthert in his evidence said:

> "My reason for making that statement is simply that there are many cases where questions are raised as to how the child died and, because there is a big question mark over the circumstances, it is rather tempting to assume that ways of causing death in this fashion that we do know about are the only reasonable explanations. But in fact I think we have had examples of this — I have heard already. There are areas of ignorance. It is very easy to try and fill those areas of ignorance with what we know, but I think it is very important to accept that we do not necessarily have a sufficient understanding to explain every case."

As noted by the Court in *Cannings* and *Kai-Whitewind* these observations apply generally to infant deaths.

Professor Whitwell

136   We have left Prof. Whitwell's evidence until last when dealing with the evidence in this appeal. She was one of the team of doctors who co-authored Geddes III with Dr Geddes. In our judgment her view must necessarily be considered in the light of Dr Geddes' concessions in respect of Geddes III.

137   In this case having examined all the material, Prof. Whitwell produced a report in which she referred to the fact that the major pathology was of hypoxic-ischaemic trauma damage which she said might be secondary to trauma or other cause of cardio-respiratory arrest. She went on to raise the question of the degree of force necessary to produce localised neck injuries. Her opinion expressed in the final paragraph of her report was that the injuries to the brain may have arisen in the background of a "shaking" incident but there was a possibility of an underlying natural cause of the collapse. She said the neuropathological findings may be open to several interpretations.

138   In evidence she gave some support to Dr Squier's opinion that bleeding and injuries to the nerve roots could have been caused by herniation. But she agreed in cross-examination that the most significant factor in her opinion was a stretching injury to the nerve roots.

The submissions

139   Mr Horwell submitted that the new evidence did not undermine the conviction. He asked the Court to accept that the triad had survived intact. He pointed to the fact that at 1.00am on December 5, 1998 Dr Barber examined Patrick and found

him to be well. At 2.30am Patrick was found to be suffering cardio-respiratory arrest. Mr Horwell submitted that the only credible explanation for this sudden collapse was shaking by Harris. The triad of injuries was established and there was no credible alternative cause of these injuries. In addition, Dr Rorke-Adams' evidence of injuries to the brain should be accepted. He submitted that her evidence together with the evidence of the doctors dealing with the ocular injuries demonstrated that unlawful force had been used. He argued that Harris was asking the court to accept that the cause of death was a series of coincidences involving two unlikely syndromes. He invited the Court to find that all suggested causes of Patrick's collapse and death other than the triad had been disproved. The conviction was therefore safe.

140   Mr Mansfield Q.C. submitted that there were disagreements between the experts as to the cause of death. He rightly pointed out that it was not for Harris to prove an alternative cause of Patrick's death. He submitted that this court could not decide matters which a jury should decide such as the differences of opinion expressed by Dr Squier and Dr Rorke-Adams. Finally, he submitted that in a case such as this, where the clinical evidence and the history given by the mother, ran completely contrary to a finding of unlawful force, the Court was entitled to accept that this was one of those cases where the explanation for Patrick's injuries and his death was just not known; and/or that the amount of force used by her was no more than any mother might use to revive her baby and therefore not unlawful.

Conclusion in this appeal

141   In considering all the evidence in this appeal we have kept well in mind that our task is to decide whether the conviction is safe. We also bear in mind Lord Bingham's test in *Pendleton* in a case of any difficulty (which in our view this is) of "asking whether the evidence, if given at the trial might reasonably have affected the decision of the trial jury to convict." This approach, in our judgment, merits careful consideration in this appeal.

142   We have already stated that so far as the evidence relating to an alternative cause of death based on a possible infection is concerned, in our judgment, this evidence does not form any basis for holding that the conviction is unsafe.

143   So far as the other issues are concerned, the evidence at trial and the evidence adduced by the Crown in this appeal, provide a strong case against Harris. Mr Horwell's submission that the triad is established and that any attempt to undermine it is based on speculation is a powerful one. Nevertheless strong as is the case against Harris we have concerns about the safety of the conviction.

144   First, in order to dismiss the appeal, we would have to accede to Mr Horwell's submission that we should reject Dr Squier's evidence in its entirety. If Dr Squier may be right, such evidence of subdural bleeding as she accepts was present was small; untypical of the usual thin-film subdural haemorrhages found in triad cases; in the sense that it was not found at the top of the head and probably not caused by trauma. Secondly, if Dr Squier is, or may be, right there is no pathological evidence of trauma. At one stage Mr Horwell in cross-examination, suggested to Dr Squier that she had lost objectivity in her evidence in this appeal. This was a

bold assertion and one which we find difficult to accept. It was put at the end of her evidence when Dr Squier was describing subdural haemorrhages in another case which she said represented bleeding seeping from the dura into the subdural space (see para.71 to 73 above). As we have said already we find it impossible to conclude that on this issue Dr Squier's evidence is plainly wrong and that Dr Rorke-Adams must be correct.

145   The importance of Dr Squier's evidence is that it throws doubt on the significance of such subdural haemorrhages as there are; and it throws doubt on the evidence of injuries to the brain described by Dr Rorke-Adams. We are far from saying that we accept Dr Squier's evidence in preference to that of Dr Rorke-Adams. Indeed, in view of the weight of evidence disputing her opinions we have reservations about whether Dr Squier can be right. But equally, in all the circumstances of this case, the differences between them are ones which the jury would have had to have assessed in the light of all the evidence in the case.

146   Secondly, although the evidence of the findings of retinal haemorrhages is powerful supporting evidence of shaking, on its own it is not diagnostic of shaking. If the subdural haemorrhages are undermined, the retinal haemorrhages findings will not fill the gap although we recognise that both can be considered together. There is also the issue of whether Dr Adams may be correct in her view that fixed and dilated pupils seen by the ambulance crew was a sign of brain swelling at that time.

147   Thirdly, although as we have already stated the amount of force required to cause the triad of injuries will in most case be more than just rough handling, the evidence suggests that there will be rare cases when injuries will not correspond to the amount of force used. It is at least possible that in such rare cases (maybe very rare cases) very little force will cause catastrophic injuries.

148   In this connection the evidence shows that in recent years the medical profession has become more aware of the degree of force necessary to cause injuries by the growing science of biomechanics. This knowledge, and to an extent Geddes I and II, in our judgment, have had the effect of moderating to some extent the conventional view that strong force is required to cause the triad of injuries. In this case Dr Bouch rejected as an explanation for the injuries he found, shaking by Harris to revive Patrick. Today he might have taken a less firm stance. This knowledge might also have acted as a counter-balance to the evidence given at trial by Prof. Green on the amount of force necessary to cause the retinal haemorrhages.

149   The above factors, which have all arisen out of post-trial material have to be assessed against the background of the clinical evidence which in our judgment is significant and important. As Dr Anslow said in his report of June 3, 2005:

> "The clinical history is perhaps the most important clinical tool available to the clinician and to reject the carer's version of events in favour of another requires the highest possible level of medical evidence. After all, the Doctor is effectively accusing the carer of lying."

Dr Anslow is not a clinician but in our judgment his words of caution are apt in cases of this sort.

150   At the outset of this judgment we have set out the clinical history. In summary, Harris was described as a careful and caring mother. She called out Dr Barber late at night because of her concerns for Patrick. Dr Barber described her as being calm and controlled at that time. The prosecution's case at trial was that in the interval between Dr Barber leaving the house and 2.30am when Harris telephoned the emergency services she must have violently and unlawfully shaken Patrick. In our judgment this history combined with the absence of findings of bruises to any part of the head, face or body; and the absence of fractures or any other sign apart from the triad of injuries, does not fit easily with the Crown's case of an unlawful assault based on the triad of injuries, itself a hypothesis.

151   The Crown relies upon the fact that Patrick was in the sole care of Harris throughout the evening of December 4–5. It is also correct that Harris admitted shaking Patrick in an effort to revive him; and bouncing him on her knee when she was telephoning the emergency services. But, those actions are not suggestive of unlawful force being used by her although it is possible that a jury might now find them to be sufficient to cause the injuries seen by Dr Bouch albeit not unlawful.

152   As we have said the Crown's evidence and arguments are powerful. We are conscious that the witnesses called on behalf of Harris have not identified to our satisfaction a specific alternative cause of Patrick's injuries. But, in this appeal the triad stands alone and in our judgment the clinical evidence points away from NAHI. Here the triad itself may be uncertain for the reasons already expressed. In any event, on our view of the evidence in these appeals, the mere presence of the triad on its own cannot automatically or necessarily lead to a diagnosis of NAHI.

153   The central issue at trial was whether Harris caused the death of her son, Patrick by the use of unlawful force. We ask ourselves whether the fresh evidence, which we have heard as to the cause of death and the amount force necessary to cause the triad, might reasonably have affected the jury's decision to convict. For all the reasons referred to we have concluded that it might. Accordingly the conviction is unsafe and this appeal must be allowed. The conviction will be quashed.

Rock

The focus of the appeal

154   The history of this matter has already been set out; we turn directly to the appeal. Certain matters are common ground. First, there is no dispute that Rock did shake Heidi; there is likewise no dispute (given the full thickness bruise to the back of the head) that she suffered an impact. Secondly, there is no realistic suggestion that disease or infection could possibly have played a role in Heidi's death. The thrust of the appeal was instead that the conviction was unsafe in the light of research subsequent to the trial, calling into question the minimum degree of force necessary to cause the pathology in this case. Rock, it was submitted, was not safely convicted of any offence; at the very least, his conviction of murder was unsafe and a conviction of manslaughter should be substituted.

155   For its part, the Crown vigorously resisted the notion that there was any real alternative to unlawful killing. Here, as elsewhere, it was to be borne in mind that the minimum degree of force in question was the degree of force necessary to cause *all* the injuries suffered; Geddes I and II did not address the minimum degree of force necessary to tear bridging veins and cause retinal haemorrhages; the "unified hypothesis" (i.e., Geddes III) which might have done so, has of course gone. The surrounding circumstances and the injuries suffered amply supported the safety of the conviction. While conceding in terms that if there had been the "triad" and no more, "that was unlikely ever in itself to be sufficient" to support a charge of murder (as distinct from manslaughter), here it was contended that there were additional features which justified the jury's verdict—bearing in mind that the intention to cause grievous bodily harm could be both rapidly formed and almost instantly regretted.

The new evidence on the appeal

156   In the view which we take of this appeal, it is unnecessary to review the new evidence at length; it suffices to summarise the position reached on the totality of the new material.

157   As to radiology, save for one area (to be mentioned shortly) there was no or no real dispute between Dr Anslow (called by Rock) and Dr Jaspan (called by the Crown). The first CT scan, taken on June 2, 1998 at about 10.21pm, some $2\frac{1}{2}$ hours after Heidi's admission into hospital, showed a minimally swollen brain but the presence of subdural blood. On June 4, some 39 hours later, the second CT scan revealed a very different picture. This showed, apart from cerebellar tonsillar herniation and established hypoxic ischaemic brain damage, a grossly swollen brain but the same small amount of subdural bleeding—notwithstanding a "huge" (Dr Jaspan's word) increase in pressure. Dr Anslow accepted that subdural bleeding at a time when there was no evidence of raised intra-cranial pressure ("ICP"), was a "very strong indicator" of trauma. On the assumption that Geddes III did not apply, he could think of no cause other than trauma to account for the subdural bleeding.

158   The only area of dispute between Dr Anslow and Dr Jaspan was whether a lesion in the corpus callosum revealed by MRI scans was caused by trauma; Dr Jaspan was firmly of the opinion that it was; Dr Anslow said that it might be an artefact. As we have already indicated such disputes between reputable experts potentially give rise to difficult issues on an appeal of this nature. In the event, notwithstanding the powerful nature of Dr Jaspan's evidence in this regard, it is unnecessary for us to resolve this dispute. We proceed on the assumption that Dr Anslow might be correct.

159   In cross-examination, Mr Mansfield Q.C. put to Dr Jaspan one of the "scenarios" developed by Dr Geddes (see below), involving a departure from the evidence given by Rock at trial. This set of facts assumed that Heidi *had* struck her head when falling and was subsequently the subject of two well-intentioned shakes by Rock. Asked whether this was a possible scenario capable of explaining the injuries sustained by Heidi, Dr Jaspan's initial (and firm) answer was

"no". He based this answer on his views as to the cause of the corpus callosum lesion. If wrong about that, he accepted that the scenario "might just be feasible". Immediately thereafter, Dr Jaspan was re-examined by Mr Horwell as follows:

"Q. If you leave the corpus callosum out of the equation, when you say it just might be feasible, what do you mean?

A. Because in medicine there is never a hundred per cent certainty. So, if I was asked is there a hundred per cent certainty that it could happen, I would have to be honest and say no, there must be almost the freak situation where that could happen.

Q. What are the chances from your clinical experience?

A. By inference, 99 per cent unlikely."

In his final submissions, Mr Mansfield Q.C. sought to suggest that these answers disclosed a major concession on Dr Jaspan's part. Having seen and heard Dr Jaspan give evidence and having reviewed the transcript of his answers, we respectfully disagree. The essence of Dr Jaspan's views remained plain and unaltered, albeit couched in rather more moderate and less graphic language than apparently deployed at trial.

160   Turning to the neuropathologists, in her report dated April 14,1999 prepared for the trial (but which remained understandably unused by the defence), Dr Geddes said this:

"I believe that both the intracranial and the intraocular bleeding are likely to have been the result of vigorous to-and-fro movements of the brain inside the skull, of the type that occurs in a shaking injury."

Subsequently, Dr Geddes has (as is well-known) revised her thinking. That said, in her evidence at trial, Dr Geddes accepted the presence of subdural haemorrhages but was unable to provide an explanation for them. She remained of the view that for violent shaking to have produced the subdural and retinal haemorrhages here, she would have expected some form of widespread diffuse axonal injury and damage to the muscles in the neck and spinal column. She accepted, however, in answer to questions from the Court, that, on any view, Heidi must have had some insult to the brain, not explained by Rock's account of events. She could not rule out impact plus shaking.

161   In her report of May 24, 2005 Dr Geddes posited three "scenarios" (to which reference has already been made) which might have caused the pathological findings in this case. She could not be certain which of the three actually happened. The first scenario involved a low-level fall in which Heidi, among other things, knocked the back of her head, resulting in hyperflexion of the neck which damaged her brain stem. The second, also involved a fall, followed by a resuscitative (i.e., well-intentioned) shake by Rock, causing damage to her brain stem. In both these scenarios, damage to the brain stem resulted in Heidi's breathing stopping, her brain swelling rapidly and consequential subdural and retinal bleeding. The third scenario involved an assault on Heidi. We are bound to observe that the suggested sequence of the first two scenarios is troubling, given the apparent conflict with the radiology evidence (see above). Moreover, Dr Geddes was closely

cross-examined as to the factual basis for the first scenario, involving a departure from Rock's own account of events—in which he was adamant that Heidi had *not* struck her head. Pressed on this point, Dr Geddes said that she was duty bound to point out that there was impact (given the bruise at the back of Heidi's head); she thought that Rock must have been wrong in his account but had not given the matter attention when writing her 1999 report; she was (notwithstanding the factual evidence) prepared to speculate to this degree in now giving her evidence to the Court.

162   Dr Rorke-Adams and Dr Geddes disagreed as to (i) the extent of subarachnoid bleeding in this case; and (ii) the cause of a "hole" or "tear" in the corpus callosum (in a location different from that which formed the subject of the disagreement between the radiologists, already referred to). Once again, it is not necessary to resolve this dispute and, we proceed on the assumption that Dr Geddes might be correct. For our part, we find the agreement between Dr Rorke-Adams and Dr Geddes that there were here subdural haemorrhages considerably more significant than the areas in which they disagreed. As Dr Rorke-Adams put it:

"Subdural haemorrhage is essentially always traumatic in origin except under very unusual circumstances . . .."

In itself, of course, that answer cannot resolve the source of the trauma nor, insofar as it was inflicted by another, the intention with which it was inflicted.

163   On the appeals, evidence was given by Dr Plunkett, who has undertaken research into "low-level" infant falls—i.e., falls of less than 10 feet. The conclusions which Dr Plunkett drew from his study were that (i) low-level falls were capable of causing serious injury or death; but (ii) that there was no inevitability about it; as he expressed it:

". . . I do not know either an upper limit or a lower limit of impact velocity below which there is no injury and above which there is always injury."

Dr Plunkett's evidence related to the cases of Rock, Cherry and Faulder. We shall have more to say of his evidence, in particular with regard to the Cherry case.

164   For the moment, we confine ourselves to Dr Plunkett's evidence with regard to the appeal of Rock. Here, basing himself on the bruise on the back of Heidi's scalp, Dr Plunkett expressed the opinion that her death was the result of an impact injury; this was an instance of a "low-velocity impact event with a bad outcome". Plainly therefore, Dr Plunkett's evidence entailed a departure from the evidence, as given by Rock; on no view, could a fall onto her bottom (as described by Rock) have explained this fatality. In Dr Plunkett's view, Heidi's head must have struck something, a matter unexplained on Rock's account.

165   We come next to the evidence of the ophthalmic experts, Prof. Luthert and Dr Adams, called by Rock and Dr Gregson, called by the Crown. It is convenient to take Dr Gregson's evidence first. He put the matter starkly; the significance of the eye injuries was crucial to this case. The retinal injuries were at the very top of the range or not far from it. There were in addition para-macular retinal folds, a

type of detached retina. In his evidence-in-chief, Dr Gregson explained this matter as follows:

"Q. The retina is completely detached from the eye?
A. The retina is folded up very much like a rug would be if you pushed it together. It is not detached in the same way as boxers get retinal detachments, but the fact that it is folded means it is not in the place that it should be."

A little earlier, Dr Gregson had observed that in children of Heidi's age, he knew of no other cause for para-macular folds other than trauma; this was so, regardless of when the para-macular folds had first appeared. Moreover, the presence of para-macular folds was indicative of severe injury—"a lot of trauma" was required. His reason for this view was as follows:

". . . the retina wants to stay attached; it does not want to fold. It requires an effort to detach it."

166   Turning to Prof. Luthert, we begin with his written material. In his report of April 14, 1999 he was of the opinion that, absent any alternative explanation, severe trauma, such as shaking combined with impact, was the most likely explanation for the pathological findings in Heidi's eyes. In his letter dated January 12, 2005 he maintained the view that such trauma (i.e., shaking, impact or both) was the most likely cause of Heidi's death and the condition of her brain and eyes. He added this:

"I do not believe that the presence of retinal haemorrhages necessarily implies a specific level of force although I think the level of force is likely to be more than would be seen in even rough normal play."

167   In his oral evidence, Prof. Luthert stated that it was difficult in an individual case to extrapolate from the severity of a retinal haemorrhage to any assumed degree of applied force. By contrast, in the generality of cases, it was to be expected that there would be a (broad) correlation between the degree of trauma and the seriousness of the injury suffered. That said, there was "not necessarily a tight correspondence between level of trauma and severity of outcome".

168   Initially in his evidence, Prof. Luthert said that it was difficult to "exclude with total confidence" the possibility that the fall described by Rock had caused the retinal injuries. Pressed, unsurprisingly, on this point, he ultimately accepted that a fall onto her bottom would not be expected to cause injuries of this nature. Although he said that he had seen "more severe" retinal injuries, he further accepted that these were "highly significant", a description which he later amplified as meaning "extremely significant and abnormal pathology". While he did not view the presence of para-macular folds as diagnostic of shaking, he agreed that they could not "in their entirety" have been artefactual—a necessary concession, as they had been noted during Heidi's lifetime. He agreed in cross-examination that the "most likely explanation" for Heidi's retinal injuries was shaking. In re-examination, Prof. Luthert said that a version of the facts, in effect based on Dr Geddes' first two scenarios, was not fanciful.

169   Returning to his written report of June 2, 2005 Prof. Luthert explained that since the original trial and following publications by Dr Geddes and Dr Plunkett, he had reconsidered the minimum degree of force required to generate the "triad". He went on to say this:

> "The minimum level of force required to produce this syndrome can not be defined, but the recent Royal College of Ophthalmologists Working Party concluded '*It is highly unlikely that the forces required to produce retinal haemorrhage in a child less than 2 years of age would be generated by a reasonable person during the course of (even rough) play or an attempt to arouse a sleeping or apparently unconscious child.*' In my opinion, it is now not possible to exclude the possibility that a well-intentioned but ill-advised shake might cause the pattern of pathology seen in Heidi. The same Working Party commented '*It seems clear that minor falls can, only exceptionally, give rise to subdural and retinal bleeding. In these cases, it may well be that the biomechanics of the impact induce the rotational forces necessary to produce the picture considered typical of SBS.*' So it is difficult to exclude with total confidence the possibility that the fall caused the injuries seen. Finally, it is also feasible that Heidi was assaulted."

In answer to questions from the Court as to this passage, Prof. Luthert asserted that he had relied on Geddes I and II but not Geddes III. Professor Luthert said that he had been a member of the Working Party and agreed with its conclusions. While he was (in effect) contemplating the infliction of some force going beyond rough play, by itself that did not determine the intention of the person inflicting the force.

170   In a nutshell, the evidence given by Dr Adams was to the following effect:

  i) The fall as described by Rock was not the cause of Heidi's retinal haemorrhages;
  ii) The injuries to Heidi's eyes were at the very top end of the scale;
  iii) The cause of those injuries was shaking or shaking and an impact;
  iv) Simply by looking at the retinal haemorrhages, it could not be said "definitively" what level of force had been applied.

171   For completeness, we note that in her reports Dr Adams had raised the question of whether a lumbar puncture might have been the cause of the retinal damage. Suffice to say that no evidence emerged to support this line of inquiry and Mr Richards gave cogent evidence, which we accept, as to its irrelevance; we say no more of this point.

Conclusions

172   At the outset, we should underline that this is *not* a case where the expert medical evidence and the presence of the "triad" stand alone. We accept of course that Rock was a man of good character and that in general, he had been very good with Heidi. But there was also evidence of some hostility towards her, prior to the events of the June 2, 1998. Perhaps more tellingly, there was the evidence

from the neighbour, Ms Banham, that, on the night, she heard Heidi screaming for a significant period of time and Rock shouting at her to "fucking shut up"; then it all went quiet. For completeness, we do not think that the reliability of Ms Banham's evidence is called into question by the mere fact of there being some unused and untested material from police officers, apparently saying that they could not hear shouting between the two houses.

173   Against that background, we come to the evidence in this case of the presence of the "triad"; namely, encephalopathy, subdural haemorrhages and retinal haemorrhages. There is, moreover, the bruise found at the back of Heidi's head.

174   How were these injuries caused? Having regard to the evidence we have summarised, it is plain that Rock's explanation—a fall in which Heidi did *not* strike her head—cannot account for them. We are, moreover, unable to accept that Rock's version of events was innocently mistaken, along the lines that he had simply not seen her strike her head. As set out above, he was adamant that he had prevented her hitting her head. We naturally have regard to the burden of proof resting on the Crown throughout. That burden may however be satisfied by reliance on such inferences which it is proper to draw from Heidi's injuries, taken together with Ms. Banham's evidence and the absence of an explanation from Rock, with whom Heidi was alone at the relevant time.

175   We turn then to the inferences which it is proper to draw. We do so with great caution, mindful both of the gravity of the matter and that (as already underlined) the mere presence of the "triad" does not automatically or necessarily lead to a diagnosis of NAHI and/or a conclusion of unlawful killing. All the facts of the individual case must be taken into account.

176   Given the assumptions that we have thought it right to make with regard to the disputes between Dr Anslow and Dr Jaspan and between Dr Geddes and Dr Rorke-Adams, encephalopathy does not take the matter further—save for the fact of its presence. The position is, however, very different with regard to subdural haemorrhages and retinal haemorrhages.

177   As has been seen, the presence of subdural haemorrhages was common ground between the relevant experts. It was also indisputable that the subdural haemorrhages preceded the development of brain swelling and that there was no evidence of any increase in subdural bleeding notwithstanding the rise in intracranial pressure following the swelling of the brain. Pausing there, these features would themselves have gone a very long way to undermine the credibility of Geddes III, had that hypothesis not in any event been withdrawn in the manner already described. Matters do not end there. Without Geddes III, Geddes I and II cannot suggest a mechanism to explain the subdural haemorrhages; strikingly, as we have seen, Dr Geddes in her evidence could not explain them. There is accordingly no realistic challenge here to the "traditional" mechanism of the tearing of bridging veins. If so, it necessarily follows that Heidi was subject to a degree of force sufficient to tear those veins.

178   We return to the retinal injuries. On the totality of the evidence, we are sure that these were at the top end of the scale (Dr Gregson and Dr Adams) and we are not deterred from that conclusion by anything said by Prof. Luthert, if indeed he ultimately disagreed. We cannot necessarily infer from the severity of those injuries,

including the presence of the para-macular folds, that any precise or specific degree of force was used; we are acutely conscious both of "thin skull" cases on the one hand and of "lucky" victims on the other. We have, however, no realistic doubt that the force used must have been—as even Prof. Luthert was minded to agree—in excess of anything generated by a reasonable person in the course of rough play. We further have no real doubt that the cause of those injuries was shaking or shaking plus an impact; if anything, we favour the latter given the presence of the bruise at the back of the head. In all the circumstances, we regard as fanciful the notion that Heidi's retinal injuries can be explained by a fall in which she struck her head and was then the subject of a well-intentioned resuscitative shake (Geddes, first and second scenarios).

179   We have not overlooked the evidence of Dr Plunkett but we are unable to regard it as of assistance in this case. First, there is no proper factual foundation for Dr Plunkett's evidence; his opinion rests on a version of events relying on Rock's account of an accidental fall but departing from it so as to account for Heidi striking her head when falling. Secondly, Dr Plunkett's suggestion that the bruise at the back of Heidi's head caused her death, lacks credibility. Quite apart from more general considerations as to the relevance of Dr Plunkett's study to cases such as these (see below, when dealing with Cherry), his thesis here does not begin to address the subdural haemorrhages and retinal injuries.

180   We are accordingly left with a powerful Crown case for unlawful killing, based on the surrounding circumstances (Rock's shouting on the night), and the nature and severity of Heidi's injuries (the subdural haemorrhages and retinal damage). All that there is to set against that case is the suggestion of accident, based on a manifestly flawed account from Rock, the one person who could have explained what happened, supplemented by a variety of speculative suggestions from the experts — necessarily lacking a sound factual base. We remind ourselves that our task is not to retry Rock; our inquiry is as to the safety of his conviction. On all the evidence, we are amply satisfied as to the safety of his conviction for unlawful killing.

181   For completeness, we are not deterred from that conclusion by the following matters:

　　i) On behalf of Rock, some play was made with the moderation in language employed by Crown experts between the trial and the appeal; in this regard, as we have seen, considerable emphasis was placed on the alleged "concession" made by Dr Jaspan, an emphasis we have already indicated we regard as misplaced. We think that the submission as to moderation of language is correct as far as it goes; but we do not think it goes very far. Doubtless, as expert thinking has evolved, so, rightly, the language has moderated and become less graphic or emotive. Those are welcome developments. But when the totality of the evidence is considered, there is nothing in any of this to suggest that the safety of Rock's conviction is undermined.

　　ii) Dr Geddes, as we have seen, was puzzled as to the absence of other injuries, if indeed Heidi had been the subject of violent shaking. We have

given this matter anxious consideration but ultimately regard it as deci-
sively outweighed by the overwhelming evidence pointing to a degree
of force (or violence) at least going beyond even rough play. There is,
as has frequently been urged on us, no precise correlation between
force inflicted and the gravity of the injuries suffered.

iii) As seen in the passages set out earlier, the Judge summed up in robust
terms. On the evidence before him, no proper criticism could be made
of those passages. Given the totality of the evidence now before the
Court, even though an alteration in expression might have been warranted, we do not think that any change to the substance of the summing-up
would have been such so as to undermine the safety of a conviction for
unlawful killing on this ground.

182   What remains is whether Rock's conviction for *murder* as distinct from *manslaughter* is safe. In *R. v Stacey* [2001] EWCA Crim 2031, a "shaking" case, the
Court said this:

"48.   Other grounds of appeal having been examined, and in the end abandoned, that leaves only the question of whether the jury was entitled to find
that she intended to do really serious harm. We are troubled about that. One
brief period of violent shaking by a frustrated mother and child-minder was
all that was required to explain this death. Apart from the bruises to the neck,
no other injuries were found. As the judge said, an intent to do serious bodily
harm may be quickly formed and soon regretted; but so may a less serious
intent, simply to stop a child crying by handling him in a way any responsible adult would realise would cause serious damage or certainly might
do so. That would only provide the mental element necessary for manslaughter.

49.   Even allowing for the jury's obvious advantage in seeing the appellant
give evidence, we have been unable to discern anything which, in our judgment, would have made it safe for the jury to convict this appellant of the
more serious charge. In our judgment, the less serious charge was the
only safe verdict. If the jury had had the additional benefit of hearing the
fresh medical evidence we have heard, they might well have come to the
same conclusion."

183   *Stacey* was of course a case on its own facts but the reasoning of the Court has,
with respect, an undoubted resonance. As already foreshadowed, the Crown's
stance, very fairly, was to accept that a verdict of murder was unlikely ever to
be justified on the basis of the "triad" standing alone; it follows that the verdict
of murder could be justified here, only, if at all, on the basis of (i) the bruise at the
back of the head and (ii) Ms Banham's evidence.

184   Elaboration is unnecessary. Those two additional features go in this case to
underpin the safety of the conviction as to unlawful killing; but they do not assist
on the question of murder or manslaughter. Necessarily therefore the conviction
of murder cannot be sustained. We are fortified in reaching this conclusion by a
consideration of the additional medical evidence we have heard. A brief period of

violence (going beyond even rough play) was all that was required to cause Hei-di's fatal injuries; such violence undoubtedly furnishes the mental element necessary for a conviction of manslaughter; but it does not necessarily demonstrate an intention to cause grievous bodily harm, the relevant intention if the conviction of murder was to be upheld.

185   Accordingly, we set aside Rock's conviction for murder and substitute a conviction for manslaughter. To this extent only, this appeal is allowed. We shall hear submissions on sentence for the offence of manslaughter.

Cherry

186   We again do not repeat the facts of this matter, which have already been set out. It will be recollected that on Cherry's account, he left the child alone for a matter of minutes downstairs while he went upstairs; when he returned minutes later, she was, as the Judge put it in the summing-up, in a "poor state" on the floor. Essentially the decision for the jury was whether they could be sure that Sarah's death was caused by an unlawful act on the part of Cherry (a formulation to which we shall return, later) or whether her death was or might have been attributable to an accidental fall from a chair some 6–8 inches high ("the chair").

187   On this appeal, Mr Mansfield Q.C.'s submissions proceeded as follows:

    i) The Crown's position had shifted between trial and appeal; at trial, this was a case of impact; now it was a case of both shaking and impact; but that was not how the matter had been placed before the jury.

    ii) There was new evidence to the effect that death or serious injury from low level falls could not be ruled out. In addition, there was a possibility that Sarah had aspirated vomit. Death could have resulted from a combination of the two. In any event, if this was a case of both shaking and impact, the innocent combination of an accidental fall followed by a resuscitative shake could not be ruled out.

    iii) Great care had to be taken in approaching the bruising on Sarah's head and body, both in the light of the new evidence and the course which the trial had taken.

    iv) In all the circumstances, the conviction was unsafe.

188   The Crown resists the appeal and contends that nothing has emerged to undermine the safety of the conviction. In a nutshell, the evidence as to low-level falls is inapplicable to a fall of the nature postulated here. Upon analysis, there was no evidence capable of suggesting that aspiration of vomit was a relevant consideration. As to the new evidence, it had all to be taken into account; Cherry could not pick and choose; the introduction of a shaking component did nothing to undermine the safety of the conviction. Evidence of Sarah's other injuries, properly and fairly considered, lent support to the Crown's case and suggested that the notion of an accidental fall was fanciful.

The new evidence on the appeal

189   We begin with the pathologists. As already observed, Prof. Whitwell conducted the post-mortem and was a prosecution witness at the trial; on the appeal, she
now gave evidence for Cherry.

190   In her witness statement for the trial, Prof. Whitwell attributed Sarah's injuries
and brain damage, taken in conjunction with the scalp bruising (already
described), to "direct blunt trauma". She went on to say this:

> "The degree of trauma necessary to produce such damage is considerable
> and the findings are not consistent with a simple fall onto a carpeted surface.
> They are consistent with the head being forcibly propelled against a hard
> surface or a blunt object contacting the head.
> Apart from the brain injuries there are a number of bruises on the body. The
> sighting of a number of these is highly suggestive of non-accidental injury
> rather than being caused accidentally—in particular the bruises to the but-
> tock, face, thigh and arm."

191   Her report of June 2, 2005, prepared for the appeal, evidences her revised
views. She said that the possibility of Sarah suffering a fatal injury as a result
of falling from the chair had to be considered afresh in the light of Dr Plunkett's
research. The "primary brain pathology" was due to lack of oxygen; this
hypoxic-ischaemic injury could have been caused as a result of primary injury
to the brain, causing Sarah to stop breathing and/or as a result of "vomiting
with inhalation of vomit into the lungs". She would "still to some extent be
unhappy as regards the scalp bruises arising in a fall but it has to be a considered
possibility that Sarah's head impacted against some other surface as well as the
ground".

192   In her oral evidence at the appeal, she explained that her change of view was
based on Dr Plunkett's work and her own experience. She had not found diffuse
axonal injury; such trauma as she found was associated with impact. The need to
explain Sarah's scalp bruising (in two separate locations) led to Prof. Whitwell
contemplating that Sarah might have struck her head *both* on the window and
then on the ground in the course of her fall; indeed, she later underlined that
two impacts were needed to explain this bruising.

193   Professor Whitwell agreed that at post-mortem, there was no evidence of
vomit or aspiration. She agreed that Sarah had up to a maximum of 22 bruises;
she was "concerned" about that number of bruises. They were probably
"more than" fair wear and tear for a 21 month old. In the absence of proper explanation, they were highly suggestive of abuse. There had been no developments in
science between the trial and the appeal to alter her view as to the relevance of the
two sites of scalp bruising. Her view at the trial (and she was the person who had
conducted the post-mortem) was that those two areas of bruising had been caused
at about the same time. She had herself identified traumatic injury to the brain.
She accepted that the subdural bleeding occurred because of the tearing of bridging veins.

194   Dr Rorke-Adams was firmly of the view that Sarah's injuries were inconsistent with a fall from the chair; she placed emphasis on the multiple areas of injury and the extent of those injuries. Sarah's injuries were caused by "trauma"; the "pattern of injury" was characteristic of both shaking and impact; it was a combination of both. Although the degree of injury could not be correlated with the degree of force, considering the injuries as a whole, they must have been caused by "strong force".

195   Pausing here, it will be apparent that there was agreement between Prof.Whitwell and Dr Rorke-Adams: (i) that there had been traumatic injury to the brain; (ii) that there were subdural haemorrhages; (iii) that those haemorrhages had been caused by the tearing of bridging veins. There was some dispute between these two witnesses as to whether further injury to the brain, which it is unnecessary to detail, was also attributable to trauma or was artefactual in origin. Impressed as we were by Dr Rorke-Adams' evidence in this regard (the coincidence relied upon by Prof. Whitwell seemed unlikely), this is another of those areas where we do not think it would be right simply to discount a reputable expert's contrary views. We therefore proceed with this appeal on the assumption (in favour of Cherry) that the brain damage suffered by Sarah did not extend beyond the areas of agreement between Prof. Whitwell and Dr Rorke-Adams, summarised above.

196   We move next to the evidence of Dr Plunkett, which it is helpful to consider here in a little greater detail than in the preceding appeal of Rock. Dr Plunkett said that there was nothing inevitable about a serious injury resulting from a fall from the chair but "the potential for serious injury or even death exists". The floor surface did not matter; it was immaterial whether it was carpet over concrete or just concrete.

197   Questioned as to his research, Dr Plunkett explained that he had worked from a database for head and neck injuries involving playground equipment, recorded by the United States Consumer Product Safety Commission ("CPSC"). Over $11\frac{1}{2}$ years, he had identified 18 fatalities from head and neck injuries involving falls. None of the children (or infants) in his study had formal retinal examinations. These cases included falls from swings, which, he agreed were complex or complicated falls. He further agreed that none of these cases were similar to a shaken baby case. The distance of a fall is said to be measured with reference to the closest part of the body to the ground at the beginning of a fall.

198   Case no.5 in Dr Plunkett's study was said to be closest to a fall from a 6–8 inch chair; this was suggested on the basis that the child in question had suffered the equivalent of a 12 inch fall. Dr Plunkett's paper described this fall as follows:

> "A 23 month-old was playing on a plastic gym set in the garage at her home . . . She had climbed the attached ladder to the top rail above the platform and was straddling the rail, with her feet 0.70 metres (28 inches) above the floor. She lost her balance and fell headfirst onto a 1-cm (3/8 inch) thick piece of plush carpet remnant covering the concrete floor. She struck the carpet first with her outstretched hands, then with the right front side of

her forehead, followed by her right shoulder. Her grandmother had been watching . . .. And videotaped the fall. She cried after the fall but was alert and talking . . . However, approximately 5 minutes later she vomited and became stuporous . . . .. A CT scan indicated a large right-sided subdural haematoma . . . .. The haematoma was immediately evacuated. She remained comatose postoperatively, developed cerebral oedema with herniation, and was removed from life support 36 hours after the fall . . .''

Dr Plunkett suggested that, as her head had been some 42 inches above the ground when the fall began and as her body length was some 30 inches, it was equivalent to her falling from a chair 12 inches high. We confess some difficulty with this reasoning but we nonetheless continue with our consideration of Dr Plunkett's evidence. We do acknowledge that we felt, as indeed Dr Anslow later expressed it, "shocked" that a fall, as captured on the video (which was shown to the Court), could have resulted in a fatality; this, indeed, may be the strength of Dr Plunkett's evidence, so far as it goes. Nonetheless, it is pertinent to record the following: (i) It transpired, as explained by Dr Plunkett in his oral evidence following the playing of the video, that the rail from which the child fell was in fact 39 inches above the floor, not 28 inches; (ii) she fell a sufficient distance for her to rotate and so as to fall onto her head with some 2/3 of her body weight contributing to the impact; (iii) there was a lucid interval after the fall (unlike the cases before us); (iv) the haematoma was large and lop-sided (again unlike the thin film haematomas encountered in cases such as the present); Dr Plunkett agreed that the mass effect of this haematoma caused the child's death. Notwithstanding all these factors, Dr Plunkett continued to maintain that the Case 5 fall was "exactly comparable" to a 12 inch fall. The velocity was relevant and what was not known was the "minimal impact velocity" required to cause these types of injuries.

199 Closely cross-examined, Dr Plunkett agreed this:

"Q. . . . your paper does not establish the proposition that any impact, no matter how minor, can lead to fatal consequences, does it?
A. That is correct.''

After some questioning from the Court, Dr Plunkett acknowledged the common sense proposition that the lesser the distance of the fall, the less likely it was to cause an injury to a vulnerable part of the body. In any event though for a time it seemed that Dr Plunkett was resistant to the suggestion, the distance of a fall is a necessarily relevant consideration. Dr Plunkett's own formula for impact velocity was as follows: Velocity (V) squared = $2 \times$ Acceleration (A) $\times$ Distance (D). From this it must follow that, all other things being equal, a reduction in D will result in a reduced V.

200 Reverting to the individual case of Cherry, Dr Plunkett asserted that the bruising on Sarah's body amounted to "normal wear and tear". We observe at once that this answer was manifestly unconvincing.

201 Standing back from Dr Plunkett's evidence, we do not say that his work does not have utility. As recorded, we were ourselves very surprised by the outcome in

case no.5, as shown on the video. However, we think that it is important to look closely at both the limits of his study and its relevance to any individual case; the true comparability of the falls he studied to the cases before the Court merits careful scrutiny. We return to this theme when indicating our conclusions on the Cherry appeal.

202   Mr Richards gave evidence for the Crown in this case as well. In his opinion, Sarah died as a result of a severe inflicted non-accidental head injury. His oral evidence included the following passage:

> "Q. You have used the word 'severe'. Degree of force required in this particular case?
> A. Far in excess of anything we see in normal life with children of this age. Children are toddling around at this age. They fall over all the time. It they suffered severe head injury from little falls, the casualty departments would be inundated with them, the intensive cares would be full of them, my operating theatres would be operating or dealing with them on a daily basis. I have not seen a child of this age suffer a severe head injury in my 24-year neurosurgical career from a minor injury as described or. . . as considered. This very short 6-inch fall."

Other than being prepared to accept never to say never, try as Mr Mansfield Q.C. might, Mr Richards did not shift in substance from this answer.

203   We turn next to the issue of aspiration of vomit. Given that, for very good reason to which we shall come, it played an ever diminishing role on the appeal, we shall take it very shortly indeed.

204   Mr Wrightson, a neurosurgeon, whose evidence on behalf of Cherry we heard by way of video-link from New Zealand, said this, in his report for the appeal:

> ". . . there is no doubt that Sarah vomited and aspirated material into her lungs. The vomiting was described by Mr. Cherry and was confirmed by those who arrived to help. A chest X-ray later in the day of injury showed 'widespread airspace shadowing throughout both lungs'. The hypoxia which this would have caused is likely to have resulted in or at least contributed to the gross cerebral swelling that was present."

In his oral evidence, Mr Wrightson said, early on, that this was "the key to the whole situation". There was no reason for Cherry to have invented the evidence he gave. As to aspiration, the ambulance personnel described a "bubbly" chest. At the hospital, copious bloodstained fluid came out from the lungs; the chest x-ray and the findings on post-mortem were likewise said to support these conclusions.

205   Under cross-examination, Mr Wrightson agreed that there was no sign of vomit at the scene; that the neighbours who attended (one of whom was a nurse) did not suggest that Sarah had vomited; that one of the paramedics had said that he did not see any signs of vomiting; that, at the post-mortem, no sign of aspiration pneumonia was found.

206   Dr Peters, a consultant paediatric intensivist, was called by the Crown. His impressively clear evidence may be summarised as follows:

i) Neurogenic pulmonary oedema ("NPO") was a condition involving fluid in the lungs as a result of something catastrophic happening to the brain. It is characteristically immediate. The description given by the para-medics was "almost a text-book" description of NPO:

> "A combination of the noisy chest, with obvious fluid, with pink frothy secretions coming out of the mouth and the child making respiratory effort to overcome this fluid in the chest are all typical. It could read like a text-book description."

ii) At no stage was there any evidence of aspirated vomit. The most relevant evidence was that of Sarah's appearance at intubation. Had aspiration been a major cause of respiratory failure then, typically, when the tube was placed into the lungs there would be a "welling up" from the chest of whatever was aspirated. No suggestion of aspirated vomit was made by the intensive care staff; to the contrary the fluid seen remained pink and frothy and became more blood-stained as time passed. This was a typical pattern of NPO. Had the fluid been erythromycin (a very common child's antibiotic which Sarah had been given), Dr Peters would have expected the paediatric staff to recognise the difference between it and blood-staining.

iii) To cause respiratory distress suddenly, massive aspiration was necessary. If so, however, it would have been apparent on intubation and subsequent care. Conversely, unless it was massive, it would not be a "credible cause" of this respiratory distress of this severity.

207   The ophthalmic evidence can be disposed of summarily. Dr Gregson, called by the Crown, fairly conceded that the retinal haemorrhages in this case were superficial only and were not typical of those discussed in the other appeals before the Court. They were not typical of shaking. In the circumstances, we do not think that the Crown case derives any support from the retinal haemorrhages. Conversely, however, we were not in any way persuaded that the absence of "typical" retinal haemorrhages somehow assisted Cherry's case on the appeal.

208   For our part, this being a case where impact as well as shaking is alleged we regard the absence of "typical" retinal haemorrhages as neutral. We say no more of this point. In the event, it is unnecessary to consider the otherwise interesting (sub-) issue as to when the retinal haemorrhages in truth first appeared.

209   Finally in this case we have considered detailed written reports from two experts in biomechanics: Dr Thibault and Dr Bertocci for Cherry and for the Crown respectively. Dr Thibault, whose approach to "injury thresholds" we have described earlier, considered that the forces applied to the head in a three foot impact fall onto carpet represented approximately 50,000 radians per second squared, whereas the injury threshold associated with subdural haemorrhage and diffuse axonal haemorrhage were between 8,000 and 12,000 radians per second squared. A three foot fall therefore, in Dr Thibault's view, is well within the physical context in which subdural bleeding and DAI may occur. Dr Thibault

identified the primary point of impact to be the occipital region. The cause of sub-dural bleeding is accepted to be rupture of bridging veins, but such a rupture could occur, in Dr Thibault's opinion, as a result of the substantial internal rotational forces that arise when a child falls and impacts her head. He concluded that whilst deliberate inflicted injury cannot be ruled out, the injuries were entirely consist-ent with the mechanics of the speculated accidental fall.

210   Dr Bertocci explained that her habitual starting point when asked to determine whether a given account fits the resulting injuries is to begin with an assessment of any bruising found on the child: "bruising represents points of force appli-cation and a roadmap to the child's exposure" to force. Dr Thibault considered that the two apparently separate sites of impact could be explained by a fall indu-cing a well-distributed contact load across the occipital region resulting in dynamic in-bending of the skull and contusion to the outer left and right margins of the total contact area. The presence of bruising on two opposite sides of the head indicated to Dr Bertocci two very different lines of force applied from dif-fering directions, and is not consistent with a fall from a chair. Further, Dr Bertocci observed that the size of the scalp bruises at 2.5cm and 3.5cm are much larger than bruises found in children injured through accidents. Finally, Dr Bertocci summarised published research and her own unit's experiments with an automotive "12 month old" crash test dummy. Her conclusion, which is again in total contrast to that of Dr Thibault, was that a 12 month old falling from a 9 inch vertical position impacting their head on a padded carpet surface would produce head accelerations that are well below published biomechanical injury thresholds. She concluded that Sarah's injuries are not attributable to a fall from a 9 inch chair.

Conclusions

211   As is apparent, encephalopathy and subdural haemorrhages are present in this case. With regard to the latter, there is no dispute here that they were caused by the tearing of bridging veins. Two elements of the "triad" are thus present. For reasons already set out, although there were retinal haemorrhages (the third ele-ment of the triad), these are neutral and do not advance the argument of either party on the appeal.

212   Next it is convenient to mention the issue of aspiration of vomit, essentially to dispose of it. We found Dr Peters' analysis of the evidence on this issue compel-ling. Mr Wrightson's views to the contrary do not survive this analysis. We accept Dr Peters' evidence and dismiss aspiration of vomit as a credible cause or con-tributory cause of Sarah's death.

213   We turn to the topic of low-level falls. We have already indicated our general views with regard to Dr Plunkett's evidence. Having given the matter anxious consideration, we are not persuaded that the postulated fall from the 6–8 inch chair was a credible cause or contributory cause of Sarah's death. Our reasons are these:

    i) On any realistic view, the fall here (if fall there was or might have been) was of a very different type and nature from those forming the subject of

Dr Plunkett's study. The factual differences between any fall here and Dr Plunkett's Case 5 (said to be the closest comparable) are marked indeed, not least with regard to the nature of the subdural bleeding found.

ii) Even if the reservations in i) above are put to one side, notwithstanding the extent of Dr Plunkett's research, there is *no* example of a 6–8 inch fall, from a static object, causing death or serious injury to a 21 month old child. As he himself agreed in cross-examination (see above), it does *not* follow from Dr Plunkett's study that any impact, no matter how minor, can lead to fatal consequences.

iii) Even if (contrary to the above) it was thought that Dr Plunkett's study did mean that a fall from the chair here was capable of furnishing a realistically possible innocent explanation for Sarah's death, it remains necessary to address the two separate sites of scalp bruising. Prof. Whitwell conducted the post-mortem; as she agreed in her oral evidence, her impression (at least at the time of the trial) was that the two separate areas of scalp bruising had been caused at about the same time. Inevitably and as Prof. Whitwell further agreed, no scientific developments since the trial could alter the relevance of these two separate sites of bruising. Accordingly, for the fall to be capable of providing an innocent explanation of these injuries, it was necessary to postulate two impacts (window and floor) in the course of the same fall. As it seems to us, this is pure speculation and stretches credibility altogether too far.

iv) We have set out earlier Mr Richards' observations (i) that if such falls did generate severe injuries, casualty departments and the like would be inundated; but (ii) that in more than 20 years of practice he had never encountered a severe head injury in a child of this age arising from a 6 inch fall. Some caution is necessary in approaching these observations; first, there is no claim that serious injury is the inevitable result of falls of this nature; secondly, "never" is an unfortunate word. Nonetheless, when this evidence based on practical experience is considered cumulatively with reasons i)–iii) above, it furnishes powerful support for the conclusion that the notion of an accidental fall in this case, causing or contributing to Sarah's death, is simply fanciful.

v) We are not swayed from our view by the evidence of biomechanics summarised earlier. This is a complex, developing and (as yet) necessarily uncertain area of scince, as illustrated by the stark divergence of opinion between Dr Bertocci and Dr Thibault. Be that as it may, Dr Thibault's views are altogether too difficult to reconcile with evidence of primary fact in this case, for the conviction to be regarded as unsafe by reason of the biomechanical evidence.

214   Pulling the threads together, this is a case of a sudden collapse of a 21 month old child. Cherry was alone at home with her. His factual account cannot explain her injuries and death. Upon analysis, the possible explanations advanced on his behalf on the appeal do not carry credibility. The case cannot be one of SIDS, given, as is undisputed, her traumatically caused subdural haemorrhaging. As

it seems to us, in the light of those subdural haemorrhages and the separate sites of scalp bruising, the inference can properly be made that her injuries and death were attributable to a combination of shaking and impact. On any realistic view (and in this case we are of course only concerned with a count of manslaughter), the force involved must have been such that the risk of some harm to Sarah would have been foreseeable to all sober and reasonable people. In the circumstances, unless there is anything in the argument as to the shift in the Crown's case between trial and appeal rendering the conviction unsafe (see below), we are amply satisfied of the safety of Cherry's conviction for manslaughter.

215   We are fortified in this conclusion by the evidence as to up to 22 bruises on Sarah's body. As Prof. Whitwell was driven to agree, these were highly suggestive of abuse, in the absence of proper explanation of which there was and has been none. In approaching this evidence, we have thought it right to proceed with caution; as the summing-up suggests, at the trial, Cherry was treated as a good stepfather and there had been no suggestion of any improper behaviour towards Sarah or any of the other children. But on the state of the evidence at the trial, there may have been no need for the Crown to explore this wider area. Cherry, having introduced new lines of inquiry on the appeal, cannot, we think, complain at all the evidence being revisited. While even then we would have hesitated long and hard before treating this question of bruising as determinative of the appeal, in this appeal we see no unfairness in taking it into account as an additional reason pointing towards the safety of the conviction.

216   Finally, we turn to Mr Mansfield's submission that the conviction was unsafe because of the shift in the Crown's position between trial and appeal; at trial, this had been a case of impact; now it was one of both shaking and impact. Cherry did not have a fair opportunity to deal with the "new" case; nor did the jury consider it. With respect, we cannot agree.

217   First, as a matter of principle and as already foreshadowed in dealing with the evidence of bruising to Sarah's body, once an appellant has introduced new evidence on the appeal, he can hardly complain if such evidence is answered or rebutted by the Crown. Unavoidably, in such a process, the nature of the case may take on a different hue and there may be some change in the manner in which the Crown puts its case. But it cannot be, that on this ground alone, a conviction must be regarded as unsafe; fresh evidence, once admitted, may serve to confirm, not only to undermine, the safety of a conviction. Accordingly, if on all the evidence before this Court, the only reasonable conclusion is that, considered in the round, the conviction is safe, the Court should give effect to that conclusion: *R. v Hanratty (Dec'd)* [2002] 2 Cr.App.R. 30 (p.419), at [101]–[104].

218   Secondly, however, this principle is qualified by consideration of fact and degree. In an individual case where an issue of this kind arises, it may be that the Crown's change of position between trial and appeal is such that the conviction cannot be considered safe. Whether it does or not will necessarily depend on the facts of the particular case. Here, we see nothing in the development of the Crown's case on the appeal that renders Cherry's conviction unsafe. The essential question for the jury was whether Sarah's death was accidental or the result of

some unlawful act on the part of Cherry. That was the fundamental divide; in this case, given the nature of Cherry's evidence, the mechanism was necessarily of secondary importance. It is true that the mechanism favoured by the Crown at trial was one of impact. It is further true that on appeal the Crown's case as to mechanism has evolved to one of a combination of shaking and impact. That evolution, however, cannot have caused Cherry any prejudice. Moreover, any suggestion here that a well-intentioned shake was capable of giving rise to a possible defence depended on the credibility of the explanations we have already dismissed, namely those relating to the low-level fall and/or the aspiration of vomit.

219   In all the circumstances, we are fully satisfied as to the safety of the conviction. This appeal must be dismissed.

Faulder

Appeal

220   Faulder's Notice of Appeal relies upon two post-trial developments. Firstly the publication of Geddes I and II which, it is said, provides a basis for questioning the explanations previously advanced for N's injuries, and, secondly, a judgment given by Mr Justice Eady in a libel case, *Reed and Lillee v Newcastle CC* [2002] EWHC 1600 (QBD) in which Dr San Lazaro, a key prosecution expert witness in the Faulder case, had been severely criticised. In addition the Notice of Appeal relies upon a new explanation, the MORO reflex, which might explain N's sudden movement and subsequent fall from Faulder's outstretched arm. Finally, the Notice relies upon fresh expert evidence from Prof. Whitwell, which calls into question the Crown's view at trial that this was primarily a shaking injury, her opinion being that there was evidence of a number impacts (which might fit Faulder's account) and that the primary cause of collapse was likely to be cessation of breathing and consequent brain damage, rather than primary brain damage due to direct trauma.

221   The "Statement of Reasons" supporting the Criminal Cases Review Commission decision in Faulder's case refers to the trial evidence given by Dr San Lazaro and Dr Alexander to the effect that N's primary injury was as a result of direct impact between the brain and the skull, which would require massive and violent force comparable to a child being hit by a car travelling at 40mph. As the Commission's statement observes, "within this paradigm, Mr Faulder's explanation is inadequate." The Commission refers to Geddes I and II and postulates that Faulder's explanation becomes more plausible if the cause of N's collapse is cessation of breathing. The Commission concludes that:

a) had the jury been aware of the new evidence they might not have been certain that Faulder's account was untrue; and

b) the medical evidence now available provides a possible alternative explanation for N's injuries and challenges the prosecution case that the injuries must have been caused by shaking.

The injuries

222   In Faulder's case the injuries and symptoms relating to N that require consideration are:

Bruises
   i) Area of erythema (ill defined flushing of the skin) that was "grazed/bruised" located directly on top of the head;
   ii) A triangular fresh bruise 2cm by 2cm above the forehead;
   iii) A 2cm linear bruise on the left side of the head above the ear;
   iv) A small deep blue bruise over the right forehead;
   v) A second small deep blue bruise over the right forehead but more centrally sited;
   vi) Marked swelling over the top of the occipital bone in the midline.
   Subdural haemorrhage
   vii) Thin fresh subdural haemorrhage along the falx with a thin layer of subdural blood over the surface of the brain (seen on the first CT scan at 7.44 am on the morning after admission, it remained largely unchanged in subsequent scans);
   Brain swelling and HII
   viii) In the first scan (12 hours after the 999 call) there is no significant brain swelling or injury. Subsequent scans over the following three days show developing brain swelling and hypoxic-ischaemic injury in both cerebral hemispheres.

223   It is of note that in Faulder's case there is no evidence of retinal haemorrhaging or primary brain injury.

224   In the course of Faulder's appeal we have considered evidence from the following experts on behalf of the appellant: Professor Whitwell, Dr Plunkett and Dr Sunderland. In response the Crown have particularly relied upon evidence from Dr Jaspan, Mr Richards, Prof. Jenny, Dr Lawler and Dr Rorke-Adams.

Appellant's experts

225   For the appellant Prof. Whitwell, relying upon the Geddes I and II research, considered that the hypoxic-ischaemic injury to the brain could arise as a result of oxygen starvation caused by a sudden bending and stretching of the nerve tracts in the cranio-cervical region. As N survived, there was obviously no opportunity to use the βAPP test for axonal damage to confirm this opinion. In N's case the damage may have been ischaemic and localised, but the mechanism was the same as in the case of hypoxia. The Professor, who is a pathologist, rightly conceded that in this case, which did not result in death, her expertise did not permit her to comment upon the interpretation of the radiological evidence.

226   Professor Whitwell considered that the findings were all consistent with some form of impact. The injuries to the head indicated a number of impacts, the multiplicity of which gave rise to concern, but in cross examination she also questioned whether all of the external injuries were clearly present at the time of admission, or, in relation to two, arose as a result of therapeutic intervention.

She advised that the forces required to produce subdural haemorrhages in a child of this young age are unknown.

227   Dr John Plunkett's evidence was based upon his own research into young children and low level falls. He drew attention to the fact that the skull of a seven week old infant differs fundamentally from that of an older infant or adult. A scalp impact to a seven week old would cause the skull to bend inwards or deform, with a consequent deformation or movement within the brain itself. This movement, Dr Plunkett advised, could cause subdural haemorrhages and functional brain damage, for example breathing difficulties. Both Dr Plunkett and Prof. Whitwell accepted that the subdural haemorrhages were assumed to have been caused by tearing of bridging veins. The minimal impact velocity needed to cause these injuries is not known, but as N did not have any skull fracture or brain contusion, Dr Plunkett postulated that the impact velocity was extremely low. In this manner, Dr Plunkett considered that all of N's injuries could be explained by the account of the fall given by Faulder. Dr Plunkett did not however accept that N had as many as six external head injuries believing that there were only three. In particular Dr Plunkett considered that marked swelling seen on the scans was a manifestation of the triangular shaped bruise seen earlier over the top of the occipital bone which, he explained, had migrated to the back of the head by reason of gravity. This explanation and the further explanation proffered by Prof. Whitwell that the two forehead bruises were caused during treatment, were rejected by each of the relevant experts for the Crown. In so far as may be necessary we were not persuaded by Dr Plunkett or Prof. Whitwell on these issues and, having seen the relevant photographs, scans and medical notes, have no difficulty in finding that there were indeed six separate sites of external head injury as listed above at para.219.

228   Dr Sunderland's written report to the CCRC introduced the "MORO Reflex" (a recognised automatic response seen in babies under eight weeks old) as an explanation for N arching his back or throwing his arms out. It was therefore surprising that it was only after a substantial number of questions in cross examination that Dr Sunderland responded to junior counsel for the Crown by saying "I am allowing you to develop your proposition. At some point I must help you. I do not think the MORO reflex is relevant to Faulder. But I am cutting in, you develop your proposition." We found Dr Sunderland's contribution in this regard fell short of that which is required by the court from an expert witness.

229   Dr Sunderland, having had Faulder's detailed account put to him, stated that a baby of N's age could have behaved in the manner described.

230   Dr Thibault, an expert in biomechanics who was, as we have said, not available to give oral evidence, produced an analysis of the evidence which concluded that Faulder's account accorded with a biomechanical analysis of the injuries. Dr Thibault's opinion is however upon the basis that there were only two impacts: one being the linear bruise above the left ear (number (iii) in our list) and the other which caused both of the marks above the right eye (numbers (iv) and (v)). Dr Thibault discounted the swelling on the back of the head (number (vi)) which is only visible on the scan on the basis that if this had been traumatic one would have expected the treating clinicians to have noted it and, further, there

is no note of any surface marking at the same location indicating an impact. The report does not consider the area of erythema located directly on top of the head ((i)) or the triangular fresh bruise 2cm by 2cm above the forehead ((ii)), these marks are shown in the photographs, however the photographs were not made available to Dr Thibault.

231   Dr Thibault considered that the linear bruise was consistent with contact with part of the high chair, whereas the two marks on the forehead were consistent with impact on a flat surface, for example the floor. The fall as described by Faulder would, according to Dr Thibault, have been sufficient in magnitude to deform the skull and cause shifting and deformation of the underlying bridging veins and neural tissue thereby producing acute SDH. He also postulated the temporary deformation causing a temporary herniation at the cranio-cervical junction leading to consequent interference with the respiratory system and thereby hypoxic-ischaemic injury.

Crown's experts

232   For the prosecution Dr Jaspan described the existence of the subdural haemorrhages and the development of what became extensive hypoxic-ischaemic injury in both cerebral hemispheres. He considered that the most substantial impact was that which caused swelling to the right parietal region, with the other bruises resulting from injuries of lesser magnitude. Dr Jaspan, in a balanced report, drew attention to the fact that only four of the eight elements that would normally constitute a diagnostic 'full house' for inflicted injury were present in this case, namely: unexplained encephalopathy, scalp bruising, subdural haemorrhages and secondary hypoxic-ischaemic injury. He therefore considered that accidental trauma could not be entirely excluded, but some form of inflicted injury was the most likely cause.

233   Mr Richards, who in his written evidence questioned whether a seven week old baby would have come to fall in the manner described by Faulder, in oral evidence came to accept that N may have fallen from Faulder's arm in an ordinary "gravity roll", which did not depend upon any overt momentum from the child himself other than throwing his arms up because he felt unstable. If such a fall took place, Mr Richards would have anticipated a hairline skull fracture or a fractured clavicle. On the other hand, such a fall was unlikely to cause such severe brain substance injury and subdural haemorrhages. He concluded that it was highly likely that N suffered inflicted NAHI.

234   Professor Jenny clearly identified the six external head injuries found on N. Her evidence on this point, which we accept, was confirmed by Dr Lawlor. Professor Jenny's opinion was that N had sustained multiple blunt injuries to the head which were not accounted for by the history of a fall given by his father. Professor Jenny disagreed with the prosecution experts at trial, who had concentrated upon shaking rather than some form of impact causing the injuries.

235   When considering the triad as a diagnostic tool Prof. Jenny regarded the presence of characteristic retinal haemorrhaging as being particularly important in identifying shaking as the mechanism of trauma. She explained that "you really

have difficulty diagnosing Shaken Baby Syndrome, as opposed to abusive head trauma, if you do not have those retinal haemorrhages, because they seem to be very characteristic of that particular biomechanical event".

236   Dr Rorke-Adams' conclusion was to the same effect, namely that N was subjected to blunt force trauma to the head. She too expressly disagreed with the crown's experts at trial. Dr Rorke-Adams considered that there was discordance between Faulder's account and the severity of the injuries to N.

237   Dr Rorke-Adams, relying firstly upon her interpretation of the CT scans and secondly upon the fact that N experienced a left-sided paralysis after the incident, considered that the primary injury was to the right side of the brain, and therefore was focussed on a particular location rather than being diffuse and evenly distributed throughout the brain. Dr Rorke-Adams was the only witness to put forward this interpretation of the evidence. As a pathologist Dr Rorke-Adams was at a similar disadvantage to Prof. Whitwell in this case. Equally, Dr Rorke-Adams is not a radiologist. Dr Jaspan in a very thorough report on the series of scans does not identify any particular difference in presentation between the two sides of the brain. We are therefore cautious about placing undue weight about Dr Rorke-Adams's conclusion that there was a focal (as opposed to a diffuse) brain injury.

238   Dr Rorke-Adams conclusion in favour of a focal injury to one part of the brain is the main reason for her dismissing Prof. Whitwell's proposition that the brain injury may be secondary to a stretching injury at the cranio-cervical junction. Given our caution about Dr Rorke-Adams' view on this point, it follows that we do not feel able to dismiss Prof. Whitwell's opinion on that basis as being untenable.

239   The prosecution expert on biomechanics, Dr Bertocci, due to the short notice available to her, did not make observations about this case.

Changes in the Crown's case

240   The appellant asserts that the Crown's case against him at trial has now been changed in three significant respects relating to (1) his account of the fall, (2) whether there was a primary injury to the brain itself and (3) whether the injury was caused by shaking or impact.

(1) The appellant's account of the fall

241   The appellant has consistently given an account of N's fall from his outstretched arm to the effect that N's head was cupped in his hand and N's body ran along his forearm. At some stage N arched his back, slipped off the arm and fell, catching his back on a push-chair and his head on the bar of a highchair before hitting the floor headfirst. At trial, Dr San Lazaro did not accept that a seven week old child could make sufficient jerking, arching or rolling movement to propel itself from a carer's arm. That was also the position of a number of the Crown's experts on paper at the start of this appeal. During oral evidence, as we have already noted, Mr Richards came to accept that N may have fallen in the manner described by Faulder simply as a result of a gravity

roll from his insecure position lying along Faulder's arm. It follows that the prosecution expert testimony is no longer entirely at odds with Faulder's account on this point.

(2) Causation of brain injury

242   At trial, Dr Alexander considered that the fall described by Faulder bore no relationship to the severity of the brain injury. His opinion was that the subdural haemorrhages and brain injury were the result of shaking and were the sort of injuries seen "in older children who have been hit by a car at 40mph, spun round and eventually hit the floor". He described the mechanism for the brain injury by imagining that the brain was similar in substance to porridge, with the shaking causing the brain to accelerate and decelerate many times causing a spinning effect which was "just like putting a food mixer inside the brain." He further postulated that the trauma to the brain may have interfered with breathing, thereby causing further brain damage. Dr San Lazaro, at trial, explained that only "very severe forces" or "severe massive deceleration forces" would account for the brain injuries which were caused by "violent shaking and slamming down". In the CCRC report for this appeal, Dr Lazaro and Dr Alexander are quoted as stating in letters written to the CCRC in 2001 that N's injuries included "brain contusions".

243   At trial, Dr Gholkal, a consultant radiologist, did not positively identify any primary brain injury.

244   Before us, with the exception of Dr Rorke-Adams, whose opinion relating to a localised focal brain injury we have already described, none of the Crown's experts suggested that there was evidence of direct trauma to the brain. Dr Jaspan identifies secondary hypoxic-ischaemic injury and asserts that there is no evidence of primary brain injury or brain contusions.

245   N survived these events and thus the only direct evidence of the condition of his brain is radiological. Given the careful and clear evidence of the prosecution radiologist, Dr Jaspan, on this point we consider that the opinion of both Dr San Lazaro and Dr Alexander that there was primary brain injury is not tenable.

(3) Shaking or Impact

246   At trial both Dr Alexander and Dr San Lazaro advised that these injuries were caused by very severe shaking. We have already observed that a number of the Crown's experts on appeal have expressly disagreed with this conclusion. They regard this as a case of N being the victim of a number of blunt impact blows to the head.

247   This significant change in the case being put against Faulder is of consequence in at least two respects. Firstly, he has never been required to consider, and neither was the jury required to consider, the allegation that he hit N at least five or six times around the head. Secondly, the degree and type of force now relied upon must differ from the "hit by a car at 40mph" description put forward at trial.

248   Whilst we note that the judge in describing the central issue in the case to the jury focused upon the defendant's intention ("did the defendant deliberately

injure the child?") rather than upon any particular mechanism for injury. The expert evidence presented to the jury was that the severity of primary brain injury could not be explained by Faulder's account. Before us the position is different in that the injury to the brain substance is broadly accepted to be secondary hypoxic-ischaemic injury. The primary injuries being the external bruising and swelling, the subdural haemorrhages and unexplained encephalopathy (brain failure). Whilst Faulder's account is not accepted by the Crown, it is nevertheless an account of a series of impacts and is therefore significantly closer to the case now put by the Crown than was the position at the trial.

249   An essential question raised in Faulder's appeal is therefore what effect, if any, this change of mechanism and force has upon the central issue of the defendant's intention.

250   In summary the prosecution's position at the conclusion of the appeal differed from the Crown case at trial in the following material respects:

   a) Faulder's account of N falling from his outstretched arm is now accepted as a possible event;
   b) The brain injury is now seen to be a secondary hypoxic-ischaemia rather than as a result of primary intra-cranial trauma;
   c) The mechanism for injury is now stated to be a number of blunt force impacts to the head, rather than the massive violent shaking mechanism put forward at trial.

Dr San Lazaro

251   The Amended Grounds of Appeal rely in part upon the fact that Dr San Lazaro's credibility and impartiality have subsequently been seriously challenged in the case of *Lilley and Reed v Newcastle CC* (above). It is indeed the case that Eady J. considered Dr San Lazaro's role in a substantial child sexual abuse investigation and, having heard her give evidence, found that, in order to meet what she perceived to be the needs of the children she examined, she was prepared to throw "objectivity and scientific rigour to the winds in a highly emotional misrepresentation of the facts". She was, according to Eady J.'s findings, "unbalanced, obsessive and lacking in judgment".

252   In the event this point was not raised in the appellant's Skeleton Argument filed at the start of the appeal hearing and did not feature in the written closing submissions. Mr Mansfield Q.C. told us that he was effectively not relying upon this ground in support of Faulder's appeal. We consider that this was a realistic concession. There is no challenge to the primary evidence of fact given by Dr San Lazaro. If Dr San Lazaro had remained the leading Crown expert in the case, there might well have been some concern arising from Eady J's findings, however the wealth of medical evidence that has now been acquired indicates that even were her evidence to be totally ignored there is a substantial body of expert opinion that supports the Crown's case as it is now cast.

Overview of Faulder's case

253   We now seek to draw together the various central issues in Faulder's appeal. Before doing so, it is helpful to highlight the fact that there are now no less than five different explanations for N's injuries that have been put forward by experts either at trial or on appeal, they are:

a) Shaking and slamming down involving very severe force (Dr San Lazaro and Dr Alexander at trial);
b) Non-specific inflicted head injury (Dr Jaspan and Mr Richards) involving secondary, but not primary, brain injury (Dr Jaspan);
c) Multiple (at least six) blows to the head (Prof. Jenny and Dr Rorke-Adams) causing primary localised brain injury (Dr Rorke-Adams);
d) A bending and stretching injury to the respiratory nerves in the cranio-cervical junction causing a secondary brain damage. On the basis that the minimum degree of force required to cause subdural haemorrhages is unknown, all the symptoms could have been caused in the fall described by Faulder (Prof. Whitwell);
e) A blow to the skull during the fall from Faulder's arm, causing the baby's skull temporarily to deform and directly injure the underlying brain substance, which may then hinder respiration and cause secondary brain damage (Dr Plunkett).

254   On the evidence that is now before the court, there is unanimity that what occurred was primarily an impact injury. The central questions remaining are:

i) What is the minimum degree of force required to cause these injuries? and
ii) Might the injuries have been incurred by a fall as described by Faulder?

255   For the reasons that we have already given, we conclude that there were six separate sites of injury found on N's head when he was examined at hospital. This is an important finding as whilst three or possibly four impacts could conceivable fit with Mr Faulder's account, it is not possible to stretch the sequence of events he describes to explain all six injuries.

256   Coming to a conclusion about the external head injuries is, however, a very much more straightforward task compared to consideration of the internal injuries. Having heard all of the evidence we are not in a position to reject Prof. Whitwell's opinion that the key event was a nerve injury at the cranio-cervical junction. That opinion is based on the Geddes I and II research, which has been largely accepted by the scientific community. If that opinion is correct, then the severity of the brain injury does not arise from the degree of force used, but from the extent to which the brain is starved of oxygen and/or blood. Questions of degree of force, on the Whitwell basis, are confined to the minimum force needed (a) to cause the cranio cervical junction nerve damage and (b) the subdural haemorrhage.

257   We have already expressed our overall conclusions upon the necessary degree of force in triad cases by stating four general propositions (paras 72–80). Apply-

ing those propositions to Faulder's case we are therefore mindful that there will be rare cases where comparatively minor falls may generate serious injuries and that an infant may be particularly vulnerable to injury at the site of the craniocervical junction as postulated by Prof. Whitwell in this case.

258   In not rejecting Prof. Whitwell's opinion, we have particularly borne in mind Dr Jaspan's cautious analysis ("an unequivocal stance cannot be taken"). Dr Jaspan considered that only four of a possible eight signs for NAHI were present. We would add that of those four, only two are direct evidence of a primary event involving force (scalp bruising and subdural haemmorhage) whereas the other two are, or could be, secondary consequences of the primary event (unexplained encephalopathy and secondary hypoixic-ischaemic injury).

259   There are no retinal haemorrhages in this case. On Prof. Jenny's evidence, that would be a cause for concern were the Crown's case to have remained one of pure shaking, but is a lesser matter of note in the context of an impact injury.

260   We have already considered Dr Plunkett's evidence in relation to the appeals of Rock and Cherry (in particular we summarise our view at para.201). It is, as we have said, important to look closely at the relevance of Dr Plunkett's research to each individual case. In relation to Faulder's appeal we are troubled by Dr Plunkett declining to accept that N had more than three sites of injury. Our approach has been to evaluate each case by considering all of the symptoms as a whole, as well as individually. Dr Plunkett's inability to include and account for the six sites of injury must devalue, but not eliminate, the importance of his evidence in this particular case.

261   The jury were directed to treat Faulder as a man of good character and that is a factor that we too bear in mind. We also have particular regard to the fact that, unlike the Crown case, his account of the key event has been consistent throughout.

262   If the number of external marks of impact had been four or less we would have little hesitation in holding that there is sufficient within the evidence of Prof. Whitwell, when set against the conflicting and contradictory evidence that has, when looked at as a whole, been presented by the Crown, to render this conviction unsafe.

263   We have approached each of these cases by attempting to look at the evidence as a whole. Do the two or three external marks that fall outside Mr Faulder's account tip the balance in favour of dismissing the appeal?

264   In considering this question we are conscious of the fact that this was not a matter that the jury were ever asked to contemplate in this case. In the same regard we consider it is relevant to question how fair it is for the Crown to change its case so radically from "very severe shaking" to "at least six blows to the head" in an attempt to uphold the conviction.

265   In conclusion we are struck in this appeal by the very radical change in the Crown case; the jury considered one case, shaking, yet that case is now rejected and we have been asked to consider a totally different allegation of multiple blows to the head. During the summing up at trial the jury were told that Dr San Lazaro was "very, very experienced" and "specialises in child protection and abuse" cases. They were also reminded that Dr San Lazaro had said "I am as

certain as you can be in medicine" in her opinion that this was a shaking injury. This "certain" opinion from the Crown's principal witness is now rejected by Crown experts who are equally firm in their own opinion. We have to consider the evidence in its totality, both at trial and before us. There are, as we have observed, now five different explanations put forward by experts for N's injuries.

266   In relation to Cherry's appeal we have stressed that the mere fact that there has been some change in the manner in which the Crown puts its case will not automatically lead to a conclusion that the conviction is unsafe. It will be a matter of fact and degree to be considered in each individual case. In contrast to Cherry's case, the turnaround in the Crown's case in Faulder could hardly be more substantial. This factor, coupled with the introduction of potentially credible alternative explanations presented by the defence experts, drives us to the conclusion that, despite the number of bruises found, this conviction must now be considered unsafe. We therefore allow the appeal and quash the conviction.

Final Comments

267   In earlier sections of this judgment we have made comments on the triad of injuries, the "unified hypothesis"—Geddes I, II, III, and some general issues. We do not think it possible or desirable to add anything further to those observations. In our judgment, these appeals demonstrate that cases of alleged NAHI are fact-specific and will be determined on their individual facts.

268   We have been asked by Mr Horwell to give some guidance in respect of expert witnesses in cases such as these. In his final submissions Mr Horwell submitted that these appeals demonstrated that there had been a significant failure within the criminal justice system to control and manage expert evidence. He argued that there must be a change in approach and invited the court to consider giving guidance.

269   Whether or not there has been a failure by the criminal justice system to control and manage expert evidence we are reluctant to give any new guidance on expert evidence arising from the facts of these cases. It may, however, be helpful to reiterate current guidance.

270   As to expert evidence generally, the evidential rules as to admissibility are clear (see for example *R. v Bonython* (1984) 38 S.A.S.R. 45 and *R.v Clarke* (RL) [1995] 2 Cr.App.R. 425 (facial mapping)). We see no reason for special rules where medical experts are involved. There is no single test which can provide a threshold for admissibility in all cases. As *Clarke* demonstrates developments in scientific thinking and techniques should not be kept from the Court. Further, in our judgment, developments in scientific thinking should not be kept from the Court, simply because they remain at the stage of a hypothesis. Obviously, it is of the first importance that the true status of the expert's evidence is frankly indicated to the court.

271   It may be helpful for judges, practitioners and experts to be reminded of the obligations of an expert witness summarised by Cresswell J. in the *National Justice Cia Naviera SA v Prudential Assurance Co Ltd (Ikarian Reefer)* [1993] 2

Lloyds Rep. 68 at 81. Cresswell J. pointed out amongst other factors the following, which we summarise as follows:

(1) Expert evidence presented to the court should be and seen to be the independent product of the expert uninfluenced as to form or content by the exigencies of litigation.

(2) An expert witness should provide independent assistance to the court by way of objective unbiased opinion in relation to matters within his expertise. An expert witness in the High Court should never assume the role of advocate.

(3) An expert witness should state the facts or assumptions on which his opinion is based. He should not omit to consider material facts which detract from his concluded opinions.

(4) An expert should make it clear when a particular question or issue falls outside his expertise.

(5) If an expert's opinion is not properly researched because he considers that insufficient data is available then this must be stated with an indication that the opinion is no more than a provisional one.

(6) If after exchange of reports, an expert witness changes his view on material matters, such change of view should be communicated to the other side without delay and when appropriate to the court.

272   Wall J., as he then was, sitting in the Family Division also gave helpful guidance for experts giving evidence involving children (see *In re AB (Child Abuse: Expert Witnesses)* [1995] 1 F.L.R. 181). Wall J. pointed out that there will be cases in which there is a genuine disagreement on a scientific or medical issue, or where it is necessary for a party to advance a particular hypothesis to explain a given set of facts. He added (see p.192):

"Where that occurs, the *jury* will have to resolve the issue which is raised. Two points must be made. In my view, the expert who advances such a hypothesis owes a very heavy duty to explain to the court that what he is advancing is a hypothesis, that it is controversial (if it is) and placed before the court all material which contradicts the hypothesis. Secondly, he must make all his material available to the other experts in the case. It is the common experience of the courts that the better the experts the more limited their areas of disagreement, and in the forensic context of a contested case relating to children, the objective of the lawyers and the experts should always be to limit the ambit of disagreement on medical issues to the minimum."

We have substituted the word *jury* for *judge* in the above passage.

273   In our judgment the guidance given by both Cresswell J. and Wall J. are very relevant to criminal proceedings and should be kept well in mind by both prosecution and defence. The new Criminal Procedure Rules provide wide powers of case management to the Court. Rule 24 and Para.15 of the Plea and Case Management form make provision for experts to consult together and, if possible, agree points of agreement or disagreement with a summary of reasons. In

cases involving allegations of child abuse the judge should be prepared to give directions in respect of expert evidence taking into account the guidance to which we have just referred. If this guidance is borne in mind and the directions made are clear and adhered to, it ought to be possible to narrow the areas of dispute before trial and limit the volume of expert evidence which the jury will have to consider.

274   We see nothing new in the above observations.

275   Lastly, we wish to express our gratitude to all counsel, solicitors and the many expert witnesses for the prodigious amount of work and time which they have given to these appeals. Cases of this sort raise difficult and complex medical issues. The Court is very dependent upon the skill of the advocates and the ability of the witnesses to elucidate the evidence and inform the court on the issues involved. We have received enormous assistance from all concerned and pay tribute to their efforts.

Appeal of Harris allowed; conviction quashed
Appeal of Rock allowed; conviction of manslaughter substituted.
Appeal of Cherry dismissed.
Appeal of Faulder allowed; conviction quashed.

R. v HENRY

COURT OF APPEAL (Lord Justice Maurice Kay, Mr Justice Silber and
Judge John Saunders Q.C.): May 12; June 29, 2005

[2005] EWCA Crim 1681; [2006] 1 Cr.App.R. 6

_LT_ Admissibility; Medical evidence; Mens rea; Mental disorder

H1 EVIDENCE
Expert medical evidence
Admissibility—Defendant having IQ of 75—Whether expert evidence admissible as to defendant's ability to form mens rea.

H2   The appellant was charged with soliciting to murder and conspiracy to murder. His defence was that he had not intended to harm the proposed victim, that his co-defendant was manipulative and he had played along with her in order to pacify her. Prior to and during his trial neither the appellant's solicitor nor his counsel had reason to question the appellant's cognitive skills or intelligence, however, after his conviction, in anticipation of sentence, a report was commissioned from a psychologist. He concluded that the appellant had an IQ of about 75, which placed him with a mental age of approximately 12 years, and that the appellant was an impulsive individual who tried to please others and help them and who was easily imposed upon. A forensic psychologist instructed by the Crown came to similar conclusions. The appellant appealed on the ground that the reports amounted to fresh evidence which, had they been available at the time of the trial, would have been adduced on the issue of the appellant's intention.

H3   **Held,** dismissing the appeal, that the appellant did not suffer from a mental illness nor, with an IQ of 75, was he regarded as mentally defective. An intention that someone should be killed was a visceral matter of no great complexity and it was not a matter which lent itself to expert evidence in relation to a person such as the appellant. Accordingly, the experts' reports did not contain admissible evidence on the issue of intention, nor were they admissible as supporting the credibility of the appellant's account of a lack of the requisite intention (post, paras [14]–[15], [17]).

H4   _R. v Toner_ (1991) 93 Cr.App.R. 382, CA distinguished.
       R. v Masih [1986] Crim.L.R. 395, CA considered.

H5   (For expert evidence, see _Archbold_ 2005, paras 4–326 to 4–328, 17–99 and 17–100)

Appeal against conviction

H6   On November 4, 2003 in the Central Criminal Court (Judge Barker) the appellant, Nigel Henry, was convicted of soliciting to murder and conspiracy to murder and was later sentenced to concurrent terms of four years' imprisonment. He appealed against conviction by leave of the single judge.

H7   The facts and grounds of appeal appear in the judgment of the court.

H8   *Godfrey Carey Q.C.* (instructed by Osibanjo Ete & Co) for the appellant.
Edward Brown (instructed by the Crown Prosecution Service) for the Crown.

Cur. adv. vult.

June 29.   Maurice Kay L.J. handed down the judgment of the court.

1   On November 4, 2003 in the Central Criminal Court the appellant was convicted of soliciting to murder and conspiracy to murder and was later sentenced to concurrent terms of four years' imprisonment. His co-defendant, Donna Bailey, was convicted of the same offences and sentenced to concurrent terms of six years' imprisonment. He appeals against conviction by leave of the single judge.

2   The factual background is unusual. Donna Bailey met and befriended a fellow student, Anna, but that friendship diminished and they eventually fell out following a row in February 2003. The case for the prosecution was that Donna Bailey became obsessed with Anna to the point that she and the appellant planned to have her killed by a hitman or (later) to do the job themselves. The offence of incitement was evidenced by contact they had with a man called Headley who introduced them to Robinson. They told Robinson that they wanted a woman killed and they gave him a post-it sticker with Anna's address on it. Robinson mentioned a price of £5000 and told them to come back to him when they had raised the money. On the following day, when he was stopped by the police for breach of bail conditions in respect of an unconnected matter, Robinson told the police about his meeting with Donna Bailey and the appellant. He made a witness statement and was introduced to an undercover police officer called George.

3   A week later Robinson and George visited Donna Bailey and the appellant. George was introduced as a hitman from Birmingham. The appellant told Robinson and George that the job was cancelled because of the expense and that he and Bailey would be doing it themselves. Most of the conversation on this occasion was tape recorded on a concealed device. After it had ended, Bailey and the appellant were arrested and the house was searched. Several incriminating items were found, including handwritten notes, maps, plans and details of observations carried out at Anna's address. A bag containing a syringe filled with liquid, a mask, gloves and binoculars was also found. The liquid was domestic cleaning fluid. Much of the handwriting was that of the appellant, as it was also on the post-it which had been handed to Robinson a week earlier and which he had handed to the police. On the basis of all this (and we are abbreviating the evidence for present purposes), the prosecution asserted that Bailey and the appellant had first sought to incite Robinson but had changed their

minds because of the cost and had thereafter conspired together to murder Anna. It was common ground between the prosecution and the appellant that he was a weaker person than Bailey.

4 The appellant's defence was that he had never intended that Anna should come to any harm. Bailey was a lying and manipulative obsessive and he had simply played along with her in order to pacify her. Anything written by him was at her dictation. He had not thought that she was serious. When he had told Robinson and George that they were now going to do the job themselves, he was just trying to get rid of them. He had already threatened to call the police if Bailey did not cancel the plan which had previously been imparted to Robinson.

5 Donna Bailey's defence was that she had had no thought of having Anna killed but that at the first meeting with Robinson the appellant had suddenly come out with the idea. She sought to distance herself from the handwriting, denying that it had been done at her dictation. It was the appellant who had lined up the hitman and, when Robinson and George had paid a visit a week later, she had just said things to get rid of them.

6 On behalf of the appellant, Mr Carey Q.C. made no criticism of any ruling or the summing up by the trial judge. He seeks to advance the appeal in this way. Prior to and during the trial, neither Mr Carey, nor his junior nor his instructing solicitor had had cause to question the cognitive skills or intelligence of the appellant as a factor relevant to criminal liability. He presented in a plausible manner except that at one stage prior to the commencement of the trial he had started to behave in a peculiar manner and a psychiatric assessment was called for on the issue of fitness to plead. The assessment resolved that issue and did not raise any medical issue relevant to criminal liability. Accordingly, the trial proceeded without concern in that regard. The appellant continued to present in a plausible way.

7 After conviction and in anticipation of sentence a report was commissioned from Dr L.F. Lowenstein, a psychologist. It was prepared for use in mitigation but, following sentence, it became the foundation of this appeal against conviction. When leave to appeal was granted, the prosecution instructed Professor Gisli Gudjonsson, a forensic psychologist, and his report is now relied upon by Mr Carey. The reports are mutually consistent. They lead to the appeal being put in this way. They amount to fresh evidence, not anticipated or realised at the time of the trial but which, if then available, would have been adduced on behalf of the appellant on the issue of his intention. As the jury did not have the benefit of this evidence, and as it is credible but was not reasonably discoverable at the time of the trial, the conviction is unsafe. On behalf of the prosecution, the central submission of Mr Brown is that, on the issue of intention, the evidence of the psychologists would not have been admissible at trial and does not affect the safety of the conviction. By s.23(2)(c) of the Criminal Appeal Act 1968, the admissibility of the evidence at trial is a relevant matter in relation to its receipt in evidence on appeal. Before we address the question of admissibility, it is necessary to summarise the findings of the psychologists.

8 Dr Lowenstein found the appellant to be an extroverted personality with a number of neurotic traits or psychological problems. He is also an impulsive indi-

vidual who tries to please others and help them. Testing of his intellectual abilities produced "roughly a 75 IQ score" and would place him with the mental age of approximately 12 years. Dr Lowenstein concluded as follows:

"1. Mr Henry is a fairly disturbed individual who gives an impression of his intellectual capabilities which is totally wrong. He has a tendency to fail to see the significance of acting by himself leading him into difficulties.
2. He is easily imposed upon as may be noted by the influence his girlfriend had upon him to commit certain acts which led to his conviction. This is again partly attributable to his low intellectual ability to reason matters out as well psychological problems which would make him susceptible to fall under the influence of others.
3. Mr Henry falls into the category of just being above the mentally defective area or what is commonly termed 'borderline' defective area of intellectual ability . . . Mr Henry is a strange man with a Walter Mitty-type of attitude to viewing himself as a clever individual capable of carrying out a crime of a very serious nature and yet not having the mental capacity to see matters through logically and reasonably . . . It is unfortunate for him that he has a bearing of an intellectual but the capacity of someone of virtually mentally defective ability. While this does not excuse his offences, it does or could provide mitigation."

9   As we have related, Dr Lowenstein was instructed to prepare a report for possible use in mitigation rather than exculpation. Professor Gudjonsson, on the other hand, was instructed by the Crown Prosecution Service to prepare a report specifically in relation to this appeal against conviction. He carried out a more extensive assessment of the appellant's intellect and concluded:

"1. The current intellectual assessment . . . indicates that Mr Henry is functioning in the borderline range of learning disability. His full scale score of 71 falls at the bottom 3% of the general population. This suggests a significant intellectual impairment . . .
2. I found no evidence that Mr Henry is currently mentally ill nor is there evidence that he has ever been mentally ill . . . he seems to have serious emotional problems, including a high level of anxiety, proneness towards agitation, self-defeating personality structure, dependence needs and extremely poor self-esteem . . .
3. In summary, Mr Henry is a psychologically vulnerable individual, whose intellectual abilities are very limited, in social interactions he undoubtedly tried to cover up his limited abilities and he superficially presents as intellectually brighter than he actually is . . . It is likely that these problems interfere with his effectively coping with stress and demands placed upon him by others (eg Miss Bailey involving him in arranging a hit-man to deal with [Anna]."

10   We now turn to the authorities. In *R. v Turner* (1974) 60 Cr.App.R. 80; [1975] Q.B. 834, Lawton L.J. said (at pp.83 and 841):

"An expert's opinion is admissible to furnish the Court with scientific information which is likely to be outside the experience and knowledge of a judge or jury. If on the proven facts a judge or jury can form their own conclusions without help, then the opinion of an expert is unnecessary."

This approach has been followed in subsequent cases. A good example of a case in which the issue of expert evidence in relation to intent was considered is *R. v Masih* [1986] Crim.L.R. 395 (Court of Appeal, Criminal Division, January 27, 1986) in which Lord Lane C.J. said:

"Generally speaking, if a defendant is mentally defective, or otherwise comes in the last class, '69 and below mental defective', then in so far as that defectiveness is relevant — relevant that is to the particular case — it may be that expert evidence should be admitted about it. That is in order to enlighten the jury upon a matter which is abnormal, and therefore *ex hypothesi*, presumably, outside their own experience. If it is admitted it should be confined to the assessment of the defendant's Intelligence Quotient, and to an explanation of any relevant abnormal characteristics which such an assessment involves . . . Where the defendant however is within the scale of normality, albeit, as this man was, at the lower end of that scale, expert evidence, in our judgment, is not as a rule, necessary and should be excluded."

The IQ of the appellant in that case was assessed at 72, virtually the same as that of the appellant in the present case. The cut-off point of 69 has sometimes been criticised as arbitrary but it has psychological significance and, as the late Prof. J.C. Smith said in his commentary in the Criminal Law Review, it does have the advantage of being "a clean rule", even if "a rather stringent one".

11   The current edition of *Archbold* 2005, para.17–99 states that

". . . it is possible to discern a relaxation of the attitude of the Court of Appeal in the last 25 years."

12   The case cited as authority for this statement is *R. v Toner* (1991) 93 Cr.App.R. 382. However, there the issue was the possible effect of hypoglycaemia on the formation of an intention. Russell L.J. said (at p.387):

". . . we do not know what, if any, effect mild hypoglycaemia can have upon a man's ability to form an intent, and without that expert evidence the jury were deprived of assistance in a field where their ordinary experience did not enable them to judge for themselves."

In other words, unlike borderline intellectual impairment, in relation to which *Masih* decided that the jury *can* judge for itself, hypoglycaemia is a medical matter outside the ordinary experience of the jury. We see *Masih* and *Toner* as cases on different sides of an identified line and wholly consistent with each other.

13   The one area in which a different approach is clearly discernible is that of the reliability of confession evidence. There one can see an increased willingness to admit expert evidence. See, for example, *R. v Silcot and others*, The Times,

December 9, 1991, in relation to the appellant *Raghip*. However, in *R. v Coles* [1995] 1 Cr.App.R. 157, Hobhouse L.J. observed (at p.168F) that the Court in *Silcot* had expressly drawn a distinction between expert evidence going to the reliability of a confession and expert evidence going to *mens rea*. In *Coles* the disputed expert evidence was that of a psychologist on the capacity of the appellant to foresee the risks involved in his actions. The Court held that it had been rightly excluded and that (*ibid*)

> "unless some factor of the mental health or psychiatric state of the defendant is raised, such evidence is not admissible."

14   Where does all this lead? In our judgment, the evidence of Dr Lowenstein and Prof. Gudjonsson is no more admissible on the issue of intention in the present case than the disputed evidence was in *Masih* and *Coles*. This is not a case of mental illness nor is it a case in which the IQ of the appellant is below that considered by the Lord Chief Justice to be the threshold for admissibility in *Masih*. Whilst it is true that persons with an IQ as low as that of the appellant form a small part of the population at large, sadly they form a somewhat larger part of those charged with criminal offences. An intention that someone should be killed is a visceral matter of no great complexity. In our judgment, it is not a matter which, on the authorities, lends itself to expert evidence in relation to a person such as this appellant. Moreover, it is not without significance that, in any event, the reports of Dr Lowenstein and Prof. Gudjonsson do not opine that the intellectual impairment of the appellant acted or may have acted as a contra-indication of the specific intention. Indeed, to the extent that they portray the appellant as easily led and ineffective in coping with stress and demands placed upon him by someone such as Donna Bailey, their views are entirely consistent with the prosecution case.

15   For all these reasons, we are satisfied that the convictions of the appellant are not unsafe by reason of the reports of Dr Lowenstein and Prof. Gudjonsson which do not contain admissible evidence on the issue of intention. Nor, in our judgment, are they admissible as supporting the credibility of the appellant's account of a lack of the requisite intention. Outside the special area of confessions to which we have referred, it is not generally permissible for a defendant to adduce expert evidence on the credibility of his defence. It is stated in the current edition of *Archbold* (at para.4–326)

> "Nor, save in exceptional circumstances (e.g. *Lowery v R.* [1974] A.C. 85, PC), can psychiatric evidence be admitted to prove the probability of the accused's veracity."

We agree. *Lowery* is heavily relied upon by Mr Carey in the present case. However, it was considered in *Turner* and subsequent cases on these issues (but not in other respects: see *R. v Randall* [2003] UKHL 69; [2004] 1 Cr.App.R. 26 (p.375); [2004] 1 W.L.R. 56,) to be exceptional and fact-specific. Alternatively, it has been viewed as distinguishable in law:

16   We record that the written submissions on behalf of the appellant included an alternative argument to the effect that the reports of the psychologists would have

made it possible to seek to exclude the evidence of the meeting with Robinson and George by reference to s.78 of the Police and Criminal Evidence Act 1984, on the basis that the tape recording was analogous to an unreliable confession. We are wholly unpersuaded by this submission. Indeed, no real reliance was placed on it in oral argument.

17 It follows from what we have said that, notwithstanding the succinct and elegant submissions of Mr Carey, the convictions of the appellant are not unsafe and his appeal is therefore dismissed.

Appeal dismissed.

R. v HIGHTON
R. v VAN NGUYEN
R. v CARP

Court of Appeal (Lord Chief Justice (Lord Woolf), Lord Justice
Moore-Bick and Mr Justice Richards): July 11 and 28, 2005

[2005] EWCA Crim 1985; [2006] 1 Cr.App.R. 7

⟨LT⟩ Admissibility; Bad character; credibility; propensity

H1   EVIDENCE
   Bad character
   Evidence of defendant's bad character admitted following attack on another's
character—Whether capable of showing propensity to commit offences of kind
charged or solely relevant to credibility—Criminal Justice Act 2003 (c.44),
s.101.

H2   In the first case, the appellant was charged with kidnapping, robbery and theft.
At trial, he accused the complainants of lying and, as a result, the judge allowed
details of his previous convictions to be admitted pursuant to s.101(1)(g) of the
Criminal Justice Act 2003. The judge indicated in the course of argument that
he would not direct the jury that they could take those previous convictions
into account when deciding whether the appellant had a propensity to commit
offences of the kind charged. However, in summing up, the judge directed the
jury that, in addition to taking into account the previous convictions when considering the appellant's credibility, that same evidence was relevant to an
important matter in issue, namely whether he had a propensity to commit
offences of the kind charged. The appellant was convicted and he appealed.

H3   In the second case, the appellant was charged with cultivating a controlled
drug, cannabis. He accepted that he was aware that plants that were controlled
drugs were being grown in the premises in which he was living but he contended
that he had not known that they were cannabis plants and that he was not involved
in their cultivation. At trial, the judge allowed evidence that the appellant was a
heroin user to be admitted, pursuant to s.101(1)(d) of the 2003 Act, on the ground
that it was relevant to an important matter in issue, namely whether he knew that
the plants were cannabis. The appellant was convicted and he appealed.

H4   In the third case, the appellant was charged with two counts of common
assault. At trial, he contended that he had acted in self defence and he was allowed
to cross-examine the complainant about her violent background, pursuant to
s.100 of the 2003 Act. As a result, the judge ruled that details of the appellant's
previous convictions could be admitted under s.101(1)(g). The judge directed the
jury that evidence of those previous convictions could be used in deciding

whether the appellant's evidence was truthful and in considering whether he had
committed the offences charged. The appellant was convicted and he appealed.

H5 **Held,** (1) dismissing the appeals in the first and third cases, that a distinction
had to be drawn between the admissibility of evidence of bad character, which
depended upon it getting through one of the "gateways" in s.101 of the 2003
Act, and the use to which it could be put once it was admitted. The use to
which it could be put depended upon the matters to which it was relevant rather
than upon the gateway through which it was admitted. Evidence which was
admitted under s.101(1)(g) because the defendant had made an attack on another
person's character could, depending on the particular facts, be relevant not only
to credibility but also to propensity to commit offences of the kind charged. In
those circumstances, it was important that the trial judge should exercise care
to give the jury the appropriate warnings as to the relevance of such evidence.
Protection was also provided for the defendant by the terms of s.101(3), whereby
the evidence could be excluded if it would cause unfairness. In that context, there
was a very close relationship between the requirements of fairness and the general requirement of the rules of evidence that, unless evidence was relevant, it
should not be admitted. In the first case, on the facts, the evidence of the appellant's previous convictions was properly admitted under s.101(1)(g) and any
application to exclude it under s.101(3) would have been doomed to fail. In
view of the indication given by the judge during the trial, the judge erred in summing up in the terms that he did. However, the appellant's previous convictions
did provide evidence of a propensity to commit offences of the kind charged and
the judge had carefully directed the jury as to the limits of the value of bad character evidence. In all the circumstances, therefore, the conviction was not unsafe.
In the third case, the previous convictions of the appellant were properly admitted
under s.101(1)(g); they did provide evidence of a propensity to commit offences
of the kind charged and the judge gave the jury the necessary warnings as to the
use of that evidence. Accordingly, the conviction was safe (post, paras [10]–[12],
[20]–[24], [53]–[54], [59]).

H6 (2) Allowing the appeal in the second case, that once the appellant had admitted that he thought the plants were a controlled drug of some kind, the only issue
was whether he was involved in growing them and, since any knowledge he
might have had of the precise nature of the plants was not likely to shed much
light on that question, the judge was wrong to hold that the evidence of the appellant's heroin addiction was admissible under s.101(1)(d) as relating to an
important matter in issue. Further, having admitted that evidence, its relevance
was not explained to the jury and the focus of the trial was distorted because of
the emphasis on it. Accordingly, in all the circumstances, the conviction was
unsafe (post, paras [39]–[43]).

H7 *Per curiam.* Judges may consider that it is a sensible precaution, when making
rulings as to the use of evidence of bad character, to apply the provisions of s.78 of
the Police and Criminal Evidence Act 1984 and exclude evidence where it would
be appropriate to do so under s.78, pending a definitive ruling to the contrary.
Adopting this course will avoid any risk of injustice to the defendant and should

avoid any risk of the court failing to comply with Art.6 of the Convention for the Protection of Human Rights and Fundamental Freedoms (post, paras [13]–[14]).

H8   The exclusion of evidence under the provisions of s.101(3) depends on there being an application by the defendant. If no such application is made, no criticism can be made of the judge for failing to act of his own motion under this section (post, para [23]).

H9   (For evidence of bad character, see *Archbold* 2005, para.13–55 and following).

Appeals against conviction

H10   *R. v Highton*

On February 28, 2005, in the Crown Court at Oxford (Judge Morton Jack), the appellant, Edward Paul Highton, was convicted of two counts of kidnapping, two offences of robbery and one count of theft. He was sentenced to four and a half years' imprisonment on each count to run concurrently. His application for leave to appeal against conviction was referred directly to the Court of Appeal by the Registrar. The full court granted leave.

The facts and grounds of appeal appear in the judgment of the court.

H11   *R. v Van Nguyen*

On February 16, 2005, in the Crown Court at Manchester (Judge Ensor) the appellant, Dong Van Nguyen, was convicted of cultivating a controlled drug, namely a plant of the genus cannabis. He was sentenced to 30 months' imprisonment. In addition, an order was made for the forfeiture and the destruction of the cannabis. His application for leave to appeal against conviction was referred directly to the Court of Appeal by the Registrar. The full court granted leave.

The facts and grounds of appeal appear in the judgment of the court.

H12   *R. v Carp*

On February 9, 2005 in the Crown Court at Taunton (Mr Recorder Marston) the appellant, Anthony Mark Carp, was convicted of two counts of common assault. He was sentenced in respect of the first assault to two months' imprisonment suspended for two years and in relation to the second offence, he was sentenced to four months' imprisonment, consecutive to the sentence for the first offence, suspended for two years. He was also ordered to pay £400 towards the costs of the prosecution. He appealed against conviction by leave of the single judge.

The facts and grounds of appeal appear in the judgment of the court.

H13   *Peter Du Feu* (assigned by the Registrar of Criminal Appeals) for Highton.
Fiona Horlick (instructed by the Crown Prosecution Service, Thames Valley) for the Crown.
Michael Goldwater (assigned by the Registrar of Criminal Appeals) for Van Nguyen.
William Baker (instructed by the Crown Prosecution Service, Manchester) for the Crown.
Terry Munyard (assigned by the Registrar of Criminal Appeals) for Carp.

Peter Ashman (instructed by the Crown Prosecution Service, Taunton) for the Crown.

Cur. adv. vult.

July 28.   Lord Woolf C.J. handed down the judgment of the court.
This is the judgment of the Court:

The general position

1   We are hearing these three appeals together because they each concern the bad character provisions contained in the Criminal Justice Act 2003 (the "2003 Act"), Pt XI, c.1, ss.98–113. There are already three previous decisions of this Court dealing with these provisions. The cases are those of *R. v Hanson and others* [2005] EWCA Crim 824; [2005] 2 Cr.App.R. 21 (p.299); *R. v Bovell and Dowds* [2005] EWCA Crim 1091; [2005] 2 Cr.App.R. 27 (p.401) and *R. v Edwards, Fysh, Duggan and Chohan* [2005] EWCA Crim 1813; [2006] 1 Cr.App.R. 3. The principal issue which arises on these appeals is whether evidence admitted under s.101(1)(g) as a result of an attack by the defendant on another person's character is admissible as evidence of a propensity to commit offences of the kind with which the defendant is charged, or is only admissible in relation to his credibility, that is, as evidence tending to show that he is likely to be untruthful. That issue did not arise in those earlier appeals and this judgment is the first judgment relating to it.

2   The issue arises because s.101 of the 2003 Act identifies seven different gateways, at least one of which must be complied with before evidence of a defendant's bad character is admissible in criminal proceedings. However, the 2003 Act does not expressly identify the purpose for which the bad character evidence can be used if it passes through one of those gateways and is therefore admissible. Two different interpretations are contended for by counsel appearing for the appellants and the Crown. The appellants contend that the purposes for which admissible evidence of bad character can be used are confined by the terms of the gateway through which the evidence is admitted. The Crown, on the other hand, contends that once the evidence becomes admissible by passing through any gateway, it can be used for any purpose for which bad character evidence is relevant in the particular case.

3   The dimensions of the issue are apparent when the relevant provisions of the sections of the 2003 Act are considered. They start with s.101(1) itself.

> Defendant's bad character
> "101   (1)   In criminal proceedings evidence of the defendant's bad character is admissible if, but only if—
> > (a)   all parties to the proceedings agree to the evidence being admissible,

(b) the evidence is adduced by the defendant himself or is
given in answer to a question asked by him in cross-
examination and intended to elicit it,

(c) it is important explanatory evidence,

(d) it is relevant to an important matter in issue between the
defendant and the prosecution,

(e) it has substantial probative value in relation to an important matter in issue between the defendant and a co-
defendant,

(f) it is evidence to correct a false impression given by the
defendant, or

(g) the defendant has made an attack on another person's
character.

(2) Sections 102 to 106 contain provisions supplementing subsection (1).

(3) The court must not admit evidence under subsection (1)(d) or
(g) if, on an application by the defendant to exclude it, it
appears to the court that the admission of the evidence
would have such an adverse effect on the fairness of the proceedings that the court ought not to admit it.

(4) On an application to exclude evidence under subsection (3)
the court must have regard, in particular, to the length of
time between the matters to which that evidence relates and
the matters which form the subject of the offence charged."

4   The meaning of the words "the defendant's bad character" is dealt with in s.98
which provides:

'Bad character'
"98 References in this Chapter to evidence of a person's 'bad character'
are to evidence of, or of a disposition towards, misconduct on his part,
other than evidence which—
(a) has to do with the alleged facts of the offence with which the
defendant is charged, or
(b) is evidence of misconduct in connection with the investigation or
prosecution of that offence."

The interpretation section, s.112, provides:

"(1) In this Chapter:
'bad character' is to be read in accordance with s.98;
'criminal proceedings' means criminal proceedings in relation to
which the strict rules of evidence apply; and
'misconduct' means the commission of an offence or other reprehensible behaviour.

Section 99 abolishes the common law rules governing the admissibility of evidence of bad character in criminal proceedings but the abolition is subject to s.118 (1), in so far as it preserves the rules under which, in criminal proceedings, a person's reputation is admissible for the purposes of good or bad character."

5   It is next necessary to refer to s.102 which is linked to s.101(1)(c). Section 102 provides:

"For the purposes of section 101(1)(c) evidence is important explanatory evidence if—
    (a) without it, the court or jury would find it impossible or difficult properly to understand other evidence in the case, and
    (b) its value for understanding the case as a whole is substantial."

6   Next, we come to s.103 which played a significant part in the argument. It is linked to s.101(1)(d). It reads:

"(1) For the purposes of section 101(1)(d) the matters in issue between the defendant and the prosecution include—
    (a) the question whether the defendant has a propensity to commit offences of the kind with which he is charged, except where his having such a propensity makes it no more likely that he is guilty of the offence;
    (b) the question whether the defendant has a propensity to be untruthful, except where it is not suggested that the defendant's case is untruthful in any respect.
(2) Where subsection (1)(a) applies, a defendant's propensity to commit offences of the kind with which he is charged may (without prejudice to any other way of doing so) be established by evidence that he has been convicted of—
    (a) an offence of the same description as the one with which he is charged, or
    (b) an offence of the same category as the one with which he is charged.
(3) Subsection (2) does not apply in the case of a particular defendant if the court is satisfied, by reason of the length of time since the conviction or for any other reason that it would be unjust for it to apply in his case.
(4) For the purposes of subsection (2)—
    (a) two offences are of the same description as each other if the statement of the offence in a written charge or indictment would, in each case, be in the same terms;
    (b) two offences are of the same category as each other if they belong to the same category of offences prescribed for the purposes of this section by an order made by the Secretary of State.
(5) A category prescribed by an order under subsection (4)(b) must consist of offences of the same type.

(6) Only prosecution evidence is admissible under section 101(1)(d)."

7   Section 104 deals with matters in issue between the defendant and co-defendant (dealt with in s.101(1)(e)). Section 105 deals with evidence to correct a false
impression (dealt with in s.101(1)(f)) and s.106 deals with attacks on another person's character (dealt within s.101(1)(g)). These sections did not feature in
argument and it is not necessary to refer to them further.

8   If, however, we return to s.103(1), it is to be noted that it deals with propensity.
The argument before us was as follows: as s.101(1)(d) is the only gateway that is
referred to in s.103(1), the reference it contains to propensity makes it clear that it
is only if the evidence is admitted under s.101(d) that bad character evidence can
be used to show a propensity on the part of the defendant to commit the offences
of which he is charged or a propensity to be untruthful.

9   In our view, however, the force of this argument is diminished for a number of
reasons. First, s.103(1) prefaces s.103(1)(a) and (b) with the word "include".
This indicates that the matters in issue may extend beyond the two areas mentioned in this sub-section. More importantly, while this argument can be
advanced in relation to s.101(d), it can also be advanced in respect of the other
parts of s.(1), in particular in relation to s.101(1)(a) and (b). In addition,
s.101(1) itself states that it is dealing with the question of admissibility and
makes no reference to the effect that admissible evidence as to bad character is
to have. We also consider that the width of the definition in s.98 of what is evidence as to bad character suggests that, wherever such evidence is admitted, it
can be admitted for any purpose for which it is relevant in the case in which it
is being admitted.

10   We therefore conclude that a distinction must be drawn between the *admissibility* of evidence of bad character, which depends upon it getting through one of
the gateways, and the *use* to which it may be put once it is admitted. The use to
which it may be put depends upon the matters to which it is relevant rather than
upon the gateway through which it was admitted. It is true that the reasoning that
leads to the admission of evidence under gateway (d) may also determine the matters to which the evidence is relevant or primarily relevant once admitted. That is
not true, however, of all the gateways. In the case of gateway (g), for example,
admissibility depends on the defendant having made an attack on another person's character, but once the evidence is admitted, it may, depending on the
particular facts, be relevant not only to credibility but also to propensity to commit offences of the kind with which the defendant is charged.

11   This approach underlines the importance of the guidance that was given in the
case of *Hanson and others* as to the care that the judge must exercise to give the
jury appropriate warnings when summing up. (We refer in particular to [18] of
that judgment and [3] of the judgment of *Edwards* and its commendation of
the summing up of Judge Mort in the case of *Chohan*). In *Edwards* the Vice-President, Rose L.J. said:

"What the summing up must contain is a clear warning to the jury against
placing undue reliance on previous convictions, which cannot, by themselves, prove guilt. It should be explained why the jury has heard the

evidence and the ways in which it is *relevant* to and may help their decision. Bearing in mind that *relevance* will depend primarily, though not always exclusively, on the gateway in s.101(1) of the Criminal Justice Act 2003, through which the evidence has been admitted. For example, some evidence admitted through gateway (g), because of an attack on another person's character, may be relevant or irrelevant to propensity, so as to require a direction on this aspect." (para.3) (emphasis added)

12   Protection is also provided for the defendant at the stage of admissibility by the terms of s.101(3) if the admission of the evidence could cause unfairness, and by the reference in s.103(3) to convictions which it would be unjust to admit as evidence of a propensity to commit offences of the kind with which he is charged because the Court is satisfied, "by the reason of the length of time since the conviction or for any other reason" that it would be unjust for s.103(2) to apply. In this context, there is a very close relationship between the requirements of fairness and the general requirement of the rules of evidence that, unless evidence is relevant, it should not be admitted.

13   Those provisions protect against unfairness arising out of the admission of bad character evidence under s.101(1)(d) or (g). The question also arises as to whether reliance can be placed on s.78 of Police and Criminal Evidence Act 1984 ("PACE"). The application of s.78 does not call directly for decision in this case. We, therefore, do not propose to express any concluded view as to the relevance of s.78. However, it is right that we should say that, without having heard full argument, our inclination is to say that s.78 provides an additional protection to a defendant. In light of this preliminary view as to the effect of s.78 of PACE, judges may consider that it is a sensible precaution, when making rulings as to the use of evidence of bad character, to apply the provisions of s.78 and exclude evidence where it would be appropriate to do so under section s.78, pending a definitive ruling to the contrary. Adopting this course will avoid any risk of injustice to the defendant.

14   In addition, as s.78 serves a very similar purpose to Art.6 of the European Convention on Human Rights, following the course we have recommended should avoid any risk of the court failing to comply with Art.6. To apply s.78 should also be consistent with the result to which the court would come if it complied with its obligation under s.3 of the Human Rights Act 1998 to construe ss.101 and 103 of the 2003 Act in accordance with the Convention.

The appeal of Highton

The facts

15   Having given this general guidance, we turn to the appeal of Edward Paul Highton. Highton is now 24 years of age. On February 28, 2005 at Oxford Crown Court, he was unanimously convicted of two counts of kidnapping, two offences of robbery and one count of theft. He was sentenced to four and a half years' imprisonment on each count to run concurrently. Highton's application for leave to appeal against conviction was referred directly to this Court by the

Registrar. We give Highton leave to appeal. Highton had a co-accused, Dean Wilson. He was also convicted of the counts on which Highton was convicted. In addition, he pleaded guilty to a separate offence of theft. He received a total of six and a half years' imprisonment.

16   The prosecution's case was that on September 29, 2004 the two victims, Stephen Duckett and Alan McPherson, were kidnapped by Dean Wilson in Milton Keynes and forced to drive to Highton's house in Oxford. At that house, they were robbed at knife-point and thereafter, taken to a cash point where Highton withdrew and stole £330 from Duckett's account. It was said by the Crown that Highton and Wilson were engaged in a joint enterprise.

17   The defence's case was that the two victims went to Oxford voluntarily to buy drugs. Neither the robberies nor the kidnapping took place, and the cash was stolen by the dealer from whom the victims were trying to buy the drugs. They said that the victims had originally lied to the Police in their statements, stating that Highton had been present in Milton Keynes at the alleged kidnapping, which they stated was at random by two strangers. Not surprisingly in these circumstances the credibility both of the defendants and of the complaints, that is to say who was speaking the truth, was one of the main issues at the trial.

18   Wilson and Highton both had previous convictions, details of which were allowed to go before the jury. Wilson had convictions for various offences of dishonesty and for offences of violence, including convictions for two robberies in 2002. Highton also had convictions for offences of dishonesty and for offences of violence, including four offences of assault occasioning actual bodily harm, one of causing grievous bodily harm, two relating to the possession of offensive weapons, and one of affray, all in the period 1998 to 2004.

19   The grounds of appeal were:

    a) that the judge wrongly admitted the appellant's previous convictions under s.101(g) of the 2003 Act.

    b) that he also wrongly directed the jury as to the significance of the appellant's conviction in relation to the issue of propensity.

Our conclusions

20   There was no answer to the contention that this was a case that fell within s.101(1)(g). Mr Du Feu based his argument upon s.101(3). He argued that the judge should exclude evidence as to Highton's previous convictions as a matter of discretion under that subsection. Against the co-defendant, Wilson, the prosecution also relied on s.101(1)(d). Section 101(1)(d) was never clearly relied upon by the prosecution against Highton. Furthermore, at the end of the argument, Judge Jack said with regard to Highton "he is not at risk from a propensity argument".

21   However, when the judge came to sum up, he unfortunately does not appear to have recalled his exchange with Mr Du Feu, since when dealing with the evidence as to bad character he told the jury:

"Well, plainly that is a substantial attack on the prosecution witnesses' character, and in those circumstances, the law says that it is only right that you should hear what character those who are making such an attack bear. But you also heard about their characters because it may help you to resolve an issue in the case, which is this: the prosecution argue that the *defendants* have a propensity to commit offences of the sort that you are considering. You may therefore use the evidence of the defendant's bad character in relation to those two matters which explains why you have heard about it, but only if you find it helpful to do so."

22   The evidence having been properly admitted through the s.101(1)(g) gateway, for the reasons we have explained, it can be, in the appropriate circumstances, relied upon as evidence of a propensity to commit offences of the kind with which the defendant is charged as well as as evidence going to the defendants' credibility. However, in the course of the exchange which took place between the judge and Mr Du Feu during argument, the judge led counsel and the appellant to believe that he would not direct the jury that they could take his previous convictions into account when deciding whether he was guilty of the offences with which he was charged. In those circumstances, the judge was in error in summing up in the terms that he did.

23   This was not a case where the judge was required to exclude the previous convictions under s.101(3). Mr Du Feu candidly acknowledged that he did not ask the judge to exclude the evidence, but any such application would have been doomed to fail. It may be worth pointing out, however, that the exclusion of evidence under the provisions of s.101(3) depends on there being an application by the defendant. If no such application is made, no criticism can be made of the judge for failing to act of his own motion under this section.

24   The appellant's previous convictions, which included convictions for offences of violence and for the possession of offensive weapons, did provide evidence of a propensity to commit offences of the kind with which he was charged. In addition, the judge did direct the jury carefully as to the limits of the value of character evidence. In the result, therefore, we have come to the conclusion that, while the judge did make the error that we have identified in this summing-up, the error was not such as to make the verdicts of the jury unsafe. Accordingly, Highton's appeal is dismissed.

The appeal of Dong Van Nguyen

The background to the appeal

25   On February 16, 2005, at the Crown Court at Manchester before Judge Ensor, Dong Van Nguyen was convicted of cultivating a controlled drug, namely a plant of the genus *cannabis*. He was sentenced to 30 months' imprisonment. In addition, an order was made for the forfeiture and the destruction of the cannabis. We gave Mr Van Nguyen leave to appeal, his application for leave having been referred to the Court by the Registrar.

26   Mr Van Nguyen was jointly indicted with his brother. The brother pleaded
guilty to the same offence.

27   Number 19 Halliwell Street West, in Manchester, is the property of a Housing
Association. The tenancy was in the name of the appellant's father, who had
become a tenant on April 15, 2004.

28   On May 15, 2004, the appellant had a visit from a Police Constable Ludlow
who was investigating the appellant's complaint of having had £10 stolen in a
public lavatory. The police constable did not enter the premises but spoke to
the appellant on the doorstep.

29   On August 11, 2004 the police called again at the premises. On this occasion, it
was to search for a wanted man who used to live at the premises. The reason for
the visit was unconnected with this appeal. When the police arrived, they saw the
appellant run upstairs to the loft. He remained there until he was approached by
officers.

30   Upon entry into the house, the police found a large quantity of cannabis and
other material. They also found a total of 193 cannabis plants in various stages
of maturity. A large number were little more than seedlings, but there were 85
large mature plants which the police estimated would have yielded 1.3kg of cannabis at a value of between £3,800 and £6,400 pounds. The plants were in the
dining room and in one of the upstairs bedrooms. These rooms had been converted into growing rooms and had been fitted with lighting, heating equipment,
fans, silver foil and various electrical equipment. In addition, two empty containers of methadone were found. But fingerprints of the appellant were not
found on any of the cannabis plants or the equipment used in the cultivation process. Fingerprints of the appellant's brother were, however, found. It was the
appellant's case that he had no knowledge that the plants were cannabis plants,
he was not involved in the cultivation and he had been living in the premises
for only three weeks. However, in the circumstances, he could hardly deny he
was aware that plants that were controlled drugs were being grown in the premises and did not do so. This meant that the only live issue in the cases was whether
the appellant was engaged in the cultivation of the plants. Was this joint enterprise or was it solely the activity of the brother?

31   At the outset of the trial, Mr Goldwater, who appeared on behalf of the appellant, made an application to Judge Ensor, the trial judge, to exclude from the
evidence evidence of an interview which had taken place between the appellant
and the police. This was evidence that indicated that he took heroin and used
methadone. Mr Baker, on behalf of the prosecution, contended that the evidence
was relevant and admissible at common law and admissible under the provisions
of s.101(1)(d) of the 2003 Act. He argued that the important issue to which it was
relevant, was whether the appellant knew that the plants were cannabis, and the
fact that the appellant was very conversant with the drug scene made it more
likely that he would know that they were cannabis. He contended that there
was an obvious link between those who took drugs of any kind and those who
took cannabis. The judge accepted the prosecution's submissions and allowed
the evidence to be given.

32   As a result of the evidence being admitted, during the course of the defendant's cross examination, the prosecution suggested that his heroin addiction meant that he would be desperate for money to fund his habit and that was the reason for his becoming involved in the cultivation of cannabis.

33   In addition, the appellant had previous convictions consisting of four offences of shoplifting in 2001. The prosecution served notice to introduce these convictions under the provisions of s.101. The introduction was not resisted and in the event they were introduced by the appellant himself when he gave evidence. This was no doubt because the appellant wished to establish that he had no convictions for drug offences. However, the prosecution suggested that the shoplifting offences were carried out to fund his addiction. There was no evidence to support this assumption. There was no evidence, for example, that the goods which were stolen had a significant re-sale value.

34   The appellant was also cross-examined on the basis that his connections with drug dealers through his purchases of heroin would mean that he had ready means of access to persons who could dispose of the cannabis crop.

35   Finally, the prosecution relied on the complaint which the appellant made of being robbed of £10 and which resulted in PC Ludlow making the initial call to the house. The prosecution alleged the robbery demonstrated that the defendant, at the time, had been trying to buy drugs in the toilet. This it was suggested, showed that he was the sort of person who did heroin deals in the lavatories of public houses and that the person from whom he was buying heroin could be the dealer in the cannabis that was being cultivated.

36   Mr Goldwater contended with some justification that, since the appellant accepted that he thought the plants were probably some form of controlled drug, the offence for which he was charged did not depend on it being established that he knew the drug that was being grown was cannabis. What was critical was that the appellant was engaged in the cultivation of cannabis.

The summing-up

37   The very experienced trial judge summed up to the jury that they had to be satisfied that "cannabis was being cultivated, the defendant played a part in the cultivation and that he knew it was cannabis." He also made it clear that the case for the prosecution was that this was a joint enterprise between the appellant and his brother. The judge also gave a perfectly adequate direction about the relevance of lies which the appellant had undoubtedly told.

38   Mr Goldwater's complaint about the trial and the summing-up following the initial ruling is that, because of the emphasis that was being placed upon the fact that the appellant was a heroin consumer, the real issue was being lost sight of. The issue was not whether he knew that the plants were cannabis but solely whether he was engaged in the cultivation of the plants which he accepted he appreciated were probably some form of drug. He submits accurately that the judge failed to give the jury any assistance as to how to approach the defendant's admission that he was a heroin user, its relevance or the weight to be attached to it.

Conclusion

39   In our view Mr Goldwater's submission is well-founded. Once the appellant had admitted that he thought the plants were a controlled drug of some kind and thereby ruled out any possibility of a defence under s.28(3) of the Misuse of Drugs Act 1971, it did not matter for the purposes of proving the offences whether he knew they were cannabis. The only issue was whether he was involved in growing them and we do not think that any knowledge he might have had of the precise nature of the plants was likely to shed much light on that question. In our view, therefore, the judge was wrong to hold that the evidence was relevant to an important issue between the defendant and the prosecution so as to render it admissible under s.101(1)(d).

40   Another criticism that is made of the judge's ruling was that he did not take into account s.101(3), namely the adverse affect on the fairness of the proceedings. By s.110 of the 2003 Act, the court must give reasons for any ruling on the admissibility of evidence under s.101 and on any application made under s.101(3) to exclude evidence on the grounds of unfairness. In the present case the judge's ruling clearly dealt with the question of admissibility, but he made no mention of s.101(3) in the ruling, nor did he give any reasons for holding that it would not be unfair to admit it. However, it had been the subject of argument and we do not accept that the admission of evidence that the appellant was a heroin addict was unduly prejudicial, provided that the jury was given a proper direction about its place in the case as a whole. The judge may have been technically wrong to regard the situation as one where the evidence could be admitted under s.101(1)(d) as relating to an important matter in issue, but it certainly assisted in understanding the issues in the case.

41   There is the further problem that, having allowed the evidence of the appellant's heroin addiction to be put before the jury, its relevance was not explained to the jury. In our judgment, there is force in Mr Goldwater's submission that the fact that a person is addicted to heroin does not mean that he is more likely to recognise a cannabis plant than someone who is not addicted to heroin. More importantly, the fact that he is addicted and therefore a user of drugs in their processed form, is not evidence he was engaged in their cultivation or even that he has an enhanced ability to identify a particular controlled drug.

42   What is unfortunate about the trial is that once the evidence of the appellant's heroin addiction was placed before the jury, it became the centre of focus of the trial. It was a major subject of cross-examination and played a disproportionate part in the trial, not least because of the nature of the cross-examination of the appellant when he gave evidence.

43   The fact was that the only evidence that the appellant was engaged in cultivation was that he lived in the house were cultivation was taking place and behaved as though he had something to hide when the police arrived at the house. Having regard to this, it was incumbent upon the judge to clearly explain to the jury that the appellant's heroin addiction was no more than background to the offence alleged. A warning of its limited relevance did not appear in the summing-up, which indeed contained no guidance on the use to which the evidence

might be put. It should have done so because the focus of the trial was distorted as a result of the cross-examination which took place and the emphasis on the appellant's addiction. Accordingly, we have come to the conclusion that this conviction is unsafe.

The appeal of Anthony Carp

The background

44   On February 9, 2005 at the Crown Court at Taunton, Anthony Carp was convicted of two counts of common assault. He was sentenced in respect of the first assault to two months' imprisonment suspended for two years and in relation to the second offence, he was sentenced to four months' imprisonment, consecutive to the sentence on count 1, suspended for two years. He was also ordered to pay £400 towards the costs of the prosecution.

The facts

45   The victim of both assaults had cohabited with the appellant for many years. At the time of the two alleged incidents, and for some time previously, she and the appellant had been living together in the appellant's house. There is no doubt that the relationship at times was stormy. The appellant had obtained an injunction against the complainant as he claimed that she had been violent towards him.

46   On New Year's Eve 2003, the couple had an argument in a public house. They both made their separate ways home where the row continued. The complainant alleged that she was slapped by the appellant who also punched her in the face. This was the first assault. On January 9, 2004 there was another incident in the home in which the complainant alleged that she had been assaulted by the appellant who had punched her in the face. On both occasions, the complainant had been drinking.

47   It was the appellant's case that he had acted in self defence.

48   At the start of the prosecution's evidence, the defence applied under s.100 of the 2003 Act to cross-examine the complainant about her violent background. The Recorder granted the application. At the commencement of the appellant's case, the Recorder also ruled that a number of the previous convictions of the appellant could be admitted in evidence under s.101(1)(g). They included a number of offences of violence (including wounding with intent, assault occasioning actual bodily harm, and assault on a police officer) in the period 1982 to 1993; offences of theft, handling and deception dealt with in 1993; and two drink-related driving offences (failing to provide a specimen, and driving with excess alcohol) in 2000 and 2004.

49   In his evidence, the appellant admitted that he had been a tearaway in the past but he did not attack women. A baby-sitter who was regularly employed by the complainant and the appellant gave supporting evidence of an incident in September 2003. On that occasion the complainant had returned home very drunk. She abused the appellant and physically assaulted him by hitting him on the head with a cordless phone and slapping him.

50   The appellant now appeals against his conviction by leave of the single judge. In support of the appeal, he relies on three grounds:

    i) that evidence of the convictions admitted under the s.101(1)(g) is relevant only in relation to credibility, as would have been permissible if the case were being determined under the old law;

    ii) that if evidence of previous convictions admitted under s.101(1)(g) can be relevant to propensity in either sense, the judge should not have admitted evidence of the convictions for theft and deception;

    iii) the Recorder failed properly to direct the jury as to the relevance of previous convictions or to warn them of the dangers of placing too much reliance on them.

51   At the start of the presentation of the case for the prosecution, counsel for the defence applied under s.100 of the 2003 Act to cross-examine the complainant about her violent background. That background included a significant psychiatric history, incidents of self-harm, at least one incident of violence towards the appellant and the grant of an injunction restraining the complainant from using violence against the appellant. The application under s.100 was granted by the Recorder. As the evidence of the complainant's character was admitted under s.100, an application by the prosecution under s.101(1)(g) of the 2003 Act was irresistible and the Recorder ruled that the previous convictions were admissible.

52   In his summing-up, the Recorder said, having referred to the complainant's conduct:

"You also heard that the defendant has previous convictions for a number of offences of violence. Last being April 1993. A number of offences of dishonesty, last of those also being in 1993 and two drink-related offences, which took place during the time of the defendant's relationship with Miss Byron. This has been given in evidence because the defendant has attacked the character of Miss Byron and it is right in those circumstances that you should know the character of the person making the attack as well. You may use the evidence of the defendant's bad character, his previous convictions in the following ways. First, if you think it is right you may take it in to account when deciding whether or not the defendant's evidence is truthful. A person with previous convictions for dishonesty may be less likely to tell the truth but of course it doesn't follow that he is incapable of doing so. You must decide to what extent if at all his character helps you when judging his evidence. If you think it is right you can also take into account when deciding whether or not the defendant committed the offences — with which he is now being charged — his previous convictions. These allegations are of violence and Miss Byron has also said that she had been drinking when he had allegedly committed these offences. You have got to decide to what extent if at all his convictions help you when you are considering whether or not he is guilty, but bearing in mind that his bad character itself cannot prove anything, it cannot prove anything. It cannot prove his guilt on its own. It would therefore be wrong to jump to the conclusion that he is guilty just because of his bad character."

Conclusion

53   Since the appellant had attacked the character of the complainant, evidence of his bad character became admissible under s.101(1)(g), subject only to the judge's duty to exclude it under s.101(3) if he considered that to admit it would render the proceedings unfair. Here the convictions which were relied on did not occur so long ago that it could be said that in the circumstances the evidence was so prejudicial that it must have been wrong for the evidence to be admitted. The Recorder exercised his discretion and there is no basis upon which this Court can properly interfere with the exercise of the Recorder's discretion.

54   As we have already made clear, the fact that the evidence of the appellant's bad character was admitted under s.101(1)(g) does not prevent the evidence from being used for purposes other than establishing the appellant's credibility. It could be used to show that he was more likely to commit the offences with which he was charged. That is to say, the evidence could be used to show a propensity on his part to commit the sort of assaults with which he was charged, subject to the question of relevance and the evidence not being unduly prejudicial.

55   The appellant relies on paras [7] to [13] of the judgment of the Rose L.J. in *Hanson*. We do not consider that the guidance given by Rose L.J. in these paragraphs is inconsistent with the approach adopted by the Recorder, but it is necessary to deal with one particular aspect of the appellant's case which arises out of what was said in para.[13] of the judgment in that case.

56   Although the second ground of appeal in this case is apparently directed to the admissibility of the appellant's previous convictions, it is apparent from counsel's skeleton argument and the advice on appeal that what it is really directed to is the use of which that evidence may properly be put. Mr Munyard submitted that the Recorder was wrong to direct the jury that they could take the appellant's bad character into account when deciding whether his evidence was truthful without any further qualification. In *Hanson* the court pointed out that convictions for dishonesty (and the same applies to convictions for other kinds of offences) do not necessarily provide reliable evidence of a propensity to be untruthful: it all depends on the nature and circumstances of the conviction. Accordingly, it is said, the Recorder should have warned the jury that they could not place any weight on the fact that the appellant had previous convictions when considering whether they could believe what he said.

57   Since the appellant's previous convictions included three offences of obtaining by deception in addition to offences of theft, this is not a particularly meritorious point. In our view his convictions for obtaining by deception were evidence of a propensity to be untruthful and in that context his convictions for theft added little. (The Recorder did not suggest that previous convictions for offences of violence were relevant in this context). It would have been better, therefore, if

the Recorder had given the jury more detailed guidance on the relevance of the appellant's convictions to the issue of his truthfulness, but in the circumstances of this case we do not think that his failure to do so affected the outcome of trial so as to render his convictions unsafe.

58   In the course of argument Mr Munyard submitted on behalf of the appellant that the Recorder was wrong to have admitted evidence of his two drink-related driving offences. The Recorder was asked to exclude them in the exercise of his powers under s.101(3), but he decided that in all the circumstances they were relevant to the offences with which the appellant was charged and that it would not be unfair for them to be admitted. We can see no grounds on which the exercise of his discretion in this matter can properly be challenged.

59   In para.[18] of the judgment in *Hanson*, Rose L.J. emphasises the need for warnings to be given to a jury not to place undue reliance on previous convictions. In particular, the jury should be directed that they should not conclude that the defendant is guilty or untruthful merely because he has convictions. Looking at the language used by the Recorder, we find that the Recorder gave the necessary warnings in a manner which adequately brought home to the jury the need to take proper care when deciding how much weight, if any, to place on the appellant's previous convictions. In particular he dealt separately with issues of truthfulness and guilt and indicated how different convictions might be relevant to those issues. We therefore do not accept that there is any substance in any of the grounds of appeal relied upon by the appellant and dismiss his appeal.

Highton's appeal against conviction dismissed.
Van Nguyen's appeal against conviction allowed; conviction quashed.
Carp's appeal against conviction dismissed.

R. v ALI AND OTHERS
R. v BHATTI

COURT OF APPEAL (Lord Justice Hooper, Mr Justice Tugendhat and
Sir Douglas Brown): April 19, 20, 29; June 7, 2005

[2005] EWCA Crim 87; [2006] 1 Cr.App.R. 8

⟨LT⟩ Conspiracy; Criminal conduct; Drug trafficking; Jury directions; Money
laundering; Proceeds of crime; Proof; Unfair evidence

H1   CONSPIRACY
      Concealing the proceeds of crime
      Defendants charged with conspiracy to conceal, disguise or remove from the
      jurisdiction bank notes, knowing or having reasonable grounds to suspect the
      money to be the proceeds of drug trafficking or criminal conduct—Whether sus-
      picion as to the character of the money sufficient for offence of conspiracy—
      Criminal Law Act 1977 (c.45), s.1(1)(a), (2) (as substituted by Criminal Attempts
      Act 1981 (c.47), s.5)—Criminal Justice Act 1988 (c.33), s.93C(2) (as inserted by
      Criminal Justice Act 1993 (c.36), s.31)—Drug Trafficking Act 1994 (c.37),
      s.49(2)

H2   The first three appellants were convicted of offences of conspiracy to conceal,
      disguise or remove from the jurisdiction bank notes, knowing or having reason-
      able grounds to suspect that in whole or in part they represented another person's
      proceeds of drug trafficking, contrary to s.49(2) of the Drug Trafficking Act
      1994[1] and s.1(1) of the Criminal Law Act 1977[2]. The money was alleged to
      have been laundered through a money transfer business ("Hawala banking")
      used for the remittance of money by people of Asian origin to their country of
      origin.
H3   At a separate trial, arising out of the same investigation by Customs and
      Excise, the fourth appellant was convicted of an offence of conspiracy to contra-
      vene s.49(2) of the 1994 Act or, alternatively, s.93C(2) of the Criminal Justice Act
      1988,[3] and s.1(1) of the Criminal Law Act 1977, by concealing, disguising or
      removing from the jurisdiction bank notes knowing or having reasonable
      grounds to suspect that in whole or in part they represented another persons' pro-
      ceeds of drug trafficking or other criminal conduct. He was also convicted of a
      similar conspiracy to contravene the 1988 Act but not the 1994 Act.
H4   The appellants appealed against conviction on the ground, inter alia, that the
      counts on the indictment were bad in law in that the particulars of the offence

---

[1] Drug Trafficking Act 1994, s.49: see, post, para.[69]
[2] Criminal Law Act 1977, s.1: see, post, paras [81] and [82]
[3] Criminal Justice Act 1988, s.93C (as inserted by the Criminal Justice Act 1993, s.31): see, post,
para.[79]

did not allege an agreement that was capable of amounting to a conspiracy contrary to s.1 of the 1977 Act. It was submitted that although the substantive offences relevant to this appeal could have been committed if a person merely had reasonable grounds to suspect that the property was the proceeds of drug trafficking or of other criminal conduct, the offence of conspiracy could only be committed if the person *knew* that fact and the judge in each trial should have directed the jury to that effect. It was argued for the defence first that a count of conspiracy to contravene s.49(2) or s.93C(2) fell foul of s.1(1)(a) of the 1977 Act, following *R. v Montila* [2005] 1 Cr.App.R. 26 (p.425), if it included the words "reasonable grounds to suspect" or even just "suspect"; and secondly, in the light of *Montila*, such a count fell foul of s.1(2) of the 1977 Act because that subsection required the defendant and a co-conspirator to know or intend at the time of the agreement that the fact that property was the proceeds of drug trafficking or other criminal conduct "shall or will exist at the time when the conduct constituting the offence is to take place". Reliance was placed on *R. v Harmer* [2005] EWCA Crim 1 to support both arguments. For the Crown, it was contended that the obiter dictum in *Harmer* relied on by the appellants was wrong and that the law had been laid down in *R. v Rizvi and Chisti* [2003] EWCA Crim 3575 and approved in *R. v Sakavickas* [2005] 1 Cr.App.R. 36 (p.584), which was not cited to the court in *Harmer*, namely that it was the existence of suspicion, objective or subjective, that the property was criminal property, as opposed to the fact that it was criminal property, which was a fact or circumstance necessary for the commission of the offence.

H5   **Held,** that (1) the judge had directed the jury that they could not convict unless sure that at least part of the bank notes delivered to the Hawala bank were the proceeds of drug trafficking, so that on the jury's verdict the appellants had agreed to deal with banknotes which were actually (in part at least) the proceeds of drug trafficking and which they (at least) suspected were at least in part the proceeds of drug trafficking. Accordingly, at the time that they reached the agreement to deal with the banknotes which they suspected were the proceeds of drug trafficking, the offence against s.49(2) would necessarily have been committed if they did deal with them. In the light of the judges' direction, s.1(1)(a) of the 1977 Act was satisfied and that argument failed (post, para.[106], [111]).

R. v Harmer [2005] EWCA Crim 1 [23] doubted (post, paras [103], [110]).

H6   (2) allowing the appeals, that following *Montila* the substantive offences under s.49(2)and s.93C(2) required proof that the defendant was in fact dealing with the proceeds of drug trafficking or of other criminal conduct and, following *Harmer*, s.1(2) of the 1977 Act required that the jury only convict of conspiracy if the defendant knew that he was dealing with the proceeds of drug trafficking or of other criminal conduct. *Harmer* reflected the law as it stood after the decision in *Montila*. Accordingly, the jury should not have been directed that they could convict if a defendant only suspected that at least part of the money he was dealing with was the proceeds of drug trafficking or other criminal conduct (post, paras [138], [139], [148]).

H7   *R. v Montila* [2004] UKHL 50; [2005] 1 Cr.App.R. 26 (p.245); [2004] 1 W.L.R. 3141, HL, and *R. v Harmer* [2005] EWCA Crim 1 applied.

R. v Sakavickas [2004] EWCA Crim 2686; [2005] 1 Cr.App.R. 36 (p.584); [2005] 1 W.L.R. 857, CA, distinguished.

R. v Rizvi and Chisti [2003] EWCA Crim 3575 and *R. v Singh* [2003] EWCA Crim 3712 not followed.

H8   (For the offence of conspiracy under s.1 of the Criminal Law Act 1977, see *Archbold* 2005, para.34-2. Section 93C(2) of the Criminal Justice Act 1988 and s.49(2) of Drug Trafficking Act 1994 have now been repealed, but can be found in editions of *Archbold* prior to 2004.)

Appeals against conviction

H9   On June 18 and 19, 2003 in the Crown Court at Leeds (Judge Wolstenholme) the appellants, Liaquat Ali and Akhtar Hussain were convicted of two counts (counts 1 and 4) and Mohsan Khan was convicted of one count (count 1) of conspiracy to contravene s.49(2) of the Drug Trafficking Act 1994, contrary to s.1(1) of the Criminal Law Act 1977, by concealing, disguising or removing from the jurisdiction bank notes, knowing or having reasonable grounds to suspect that, in whole or in part, they represented another persons' proceeds of drug trafficking. Ali and Hussain were each sentenced to concurrent terms of 12 years' imprisonment on each count and Khan was sentenced to eight years' imprisonment.

H10   On October 12, 2004 in the Crown Court at Leeds (Judge Wolstenholme) the appellant, Shahid Bhatti, was convicted of two counts of conspiracy to contravene s.49(2) of the Drug Trafficking Act 1994 or, alternatively, s.93C(2) of the Criminal Justice Act 1988 contrary to s.1(1) of the Criminal Law Act 1977 by concealing bank notes, knowing or having reasonable grounds to suspect that, in whole or in part, they represented another person's proceeds of drug trafficking or other criminal conduct. He was sentenced to six years' imprisonment on count 3 and four years' imprisonment concurrent on count 4. He was acquitted of counts 1 and 2 which charged alternative conspiracies to count 3.

H11   The facts and grounds of appeal appear in the judgment of the Court.

H12   *William Clegg Q.C.* (instructed by Byrne and Partners) for Ali.
Balbir Singh (assigned by the Registrar of Criminal Appeals) for Hussain.
Nadim Bashir (assigned by the Registrar of Criminal Appeals) for Khan.
Peter Collier Q.C. (assigned by the Registrar of Criminal Appeals) for Bhatti.
Martin Bethel Q.C. and *Andrew Haslam* (instructed by Revenue and Customs Prosecutions Office) for the Crown.

Cur. adv. vult.

June 7   Hooper L.J. handed down the judgment of the Court

1   This is the judgment of the Court to which all members have contributed.

2   On the June 18 and 19, 2003 in the Crown Court at Leeds, before Judge Wolstenholme the appellants Liaquat Ali and Akhtar Hussain were convicted of two
counts of conspiracy, counts 1 and 4. The jury were discharged from reaching verdicts on counts 2, 3, 5 and 6. On June 19, the appellant Mohsan Khan was
convicted of conspiracy, count 1. The jury were discharged from reaching verdicts on counts 2 and 3. Counts 1 and 4 charged conspiracies to contravene
s.49(2) of the Drug Trafficking Act 1994, contrary to s.1(1) of the Criminal
Law Act 1977. There was a fourth accused, Arshad Mahmood, who was acquitted.

3   In count 1 it was alleged that between September 1997 and February 2001 they
had conspired together and with Ghulam Mustafa Khan, Raja Munawar Khan
and other persons unknown. On count 4 it was alleged that between the same
dates Ali and Hussain (but not Mohsan Khan) had conspired together and with
Faisal Malik, Imran Syed, Abdul Mitha, James Carr and Asif Memon and with
other persons unknown.

4   It was alleged in substance that the conspirators had concealed, disguised or
removed from the jurisdiction bank notes knowing or having reasonable grounds
to suspect that in whole or in part they represented another person's proceeds of
drug trafficking (in short, money laundering). The difference between the two
counts was that in count 1 the bank notes were alleged to have come from Ghulam
Mustafa Khan and in count 4 from Asif Memon.

5   The money was in each case alleged to have been laundered through a firm
called Watan Travel. This firm had a travel agency and money transfer business
which was not alleged to be unlawful. The money transfer business was of the
kind known as Hawala banking, used for the remittance of money, usually deposited in the form of bank notes, by people of Asian origin to their country of origin.
Watan Travel was an agent of Pakistan International Airlines. It had a shop in
Bradford operated by Hussain and Mamood and one in Birmingham run by Ali.

6   On June 19, 2003 Liaquat Ali and Akhtar Hussain were each sentenced to 12
years' imprisonment concurrent on each count and Mohsan Khan was sentenced
to eight years' imprisonment. Each now appeals against conviction by leave of
the single judge.

7   On October 12, 2004 at the same court and before the same judge Shahid Nazir
Bhatti was convicted of two counts of conspiracy. On count 3 he was sentenced to
six years' imprisonment and on count 4 to four years' imprisonment concurrent.
He was acquitted of counts 1 and 2, which charged alternative conspiracies to
count 3.

8   Count 3 charged Shahid Bhatti with conspiracy to contravene s.49(2) of the
Drug Trafficking Act 1994 or alternatively s.93C(2) of the Criminal Justice
Act 1988, contrary to s.1(1) of the Criminal Law Act 1977. It was alleged that
Shahid Bhatti conspired with his father Nazir Bhatti, and with Faisal Malik,
Imran Syed, James Carr and Asif Memon and other persons unknown to conceal
bank notes knowing or having reasonable grounds to suspect that, in whole or in
part, they represented another person's proceeds of drug trafficking or other
criminal conduct. In count 4 Shahid Bhatti was charged with conspiring together
with his father and a George Cockerill to conceal bank notes knowing or having

reasonable grounds to suspect that, in whole or in part, they represented another person's proceeds of criminal conduct, other than the proceeds of drug trafficking. The period alleged in each count for the conspiracy is July 1, 1999 to February 12, 2001. The money was alleged to have been laundered through Bradford Travel and the associated Bradford Currency Exchange which were run by Shahid Bhatti and his father.

9   Count 1, of which Shahid Bhatti was acquitted, was in similar terms to count 3 but alleged that the proceeds were the proceeds of drug trafficking.

10   Count 2, of which Shahid Bhatti was acquitted, was in similar terms to count 3 but alleged that the proceeds were the proceeds of criminal conduct other than drug trafficking.

11   Shahid Bhatti applies for leave to appeal against conviction.

12   These two trials were the second and third trials arising out of an investigation by HM Customs and Excise culminating in arrests made in February 2001. In the first of the three trials four defendants were convicted, namely Amer Ramzan, together with Faisal Malik, Imran Syed (he on his plea of guilty) and James Carr. It was because the latter three had been convicted at the first trial that the case against them was not pursued in the second and third trials, in which they were named in some of the counts as co-conspirators. In the first trial it was alleged that the bank notes had been laundered through the Halifax office of Ramzan Travel which was run by Amer Ramzan.

13   There have been a number of issues raised or sought to be raised at this hearing. Those which were advanced until the day before this hearing are:

    i) Whether the judge was right to have permitted the prosecution to adduce evidence in the second and third trials of the convictions in the first trial of Malik and Carr. On this point Ali, Hussain and Khan have the leave of the single judge. Shahid Bhatti applied for leave to appeal on this point and we granted that leave on April 20, 2005.

    ii) Whether the judge was right to have permitted the prosecution to adduce at the second trial evidence of an expert. His evidence was to the effect that samples of bank notes recovered from Watan Travel were found upon testing to be contaminated with drugs. On this point Ali and Hussain have the leave of the single judge. Mohsan Khan does not advance this point.

    iii) Mohsan Khan renewed his application, refused by the single judge, to appeal on the ground that the trial judge ought not to have allowed the prosecution to adduce certain observation evidence linking Mohsan Khan to Ramzan. It was accepted that the fate of this point followed the fate of the first point.

    iv) Mohsan Khan also renews his application refused by the single judge to appeal against sentence.

    v) Shahid Bhatti applies for leave to appeal on a second ground namely that the trial judge should have stopped the trial at the end of the prosecution case.

vi) Shahid Bhatti applies for leave to appeal on a third ground namely that the verdicts of the jury were inconsistent.

For lack of time, we had to adjourn argument on the latter two grounds until the hand-down of this judgment.

14   In a skeleton argument dated April 17, 2005 that is the day before the start of this hearing, Ali applied for leave to argue a further ground of appeal, namely that the counts on the indictment on which he was convicted were bad in law in that the particulars of the offence did not allege an agreement that was capable of amounting to a conspiracy contrary to s.1 of the Criminal Law Act 1977. We granted leave to all three appellants in respect of this ground on April 20, 2005. This was linked to an argument advanced for Shahid Bhatti on the form of the indictment. We granted leave to Bhatti on this ground.

15   The three trials could in principle have all been combined into one. The reason for not doing this (we were told) was that the cases would then have become too long and difficult to manage efficiently.

16   All three trials arise out of the deposit of millions of pounds in cash which the three separate businesses referred to above, for the purpose of making corresponding payments abroad, mainly in Dubai and Pakistan, in US dollars or rupees. The three trials correspond to the three businesses: Ramzan, Watan and Bradford.

17   Each of the businesses operated a service for transmitting money from the UK mainly to Pakistan for the benefit of the Asian community here. The Crown accepted that the making of these cash remittances to a very substantial extent did not involve the proceeds of drug trafficking or any other crime. There were remittances totalling some £120 million which the Crown did not allege to be the proceeds of any crime. But the Crown alleged that sums amounting to £170 million did represent the proceeds of crime. They identified a number of individuals as sources from whom the defendants received the cash. The most significant of these was Asif Memon from whom some £80.6 million was received in cash by Watan in the period of less than two years identified in the indictment. The next most significant was GM Khan from whom £46.5 million was received in cash by Watan in the period. These two were therefore identified in the counts of the indictments referred to above. For reasons of case management there were no separate counts identifying the other sources. But the jury bundles did include documents identifying the other sources, and the sums involved. These included Altaf K £30 million, Bashir £5.2 million, Moti £4 million, Gazi £3.2 million, Luton £805,000, Multinet £221,000 and Ramzan £210,000.

18   Until 1999 Watan Travel had had banking facilities with the Midland Bank. Through these facilities the money was converted into US dollars and transferred abroad, principally to the New York bank accounts of a Dubai based currency exchange business called World Link Exchange. Midland Bank became concerned about compliance with money laundering legislation and the business was transferred to Giro Bank. They offered a less advantageous facility. Asif Memon was alleged to be an official of World Link Exchange. Faisal Malik

and Imran Syed delivered the £80.6 million on his behalf to Watan Travel in cash. Some of that was collected from James Carr in boxes at a meeting point near the M62 which had been observed by officers.

19   GM Khan carried on business in Islamabad, Pakistan and in that period, on the prosecution's case, the £46.5 million in cash was delivered on his behalf to the business of Watan Travel at their offices either in Bradford or Birmingham. One of those carrying the cash was Mohsan Khan.

20   In the case of Shahid Bhatti, the Crown's case was that between July 1, 1999 and February 12, 2001 over £71 million went through the Bradford Travel business. Of this £29 million represented what the prosecution accepted to be traditional Hawala banking which they did not allege to be the proceeds of drug trafficking or other crime. The balance of £42 million was alleged to be the proceeds of drug trafficking or other criminal conduct. Of this £3.7 million was involved in count 4 and £38 million in counts 1 to 3.

21   Hawala banking is an arrangement by which individuals (or intermediaries who have collected money from individuals) deposit money, usually in the form of modest amounts of cash, with a Hawalader in, for example, the UK to be remitted to beneficiaries abroad, commonly in the country from which the remitters' families originate, for example Pakistan. The UK Hawalader will have a Hawala contact in Pakistan who will pay a sum in rupees, at a rate of exchange which may have been agreed with the remitter in advance. The payment will commonly be made more quickly, more cheaply and with less formality than any corresponding service that might be available through the medium of the commercial banks. There is commonly a family relationship between the UK Hawalader and his contact in Pakistan which enables the transaction to be completed with a greater reliance on trust than is necessary in other commercial financial dealings. The accounts between the Hawalader and the contact in Pakistan could be settled by remittances in US dollars which might be paid into accounts held outside Pakistan, for example in New York or Dubai.

22   For ordinary Hawala there must be records to show the identities of the individuals from whom the money had originally been collected in the UK and of those to whom it was ultimately to be paid in Pakistan. In relation to the bank notes alleged to be the proceeds of drug trafficking this essential information was conspicuously lacking, whether in the records of Watan Travel, or the records of Malik or for that matter Carr. What was recorded was the name of the source, such as GM Khan or Asif, and the name of an intermediate transferee such as World Link Exchange. The defence case was that this was what they called corporate Hawala. They said that is ordinary Hawala money which had been collected from individuals by intermediaries, and that the intermediaries did not communicate to the defendants the source or ultimate destination of the funds for reasons of commercial confidentiality

23   Amongst the evidence relied on by the prosecution that this was not ordinary Hawala money was:

   i) the difference in the records available in respect of the remittances which they did not allege to be of the proceeds of crime, and of the remittances that they did allege to be;

  ii) the very large sums involved;

 iii) observation evidence of the transport in boxes and bags of what the Crown alleged to be the bank notes, the deliveries corresponding with entries (limited as they were) in the books kept by the defendants. The defence case on the contents of the bags observed to be carried by Mohsan Khan included explanations such as that they contained clothes and other things he had been buying and which the surveillance officers had not seen him buy, and that his visits to Watan Travel were to pay cash for airline tickets.

The admission of the convictions of Faisal Malik and others.

24   At almost the start of the second trial, on May 1, 2003 the judge ruled that the prosecution could adduce evidence that Faisal Malik and James Carr but not Amer Ramzan had been convicted the previous June of conspiracy with Asif Memon to launder the proceeds of drug trafficking through the business of Ramzan Travel.

25   The judge reached the same conclusion in the Shahid Bhatti trial and that is also appealed. At the conclusion of the argument we indicated that the appeals against the rulings failed. We said that we would give reasons later, and the reasons are as follows.

26   No distinct submissions were made on behalf of Shahid Bhatti and it is therefore sufficient to address the arguments made on behalf of Ali, Hussain and Khan.

27   The admissibility of evidence of the convictions of persons other than a defendant is provided for by the Police and Criminal Evidence Act 1984. That provides:

> "74 (1) In any proceedings the fact that a person other than the accused has been convicted of an offence by or before any court in the United Kingdom . . . shall be admissible in evidence for the purpose of proving, where to do so is relevant to any issue in those proceedings, that that person committed that offence, whether or not any other evidence of his having committed that offence is given . . ..
>
> 75 (1) Where evidence that a person has been convicted of an offence is admissible by virtue of section 74 above, then without prejudice to the reception of any other admissible evidence for the purpose of identifying the facts on which the conviction was based—
>
> > (a) the contents of any document which is admissible as evidence of the conviction; and
> >
> > (b) the contents of the information, complaint, indictment or charge-sheet on which the person in question was convicted, shall be admissible in evidence for that purpose . . ."

28   All the defendants objected to the admission of those convictions on the grounds of relevance, under s.74, and on the further ground that the admission of the evidence would be unfair and should be excluded under s.78, which provides:

> "(1) In any proceedings the court may refuse to allow evidence on which the prosecution proposes to rely to be given if it appears to the court that, having regard to all the circumstances, including the circumstances in which the evidence was obtained, the admission of the evidence would have such an adverse effect on the fairness of the proceedings that the court ought not to admit it . . .."

29   The basis on which the prosecution submitted that the conviction was relevant was as follows. The principal courier of cash to Watan Travel on account of Asif Memon was Faisal Malik, assisted by Imran Syed and Abdul Mitha. Malik kept a book which had been seized by Customs and was an exhibit. In that book he recorded collections and deliveries of cash. Entries in the book for deliveries corresponded to entries in the Watan Travel books for receipts. The books showed that the money recorded as collected by Malik and his associates went mainly to Watan Travel up to August 1999 and thereafter went mainly to Ramzan Travel. All of it then went to World Link Exchange. On one occasion cash delivered by Carr to Malik was divided by Malik into separate onward deliveries to Watan Travel and Ramzan Travel. On another occasion the money from Carr was split between Watan Travel and Bradford Travel. It was the cash delivered by Malik and his associates to Ramzan Travel which was the subject of the first trial which resulted in the convictions the prosecution proposed to adduce. The evidence of Malik's activities was in any event before the jury in the second trial in which this application was made. The question was whether the convictions should also be before the jury.

30   It is significant, in view of the fact that the conviction in the first trial is one for conspiracy, that the jury had been directed at the first trial to find a defendant guilty of that offence only if they were satisfied that at least some of the cash represented the proceeds of drug trafficking. The prosecution submitted that it followed from the form of the direction, and from the fact of the conviction, that the jury were sure that some or all of the money which Malik and his associates delivered to Ramzan was the proceeds of drug trafficking. The prosecution submitted that the convictions were relevant because they went to the issue of whether the bank notes that went to Watan Travel were the proceeds of drug trafficking. The prosecution submitted that the convictions supported the inference that some or all of the money delivered by Malik and his associates to Watan Travel was also the proceeds of drug trafficking. The prosecution did not contend that the convictions proved anything in relation to the state of mind of the defendants at the second trial. They were put in only on the issue of whether the Asif Memon money was the proceeds in whole or in part of drug trafficking.

31   The defendants submitted to the judge, as they have to us, that the bank notes were different in each delivery, and that the convictions were in any event consistent with some of the bank notes delivered to Ramzan Travel not being the

proceeds of drug trafficking. So, it was said, it did not follow from the earlier convictions that the bank notes delivered to Watan Travel were the proceeds of drug trafficking. This is obviously correct, so far as it goes, as the judge accepted.

32   It was also submitted that strictly it is not a necessary ingredient of the offence of conspiracy that the cash in question in fact represented the proceeds of drug trafficking, only that the defendant must at least have reasonable grounds to believe such to be the case. This is also correct. But what was not disputed at the second trial was that, as a matter of fact, the jury in the first trial had been given the direction mentioned above, namely to find a defendant guilty of that offence only if they were satisfied that at least some of the cash represented the proceeds of drug trafficking.

33   The judge permitted the evidence to be adduced in relation to the couriers, Malik and Carr, but not in relation to Ramzan. In his summing up he explained the relevance of the evidence to the jury as follows:

> "The relevance of this evidence is not to demonstrate what these defendants knew or suspected about the origin of the money, but that taken with the other evidence, it may tend to show that people in possession of these amounts of cash were connected with traffickers in drugs and therefore that the Asif cash delivered to Watan Travel is likely to represent in whole or in part the proceeds of earlier drug trafficking."

34   This was an "issue" within the section as explained in *R. v Robertson* (1987) 85 Cr.App.R. 304. The judge gave other directions on the subject, some to a similar effect, and some additional, including a direction that it was not evidence relevant to Mohsan Khan (who was the courier from GM Khan, not Asif Memon). In his ruling the judge noted that even without the convictions of Malik and Carr, a prima facie case on the issue of whether the money was at least in part the proceeds of drug trafficking had been made out and called for an answer from the defence.

35   Before us it was submitted that the conviction proved only the propensity of Malik and Carr to handle the proceeds of drug trafficking, and that evidence of propensity was not admissible. But the rule excluding evidence of propensity relates to the defendant at a trial, not to others who are not defendants.

36   Further it is submitted that the convictions, even when considered in conjunction with the terms of the indictment, do not show that Malik and Carr were found to have dealt with what was in fact the proceeds of crime. This could be proved, if at all, only by also proving the terms of the direction to the jury. This is a step too far, it is submitted, there being no reported case in which a jury has had the basis for a plea or conviction adduced in evidence before it.

37   The possible significance of a basis of plea or conviction to evidence sought to be adduced under s.74 was touched on in *R. v Mahmood and Manzur* [1997] 1 Cr.App.R. 414, but the question we have to decide did not have to be decided in that case.

38   Where there is a conviction for robbery or burglary the indictment commonly will not identify the stolen property unambiguously. In a subsequent trial of a handler (or of some other person whose criminal responsibility depends on par-

ticular property having been stolen), it may be relevant to establish precisely what property was the subject of the earlier conviction. In practice this may well be entirely non-contentious.

39   Section 75 of the 1984 Act expressly makes some provision for solving the problem of identifying the facts on which a conviction is based. It provides specifically for the admissibility of certain documents such as the indictment. It also provides that that is "without prejudice to the reception of any other admissible evidence for the purpose of identifying the facts on which the conviction was based". So the question is whether, in principle, the terms of the direction to the jury would be such evidence. We see no reason why it should not be. In practice, the point is likely to be dealt with by admissions.

40   That does not conclude the point before us, because the terms of the direction to the jury were not put before the jury in this case. If the point had been foreseen, they could have been. This could have been done all the more readily because the judge had put the essential part of his directions in writing. But as noted above, this point was not taken at the time, and Mr Clegg Q.C. who advances the point to us on behalf of Ali was not counsel at the trial. Everybody on May 1, 2003 knew about the earlier trial, it was the same judge and counsel for the prosecution. The matter proceeded on the footing that it was common ground that the jury in the first trial had been directed as the judge described. It was thus not necessary for the prosecution to take the matter any further.

41   So far as fairness is concerned, it was submitted to us that the evidence of the convictions might cause the jury to take the forbidden line of reasoning, namely that because Malik and Carr were guilty in the first trial in relation to money delivered to Ramzan, therefore they were also (as named co-conspirators) guilty in relation to the money delivered to Watan Travel (the subject of the second trial).

42   Given the careful and repeated directions which the judge proposed to give, and did give, to the jury in the second trial as to what the evidence was and was not to be used for, we can see no error in his decision under s.78. The point on unfairness was a strong point in relation to Amer Ramzan. The fact that he was convicted on the basis that he was the person to whom the bank notes were delivered and who had laundered them might have led the jury to conclude that the defendants in this case were guilty. But the judge accepted this submission and excluded the evidence of Ramzan's conviction.

43   We turn to the ground of appeal that concerns the contaminated bank notes.

44   Ali and Hussain have leave to argue that the judge wrongly admitted evidence of contamination of bank notes. The evidence as to contamination came from an expert scientist Mr Fletcher Burton. There was in the end no challenge to his expertise. This ground is based on the contention that the bank note contamination evidence is wholly irrelevant and therefore inadmissible.

45   Mr Burton, who is a chemist, works for a laboratory which specialises in the analysis of bank notes for the presence of drugs. Since 1995 his laboratory has regularly analysed cash in general circulation for traces of drugs. The cash is taken at random from banks in different parts of the country, the amount being analysed each time being £2,000. From that his experience is that chemical evi-

dence of cocaine and heroin is quite rarely found on bank notes in general circulation the average being three notes in every hundred. In the present case in
January and February 2001 Customs and Excise officers seized cash that had
passed through Watan Travel and Mr Burton analysed it to see if there was any
difference in the degree of cocaine and heroin contamination found in the
notes and the average for notes in general circulation. The first cash that was
tested showed a contamination rate around 3 per cent. But the second amount
of cash collected from Watan produced on analysis a very different picture.

46   The cash collection was £25,000 and Mr Burton analysed £9,400 worth made
up of 622 individual notes. A graph was before the jury showing the result of the
analysis of 170 notes 35 per cent of which were contaminated to a significant
degree. The percentage for the third batch of cash tested was that 25 per cent
of the notes were found to be contaminated to a significant degree. The fourth collection which was analysed resulted in a finding that 22 per cent of the notes were
contaminated to a significant degree. The percentage for the fifth examination of
cash was 22 per cent. For the sixth examination the percentage was 10 per cent .
Examination was made, of money seized from a safe at Watan Travel on the day
of the arrests. Analysis of the 166 bank notes found showed contamination of 23
per cent. He also tested some cash taken from Birmingham which was consistent
with the percentage in cash in general circulation. The same result was achieved
on examination of a substantial amount of cash taken from the home of Hussain.

47   Finally Mr Burton examined £2,175 consisting of 130 separate bank notes
found in Mohsan Khan's briefcase. The graph for this examination showed 20
per cent contamination.

48   In summing up, almost at the end, the judge took the jury in detail through the
various charts of percentages.

49   In ruling on defence objections to the admissibility of this evidence the judge
said:

> "The Crown concede that it cannot be proved that that cash came either
> from the Asif monies or the Ghulam Mustapha Khan monies, both monies
> being the subject of the two particular conspiracies on the indictment, but
> the Crown have put the case on the basis that monies sent abroad in a similar
> manner on behalf of other named parties are also the proceeds of drug traf-
> ficking. The Crown concede that they cannot exclude the possibility that
> some or all of these samples relate to cash deposited in the course of Hawala
> business conducted by the defendants which before this jury the Crown have
> not sought to impugn. However, the Crown have to prove, as an element of
> the offence here, that some of the monies represent the proceeds of drug traf-
> ficking. All these samples concern cash put through the system by the
> defendants and I accept Mr. Bethel's submission that it is logically relevant
> to proving or helping to prove that cash transmitted by Watan Travel was the
> proceeds of drug trafficking."

50   The judge said he regarded arguments advanced by counsel as going to the
weight to be attached to the evidence and not to admissibility.

51   Having taken the jury through the detail of the evidence the judge said [426]:

"Now what do you make of all this? As I have already said, it is important to remember that none of this cash came from the Asif monies, the subject of count 4 and that it cannot be proved any of it came from the GM monies, the subject of count 1. All that is proved is that the cash examined by Mr. Burton was cash going through the Watan Travel business, apart from the cash in Mohsan Khan's briefcase (427). The prosecution concede that if this is drug money, it could be drug money that went through the business as ordinary Hawala cash. What it proves, you may think, if you accept this scientific evidence, and having accepted it you draw the conclusion that this cash must have been in contact, directly or indirectly with people who have been in contact with drugs, what it proves is that such money was going through the business of Watan Travel in late January, early February, as shown by five out of the six random samples of cash taken and that Mohsan Khan had such money in his briefcase (428). Does it support the prosecution case that the Asif and GM monies represented the proceeds of drug trafficking? Well, Mr. Thomas has suggested to you that the evidence proves nothing and that it is simply prejudicial and certainly you will bear in mind that it does not relate to the Asif or GM monies and the prosecution do not suggest that this evidence is decisive, it is simply part of a picture and the whole picture has been put before you. It is for you to decide the extent to which, if at all, this evidence is helpful to you on the very important issue of whether the Asif monies and the GM monies must have been as the prosecution contend, at least in part the proceeds of drug trafficking."

52   Mr Clegg Q.C. who made the principle submissions on this point said that the evidence lacked any probative value whatsoever. That the cash could have come from a legitimate source could not be excluded. It could for example be money from genuine Hawala customers who were nevertheless drug users.

53   Mr Clegg Q.C. referred to the passages of the summing up we have already referred to. In particular the first sentence of [427] "the prosecution concede that if this is drug money, it could be money that went through the business as ordinary Hawala cash." That concession having been made, the evidence was completely irrelevant and the jury had been asked to draw a wholly improper inference from this evidence. The judge was asking the jury that which logic, common sense and the law did not permit.

54   His understanding of the Crown's attitude in closing was that this evidence was described as of little evidential value.

55   Mr Singh submitted that it was impermissible for the judge to invite the jury to look at the whole picture. He referred to the case of *R. v Boyson* [1991] Crim. L.R. 274. This court (Watkins L.J., Hirst and Popplewell JJ.) indicated that it did not approve the growing practice of allowing evidence to go before a jury which is irrelevant, inadmissible, prejudicial or unfair simply because it is convenient for the jury to have "the whole picture".

56   Mr Bethel first dealt with a point briefly raised by Mr Clegg as to the admissibility of the test results on the cash in Mohsan Khan's briefcase. Mr Bethel said it

was plainly relevant. Mohsan Khan was a carrier of cash for GM Khan and over £2,000 had been found on his arrest. The jury could infer he had collected that for GM Khan and it was destined for him. Mohsan Khan had given an explanation that it represented the proceeds of a take-away business. That was for the jury to consider and it was plainly admissible in the case.

57   He said the Crown's case was that money from drugs was not confined to GM Khan and Asif Memon monies but included all the cash not supported by documents listed at divider eight in the respondents bundle.

58   While accepting that it was possible that some had come from Hawala money the evidence was rightly admitted on a limited basis. It was admissible to give the general picture particularly with repeated emphasis by the judge that the money tested could not have come from the GM Khan or Asif Memon deposits.

59   The judge had stressed that the evidence only went to the origin of the money and repeatedly stressed that the prosecution had to prove separately knowledge or suspicion. This was significantly the most important part of the case.

60   The jury had clearly paid attention because they acquitted Mahmood since they could not have been satisfied on the question of knowledge or suspicion.

61   The judge warned the jury carefully about the limitations of this evidence. Mr Bethel conceded it would have been better with hindsight if the judge had not summed up the evidence in such detail and reminded the jury of it graph by graph. However, he submitted that the safety of the conviction was not affected.

62   In our judgment this ground fails. The fallacy in Mr Clegg's attractive argument lies in the fact that what the Crown contended was non Hawala cash, was not confined to the two Hawaladers identified in count 1 and count 4, i.e. GM Khan and Asif Memon. The others who received this money, as can be seen from the totals in Dubery P at 79, were given over £44 million with no documentary support or verification. This money, unlike the GM Khan and Asif Memon cash was received at times relevant to the cash sampling.

63   While the prosecution made the sensible concession that cash from Hawala transactions could possibly have been excessively contaminated, it was open to the jury as a matter of common sense to infer that it was far more likely that the genuine Hawala cash would be either not contaminated or lightly contaminated. The cash which was contaminated was likely to come from non Hawala money. It was in our view legitimate for the jury to have regard to the contamination evidence and conclude that the evidence gave them some, but limited assistance in the way the judge offered for their consideration in the summing up.

64   On its own it might not have the greatest importance but the jury would consider it alongside the devastating evidence of collection and delivery of cash: by way of example the hundreds of thousands of pounds delivered in cardboard boxes from Liverpool by car at pre-arranged venues.

65   We agree with Mr Clegg that the emphasis given to the evidence at the end of the summing up was, with hindsight, unfortunate. It would, as Mr Bethel conceded, have been better if the judge had not spent so long reminding the jury of the detail of the charts. However, looking at the summing up on this topic in the round, we do not think that it can in reality be argued that any imbalance in the summing up at this point was such as to render the convictions unsafe.

66   We turn to the ground newly raised on behalf of Ali, Hussain and Khan and
raised in a different form in the Bhatti grounds, namely, the conspiracy counts
were bad in law in that the particulars of the offences did not allege an agreement
that was capable of amounting to a conspiracy contrary to s.1 of the Criminal Law
Act 1977. The thrust of the argument is that although the substantive offences relevant to this appeal are committed if a person merely has reasonable grounds to
suspect that the property is the proceeds of drug trafficking or of other criminal
conduct, the offence of conspiracy can only be committed if the person *knows*
that.

67   Count 4 in the Ali, Hussain and Khan indictment read (other counts charging
similar conspiracies in the Ali trial and in the Bhatti trial were framed using the
same general language):

> **"Statement of offence**
> CONSPIRACY to contravene section 49(2) of the Drug Trafficking Act
> 1994, contrary to section 1(1) of the Criminal Law Act 1977.
> *Particulars of offence*
>
> Liaquat Ali, Akhtar Hussain and Arshad Mahmood [acquitted] on a day
> between the 1st day of September 1997 and the 13th day of February 2001
> conspired together with Faisal Malik, Imran Syed, Abdul Mitha, James
> Carr and Asif Memon and with other persons unknown to conceal, dis-
> guise or remove from the jurisdiction property namely, a quantity of
> bank notes, knowing or having reasonable grounds to suspect that, in
> whole or in part, directly or indirectly, they represented another person's
> proceeds of drug trafficking for the purpose of assisting another to avoid
> prosecution for a drug trafficking offence or the making of a confiscation
> order or avoiding the enforcement of a confiscation order in contra-
> vention of Part II of the Drug Trafficking Act 1994."

68   We set out the various statutory provisions directly or indirectly relevant to this
appeal, underlining references to the required mental element of knowing, suspecting or having reasonable ground to suspect.

69   Section 49 of the Drug Trafficking Act 1994 Act provides:

> "(1) A person is guilty of an offence if he —
>   (a) conceals or disguises any property which is, or in whole or in part
>   directly or indirectly represents, his proceeds of drug trafficking,
>   or
>   (b) converts or transfers that property or removes it from the jurisdic-
>   tion,
>   for the purpose of avoiding prosecution for a drug trafficking offence
>   or the making or enforcement in his case of a confiscation order
> (2) A person is guilty of an offence if, knowing or having reasonable
>   grounds to suspect that any property is, or in whole or in part directly
>   or indirectly represents, another person's proceeds of drug trafficking,
>   he —
>   (a) conceals or disguises that property, or

> (b) converts or transfers that property or removes it from the jurisdiction,
>
> for the purpose of assisting any person to avoid prosecution for a drug trafficking offence or the making or enforcement of a confiscation order."

70   The predecessor to s.49 was s.14(1) and (2) of the Criminal Justice (International co-operation) Act 1990 (see *R. v Montila* [2004] UKHL 50; [2005] 1 Cr.App.R. 26 (p.425); [2004] 1 W.L.R. 3141 for the international and domestic history of the offences of the laundering of drugs money).

71   Section 50(1) provides:

> "Subject to subsection (3) below, a person is guilty of an offence if he enters into or is otherwise concerned in an arrangement whereby—
>> (a) the retention or control by or on behalf of another person (call him "A") of A's proceeds of drug trafficking is facilitated (whether by concealment, removal from the jurisdiction, transfer to nominees or otherwise), or
>> (b) A's proceeds of drug trafficking—
>>> (i) are used to secure that funds are placed at A's disposal, or
>>> (ii) are used for A's benefit to acquire property by way of investment, and he knows or suspects that A is a person who carries on or has carried on drug trafficking or has benefited from drug trafficking."

72   Section 50(4) provides:

> "4) In proceedings against a person for an offence under this section, it is a defence to prove—
>> (a) that he did not know or suspect that the arrangement related to any person's proceeds of drug trafficking;
>> (b) that he did not know or suspect that by the arrangement the retention or control by or on behalf of A of any property was facilitated or, as the case may be, that by the arrangement any property was used as mentioned in subsection (1)(b)."

73   Section 51(1) provides:

> "A person is guilty of an offence if, knowing that any property is, or in whole or in part directly or indirectly represents, another person's proceeds of drug trafficking, he acquires or uses that property or has possession of it."

74   The offences created by these sections are punishable by 14 years' imprisonment.

75   By virtue of s.52(1) a person is guilty in certain circumstances of an offence if he knows or suspects that another person is engaged in drug money laundering and does not disclose the information to a constable as soon as is reasonably practicable after it comes to his attention. Similar language is used in s.53, which prohibits "tipping off".

76   All these provisions of the Drug Trafficking Act 1994 were repealed and replaced by the Proceeds of Crime Act 2002.

77   Sections 93A, B, C and D of the Criminal Justice Act 1988 (as inserted by the Criminal Justice Act 1993 and now repealed and replaced by Pt 7 of the Proceeds of Crime Act 2002) correspond respectively to ss.50, 51, 49 and 53 of the Drug Trafficking Act 1994. The relevant differences are that the s.93 offences relate to criminal conduct. That is defined in s.93A(7) as:

> "conduct which constitutes an offence to which this Part of this Act applies or would constitute such an offence if it had occurred in England and Wales or (as the case may be) Scotland."

78   Section 71(9) (c) of the Criminal Justice Act 1988 provides that an offence to which this Part of this Act applies includes any indictable offence other than a drug trafficking offence (or certain terrorist offences).

79   Section 93C, with which this appeal is concerned, provides:

> "(1) A person is guilty of an offence if he—
>   (a) conceals or disguises any property which is, or in whole or in part directly or indirectly represents, his proceeds of criminal conduct; or
>   (b) converts or transfers that property or removes it from the jurisdiction,
>   for the purpose of avoiding prosecution for an offence to which this Part of this Act applies or the making or enforcement in his case of a confiscation order.
> (2) A person is guilty of an offence if, <u>knowing or having reasonable grounds to suspect</u> that any property is, or in whole or in part directly or indirectly represents, another person's proceeds of criminal conduct, he—
>   (a) conceals or disguises that property; or
>   (b) converts or transfers that property or removes it from the jurisdiction,
>   for the purpose of assisting any person to avoid prosecution for an offence to which this Part of the Act applies or the making or enforcement in his case of a confiscation order."

80   Section 93A, which we shall have to also consider provides in so far as relevant:

> "If a person enters into or is otherwise concerned in an arrangement whereby —
>   (a) the retention or control by or on behalf of another (A) of A's proceeds of criminal conduct is facilitated . . .
>   <u>knowing or suspecting</u> that A is a person who is or has been engaged in criminal conduct, or who has benefited from criminal conduct, he is guilty of an offence."

81   The other statutory provision which we shall have to consider in detail is s.1(1) of the Criminal Law Act 1977, which reads:

> "Subject to the following provisions of this Part of this Act, if a person agrees with any other person or persons that a course of conduct shall be pursued which, if the agreement is carried out in accordance with their intentions, either—
>> (a) will necessarily amount to or involve the commission of any offence or offences by one or more of the parties to the agreement, or
>> (b) would do so but for the existence of facts which render the commission of the offence or any of the offences impossible,
> he is guilty of conspiracy to commit the offence or offences in question."

82   That subsection is subject to s.1(2) of the Act which provides:

> "Where liability for any offence may be incurred without knowledge on the part of the person committing it of any particular fact or circumstance necessary for the commission of an offence, a person shall nevertheless not be guilty of conspiracy to commit that offence by virtue of subsection (1) unless he and at least one other party to the agreement intend or know that that fact or circumstance shall or will exist at the time when the conduct constituting the offence is to take place."

It is worth noting that cl.48(2) of the Draft Criminal Code for England and Wales provides that "recklessness with respect to a circumstance suffices where it suffices for the offence itself" (see Law Commission Report No.177 and commentary thereon at 241, where it is stated that this "sub-section states for conspiracy a rule in similar terms to that stated in 49(2) for attempt").

83   Mr Clegg submits that by virtue of the decision in *Montila* and of s.1(1) and (2), a person cannot be guilty of a conspiracy to commit an offence against s.49(2) or a conspiracy to commit an offence against s.93C(2) unless he and another conspirator know at the time of the agreement that the property is the proceeds of drug trafficking (s.49(2)) or of other criminal conduct (s.93C(2)).

84   The first issue which we propose to consider relates to the meaning of the expression "reasonable grounds to suspect". It or a similar expression is very familiar. Section 24 of the Police and Criminal Evidence Act 1984 provides:

> "(4) Any person may arrest without a warrant—
>> (a) anyone who is in the act of committing an arrestable offence;
>> (b) anyone whom he has reasonable grounds for suspecting to be committing such an offence.
> (5) Where an arrestable offence has been committed, any person may arrest without a warrant—
>> (a) anyone who is guilty of the offence;
>> (b) anyone whom he has reasonable grounds for suspecting to be guilty of it.
> (6) Where a constable has reasonable grounds for suspecting that an arrestable offence has been committed, he may arrest without a war-

rant anyone whom he has reasonable grounds for suspecting to be guilty of the offence.

(7) A constable may arrest without a warrant—

    (a) anyone who is about to commit an arrestable offence;

    (b) anyone whom he has reasonable grounds for suspecting to be about to commit an arrestable offence."

85   For the purposes of these and similar provisions a person has reasonable grounds for suspecting X if he suspects X and there are reasonable grounds for suspecting X (see *Archbold*, 2005, paras 15–23 to 24).

86   If that definition were to be applied to the provisions in issue in this appeal, the offence would be committed if the defendant suspected that the property was the proceeds of drug trafficking or of other criminal conduct and that suspicion was a reasonable one. It seems unlikely that the draftsman intended that result—interpreted in that way it would be more difficult to obtain a conviction of the offences in ss.49(2) of the 1994 Act and 93C(2) of the 1988 Act. Whereas for the other offences knowledge or suspicion would be sufficient, for these two offences knowledge or a *reasonable* suspicion would be required.

87   Mr Collier Q.C. submitted that, if suspicion were sufficient (which he does not accept) the judge should have directed the jury that if they were sure that the defendant and a co-conspirator suspected at the time of the agreement that the property was the proceeds of drug trafficking, then the prosecution must also prove that the suspicion was reasonable.

88   If the draftsman intended to include liability for negligence, as well as for knowledge and suspicion, then one would have expected the use of an expression such as: or "he knows or suspects or ought to know or suspect that the property is the proceeds of drug trafficking or of other criminal conduct". Section 49(2) would then read:

> "A person is guilty of an offence if, when he knows or suspects or ought to know or suspect that any property is, or in whole or in part directly or indirectly represents, another person's proceeds of drug trafficking, he—
>
>   (a) conceals or disguises that property, or
>
>   (b) converts or transfers that property or removes it from the jurisdiction . . .".

89   That does not however solve a further problem. The section requires the defendant to conceal or disguise "for the purpose of assisting any person to avoid prosecution for a drug trafficking offence". It is difficult to see how a person who only ought to have known or suspected can have as the purpose of the concealment "assisting any person to avoid prosecution for a drug trafficking offence . . .".

90   The judge recognised this difficulty at [52] of the Ali, Hussain and Khan summing-up, to which we turn shortly.

91   Between those two competing possible interpretations is a middle way, which was adopted by Tuckey L.J. in *R. v Rizvi and Chisti* [2003] EWCA Crim 3575. The effect of the decision is that if "the facts or circumstances" proved by the

prosecution ought to have given rise to the suspicion that the property is the proceeds of drug trafficking (s.49(2)), then the defendant has reasonable grounds to suspect that the property is the proceeds of drug trafficking.

92   The judge in the Ali, Hussain and Khan summing-up (the Bhatti summing-up is to a like effect) reminded the jury of the words of the indictment and of s.49(2). He continued:

> "51. Now as a matter of strict law a person would be guilty of this offence even if he did not know or even suspect that the money represented the proceeds of drug trafficking or other criminal conduct provided he had reasonable grounds to suspect that might be the case because that is what the Act of Parliament says that having reasonable grounds to suspect is sufficient.
>
> 52. Having said that you may think it is difficult to envisage a situation where you could be sure a person's purpose was to assist somebody to avoid prosecution or a confiscation order unless he actually suspected, as opposed to simply having reasonable grounds to suspect, that the money had the requisite criminal origin.
>
> 53. Now, as I have said, to help you with all this I have put into writing what needs to be proved. We will have a quick look at it now and then when I start on Monday I will go over it again, but we will have a quick look at it now, if you will bear with me, because it brings together, I hope, the directions I have been giving you.
>
> (Document handed to jury)
>
> 54. Members of the jury, it is six pages long but today we will just look at page 1, which relates to count 1.
>
>> Before you can convict any of these defendants of count 1 you must be sure:
>>
>> That at least part of the bank notes delivered to Watan Travel on behalf of Ghulam Mustapha Khan was the proceeds of drug trafficking; and
>>
>> That there was in fact a conspiracy, that is an agreement between two or more persons to commit the offence of money laundering the proceeds of drug trafficking; and
>
> That the defendant whose case you are considering is a party to that agreement in the sense that;
>
>> He agreed with one or more of the other persons referred to in the count that the agreement would be carried out; and that he knew or suspected that at least part of the money he was dealing with was another person's proceeds of drug trafficking; and that he knew that the purpose of the agreement was to assist another person to avoid prosecution for a drug trafficking offence or the making or enforcement of a confiscation order."

93   Thus the judge, as the written directions show, told the jury to convict a defendant only if he knew or *suspected* that at least part of the money he was dealing with
was another person's proceeds of drug trafficking.

94   We note that the "other persons" whose proceeds were being laundered were
named in the indictments as co-conspirators (in the Liaquat Ali case, Ghulam
Mustapha Khan in count 1 and Asif Memon in count 4). No point is taken on
that. It is worth noting, however, that a person who launders his own proceeds
of drug trafficking commits an offence under s.49(1) and not s.49(2). (The indictment in this case is worded, in this respect, in the same way as in *R. v Sakavickas*
[2004] EWCA Crim 268; [2005] 1 Cr.App.R. 36 (p.584); [2005] Crim. L.R. 2005,
to which we turn below.)

95   In the light of that direction it is not necessary for us in this case to resolve the
issue raised by the words "reasonable cause to suspect". Mr Bethel Q.C. told us
that any decision on the meaning of these words could have a substantial effect on
a number of convictions. It is necessary however to deal with the submission of
Mr Collier Q.C. set out in [88] above. We have no doubt that even if Mr Collier
were right, the failure to direct the jury in either case that the suspicion had to be
reasonable would not affect the safety of the convictions on the facts of these
cases. If the jury only found suspicion, it is inconceivable, on the facts of this
case, that the jury would not also have found the suspicion reasonable.

96   Mr Clegg has two arguments in support of his submission that a person cannot
be guilty of a conspiracy to commit an offence against s.49(2) or a conspiracy to
commit an offence against s.93C(2) (or indeed the other offences) unless he and
another conspirator know at the time of the agreement that the property is the proceeds of drug trafficking (s.49(2)) or of other criminal conduct (s.93C(2)). First, a
count of conspiracy to commit an offence against s.49(2)or 93(C)(2) is bad in law
if it includes the words "reasonable grounds to suspect" or even just "suspect".
He submits that such a count falls foul of s.1(1)(a) of the Criminal Law Act 1977
in the light of *Montila*. He submits that an agreement to conceal etc the property
will not necessarily amount to or involve the commission of the substantive
offence of money laundering if the state of mind of the conspirators is only suspicion (objective or subjective). Secondly, in the light of *Montila*, such a count
falls foul of s.1(2) of the Criminal Law Act 1977. That sub-section requires the
defendant and another co-conspirator to intend or know at the time of the agreement that the fact that the property is the proceeds of drug trafficking (s.49(2)) or
of other criminal conduct (s.93C(2)) "shall or will exist at the time when the conduct constituting the offence is to take place". Mr Collier merely expressed his
agreement with the first argument but further developed the second argument.

97   In *Montila* the House of Lords decided that for the offences under subs.49(2) of
the 1994 Act subs.93C(2) of the 1988 Act it must be proved that the property was
in fact the proceeds of respectively drug trafficking or of other criminal conduct.
It is not enough that the defendant has reasonable grounds to suspect that the
property is the proceeds of drug trafficking or of other criminal conduct when
in fact it is not (or cannot be proved to be so). Lord Hope of Craighead giving
the considered opinion of the Committee said ([2005] 1 Cr.App.R. 26 (p.425)):

"27 Subsection (2) states that a person is guilty of an offence 'if knowing or having reasonable grounds to suspect that any property is . . . another person's proceeds of drug trafficking [section 49(2) of the 1994 Act] of criminal conduct [section 93C(2) of the 1988 Act]' he does one or other of the things described to 'that property' for the purpose which the subsection identifies. A person may have reasonable grounds to suspect that property is one thing (A) when in fact it is something different (B). But that is not so when the question is what a person knows. A person cannot know that something is A when in fact it is B. The proposition that a person knows that something is A is based on the premise that it is true that it is A. The fact that the property is A provides the starting point. Then there is the question whether the person knows that the property is A.

28 The opening words of the subsection thus provide a strong indication that it is directed to activities in relation to property which is in fact 'another person's proceeds of drug trafficking' or 'another person's proceeds of criminal conduct', as the case may be. A further indication is to be found in the absence of any defence if the property which the defendant is alleged to have known or had reasonable grounds to suspect was another person's proceeds turns out to be something different. Subsequent events may show that the property that he was dealing with had nothing whatever to do with any criminal activity at all, but was the product of a windfall such as a win on the National Lottery. On the Crown's argument it is enough for it to be proved that he had the mens rea at the time when he was dealing with the property and that he was doing what he did for the purpose that the subsection identifies.

29 Further indications that when the subsection refers to 'another person's proceeds' it proceeds on the basis that the property in question is in fact proceeds of the kind described are to be found in the surrounding context. . . ."

98   At one point in his argument Mr Clegg appeared to be submitting that the effect of *Montila* is that a person can only commit a conspiracy to commit an offence against s.49(2) or 93C(2) if the property actually exists. Thus, he submitted, if A and B agreed to deal with (a convenient expression to describe conceal, disguise, etc.) the supplier's proceeds of a supply of drugs which they expect to take place tomorrow, they would not be guilty of conspiracy. He accepted after further time to consider the point, that this could be an effective conspiracy even if the supply did not take place. If the prosecution proves that the property which is the subject of the agreement would be, to the knowledge (belief would be a better word) of the co-conspirators, the proceeds of drug trafficking or of other criminal conduct at the time when the conduct constituting the substantive offence is to take place, then the offence of conspiracy would be made out (if the other ingredients are satisfied). This follows from s.1(2) which refers to knowledge (belief would be a better word) that the fact or circumstance shall or will exist at the time when the conduct constituting the offence is to take place.

99   Mr Clegg relies upon *R. v Harmer* [2005] EWCA Crim 1, which he says supports both of his arguments. The ratio supports his first argument, so he submits,
and the obiter dictum supports his second.

100   *Harmer* was convicted of conspiracy to convert or transfer property, namely
currency, which he and his co-conspirator (Hadley) had reasonable grounds to
suspect in whole or in part represented another person's proceeds of criminal conduct and/or drug trafficking. The count as left to the jury reflected an earlier
amendment:

> "7. . . . [T]he words 'knew or' had been deleted from the Particulars before
> the words 'had reasonable grounds to suspect'. Thus, the prosecution had
> accepted that they could not establish that the various amounts of money
> were the proceeds of crime; and . . . they were not alleging that the appellant
> and Hadley knew that the money was another person's proceeds of criminal
> conduct or drug trafficking. The case rested alone on the allegation that the
> appellant had reasonable grounds to suspect this."

101   The facts were:

> "9. Between April and September 2001, the Customs and Excise conduc-
> ted surveillance on the appellant and Hadley. They observed regular
> meetings between them, when they arrived at and departed from various
> places, such as a local hotel and station car parks. On occasions, packages
> were passed between them. They were also seen to meet others, including
> Hooshang Lanjani, Kaushik Taylor and Paul Kennedy. After his meetings
> with Hadley, the appellant was seen on the same day visiting various
> branches of Barclay's Bank in Essex, where he made cash deposits of up
> to £20,000 into various corporate bank accounts. Large amounts of
> money were then regularly transferred to bank accounts in Spain. Each of
> these Spanish accounts was bogus. They had been opened using passports
> with photographs of Walter Callinan or Barry Smith, who was Paul Kenne-
> dy's father-in-law.
> The prosecution case was that the purpose of the meetings was to facilitate
> money laundering. It was alleged that from the 1st December 2000 to the
> 29th September 2001 the appellant and Hadley had conspired with others
> to launder the proceeds of another person's crime or drug trafficking. It
> was alleged that during this period over £1.2m was transferred out of the jur-
> isdiction from accounts to which the appellant was a signatory. Before it was
> transferred abroad, the money had been transferred between different cor-
> porate bank accounts in order to mix it up and make it difficult to trace."

102   May L.J. giving the judgment of the Court allowing the appeal said:

> "14. At no stage did the judge direct the jury that the prosecution also had to
> prove that the relevant money *was* the proceeds of criminal conduct or the
> proceeds of drug trafficking. His omission to do so was in accordance with
> the understanding of the legal requirements of the substantive offences
> under section 93C of the 1988 Act and section 49 of the 1994 Act, as it

was before the House of Lords decision in *Montila*. As we have said, the prosecution had accepted that they could not prove this. Their evidence was very strong as to the suspicious movement of what in general may have looked like illicitly obtained money. But they called no evidence to attempt to establish its provenance. As Mr Ross, for the prosecution, said, the evidence might have surely sustained an inference that the provenance of the money was illicit, but the jury were not invited to draw such an inference, nor did the judge direct them as to that possibility. Whether the evidence might have surely sustained an inference that the provenance of the money was drug trafficking on the one hand or criminal conduct on the other is not clear to us.

15. Indeed, the prosecution had, so it seems, three related difficulties. First, they were unable to establish the criminal provenance of the various amounts of money. Second, they were unable to establish the person or persons whose proceeds of crime it was. Third, they were unable to establish whether it was the proceeds of drug trafficking or of criminal conduct. The first of these difficulties is central to what is now the main ground of appeal in the present case. . . .''

103   Having summarised the decision in *Montila* and set out s.1 of the Criminal Law Act 1977, May L.J. continued:

"23. [For the appellant] Mr Kane's central submission is that the statutory definition of conspiracy comprising section 1(1)(a) of the 1977 Act embraces an agreement whereby the conspirators intend and agree to commit 'an offence or offences'. *Montila* decides that converting or transferring property which a defendant has reasonable grounds to suspect represents another person's proceeds of crime is not an offence, unless the Crown also prove that the property is the proceeds of crime. The Crown, therefore, did not establish in the present case that the appellant was guilty of conspiracy under section 1(1)(a), since they did not establish that the object of the agreement was an offence. In our judgment, this is clearly a correct construction of the sub-section. . . . Mr Kane's . . . point appears to have been conceded by the prosecution before this court in *R v El Kurd*[2001] Crim. LR 234 — but see paragraph 39 of *Montila*. We also note that this court said in paragraph 33 of its judgment in *R v Hussain*[2002] EWCA Crim 06; [2002] 2 Cr App R 26 page 363 at 375 of equivalent conspiracy charges:

'. . . as we have already said, the Crown have to establish the Conspiracy Offence comprised in the making of the agreement. They do not have to establish as such that one or other of the Agreed Offences was committed, although they may incidentally do so as part of the evidence from which they would ask the jury to infer the agreement. They do have to establish that the Agreed Offences would, if the agreed course of conduct was carried out, be offences.'

24. . . .Mr Ross submits that the Crown can rely in answer to Mr Kane's submission on section 1(1)(b) of the 1977 Act. A person, who agrees with another person to convert or transfer property which he has reasonable grounds to suspect represents another person's proceeds of crime, does agree that a course of conduct will be pursued which, if the agreement is carried out in accordance with their intentions, would necessarily amount to or involve the commission of an offence or offences, but for the existence of facts which render the commission of the offence or any of the offences impossible, if nevertheless the property does not represent the proceeds of crime. He submits that there is no difference in principle between a person who agrees to convert or transfer property which he has reasonable grounds to suspect is the proceeds of crime, when it is not, and a person who agrees to import a package which he believes to contain prohibited drugs, but where customs officers have removed the drugs which were previously there. These examples are not, in our judgment, equivalent. With the second, if the drugs had been there as the importer believed, an offence would have been committed. The prosecution can readily prove this. With the first, the offence would be an offence if the prosecution could prove that the property was the proceeds of crime. But in the present case they could not prove this. The substantive offence was not impossible to commit. It was simply that the prosecution could not prove that it had been committed. This is not a case where the prosecution could prove the agreement alone, apart from what they could show might be the substantive offence. They had to ask the jury to infer the agreement from the subsequent putting of it into operation. Although the offence of conspiracy comprises an agreement to commit an offence (not the subsequent committing of the agreed offence), the agreement has to have a material object. In the present case, the appellant was not alleged to have been party to an abstract agreement to convert or transfer theoretical property which might turn out opportunistically to be the proceeds of crime. The alleged agreement concerned the particular money to which the Crown's evidence related and was, on the Crown's case, to be inferred from that evidence."

104   In the light of [24] it could be said that the Court's decision is limited to the facts. This not being "a case where the prosecution could prove the agreement alone, apart from what they could show might be the substantive offence" and given that the prosecution "had to ask the jury to infer the agreement from the subsequent putting of it into operation", the inability to prove that the various amounts of money were the proceeds of crime was fatal to the charge of conspiracy (as it would be to the substantive offence after *Montila*).

105   However that would overlook what was said at [23] where the Court adopted the interpretation by Mr Ross of the sub-section as clearly the correct construction: the prosecution had not established that the appellant was guilty of conspiracy under s.1(1)(a), since the prosecution did not establish that the object of the agreement was an offence. If a person agrees with another to deal with property which he only has reasonable grounds to suspect is the proceeds of

drug trafficking or other criminal conduct, the prosecution will not have established that, if the agreement is carried out in accordance with their intentions, it will necessarily amount to or involve the commission of any offence or offences by one or more of the parties to the agreement. It will only necessarily amount to or involve the commission of any offence or offences if the defendant and another co-conspirator *know* this, because a person can only know that property is the proceeds of drug trafficking or other criminal conduct when it is (or will be) the proceeds of drug trafficking or other criminal conduct.

106   In this case the judge, who skillfully anticipated *Montila*, directed the jury (for example) in relation to count 1 in the Liaquat Ali case, that they could not convict unless sure that at least part of the bank notes delivered to Watan Travel on behalf of Ghulam Mustapha Khan were the proceeds of drug trafficking. He gave a similar direction in relation to other counts. Thus, on the jury's verdict, the defendants agreed to deal with the banknotes which were (in part at least) the proceeds of drug trafficking and which they (at least) suspected were at least in part the proceeds of drug trafficking. At the time that they reached the agreement to deal with the banknotes which they suspected were the proceeds of drug trafficking, the offence against s.49(2) would necessarily be committed if they did deal with them.

107   Let us take two examples:

> Example (1): D1 runs a Hawala bank. D2 comes in with £750,000 in cash which he tells D1 belongs to C. It is in fact C's proceeds of drug trafficking and D2 knows that but does not tell D1 that. D1 merely suspects that the cash is C's proceeds of drug trafficking. D1 and D2 agree that the money is to be sent to Pakistan and their purpose in so doing is to assist C to avoid prosecution (in the case of D1 his purpose, presumably, is to assist D2 if his suspicions about the source of money are well founded). If the agreement is carried out in accordance with their intentions, the course of conduct which they agree to pursue (sending the money to Pakistan) will necessarily involve the commission of the substantive offence by D2 who will have the required knowledge (s.1(1) only requires that the course of conduct will if carried out in accordance with the conspirator's intentions necessarily amount to the commission of an offence by one of the parties).
>
> Example (2): the same facts as example (1) but D2 only suspects that the cash brought into the Hawala bank is the proceeds of drug trafficking albeit that it is in fact the proceeds of drug trafficking. If the agreement is carried out in accordance with their intentions, the course of conduct which they agree to pursue (sending the money to Pakistan) will, so it seems to us, necessarily involve the commission of the substantive offence by both of them. D1 and D2 will have the necessary suspicion and the money with which they are agreeing to deal with is in fact the proceeds of drug trafficking.

108   The second example reflects this case (assuming that the jury were sure of "suspicion" but not sure of "knowledge" on the part of the defendants)—subject to one caveat. The two examples envisage an agreement being formed about the

particular cash brought into the Hawala bank. In reality the agreement is likely to have been formed earlier—D1 and D2 have agreed that D1 will send to Pakistan C's money if D2 brings it in to the Hawala bank. That should not however make any difference in the light of the concession rightly made by Mr Clegg to which we refer in [98] above.

109   Likewise if D1 and D2 agree to receive goods which are (or will be) stolen believing (only) that they are (or will be stolen), then, if the course of conduct (handling) is carried out in accordance with their intentions, that will necessarily amount to the commission of an offence by both parties (that still leaves the s.1(2) problem to which we turn next).

110   Not without some hesitation in what is a difficult area, we think that the passage in [23] of *Harmer* to which we referred in [105] above is open to doubt.

111   In our view this first argument fails because the jury were directed to convict only if sure that (at least) part of the money was in fact the proceeds of drug trafficking. In the light of that direction s.1(1)(a) is, in our view, satisfied.

112   We turn to the second argument. It follows from *Montila*, so it is submitted on behalf of the appellants, that for the purposes of s.1(2), the fact that the property is or will be the proceeds of drug trafficking or of other criminal conduct is a fact upon which the sub-section bites. To the extent to which the substantive offence imposes liability without knowledge on the part of the person committing it of any particular fact or circumstance necessary for the commission of an offence, a person shall nevertheless not be guilty of conspiracy to commit that offence unless he and at least one other party to the agreement intend or know that that fact or circumstance shall or will exist at the time when the conduct constituting the offence is to take place. Knowledge of the fact that the proceeds are or will be the proceeds of drug trafficking or of other criminal conduct is required—suspicion is insufficient.

113   It is necessary to consider another passage in *Harmer*, a passage which it is agreed is obiter:

> "25. There is a further answer to Mr Ross' submission, which, in our judgment, is fatal to it. It derives from the late Professor Sir John Smith QC's commentary on *Hussain* in [2002] Crim. L.R. 407 at 409 where he said:
>
>> '*Agreement to commit crime A or B as circumstances dictate*. The parties agree to launder money illicitly obtained — i.e. obtained contrary to section 49(2) of the 1994 Act or (a different crime) contrary to section 93C(2) of the 1988 Act. The difficulty here lies in the very strict *mens rea* requirements of statutory conspiracy. Recklessness is not enough. The effect of section 1(2) (not mentioned in *Siracusa, El Kurd* or the judgment in the present case) is that D is not guilty of conspiracy to commit an offence by virtue of section 1(1)—
>>
>>> 'unless [D] and at least one other party to the agreement intend or know that [all the facts and circumstances necessary for the commission of the offence] shall or will exist at the time when the conduct constituting the offence is to take place'.

Can it be said that the parties 'intend or know' that the money will be the proceeds of drug trafficking? Or that they 'intend or know' that it will be the proceeds of criminal conduct other than drug trafficking? If it is one or the other, they cannot know both, so they cannot know either. A person who believes that there is a 50/50 chance that something is so can hardly be said to 'know' that it is so; and 'intend' appears to be irrelevant where the parties know they have no control over the existence of fact or circumstances—as here.

26. This commentary addresses the more complicated problem, alluded to earlier in this judgment and discussed in *El Kurd* and *Hussain*, when the prosecution cannot establish that the provenance of obviously illicit money is criminal conduct on the one hand or drug trafficking on the other. But the commentary emphasises the statutory requirement that, where, as in the present case, the substantive charge would only be that the defendant had reasonable grounds to suspect that the money was the proceeds of crime (i.e. the offence would be incurred without knowledge on the part of the person committing it), he is not to be guilty of conspiracy unless he and at least one other party to the agreement intend or know that the money will be the proceeds of crime when the agreed conduct takes place. This intention or knowledge is precisely what the prosecution in the present case accepted they could not prove when the words 'knew or' were omitted from the particulars of count 2. If the prosecution cannot prove that the money was the proceeds of crime, they cannot prove that the appellant knew that it was. So section 1(2) of the 1977 Act applies and is not satisfied. Mr Ross drew our attention in this context to paragraphs 27, 28 and 34 of the judgment of this court in *R. v. Singh* [2003] EWCA Crim 3712 (18 December 2003). This decision preceded *Montila* and, in so far as it might be seen to support Mr Ross' argument, does not in our view survive *Montila*."

114   The Court then went on to consider a possible solution, charging an attempt to commit a conspiracy. The Court said that it "found the concept of attempting to make an agreement an odd one". It rejected that solution given that:

"the case was simply not conducted and the judge did not direct the jury with an eye to attempt; and it is not possible to say that the jury must have been satisfied of facts which proved the appellant guilty of attempting to commit the indicted offence the case was not conducted in that way."

115   Mr Clegg relies on this passage in *Harmer*. If it is a correct analysis of s.1(2), then he submits that these appeals must succeed. He points out that, although the Court in [26] referred to "reasonable grounds to suspect" (not relied upon by the judge in the instant cases), the underlined passage, he submits, shows that "suspicion" is also insufficient if the charge is one of conspiracy. Mr Bethel does not dispute this analysis. He submits, however, that *Harmer* is wrong, that the law was laid down in *Rizvi and Chisti*, approved in *Sakavickas* (not cited to the

Court in *Harmer*) and that this Court is bound to follow those decisions and not *Harmer*.

116   In *Rizvi and Chisti* the appellants had been convicted on a count which stated:

> "Conspiracy to deal with the proceeds of drug trafficking, and/or criminal conduct, contrary to section 1(1) of the Criminal Law Act."

117   The two substantive offences were s.49(2)(b) of the Drug Trafficking Act 1994 and its mirror provision, s.93C(2)(b) of the Criminal Justice Act 1988. So it was alleging a statutory conspiracy. The particulars of the offence were:

> "Between the 1st day of February 2001 and the 21st day of April 2001, knowing or having reasonable grounds to suspect that certain property, namely quantities of banknotes, in whole or in part, directly or indirectly, represented another person's proceeds of drug trafficking, and/or criminal conduct, conspired with each other and with others, to convert the said property for the purpose of avoiding prosecution for a drug trafficking offence, or for the purpose of avoiding prosecution for an offence to which Part VI of the Criminal Justice Act 1988 applies, or the making of a confiscation order, or avoiding the enforcement of a confiscation order."

118   It was submitted by counsel for the appellant that:

> ". . . the learned judge misdirected the jury that they could convict on the basis that they were sure that a particular defendant had reasonable grounds to suspect that the monies came from the proceeds of drug trafficking or other crime. This is contrary to section 1(2) of the Criminal Law Act 1977, which provides that where liability for any offence may be incurred without knowledge on the part of the person committing it of any particular fact or circumstances necessary for the commission of the offence, there can be no criminal liability . . ."

119   The Court set out s.1(2) and continued:

> "11. . . . So far as actual knowledge is concerned, there is no question of a defendant being convicted of an offence without knowledge on his part. The more difficult question is what the effect of section 1(2) is on a person who has reasonable grounds for suspicion that the money is 'hot'.
>
> 12.   In this situation again it seems to us that there is no question of liability without knowledge of any particular fact or circumstance. In other words the liability is not absolute. It depends upon the defendant's knowledge of the facts or circumstances which ought to give rise to the suspicion. On this analysis, there is no lack of knowledge of 'any particular fact or circumstance' for the purposes of section 1(2).
>
> 13.   We do not think there is anything in *Anderson* (1985) 81 Cr App R 253, or its consideration in *Siracusa* (1990) 90 Cr App R 340 to which Mr Campbell Clyne referred which casts doubt on that conclusion. A defendant is

guilty of conspiracy if he agrees to commit the offences created by the two
sections knowing or having reasonable grounds for suspecting that the
money is 'hot'."

120   In *Sakavickas* he and Reichwald had been convicted of conspiracy to commit
an offence contrary to s.93A of the Criminal Justice Act 1988. We have already
set out the terms of that section ([80] above). It should be noted that the required
mental element is "knowing or suspecting". In other words the same mental element as the judge directed the jury to find before conviction in the instant cases.

121   Summarising the facts, the Court said ([2005] 1 Cr.App.R. 36 (p.584)):

> "2. In substance what was alleged was that a bank account operated by
> Reichwald was used to deal with the cash proceeds of cigarettes smuggled
> by Sakavickas and his associates out of Eastern Europe into the United
> Kingdom."

122   The judge had, like the trial judge in the instant cases, directed the jury at [10]:

> "Have the Crown made you sure that the money, or part of it, was the pro-
> ceeds of crime which involved Sakavickas and others? The Crown have
> nailed their colours to that mast. The money that they say you are concerned
> with is money coming from crime which involves Sakavickas and others. If
> they do not convince you of that it is not guilty all round. That is the first
> hurdle they have to cross."

123   The judge continued:

> "Secondly, have the prosecution made you sure that the defendants knew or
> suspected that Sakavickas and others were engaged in criminal conduct or
> were benefiting from such conduct? Thirdly, have they proved to you that
> the defendant agreed with others to help retain control of and the benefit
> of those criminal proceeds, knowing or suspecting that they were indeed
> criminal proceeds?"

124   It was submitted on behalf of the appellant Reichwald by Mr Rees Q.C. that:

> "[The judge's] direction as to the third element of the offence was mistaken
> because as conspiracy was alleged it was not enough to show that the alleged
> offender suspected that Sakavickas and others had obtained the money
> under consideration by means of crime. It had to be shown that the alleged
> offender knew that to be the case. That is said to be the effect of section 1(2)
> of the Criminal Law Act 1977 in the circumstances of this case."

125   It is important to set out the reasons given by Kennedy L.J. for dismissing the
appeal:

> "13. To support that basic submission Mr Rees drew our attention to some
> legal commentaries, mainly emanating from the late Professor Sir John
> Smith QC, and to some decisions of this Court. He started with the legal
> commentaries. In an article in the Criminal Law Review on Conspiracy
> under the Criminal Law Act 1977, [1977] Crim LR 598, Professor Smith

examined the wording of section 1(2) and said at 603 that the provision is intended to ensure that strict liability and recklessness have no place in conspiracy. The subsection, he said, is intended to codify the principles of the *mens rea* of conspiracy as stated in *R. v Churchill (No 2)* [1967] 2 AC 224. In that case their Lordships held that a defendant could not be liable for a conspiracy to commit a strict liability offence unless he had knowledge of the facts which rendered the implementation of the agreement unlawful. Before us it seems to be common ground that this was the purpose of the subsection, but, whatever may have been the original intention, it was Professor Smith's contention that section 1(2) as enacted became applicable to conspiracy to commit any crime, a view not shared by all other academic commentators. It seems to us relevant to observe that Prof Smith took this view principally because he thought that, unless the subsection were given this broad construction, defendants could be liable for a statutory conspiracy without appreciating all the elements of the offence which rendered the envisaged course of conduct unlawful, provided one of the conspirators had the appropriate mens rea. As we point out below, the House of Lords has held in *R. v Anderson* (1985) 81 Cr.App.R. 253; [1986] A.C. 27 that this premise is incorrect.

14. The wording of subsection 2 is not easy. It applies —

'Where liability for any offence may be incurred without knowledge on the part of the person committing it of any particular fact or circumstance necessary for the commission of the offence.'

Mr Rees points out that liability under section 93A of the 1988 Act can be incurred without knowledge on the part of the alleged offender that the money which he is said to be helping to launder is in fact the proceeds of criminal conduct by someone else. It is enough if he suspects that to be the position. Mr Rees goes on to submit that in the words of section 1(2) the illegal provenance of the money is a 'fact or circumstance necessary for the commission of the offence'. Section 1(2) is therefore applicable to an offence contrary to section 93A, and the subsection states that where it is applicable a person shall not be guilty of conspiracy to commit (the section 93A offence)—

'Unless he and at least one other party to the agreement (i.e. the conspiracy) intend or know that that fact or circumstance (i.e. that the money to be laundered is or will be the proceeds of someone else's crime) shall or will exist at the time when the conduct constituting the offence (i.e. the section 93A Act offence) is to take place.'

That conduct is the entering into or otherwise being concerned in an arrangement to launder.

Our initial response

15. The starting point for the analysis is the opinion of Lord Bridge, with which the rest of their Lordships concurred, in *R. v Anderson* (1985) 81 Cr.App.R. 256; [1986] A.C. 27. His Lordship considered the effect of section 1(1) of the 1977 Act. He observed that an essential ingredient in the crime of conspiring to commit a specific offence or offences under section 1(1) of the Act of 1977 is that the accused should agree that a course of conduct be pursued which he knows must involve the commission by one or more of the parties to the agreement of that offence or those offences.'(p.39E) It is not sufficient that another conspirator appreciates that the course of conduct will involve acts infringing the criminal law; the defendant himself must do so. On this analysis, therefore, there is no question of a defendant being held liable if, on implementation of the agreement, he could not be liable for the substantive offence. It is not necessary, therefore, for subsection (2) to be invoked to achieve that particular objective.

16. In our view the judge summed up in accordance with this principle. He required the jury to be sure that the agreed course of conduct, if implemented, would involve commission by the appellants of the substantive offence. They therefore had to have the necessary mens rea for that offence. Mr Rees accepts, as we understand it, that the judge's direction required that his client did, on the assumption that the agreement was implemented, have the mens rea necessary to satisfy the substantive offence. He contends, however, that for a statutory conspiracy the effect of section 1(2) is to alter the required state of mind so that knowledge and not merely suspicion of in this case (to put it shortly) the criminal character of Sakavickas is required. The premise of the argument, as we have said, is that his criminal character is a relevant 'fact or circumstance' within the meaning of subsection 2.

17. We reject that argument. The fundamental weakness, as it seems to us, is that it fails to recognise that for the purposes of section 93A the existence of suspicion on the part of the alleged offender (as an alternative to actual knowledge) of the criminal character of Sakavickas is a fact to be proved by the prosecution. It is the suspicion, as opposed to the fact, that Sakavickas was engaged in criminal conduct which is, for the purposes of section 1(2) of the 1977 Act, a 'fact or circumstance necessary for the commission of the offence'. True it is that the defendant must have knowledge of the suspicion, but he will of course inevitably have knowledge of his own state of mind. (The position would be otherwise if the statute required reasonable grounds for suspicion, for then the defendant would have to have knowledge of the reasonable grounds. An illustration of this is the *Rizvi and Chisti* case, discussed below.)

18. Accordingly, an offence contrary to section 93A is not an offence where liability can be incurred without knowledge on the part of the alleged offender of any fact or circumstance necessary for the commission of the offence. The prosecution must prove the suspicion of the defendant and in so doing they inevitably prove knowledge of that suspicion. It is not there-

fore an offence to which section 1(2) of the 1977 Act applies. We would add that in any event, even if subsection 2 were applicable, in our judgment the directions of the judge were consistent with it precisely because establishing suspicion also establishes knowledge of that suspicion.

The authorities

19. We turn therefore to the authorities which we asked to consider to see whether they assist as to the conclusion which we have tentatively expressed.

20. In *R. v Mir and Beg* (unreported) April 22, 1994 the offence under consideration was conspiracy to commit aggravated arson. Section 1(2) of the 1977 Act was found to be relevant to that offence, and the court held that in those circumstances it was necessary to establish against each defendant subjectively the element of recklessness. In *Browning and Dixon* 6th November 1998 the same approach was adopted in relation to a conspiracy to commit criminal damage, being reckless as to whether life would be endangered.

21. In *R. v Rizvi* [2003] EWCA Crim 3575 the conspiracy alleged was in the form approved in *R. v Hussain, Bhatti and Bhatti* [2002] Cr.App.R. 363. Under the relevant statutory provisions in play in that case it was necessary for the prosecution to show that the defendant knew or had reasonable grounds to suspect that certain property had an illegal provenance. It was submitted that because of the provisions of section 1(2) of the 1977 Act the judge was wrong to direct the jury that each defendant had to know or have 'reasonable grounds for suspicion that the money was hot'. The point taken by counsel for the appellant was that a person may have reasonable grounds for suspicion without ever in fact becoming suspicious. As to that Tuckey LJ said at paragraph 12—

> 'There is no question of liability without knowledge of any particular fact or circumstance. In other words the liability is not absolute. It depends upon the defendant's knowledge of the facts or circumstances which ought to give rise to the suspicion. On this analysis there is no lack of knowledge of "any particular fact or circumstance" for the purposes of section 1(2).'

Although relating to different statutory provisions, that, as it seems to us, is entirely in accordance with the view which we have tentatively expressed, and Mr Rees recognised that the decision in *Rizvi* does make it very difficult for him to succeed in the present case.

22. Finally our attention was invited to the decision of this Court in *R. v Singh (Gulbir Rana* [2003] EWCA Crim 3712. Once again the charge followed the form approved in *Hussain* but included the assertion that the defence knew or had reasonable grounds to suspect that the money was from an illicit source. The Court at paragraph 34 held that to be an immater-

ial averment, but *Rizvi*, which had been decided about 3 weeks earlier, does not appear to have been cited, and before us Mr Jeremy for the Crown did not attempt to place any particular reliance upon the decision in *Singh*.

Conclusion

23. It is therefore clear that the authorities, and in particular *Rizvi*, afford some support for the conclusion which we set out tentatively earlier in this judgment, and which we now adopt. As section 1(2) of the 1977 Act did not apply to the offence alleged in this case the appeal of each appellant must fail. Mr Kivdeh for Sakavickas could only have any hope of success if the appeal of Reichwald were to succeed and even then he had to face the almost insurmountable problem that the only conceivable inference from the verdict of the jury is that Sakavickas did know of his own criminal character and of the tainted source of the money, as, it seems, did the other conspirators, as indicated by their pleas of guilty. It follows that the appeals fail."

126   We turn to *Browning and Dixon*, which was cited by Kennedy L.J. in *Sakavickas* and in which *Mir and Beg*, also cited by Kennedy L.J., was followed.

127   The substantial point in *Browning and Dixon* related to the mens rea necessary to support a charge of conspiracy to commit criminal damage being reckless as to whether life would be endangered. Dixon and Browning were jointly indicted in alternative counts of conspiracy to commit criminal damage:

"Both charges were laid under section 1(1) of the Criminal Law Act 1977 but the first reflected the substantive offence of aggravated criminal damage under section 1(2)(b) of the Criminal Damage Act 1971 and the second and alternative charge reflected the simple offence of criminal damage under section 1(1) of the same Act. The particulars of the first count were that they between 1st January 1996 and 26 September 1996 conspired together and with Michael James Ashton and other persons unknown to damage a railway line belonging to Railtrack intending to destroy or damage such property and being reckless as to whether the life of any person who travelled upon the railway would thereby be endangered. The second and alternative count charged a conspiracy between themselves, Michael James Ashton and others unknown to damage a railway line belonging to Railtrack intending to destroy or damage such property or being reckless as to whether such property would be destroyed or damaged."

128   Mantell L.J. giving the judgment of the Court said:

"The point taken is that the judge mis-directed the jury in inviting them to consider whether or not Dixon had been reckless as to whether the life of any person who travelled upon the railway would be endangered by reference to what would have been the appreciation of the risk by an ordinary prudent bystander. That, submits Mr Sweeney is to apply an objective test and what was necessary to support count 1 was proof that Dixon along with at least one other conspirator himself appreciated the risk — that is to say that the test is a subjective one. The judge's direction begins at p.5 of the transcript of the summing up and continues through to p.8. It begins by explaining that it is the agreement which constitutes the offence and that the fulfilment of the purpose of the conspiracy is immaterial. It makes plain that it is what is in the minds of the conspirators at the time of the making of the agreement which is important and not what they might be thinking when the unlawful act is carried out. The direction goes on to distinguish between counts 1 and 2 and then to isolate those matters which the prosecution had to prove to bring home count 1. At the bottom of p.6 the direction concentrates on the mental element which distinguishes count 1 from count 2. The judge explained that the prosecution had to prove,

'That the defendant was reckless as to whether the life of any person who travelled on that piece of damaged track would thereby be endangered' and then went onto explain that if [that] element or ingredient had not been proved but that all the others had that it would be open to the jury to convict on the alternative contained in count 2. He then went on in the course of his direction at p.7 to explain what was meant by recklessness.

[The trial judge then gave the *Caldwell* [(1981) 73 Cr.App.R. 13] test for recklessness which is now no longer the right test following *R. v G* [2004] 1 Cr.App.R. 21 at 237; [2004]1 AC 1034]

Mr Sweeny submits that the direction in those terms was to apply a test which might be appropriate in consideration of the substantive offence (see *R v Sangha* (1988) 87 Cr.App.R p.88) but which was inappropriate to a charge of conspiracy.

[The Court then referred to Professor Smith's article in the 1977 Criminal Law Review 598 and 638]

Fortunately we do not need to become embroiled in the debate because on a previous occasion this court has had an opportunity of considering the effect of section 1(2) of the Criminal Law Act in circumstances very similar to those in the instant case. In *R v Mir and Beg* (unreported) 22nd April 1994 the court had to consider the appropriate direction where the charge was one of conspiracy to commit aggravated arson. The particulars of the offence were that the appellants and others had conspired together without lawful excuse to destroy or damage by fire a building intending to destroy or damage such property and being reckless as to whether the life of another would thereby be endangered. Apparently those involved had brought petrol onto the premises and were caught red-handed before the fire could be started. The risk to life arose out of the fact that there was gas present and an explosion could well have occurred as a result of the fire. In dealing with the accused's perception of the risk of danger to others the judge directed the jury as follows:

'Of course it is for you as reasonably prudent persons. The fact that the defendants in question, the defendant whose case you are considering, personally did not foresee the risk is neither here nor there. The test is would the risk be obvious to a reasonably prudent person without any particular specialised knowledge as represented by you members of the jury?'

The court agreed with the submission of counsel that section 1(2) of the Criminal Law Act 1977 was relevant to the case and that it was necessary for the Crown to prove as a subjective ingredient that the appellants intended or knew that the agreed course of conduct to be pursued would or might create an obvious risk that the life of another would be endangered and then in giving the judgement of the court Lord Justice Farquharson said this at p.9 of the transcript:

'We accept Mr Fortson's submissions on these facts, if the prosecution was to succeed on count 1 against the appellants and the others accused it was necessary to prove:
They knew and agreed that the gas would be employed;
They knew that the use of gas would in the circumstances create an obvious risk to life;
That they recognised the risk; and
That they still proceeded to take the risk. It follows that it was for the prosecution to prove that knowledge subjectively and not by any objective standard.'

The court then held that the passage which we have recited from the summing up was a misdirection and quashed the convictions on that count.

We are unable to make any sensible distinction between the case of *Mir & Beg* and the present case. If we follow the same reasoning, as we are bound to do, the result must be the same. Consequently we have decided to quash Dixon's conviction on count 1."

129   We now take a closer look at these cases, starting with the criminal damage cases referred to in *Sakavickas*. Professor David Ormerod in his commentary on *R. v Sakavickas* in [2005] Crim. L.R. 293 writes:

"[These cases seem] to support the approach in the present case because it adopts a degree of *mens rea* less than knowledge as to a fact. It is submitted however that the cases offer no such support. They are based on the false assumption that the substantive offence requires proof of a fact that life is endangered. It does not: *Parker* [1993] Crim LR 856. Since life endangerment is not 'a circumstance' that needs to exist for the full offence, it is unnecessary in a conspiracy to prove that Ds knew of or intended it; recklessness as to this element will suffice on a conspiracy charge. It is submitted therefore that the decisions in *Mir* (1994) 22 April, *Browning* (1998) unreported, on which the court in the present case places reliance (and *Ryan* The Times, October 13, 1999) offer no support for the interpretation adopted."

130   We agree.

131   As to *Rizvi and Chisti*, Prof. Ormerod wrote in the same commentary:

". . . The Court of Appeal held that 'a defendant is guilty of conspiracy if he agrees to commit the offences created by the two sections knowing or having reasonable grounds for suspecting that the money is 'hot' [para 13]. The conspirator's knowledge, it was held, must be established only as regards the facts on which his suspicion was formed, and not as to the fact of the provenance of the money. With respect, there is an enormous gulf between what s1(2) requires on a natural reading — *knowledge* of the circumstance of the money being 'hot'— and knowledge of a fact that gives rise to a suspicion that it is 'hot'. To take a very different example, the fact that D knows goods on offer are ridiculously cheap which causes him to suspect they may be stolen, does not amount to him having *knowledge* of the fact or circumstance that they are stolen. Support for this view can be gained from the Draft Criminal Code, which defines knowledge with respect to a circumstance as 'being aware that it exists or will exist' and avoiding 'taking steps that might confirm the belief that it exists or will exist' (cl.18.). Support also derives from *Montila* in the House of Lords at para. [27]

'A person may have reasonable grounds to suspect that property is one thing (A) when in fact it is something different (B). But that is not so when the question is what a person knows. A person cannot know that something is A when in fact it is B. The proposition that a person knows that something is A is based on the premise that it is true that it is A. The fact that the property is A provides the starting point. Then there is the question whether the person knows that the property is A.'

Any support that *Rizvi* does offer to the interpretation in the present case must now be seriously undermined because it was based on an erroneous interpretation of the substantive law. The Court of Appeal had held in *Montila* that it was unnecessary for proof of the substantive offences under ss.49(2) of the 1994 Act and s.93C of the 1988 Act to establish that the money in issue was in fact illicit; it was sufficient that the accused thought it was: [2003] EWCA Crim 3082. This harsh approach has been overruled by the House of Lords in *Montila* [2004] UKHL 50. While it was extant, which included the period of the decisions in the present case and *Rizvi* this view meant that the substantive offence under s93C could be established without proof of the fact or circumstance of illicit provenance."

132   We take the view that Prof. Ormerod is right and that *Rizvi and Chisti* is no longer good law in the light of *Montila*.

133   We would add a further comment about *Rizvi and Chisti*. If, as decided in *Rizvi and Chisti*, it is sufficient to establish the conspirator's knowledge only as regards the facts which ought to have given rise to the suspicion that the money was the proceeds of drug trafficking (or of other criminal conduct), then it is difficult to see how the jury could be sure that the purpose of the alleged conspirators in dealing with the money was to avoid any person's prosecution for a drug trafficking offence (the point made by the judge in the instant case, see [89] and [90] above).

In addition to a standard conspiracy direction, the judge would presumably have to identify for the jury those material facts (and circumstances) which a jury would be entitled to conclude ought to have given rise to the suspicion that the money being dealt with was the proceeds of drug trafficking. The judge would then say: "If you are sure about those facts and if you are sure that the defendant had knowledge of them, are you sure that the facts ought to have given rise to that suspicion?". If the answer to that question is "Yes", the jury would then have to be told that they must also be sure that the purpose of the defendant whose case they are considering was to avoid any person's prosecution. But if a defendant neither knew nor suspected, it is difficult to see how the jury could conclude that he had that purpose.

134   We turn to *Sakavickas*. To the extent to which the Court relied on *Rizvi and Chisti*, we take the view, as we have said, that *Rizvi and Chisti* is no longer good law.

135   The offence alleged against the defendants in *Sakavickas* was, as we have said, a conspiracy to commit an offence against s.93A of the Criminal Justice Act 1988. Quite why it was necessary to charge conspiracy, given the wide terms of the substantive offence, we are not sure.

136   Section 93A, on the facts in the Sakavickas appeal, made it an offence if Reichwald agreed to enter into an arrangement whereby the retention by *Sakavickas* of his proceeds of criminal conduct was facilitated, knowing or suspecting, at the time, that *Sakavickas* is a person who is or has been engaged in criminal conduct.

137   It was submitted on behalf of Reichwald, in reliance upon s.1(2) of the Criminal Law Act 1977, that he was guilty of conspiracy only if he, at the time, *knows* that Sakavickas is a person who is or has been engaged in criminal conduct. That the Court held was wrong. The Court decided that the prosecution "must prove the suspicion of the defendant and in so doing they inevitably prove knowledge of that suspicion". Section 93A "is not therefore an offence to which s.1(2) of the 1977 Act applies". Professor Ormerod argues in the Commentary to which we have referred that: "This is clearly not how s.1(2) was intended to be interpreted".

138   Although, as Mr Bethel rightly submits, in *Sakavickas* the judge had directed the jury, in accordance with s.93A, that the prosecution must prove that the money was the proceeds of criminal conduct, counsel does not appear to have argued that, nor the Court considered whether, s.1(2) of the 1977 Act "bit" on this fact. Counsel did not argue that Reichwald had to know that the money, the retention of which he was facilitating, was the proceeds of drug trafficking.

139   That distinguishes this case. Following *Montila*, the substantive offences under s.49(2)and 93C(2), require proof that the defendant is in fact dealing with the proceeds of drug trafficking or of other criminal conduct. Following *Harmer* s.1(2) of the 1977 Act bites on that and the jury may only convict of conspiracy if the defendant knew that he was dealing with the proceeds of drug trafficking or of other criminal conduct.

140   Mr Bethel has not submitted that, if *Harmer* is right and to be followed, the convictions for conspiracy are nevertheless safe.

141   We must now consider one further case, *R. v Singh* [2003] EWCA Crim 3712, referred to by Mr Bethel. It was not cited in *Harmer*. The appellant was convicted on three counts of conspiracy to convert, transfer and remove from the jurisdiction the proceeds of drug trafficking and/or of other criminal conduct. The particulars of the counts read:

> ". . . conspired together and with persons unknown, knowing or having reasonable grounds to suspect that certain property, namely banknotes, was, or in whole or in part directly or indirectly represented, another person's proceeds of drugs trafficking and/or criminal conduct, to convert or transfer or remove from the jurisdiction that property for the purpose of assisting any person to avoid prosecution for a drug trafficking offence and/or for an offence to which Part IV of the Criminal Justice Act 1988 applies, or for the purpose of avoiding the making or enforcement of a confiscation order, in contravention of . . . the Drug Trafficking Act 1994 and/or . . . the Criminal Justice Act 1988."

142   Mr Krolick, on behalf of the appellant, submitted, in the light of s.1 of the 1977 Act:

> "that the formula in the indictment, 'knowing or having reasonable grounds to suspect', whilst apt for an allegation of the specified substantive offences of concealing or transferring proceeds respectively of drug trafficking under section 49(2)(b) of the 1994 Act and of criminal conduct under section 93C(2)(b) of the 1988 Act, was not sufficient for an allegation of statutory conspiracy to commit either of those offences."

143   Auld L.J. giving the judgment of the Court rejected the argument saying:

> "34. . . . the inclusion in the particulars of the words 'knowing or having reasonable grounds to suspect that certain property, namely banknotes, was, or in whole or in part directly or indirectly represented, another person's proceeds of drug trafficking and/or criminal conduct' . . . are an immaterial averment."

144   The particulars of the indictment "could have been drafted so as to give effect to s.1(2) of the 1977 Act and as a mercy to the jury, namely that the appellant and his co-accused":

> ". . . conspired together and with persons unknown to convert or transfer or remove from the jurisdiction certain property, namely banknotes, which in whole or in part directly or indirectly represented, another person's proceeds of drug trafficking and/or criminal conduct, with the intention of assisting any person to avoid prosecution for a drug trafficking offence and/or for an offence to which Part IV of the Criminal Justice Act 1988 applies, or for the purpose of avoiding the making or enforcement of a confiscation order . . ." etc.

145   Auld L.J. concluded:

"35. . . . there is no point of substance in Mr. Krolick's complaint that something short of knowledge was alleged in the indictment when, given the thrust of the prosecution case, knowledge of the precise provenance of the banknotes money was not at the heart of this conspiracy, but intention to launder illicitly obtained money was."

146   In *Sakavickas* Kennedy L.J. said of *Singh*:

"22. Finally our attention was invited to the decision of this Court in *Gulbir Rana Singh* [2003] EWCA Crim 3712. Once again the charge followed the form approved in *Hussain* but included the assertion that the defence knew or had reasonable grounds to suspect that the money was from an illicit source. The Court at paragraph 34 held that to be an immaterial averment, but *Rizvi*, which had been decided about 3 weeks earlier, does not appear to have been cited, and before us Mr Jeremy for the Crown did not attempt to place any particular reliance upon the decision in *Singh*."

147   It seems to us that *Singh* does not survive *Montila*. An intention to launder illicitly obtained money is not enough. The money must be proved to have been the proceeds of drug trafficking or other criminal conduct. On to that requirement, s.1(2) of the 1977 Act bites.

148   In the light of our analysis of the cases and of our decision that *Harmer* reflects the law as it stands after *Montila*, the jury should not have been directed to convict if a defendant only suspected that at least part of the money he was dealing with was another person's proceeds of drug trafficking.

149   For these reasons the appeals are allowed.

150   Finally we wish to say something about the use of conspiracy counts. In the case of Ali, Hussain and Khan the prosecution's overall case was that they dealt with nearly £171 million in bank notes, which were the proceeds of eight other persons' drug trafficking. The dollar equivalent of those banknotes, on the prosecution's case, was remitted by the defendants abroad. As we have seen the defendants claimed that the money was being sent to Pakistan as part of a genuine Hawala business and not to pay the suppliers of drugs. Why then could the prosecution not charge the substantive offences? The answer Mr Bethel gave was that each delivery of money would be a separate offence and would have to be charged separately, given the rules against duplicity (see r.4(2) of the Indictment Rules 1971). Thus to charge substantive offences would have led to an overloaded or unrepresentative indictment.

151   The consequence of the present decision is (if we are right), that the prosecution has a heavier burden to discharge than it would have in order to prove the substantive offence. Although there are issues of duplicity with a conspiracy count (see *Singh*, [23]–[24]), a conspiracy count can be presented to overcome those difficulties.

152   Sections 17 and following of the Domestic Violence, Crime and Victims Act 2004 (not yet in force) provides one solution to the problem caused by the duplicity rule. Another solution would be to amend r.4(2), which can now be done by the Criminal Procedure Rules Committee together with the Lord Chan-

cellor and the Home Secretary (see s.2 of the Indictments Act 1915 as amended by the Courts Act 2003, s.109(1), Sch.8, para.67). We invite the Committee to consider the matter.

Appeals allowed.
Convictions quashed

The Court of Appeal certified under s.33(2) of the Criminal Appeal Act 1968 that a point of law of general public importance was involved in its decision, namely: "On an indictment alleging either a conspiracy to commit an offence contrary to s.93C(2) of the Criminal Justice Act 1988 or an offence contrary to s.49(2) of the Drug Trafficking Act 1994: (i) does s.1(2) of the Criminal Law Act 1977 apply to a conspiracy to commit such an offence? (ii) If s.1(2) does apply to such a conspiracy is its effect that actual knowledge of the origin of the property must be proved or is it sufficient to prove the facts or circumstances giving rise to suspicion or reasonable grounds for suspicion as to its origins?"

Leave to appeal to the House of Lords refused.

R. v AL–KHAWAJA

COURT OF APPEAL (Lord Justice Scott Baker, Mr Justice Jack, Mr Justice David Clarke): September 6; November 3, 2005

[2005] EWCA Crim 2697; [2006] 1 Cr.App.R. 9

(LT) Admissibility; Death; Right to examine witnesses; Witness statements

H1   EVIDENCE
    Witness
    Prosecution witness dying before trial—Judge allowing witness statement to be read to jury—Whether defendant's Convention right to fair trial breached—Human Rights Act 1998, Sch.1, Pt I, Art.6(3)(d)

H2   The appellant was accused of sexually assaulting two females and was charged with two counts of indecent assault. By the time of the trial the first complainant had died. The prosecution case was that the allegations of the two complainants were mutually supportive. The Crown also relied on allegations of sexual assault which were not charged on the indictment made by two other women. No suggestion was made that the four women knew each other or were aware of the details of the others' allegations. The prosecution applied to admit in evidence the witness statement made by the first complainant. The judge held it was in the interests of justice for the statement to be admitted pursuant to ss.23, 25 and 26 of the Criminal Justice Act 1988.[1] The appellant was convicted. The appellant appealed on the ground that since it had not been possible to cross-examine the first complainant it had been a breach of Art.6(3)(d) of the Convention for the Protection of Human Rights and Fundamental Freedoms[2] to admit her statement in evidence.

H3   **Held,** dismissing the appeal, that where a witness who was the sole witness of a crime had made a statement to be used in its prosecution and had died, there was a strong public interest in the admission of the statement in evidence so that the prosecution might proceed. Although that public interest did not override the requirement that the appellant have a fair trial, the provision in Art.6(3)(d) that a person charged should be able to examine the witnesses against him was just one specific aspect of a fair trial. If the opportunity was not provided the question was whether the proceedings as a whole, including the way the evidence was taken, were fair. In the present case the complainant had not absented herself through fear or otherwise, nor had she exercised a right to keep silent. The reason was death which brought considerations of its own. In the circumstances the

---

[1]   Criminal Justice Act 1988, ss.23, 25, 26: see post, paras [13], [14], [15].
[2]   Human Rights Act 1998, Sch.1, Pt I, Art.6(3): "Everyone charged with a criminal offence has the following minimum rights . . . to examine or have examined witnesses against him . . ."

rights of the appellant under Art.6 of the Convention had not been infringed by the admission of the statement and his trial had not been unfair (post, paras [26]–[28], [31]).

H4　　　*R. v Sellick* [2005] EWCA Crim 651; [2005] 2 Cr.App.R 15 (p.211); [2005] 1 W.L.R. 3257, CA, considered.

H5　　　(For ss.23, 25 and 26 of the Criminal Justice Act 1988, see *Archbold* 2005, paras 9–127, 9–129 and following. For Art.6(3)(d) of the Convention, see *ibid.* paras 16–57)

Appeal against conviction

H6　　　On November 30, 2004 in the Crown Court at Lewes (Judge Hayward) the appellant, Imad Al-Khawaja, was convicted of two counts of indecent assault on a female, contrary to s.14(1) of the Sexual Offences Act 1956. He was sentenced to 15 months' imprisonment on the first count and to 12 months' on the second count to be served consecutively, making a total of two years, three months' imprisonment.

H7　　　The facts and grounds of appeal appear in the judgment of the Court.

H8　　　*Joel Bennathan* (assigned by the Registrar of Criminal Appeals) for the appellant. *Sonia Woodley Q.C.* (instructed by the Crown Prosecution Service, Lewes) for the Crown.

Cur. adv. vult.

November 3　Jack J.: handed down the judgment of the Court

Introduction

1　　　The primary point on this appeal was whether the admission of a written statement made by the complainant in a charge of indecent assault, who had since died, was a breach of the defendant's human rights under Art.6 of the European Convention. We dismissed the appeal, reserving our reasons which we now give.

2　　　On November 30, 2004 at the conclusion of his trial at the Crown Court in Lewes before Judge Hayward the appellant, Imad Al-Khawaja, was convicted of two counts of indecent assault on a female contrary to s.14(1) of the Sexual Offences Act 1956. He was later sentenced to 15 months' imprisonment on the first count and to 12 months' on the second count to be served consecutively. He appealed against his convictions by leave of the single judge.

3　　　The appellant was a consultant physician in rehabilitative medicine and practised at the Sussex Rehabilitation Centre at Brighton Hospital. His treatments included hypnotherapy. He was alleged to have assaulted two female patients who had been referred to him for treatment. The first, Susan T, had been referred to him by her GP in October 2002. She suffered from multiple sclerosis and was wheelchair bound. It was alleged that the appellant assaulted her on her second visit to him on June 3, 2003. Most sadly, she committed suicide prior to the trial. There was no suggestion that this was a consequence of the alleged assault. In a pre-trial ruling given on March 22, 2004 Judge Rennie directed that her witness statement could be read in evidence at the trial pursuant to ss.23, 25 and 26 of the Criminal Justice Act 1988. This ruling lay at the heart of the appeal.

4 The submission was that the judge was wrong to have allowed the statement to be read. It was also submitted that in his summing up the trial judge did not give an adequate direction to the jury as to the consequential disadvantage to the appellant. It was said that this made the conviction on the first count unsafe, and also tainted the conviction on the second count.

5 The second count concerned a different patient, Vivienne U, who suffered from dystonia, an involuntary movement, in her neck. She was referred to the appellant by her consultant neurologist in October 2002. The indecent assault on her was said to have occurred on her third visit to the appellant on June 12, 2003. That was nine days after the assault on Miss T.

6 On July 9, 2003 the appellant was arrested as a result of a complaint by Miss U. He declined to answer questions when interviewed by the police, saying, that, before he could answer he needed access to medical records and to enquire as to patient confidentiality. He was given police bail until September 11, and he then produced a written statement in answer to Miss U's allegations. He was then, on the same day, arrested in connection with a complaint made by Miss T. The same course followed, and on November 21, he produced a written statement in answer to her allegations. Each statement contained a complete denial.

7 The prosecution case was that the allegations of the two complainants were mutually supportive. The prosecution also relied on the strikingly similar evidence from two other women, Kirsty K who was a physiotherapist at X Hospital, and Debra D who was an unofficial patient of the appellant, in each case relating to what the appellant had allegedly done to them. Those incidents were not charged on the indictment. Miss K and Miss D both said in evidence that they had known that allegations had been made against the appellant before they made their statements to the police. However, there was nothing to suggest that the four women knew each other or were aware of the details of the others' allegations.

8 The prosecution also called evidence of a "recent complaint" by Miss T. Basil F provided help around the house and garden for Miss T and her sister—who also suffered from multiple sclerosis. He had visited them on June 3, 2003 the day of the alleged assault. He knew that Miss T had been to see a doctor that day. When they were alone, she told him that she had been sexually abused. She said that the appellant had said she was a beautiful woman and that he could give her a climax. She did not refer to hypnosis. She was calm, but appeared angry.

9 Sandra H was a neighbour who did chores and shopping for Miss T. She let herself into the house at about 7pm on June 5. Miss T was on the telephone. After the call she looked upset, ashen and anxious. She said that she had been to see a hypnotist who had just been on the telephone and had suggested that he should visit her at home. She became upset and told Mrs H that the appellant had made her do things to herself, which she described.

10   We need not refer in any detail to the evidence by way of Miss T's statement or
to the oral evidence of Miss U, Miss K and Miss D. It is enough to say that in each
case, if their evidence was truthful, the appellant had behaved improperly while
they were aware of what was happening to them but under hypnosis. On that
basis, he committed serious indecent assaults on Miss T. He committed a lesser
indecent assault on Miss U. He made improper suggestions to Miss K and to Miss
D. We should mention that Miss T did not make her statement until September 20,
2003.

The admission of the statement

11   At the preliminary hearing Judge Rennie approached the question whether
Miss T's statement should be admitted in evidence on what we would describe
as classic English domestic law lines. He was not referred to Art.6 of the
European Convention, or to any of the case law concerning the Article and the
admission of evidence from a person who could not be questioned on behalf of
a defendant. He did not avert to it himself. The argument which we have to consider was raised for the first time in this court by Mr Joel Bennathan, who did not
represent the appellant in the Crown Court.

12   At the time of Judge Rennie's ruling and the trial, the relevant statutory provisions were to be found in ss.23 to 28 of the Criminal Justice Act 1988. They
have now been replaced by the hearsay provisions contained in Ch.2 of Pt 11
of the Criminal Justice Act 2003. Those apply to all trials held on or after
April 4, 2005. Section 116 of that Act applies where, among other situations, a
witness in unavailable because he is dead. Subsection (4) is broadly similar to
s.26 of the 1988 Act.

13   Section 23 of the 1988 Act provided for the admission of first hand documentary hearsay. So far as relevant here, it read:

> ". . . a statement made by a person in a document shall be admissible in
> criminal proceedings as evidence of any fact of which direct oral evidence
> by him would be admissible if—
>
> (i) the requirements of one of the paragraphs of subsection (2) below are
>   satisfied;
>   or
> (ii) the requirements of subsection (3) below are satisfied.
> (2) The requirements mentioned in subsection (1)(i) above are—
>   (a) that the person who made the statement is dead or by reason of his
>   bodily or mental condition unfit to attend as a witness;
>   (b) that—
>   (i) the person who made the statement is outside the United Kingdom;
>   and
>   (ii) it is not reasonably practicable to secure his attendance; or
>   (c) that all reasonable steps have been taken to find the person who made
>   the statement, but that he cannot be found
> (3) to (5) . . ."

Subsection (3) related to persons not giving evidence through fear.

14   Section 25 provided the general principles to be followed. It stated:

> "25 (1) If, having regard to all the circumstances—
>   (a) the Crown Court
>   (i) on a trial on indictment;
>   (ii) to (iv) . . .
>   (b) . . .
>   (c) . . .
> is of the opinion that in the interests of justice a statement which is admissible by virtue of section 23 or 24 above nevertheless ought not to be admitted, it may direct that the statement shall not be admitted.
> (2) Without prejudice to the generality of subsection (1) above, it shall be the duty of the court to have regard—
> (a) to the nature and source of the document containing the statement and to whether or not, having regard to its nature and source and to any other circumstances that appear to the court to be relevant, it is likely that the document is authentic;
> (b) to the extent to which the statement appears to supply evidence which would otherwise not be available;
> (c) to the relevance of the evidence that it appears to supply to any issue which is likely to have to be determined in the proceedings; and
> (d) to any risk, having regard in particular to whether it is likely to be possible to controvert the statement if the person making it does not attend to give oral evidence in the proceedings, that its admission or exclusion will result in unfairness to the accused or, if there is more than one, to any of them."

However, where s.26 applied, s.25 would largely be superseded in practical effect by the provisions of s.26.

15   Section 26 related to documents prepared for criminal proceedings. It provided:

> "26. Where a statement which is admissible in criminal proceedings by virtue of section 23 or 24 above appears to the court to have been prepared, . . ., for the purposes—
>   (a) of pending or contemplated criminal proceedings; or
>   (b) of a criminal investigation,
> the statement shall not be given in evidence in any criminal proceedings without the leave of the court, and the court shall not give leave unless it is of the opinion that the statement ought to be admitted in the interests of justice; and in considering whether its admission would be in the interests of justice, it shall be the duty of the court to have regard—
>   (i) to the contents of the statement;
>   (ii) to any risk, having regard in particular to whether it is likely to be possible to controvert the statement if the person making it does not attend to give oral evidence in the proceedings, that its admission or

exclusion will result in unfairness in the accused or, if there is more
that one, to any of them; and

(iii) to any other circumstances that appear to the court to be relevant.
. . ."

Schedule 2 to the Act is given effect to by s.28(2) to supplement the foregoing
provisions. It provides in particular for the credibility of the maker of a statement
to be challenged.

16   Judge Rennie ruled on the statement of Miss T in the following way. First, he
recorded that it was agreed that by reason of her death the statement was eligible
to be admitted in evidence under s.23. Next, he noted that the defence to each allegation was that it was untrue both as to the alleged indecent touchings and as to
the indecent comments which it was alleged were also made. He observed that the
appellant was very likely to feel that he had no realistic alternative but to give evidence in order to defend himself on the second count relating to Miss U, and so
the reading of the statement would not have the effect of making it very difficult
for him not to give evidence, for that was already so. He also noted that collusion
between the two complainants was not alleged, and so that need not be investi-
gated by cross-examination. He referred to s.5 and its provision that he should
not admit the statement if it was not in the interests of justice to do so. He then
went on to s.26, reminding himself that it required him, when considering the
interests of justice, to have regard to the contents of the statement; and, in summary, whether it would be possible to controvert the statement, and whether its
admission would result in unfairness to the defendant, and other relevant circumstances. He observed that the statement was crucial to the prosecution's case on
count 1, because without it there was no evidence of an assault. He concluded that
inconsistencies which existed between Miss T's statement and what Mr F and
Mrs H said could be explored with Mr F and Mrs H. He also referred, in the context of inconsistencies, to the evidence of a third witness, whom he identified as
Pauline. Miss T's credibility could be tested by that means. He also mentioned
expert evidence to be called on behalf of the Crown and on behalf of the appellant
about the altered perception that can occur under hypnosis, saying that it was to
the appellant's benefit that any such evidence favourable to the appellant could
not be contradicted by Miss T. He found the gravity of the allegation to be a neutral circumstance. He concluded that he was satisfied and sure that, having in
mind the statutory tests, it was in the interests of justice for Miss T's statement
to be admitted in evidence. He ended by referring to the direction which it
would be necessary for the trial judge to give at the trial to the jury concerning
the statement.

17   Mr Bennathan did not criticise the judge's approach to the application of the
statutory provisions as a matter of English domestic law. His submission was
that consideration of the application of Art.6 and relevant Convention jurisprudence should have led to a decision not to admit Miss T's statement in
evidence. Article 6(1) requires that "in the determination of . . . any criminal
charge against him, everyone is entitled to a fair . . . hearing . . .." More particularly, Art.6(3)(d) provides:

"(3) Everyone charged with a criminal offence has the following minimum rights:

(d) to examine or have examined witnesses against him and to obtain the attendance of and examination of witnesses on his behalf under the same conditions as witnesses against him."

18 Mr Bennathan submitted that it was a breach of Art.6(3)(d) for the statement to be read because Miss T could not be cross-examined: it was irrelevant that she had died. He relied on a passage from the decision of the European Court of Human Rights in *Kostovski v The Netherlands* (1990) 12 E.H.R.R. 434 at [41]:

"As a rule, these [Article 6] rights require that an accused should be given an adequate and proper opportunity to challenge and question a witness against him, either at the time the witness was making his statement or at some later stage of the proceedings."

Kostovski had been convicted of armed robbery on the basis of the evidence of anonymous witnesses whom he had no opportunity to question, and, not knowing who they were, he could not attack their credibility.

19 Mr Bennathan also relied on the European Court's decision in *Luca v Italy* (2003) 36 E.H.R.R. 807, which reads:

"40. As the Court has stated on a number of occasions, it may prove necess-ary in certain circumstances to refer to depositions made during the investigative stage (in particular, where a witness refuses to repeat his depo-sition in public owing to fears for his safety, a not infrequent occurrence in trials concerning Mafia-type organisations). If the defendant has been given an adequate and proper opportunity to challenge the depositions, either when made or at a later stage, their admission in evidence will not in itself contravene Art.6(1) and (3)(d). The corollary of that, however, is that where a conviction is based solely or to a decisive degree on depositions that have been made by a person whom the accused has had no opportunity to examine or to have examined, whether during the investigation or at the trial, the rights of the defence are restricted to an extent that is incompatible with the guarantees provided by Article 6."

Luca had been convicted on the basis of statement made to the police by a fellow drug dealer who had exercised his right of silence when brought to court.

20 The conjunction of Art.6 and ss.23 to 26 of the 1988 Act in the light of decisions of the European Court has been considered by this court on a number of occasions, and in each case, so far as we are aware, it has been held that the admission of the statement did not infringe Art.6. There is, however, no decision of this court, so far as we are aware, which has considered the situation where, as here, the witness cannot be examined on behalf of the accused because the wit-ness has died since giving the statement. We believe that there is likewise no such decision of the European Court.

21 Recently this court reviewed the European and English decisions in the case of *R. v Sellick* [2005] EWCA Crim 651; [2005] 2 Cr.App.R. 15 (p.211). We need not

repeat that process. In *Sellick* the accused was charged with murder. The trial judge gave leave for four statements to be read, two of them on the basis that he was sure that the makers had been kept away through fear, and two of them on the basis that reasonable steps had been taken to trace them but had failed. In respect of one of the latter he held that it was highly probable that he was kept away by fear. The fourth witness was described by this court as of little importance.

22   As a preliminary to a review of the decisions of the European Court, Waller L.J. giving the judgment of the court observed, first, that the jurisprudence had begun its development with cases arising under the inquisitorial process of criminal prosecution existing in many European countries, and without regard to such safeguards as are built into the English adversarial procedure. He noted that under the English procedure there was one moment only, namely at the trial itself, when a prosecution witness could be examined on behalf of a defendant, a point which had not been examined in the European cases, and which was particularly relevant in a case where the witness had been kept away by fear. He stated that it had to be borne in mind that questions whether Art.6 had been infringed were very fact sensitive. Having reviewed eight cases decided by the European Court he drew from them four propositions:

"(i)   The admissibility of evidence is primarily for the national law;

(ii) Evidence must <u>normally</u> be produced at a public hearing and as a <u>general rule</u> Article 6(1) and (3)(d) require a defendant to be given a proper and adequate opportunity to challenge and question witnesses;

(iii) It is not necessarily incompatible with Article 6(1) and (3)(d) for depositions to be read and that can be so even if there has been no opportunity to question the witness at any stage of the proceedings. Article 6(3)(d) is simply an illustration of matters to be taken into account in considering whether a fair trial has been held. The reasons for the court holding it necessary that statements should be read and the procedures to counterbalance any handicap to the defence will all be relevant to the issue, whether, where statements have been read, the trial was fair.

(iv) The quality of the evidence and its inherent reliability, plus the degree of caution exercised in relation to reliance on it, will also be relevant to the question whether the trial was fair."

23   Those conclusions are in particular assisted by a passage from the European Court's judgment in *Doorson v The Netherlands* (1996) 22 E.H.R.R. 330, under the heading "The Court's general approach", as follows:

"66. As the requirements of Article 6(3) are to be seen as particular aspects of the right to a fair trial guaranteed by Article 6(1) the Court will examine the complaints under Article 6(1) and (3)(d) taken together.

67.   The Court reiterates that the admissibility of evidence is primarily a matter for regulation by national law and as a general rule it is for the national courts to assess the evidence before them. The Court's task under

the Convention is not to give a ruling as to whether statements of witnesses were properly admitted as evidence, but rather to ascertain whether the proceedings as a whole, including the way in which evidence was taken, were fair."

24   The finding that the three important witnesses in *Sellick* were absent through fear, was an essential part of the Court's reasoning, for the inducing of that fear was to be attributed to the defendants or those acting on their behalf. It could be asked why it was unfair to the defendants that the statements of the witnesses whose absence they had caused should be read. There is no equivalent factor here.

25   The important factors in the present case are the following. The witness, Miss T, could not be examined on behalf of the appellant because she had died. She was the only witness whose evidence went directly to the commission of an indecent assault on her by the appellant. If her statement had been excluded, the prosecution would have had to abandon the first count. The appellant was able to attack the accuracy of Miss T's statement by exploring the inconsistencies between it and the witnesses, Mr F and Mrs H, and through the expert evidence relating to "altered perception" under hypnosis. The relevant sections of the 1988 Act contained provisions designed to protect defendants, which were properly considered by the judge, before the statement was admitted in evidence. Lastly, the tribunal of fact, here the jury, could and should take proper account of the difficulties which the admission of a statement might provide for the appellant, which should be provided by an appropriate direction to the jury.

26   Where a witness who is the sole witness of a crime has made a statement to be used in its prosecution and has since died, there may be a strong public interest in the admission of the statement in evidence so that the prosecution may proceed. That was the case here. That public interest must not be allowed to override the requirement that the defendant have a fair trial. Like the court in *Sellick* we do not consider that the case law of the European Court of Human Rights requires the conclusion that in such circumstances the trial will be unfair. The provision in Art.6(3)(d) that a person charged shall be able to have the witnesses against him examined is one specific aspect of a fair trial: but if the opportunity is not provided, the question is "whether the proceedings as a whole, including the way the evidence was taken, were fair— *Doorson*, [19]". This was not a case where the witness had absented himself, whether through fear or otherwise, or had required anonymity, or had exercised a right to keep silent. The reason was death, which has a finality which brings in considerations of its own, as has been indicated at the start of this paragraph.

27   It was suggested by Mr Bennathan that one important consequence of the absence of Miss T, which made it unfair for her statement to be admitted, was that "there were real areas that the defence would have sought to explore about the complainants' knowledge of each other's complaints." This ignores the stance taken on behalf of the appellant both at the hearing before Judge Rennie when he ruled the statement admissible, and at the trial, not to explore the possibility of collusion between the witnesses: collusion was not suggested.

Further, as we have stated, there was nothing to suggest that the women knew the details of each other's allegations.

28   We have concluded that the rights of the appellant under Art.6 were not infringed by the admission of the statement. We consider that his rights were sufficiently protected in the circumstances of his case. His trial was not unfair. We refer to the matters we have set out in [25], [26] and [27]. That conclusion must be subject to the question whether the trial judge gave an appropriate direction to the jury as to the statement. It is well established that such a direction must be given.

The direction to the jury

29   In *R. v McCoy*, unreported, December 10, 1999 this court stated:

> "If a statement of a critical witness is to be read to a jury, perhaps especially in an alibi case where identification is the true issue, it must be incumbent on the trial judge to ensure that the jury realise the drawbacks which are imposed on the defence if the prosecution statement is read to them. It is not enough simply to say that counsel has not had the opportunity of cross-examining. The lay jury may not appreciate the significance of that fact. The judge must at least explain that it means that they may feel quite unable to attach anything like as much weight to the evidence in the statement, as they might if it were tested in cross-examination; and where appropriate it would be necessary, certainly desirable, for the judge also to indicate to the jury by way of illustration the sort of matters that might well be put in cross-examination in the particular case. None of that was done in this case."

The need for an appropriate direction was also emphasised in *Sellick*, where the direction given at the trial by Butterfield J. is set out in [67] of the judgment.

30   The directions given here were as follows:

> "Count 1 concerns Susan T. Her statement was, of course, read to you. As I explained at the time, normally witnesses have to come to court to give evidence, particularly if that evidence is very much in dispute, but there are circumstances or reasons when a witness's statement can be read. The death of the witness is one of those reasons. We know, tragically, that Miss T committed suicide. She had become increasingly depressed about the multiple sclerosis, the MS that she was suffering from, and the increasing disability it was causing to her.
>
> It is very important that you bear in mind when considering her evidence that you have not seen her give evidence; you have not heard her give evidence; and you have not heard her evidence tested in cross-examination by Mr Seabrook who would, undoubtedly, have had a number of questions to put to her."

and:

"So far as Count 1 is concerned, members of the jury, the alleged assault, the touching of Miss T's lips, her mouth, her breasts and her bottom for the defendant's sexual gratification, bear in mind, as I said, that this evidence was read to you. The allegation is completely denied, and as I have said, Mr Seabrook would have had a number of questions for Miss T, and you must take that into account when considering her evidence. The prosecution suggest that her evidence is supported by the evidence of Miss U, Miss K and Miss D."

31   We consider that it would have been better if the judge had stated explicitly that the appellant was potentially disadvantaged by the absence of Miss T and that in consequence of the inability to cross-examine her and of the jury to see her, her evidence should carry less weight with them. Nonetheless, in the circumstances of this case it must have been wholly clear to the jury from the directions the judge did give, that this was the purpose of his remarks. We therefore consider that the jury were given an adequate direction as to the consequences of Miss T's statement being in evidence in her absence, and that this is not a factor which might make the appellant's trial unfair and in breach of Art.6. We should also say that overall the evidence against the appellant was very strong. We were wholly unpersuaded that the verdicts were unsafe.

Appeal against conviction dismissed.

R. v H (JR) (CHILDHOOD AMNESIA)

COURT OF APPEAL (Lady Justice Smith, Mr Justice Hughes and Mr Justice Wakerley):   June 30; July 1, 2005.

[2005] EWCA Crim 1828; [2006] 1 Cr.App.R. 10

(LT) Admissibility; Expert evidence; Fresh evidence; Witnesses

H1   EVIDENCE
       Expert psychological evidence
       Convictions for offences of sexual abuse dependent upon childhood memory—Doubt cast on reliability of memory in expert psychological report—Whether evidence relevant and admissible—Whether evidence furnished information likely to be outside knowledge and experience of jury—Warning appropriate to be given to jury if evidence admitted

H2   The appellant JRH was convicted on counts of the indictment alleging, inter alia, indecent assault upon his daughter when she was aged four or five. Her witness statement, made when she was aged 19, gave a detailed narrative account of the incidents including a description of her own emotional reaction to what had occurred. Following an unsuccessful appeal against conviction, the Criminal Cases Review Commission referred the case to the Court of Appeal together with the appeal of TG, convicted separately of offences of indecent assault and rape on the same complainant. Under s.23 of the Criminal Appeal Act 1968 the Court agreed to hear evidence from a psychologist and expert in the field of memory formation and development. The gist of his evidence was that memories of early childhood were qualitatively different from memories of later events; that adults could not usually remember events of early childhood so as to be able to give a coherent narrative account, the only recall being one which was fragmentary, disjointed and idiosyncratic; and that this "period of childhood amnesia" lasted until the age of about seven. Therefore evidence of an event said to have occurred at an early age containing detail and extraneous facts might well be unreliable yet, nonetheless, apparently credible.

H3   **Held,** allowing JRH's appeal, ordering a retrial and adjourning TG's appeal, (1) that the evidence in question was true expert evidence, suitable for admission at a criminal trial, in that it provided information likely to be outside the knowledge and experience of the jury. The evidence would therefore be received under s.23 of the Criminal Appeal Act 1968. Moreover, in the case of JRH, if the new evidence had been put before the jury, it was possible that they would have reached different conclusions and would have acquitted JRH of more or even all counts. Therefore JRH's appeal was allowed and the convictions on counts 1 to 5 and 7 were quashed. A retrial was ordered (post, paras [36], [38], [44], [46]).

(2) The appeal of TG would be adjourned pending the outcome of the retrial of JRH (post, para.[46]).

(3) Where such evidence was admitted it was incumbent on the trial judge to warn the jury that, if they accepted it, they should approach the evidence of the witness to whom it related with special caution and that the evidence although apparently convincing might nonetheless be mistaken (post, para.[42]).

H4   *Per curiam* The expert evidence considered by the court was unlikely to be helpful in any but the most unusual case of child sexual abuse. The ability of a witness to remember events will, in the absence of special considerations, ordinarily be well within the ordinary experience of jurors. The admission of expert evidence will be relevant only in those rare cases in which the complainant provides a description of very early events occurring during the period of childhood amnesia which appears to contain an unrealistic amount of detail (post, paras [47], [48]). *R. v Turner* (1974) 60 Cr.App.R. 80; [1975] Q.B. 834, CA considered.

H5   (For expert evidence generally, see *Archbold* 2005, para.10–61 *et seq.*)

Appeals against conviction

H6   On November 14, 2000 in the Crown Court at Leeds (Harrison J.) the appellant, JRH, was convicted of two counts of indecent assault (counts 1 and 2) and four counts of rape (counts 3, 4, 5 and 7). He was acquitted of a further count of rape (count 6). He was sentenced to a total of 12 years' imprisonment. On January 12, 2001 in the Crown Court at Bradford (Harrison J.) the appellant, TG, was convicted of five counts of indecent assault and three counts of rape of the same complainant. He was sentenced to a total of eight years' imprisonment. In July 2002, following a joint hearing, the Court of Appeal, Criminal Division, dismissed the appeals of both JRH and TG. TG died in prison in August 2002. In September 2004 the Criminal Cases Review Commission referred both cases to the Court of Appeal, Criminal Division, under s.9(1) of the Criminal Appeal Act 1995 on the basis of fresh evidence. The mother of the deceased appellant, TG was given leave, under s.44A of the Criminal Appeal Act 1968, to pursue the appeal.

H7   The facts and grounds of appeal appear in the judgment of the Court.

H8   *James Goss Q.C.* and *Sophie Drake* (instructed by Eaton Smith, Huddersfield) for JRH.
Malcolm Swift Q.C. (assigned by the Registrar of Criminal Appeals) for TG.
Jeremy Richardson Q.C. (instructed by the Crown Prosecution Service, Leeds) for the Crown.

Cur. adv. vult

July 1, 2005   Smith L.J.: handed down the following judgment of the Court

1   There are before the court two appeals against conviction for offences of sexual abuse which have been referred to this court by the Criminal Cases Review

Commission ("CCRC"). On November 14, 2000 at Leeds Crown Court, after a trial before Harrison J. and a jury, the appellant JRH was convicted by majorities of 10:1 of two counts of indecent assault (counts 1 and 2) and four counts of rape of his daughter, JH (counts 3, 4, 5 and 7). He was sentenced to 12 years' imprisonment. He was acquitted of count 6, also an allegation of rape.

2   On January 12, 2001 at Bradford Crown Court, after a trial before Harrison J. and a jury, the appellant TG was convicted of five counts of indecent assault and three counts of rape of JH. He was sentenced to eight years' imprisonment.

3   In July 2002 the Court of Appeal, Criminal Division, dismissed both men's appeals against conviction following a joint hearing.

4   G died in prison in August 2002.

5   Both cases were referred to the CCRC, which, in September 2004, referred them to this Court under s.9(1) of the Criminal Appeal Act 1995, on the basis of fresh evidence said to be admissible pursuant to s.23 of the Criminal Appeal Act 1968, as amended. The referred appeals were heard together on June 30, 2005. At the commencement of the hearing the Court gave leave under s.44A of the Criminal Appeal Act 1968 for MG, the mother of the deceased appellant TG, to pursue the appeal. At the conclusion of the hearing, JRH's appeal was allowed in respect of all six counts of which he had been convicted and a retrial was ordered on all counts. The appeal of TG was adjourned pending the outcome of the retrial of JRH. We now give reasons for those decisions.

6   Because there will be a further trial, we shall confine ourselves to an account of the facts which is just sufficient to explain our reasons.

The factual background: allegations against JRH

7   JH was born in September 1979. She claimed to have memories going back to a time before she was three years old. In her police statement, she recounted in some detail an account of an event when her father had been angry with her and had taken her upstairs to her bedroom. She would have been just three at the time. She suggested that the way her father had carried her, with his hand between her legs, was indecent. However, this incident did not figure as an allegation on the indictment.

8   Counts 1 and 2 alleged that JH's father had indecently assaulted her when she was aged four or five. She described two incidents, both of which took place in her parents' bedroom. In her witness statement made at the age of 19, she gave a very detailed narrative account of an incident in which her father made her masturbate him. She included much detail about the circumstances leading up to the incident and about her own emotional reaction to what had happened. In evidence at trial, she said only that her father had made her masturbate him on several occasions.

9   In respect of the second allegation, her witness statement contained a detailed narrative account of how her father had touched her vagina, then inserted his finger into it and then progressed to kissing it. Her account again included considerable detail about the surrounding circumstances, including a recollection of what she and her father were wearing. In evidence, she said only that

she could remember her father touching and kissing her vagina on a number of occasions and sometimes putting his finger inside it.

10   Counts 3, 4 and 5 all alleged rape when JH was between the ages of 8 and 10. In her statement, she gave very detailed narrative accounts of three specific incidents of sexual intercourse, one of which took place in her parents' bedroom, one at her grandparents' house and one at her father's place of work. In evidence, her account of the first such incident was general and described what usually happened when her father raped her.

11   In respect of counts 1 to 5, the detailed accounts in the police statement were not adduced in evidence. There was no real inconsistency between what JH said in evidence and what she had said in her witness statement. No doubt counsel for JRH would not have wished to explore the detail given in the statement as there would have been a danger that the detail would have been accurately repeated and would have impressed and convinced the jury.

12   In respect of count 6, JH described in her statement how, when she was about 10, her father took her to a room in a building to which she had never been before. There she saw four men whom she did not know. She gave a detailed description of the layout of the room and the furniture. She also described each man and his clothing, in two cases descending into some detail. She then described, again in detail, how her father had had intercourse with her in the presence of the four men and how, after that, her father had forced her to have oral sex with him, had ejaculated into her mouth and had told her to swallow. The men watching were laughing. She then described how she was touched by some of the other men and had to masturbate one of them.

13   In evidence her account differed in two important respects from her previous statement. She said that she had not had to have oral sex with her father and had no recollection of ejaculate in her mouth. Also she added an allegation that the other men had inserted objects into her vagina, which had not previously been mentioned.

14   In respect of that count, JH was cross-examined closely about the differences between her police statement and her evidence, and, as we have said, JRH was acquitted on that count.

15   In respect of the seventh count, JH said that on numerous occasions up to the age of about 11 her father would rape her in his bedroom at home. She described what would usually happen on such occasions. She said that intercourse then ceased, but that inappropriate, sometimes indecent, touching continued until she was about 17.

16   There was a good deal of evidence about the events of JH's teenage years. She began to harm herself from the age of about 13. Her brother, her only sibling, to whom she was very close, died when she was 15. She was deeply upset. In the ensuing years, she became closely involved with a Pentecostal church. In due course she began to receive counselling.

17   Despite all these difficulties, she did well academically at GCSE and A level, and obtained entrance to medical school. At the age of 18, she left home and went to live with another family in a different part of the country. Soon afterwards, in November 1998, she made a formal allegation of sexual abuse by TG, who had

been her music teacher at junior school. A month later she made a statement against her father, JRH. She was 21 when she gave evidence at trial.

18   On arrest, JRH, who was of good character, answered all questions and denied any improper conduct. He gave evidence at trial in accordance with his answers in interview. The defence called an expert, who expressed the opinion that JH's allegations were the result of false memory syndrome.

The factual background: the evidence against TG

19   TG was a peripatetic music teacher who visited JH's school. From September 1989, when she was just 10 and in her third year at the school, JH had weekly music lessons from TG, initially as part of a group and then eventually on a one-to-one basis. She alleged that, during such lessons, TG began to touch her inappropriately. One day, he made her sit in a chair and masturbate him. Then he forced her to have oral sex, ejaculated in her mouth and told her to swallow it. This, she said, happened on a number of occasions and was covered by counts 1 and 2 on the indictment. She also alleged that on several occasions TG inserted coloured objects into her vagina. This, she said, was very painful.

20   Counts 4 and 5 alleged indecent assaults when she was in the fourth year at school, one of which entailed licking her vagina.

21   Counts 6 to 8 alleged rape, also during her fourth year at the school. In her statement, JH gave detailed descriptions of three specific incidents of rape, the first of which took place during the winter of that year. She said that penetration was extremely painful. Such incidents, she said, had taken place on more occasions than she could remember. She said that TG had stopped visiting the school at the Easter of her fourth year. The abuse then stopped.

22   When arrested, TG, who was of good character, answered all questions in interview, denying any impropriety and gave evidence at trial to the same effect. The defence did not call the expert on false memory syndrome, but did call a number of character witnesses. As we have said, TG was convicted on all counts.

The first appeal

23   No complaint was made by either appellant about the conduct of his trial or the summing-up. H's appeal relied to a large extent on a submission that the jury appeared to have accepted the expert evidence of false memory syndrome in respect of count 6 and it was therefore worrying that they had convicted on other counts. Various inconsistencies in JH's evidence were pointed out, and it was submitted that the evidence could not safely be relied upon without support from an independent source. The Court rejected that argument.

24   TG's appeal relied mainly on criticism of the tactics adopted by TG's trial counsel, who had been replaced. The Court rejected that argument. However, at the end of the judgment, Buxton L.J. said that the Court had anxiously considered whether there was a lurking doubt about the safety of both convictions because it was a striking coincidence that JH had been sexually abused by two men over the same period of time in circumstances where it was accepted that there was absolutely no connection between the two men. There were also a num-

ber of similarities between JH's evidence in respect of both men. However, the
court concluded that the allegations in the two cases were not sufficiently similar
to give rise to a fear that one or other or both had been fabricated or were otherwise unreliable. The Court was not prepared to interfere with the conclusions of
two separate juries, reached on the basis of impeccable directions and after the
most careful of trials.

The present appeals: fresh evidence—Professor Martin Conway

25   In the present appeals counsel sought to introduce the expert evidence of Prof.
Martin Conway, an academic psychologist, now Professor of Cognitive Psy-
chiatry at the University of Leeds. For about 25 years, he has worked and
published extensively in the field of memory formation and development. He
has a specialist interest in autobiographical memory.

26   In a report, which comprised answers to questions asked of him by the CCRC,
he had expressed the view that some parts of JH's evidence should be regarded as
unreliable. Mr Richardson Q.C., who appeared for the Crown, quite rightly
objected to those parts of his evidence as being inadmissible on the ground
that such evidence usurped the function of the jury. However, as Mr Goss Q.C.
for JRH submitted, there was within the report an explanation of the formation
of childhood memory and the features usually to be found in memories of childhood experience, which amounted to true expert evidence. They were capable of
providing a jury with information on matters that would be outside their usual
knowledge and experience. Mr Goss submitted that this evidence would potentially assist a jury in its approach to the reliability of JH's evidence,
particularly the evidence of her memories of very early childhood.

27   We agreed to hear Prof. Conway *de bene esse* in order to see whether, after oral
explanation of his views and cross-examination, his evidence amounted to expert
evidence which would, if available, have been admissible at the trial of JRH and
that its relevance to the issues in the case was such that it might afford grounds for
allowing the appeal.

28   It had been conceded by the Crown that, in other respects, the requirements of
s.23 of the Criminal Appeal Act 1968 were satisfied: the evidence was credible
and there was a reasonable explanation for the defence's failure to call Prof. Conway at the trial. Although much of his work was in the public domain in 2000, Mr
Richardson accepted that it was not well known.

29   We do not propose to set out the whole of Prof. Conway's evidence. The gist of
it was that memories of early childhood are qualitatively different from memories
of later events. Adults cannot usually remember events of early childhood so as to
be able to give a coherent narrative account. They may remember an event, and
sometimes a visual image, but the recall will be fragmentary, disjointed and idiosyncratic. This period in early childhood of which the adult will have an
impoverished memory is called the "period of childhood amnesia". Usually
childhood amnesia extends to the age of about seven. Adult memory of events
relating to later childhood becomes gradually richer, more detailed and more
organised.

30   In the course of his research, the professor had never come across a person who had been able to provide a detailed narrative account of an event that had taken place at the age of four or five. A child of four might well remember something that had happened when he was three, but by the time he was seven or eight he would have forgotten it and it would not be recaptured. It was possible that, if a child was regularly reminded about an event which occurred when he was very young, he might retain the memory of it. If the child had a traumatic experience, one would expect that, as an adult, he or she might recall a few—usually three or four—intrusive and disjointed features of the event. However, where the childhood event was merely unpleasant, such as a painful medical procedure or an accident such as falling off a bicycle, the adult might well remember the salient or central feature of the event but would not remember the surrounding or extraneous details. He would not be able to give an accurate and reliable narrative account.

31   Professor Conway's explanation for this state of affairs was that, during the first five years of life, the frontal lobes of the brain were in a very rapid state of change and development and material was not retained in the memory. He said that, so far as he knew, all psychologists working in the field of memory formation agreed with what he had said about the effect of childhood amnesia, although not all agreed with his view about why it occurred.

32   It was Prof. Conway's opinion that, if evidence of an event said to have occurred at an early age was very detailed and contained a number of extraneous facts, it might well be unreliable. It may be that the central feature of the event had indeed occurred, although research showed that, when seeking to remember life events from childhood, it was quite common for people genuinely to believe that they could remember events which were known not to have taken place.

33   In an adult account of a childhood event some surrounding detail might well be accurate if it was derived from conceptual knowledge, which are things that the adult knows about his childhood, such as which school he went to, where he lived, or the layout of his home. However, details which do not come from conceptual knowledge may well be false or unreliable. In effect they may well have been added on to the true memory at some later time.

34   Professor Conway considered that a narrative account of an event which was said to have taken place during the years of childhood amnesia should be treated with caution, especially if it contained a number of details that were extraneous to the central feature of the event.

35   Professor Conway also said that the effect of giving an account which contained details was to enhance its credibility to the ears of the listener. Research showed that listeners responded differently to two accounts of essentially the same event. If the account included a detail, the listener was more likely to believe and accept it than if that detail were omitted. The detail might not make any difference to the information being conveyed; it might be quite without value, but its effect would be to enhance the listener's perception. What this came down to, although Prof. Conway did not articulate it in quite this way, is that there is a danger that if a witness gives an account of a childhood event which contains detail about which he feels confident but may well be unreliable because of child-

hood amnesia, the listeners (namely a jury) might find the account more convincing than they safely should.

36   We came to the conclusion that Prof. Conway's evidence was true expert evidence, suitable for admission at a criminal trial, in that it provided information likely to be outside the knowledge and experience of the jury. We also considered that, in the exceptional circumstances of this case, where JH had provided quite remarkably detailed accounts of events which she claimed had taken place at the ages of three, four and five, his evidence was relevant and was capable of affording a ground for allowing the appeal of JRH, in that it might affect a jury's view of JH's reliability as a witness. We decided, therefore, to admit the evidence.

Fresh evidence: post trial medical records

37   There was also fresh evidence put before the court in the form of documents found within JH's post-trial medical records. JH has undergone psychiatric treatment since 2001. A letter of referral written in 2003 by a Dr B seeking to arrange psychotherapy for JH with Miss G contained an account of JH's childhood abuse. It appears from this letter that JH had said things to Dr B that were inconsistent with her earlier evidence and that one statement made to Dr B was demonstrably untrue. A report of the first two consultations between JH and Miss G likewise appear to show that JH has given her at least an exaggerated or over-dramatised account of past events.

38   Mr Richardson agreed this evidence "for what it was worth", as he put it. He accepted that it was credible, relevant to the issues and was capable of affording a ground of appeal. Self-evidently it had not been available at the trial. We agreed to receive the evidence under s.23.

Submissions

39   Mr Goss for JRH submitted that if, hypothetically, the evidence of Prof. Conway and the medical records had been available at the trial, it was likely that the jury would have taken a different view of JH's reliability as a witness. Her evidence in relation to the very early allegations in counts 1 and 2 might have been seriously undermined. The effect might have extended to the later counts. When these new factors were taken into account, in addition to the inconsistencies in her evidence that were established at the trial and the inherent implausibility of her being abused by two completely unconnected men at the same time, the result might well have been an acquittal on all counts.

40   Mr Swift Q.C., who appeared on behalf of TG, accepted that JH's evidence against TG could not have been affected by Prof. Conway's evidence about childhood amnesia. The allegations against TG related to a time when JH was 10 and 11. However, he submitted that, if it could be shown that JH's evidence against JRH had been unreliable, there might well be an effect on the jury's view of the case against TG. Moreover, the medical records cast doubt on JH's reliability as a witness generally, even though she had not said anything to her doctors about abuse by TG. Indeed the fact that she had omitted to mention him at all might be

of some significance. Mr Swift submitted that the new evidence rendered TG's convictions unsafe.

41   In respect of JRH, Mr Richardson submitted that, even with this additional material, the case against JRH was overwhelming. JH had obviously been an impressive witness. The jury had also heard JRH at some length and had convicted him. There was no reason to fear that the result would have been different even if the new material had been available.

42   However, he agreed with the proposition put to him by Wakerley J. that the effect of Prof. Conway's evidence was such that it would have been incumbent on the judge to warn the jury that, if they accepted the evidence, they should approach JH's evidence with special caution. This would be because the detailed narrative accounts that she had given of the early incidents would, if Prof. Conway's evidence were accepted, be inherently unreliable and yet might well sound particularly convincing. Mr Richardson accepted that an appropriate warning would be similar to the warning that is usually given in identification cases, where the judge warns the jury of the danger that a witness might be very convincing, because he or she was quite sure that the identification was correct, and yet could still be mistaken. He also accepted that if, such a warning had been necessary but had not been given, that might well render a conviction unsafe.

43   Very fairly and realistically, Mr Richardson accepted that when, in addition, the fresh evidence of the medical records was brought into consideration, this court might feel real doubt about the safety of JRH's convictions. In respect of TG, Mr Richardson submitted that the new evidence was of lesser effect than in the case of JRH and that the verdicts in his case were safe. However, he accepted that, unless and until it was known how a jury would react to the new evidence if adduced by H, it would not be possible to say what effect the new evidence might have in respect of TG.

Conclusion

44   In the case of JRH, it is our view that, if the new evidence had been put before the jury, it is possible that they would have reached different conclusions and would have acquitted JRH of more or even all counts. We cannot say that they would have done: the new evidence falls far short of showing that JH was not abused. But we are persuaded that it might have made a crucial difference, particularly when considered together with the inconsistencies in evidence that were noted at the trial and the striking coincidence that JH should have been abused at the same time by two men completely unconnected with each other. We have concluded that the appeal should be allowed and that the convictions on counts 1 to 5 and count 7 of the indictment should be quashed.

45   We granted Mr Richardson's application for a retrial. Provided that the prosecution is satisfied that it is not against JH's interests that she should have to give evidence again, as to which independent advice will be taken, we consider that it is in the public interest that JRH should be retried for what are very grave allegations of abuse.

46   So far as TG is concerned, the basis for allowing his appeal is less clear. Professor Conway's evidence is not irrelevant to TG's case but is of less direct relevance than to JRH's case. The evidence of the medical records is also of less direct relevance to TG, although it is by no means irrelevant. Bearing in mind that TG is dead, that there is no possibility of a retrial and therefore no urgency to resolve his posthumous appeal, we decided to adjourn our decision pending the outcome of the retrial of JRH. We consider that the jury's reaction to Prof. Conway's evidence, the view that they take of JH in the light of that evidence and the warning which we anticipate the judge will have to give are matters that will affect the strength of the appeal in TG's case. Mr Swift did not seek to dissuade us from this course, unusual though it is. Accordingly, TG's appeal stands adjourned.

47   We would not wish to leave this case without sounding a note of caution about the introduction of evidence of the kind given by Prof. Conway in this case. It will only be in the most unusual of circumstances that such evidence will be relevant and admissible at the trial of allegations of child abuse. The evidence would be relevant only in those rare cases in which the complainant provides a description of very early events which appears to contain an unrealistic amount of detail. That, in the experience of this court, does not happen often.

48   The principles set out in *R. v Turner* (1974) 60 Cr.App.R. 80; [1975] Q.B. 834; should be kept firmly in mind. Expert evidence is only admissible when it is likely to assist the jury on a topic which falls outside its ordinary experience. A witness's ability to remember events will, absent the special considerations arising from the period of early childhood amnesia, ordinarily be well within the experience of jurors. We would not wish it to be thought that the introduction of evidence such as that heard from Prof. Conway will be helpful in any but the most exceptional case.

Appeal by JRH allowed, conviction quashed, retrial ordered.
Appeal by TG adjourned pending outcome of JRH's retrial.

R. v LAHAYE

COURT OF APPEAL (Sir Igor Judge P., Mr Justice Roderick Evans and
Sir Charles Mantell): October 12, 2005

[2005] EWCA Crim 2847; [2006] 1 Cr.App.R. 11

LT Alternative charges; Grievous bodily harm; Indictments; Wounding with
intent

H1 **ASSAULT**

Alternative verdict

*Defendant charged on indictment with single count of wounding with intent—
Jury directed on availability of verdict on lesser offence of wounding—Jury
acquitting defendant of count on indictment but finding defendant guilty of
wounding—Whether judge correct to leave lesser offence for consideration by
jury—Whether better practice to include count on indictment alleging lesser
offence—Offences Against the Person Act 1861 (24 & 25 Vict.c.100), ss.18,
20— Criminal Law Act 1967 (c.58), s.6(3)*

H2 The appellant and P were neighbours. After angry words passed between them
in the street P ran into his house and came out carrying two knives and attacked
the appellant. P was subsequently convicted of an offence in relation to this
attack. The following day there was a further altercation between the appellant
and P in the course of which P sustained three stab wounds. The appellant was
charged with an offence of wounding with intent, contrary to s.18 of the Offences
against the Person Act 1861. The prosecution case was that he had deliberately
stabbed P in revenge for what P had done to him the previous evening. There
was a good deal of evidence to support that case. The defence case was that P
had lunged at the appellant with a large knife and the appellant had grabbed
P's arm to prevent any further stabbing action. He denied that he had tried to
stab P. At the trial neither prosecuting nor defence counsel were anxious to
leave to the jury an alternative count of the lesser offence of wounding, contrary
to s.20 of the 1861 Act. The judge nevertheless directed the jury that if they were
not sure that the appellant had the necessary intention to cause really serious
injury, the verdict would be not guilty of wounding with intent but guilty of
unlawful wounding. The appellant was convicted of the lesser offence and
appealed against conviction on the ground that the alternative offence under
s.20 should not have been left to the jury.

H3 **Held,** dismissing the appeal, that s.6(3) of the Criminal Law Act 1967 enabled
a defendant to be convicted of an offence contrary to s.20 of the 1861 Act as an
alternative to a charge and single count alleging contravention of s.18. The authorities also established that a verdict under s.20 was normally available when an

offence under s.18 was alleged. The judge was concerned to enable the jury to return a true verdict and summed up in a way which could not be criticised. There was no improper prejudice or unfairness (post, paras [16]–[18]).

H4   *Per curiam.* In circumstances where, as a matter of law, s.20 is available as an alternative to s.18, and the application of s.6(3) of the 1967 Act means that that alternative would be available even if s.20 were not alleged, it would be better practice for the s.20 count to be included on the face of the indictment (post, para.[21]).

H5   (For the general rule as to verdicts for lesser offences, see *Archbold* 2006, paras 4–453 and 4–454; for s.6(3) of the Criminal Law Act 1967, see *ibid* paras 4–455 and 4–456).

Appeal against conviction

H6   On August, 4 2004, in the Central Criminal Court (Judge Morris Q.C.) the appellant, Dean John Lahaye, was convicted of wounding, contrary to s.20 of the Offences Against the Person Act 1861, as an alternative to a single count in the indictment alleging wounding with intent, contrary of s.18 of the 1861 Act. He was sentenced to two years' imprisonment.

H7   The facts and grounds of appeal appear in the judgment of the court.

H8   *John Cooper* (assigned by the Registrar of Criminal Appeals) for the appellant. *Nicholas Corsellis* (instructed by the Crown Prosecution Service) for the Crown.

Sir Igor Judge P. gave the judgment of the Court

1   This is an appeal against conviction with leave of the full court by Dean Lahaye. He appeared at the Central Criminal Court before Judge Morris Q.C. and a jury on a single count alleging wounding with intent, contrary to s.18 of the Offences Against the Person Act 1861. In the result he was convicted of wounding, contrary to s.20 of the same Act. He was subsequently sentenced to two years' imprisonment.

2   The facts of the case can be summarised shortly. The appellant was a man of previous good character. The victim, David Probert, had previous convictions. They were neighbours. On September 5, 2002 Probert became abusive to the appellant. The appellant was troubled about Probert's habit of throwing bottles which smashed onto the pavement. After some words had passed between them, Probert ran into his house and came out carrying two knives. He attacked the appellant in the street. In the violence which then ensued he caused a stab wound to the appellant's arm which required seven stitches. He was subsequently sentenced to 18 months' imprisonment for this attack. Later that evening he was arrested in connection with an assault on his wife. During the course of his arrest he behaved abusively and violently towards the police. He was released from police custody the next day.

3   Shortly after midday the appellant and Probert came across each other again. There was an altercation in the course of which Probert sustained three stab wounds: one to the back of the left of his chest which penetrated the pericardium and just missed his heart, another to the diaphragm and another to the surface of the left lobe of his liver. Probert required surgery and intensive care. He was detained in hospital for some time.

4   The prosecution case was straightforward. The appellant had deliberately stabbed Probert in revenge for what Probert had done to him on the previous evening. There was a good deal of evidence to support that case. One eyewitness, for example, identified the man (who, on his account, was the appellant) holding a knife with a long blade which was seen coming out from Probert's abdomen. Another witness described seeing the man who was the appellant taking a long, thin object, which the Crown said was this knife, from within his jacket and coming into close contact with Probert. Yet another witness described hearing an argument, which became increasingly aggressive and unpleasant, and words to this effect, "You stabbed me, you fucker. I'm going to stab you".

5   The defence case was that all this evidence was wrong. The appellant gave evidence that he had reported the earlier incident in which he had been stabbed to the police and that, not surprisingly, he had been frightened by what had happened. His injuries required that his arm should be put in a sling. He had seen the victim's wife and went out into the street. He called for her to come out, but she disappeared. He then realised that Probert was in the same street with him. Given what had happened earlier, he was surprised to find him there and not at the police station or in police custody. His case was that Probert had lunged at him with a large knife and in doing so he had cut his (the appellant's) pocket. Faced with that, he took his arm out of his sling, grabbed hold of Probert's arm and struggled to prevent any further stabbing action. His evidence was that he thought he was going to be killed. He denied that anything had been said about the stabbing incident on the previous evening. Somehow at some point in the struggle Probert had fallen. At that stage the appellant had a knife in his hand, but he could not remember how it came to be in his hand. He denied adamantly that he had tried to punch or to stab the victim.

6   On this brief summary of his case, as it seems to us, issues of self-defence and accident arose. Importantly, it was plain from his evidence that, whatever else he was saying, he was saying that he had no intention that Probert should suffer any harm, let alone really serious bodily harm. He called a number of witnesses to give evidence on his behalf. It is unnecessary for the purpose of understanding the issue in this appeal to recite that evidence.

7   At the close of the evidence, and before speeches, Mr Cooper, who appeared at the Old Bailey and has appeared before us in support of this appeal, raised with the judge the issue of an alternative verdict under s.20. He put his submission to the judge in this clear way:

> ". . . my initial view is, subject to your Lordship's, that this is a section 18 or nothing, as it were."

He made the point that the Crown had not regarded this as a s.20 case. When the judge asked counsel for the Crown, Mr Corsellis, who also appeared below and before us, agreed. Mr Cooper suggested that the Crown had put its case forward against the appellant as a deliberate action by him, and that they had accordingly tied their colours to the mast of s.18 or nothing.

8   On closer analysis that is not entirely accurate. The judge rightly understood that the Crown's purpose was to seek to avoid what in the Crown's view would have been an inappropriate verdict of wounding, contrary to s.20. To leave that option to the jury would decrease the prospect of what the Crown believed would be an appropriate conviction under s.18. At the same time, as it seems to us, the defence were not anxious for s.20 to be left to the jury because that might reduce the prospect of an acquittal overall. In short, there were tactical considerations afoot. No issue of principle was involved. We understand the forensic positions being taken by each side.

9   However, the judge had a different duty. Among others, his duty was to assist the jury to return whatever verdict was properly open to them and which they regarded as a true verdict according to the evidence. As the discussion developed, the judge pointed out that there might be "a number of reasons why a jury would be satisfied as to the intent but, if they were not satisfied as to the intent . . . it would be open on the face of it to acquit of section 18 and convict of section 20". He acknowledged that that was not the way the Crown wanted the case put, and might well not be how the defence wanted the case put but, "out of fairness to the defendant, it seems to me that the matter ought to be left to the jury, unless you wish to argue to the contrary".

10   Having expressed himself in that way, the judge invited further submissions. Mr Cooper did not at that stage suggest that the case for the appellant would have been conducted differently if he had appreciated that s.20 would be left to the jury. We do not see how he properly could have done so. The appellant's case was that he had never at any time been an aggressor. That was the case that Mr Cooper had put on his behalf to witnesses who inculpated him in this crime, and he called evidence, including the appellant himself, to support. In other words, the factual case presented by the applicant was identical to the case which would have been presented if a specific count under s.20 had been included in the indictment.

11   When the judge came to sum up the case, he dealt with the matter very clearly and simply. He pointed out to the jury, and directed them, that in relation to s.18 there were three specific ingredients to be considered. Then he came on to the fourth ingredient, which only arose if the jury were satisfied so as to be sure that what had happened represented deliberate, non-accidental action by the appellant, which was unlawful and not in self defence. The judge said:

> ". . . when the defendant stabbed Mr Probert, he intended to cause him really serious injury."

He then gave an appropriate direction about that ingredient. Having done so, he went back to the position which could arise if the jury were sure of the first three ingredients: that Probert had been wounded; that the appellant had inflicted those wounds by deliberate acts; and that the stabbing was unlawful because it was not in reasonable and necessary self defence. He directed the jury that if they were not sure that the appellant had the necessary intention to cause really serious injury, the verdict would be not guilty of wounding with intent but guilty of unlawful wounding, "which is the lesser offence and which does not involve the intention to cause really serious injury."

12   The essence of this appeal arises from Mr Cooper's complaint that the s.20 alternative should not have been left to the jury. He submitted that this was not a case in which that alternative would have been available on the evidence; it was not the case the Crown was putting, and it therefore was not the case that the appellant had had to meet. He suggested that if he had appreciated at an earlier stage that the judge would leave s.20 to the jury, he would (or might) have conducted the case in a different way.

13   The current statutory arrangement for alternative verdicts is provided by s.6(3) of the Criminal Law Act 1967. For the purposes of this judgment it is unnecessary to recite its terms.

14   We have had our attention drawn to a very large number of authorities. For the purposes of this judgment we do not propose to recite them. We have considered their impact. We note in passing that in *R. v Saunders* (1987) 85 Cr.App.R. 334; [1988] A.C. 148 the House of Lords considered the application of s.6(2) of the 1967 Act which, as the text shows, is expressly concerned with verdicts of manslaughter when the indictment alleges murder. There is a sentence in the speech of Lord Ackner which suggests that the principles of the common law in relation to murder (and treason) were not abrogated by s.6(2). However, it is difficult to envisage circumstances in any other cases in which the common law continues to permit an alternative verdict in circumstances which would not be encompassed by s.6(3). So the starting point, and subject to possible exceptional cases (which it is difficult to imagine as we sit here now), the end point remains s.6(3).

15   Any analysis of the authorities drawn to our attention suggests that the critical question to the understanding of the judgment in each case requires attention to be given to whether the ground of complaint arose because the appellant was convicted of a serious offence, when the judge failed to leave the alternative verdict of a lesser offence to the jury, or whether the argument arose when the defendant charged with a major offence was convicted of a lesser offence. *R. v Fairbanks* (1986) 83 Cr.App.R. 251; [1986] 1 W.L.R. 1202 is a classic example of the first situation. The error made by the judge arose from his failure to direct the jury that a verdict of careless driving was available to them when the indictment charged causing death by reckless driving. In the same context the reasoning in *Fairbanks* was applied in the House of Lords in *R. v Maxwell* (1990) 91 Cr.App.R. 61; [1990] 1 W.L.R. 401, where Lord Ackner observed at 68 and 408:

> "The court, before interfering with the verdict, must be satisfied that the jury may have convicted out of a reluctance to see the defendant get clean away with what on any view was disgraceful conduct. If they are so satisfied, then the conviction cannot be safe or satisfactory."

16   In the present appeal we are confronted with an instance of the second situation, that is that the judge left the lesser offence to the jury when it was not expressly alleged in the indictment. The effect of the decisions of the House of Lords in *R. v Wilson* (1983) 77 Cr.App.R. 319; [1984] A.C. 242 and *R. v Mandair* (1994) 99 Cr.App.R. 250; [1995] 1 A.C. 208 has deprived a number of earlier decisions, such as *R. v Springfield* (1969) 83 Cr.App.R. 608; *R. v McCready* (1978) 67 Cr.App.R. 345; [1978] 1 W.L.R. 1376 and *R. v Field* (1993) 97 Cr.App.R. 357, of any continuing authority in this area. In summary, s.6(3) of the 1967 Act enables a defendant to be convicted of an offence contrary to s.20 of the 1861 Act as an alternative to a charge and single count alleging contravention of s.18.

17   The proper operation of the powers granted by s.6(3) requires that, like any other aspect of the trial process, the defendant should not be unfairly prejudiced. In this particular context the principle would normally be contravened if the defendant were suddenly to find himself facing an allegation not previously advanced nor even contemplated, and deprived of a sufficient opportunity to prepare and present his defence to the lesser charge.

18   We return to the facts of this case and apply those principles to them. As we have indicated, the factual case presented by the appellant in the course of this trial was identical to any case which would have been presented if a specific count under s.20 had been included in the indictment. We have examined Mr Cooper's contention about potential prejudice. The reality is that we can see no improper prejudice. None was identified by Mr Cooper when the issue was canvassed with the judge. In truth, all that happened here was that the judge was ahead of the forensic tactical battle. He allowed neither side to take advantage of the other. His concern was to enable the jury to return a true verdict. Knowing that s.20 would be left by the judge to the jury, both sides addressed the jury in their closing speeches with an ample opportunity to, and no doubt they sought to, persuade the jury of the validity of their case—in the case of the Crown that s.18 was the correct verdict; and in the case of the appellant, that an acquittal would be right. The judge then summed up the case in the way we have already indicated, and, subject only to this point, in a way which was not criticised.

19   We have looked closely to see whether there was any possible prejudice or that any glimmer of unfairness has been demonstrated in the course taken by the judge. We can see none. Accordingly, this appeal must be dismissed.

20   We are, however, troubled at the absence of a count under s.20. As we have indicated, the authorities establish beyond doubt that a verdict under s.20 is normally available when s.18 is alleged. However we can see no advantage (and none has been drawn to our attention) by the omission of a s.20 count, which in virtually every case will be available to the jury and which the judge at trial will almost inevitably have to address, because whether s.20 is alleged or not, it is the judge's duty to cut to the heart of the matter. If s.20 would be available in any event, we can see no reason why it should not be alleged at the outset. We see no disadvantage to the Crown. If their case is that the jury should convict of s.18, they will present their evidence and the arguments to sustain that con-

clusion. On the other hand, the jury may take a different, less severe view and should be trusted to reach the appropriate verdict according to the evidence.

21   In circumstances where as a matter of law s.20 is available as an alternative to s.18, and where the application of s.6(3) of the 1967 Act means that that alternative would be available even if s.20 were not alleged, we consider that it would be better practice for the s.20 count to be included on the face of the indictment.

Appeal against conviction dismissed.

R. v PLEYDELL

COURT OF APPEAL (Lord Justice May, Mr Justice David Steel and
Mr Justice Walker): May 20, 2005

[2005] EWCA Crim 1447; [2006] 1 Cr.App.R. 12

(LT) Admissibility; Blood samples; Causing death by dangerous driving; Controlled drugs; Relevance

H1   ROAD TRAFFIC
Dangerous driving
Causing death by—Evidence of drug consumption—Whether admissible—
Whether quantitative evidence necessary—Whether necessary to establish likely
or actual adverse effect on driver

H2   The appellant lost control of the vehicle he was driving and collided with a
parked car, as a result of which a person was killed. The appellant was taken to
a police station and, about three hours after the accident, he gave a sample of
blood which was found to contain traces of cocaine. He was charged with causing
death by dangerous driving. At trial the judge acceded to a prosecution application to adduce evidence of consumption of cocaine by the appellant. A
forensic toxicologist gave evidence that cocaine could affect a person's ability
properly to drive a car. He also said that cocaine could be detected in blood
samples three to six hours after use. He concluded that the appellant had used
the drug shortly before the accident. The appellant denied having taken cocaine
on the day of the accident and could not explain why there had been traces of
cocaine in his blood. He was convicted. He appealed against conviction on the
ground that there had been no evidence as to the quantity of cocaine he had
taken nor expert opinion as to the actual impact on his driving rather than the
potential impact, and therefore the evidence that he had taken cocaine was prejudicial and inadmissible.

H3   **Held,** dismissing the appeal, that if the jury was persuaded that the appellant
had taken a drug, that was a fact relevant to the issue of whether he had driven
dangerously. The material adduced by the prosecution was that he had taken
cocaine, that he had taken it shortly before the accident, that he had lied about
the timing of that and that the drug, while short lasting, had a tendency or capacity
to impair driving ability. The prosecution was correct in asserting that the jury
was entitled to view the consumption of the cocaine *per se* as relevant to the
issue of driving dangerously, in contrast to modest consumption of alcohol. In
the circumstances, the decision by the trial judge to admit the evidence relating
to the presence of cocaine in the blood sample of the appellant was fully justified
and correct (post, paras [28]–[32]).

H4   *R. v Woodward* [1995] 2 Cr.App.R. 388; [1995] 1 W.L.R. 375, CA distinguished.

H5   (For evidence of alcohol or drugs in driving offences, see *Archbold* 2006, para.32-20)

Appeal against conviction

H6   On September 17, 2004 in the Crown Court at Lewes (Judge Niblett) the appellant, Michael Aaron Pleydell, was convicted of causing death by dangerous driving. On November 1, 2004 he was sentenced to three years' imprisonment, disqualified from driving for five years and ordered to take an extended re-test. He pleaded guilty to using a vehicle without insurance and his licence was endorsed. No verdict was given on an alternative count to that which he was convicted, namely causing death by careless driving when unfit through drink or drugs.

H7   The facts and grounds of appeal appear in the judgment of the Court.

H8   *Rowan Jenkins* (assigned by the Registrar of Criminal Appeals) for the appellant. *Stephen Shay* (instructed by the Crown Prosecution Service) for the Crown.

1   The appellant is aged 27. On September 17, 2004 in the Crown Court at Lewes, before Judge Niblett and a jury, he was convicted of causing death by dangerous driving. On November 1, he was sentenced to three years' imprisonment, disqualified from driving for five years and ordered to take an extended re-test. In addition he pleaded guilty to using a vehicle without insurance for which his licence was endorsed. No verdict was given on an alternative count to that which he was convicted, namely causing death by careless driving when unfit through drink or drugs. He appeals against conviction by leave of the single judge.

2   The heart of this appeal relates to a ruling made at the beginning of the trial permitting the Crown to adduce evidence of consumption of cocaine by the appellant. But it is desirable to outline what emerged during the course of the trial.

3   At about 22.45 on September 30, 2003 the appellant was driving a car along Carew Road in Eastbourne. He had a passenger who was a friend in the passenger seat. As he drove along the appellant lost control of the vehicle and it collided with a parked car. The passenger side of the vehicle bore the force of the impact and as a result his passenger suffered multiple injuries.

4   After this accident the appellant almost immediately drove to Eastbourne District General Hospital, where he arrived at about 22.50. He told a security officer that his "mate" was trapped in the car and needed help. The appellant was clearly very distressed. His passenger was inside the car, still alive and moaning. He was removed and treated but he died some two hours later.

5   A police officer examined the vehicle and concluded (and there was no controversy about it), that there was no fault or defect which caused or contributed to the
collision.

6   The prosecution case was that having taken cocaine, the appellant caused the
death of the passenger by driving a motorcar dangerously. The defence case was
simply that the appellant's driving was not dangerous and he had not consumed
cocaine immediately prior to the incident.

7   Evidence relating to reconstruction of the accident was provided both by the
Crown and the defence. A police constable who was a traffic officer and collision
investigator examined the scene. He reported that, at the relevant junction,
between Mill Gap Road and Carew Road the road surface was raised creating
a bump. He found two sets of tyre scuff marks in Carew Road, which he concluded were made by a vehicle starting to slide sideways, indicating that the driver
had lost control of the vehicle. The pattern of these two separate sets of skid marks
indicated a vessel spinning out of control. The result had been that the front passenger side of the appellant's car had collided with the rear of a stationary
Volkswagen, which in turn was forced to move on impact into a telegraph pole
and then into its final resting position.

8   The conclusion of the officer was that the first set of tracks revealed that the car
had been travelling at 49mph, plus or minus 10 per cent, i.e. a minimum of
44mph. In cross-examination, he expressed the opinion that the loss of control
was caused by excessive speed, together with the bump in the road.

9   The defence called a Douglas Wragge as a consultant engineer who also examined the scene and the vehicle. He agreed there was no apparent fault or defect
which caused or contributed to the collision.

10   So far as the scuff marks were concerned, it was his opinion that there was an
equal chance or possibility of the first set of marks being made by a different car.
Otherwise his evidence was similar to that adduced on behalf of the Crown. There
was also evidence relating to the question of impairment through drugs or alcohol
and medical evidence.

11   The Crown called a PC Allcorn who gave evidence that he spoke to the appellant at hospital. The appellant agreed that he had been the driver. He was clearly
concerned about his passenger. The police officer described how the appellant's
manner changed from being morose to animated, excitable and talkative. He said
he detected the smell of alcohol on the appellant's breath and tried to obtain a
sample. But he was unable to do so because of the appellant's distressed state.

12   A Dr Sparkes, a forensic medical examiner, gave evidence that he took a blood
sample from the appellant at the police station. This was about three hours after
the accident. The appellant was compliant but was clearly suffering from acute
stress reaction. The symptoms being that he was subdued, pre-occupied, shaking
and breaking down in tears from time to time. Indeed, at one point, he was physically sick. He did not display any signs of irritability and he was not on the face
of it dopey. Dr Sparkes concluded in fact that the appellant was not fit for interview at that time.

13   There was a statement from Dr Chatterton, a forensic toxicologist, which was
read. It analysed the appellant's blood sample that had been taken by Dr Sparkes.

No alcohol was detected but screening tests gave positive indications for the presence of cannabis and cocaine. We will revert, in a moment, to the detail of his discussion of the significance of those findings.

14   The defence evidence included the calling of Dr Christopher Williams, a consultant neuropsychologist, who gave evidence that following the incident the appellant was suffering from pre-imposed traumatic amnesia, in particular, covering the period of seconds prior to impact and seconds thereafter. The appellant, in his judgement, suffered from acute reaction to the trauma of collision. This explained his behaviour at the hospital and the police station after the accident.

15   In interview, the appellant denied driving whilst under the influence of cocaine. He initially denied ever using cocaine but subsequently admitted he had taken the drug previously.

16   The appellant gave evidence at the trial. He referred to the fact that he had been prescribed anti-depressant drugs that he was taking from time to time. He had borrowed the vehicle from a friend. He had driven that vehicle before and was familiar with Carew Road having driven on it on numerous occasions. On the day in question, he had left work at 18.30 and met a friend for a drink. He had taken cocaine by snorting and cannabis by smoking at a party the previous Saturday night/Sunday morning, the incident having taken place on the following Tuesday. The impact of cocaine on him as he described it made him jovial, chatty and in a good mood. He occasionally had taken cannabis and cocaine previously. He did not take any substance after the party and certainly not on the Monday or the Tuesday.

17   In cross-examination, he accepted that he had lied to the police in his first interview. He denied ever using cocaine because it was not a particularly clever thing to do. He could not explain why there were traces of cocaine in his blood. He had taken the drug five to six times previously. It made him talkative and erased his fears. He would never take it shortly before driving a car. He did not think it would affect his driving but would not take the risk. He would not take cocaine the night before work because it would affect his faculties. He was a competent driver. It was possible that he was driving at 44mph. If so, that was too fast.

18   The grounds of this appeal, on which the single judge gave leave, relate to a decision of the judge to allow the Crown to adduce the evidence of cocaine being identified in the appellant's blood sample. This application took place at the beginning of the trial, or perhaps immediately after the Crown's opening.

19   In support of the application to exclude the evidence of the trial, and indeed in support of this appeal, the appellant relies on the decision of this Court in *R. v Woodward* [1995] 2 Cr.App.R. 388; [1995] 1 W.L.R. 375. That case concerned a charge of causing death by dangerous driving. The appellant driver was injured in the accident, and accordingly no specimen of breath, blood or urine was taken. The primary evidence of drinking came from two statements that were within the prosecution file from two friends of the appellant who had been to the same function that he had attended and who spoke of the appellant having drunk variously between two and six pints of lager. At the outset of the trial leave was given to the prosecution to adduce that evidence. But in the event the two friends did not come

up to proof. The only evidence adduced at the trial was that the appellant had been seen with a glass in his hand. The appellant did not give evidence. In his summing-up the judge reminded the jury that the appellant had consumed alcohol, but did not instruct them to disregard that fact.

20 This Court held, first, that on a prosecution for causing death by dangerous driving, the fact that the driver was adversely affected by alcohol was a relevant circumstance in determining whether he was driving dangerously. Secondly, although the evidence had, on the facts of that case, been properly admitted, since the evidence at the trial went no further than to show the applicant had had a glass in his hand and had been drinking to some unidentified extent the judge should have told the jury to disregard those facts.

21 As regards to the first proposition, the Court in *Woodward* was referred back to a decision of this Court in *R. v McBride* (1961) 45 Cr.App.R. 262; [1962] 2 Q.B. 167, where a Court of five judges had been assembled and a reserved judgment was given by Ashworth J., which contained the following passages at 266 and 172:

> "'. . . if a driver is adversely affected by drink, this fact is a circumstance relevant to the issue whether he was driving dangerously. Evidence to this effect is of probative value and is admissible in law. In the application of this principle two further points should be noticed. In the first place, the mere fact that the driver had had drink is not of itself relevance: in order to render evidence as to the drink taken by the driver admissible, such evidence must tend to show that the amount of drink taken was such as would adversely affect a driver or, alternatively, that the driver was in fact adversely affected. Secondly, there remains in the court an overriding discretion to exclude such evidence if, in the opinion of the Court its prejudicial effect outweighs its probative value.'"

The decision in *McBride* was followed in *R. v Thorpe* (1972) 56 Cr.App.R. 293; [1972] 1 W.L.R. 342, where at 296 and 344, the Lord Chief Justice, Lord Widgery, after quoting the passage we have just quoted from *McBride* went on to say:

> "The principle which is enshrined in that paragraph is quite clearly this. It would be prejudicial and not probative for the prosecution to seek to show merely that the accused had been in a public-house on the evening in question or had been seen with a glass of beer in his hand. If evidence of that kind were allowed to be admitted, it might prejudice the mind of the jury and it would have no probative value at all. What this Court was saying in *McBride* (supra) was that such evidence is not admissible unless it goes far enough to show that the quantity of alcohol taken is such that it may have some effect on the way in which the man drives."

These decisions under earlier legislation in the same field were held nonetheless to apply to the statutory offence with which the present appellant was charged. The conclusion of the Court in *Woodward* is set out at 396 and 382:

"At the stage when the ruling was given, the learned judge had before him
the witness statement of Mr Kingsland. When that witness came to give evidence, however, he did not come up to proof. As already pointed out, neither
nor Marion Huxter gave any evidence as to the amount drunk by the appellant over the evening. There was no breath or blood test, nor was there any
other evidence of what the appellant had consumed. Accordingly, at the end
of the prosecution case the evidence went no further than to show that the
appellant had been seen with a glass in his hand and had been drinking.
On the principles laid down in *McBride* that would not have amounted to
relevant evidence. No application was made to the trial judge to discharge
the jury. The appellant did not give evidence, so when the learned judge
came to sum up, there was still no relevant admissible evidence with regard
to drink.

Mr Francis's second ground of appeal is that in those circumstances it was
incumbent upon the learned judge to give the jury a clear direction. He ought
to have told them that such evidence as they had had of the appellant's drinking was irrelevant to the issues before them and that they should put it out of
their minds. The learned judge did not do that."

22   For the purposes of the application before the trial in the present case, the
Crown relied on the forensic analysis of the blood sample taken by Dr Sparkes,
which was, taken somethree hours after the accident. Whilst no alcohol was
detected, the screening tests gave positive indication for the presence of both cannabis and cocaine. The prosecution did not propose to suggest that the defendant
was, or might have been under the influence of cannabis at the material time,
albeit he had admitted that he had consumed such on the preceding Saturday
night. It was, however, the prosecution's intention to seek to admit the material
relating to the presence of cocaine and its potential impact. The significance of
the cocaine indicator was spelt out in a report of Dr Chatterton, to which we
have already briefly referred. In that report, which in due course was read at
the trial and was not challenged, the author, having referred to the indication
of cocaine, commented that it was not accurately quantified as there was insufficient blood sample remaining for any such test. But so far as cocaine was
concerned, he went on:

"Cocaine is a Class A controlled drug. The forensic science service can
detect unchanged cocaine in blood samples typically for 3 to 6 hours after
use depending on the dose and the method of drug administration. Cocaine
is a drug of addiction and is abused by either inhalation through the nose or
smoking a form of cocaine known as crack. Cocaine is rapidly and extensively metabolised in the human body and therefore the presence of
unchanged cocaine in the blood sample demonstrates the recent use of
this drug by him. Cocaine is a powerful stimulant drug that can produce
hyperactive and feelings of euphoria, self-confidence and strength. Larger
doses induce delusions, paranoia, acute anxiety and a tendency to be violent
or aggressive. Persons under the influence of cocaine may experience blur-
red vision and demonstrate increased risk-taking behaviour. The stimulant

effects of cocaine typically last for half to 1 hour after which there may be a strong compulsion to take more of the drug. After the stimulant effects of the drug have worn off the user may exhibit signs of irritability and drowsiness. Cocaine may therefore adversely affect a person's ability to properly drive a mechanically propelled vehicle."

His conclusion was simply this:

"These experimental findings demonstrate that [the appellant] had used cocaine and cannabis at some time prior to the alleged incident. Each of these drugs has the capacity to impair driving ability. The combined use of these drugs may exacerbate their individual effects."

23   In this appeal, the appellant places strong emphasis on the fact that there was no quantitative analysis nor expert expression of opinion as to the actual impact on the defendant's driving ability rather than the potential impact. In his initial interview the appellant admitted consuming cannabis on the Saturday night but denied taking cocaine. This, despite the fact that it had been disclosed to him that the sample taken by Dr Sharpe had revealed traces of both cannabis and cocaine.

24   When that was put to him, he replied:

"Well that's impossible that's absolutely impossible.
Is it?
Yes, I wouldn't take cocaine."

Then he was asked a few questions later:

"Let's assume it breaks down in 6 hours, it would have meant you'd taken cocaine two-and-a-half prior to the crash.
No, that is ridiculous.
Have you ever taken cocaine?
I have done in the past, not then, absolutely not. Explain to me then how it is found in your blood sample.
I don't know. I really don't. Hopefully you can tell me that."

25   A page later in the interview, however, he admitted that he, in the past, had taken cocaine.

"When was the last time you took any cocaine?
Probably the weekend actually truthfully probably the weekend.
So we're talking 36 hours before.
I'm much as a loss to you to come up with that."

The interview then went on to consider the implications of admission.

26   Against that background it was accordingly the defence's submission before the trial, at the time when the application to exclude the evidence was made, that the situation that had been revealed fell squarely within the scope of the decisions in *McBride*, *Thorpe* and *Woodward*; namely the mere fact that a drug had been taken was no more than prejudicial. Absent material demonstrating

that the quantity of the drug was such as to show that the appellant would be
adversely affected, it was inadmissible.

27   The prosecution contended, first, that the decision in *Woodward* was distinguishable because cocaine was illegal and alcohol was not. Secondly, the
law recognised a level of permissible drinking on the basis that the risk of
material impact on driving skills, at low levels of alcohol consumption, were
very small. Per contra, no such allowance was or could be made for a Class A
drug which had the effects which Dr Chatterton described in his report. Thirdly,
that the evidence supported the proposition that the appellant had recently
ingested cocaine and, accordingly, was likely to have been adversely affected
in his ability to drive.

28   The judge accepted the Crown's submissions. In our judgment, he was right to
do so. Whilst we are not persuaded that the mere fact that cocaine is an illegal
drug is of any direct significance, an issue for the jury was whether the appellant
was adversely affected by drugs. If the jury were duly persuaded, it was in turn a
fact relevant to the issue of whether he had driven dangerously (and, of course,
fully relevant to the second count of causing death by careless driving under
the influence of drugs).

29   The material available at the beginning of the trial, when this application was
made, indeed the material which was in due course adduced by the prosecution,
was, first, to the effect that the appellant had taken cocaine, secondly, that he had
taken it shortly before the accident, thirdly, that he had lied about the timing of
this, and fourthly, that the drug, whilst short-lasting had a tendency or a capacity
to impair driving ability.

30   In short, in our judgment, the mere fact that he had taken a drug, very shortly
before the incident, if such could be established by the prosecution, was potentially relevant. The whole purpose of taking a drug of the kind that is
identified in the blood sample would have been to achieve a material impact,
albeit short lived. Quantification of the precise amount of cocaine consumed
would not take matters any further.

31   In our judgment, therefore, the Crown were correct in asserting that the jury
was entitled to view the consumption of the cocaine *per se* as relevant to the
issue of driving dangerously, in contrast to perhaps modest consumption of
alcohol. Indeed it is notable, albeit irrelevant for the purposes of considering
admissibility of the evidence, that such a view is shared by the appellant himself.
He had taken cocaine on earlier occasions and as we recorded, he recorded it as
making him jovial, chatty and in a good mood. When he was invited to consider
whether he had been lying in saying that he had not taken cocaine shortly before
the incident, he said this, as recorded in the summing-up:

> "As far as cocaine was concerned, he was challenged by Mr Shay and he
> said: 'I cannot explain why there were traces of cocaine found in my
> blood. At first I denied to the police ever taking cocaine because it was
> not particularly clever thing to do. I agree I initially lied to the police but
> then I told the truth and later admitted it.' He said he had taken cocaine
> maybe five or six times in his life, it just makes him talkative and erases

his fears; he snorted it. He has never taken cocaine shortly before driving a car. He would never have done so. He cannot imagine, he told you, that it would make any difference when driving a car but he wouldn't want to risk it. 'I should imagine' he said 'it would depend on the quantity taken', but it has never happened to him so he doesn't know. He wouldn't have taken cocaine that night because he was working the next morning, and the reason he would not have done so, he told you, is because it would have affected his faculties."

32   In all these circumstances the decision of the trial judge to admit the evidence relating to presence of cocaine in the blood sample of the appellant was fully justified and correct. Accordingly there is nothing in this appeal and it must be dismissed.

Appeal against conviction dismissed.

R. v ROBINSON

COURT OF APPEAL (Lady Justice Smith, Mr Justice Nelson and Mr Justice Henriques): July 11, 2005

[2005] EWCA Crim 1940; [2006] 1 Cr.App.R. 13

⟨LT⟩ Admissibility; Probative value; Relevance; Voice recognition

H1 EVIDENCE
Voice identification
Widow of deceased having received telephone call with threats at time of her husband's disappearance—Such person upon hearing a defendant speaking at trial purportedly recognising his voice as that of the caller—Some of co-defendants, but not Crown, applying for evidence to be adduced—Whether evidence of such voice recognition admissible—Appropriate test as to admissibility

H2   The appellant, R, was tried, with others, upon an indictment charging, inter alia, offences of murder, blackmail and doing acts tending and intended to pervert the course of justice. The deceased's widow attended the trial. Upon hearing R speak at the trial she believed that she recognised his voice as that of the man who had telephoned her on the night of her husband's disappearance. She left court to seek out the officer in the case and provided a written statement. The Crown indicated that it would not be seeking to adduce the evidence. However, two of the co-defendants applied for the evidence to be adduced whereas the third co-defendant opposed the application. Following legal argument, the judge ruled that the evidence was not admissible. In the event, a difficulty arose with the jury so that it had to be discharged. A second trial took place subsequently before a different judge. At the re-trial the judge was also asked to rule as to the admissibility of the contested voice recognition evidence. The judge stated that he had to ask himself two questions, namely whether the material was relevant, and whether the material possessed some weight so that it could properly be described as probative. The judge ruled that the evidence was admissible. R was convicted of murder, blackmail and doing acts tending and intended to pervert the course of justice, and appealed against conviction.

H3   **Held,** dismissing the appeal, that the judge had been right to say that he had only two questions to answer, namely whether the evidence was relevant, and, whether, if it was, it satisfied the basic test of admissibility. The appropriate test was to ask whether the evidence was such that no reasonable jury, properly warned as to its defects, could place any weight upon it; or, putting it the other way around, if the evidence was such that a jury properly warned could place some weight on it, it should be admitted. This basic threshold of admissibility was a low threshold, and the matter was a matter of judgment for the particular judge. On the facts of the instant case the voice recognition evidence had some probative value when taken in conjunction with the other evidence in the case, and the judge had been right to admit it (post, paras [17]–[20], [22]–[24]).

H4 *Per curiam.* There is some force in observations made by counsel about the problems associated with voice recognition evidence and the other associated difficulties in this particular case. However, it seems to the Court that these problems are no different in their general nature from the problems frequently encountered with visual identification. In "fleeting glimpse" cases where conditions are poor it is commonplace for the judge to have to give a detailed warning about the dangers of reliance on the evidence, yet those problems are not usually perceived to be such as should result in the evidence being regarded as inadmissible, as having no weight at all. The evidence might well be excluded under s.78 of the Police and Criminal Evidence Act 1984, but that is a different matter (post, para.[21]).

H5 (For voice identification evidence, see *Archbold* 2005, paras 14–52).

Appeal against conviction

H6 On May 28, 2003 at the Central Criminal Court (Judge Forrester) the appellant, Wayne Robinson, was convicted of murder, blackmail and doing acts tending and intended to pervert the course of justice. He was sentenced to concurrent terms respectively of life imprisonment, 10 years' and four years' imprisonment.

H7 The facts and grounds of appeal appear in the judgment of the Court.

H8 *Henry Grunwald Q.C.* (assigned by Registrar of Criminal Appeals) for the appellant.
Alan Suckling Q.C. and *Ian Darling* (instructed by the Crown Prosecution Service, Ludgate Hill) for the Crown.

Smith L.J.: delivered the following judgment of the Court

1 On May 28, 2003 at the Central Criminal Court the appellant was convicted by a jury and was sentenced by Judge Forrester to life imprisonment for murder; to 10 years' imprisonment concurrent for an offence of blackmail; and to four years concurrent for doing acts tending and intended to pervert the course of justice. He now appeals against that conviction by leave of the full court.

2 Also standing trial with him at the central court were three others: Damien Chin, Matthew Walters-Kitson (to whom we shall refer as Kitson) and André Brown. All four men were convicted of murder as on the basis of joint enterprise; all four were also convicted of perverting the course of justice. The jury failed to agree as to whether Chin and Brown were guilty of blackmail, and they were discharged. In respect of that matter Kitson was convicted of blackmail and also of having a firearm in his possession with intent to cause fear of violence.

3 The victim of the murder was Edward Hamilton, who was a drug dealer. His partially burned body was found in Bow cemetery on February 10, 2002. He

had suffered severe head injuries sufficient to cause death. One blow had been struck by a handgun. The victim's car was found parked in a street nearby. Bloodstains inside that vehicle suggested that he had been assaulted while in the rear seat of the car and had been bleeding heavily when he got out.

4   The Crown case was that the appellant, the three co-accused and one other man, a man named Steve, who was not before the court, had planned to rob the deceased. Hamilton had been lured to a rendezvous at a flat known as Winchester House following telephone calls on February 8. From there the deceased had been taken to Bow cemetery late at night. The Crown contended that two cars had been used, travelling in convoy. One was the deceased's Honda, the other a Ford Escort. Two telephone calls were made late at night using the deceased's mobile phone to the mobile phone of the deceased's wife, Mrs Hamilton. In those calls demands for money were made which amounted to blackmail. These calls could be traced. They had been made in the area near Bow cemetery. The Crown case was that, shortly after those calls had been made, Hamilton was murdered and attempts were made to destroy the body by dousing it in petrol and burning it.

5   The deceased's wife reported him as missing on February 9. She told the police that she had received two telephone calls at about 02:00 that morning. She had been very frightened by them and had fled the house. A male voice with a strong Jamaican accent had told her that they had her husband and they wanted his money and that she knew where his money was. The man said that her husband would be killed.

6   In the first telephone call she heard her husband speak to her very briefly, before the line went dead. A few minutes later there was a second call, where the same voice repeated much of the same things. She could hear her husband's voice in the background. Her evidence about those telephone calls, to which we will return later, lies at the heart of this appeal.

7   About an hour-and-a-half after those telephone calls were made, the city of London police, who were quite unaware of the previous events about which we have spoken, pursued a Ford Escort car with three occupants on account of some alleged infringement of traffic rules. During the chase a Webley handgun was thrown out of the car. The car was stopped. The appellant was driving it and Kitson and Brown were present as passengers. The deceased's mobile phone was in the car.

8   The discarded Webley bore traces of the deceased's blood and Kitson's fingerprints. The clothing of all three men bore significant traces of the deceased's blood, including airborne blood on their trousers. There was a petrol can in the boot. The three occupants of the car were arrested and interviewed and gave accounts of their movements that night. Chin was not with them in the car. He voluntarily gave himself up into police custody some weeks later. He too was interviewed.

9   The prosecution evidence, the details of which do not need to be recounted for the purposes of this appeal, comprised forensic evidence, evidence of the use of several mobile telephones found in the car, including the deceased's telephone,

and the interview evidence of the various defendants which the prosecution said contained a large number of lies.

10   At the trial the defendants ran different defences, some of which entailed blaming each other: in effect these were cut-throat defences. The details of these defences again do not matter for present purposes.

11   A trial took place before Judge Goddard Q.C. The evidence of Mrs Lalita Hamilton, the deceased's widow, was not challenged significantly and was read to the jury. Mrs Hamilton attended much of the trial, sitting not in the public gallery but in the well of the court. She was present when each of the defendants gave evidence. Soon after this appellant began to give his evidence (he was the fourth on the indictment and last to go into the witness box) she got up, went out of court and sought out the officer in the case. She told him that when the appellant had begun to speak she believed that she recognised his voice as the man who had demanded money from her on the telephone on the night of her husband's disappearance. She said that she was not sure of this. It was difficult to be sure because when the appellant spoke in court he did so in calm and quiet tones, whereas the voice on the telephone had been threatening and abusive. The telephone call had taken place some nine or ten months earlier. This was the first opportunity which she had had to hear the appellant's voice. Nonetheless, despite those difficulties, she believed that the voice on the telephone may have been that of the appellant. The police officer took a statement of her new evidence and it was shown to counsel.

12   Counsel for the Crown indicated that the Crown would not seek to adduce the evidence. Counsel for Chin and Kitson applied for it to be adduced; in particular Chin had said in evidence that he had been at the cemetery with the other three in the early hours of the morning but that he had not participated in anything that took place there. He had heard the appellant suggest that Mrs Hamilton should be telephoned. Plainly Mrs Hamilton's evidence was potentially helpful to him. It was also potentially helpful to Kitson. Counsel for Brown opposed the application, as did counsel for the Crown, contending that the evidence did not pass the threshold of admissibility. For obvious reasons, counsel for the appellant also opposed the application to admit.

13   The judge decided not to admit the evidence. She said this:

> "It is relevant to an issue ie who spoke on the telephone and as between defendants that is the only issue I have to consider.
> If the evidence has some weight it is for the jury to consider.
> However Mrs Hamilton said she could not be absolute that it was the voice. Robinson spoke softly and clearly in court, the man on the telephone was abusive and had a heavy Jamaican accent. Further in February she took the call when she had awoken from sleep.
> In my judgment given the circumstances, Mrs Hamilton's own reservations, the difficulties of voice recognition, the evidence has no or such little weight that the jury cannot be asked to consider it."

14   Accordingly, for the purposes of that trial there was an end to the matter. However, shortly before counsel was due to address the jury a problem arose within

the jury and the jury had to be discharged. The problem was not in any way related to Mrs Hamilton's new evidence.

15   The second trial took place some months later before Judge Forrester. Again the Crown said that they would not seek to adduce Mrs Hamilton's fresh evidence. Counsel for Chin and Kitson applied for it to be admitted. They wished to cross-examine her. Counsel for Brown, counsel for the Crown and of course counsel for the appellant opposed the application. Judge Forrester took a different view from that taken by Judge Goddard Q.C. He said, after summarising the submissions of counsel:

> "No one suggests that the witness is other than an honest person carefully doing her best, as her statement of 9th December suggests. It is of course well known to this court that even honest witnesses can make mistakes on the question of identification, whether it be voice identification or the more familiar type of identification on the face of an individual. There is a body of learning that voice recognition may be more difficult than any other form of identification. I am referred to the relevant passage in Archbold at paragraph 14–52, page 1333 of the current edition.
>
> Had the prosecution sought to introduce this material I would have refused the application, but that is not the position here. The position here is that counsel for two defendants apply to be at liberty to cross-examine a prosecution witness on the basis that she supports or may support their defences, and therefore to deploy this material in the defence of their clients. That is the basis for the application, and it is important to bear that in mind. It is in these circumstances that the matter is not one for my discretion.
>
> What I must do is to ask myself two questions. Firstly, is the material relevant? There is no difficulty about that: the material is relevant—indeed important, submits Mr Feinberg [who appeared for Chin]—but whether important or not, undoubtedly, it has relevance in the case. The second question is this: does the material possess some weight so that it can properly be described as probative? At the end of the day that is the important question here. In my judgment, on the arguments put before me, I have decided that the material carries sufficient weight for the jury to consider, and therefore she [Mrs Hamilton] may be cross-examined by defence counsel and, if appropriate, reexamined by Crown counsel on this point."

16   The judge then said that once admitted, depending on how the evidence was given in practice, he might have to give a direction to the jury about the dangers of relying on the evidence. In the event the evidence was given orally in the same terms as Mrs Hamilton's statement. There was no attempt at exaggeration. At the close of cross-examination she had reiterated her view that she could not be sure that the voice on the telephone had been that of the appellant but she believed that it may have been. The judge gave an impeccable direction about the dangers of reliance on voice identification evidence, about which no complaint is or could be made.

17   In this appeal the full court granted leave to argue that the judge had been wrong to admit the evidence. Given that two very experienced judges at the Cen-

tral Criminal Court had reached different conclusions, we can see immediately that the point was arguable. It is a short point because there is a large measure of agreement. It is agreed between counsel that the judge had been right to say that he had only two questions to answer: was the evidence relevant? If it was, did it pass the threshold of admissibility? If it did, he had no discretion to exclude it.

18   Section 78 of the Police and Criminal Evidence Act 1984, which gives the judge a discretion to exclude evidence on the ground that its prejudicial effect outweighs its probative value did not apply. That section applies only where the Crown seeks to adduce evidence. If the application is made by a defendant, the evidence must be admitted if it satisfies the basic test of admissibility.

19   What is that basic test? It does not appear that a test was formulated for either Judge Goddard Q.C. or Judge Forrester. Mr Suckling Q.C., who appears for the Crown before us, suggested a test at our invitation. Mr Grunwald Q.C., who appears for the appellant, did not seek to object to it. We found it helpful. It is this:

> "Is the evidence such that no reasonable jury, properly directed as to its defects, could place any weight upon it?"

Put the other way round: if the evidence is such that a jury properly warned could place some weight on it, it should be admitted. It is our view that this basic threshold of admissibility is a low threshold.

20   Mr Grunwald reminded us of all the problems associated with this evidence. In particular he reminded us that there had been a nine-month delay between the telephone calls to the time at which the voice identification had taken place. There were differences in tone and content and manner of speaking between the telephone call and the appellant's evidence in court—the one being calm and quiet and rational, the other loud, abusive and threatening. Mrs Hamilton herself had pointed out those differences. Mr Grunwald also reminded us that the witness, Mrs Hamilton, had not heard the voice before these calls. She was not able to recognise the appellant's voice on that occasion; she had never spoken to him. We were told by Mr Grunwald that Mrs Hamilton had had a very brief opportunity at the magistrates' court to hear this appellant speak, but it appears that he spoke only to identify himself. The first occasion on which she heard him speak any sentences was during his evidence at the first trial. Mr Grunwald reminded us that the calls had lasted only a short time and had taken place in circumstances that were not conducive to good recognition: they were made late at night; Mrs Hamilton had only just been awakened from sleep by the sound of the telephone, and the experience was shocking and frightening for her. The calls, Mr Grunwald reminded us, had been made over a telephone with its inevitable distortions. Finally, Mrs Hamilton had accepted in her statement that she could not be certain of her identification. She had said that she believed that it may be the appellant's voice. Mr Grunwald submitted that these problems, coupled with the inherent difficulties associated with voice recognition, were such that no jury could place any weight upon this evidence, even when properly directed as to the dangers.

21   We see the force of his observations about the problems associated with voice recognition evidence and the other associated difficulties in this particular case. However, it seems to us that these problems are no different in their general nature from the problems frequently encountered with visual identification. In fleeting glimpse cases where conditions are poor it is commonplace for the judge to have to give a detailed warning about the dangers of reliance on the evidence, yet those problems are not usually perceived to be such as should result in the evidence being regarded as inadmissible, as having no weight at all. They might well be excluded under s.78, but that is a different matter, as we have said.

22   Mr Suckling reminded us that it was accepted that Mrs Hamilton was an honest and sensible witness, who had not sought in any way to exaggerate her degree of certainty. The fact was that she had sat and listened to the evidence of the other three defendants without stirring herself in any way. Within a few minutes of this appellant starting to speak she had left the court to find the officer in the case to tell him that she believed that she recognised the voice. It seems to us that her reaction to the commencement of this appellant's evidence is a matter of some significance.

23   In the end, as Judge Forrester said, this was a matter of judgment for him, as it had been for Judge Goddard Q.C. The test formulated helpfully by Mr Suckling, although objective in its terminology, does leave room for a difference of view. We have considered the matter very carefully and have each come to the same conclusion: that in our view Judge Forrester was right to say that the evidence was admissible. As was agreed, the evidence was plainly relevant. In our view it also passed the threshold of admissibility. It was certainly not frivolous: far from it. Everyone has accepted, including Mr Grunwald before this Court, that this was a patently honest witness doing her best to assist the court in difficult circumstances.

24   It seems to us that, although this evidence could not of itself have proved that the appellant was the maker of the call, it had some probative value when taken in conjunction with other evidence in the case; and that was so despite the fact that Mrs Hamilton was not herself sure of the identification. She herself had acknowledged the difficulties of the situation she had been in, receiving a call in the middle of the night in frightening circumstances. She acknowledged and recognised the difference in tone and content between the voice on the phone and the voice heard in court. Yet, despite her recognition of those difficulties, she still felt sufficiently struck by the recognition to go immediately to find the officer in the case. For those reasons, we have come to the conclusion that the judge was right to admit the evidence. That being so, and this being the only ground of the appeal, the appeal must fail.

25   We add that as an alternative submission Mr Suckling contended that even if the evidence had been wrongly admitted the conviction was still safe as the evidence against this appellant was overwhelming. Mr Grunwald submitted to the contrary. He contended that it was not.

26　　　It is of course not necessary for us in the circumstances to reach any conclusion on this issue. We say only that it appears to us that the case against this appellant was very strong. For those reasons the appeal is dismissed.

Appeal against conviction dismissed.

R. v ROGERS (PHILIP)

Court of Appeal (Lord Chief Justice (Lord Phillips of Worth
Matravers), Mrs Justice Rafferty and Mr Justice Mackay):
October 26; November 10, 2005

[2005] EWCA Crim 2863; [2006] 1 Cr.App.R. 14

⟨LT⟩ Offensive behaviour; Racially aggravated offences

H1 PUBLIC ORDER
Racially aggravated offence
*Appellant acting aggressively and calling Spanish women "bloody
foreigners"—Appellant charged with racially aggravated abusive or insulting
words or behaviour—Whether "foreigners" describing racial group—Whether
words used capable of demonstrating hostility towards victims based on membership of racial group—Crime and Disorder Act 1998 (c.37), ss.28(4), 31(1)(a)*

H2   The appellant, who was 52 years old, was returning home after having a drink
when he encountered three young Spanish women, whom he heard speaking in a
foreign language or with a foreign accent. An altercation took place, in the course
of which he called the women "bloody foreigners" and told them to "go back to
your own country". He then pursued them to a kebab house in an aggressive manner. He was charged with using racially aggravated abusive or insulting words or
behaviour with the intent to cause fear or provoke violence, contrary to s.31(1)(a)
of the Crime and Disorder Act 1998. At the close of the prosecution case, the
appellant submitted that there was no case to answer under s.28[1] of the Act in
that the words used were not capable of demonstrating hostility based on membership of a racial group because "foreigners" did not constitute a racial group,
as defined in s.28(4) as a group defined by reference to race, colour, nationality or
ethnic or national origins. The judge rejected that submission. The appellant was
convicted and he appealed.

H3   **Held,** dismissing the appeal, that a racial group within the definition in s.28(4)
did not have to be distinguished by particular racial characteristics; that the definition in s.28(4) was sufficiently wide to embrace within a single racial group all
who were foreign; and that, accordingly, "foreigners" did constitute a racial
group as defined in s.28(4) and the judge had been right to allow the jury to determine whether the appellant had demonstrated hostility towards his victims
because they were foreigners (post, paras [19]–[20], [23], [25]).

H4   *Attorney General's Reference (No.4 of 2004)* [2005] EWCA Crim 889; [2005]
2 Cr.App.R. 26 (391); [2005] 1 W.L.R. 2810, CA applied.

---

[1]   Crime and Disorder Act 1998, s.28: see, post, para.[5].

H5   *Director of Public Prosecutions v M (A Minor)* [2004] EWHC 1453 (Admin);
[2004] 1 W.L.R. 2758, DC approved.

H6   Dicta in *R. v White (Anthony)* [2001] EWCA Crim 216; [2001] 1 W.L.R. 1352,
paras [17], [19], CA not followed.

H7   *Per curiam.* The very width of the meaning of racial group for the purposes of
s.28(4) gives rise to a danger that charges of aggravated offences may be brought
where vulgar abuse has included racial epithets that did not, when all the relevant
circumstances are considered, indicate hostility to the race in question. Section
28 is designed to address racist behaviour and prosecutors should not bring
charges based on its provisions unless satisfied that the facts truly suggest that
the offence charged was aggravated by racism (post, para.[24]).

H8   (For the Crime and Disorder Act 1998, s.31, see *Archbold* 2005 paras 29–38a
and 29–38b and for s.28 see *ibid.* para.5–84)

Appeal against conviction

H9   On February 23, 2005 in the Crown Court at Winchester (Judge Boney Q.C.)
the appellant, Philip Rogers, was convicted of using racially aggravated abusive
or insulting words or behaviour with intent to cause fear or provoke violence,
contrary to s.31(1)(a) of the Crime and Disorder Act 1998. He was sentenced
to a community punishment order for 80 hours.

H10   The facts and grounds of appeal appear in the judgment of the court.

H11   *Mark Florida-James* (assigned by the Registrar of Criminal Appeals) for the
appellant.
Richard Wilcox (instructed by the Crown Prosecution Service, Winchester) for
the Crown.

Cur. adv. vult.

November 10   Lord Phillips of Worth Matravers C.J. handed down the judgment of the Court

1   On February 23, 2005 at the Crown Court at Winchester the appellant was convicted of using racially aggravated abusive or insulting words or behaviour with
the intent to cause fear or provoke violence, contrary to s.31(1)(a) of the Crime
and Disorder Act 1998. He was sentenced to a community punishment order for
80 hours. Against that conviction he now appeals with the permission of the full
court. The appeal raises a point of law on the construction of s.31(1)(a).

2   The jury were not required to return a verdict on an alternative count of using
abusive words and behaviour with the intent to cause fear or provoke violence
contrary to s.4 of the Public Order Act 1986.

3   The result of this appeal cannot affect the appellant's sentence, for he was
given an identical sentence, to run concurrently, in relation to two other counts
that arose out of the same incident.

The facts

4   For the purpose of this appeal the facts can be very shortly stated. The appellant, a man aged 52, is incapacitated as a result of arthritis. On February 23, 2005 he was on his way home along the pavement on a motorised "mobility scooter". He had been drinking. He encountered three young Spanish women. An altercation took place in the course of which he abused the three women by calling them "bloody foreigners" and telling them to "go back to your own country". He then pursued them to a kebab house in an aggressive manner.

The issue

5   The following are the relevant provisions of the Crime and Disorder Act 1998:

"28.— (1) An offence is racially aggravated for the purposes of sections 29 to 32 below if—
　　　(a) at the time of committing the offence, or immediately before or after doing so, the offender demonstrates towards the victim of the offence hostility based on the victim's membership (or presumed membership) of a racial group; or
　　　(b) the offence is motivated (wholly or partly) by hostility towards members of a racial group based on their membership of that group.
　(2) In subsection (1)(a) above—
　　　'membership', in relation to a racial group, includes association with members of that group;
　　　'presumed' means presumed by the offender.
　(3) It is immaterial for the purposes of paragraph (a) or (b) of subsection (1) above whether or not the offender's hostility is also based, to any extent, on—
　　　(a) the fact or presumption that any person or group of persons belongs to any religious group; or
　　　(b) any other factor not mentioned in that paragraph.
　(4) In this section 'racial group' means a group of persons defined by reference to race, colour, nationality (including citizenship) or ethnic or national origins.
31.— (1) A person is guilty of an offence under this section if he commits—
　　　(a) an offence under section 4 of the Public Order Act 1986 (fear or provocation of violence);
　　　(b) an offence under section 4A of that Act (intentional harassment, alarm or distress); or
　　　(c) an offence under section 5 of that Act (harassment, alarm or distress),
　　　which is racially aggravated for the purposes of this section."

6   The prosecution's case was that by calling the Spanish women "bloody foreigners" and telling them to "go back to your own country" the appellant

demonstrated towards the women hostility based on their membership of a racial group. At the end of the prosecution evidence counsel for the appellant submitted that there was no case to answer under s.28 in that the words used by the appellant were not in law capable of demonstrating hostility based on membership of a racial group, because foreigners did not constitute a racial group as defined by s.28(4). The judge rejected the submission of no case to answer, holding that the issue raised had been resolved in favour of the prosecution by the decision of the Divisional Court in *DPP v M (A Minor)* [2004] EWHC 1453 (Admin); [2004] 1 W.L.R. 2758. We shall turn without more ado to examine that decision.

7   The defendant in that case had been involved in a violent altercation with a Turkish chef in a kebab house. In the course of argument he used the phrase "bloody foreigners". He was charged with racially aggravated criminal damage under the 1998 Act. The magistrates held that the words "bloody foreigners" were not capable of being construed as expressing hostility based on the victim's membership (or presumed membership) of a racial group. In a case stated they posed the question of whether this was correct.

8   The Divisional Court, consisting of Auld L.J. and Richards J. held that they were not. Auld L.J. gave the only judgment, with which Richards J. agreed. Auld L.J. concluded, in [37], that:

> "as a matter of construction in the context of the case the word 'foreigners' was capable of describing a 'racial group' defined by reference to national-ity and/or national origins within the meaning of section 28(4) of the 1998 Act."

9   The essence of Auld L.J.'s reasoning appears in the following passages of his judgment:

> "30. In my view, looking at the operation of section 28, as we must in the context of racial hostility directed by someone in this country to someone whose, or whose family's, origin is not in this country, it is inescapable that the word 'foreigner' may, depending on the context, qualify as demon-stration within section 28(1)(a) of a 'group of persons defined <u>by reference</u> to race . . . or national origins' within the definition in section 28(4), a min-ority, albeit now a substantial minority, in national terms in the population of this country.
>
> 31. It is perhaps of significance that section 28(4) reads 'by reference to race', et cetera, not 'by their race', or even 'by reference to their race'. I agree with Mr Parker that the Director can satisfy the definition in that pro-vision in a non-inclusive, as well as inclusive, sense according to the circumstances of the words used, or the act done, and the context of the case. In addition, as *White* and *McFarlane* show, the size of the group is, in any event, immaterial to the definition since hostility can be expressed by the use of pejorative words, such as that here or those in *White* and *McFarlane*, towards groups large or small based on colour or origin, and can be equally hurtful regardless of the number of people with whom the victim shares the non-inclusiveness of being a foreigner.

32. The non-inclusion in 'home' racial groups as a species of 'racial group' in the *Queen Mary College* case—whilst the product there of express statutory provision to that effect, absent here—in my view, supports the logic of giving a broad interpretation to the expression 'racial group' in this context. 33. To that extent the magistrates were correct, as I read the opening words of their opinion, to accept in principle, or as they put it 'as a matter of semantics', that the words 'bloody foreigners' could, depending on the context, describe a person within a 'racial group' as defined in section 28(4)."

10   The reasoning of the Divisional Court in *DPP v M (A Minor)* was relied upon by this court, again presided over by Auld L.J., in *Attorney General's Reference (No.4 of 2004)* [2005] EWCA Crim 889; [2005] 2 Cr.app.R. 26 (p.391); [2005] 1 W.L.R. 2810. We shall refer to this case as *Reference No.4*. The case involved an assault by the defendant on an Indian doctor, in circumstances where she had referred to him as "an immigrant doctor". The issue was whether this phrase was capable in law of demonstrating hostility based upon the doctor's membership of a "racial group" as defined by s.28 of the 1998 Act. The trial judge had directed the jury that it was not. The Court of Appeal held that it was.

11   We can, we think, summarise the reasoning of the trial judge as follows: Referring to a person as an immigrant infers no more than that the person belongs to that very large mass of people who are not British in origin. That mass of people cannot properly be described as a "racial group". It follows that referring to a person as an "immigrant" cannot indicate hostility based on that person's membership of a racial group.

12   Counsel for the Attorney General's submissions were summarised by Auld L.J. as follows:

> "12. Mr Jafferjee submitted that, in the light of these pointers and authorities, the Attorney General's broad approach to construction of the term 'racial group' in the 1998 Act supports the proposition that the use of the term 'immigrant' is, not only caught by the term 'national origins', but also by the word 'nationality'. He added that in the case of Dr. Newal—who appears to have had a pronounced Indian accent when speaking English and whose physical appearance in terms of colour was obviously not white—it would have been open to a jury to conclude as a matter of evidence that the reference to him as an 'immigrant doctor' would have offended each of the five statutory criteria.
> 13. Mr Jafferjee usefully concluded his submissions by commenting that if the Judge's ruling were to be upheld, it would have the absurd result that the law would permit a person to discriminate another even though demonstrating hostility towards that other based on the fact, or presumed fact, that he was an immigrant, but not if based on his membership or presumed membership of a group defined more precisely by reference to one or more of the statutory criteria."

13   These submissions illustrate the fact that two separate issues can arise in relation to s.28 of the 1998 Act. For an offence to be aggravated under that section

the defendant must first form the view that the victim is a member of a racial group, within the definition in s.28(4). He must then say something which demonstrates hostility towards the victim based on membership of that group. The words used may or may not expressly identify the racial group to which the defendant believes the victim belongs.

14   In *Reference No.4* it was open to the jury to conclude that the defendant had identified her victim as falling into the following racial groups from his appearance and from his accent. Indian, brown skinned. Each of those was unquestionably a racial group within the definition in s.28(4). The word that she used to display hostility was "immigrant". Whether or not "immigrants" constituted a further racial group within the definition in s.28(4), it was open to the jury to find that by using the word immigrant, the defendant was demonstrating hostility to the victim because he was Indian and brown skinned.

15   As we understand it, this was one of the points being made by Mr Jafferjee. He also made, however, a quite different point. In his submission immigrants constituted a racial group within the definition in s.28(4). If the words used by the defendant demonstrated hostility to the victim simply and solely because he was an immigrant, that would suffice to render the offence an aggravated offence.

16   Auld L.J. focussed precisely on the second point when he referred to authorities bearing directly on:

> "20. . . . the central question posed by this case, namely whether the use of a work like 'immigrant' as excluding all but 'British subjects resident in this country' renders all those excluded, for the purpose of section 28 of the 1998 Act a 'racial group'."

17   Auld L.J. first cited *R. v White (Anthony)* [2001] EWCA Crim 216; [2001] 1 W.L.R. 1352, a case to which we shall revert. He then cited extensively from [30], [31] and [33] of his judgment in *DPP v M (A Minor)*. He then set out the conclusions of the court as follows:

> "24. We adopt and apply that reasoning to the broad non-inclusive term 'immigrant doctor' in the context in which it gave rise to this reference. If anything, the non-inclusive term 'foreigner' denotes membership of an even broader racial group than does the term 'immigrant' as applied to an alleged victim in this country of a racially aggravated offence. As Lord Lester observed, the judge erred in determining the matter simply as a matter of construction of the word 'immigrant' as 'non-British', divorced of the factual context in which it was used. Whether Mrs D's use of the term 'immigrant doctor' towards Dr N was only an allegation of non-Britishness or was part of a demonstration by her of hostility to him within the terms of section 28(1)(a) of the 1998 Act because she perceived his non-Britishness to derive from his race and/or colour and/or his nationality and/or his ethnic or national origins involved a question of fact for determination by the jury on the facts of the case. In our view, the judge erred in ruling as he did that someone who is an immigrant to this country and, therefore, non-British

cannot as such be a member of a racial group within section 28(4) of the 1998 Act. In our opinion, he should have left the matter with the jury as one capable of having been racially aggravated offence."

18   We have found this passage a little confusing. On one reading it suggests that the critical question for the jury was whether the use of the word "immigrant" demonstrated hostility not simply to the large group of those who are not British, but to one or more of the racial groups to which the victim belonged, defined by his race, colour, nationality and ethnic origin. On balance, however, when *Reference No.4* is read as a whole, we believe that this court held that "immigrants" constituted a racial group within the definition in s.28(4). The same was true of foreigners.

19   This point is of critical importance on the facts of the present case. Those facts suggest that the only relevant characteristic that the appellant identified in relation to the victims of his assault was that they were foreign. There is no evidence that there was anything in their appearance that indicated a relevant racial characteristic. The appellant simply heard them speaking a foreign language, or with a foreign accent. If "foreigners" constitute a racial group within the definition in s.28(4), there was plainly a case to go to the jury that he had demonstrated hostility towards his victims because they were foreigners. The judge concluded that he was bound by *DPP v M (A Minor)* to hold that foreigners constituted a racial group and to let the case go to the jury on that basis.

20   We consider that the judge correctly applied *DPP v M (A Minor)*. That decision does not bind this court, but *Reference No.4* does, and for that reason alone this appeal must fail. Had the matter been in doubt, we would have reached the same conclusion as that stated by Auld L.J. Hostility demonstrated to foreigners because they are foreign can be just as objectionable as hostility based on a more limited racial characteristic. All who are black form a racial group, defined by reference to colour, within s.28(4), as do all who are white. This demonstrates the width of the concept of racial group in this context. It is no great extension of the concept to embrace within a single racial group all who are foreign.

21   Mark Florida-James, who appeared for the appellant, submitted that both *DPP v M (A Minor)* and *Attorney-General's Reference No.4* were in conflict with the reasoning of this court in *R. v White (Anthony)* [2001] EWCA Crim 216. The relevant issue in that case was whether calling a woman an "African bitch" was capable in law of demonstrating hostility towards the complainant, who came from Sierra Leone, as being a member of a racial group within the provisions of s.28(1)(a) of the 1998 Act. It was argued for the defence that "African" described disparate peoples that could not properly fall within the description of a racial group. The court rejected this submission. It held at [17]:

> ". . . In our judgment, the word African does describe a "racial group" defined by reference to race. In ordinary speech, the word African denotes a limited group of people regarded as of common stock and regarded as one of the major divisions of humankind having in common distinct physical features. It denotes a person characteristic of the blacks of Africa, to adopt a part of the definition in the dictionary."

22   The Court went on to distinguish "African" from "South American", observing at [19]:

> "Reference was made to South America in the course of argument and we mention it to make a distinction. Whereas the word African has a racial connotation, the expression South American, in England and Wales, probably does not. The range of physical characteristics in the populations of that continent, and the absence of prominence of any one group, is such that the use of the expression South American does not bring to mind particular racial characteristics. We would not expect there to be a common perception in England and Wales of a South American racial group."

23   It is plain that the court considered that a racial group within the definition in s.28(4) had to be distinguished by particular racial characteristics. This passage in the judgment of the court was *obiter*. We agree with Mr Florida-James that it is in conflict with the reasoning in *DPP v M (A Minor)* and *Reference No.4*. To that extent it should not be followed.

24   The very width of the meaning of racial group for the purposes of s.28(4) gives rise to a danger that charges of aggravated offences may be brought where vulgar abuse has included racial epithets that did not, when all the relevant circumstances are considered, indicate hostility to the race in question. Section 28 is designed to address racist behaviour and prosecutors should not bring charges based on its provisions unless satisfied that the facts truly suggest that the offence charged was aggravated by racism.

25   For the reasons that we have given, this appeal is dismissed.

Appeal against conviction dismissed

The Court of Appeal certified, under s.33(2) of the Criminal Appeal Act 1968, that a question of law of public importance was involved in its decision, namely: "Do those who are not of British origin constitute a racial group within s.28(4) of the Crime and Disorder Act 1998?"

Leave to appeal to the House of Lords refused.

R. v DHILLON

COURT OF APPEAL (Lord Justice Longmore, Mr Justice David Steel
and Judge Brodrick): November 7; November 23, 2005

[2005] EWCA Crim 2996; [2006] 1 Cr.App.R. 15

LT Custody; Escaping; Intention; Knowledge; Police officers; Summing up

H1   ESCAPE FROM LAWFUL CUSTODY
Elements of Offence
*Judge's direction to the jury—Whether direction articulated elements—
Whether sufficiently coherent—Significance of passage of time and difficult fac-
tual issues in summary for jury—Importance of care in making directions as to
law*

H2   The appellant was arrested in September 1998 as an illegal immigrant.
Because he had a knee injury he was examined by a doctor at the police station
and then taken to a hospital for an X-ray to be taken when he and his escorting
police somehow lost contact with each other. The appellant was charged with
escape contrary to law about six years later. The evidence from the police was
that another policeman had been assigned to take over custody from the one
who had escorted the appellant to the hospital. Accordingly, on the police
account, the second officer joined the first at the hospital waiting room. This
second officer said in evidence that the first officer had pointed out the appellant
using his name and that the appellant had responded to this. It was said that the
first officer then left. The appellant then went in for his X-ray. The second officer
said that he never regained contact with him after that despite looking for him.
However the appellant said that he had seen the first officer leave before he
went in for his X-ray but that he had not seen the second officer arrive and he
had found no police officers waiting for him when he came away from being
X-rayed so he had gone back home. At the trial the judge's direction to the
jury in relation to escape was lengthy, broken into three parts by other matters
and it intermingled questions of legal definition with discussion of both the present facts and hypothetical situations. The appellant was convicted of escape
contrary to law (but not of a number of other offences upon which the jury was
unable to return verdicts). He appealed against conviction.

H3   **Held,** allowing the appeal, that there were four elements which had to be
proved in the conviction of a person for the common law offence of escape:
that the defendant was in custody; that he knew this (or at least was reckless as
to whether he was or not); that the custody was lawful and that the defendant
intentionally escaped from that lawful custody. Where, in an escape trial, there
were factual issues as to the continuity of custody and as to whether the defendant

had been aware of the constraint upon him, it was important to identify these issues by reference to the definition of the offence. Where a case arose from events six years earlier and entailed issues of some difficulty against an unusual factual background a careful direction of law was required with a careful identification of the relevant issues; The judge's summing-up had not met these requirements and, accordingly the conviction was unsafe and would be quashed (post, paras 21, 24, 25 and 29).

H4 *Per curiam* A discussion prior to summing up about the appropiate directions of law would have ensured a focus on the specific issues which arose on the facts.

H5 (For escape at common law, see *Archbold* 2006, para. 28–191 and following.)

Appeal against conviction

H6 On December 14, 2004 in the Crown Court at Isleworth (Judge McDowall) the appellant, Pritpal Sineh Dhillon, was convicted of escape contrary to common law. The jury was unable to reach a verdict on other counts charging him with offences of dangerous driving, assault occasioning actual bodily harm and criminal damage. On December 16, 2004 he was sentenced to eight months' imprisonment. The prosecution offered no evidence with respect to the other counts and formal verdicts of not guilty were entered.

H7 The facts and grounds of appeal appear in the judgment of the court.

H8 *Piers Mostyn* (assigned by the Registrar of Criminal Appeals) for the appellant. *Peter Herrity* (instructed by the Crown Prosecution Service) for the Crown.

Cur. adv. vult.

November 23   David Steel J.: handed down the judgment of the court.

1   On December 14, 2004 at the Crown Court at Isleworth the appellant was convicted before Judge McDowall and a jury of escape contrary to common law. The jury was unable to reach a verdict with regard to other counts charging him with the offences of dangerous driving, assault occasioning actual bodily harm and criminal damage.

2   On December 16, 2004 he was sentenced to eight months' imprisonment. With respect to the other counts, the prosecution offered no evidence and formal verdicts of not guilty were entered.

3   He appeals against that conviction by leave of the single judge.

4   The background is as follows. At 07.49 on September 30, 1998, police officers arrested the appellant as an illegal immigrant. He was thereupon transported to a police station where, following examination by a doctor, he was taken by a police officer to Hillingdon Hospital in order for a suspected knee injury to be X-rayed.

5   It was the prosecution case that, after receiving treatment, the appellant escaped from police custody by leaving the hospital. It was the defence case that the appellant, having received his treatment and seeing no police officers,

simply left the hospital and went home unaware that this would be treated as an escape.

6   The evidence was in very short compass. PC Mitchell said that at 13.00 he was told to go to Hillingdon Hospital to take over the custody of the appellant from another officer. (This latter officer was not called to give evidence and indeed PC Mitchell could not remember his name). When he arrived at the A & E waiting area, he said that the appellant was pointed out to him by his colleague. His colleague was said to have observed "that is Dhillon" and the person concerned appeared to respond to his name.

7   PC Mitchell did not stay with the appellant when the latter went in to be seen by the triage nurses and then X-rayed. He had expected to see the appellant re-emerge into the waiting room following treatment. However, he lost contact with him and, after conducting a search which revealed an alternative exit, reported that the appellant was missing.

8   In his police interview the appellant gave predominantly no comment responses to the questions that were put. However, he expressly denied escaping from police guard. In his oral evidence he said that he had not been aware that he had been under police guard at the hospital. After he had been X-rayed he could see no police officers waiting for him. He therefore went over to where he knew a police officer had been but again could not find anyone and so he left the hospital.

9   The focus of this appeal, reflecting the leave granted by the single judge, was the question whether the summing up adequately directed the jury as to the ingredients of the offence of escape on the unusual facts.

10   It is convenient to begin consideration of the substance of this appeal by seeking to identify the ingredients of the offence of escape at common law which is a relatively unusual offence. Indeed the sections devoted to the offence in the standard text books perhaps lack the degree of particularity needed to assist a trial judge when embarking on such a task. It is at least clear that it is an indictable offence at common law for a prisoner to escape without the use of force from lawful custody: see *Archbold* (2005) para. 28–191. The following authorities are of some further assistance.

11   First *R. v Timmis* [1976] Crim. L.R. 129. The defendant had been stopped as a result of erratic driving and breathalysed. The test proving positive, the defendant was told that he would be taken in custody to a police station and he was placed in a police car. He was then left alone for some considerable time whereafter he got out of the car and walked into a public house on the opposite side of the road where he remained for about an hour.

12   At some stage the police followed him but could not find him, although it was not suggested he was actively seeking to conceal himself. The defendant in due course gave himself up at the police station and he was charged with escape. A motion to dismiss the ensuing indictment was refused. The note of the court's finding in this regard reads:

"The general principle was that all persons were bound to submit themselves to the process of the law once lawfully arrested. . . . Hence it was
possible that where a defendant deliberately and with the intention of evad-
ing the criminal process, breached his custody, the offence of escape could
be committed."

13   In this regard the editor's comment is to the effect:

"There seems to be no suggestion that it is an ingredient of the offence that
the accused should intend to remain at large permanently nor that he should
escape with any particular object in view. In these respects, the direction (in
the subsequent trial) might have been too favourable to the accused."

14   In *Dillon v R.* (1982) 74 Cr.App.R. 274; [1982] A.C. 484, the custody officer
had unlocked two cells and the two prisoners occupying them had escaped. He
was charged with negligence in permitting them to escape out of custody. At
the trial there was no affirmative evidence that the prisoners had ever been lawfully detained. The Crown relied on the fact that the prisoners were in actual
detention at the lock-up as raising a presumption that their detention there was
lawful.

15   On appeal to the Judicial Committee of the Privy Council, the appeal was
allowed. In the judgment of Lord Fraser of Tullybelton there is the following
passage at pp.277 and 487.

"Their Lordships are of the opinion that it was essential for the Crown to
establish that the arrest and detention were lawful and that the omission
to do so was fatal to the conviction of the defendant. . . . The lawfulness
of the detention was a necessary precondition for the offence of permitting
escape, and it is well established that the courts will not presume the existence of facts which are central to an offence . . .
It has to be remembered that in every case where a police officer commits
the offence of negligently permitting a prisoner to escape from lawful custody, the prisoner himself commits an offence by escaping and it would be
contrary to the fundamental principles of law that the onus should be upon a
prisoner to rebut a presumption that he was being lawfully detained which
he could only do by the (notoriously difficult) process of proving a negative."

16   In *E v Director of Public Prosecutions* [2002] Crim. L.R. 737, a youth court
remanded the appellant to a local authority with a requirement that the local authority detain him in secure accommodation. No such accommodation was
however available. He was brought back to the Youth Court by a member of
the youth offending team but then absconded. He was later convicted of escape.
An appeal by way of case stated contended that there was no evidence upon
which the justices could properly find that he was in lawful custody. This issue
was held to be a question of fact:

> "Custody was an English word which should be given its ordinary and natural meaning namely 'confinement, imprisonment, durance' subject to any special meaning given to it by statute. For a person to be in custody his liberty had to be subject to such constraint or restriction that he could be said to be confined by another in the sense that the person's immediate freedom of movement was under the direct control of another . . ."

17   As regards the constraints involved on the facts, and the defendant's knowledge of them, the report goes on:

> "The order made by the justices in the present case whereby the appellant was remanded was custodial in nature not only did it remand him into the care of the local authority but it also required that he be placed in secure accommodation. Such a remand was so restrictive of the appellant's liberty that it could properly be said to be custodial in nature. The lawfulness of the regime which was thereafter applied to the appellant in the period of remand was established by that order. The appellant was at all times fully aware of that fact. . . ."

18   The references to "direct control" in the earlier passage quoted above was considered in *R. v Rumble* (2003) 167 J.P. 203, where a defendant had surrendered to his bail at a magistrates' court. There was no usher and no security staff. Following imposition of a custodial sentence, the defendant escaped through the public entrance. It was submitted on an appeal that the defendant was not under "direct" control of anyone. Buxton L.J. dealt with this submission peremptorily:

> "That argument only has to be stated for it to be seen that it be extremely odd if it were correct. Once a person surrenders at the court as Mr Rumble did and was obliged by law to do, it would be very surprising indeed if the court's right to control him, and his vulnerability to the offence of escaping, depended upon the precise nature of the physical constraints imposed upon him."

19   In *H v Director of Public Prosecutions* [2003] Crim. L.R. 560, the defendant was remanded to local authority accommodation by a youth court without any security requirement. Following the remand the defendant was released from custody into the care of a member of the youth offending team. The defendant was briefly left unsupervised but, having been told not to move, absconded. The defendant was charged with escape.

20   The report records as follows:

> "In order to determine whether an order made under s.23 of the 1969 Act was custodial in nature which was a question of fact it was necessary to concentrate on the moment when it was alleged that the defendant absconded. In the instant case the justices had remanded him to local authority accommodation under s.23 without attaching conditions and that sanction gave power to the local authority to detain the defendant. He had been told not to move by the youth offending team member so that it was unrealistic to suggest he

did not know he was being detained and that he was not entitled to simply run off. In those circumstances there was ample evidence upon which the justice could have concluded that his immediate freedom of movement was under the direct control of the youth team member and that by absconding he was escaping from her custody."

21   In our judgment, these authorities demonstrate that the prosecution must in a case concerning escape prove four things

    i) that the defendant was in custody;

    ii) that the defendant knew that he was in custody (or at least was reckless as to whether he was or not);

    iii) that the custody was lawful; and

    iv) that the defendant intentionally escaped from that lawful custody.

22   The judge's directions on the law relating to escape appear at, or at least amongst, pp.16–20 of the summing up. The passage starts at p.16 as follows:

"As far as the law on the fourth count, that is escape, this is a common law offence. In other words, there is no specific Act of Parliament setting out what is an escape and what is not. The first thing, obviously, that the prosecution have to prove so that you feel sure, is that on this particular day in time, Mr Dhillon was in a lawful custody at Hillingdon Hospital.

Well, again you have heard that, however it happened in terms of what had happened earlier in that day, then there is no doubt at all that eventually Mr Dhillon was arrested. Although there is some element of dispute as to what he was arrested or told he was being arrested for. There is no dispute, as I say, that he was arrested, that I say he was held at the garage until some other transport turned up, and that he was taken to the police station, presented to the officer called the Custody Sergeant, who has to make the decision on whether he is detained or not, and he was not given bail or otherwise told to report back to the police station on some other occasion.

What we do know happened is that a doctor, a force medical examiner, Dr Lauder, came along to have a look at the police who had been involved in this incident, and Mr Dhillon himself. And you remember that yesterday afternoon you had this statement read to you."

23   The judge then inserted a long section dealing with the earlier counts of assault as regards the nature of any injury sustained by two police officers. He then reverted to the escape count at p.18 as follows:

"The point is that the doctor, as far as Mr Dhillon was concerned, said that he should be taken to—he ought to be taken to hospital to get an X-ray so that you could rule out any question of a broken bone.

Now, escape is not something that has to be anything dramatic like, sort of, suddenly using martial arts skills or digging a tunnel to get away. If you are once in lawful custody, then a simple sort of walking out or taking advantage of some carelessness, would amount to escape. And you can imagine at any location, if at a police station, for example, again hypothetical one, you have been stuck in a cell but someone forgot to close the door properly, so that you can walk out of it, and then someone has carelessly left a door open so you get into the outside.

I mean, you are not having to do anything dramatic to get out, you are taking advantage of carelessness, but that would be escape from lawful custody. You know that you are not being invited to leave or told you can go, but to come back in a week's time for an interview. At that stage you are perfectly well aware that you are detained.

Being taken off to a hospital is, obviously, in a slightly different category, because you are not being kept in a cell. But the circumstances may, I do stress, may, lead you to say, that the police here are not obligingly saying: 'Well, we will give you a lift to hospital and when the medics have finished we will give you a run back to whatever address you want to go to.'

You may think that in the circumstances of this case, the object of the exercise is to have this gentleman taken to hospital to check that he had not got broken bones, and then to bring him back to the police station so that you can continue with enquiries, interviews or anything else that is going on. But, again, and that is a factual matter that you have to be looking at.

The defence that Mr Dhillon is raising—and again I do remind you that it is not for him to make a defence good, it is for you to rule it out—is to say that: 'Yes, I was taken to Hillingdon Hospital. I knew I was going to see the medics. I was not particularly aware of anyone keeping their eye on me. When the medics called me in I was sent for X-ray and then I was tired, I wanted to have a nap, and by the time that I say I was ready to go away, there was no policeman there. I even went to where policeman was, had been, that had brought me there, to see if there was anyone there, no one there.' So, you know, what else was there to do? Just to go away to the address of his choice. Again, that is a matter that factually is a matter for you as to whether that was capable of amounting to an escape, as opposed to, for example, insisting that someone called the police to say: 'You arrested me, you haven't bailed me. Will you please come and pick me up again?' But again, as you can appreciate, the question of an escape does not have to be anything like the 'Great Escape' with, sort of, tunnels or trying to, sort, of jump the wire or anything. Simply taking advantage of carelessness, can constitute an escape. It is again a matter for you.

So I hope that is making the law plain to what the issues are in this particular case and I am now going to turn to the evidence."

24   We are bound to say that this last sentence was unduly optimistic if only because of the discursive nature of the direction—partly concerned with the ingredients of the offence of escape but largely concerned with a discussion of relevant (and irrelevant) factual material. Indeed, it represents a good example of the outcome where there has been no discussion about the appropriate directions of law prior to summing up and accordingly no focus on the specific issues that arise on the facts.

25   The shape of the evidence made it clear that there were issues relating to the
continuity of the custody following the initial arrest (in particular the handover to PC Mitchell) and relating to the appellant's awareness or otherwise of
the constraints on him. It was accordingly particularly important to identify
these issues by reference to the make-up of the offence of escape. This, in our
judgment, the summing-up conspicuously failed to do.

26   It is true that, later in the summing up, the judge reverted to the escape count.
But in discussing the evidence, the issues continued to be analysed in a inordi-
nately diffuse manner:

> "Now, members of the jury, I have already dealt with, what I call the law
> about the escape charge. You have heard again the evidence about how it
> was—I have reminded you the evidence about how it was that Mr Dhillon
> was taken to hospital by the police. Again, it is one of the criticisms about the
> way the case is prepared, that there is no evidence from the officer who took
> him there to give, what you call, the continuity to show exactly how things
> were done. Again, though it is matter for you, but you may think that if one
> police officer is being given charge of a prisoner, because that is what Mr
> Dhillon seems to have been, that he is not going to, sort of shove off without
> making sure that someone is taking over properly, because otherwise he
> could be in trouble. And, likewise, an officer who is taking over is likely
> to want to be sure as to know who is the prisoner. Because you will remem-
> ber that the officer who attended, Mr Mitchell, had had no dealings with Mr
> Dhillon.
> So again it is what, as I say, you would expect to happen. But remember the
> evidence is about what did happen and from that you only have the account
> of Mr Mitchell, saying that, he turned up and with his colleague, he could not
> remember his name or anything, pointed out to him in, I think, it was both
> physically and by word, saying: 'That is Dhillon' and that the person respon-
> ded and his understanding was, his perception was responding to his name.
> One thing that you, for example, might think it is highly unlikely that in an A
> & E waiting room, which again, you may or may not have had the experi-
> ence of being there, liable to be quite busy, that when one policeman's is
> not going to arrive and say: 'Oh, he's in here' and then walk off, because
> that would not really do.
> It is a matter for you whether you think there is any question of the evidence
> being less than satisfactory. If you think there is any doubt at all about the
> man that Mr Mitchell had his eye on being the defendant, Mr Dhillon,
> then, of course, the evidence becomes to a degree vague. All you are left
> with then is Mr Dhillon's account about being at the hospital, finishing
> with the medics, no police there, so he went—whether it was his home or
> some other address, does not matter, I mean, just went on his own sweet way.
> But again, members of the jury, this is factual assessment about what the
> officer said happened. If you say that, well, that does make you sure that
> he got the right man to keep an eye on, you then get to the point about,
> how did this happen. And Mr Mitchell's account, effectively, was that he

thought that going in to the triage, which is the sorting out whether you need immediate surgery or you can go home or here are some aspirins or painkillers and that is it, the sorting out bit.

He was expecting Mr Dhillon to re-emerge into the waiting area, he did not and then discovered to his horror there were other ways out. He had been X-rayed and so on, and he made a bit of a search, could not find anything, and then in his own terms had to contact authority and come back to face the music. Not a case of losing a mass murderer, or anything like that, where you would be frantically on the radio to get all units looking out for someone of a particular description. And again, a matter for you, but in terms of what was involved here, you may be unsurprised that you were not dealing with a police officer actually handcuffed to the suspect and sitting with him all the time and going with him when he comes to see the medics and so forth. It is in the scale of things, was not that kind of a case.

But, as I say, that is what the evidence was on that point and the basic clash is between what the officer says, which, is effect, Mr Dhillon taking advantage of his lack of precautions to make good his escape. And again you can understand that Mr Dhillon, on his own account, had still got some unfinished business in this country, before he was going to leave again. Or whether it was someone who just did something, that he was not intending to do any escaping, he was effectively thinking: 'Well, no police here, I am sure they will find me again.' Matter for you as a matter of fact what you make of it."

27   We are left rather breathless by this passage and remain concerned that the jury were not in any sense adequately instructed on the issues. Little or no controversy arose from the initial arrest (and the consequent lawful custody) or indeed from the final "escape" (in the sense of eluding any continuing custody). What was in issue was the question of the continuity of the custody and the appellant's knowledge of it.

28   Although the judge made considerable play of what might be assumed to have happened on PC Mitchell's arrival, the jury's task in assessing continuity was potentially impeded by the absence of any evidence from the police officer who took the appellant to hospital and who was later said to have effected the handover to him (a handover which on any view was relatively informal). There was a live issue as to whether the appellant was still subject to sufficient direct control at the time of his escape two hours later. By the same token, there was an issue as to the appellant's knowledge since his case was that, whilst he saw the first officer leave, he never saw the second officer arrive and could find no substitute.

29   This was a case arising from events some six years earlier. It raised issues of some difficulty against an unusual factual background. A careful direction on the law and a consequential careful identification of the relevant issues was called for. Taking the summing up both in its constituent parts and as a whole does not, in

our judgment, match up to these requirements. We are unable to conclude that the conviction was safe and it must be quashed.

Appeal allowed.
Conviction quashed

R. v HATTON

Court of Appeal (Lord Chief Justice (Lord Phillips of Worth Matravers), Mrs Justice Rafferty and Mr Justice Mackay): October 25; 26, 2005

[2005] EWCA Crim 2951; [2006] 1 Cr.App.R. 16

LT Murder; Self defence; Voluntary intoxication

H1   HOMICIDE·
Self-defence
Mistaken belief induced by voluntary intoxication—Defendant charged with murder—Self-defence claimed on basis of drunken mistake—Whether entitled to rely on mistake induced by drunkenness

H2   The appellant, who had been drinking heavily, met the victim in a nightclub. During the evening the victim, who suffered from manic depression, had been behaving in a strange fashion, falsely representing that he had been an SAS officer, striking martial art poses and exhibiting a hatred of homosexuals. The appellant and the victim went to the appellant's flat. In the early hours of the morning, the victim was battered to death with a sledgehammer. A stick, which belonged to the appellant and which had been fashioned to resemble a samurai sword, was found under his body. The appellant was charged with murder. At trial, he contended that he had no recollection of the victim's death and he denied being responsible for it, although he also said that he had a vague recollection of being involved in an altercation, that he thought that the victim had hit him with the stick and that he must have believed that he was under attack. The defence wished to suggest to the jury that, if the appellant had killed the victim, he might have acted in self-defence, in that the victim might have attacked him with the stick, perhaps under the erroneous impression that he was a homosexual, and that in his drunken state the appellant might have believed, mistakenly, that the victim was an SAS soldier attacking him with a sword. The defence sought a ruling that the reasonableness of the appellant's reaction fell to be judged according to the facts as he believed them to be. The judge ruled that it was not open to the appellant to rely, when seeking to establish self-defence, on a mistake induced by drunkenness and, therefore, the defence could not properly invite the jury to have regard to the effect on the appellant's perception of events of the drink that he had consumed. The appellant was convicted. He appealed against conviction.

H3   **Held,** dismissing the appeal, that a defendant who raised the issue of self-defence to a charge of murder was not entitled to be judged upon the basis of what he mistakenly believed to be the situation when that mistaken belief was brought about by self-induced intoxication. The judge was therefore right not to direct the jury to consider whether the appellant's drunkenness might have led him to make a mistake as to the severity of any attack to which he might have been subjected by the victim. In any event, there was no basis upon which the judge could have directed the jury to consider that the appellant might have been labouring under such a drunken mistake since the scenario put forward by the defence was pure conjecture (post, paras 23–24, 26).

H4   *R. v O'Grady* (1987) 85 Cr.App.R. 315; [1987] Q.B. 995, CA followed.

H5   (For mistake of fact induced by drink, see *Archbold* 2006, para.17–18)

Appeal against conviction

H6   On November 11, 2003 in the Crown Court at Sheffield (Holland J.) the appellant, Jonathan Hatton, was convicted of murder and sentenced to life imprisonment.

H7   The facts and grounds of appeal appear in the judgment of the court.

H8   *Alan Newman Q.C.* and *Laura Brickman* (assigned by the Registrar of Criminal Appeals) for the appellant.
Peter Kelson Q.C. and *Ian Goldsack* (instructed by the Crown Prosecution Service, Sheffield) for the Crown.

Cur. adv. vult.

October 26   Lord Phillips of Worth Matravers C.J.: delivered the reserved judgment of the court.

1   On November 11, 2003, in the Crown Court at Sheffield, the appellant was convicted of murder and sentenced to life imprisonment. He appeals against conviction with the leave of the full court. The appeal raises an important point of law as to the effect of voluntary intoxication on the defence of self-defence.

The Facts

2   Mr Richard Pashley was battered to death with a sledgehammer in the appellant's flat in Sheffield in the early hours of Sunday June 22, 2003. In the course of the previous evening the appellant consumed a large quantity of alcohol. At his trial he contended that he had no recollection of Mr Pashley's death and denied being responsible for it. He now accepts that he killed Mr Pashley. For the purposes of this appeal the material facts can be summarised as follows.

3   Mr Pashley was 49 years of age. He suffered from manic depression and to control the disinhibition which he felt when in manic mood he had been prescribed lithium. He regularly failed to take this drug and had probably failed to do so on the evening before his death. On that evening he had consumed sufficient alcohol to raise the level in his blood to twice the legal limit for driving. Earlier in the evening he had been behaving in a strange fashion, falsely representing that he had been an officer in the SAS and striking martial art poses. He had exhibited a hatred of homosexuals.

4   On the evening of June 21, the appellant consumed on his evidence over 20 pints of beer. In the course of the evening he embraced another man in a manner which led the latter to think that he was making a homosexual advance. He is not, in fact, a homosexual.

5   The appellant and Mr Pashley did not know one another, but met in the early hours of June 22, in a nightclub in Sheffield. From there they drove together in the appellant's car to his flat. At 11.30 on the morning of the 22nd the appellant made an emergency call saying that he had been out all night and had returned to find an unknown man dead in his flat. Near Mr Pashley's body was a sledgehammer. He had sustained multiple injuries to the head, chest and abdomen from at least seven blows struck with an extreme degree of force with this weapon, four to the body and three to the head. A single blow to the head would have rendered Mr Pashley unconscious. Under his body was found a stick, some five feet in length, which belonged to the appellant and which he had fashioned to resemble a samurai sword. An overhead lamp shade had been dislodged, and this could have resulted from a blow from the stick. Although the appellant said that he had no recollection of Mr Pashley's death, he said to the jury, "I have a vague recollection of being involved in an altercation and a vague recollection of the stick involved. I think I was hit with that stick. I believe Mr Pashley hit me with it. I must have believed that I was under attack".

6   Mr Alan Newman Q.C. wished to found upon the facts that we have just summarised to suggest to the jury that, if the appellant killed Mr Pashley, he might have acted in self-defence. Mr Pashley might have attacked him with the stick, perhaps under the erroneous impression that the appellant was a homosexual, and that the appellant might have used the sledgehammer to defend himself. For this defence to succeed, however, the jury would have to be persuaded that the use made by the appellant of the sledgehammer was or might have been a reasonable reaction to the suggested assault by Mr Pashley. Mr Newman wished to argue that the appellant's drunken state might have led him to believe, mistakenly, that Mr Pashley was an SAS soldier attacking him with a sword. In the absence of the jury he sought a ruling from the judge that the reasonableness of the appellant's reaction fell to be judged according to the facts as he believed them to be, even if that belief was mistaken and the mistake was caused by the drink that he had consumed. He said to Holland J. that he intended to indicate to the jury:

> "unless your Lordship rules that I cannot do so, that in considering the situation they are entitled to take into account the fact that my client has drunk large quantities of alcohol which may have given him a wholly warped perception of reality."

7   After hearing argument from prosecuting counsel, Holland J. ruled that it was not open to the appellant to rely, when seeking to established self-defence, on a mistake induced by drunkenness. This was established by the decision of this court in *R. v O'Grady* (1987) 85 Cr.App.R. 315; [1987] 1 Q.B. 995. It followed that Mr Newman could not properly invite the jury to have regard to the effect of the appellant's perception of events of the drink that he had consumed.

8   When summing up on the specific intent that the jury would have to find if they were to convict of murder, the judge directed them that if they were sure that the appellant had killed Mr Pashley, but thought that he might have been so drunk that he was incapable of forming any intent, they should acquit him of murder but convict him of manslaughter. When he came to deal with the defence of self- defence he made no mention of the effect on the appellant's perception of events of the drink that he had consumed. He referred to the appellant's belief that Mr Pashley had hit him with the stick. In that context he asked them to consider two questions: (1) "Are you sure and satisfied that when Jonathan Hatton killed Richard Pashley he did not honestly believe that it was then necessary to use force to defend himself?" (2) "if . . . he may have believed that, taking the circumstances as he believed them to be, are you sure and satisfied that the amount of force that he then used was unreasonable?"

9   Before us Mr Newman has submitted that the judge's ruling and his subsequent direction to the jury were both defective. The judge should have ruled that, if the appellant might have mistaken the nature of the attack because of his drunkenness, he was entitled in law to defend himself in a manner that was reasonable having regard to his drunken perception of the danger to which he was exposed. The judge should have directed the jury accordingly.

10   Mr Newman accepts that this submission is inconsistent with the judgment of this court in *O'Grady*. He submits, however, that the observations in that case were wrong in principle and were obiter dicta, so that we need not and should not follow them. We turn at once to that case.

11   The appellant had killed a friend in a fight in circumstances where they were both very drunk. In giving the judgment of the court, Lord Lane C.J. gave the following summary of the material parts of the summing-up by the trial judge [pp.318 and 998]:

> "The judge gave an impeccable direction on the ingredients of murder and upon the way in which intoxication may affect proof of intent to kill or to do serious bodily harm. Likewise impeccable was his direction on provocation, including the correct observation that, when considering whether a reasonable man would have been caused to lose his self-control, questions of drink are irrelevant.
>
> Finally he gave the classic direction on self-defence. He made no mention of the possibility that the appellant might by reason of intoxication have been mistaken as to the threat posed to him by McCloskey's action. This was no doubt because no one had taken the point.
>
> Counsel for the prosecution towards the close of the judge's directions saw fit to invite the judge to remedy what he plainly regarded as this lacuna in the charge to the jury. Counsel for the appellant wisely held his peace. The judge then gave this further direction:
>
>> 'It might be a view that you might take —I know not—that this defendant thought he was under attack from the other man mistakenly and made a mistake in thinking that he was under attack because of the drink that was in him. If he made such a mistake in drink he would nevertheless

be entitled to defend himself even though he mistakenly believed that he
was under attack. He would be entitled in those circumstances to defend
himself. But if in taking defensive measures, then he went beyond what is
reasonable either because of his mind being affected by drink or for any
other reason, then the defence of self- defence would not avail because, as
I told you earlier on, you are entitled to defend yourself if it is necessary to
do so, but the defensive measures that you take must be reasonable ones
and not go beyond what is reasonable.'

. . . .''

12 The jury found the appellant not guilty of murder but guilty of manslaughter.
He appealed on the ground that the judge's direction in relation to self-defence
had been deficient, but for which he might have been found not guilty of any
offence. He contended that the judge erred in not directing the jury that when
deciding whether the defendant might have acted reasonably in self-defence,
they should judge what was reasonable in the light of any mistake as to the
severity of the attack that he was under that his drunkenness might have induced.

13 Lord Lane C.J. went on to quote the following observation made by McCullough J., the single judge, when giving leave to appeal [pp.319 and 999]:

> "Given that a man who *mistakenly* believes he is under attack is entitled to
> use reasonable force to defend himself, it would seem to follow that, if he *is*
> under attack and mistakenly believes the attack to be more serious than it is,
> he is entitled to use reasonable force to defend himself against an attack of
> the severity he believed it to have. If one allows a mistaken belief induced by
> drink to bring this principle into operation, an act of gross negligence
> (viewed objectively) may become lawful even though it results in the
> death of the innocent victim. The drunken man would be guilty of neither
> murder nor manslaughter."

Lord Lane then stated the conclusion of the court in the following passage:

> "How should the jury be invited to approach the problem? One starts with
> the decision of this Court in *Williams (Gladstone)* (1984) 78 Cr.App.R. 276,
> namely that where the defendant might have been labouring under a mistake
> as to the facts he must be judged according to that mistaken view, whether
> the mistake was reasonable or not. It is then for the jury to decide whether the
> defendant's reaction to the threat (real or imaginary) was a reasonable one.
> The Court was not in that case considering what the situation might be where
> the mistake was due to voluntary intoxication by alcohol or some other drug.
> We have come to the conclusion that where the jury are satisfied that the
> defendant was mistaken in his belief that any force or the force which he
> in fact used was necessary to defend himself and are further satisfied that
> the mistake was caused by voluntarily induced intoxication, the defence
> must fail. We donot consider that any distinction should be drawn on this
> aspect of the matter between offences involving what is called specific
> intent, such as murder, and the offences of so-called basic intent, such as

manslaughter. Quite apart from the problem of directing a jury in a case such as the present where manslaughter is an alternative verdict to murder, the question of mistake can and ought to be considered separately from the question of intent. A sober man who mistakenly believes he is in danger of immediate death at the hands of an attacker is entitled to be acquitted of both murder and manslaughter if his reaction in killing his supposed assailant was a reasonable one. What his intent may have been seems to us to be irrelevant to the problem of self-defence or no. Secondly, we respectfully adopt the reasoning of McCullough J. already set out.

This brings us to the question of public order. There are two competing interests. On the one hand the interest of the defendant who has only acted according to what he believed to be necessary to protect himself, and on the other hand that of the public in general and the victim in particular who, probably through no fault of his own, has been injured or perhaps killed because of the defendant's drunken mistake. Reason recoils from the conclusion that in such circumstances a defendant is entitled to leave the Court without a stain on his character."

14   After citation of passages from *Director of Public Prosecutions v Majewski* (1976) 62 Cr.App.R. 262; [1977] A.C. 443, which he considered supported the court's conclusion, Lord Lane summarised the result by observing that the relevant passage from the summing-up erred in favour of the appellant.

15   *O'Grady* was followed in *R. v O'Connor* [1991] Crim. L.R. 135, an appeal against conviction for murder. The appellant complained that the judge had failed to mention the effect of drink on the defence of self-defence. This court ruled that when a defendant because of self-induced intoxication formed the mistaken belief that it was necessary to use force to defend himself, a plea of self-defence failed. The court held that *O'Grady* was binding on this point, noting that it had been subject to academic criticism to which we shall refer. The appeal was, however, allowed and the conviction for murder replaced by a conviction for manslaughter on the ground that the judge failed to direct the jury that self-induced drunkenness could have the effect of preventing the defendant from forming the specific intent that is an element of the crime of murder.

16   In a commentary to *O'Grady*, after the report in the Criminal Law Review, Professor John Smith commented that the decision proceeded on the basis that self-defence was a complete defence to a charge of homicide which was unfounded. A defendant who relied on a reasonable reaction to a drunken mistake to establish a defence to murder could not rely on the drunken mistake as a defence to manslaughter: see the decision of the House of Lords in *Majewski*. Professor Smith commended the recommendation of the Criminal Law Revision Committee (Fourteenth Report, Cmnd.7844, para.277) that the evidence of voluntary intoxication adduced in relation to a defence should be treated in the same way as evidence of voluntary intoxication adduced to negative the mental element in a crime of specific intent.

17   Professor Smith commented that the decision in *O'Grady* was obiter because the appellant had been convicted only of manslaughter. Professor Smith returned

to this theme in a commentary in the Criminal Law Review in *O'Connor*. He argued that this court was wrong to regard *O'Grady* as binding authority because *O'Grady* was convicted only of manslaughter, so anything said about the law of murder on appeal must have been unnecessary to the decision and obiter. Perhaps nor surprisingly, the same argument was advanced in the tenth edition of Smith and Hogan's Criminal Law at p.247, and is repeated in the current edition. Mr Newman adopted that argument. Mr Kelson Q.C. for the Crown contended that this court in *O'Connor* had been right to regard *O'Grady* as binding authority.

18   We have used the term "obiter dicta" because it is a recognised legal term of art that is not readily reproduced by an English phrase. The term describes judicial statements which are peripheral to the reason for the decision, the ratio decidendi. Halsbury's Laws, 4th Ed, dealing at para.1237 with "Judicial Decisions as Authorities" accurately states: "The enunciation of the reason or principle upon which a question before the court has been decided is alone binding as precedent". In considering whether the relevant statements of Lord Lane C.J. in *O'Grady* were obiter it is necessary to consider what was in issue and what was the reason or principle applied by the court in resolving that issue.

19   It is helpful to start by considering the development of the law in relation to self-defence up to the time of the decision in *O'Grady*. It has long been a defence to a charge of any crime of violence that the defendant was acting reasonably to defend himself against attack. Originally the test of whether the defendant's conduct was a reasonable reaction to the attack fell to be judged objectively. The test was whether what was done by the defendant was reasonably necessary to defend himself against the attack that he was facing. In *Palmer v R.* (1971) 55 Cr.App.R. 225; [1971] A.C. 814, in delivering the advice of the Privy Council, Lord Morris of Borth-y-Gest opened the door to a degree of subjectivity. He said at pp.242 and 832:

> "If the jury thought that in a moment of unexpected anguish a person attacked had only done what he honestly and instinctively thought necessary, that would be the most potent evidence that only reasonably defensive action had been taken."

20   The next material step in the development of the law was the decision of this case in *R. v Williams (Gladstone)* (1984) 78 Cr.App.R. 276. The appellant had been convicted of assault occasioning actual bodily harm by punching a man in the face. His defence was that he had honestly, albeit erroneously, believed that the man he had punched was assaulting a youth and that he had done no more than necessary to defend that youth. The judge had directed the jury that he could only rely on this defence if there were reasonable grounds for his belief. The court held that the defence would lie provided that the belief was honestly held, whether there were reasonable grounds for it or not. Giving the judgment of the court, Lord Lane C.J. held at p.281:

"The reasonableness or unreasonableness of the defendant's belief is material to the question of whether the belief was held by the defendant at all. If the belief was in fact held, its unreasonableness, so far as guilt or innocence is concerned, is neither here nor there. It is irrelevant. Were it otherwise, the defendant would be convicted because he was negligent in failing to recognise that the victim was not consenting or that a crime was not being committed and so on. In other words the jury should be directed first of all that the prosecution have the burden or duty of proving the unlawfulness of the defendant's actions; secondly, if the defendant may have been labouring under a mistake as to the facts, he must be judged according to his mistaken view of the facts; thirdly, that is so whether the mistake was, on an objective view, a reasonable mistake or not.

In a case of self-defence, where self-defence or the prevention of crime is concerned, if the jury come to the conclusion that the defendant believed, or may have believed, that he was being attacked or that a crime was being committed, and that force was necessary to protect himself or to prevent the crime, then the prosecution have not proved their case. If however the defendant's alleged belief was mistaken and if the mistake was an unreasonable one, that may be a powerful reason for coming to the conclusion that the belief was not honestly held and should be rejected.

Even if the jury come to the conclusion that the mistake was an unreasonable one, if the defendant may genuinely have been labouring under it, he is entitled to rely upon it."

21   This passage was approved by the Privy Council in *Beckford v R.* (1987) 85 Cr.App.R. 378; [1988] A.C. 130 in an appeal against conviction for murder. Giving the opinion of the Board, Lord Griffiths said at pp.385 and 144:

"It is because it is an essential element of all crimes of violence that the violence or the threat of violence should be unlawful, that self-defence, if raised as an issue in a criminal trial, must be disproved by the prosecution. If the prosecution fail to do so the accused is entitled to be acquitted because the prosecution will have failed to prove an essential element of the crime, namely that the violence used by the accused was unlawful.

If then a genuine belief, albeit without reasonable grounds, is a defence to rape because it negatives the necessary intention, so also must a genuine belief in facts which if true would justify self-defence be a defence to a crime of personal violence because the belief negatives the intent to act unlawfully."

22   We observe that neither in *Williams (Gladstone)* nor in *Beckford* did the judgments consider the possibility that action taken by a defendant acting under a mistake resulting from negligence may attract liability for a crime of which the mental element is not intent but recklessness.

23   With this background we come to *R. v O'Grady* (1987) 85 Cr.App.R. 315; [1987] Q.B. 995. At issue in that case was whether the trial judge had correctly directed the jury in relation to self-defence on a charge of murder. As Professor

Smith has pointed out, that question was approached on the express premise that where self-defence provides a defence to a charge of murder, it will equally provide a defence to an alternative charge of manslaughter. The reasoning of the court drew no distinction between murder and manslaughter. Having given judgment the court certified that its decision raised a point of law of general public importance, namely: "Is a defendant who raises the issue of self-defence entitled to be judged upon the basis of what he mistakenly believed to be the situation when that mistaken belief was brought about by self-induced intoxication by alcohol or other drugs?" That was the issue that this court addressed. It was a general issue, not restricted to the offence of manslaughter. To that issue the court gave the answer "No". We do not believe that upon a proper application of the law of precedent we can treat the general principle that was the reason for this court's decision as being mere obiter dicta so far as the law of murder is concerned. We are obliged to follow O'Grady and to reject Mr Newman's contention that the judge should have directed the jury to consider whether the appellant's drunkenness might have led him to make a mistake as to the severity of any attack to which he may have been subjected by Mr Pashley.

24   We would add this. Had we felt it open to us to differ from the ruling on the point made by this court in O'Grady, our observations would themselves have been obiter. This is because we can see no basis upon which the judge could have directed the jury to consider that the appellant might have been labouring under the kind of drunken mistake suggested by Mr Newman, namely that he was being attacked by an SAS officer with a sword. This scenario was pure conjecture on the part of Mr Newman. The only relevant evidence was the appellant's vague recollection of being hit by Mr Pashley with the stick. In these circumstances the judge expressed doubt as to whether there was a defence of self-defence to be left to the jury, and we can understand that doubt. In the event he left to the jury the question of whether they were sure that the appellant used unreasonable force having regard to the circumstances as he believed them to be. Having regard to the wounds inflicted on Mr Pashley's head and body by blows from the sledgehammer wielded by the appellant, the response of the jury to this question can occasion no surprise.

25   The decision in O'Grady has been the subject of criticism not only by academic writers but by the Law Commission. In his commentary on O'Connor Professor Smith observed: "It is not too late for the Court of Appeal to repent and establish a sound basis of the law."

26   Mr Kelson advanced some powerful arguments, essentially of pragmatism, in support of the law as it stands. But whether or not the law is soundly based must be decided elsewhere. For the reasons that we have given this appeal is dismissed.

Appeal against conviction dismissed.

The Court of Appeal certified, under s.33(2) of the Criminal Appeal Act 1968, that a question of law of general public importance was involved in its decision, namely: "Is a defendant who raises the issue of self-defence to a charge of murder entitled to be judged upon the basis of what he mistakenly believed to be the situation when that mistaken belief was brought about by self-induced intoxication by alcohol or drugs?"

Leave to appeal to the House of Lords refused.

R. v RIMMINGTON
R. v GOLDSTEIN

HOUSE OF LORDS (Lord Bingham of Cornhill, Lord Nicholls of Birkenhead, Lord Rodger of Earlsferry, Baroness Hale of Richmond and Lord Brown of Eaton-under-Heywood): July 20, 21; October 27, 2005

[2005] UKHL 63; [2006] 1 Cr.App.R. 17

Certainty; Common law; Mens rea; No punishment without law; Public nuisance

H1   NUISANCE
      Public nuisance
      Common law offence—Whether offence still existing—Whether definition complying with requirements of certainty—Whether separate acts against different individuals capable of constituting public nuisance—Whether foreseeability of actual nuisance necessary— Human Rights Act 1998 (c.42), Sch. I, Pt 1, Art.7(1)

H2   In the first case, the appellant sent 538 separate packages containing racially offensive material to a number of different people, most of whom did not know each other, over a period of about nine years. He was charged in an indictment containing a single count of public nuisance, contrary to common law. At a preparatory hearing, the judge ruled that the indictment charged the appellant with an offence still known to the law and that the prosecution was not an abuse of process because brought inconsistently with Arts 7, 8 or 10 of the Convention for the Protection of Human Rights and Fundamental Freedoms. The appellant's appeal against that ruling was dismissed by the Court of Appeal. The appellant appealed to the House of Lords.

H3   In the second case, the appellant owed an old friend money and he sent a cheque through the post in an envelope in which he included a small quantity of salt, which was intended as a joke. In the course of sorting, some of the salt leaked onto the hand of a postal worker who feared that it might be anthrax. The sorting office was evacuated and the second postal delivery for that day was cancelled. The appellant was charged with public nuisance, contrary to common law. He was convicted and the Court of Appeal dismissed his appeal against conviction. He appealed to the House of Lords.

H4   **Held,** allowing the appeals, (1) that public nuisance, as currently interpreted and applied, was committed when a person did an act not warranted by law, or omitted to discharge a legal duty, if the effect of the act or omission was to endanger the life, health, property or comfort of the public or to obstruct the public in the exercise or enjoyment of rights common to all. The offence was clear, precise, adequately defined and based on a discernible rational principle and, therefore, it met the requirements of the common law and of Art.7 of the Convention. Much conduct that had formerly been chargeable as public nuisance had become the subject of express statutory provision. Where Parliament had defined the ingredients of an offence, perhaps stipulating what should and should not be a defence, and had prescribed a mode of trial and a maximum penalty, it must ordinarily be proper that conduct falling within that definition should be prosecuted for the statutory offence and not for a common law offence which might or might not provide the same defences and for which the potential penalty was unlimited. It could not in the ordinary way be a reason for resorting to the common law offence that the prosecutor was freed from mandatory time limits or restrictions on penalty. Accordingly, the circumstances in which, in future, there could properly be resort to the common law crime of nuisance would be relatively rare. However, the offence continued to exist since only Parliament, not the courts, had the power to abolish existing offences (post, paras 12, 28–31, 36, 41, 43–45, 52–54, 58,60).

H5   *R. v Misra and Srivastava* [2004] EWCA Crim 2375; [2005] 1 Cr.App.R. 21 (p.328), CA, approved.

H6   (2) That a core element of the crime of public nuisance was that the defendant's act should affect a section of the public rather than just individuals. The offence did not extend to separate and individual telephone calls or postal communications, however persistent and vexatious. An individual telephone call or postal communication could not become a criminal public nuisance merely by reason of the fact that it was one of a series. Accordingly, the sending through the post of racially offensive material to individual members of the public, as alleged against the appellant in the first case, did not cause common injury to a section of the public and, therefore, the appellant could not be charged with public nuisance (post, paras 38, 47–49, 58, 60).

H7   *R. v Johnson (Anthony)* [1996] 2 Cr.App.R. 434; [1997] 1 W.L.R. 367, CA overruled.

H8   (3) That the mens rea which had to be proved against a defendant to convict him of causing a public nuisance was that he knew, or ought to have known, because the means of knowledge were available to him, that the nuisance would be the consequence of what he did or omitted to do. The public nuisance alleged against the appellant in the second case was the escape of the salt from the envelope, which led to the evacuation of the sorting office, but the escape of the salt was not a result which the appellant intended nor was it a result which he knew would occur, since it would have rendered his intended joke entirely futile. It could not be inferred that the appellant should reasonably have known that the salt would escape, at any rate without detailed consideration of the type of envelope used and the care taken in sealing it, which had not taken place either at trial or on appeal, where the emphasis had been on a foreseeable consequence if there were an escape rather than on the foreseeability of an unintended escape. Accordingly, it had not been proved that the appellant knew or reasonably should have known, because the means of knowledge were available to him, that the salt would escape in the sorting office or in the course of post and, therefore, his conviction must be quashed (post, paras 39–41, 43, 56–58, 60).

H9   Decision of the Court of Appeal (Criminal Division) [2003] EWCA Crim 3450; [2004] 1 Cr.App.R. 27 (p.388); [2004] 1 W.L.R. 2878 reversed.

H10   (For the common law offence of causing a public nuisance, see *Archbold* 2006, para. 31–40 and following. For Arts 7, 8 and 10, see *ibid.* paras 16–97, 16–101 and 16–119 respectively.)

Appeals from the Court of Appeal (Criminal Division)

H11   On April 1, 2004 the House of Lords (Lord Bingham of Cornhill, Lord Rodger of Earlsferry and Lord Carswell) granted the appellants, Anthony Rimmington and Harry Chaim Goldstein, leave to appeal from a decision on November 28, 2003 of the Court of Appeal (Criminal Division) (Latham L.J., Moses J. and Sir Edwin Jowitt) dismissing their appeals, in Anthony Rimmington's case from a ruling on September 3, 2002 by Leveson J. at the Central Criminal Court that the offence of causing a public nuisance was known to the common law and that the prosecution was not an abuse of process, and in Harry Goldstein's case against his conviction on October 3, 2002 in the Crown Court at Southwark (Judge Fingret) of causing a public nuisance.

H12   The facts are stated in the opinions of their Lordships.

H13   *James Guthrie Q.C.* and *Bernard Eaton* (instructed by Coninghams, Twickenham) for Rimmington.
David Perry and *Mark Rainsford* (instructed by the Crown Prosecution Service) for the Crown.
Jonathan Goldberg Q.C. and *Gary Grant* (instructed by Barker Gillette) for Goldstein.
David Perry and *Tracy Ayling* (instructed by the Crown Prosecution Service for the Crown.

H14   Their Lordships took time for consideration.

1   **October 27   Lord Bingham of Cornhill**   My Lords, these appeals, heard together, raise important and difficult questions concerning the definition and ingredients, today, of the common law crime of causing a public nuisance. The appellants contend that, as applied in their cases, the offence is too imprecisely defined, and the courts' interpretation of it too uncertain and unpredictable, to satisfy the requirements either of the common law or of the European Convention on Human Rights. A question also arises on the mens rea which must be proved to establish the offence.

2   The facts of the two cases are quite different. Mr Rimmington was charged in an indictment containing a single count of public nuisance, contrary to common law. The particulars were that he

> "between the 25th day of May 1992 and the 13th day of June 2001, caused a nuisance to the public, namely by sending 538 separate postal packages, as detailed in the schedule . . ., containing racially offensive material to members of the public selected by reason of their perceived ethnicity or for their support for such a group or randomly selected in an attempt to gain support for his views, the effect of which was to cause annoyance, harassment, alarm and/or distress."

No evidence has yet been called or facts formally admitted, but it is not effectively in dispute that Mr Rimmington sent the packages listed in the schedule to the identified recipients, some of them prominent public figures, between the dates specified. The communications were strongly racist in content, crude, coarse, insulting and in some instances threatening and arguably obscene. When arrested in June 2001, Mr Rimmington suggested that his campaign had been prompted by a racially-motivated assault upon him by a black male in 1992: he had decided to retaliate by causing "them" mental anguish. The indictment preferred against him was challenged at the Central Criminal Court before Leveson J., who held a preparatory hearing under s.29 of the Criminal Procedure and Investigations Act 1996 to resolve the issues of law raised by the defence. He ruled that the indictment charged Mr Rimmington with an offence known to the law and that the prosecution was not an abuse of process because brought inconsistently with Arts 7, 8 or 10 of the European Convention. Mr Rimmington's appeal to the Court of Appeal (Criminal Division) against that decision was heard by Latham L.J., Moses J. and Sir Edwin Jowitt with that of Mr Goldstein, and was dismissed: [2003] EWCA Crim 3450; [2004] 1 Cr.App.R. 27 (p.338); [2004] 1 W.L.R. 2878.

3   In the proceedings against Mr Rimmington so far, he has been anonymised as "R" in the title of the case. Where a preparatory hearing is likely to be followed by a substantive trial and there is a risk that the trial may be prejudiced by reporting of the preparatory hearing, there may be very good reason to defer full reporting of the preparatory hearing, as is recognised by s.37 of the 1996 Act. But there is no statutory warrant for withholding the name of a defendant (see s.37(9)), and in the present case there is no reason why reporting should be restricted. I would accordingly order under s.37(5) of the Act that subs.(1) shall not apply to this appeal. There should be no resort to anonymity in criminal cases without good reason and statutory authority.

4   Mr Goldstein was charged in an indictment containing one count of public nuisance contrary to common law. The particulars were that he

> "between the 16th day of October 2001 and the 20th day of October 2001 caused a nuisance to the public by posting or causing to be posted, an envelope containing salt to Unit 36, Northend Road, Wembley."

Mr Goldstein, an ultra-orthodox Jew, is a supplier of kosher foods in Manchester. He bought supplies from the company of an old friend in London, Mr Abraham Ehrlich, with whom he had a bantering relationship. Mr Goldstein owed Mr Ehrlich a significant sum of money, which the latter had pressed him to pay. Mr

Goldstein accordingly put the cheque in an envelope (addressed to Ibrahim Ehr-lich) and included in the envelope a small quantity of salt. This was done in recognition of the age of the debt, salt being commonly used to preserve kosher food, and by way of reference to the very serious anthrax scare in New York fol-lowing the events of September 11, 2001, which both men had discussed on the telephone shortly before. The inclusion of the salt was intended to be humorous, and Mr Ehrlich gave unchallenged evidence at trial that had he received the envelope he would have recognised it as a joke. But the envelope did not reach him. In the course of sorting at the Wembley Sorting Office some of the salt leaked onto the hands of a postal worker who understandably feared it might be anthrax and raised the alarm. The building, in which some 110 people worked, was evacuated for about an hour, the second delivery for that day was cancelled and the police were called. On inspecting the envelope the police were satisfied that the substance was salt. Mr Goldstein pleaded not guilty before a judge (H.H. Judge Fingret) and jury in the Crown Court at Southwark but on October 3, 2002 he was convicted. He was sentenced to a Community Punishment Order of 140 hours, and ordered to pay £500 compensation and £1850 towards the costs of the prosecution. His appeal against conviction was heard and dismissed with that of Mr Rimmington.

Nuisance

5   The origins and nature of nuisance have been the subject of detailed scholarly research which need not for present purposes be rehearsed: see Winfield, "Nui-sance as a Tort", (1932) 4 C.L.J. 189; F.H. Newark, "The Boundaries of Nuisance", (1949) 65 L.Q.R. 480; J. Loengard, "The Assize of Nuisance: Ori-gins of an Action at Common Law" [1978] C.L.J. 144. It seems clear that what we would now call the tort of private nuisance, recognised in the Assize of Nuisance, provided a remedy complementary to that provided by the Assize of Novel Disseisin. As Holdsworth succinctly puts it (*A History of English Law*, 5th ed (1942), vol.III, p.11),

> "The novel disseisin was directed to secure an undisturbed possession: the assize of nuisance to secure its free enjoyment."

By the 15th century an action on the case for private nuisance was recognised. Thus the action for private nuisance was developed to protect the right of an occu-pier of land to enjoy it without substantial and unreasonable interference. This has remained the cardinal feature of the tort, as recently affirmed by the House in *Hunter v Canary Wharf Ltd* [1997] A.C. 655. The interference complained of may take any one of many different forms. What gives the tort its unifying fea-ture (see Fleming, *The Law of Torts*, 9th ed, (1998), p.457) is the general type of harm caused, interference with the beneficial occupation and enjoyment of land, not the particular conduct causing it.

6   It became clear over time that there were some acts and omissions which were socially objectionable but could not found an action in private nuisance because the injury was suffered by the local community as a whole rather than by individ-

ual victims and because members of the public suffered injury to their rights as such rather than as private owners or occupiers of land. Interference with the use of a public highway or a public navigable river provides the best and most typical example. Conduct of this kind came to be treated as criminal and punishable as such. In an unpoliced and unregulated society, in which local government was rudimentary or non-existent, common nuisance, as the offence was known, came to be (in the words of J.R. Spencer, "Public Nuisance — A Critical Examination", [1989] C.L.J. 55, 59) "a rag-bag of odds and ends which we should nowadays call 'public welfare offences'". But central to the content of the crime was the suffering of common injury by members of the public by interference with rights enjoyed by them as such. I shall, to avoid wearisome repetition, refer to this feature in this opinion as "the requirement of common injury".

7   Unusually, perhaps, conduct which could found a criminal prosecution for causing a common nuisance could also found a civil action in tort. Since, in the ordinary way, no individual member of the public had any better ground for action than any other member of the public, the Attorney General assumed the role of plaintiff, acting on the relation of the community which had suffered. This was attractive, since he could seek an injunction and the abatement of the nuisance was usually the object most desired: see Spencer, op. cit., pp.66–73. It was, however, held by Fitzherbert J., as early as 1536 (YB 27 Hy VIII. Mich. pl.10) that a member of the public could sue for a common or public nuisance if he could show that he had suffered particular damage over and above the ordinary damage suffered by the public at large. To the present day, causing a public nuisance has been treated as both a crime and a tort, the ingredients of each being the same.

The crime of public nuisance

8   The House was very helpfully referred to a number of authoritative statements on and definitions of the crime of public nuisance. The earliest of these was Hawkins, *A Treatise of the Pleas of the Crown* (1716), Book 1, Ch.LXXV, where he raised as a first question "What shall be said to be a Common Nuisance", and began his answer

> "Sect. 1. As to the first point it seems, That a Common Nuisance may be defined to be an Offence against the Publick, either by doing a Thing which tends to the Annoyance of all the King's Subjects, or by neglecting to do a Thing which the common Good requires.
> Sect. 2. But Annoyances to the Interests of particular Persons are not punishable by a public Prosecution as Common Nuisances, but are left to be redressed by the private Actions of the Parties aggrieved by them."

He gave examples. In his Commentaries on the Laws of England (Book III, 1768, Ch.13, p.216) Blackstone distinguished between public or common nuisances, "which affect the public, and are an annoyance to all the king's subjects" and private nuisances, which he defined as "any thing done to the hurt or annoyance of the lands, tenements, or hereditaments of another". In Book IV (1769, Ch.13, p.167) he explained further:

"... common nuisances are such inconvenient or troublesome offences, as annoy the whole community in general, and not merely some particular person; and therefore are indictable only, and not actionable; as it would be unreasonable to multiply suits, by giving every man a separate right of action, for what damnifies him in common only with the rest of his fellow subjects."

9   In 1822, in the first edition of his long-lived work then called *A Summary of the Law Relative to Pleading and Evidence in Criminal Cases*, J.F. Archbold published a precedent of an indictment for carrying on an offensive trade. The requirement of common injury (as I have called it) was recognised in the particulars:

"... to the great damage and common nuisance of all the liege subjects of our said lord the King there inhabiting, being, and residing, and going, returning, and passing through the said streets and highways . . ."

He referred to such other common nuisances as using a shop in a public market as a slaughter house, erecting a manufactory for hartshorn, erecting a privy near the highway, placing putrid carrion near the highway, keeping hogs near a public street and feeding them with offal, keeping a fierce and unruly bull in a field through which there was a footway, keeping a ferocious dog unmuzzled and baiting a bull in the King's highway. He went on to deal with such common nuisances as keeping a disorderly house and a common gaming house, although these became statutory offences the same year (3 Geo IV, Cap CXIV).

10   It seems likely that the draftsman of s.268 of the Indian Penal Code (Act XLV of 1860) intended to summarise the English common law on public nuisance as then understood.

"A person is guilty of a public nuisance who does any act or is guilty of an illegal omission which causes any common injury, danger or annoyance to the public or to the people in general who dwell or occupy property in the vicinity, or which must necessarily cause injury, obstruction, danger or annoyance to persons who may have occasion to use any public right."

In the draft Code annexed to their Report by the Criminal Code Bill Commissioners in 1879, the following proposals were made:

"Section 150 *Common nuisance defined*
A common nuisance is an unlawful act or omission to discharge a legal duty, which act or omission endangers the lives safety health property or comfort of the public, or by which the public are obstructed in the exercise or enjoyment of any right common to all Her Majesty's subjects.

Section 151 *What common nuisances are offences*
Every one shall be guilty of an indictable offence, and shall be liable upon conviction thereof to one year's imprisonment, who commits any common nuisance which endangers the lives safety or health of the public, or which injures the person of any individual.

Section 152 *When a common nuisance is not to be deemed criminal*
Any one convicted upon any indictment or information for any common nuisance other than those mentioned in the preceding section shall not be deemed to have committed a criminal offence; but all such proceedings or judgments may be taken and had as heretofore to abate or remedy the mischief done by such nuisance to the public right."

In A Digest of the Criminal Law (1877, Ch.XIX, p.108) Sir James Stephen defined a common nuisance as

". . . an act not warranted by law or an omission to discharge a legal duty, which act or omission obstructs or causes inconvenience or damage to the public in the exercise of rights common to all Her Majesty's subjects."

In the eighth and ninth editions of the work, published in 1947 and 1950 respectively, this definition remained unchanged. The definition to be found in paras 31–40 of the 2005 edition of Archbold (Criminal Pleading, Evidence and Practice), save in its reference to morals, reflects the effect of these definitions:

"A person is guilty of a public nuisance (also known as common nuisance), who (a) does an act not warranted by law, or (b) omits to discharge a legal duty, if the effect of the act or omission is to endanger the life, health, property, morals, or comfort of the public, or to obstruct the public in the exercise or enjoyment of rights common to all Her Majesty's subjects."

11   In a number of countries where the law has derived from English sources, an offence of common or public nuisance, having characteristics similar to those defined above, is to be found. Thus in Canada, where common law offences have been abolished, s.180 of the Criminal Code now provides:

"180. (1) Every one who commits a common nuisance and thereby
    (a) endangers the lives, safety or health of the public, or
    (b) causes physical injury to any person,
    is guilty of an indictable offence and liable to imprisonment for a term not exceeding two years.
(2) For the purposes of this section, every one commits a common nuisance who does an unlawful act or fails to discharge a legal duty and thereby
    (a) endangers the lives, safety, health, property or comfort of the public; or
    (b) obstructs the public in the exercise or enjoyment of any right that is common to all the subjects of Her Majesty in Canada."

Section 230 of the Queensland Criminal Code provides:

"Common nuisances

   230 Any person who:

     (a) without lawful justification or excuse, the proof of which lies on the person, does any act, or omits to do any act with respect to any property under the person's control, by which act or omission danger is caused to the lives, safety, or health, of the public; or

     (b) without lawful justification or excuse, the proof of which lies on the person, does any act, or omits to do any act with respect to any property under the person's control, by which act or omission danger is caused to the property or comfort of the public, or the public are obstructed in the exercise or enjoyment of any right common to all Her Majesty's subjects, and by which injury is caused to the person of some person;

is guilty of a misdemeanour, and is liable to imprisonment for 2 years."

To similar effect is the Tasmanian Criminal Code Act 1924, s.140:

"Common nuisance defined

   140 (1) A common nuisance is an unlawful act or an omission to discharge a legal duty, such act or omission being one which endangers the lives, safety, health, property, or comfort of the public, or by which the public are obstructed in the exercise or enjoyment of any right common to all His Majesty's subjects.

      (2) For the purposes of this section the comfort of the public shall be deemed to be affected by any pollution of the environment within the meaning of the Environmental Management and Pollution Control Act 1994."

12   All of the foregoing definitions, as I read them, treat the requirement of common injury as a, perhaps the, distinguishing feature of this offence.

The authorities: (1)

13   There are many authorities on this subject, and it is necessary to be selective. In *R. v White and Ward* (1757) 1 Burr 333 the nuisance to "all the King's liege subjects" living in Twickenham and travelling and passing the King's highway was impregnating the air with "noisome and offensive stinks and smells". Each defendant, on undertaking to avoid repetition, was fined 6s 8d. A mother of a young child who took him through a public street well knowing that the child suffered from the contagious, infectious and dangerous disease of smallpox, was convicted and sentenced to three months' imprisonment in the custody of the marshal: *R. v Vantandillo* (1815) 4 M&S 73. The defendant in *R. v Moore* (1832) 3 B&Ad 184 ran a rifle range in Bayswater where customers shot at pigeons, causing a crowd to assemble outside and in neighbouring fields to shoot at the pigeons which escaped, causing noise, damage, disturbance and mischief. On conviction the defendant undertook to discontinue the shooting and no

penalty was imposed. *R. v Medley* (1834) 6 C&P 292 arose from pollution of the River Thames. Denman C.J. directed the jury that the ignorance of the directors was no defence if they had authorised a manager to conduct the works, and they were each fined £25. In *Soltau v De Held* (1851) 2 Sim NS 133, 142–143, 61 ER 291, 295, Kindersley V.C. said:

> "I conceive that, to constitute a public nuisance, the thing must be such as, in its nature or its consequences, is a nuisance—an injury or a damage, to all persons who come within the sphere of its operations, though it may be so in a greater degree to some than it is to others."

R. v Henson (1852) Dears 24, 169 E.R. 621 involved a mare which, like the child in *R. v Vantandillo* 4 M&S 73, was infected with a "contagious, infectious and dangerous disease". The defendant, having brought the mare on to the highway with knowledge of its condition, was convicted of causing a common nuisance.

14   The House was referred to *R. v Stevenson* (1862) 3 F&F 106, 176 E.R. 48, which concerned the exposing for sale of unfit meat. Similar authorities concern the bringing to market of unfit meat (*R. v Jarvis* (1862) 3 F&F 108, 176 E.R. 49) and the sending to a meat salesman of meat unfit for human consumption (*R. v Crawley* (1862) 3 F&F 109, 176 E.R. 49). It is not entirely clear that these offences were charged as common nuisances at common law. But it is clear that knowledge of the unfitness of the meat, or its intended sale for human consumption, was treated as an ingredient of the offences.

15   The issue in *R. v Stephens* (1866) L.R. 1 Q.B. 702 was whether the owner of a slate quarry was answerable for a public nuisance caused by his workmen without his knowledge and contrary to his general orders. The jury had convicted. The case is important for the observations of Mellor J. at p.708–709:

> "It is quite true that this in point of form is a proceeding of a criminal nature, but in substance I think it is in the nature of a civil proceeding, and I can see no reason why a different rule should prevail with regard to such an act as is charged in this indictment between proceedings which are civil and proceedings which are criminal. I think there may be nuisances of such a character that the rule I am applying here, would not be applicable to them, but here it is perfectly clear that the only reason for proceeding criminally is that the nuisance, instead of being merely a nuisance affecting an individual, or one or two individuals, affects the public at large, and no private individual, without receiving some special injury, could have maintained an action. Then if the contention of those who say the direction is wrong is to prevail, the public would have great difficulty in getting redress. The object of this indictment is to prevent the recurrence of the nuisance. The prosecutor cannot proceed by action, but must proceed by indictment, and if this were strictly a criminal proceeding the prosecution would be met with the objection that there was no mens rea: that the indictment charged the defendant with a criminal offence, when in reality there was no proof that the defendant knew of the act, or that he himself gave orders to his servants to do the particular act he is charged with; still at

the same time it is perfectly clear that the defendant finds the capital, and carries on the business which causes the nuisance, and it is carried on for his benefit; although from age or infirmity the defendant is unable to go to the premises, the business is carried on for him by his sons, or at all events by his agents. Under these circumstances the defendant must necessarily give to his servants or agents all the authority that is incident to the carrying on of the business. It is not because he had at some time or other given directions that it should be carried on so as not to allow the refuse from the works to fall into the river, and desired his servants to provide some other place for depositing it, that when it has fallen into the river, and has become prejudicial to the public, he can say he is not liable on an indictment for a nuisance caused by the acts of his servants. It appears to me that all it was necessary to prove is, that the nuisance was caused in the carrying on of the works of the quarry."

Blackburn J, who had presided at the trial, agreed. He said at p.710:

"All that it is necessary to say is this, that where a person maintains works by his capital, and employs servants, and so carries on the works as in fact to cause a nuisance to a private right, for which an action would lie, if the same nuisance inflicts an injury upon a public right the remedy for which would be by indictment, the evidence which would maintain the action would also support the indictment. That is all that it was necessary to decide and all that is decided."

Thus the overlap between the criminal offence and the civil tort was affirmed, and this fact was relied on to justify a strict approach to the ordinary requirement of mens rea.

16   This strict approach was acknowledged by Wright J. in *Sherras v De Rutzen* [1895] 1 Q.B. 918. Usually cited for its reference to the presumption that mens rea is an essential ingredient in every offence, this passage continues with a discussion of various exceptions where the presumption does not apply (footnotes omitted):

"Another class comprehends some, and perhaps all, public nuisances: *R. v Stephens* where the employer was held liable on indictment for a nuisance caused by workmen without his knowledge and contrary to his orders; and so in *R. v Medley* and *Barnes v Akroyd*. Lastly, there may be cases in which, although the proceeding is criminal in form, it is really only a summary mode of enforcing a civil right: see per Williams and Willes JJ. in *Morden v Porter*, as to unintentional trespass in pursuit of game; *Lee v Simpson*, as to unconscious dramatic piracy; and *Hargreaves v Diddams*, as to a bona fide belief in a legally impossible right to fish."

17   The next case which must be mentioned, *Sedleigh-Denfield v O'Callaghan* [1940] A.C. 880, was a case of private nuisance, concerned with the liability of an owner for continuing a nuisance originally caused, without his knowledge, by a trespasser. Viscount Maugham opined (at p.887):

"All that is necessary in such a case is to show that the owner or occupier of the land with such a possible cause of nuisance upon it knows or must be taken to know of it. An absentee owner or an occupier oblivious of what is happening under his eyes is in no better position than the man who looks after his property . . .."

Lord Wright at p.904 formulated what has come to be accepted as the test:

"Though the rule has not been laid down by this House, it has I think been rightly established in the Court of Appeal that an occupier is not prima facie responsible for a nuisance created without his knowledge and consent. If he is to be liable a further condition is necessary, namely, that he had knowledge or means of knowledge, that he knew or should have known of the nuisance in time to correct it and obviate its mischievous effects. The liability for a nuisance is not, at least in modern law, a strict or absolute liability."

18   The leading modern authority on public nuisance is *Attorney General v PYA Quarries Ltd* [1957] 2 Q.B. 169. This was a civil action brought by the Attorney General on the relation of the Glamorgan County Council and the Pontardawe Rural District Council to restrain a nuisance by quarrying activities which were said to project stones and splinters into the neighbourhood, and cause dust and vibrations. It was argued for the company on appeal that there might have been a private nuisance affecting some of the residents, but not a public nuisance affecting all Her Majesty's liege subjects living in the area. In his judgment Romer L.J. reviewed the authorities in detail and concluded, at p.184:

"I do not propose to attempt a more precise definition of a public nuisance than those which emerge from the textbooks and authorities to which I have referred. It is, however, clear, in my opinion, that any nuisance is 'public' which materially affects the reasonable comfort and convenience of life of a class of Her Majesty's subjects. The sphere of the nuisance may be described generally as 'the neighbourhood'; but the question whether the local community within that sphere comprises a sufficient number of persons to constitute a class of the public is a question of fact in every case. It is not necessary, in my judgment, to prove that every member of the class has been injuriously affected; it is sufficient to show that a representative cross-section of the class has been so affected for an injunction to issue."

Denning L.J. agreed. He differentiated between public and private nuisance at p.190 on conventional grounds:

"The classic statement of the difference is that a public nuisance affects Her Majesty's subjects generally, whereas a private nuisance only affects particular individuals."

He went on, at p.191, to say '

"that a public nuisance is a nuisance which is so widespread in its range or so indiscriminate in its effect that it would not be reasonable to expect one person to take proceedings on his own responsibility to put a stop to it, but that it should be taken on the responsibility of the community at large."

19   In *R. v Madden* (1975) 61 Cr.App.R. 254; [1975] 1 W.L.R. 1379 the defendant made a hoax bomb call by telephone to a steel works. The message was received by a telephonist, who informed the engineer and also the police. The police informed the chief security officer of the works, who caused eight security men to carry out a search. This lasted for just over an hour before the telephone call was found to be a hoax. The defendant was convicted at trial but succeeded on appeal, because the recorder had directed the jury to consider potential and not actual danger and discomfort, and because the requirement of common injury was not met. Giving the judgment of the court, James L.J. said at pp.256 and 1383:

"It is, in our view, still an offence known to the law of this country to commit a public nuisance. A person who makes a bogus telephone call falsely giving information as to the presence of explosives may, in our view, if there is evidence, be shown to have committed an offence of public nuisance.

In this particular case the conviction must be quashed on two grounds. First, the directions which the recorder was persuaded by the Crown to give to the jury were not right in that those directions invited the jury to consider the potential danger to the public rather than the actual danger; or the potential risk to the comfort of the public as distinct from the actual comfort of the public. Secondly, on the evidence which I have recited, it was not possible for a jury, properly directed, to have arrived at the conclusion that a considerable number of persons were affected by the action of the appellant. It is quite clear that, for a public nuisance to be proved, it must be proved by the Crown that the public, which means a considerable number of persons or a section of the public, was affected, as distinct from individual persons."

(The first of these grounds would seem hard to reconcile with the decisions in *R. v Vantandillo* 4 M&S 73 and *R. v Henson* 169 ER 621.)

20   The decision of the Court of Appeal (Criminal Division) in *R. v Soul* (1980) 70 Cr.App.R. 295 is not easy to explain. The appellant, who had agreed with others to secure the unlawful release of a restricted Broadmoor patient, was charged and convicted of conspiring to effect a public nuisance. Her appeal failed. The court rejected an argument, based on *R. v Madden* (1975) 61 Cr.App.R. 254; [1975] 1 W.L.R. 1379, that the Crown had failed to prove any actual danger. No more than, at most, passing reference was made to the requirement of common injury. A critical commentary in [1980] Crim. L.R. 234 suggested that public mischief, held by the House of Lords in *R. v Withers* (1974) 60 Cr.App.R. 85; [1975] A.C. 842 not to be an offence, could in effect be restored by judicial legislation.

21   *R. v Ruffell* (1991) 13 Cr.App.R.(S.) 204 was an appeal against sentence. The appellant had pleaded guilty to causing a public nuisance, and had been sentenced

to a suspended term of 12 months' imprisonment and a fine of £7000. The nuisance had consisted of an "acid house" party, which had attracted some thousands of people. A side road to the site had been blocked by traffic. There had been very loud music, overnight and lasting for about 12 hours. The surrounding woodlands had been littered with human excrement. The appeal against the sentence of imprisonment failed, but the fine was quashed on the ground that the appellant had no means to pay it. The facts of *R. v Shorrock* (1994) 98 Cr.App.R. 67; [1994] Q.B. 279, which also involved an "acid house" party, were a little similar. The appellant accepted that a public nuisance had been caused, but denied that he had had the requisite knowledge to be criminally liable. Thus the issue concerned the mens rea which the Crown had to prove to establish guilt. Giving the judgment of a Court of Appeal which also included Simon Brown L.J. and Popplewell J., Rattee J. reviewed the authorities and concluded that the answer was that given by the House in *Sedleigh-Denfield v O'Callaghan* [1940] A.C. 880: the appellant was guilty of the offence charged (p.289)

> "if either he knew or he ought to have known, in the sense that the means of knowledge were available to him, that there was a real risk that the consequences of the licence granted by him in respect of his field would be to create the sort of nuisance that in fact occurred."

22   *R. v Ong* [2001] 1 Cr.App.R.(S.) 117 (p.404) was an application for leave to appeal against a sentence of four years' imprisonment imposed on a plea of guilty to a court of conspiring to cause a public nuisance. The public nuisance which was planned was the extinguishment of the floodlights at a Premier Division football match between Charlton Athletic and Liverpool in order to make a fraudulent gain for a group of Far Eastern bookmakers. The plan, if implemented, would have plunged those attending the match, presumably a crowd of thousands, into darkness, and prevented them seeing the match they had paid to see. Leave was refused.

The authorities: (2)

23   I have reserved for separate consideration a line of recent authority much relied on by the Crown in the case of Mr Rimmington, but the correctness of which is challenged by him.

24   The line appears to begin with *R. v Norbury* [1978] Crim. L.R. 435, a case heard by Judge Beezley in the Crown Court at Norwich in March 1977. The defendant had over a period of some four years made 605 obscene telephone calls to 494 different women. The making of such calls was a summary offence punishable with a maximum fine of £50 under s.78 of the Post Office Act 1969, but the defendant was indicted for causing a public nuisance, an indictable offence for which there was no maximum penalty. His counsel moved to quash the indictment, I infer on the ground that the requirement of common injury was not met, but this argument was rejected. The judge ruled:

"It seems to me, dealing with the present indictment, that a repetition over a long period and on a number of occasions of telephone calls of an obscene nature, intending to cause offence and alarm and resulting in such offence and alarm to a large number of Her Majesty's subjects, selected from a telephone directory or merely by chance dialling is the very kind of act and, indeed, the very kind of series of acts which the public has an interest in condemning and has a right to vindicate."

In the light of this ruling the defendant pleaded guilty. The judge's observations, as quoted, are unexceptionable and must command unqualified assent. But they do not address the question whether separate calls to individual victims can satisfy the requirement of common injury as I have defined it in para.6 above. The commentator at [1978] Crim. L.R. 435 sounded a note of warning:

"The facts of the present case are strikingly different from the typical case of public nuisance which is obstruction of the highway. There might be some danger of public nuisance assuming the mantle of public mischief. The House of Lords has held that public mischief-even conspiracy to effect a public mischief-is not an offence known to the law: *Director of Public Prosecutions v Withers* [1975] A.C. 842; but there is no doubt that public nuisance is an offence. The question is as to how far it extends. The present case shows that it may have some potentiality for growth. Offences covering such a wide range of different matters with no obvious boundaries are only doubtfully compatible with the principle of legality-i.e. that no one should be punished for an act which was not declared by law to be an offence before the act was done."

25   The warning was not heeded. In *R. v Millward* (1986) 8 Cr.App.R.(S.) 209 the defendant had made hundreds of telephone calls (636 in a single day) to a young woman police officer with whom he had become infatuated, at the police station where she worked. He had pleaded guilty to two counts of causing a public nuisance and the appeal, which did not succeed, was against a sentence of 30 months' imprisonment. The ingredients of the offence were not in issue, and the only reference to the requirement of common injury was in the judgment of the court delivered by Glidewell L.J.:

"Quite apart from anything else, this disrupts the whole operation of the police station to which these calls are directed, because a member of the public may wish to report an urgent matter such as a criminal offence, and cannot do so or is delayed in doing so because of this kind of behaviour on the part of the appellant."

26   In *R. v Johnson (Anthony)* [1996] 2 Cr.App.R. 434; [1997] 1 W.L.R. 367, an appeal against conviction, the requirement of common injury was the central issue. The appellant had over a period of years made hundreds of obscene telephone calls to at least 13 women, and had been convicted of causing a public nuisance. It was argued on his behalf that (a) each telephone call was a single isolated act to an individual, and although that might have amounted to a private

nuisance it was wrong to group all the calls together and to regard the cumulative effect as a public nuisance, and (b) that in any event the scale and width of the conduct complained of was insufficient to constitute a public nuisance. Tucker J., giving the reserved judgment of the court, rejected the argument. He ruled, at pp.370–371 and 438:

> "In our judgment it is permissible and necessary to look at the cumulative effect of these calls, made to numerous ladies on numerous occasions in the case of each lady, and to have regard to the cumulative effect of the calls in determining whether the appellant's conduct constituted a public nuisance. In our opinion it was conduct which materially affected the reasonable comfort and convenience of a class of Her Majesty's subjects: see per Romer L.J. in *Attorney-General v PYA Quarries Ltd* . . . It was a nuisance which was so widespread in its range, or so indiscriminate in its effect, that it would not be reasonable to expect one person to take proceedings on her own responsibility, but that they should be taken on the responsibility of the community at large: see Denning L.J. . . . It was proved by the Crown that the public, meaning a considerable number of persons or a section of the public, was affected, as distinct from individual persons."

27   There was a plea of guilty in *R. v Eskdale* [2001] EWCA Crim 1159, [2002] 1 Cr.App.R.(S.) 28 (p.118). The appellant had made about 1000 obscene telephone calls, some of them very highly objectionable, to 15 women over a period of two weeks. An appeal against a sentence of nine years' imprisonment was dismissed. There was also a plea of guilty in *R. v Harley* [2002] EWCA Crim 2650, [2003] 2 Cr.App.R.(S.) 3 (p.16). Over three months in the summer of 2001 the appellant had made nearly 5000 calls to more than 1000 people. A sentence of 21 months' imprisonment was for special reasons reduced to nine months'. Sentences of 18 months' and five years' imprisonment were reduced to nine months' and 30 months' in *R. v Holliday and Leboutillier* [2004] EWCA Crim 1847, [2005] 1 Cr.App.R.(S.) 70 (p.349). The appellants were animal liberation activists who had pleaded guilty to causing a public nuisance by making a large number of telephone calls to employees and shareholders of certain companies whose activities the appellants opposed. The calls were designed to jam the company telephone switchboards, and some of them were threatening and intimidating. In *R. v Lowrie* [2004] EWCA Crim 2325, [2005] 1 Cr.App.R.(S.) 95 (p.530) the appellant appealed unsuccessfully against a sentence of eight years' imprisonment imposed on his pleas of guilty to 12 counts of causing a public nuisance. In each case the count was based on a hoax call to one of the emergency services.

The current standing of public nuisance

28   The appellants contended (1) that conduct formerly chargeable as the crime of public nuisance had now become the subject of express statutory provision, (2) that where conduct was the subject of express statutory provision it should be charged under the appropriate statutory provision and not as public nuisance,

and (3) that accordingly the crime of public nuisance had ceased to have any practical application or legal existence.

29   There is a large measure of truth in the first of these contentions. Section 79(1) of the Environmental Protection Act 1990, as amended, establishes nine categories of statutory nuisance (the state of premises, smoke emissions, fumes or gases from dwellings, effluvia from industrial trade or business premises, accumulations or deposits, animals, noise from premises, noise from vehicles or equipment in a street and other matters declared by other Acts to be statutory nuisances). Section 33 controls the dumping of waste. The Act lays down a detailed procedure for securing abatement, provides for criminal proceedings and prescribes maximum penalties for failure to comply with an abatement notice: see, generally, McCracken, Jones, Pereira and Payne, Statutory Nuisance (2001), c.2, 3, 5, 8, 9 and 10. Section 85 of the Water Resources Act 1991 makes it an offence to pollute controlled waters. It prescribes a maximum penalty of three months' imprisonment and a fine of £20,000 on summary conviction, and two years' imprisonment and a fine on conviction on indictment. By s.137 of the Highways Act 1980 it is a summary offence punishable by a fine not exceeding level 3 on the standard scale wilfully to obstruct free passage along a highway. Section 1 of the Protection from Harassment Act 1997 creates a crime of harassment, punishable summarily by imprisonment for a maximum of six months and a fine on scale 5. If the harassment involves repeated threats of violence the defendant is liable under s.4, on conviction on indictment, to five years' imprisonment and a fine. Section 32 of the Crime and Disorder Act 1998 creates an offence of racially or religiously motivated harassment and prescribes maximum penalties. Section 63 of the Criminal Justice and Public Order Act 1994 confers powers on the police to remove persons attending or preparing for a rave "at which amplified music is played during the night (with or without intermissions) and is such as, by reason of its loudness and duration and the time at which it is played, is likely to cause serious distress to the inhabitants of the locality". Breach of the statutory requirements is punishable on summary conviction by imprisonment for up to three months and a fine not exceeding level 4 on the standard scale. By s.51 of the Criminal Law Act 1977, as amended, bomb hoaxes are punishable, on conviction on indictment, by a maximum of seven years' imprisonment, with a maximum of six months' and a fine of £1000 on summary conviction. Section 114 of the Anti-terrorism, Crime and Security Act 2001 makes it an offence, attracting similar penalties, to place or send any substance or thing "with the intention of inducing in a person anywhere in the world a belief that it is likely to be (or contain) a noxious substance or other noxious thing and thereby endanger human life or create a serious risk to human health". Section 85 of the Postal Services Act 2000 makes it an offence to send by post anything which is likely to injure a postal worker or anything which is indecent or obscene. On summary conviction the offence is punishable by a fine, on conviction on indictment by imprisonment for a maximum of 12 months and a fine. By s.1 of the Malicious Communications Act 1988, enacted to give effect to the Law Commission's Report on Poison-Pen Letters (Law Com. No.147, HC 519 (1985)), as amended, it is an offence to send to another person a letter, electronic communi-

cation or article of any description which is indecent, grossly offensive, threatening or known or believed to be false. The offence is punishable on summary conviction with a maximum of six months' imprisonment and a fine on scale 5 on the standard scale. There has recently been enacted, in s.127 of the Communications Act 2003, an offence, attracting the same penalties, of improperly using a public electronic communications network. While it cannot be confidently asserted that there is no conduct which might formerly have been properly prosecuted as public nuisance which is not now the subject of express statutory provision, the appellants are in my opinion correct that the most typical and obvious causes of public nuisance are now the subject of express statutory prohibition.

30   There is in my opinion considerable force in the appellants' second contention under this head. Where Parliament has defined the ingredients of an offence, perhaps stipulating what shall and shall not be a defence, and has prescribed a mode of trial and a maximum penalty, it must ordinarily be proper that conduct falling within that definition should be prosecuted for the statutory offence and not for a common law offence which may or may not provide the same defences and for which the potential penalty is unlimited. If the directors in *R. v Medley* (1834) 6 C&P 292 who were ignorant of what had been done, or the octogenarian owner in *R. v Stephens* (1866) LR 1 Q.B. 702 who was ignorant of what had been done and whose orders were disregarded, were today to be prosecuted for causing a public nuisance rather than under the relevant statutory provision, they would have powerful grounds for objecting, and the same point applies more generally. It cannot in the ordinary way be a reason for resorting to the common law offence that the prosecutor is freed from mandatory time limits or restrictions on penalty. It must rather be assumed that Parliament imposed the restrictions which it did having considered and weighed up what the protection of the public reasonably demanded. I would not go to the length of holding that conduct may never be lawfully prosecuted as a generally-expressed common law crime where it falls within the terms of a specific statutory provision, but good practice and respect for the primacy of statute do in my judgment require that conduct falling within the terms of a specific statutory provision should be prosecuted under that provision unless there is good reason for doing otherwise.

31   It follows from the conclusions already expressed in paras 29–30 above that the circumstances in which, in future, there can properly be resort to the common law crime of public nuisance will be relatively rare. It may very well be, as suggested by J.R. Spencer in his article cited in para 6 above, at p.83, that "There is surely a strong case for abolishing the crime of public nuisance". But as the courts have no power to create new offences (see para.33 below), so they have no power to abolish existing offences. That is a task for Parliament, following careful consideration (perhaps undertaken, in the first instance, by the Law Commission) whether there are aspects of the public interest which the crime of public nuisance has a continuing role to protect. It is not in my view open to the House in resolving these appeals to conclude that the common law crime of causing a public nuisance no longer exists.

Definition

32   The appellants submitted that the crime of causing a public nuisance, as currently interpreted and applied, lacks the precision and clarity of definition, the
certainty and the predictability necessary to meet the requirements of either
the common law itself or Art.7 of the European Convention. This submission
calls for some consideration of principle.

33   In his famous polemic Truth versus Ashurst, written in 1792 and published in
1823, Jeremy Bentham made a searing criticism of judge-made criminal law,
which he called "dog-law".

> "It is the judges (as we have seen) that make the common law. Do you know
> how they make it? Just as a man makes laws for his dog. When your dog does
> anything you want to break him of, you wait till he does it, and then beat him
> for it. This is the way you make laws for your dog: and this is the way the
> judges make law for you and me. They won't tell a man beforehand what
> it is he should not do — they won't so much as allow of his being told:
> they lie by till he has done something which they say he should not have
> done, and then they hang him for it."

The domestic law of England and Wales has set its face firmly against "dog-
law". In *R. v Withers* (1974) 60 Cr.App.R. 85; [1975] A.C. 842 the House of
Lords ruled that the judges have no power to create new offences: see Lord
Reid at pp.88 and 854G; Viscount Dilhorne at pp.92 and 860E; Lord Simon of
Glaisdale at pp.95, 98 and 863D, 867E; Lord Kilbrandon at pp.106 and 877C.
Nor (per Lord Simon at pp.98 and 863D) may the courts nowadays widen existing
offences so as to make punishable conduct of a type hitherto not subject to pun-
ishment. The relevant principles are admirably summarised by Judge L.J. for the
Court of Appeal (Criminal Division) in *R. v Misra and Srivastava* [2004] EWCA
Crim 2375; [2005] 1 Cr.App.R. 328, paras [29]–[34], in a passage which I would
respectfully adopt:

> "29 To develop his argument on uncertainty, Mr Gledhill [for Dr Misra]
> focussed our attention on Art.7 of the Convention, entitled 'No punishment
> without law' which provides:

>> '7 (1) No-one shall be held guilty of any criminal offence on account of
>>   any act or omission which did not constitute a criminal offence
>>   under national or international law at the time when it was com-
>>   mitted nor shall a heavier penalty be imposed than the one that
>>   was applicable at the time the criminal offence was committed.'

> In our view the essential thrust of this article is to prohibit the creation of
> offences, whether by legislation or the incremental development of the com-
> mon law, which have retrospective application. It reflects a well-understood
> principle of domestic law, that conduct which did not contravene the crimi-
> nal law at the time when it took place should not retrospectively be
> stigmatised as criminal, or expose the perpetrator to punishment. As Lord

Reid explained in *Waddington v Miah* (1974) 59 Cr.App.R. 149 at p.151–152,

> 'There has for a very long time been a strong feeling against making legislation, and particularly criminal legislation, retrospective . . . I use retrospective in the sense of authorising people being punished for what they did before the Act came into force.'

30 Mr Gledhill demonstrated that the Convention contained repeated references to expressions in English such as 'prescribed by law': in French, the same phrase reads 'prévue par la loi'. We shall assume that the concepts are identical. Article 7 therefore sustains his contention that a criminal offence must be clearly defined in law, and represents the operation of 'the principle of legal certainty' (see, for example, *Brumarescu v Romania* (2001) 33 E.H.R.R. 35 at para.61 and *Kokkinakis v Greece* (1993) 17 E.H.R.R. 397 at para.52). The principle enables each community to regulate itself:

> 'with reference to the norms prevailing in the society in which they live. That generally entails that the law must be adequately accessible—an individual must have an indication of the legal rules applicable in a given case—and he must be able to foresee the consequences of his actions, in particular to be able to avoid incurring the sanction of the criminal law.' (*S.W. v United Kingdom: C.R. v United Kingdom* (1995) 21 E.H.R.R. 363).

31 Mr Gledhill further emphasised that in *Grayned v City of Rockford* 408 US 104 (1972) the United States Supreme Court identified 'a basic principle of due process that an enactment is void for vagueness if its prohibitions are not clearly defined. Vagueness offends several important values . . . A vague law impermissibly delegates basic policy matters to policemen, judges and juries for resolution on an ad hoc and subjective basis, with the attendant dangers of arbitrary and discriminatory application.' He pointed out that Lord Phillips M.R. had approved these dicta in *R (L and another) v Secretary of State for the Home Department* [2003] EWCA Civ 25 [2003] 1 W.L.R. 1230, para.25.

32 We acknowledge the force of these submissions, but simultaneously emphasise that there is nothing novel about them in our jurisprudence. Historic as well as modern examples abound. In the 17th century Bacon proclaimed the essential link between justice and legal certainty:

> 'For if the trumpet give an uncertain sound, who shall prepare himself to the battle? So if the law give an uncertain sound, who shall prepare to obey it? It ought therefore to warn before it strikes . . . Let there be no authority to shed blood; nor let sentence be pronounced in any court upon cases, except according to a known and certain law. . . . Nor should a man be deprived of his life, who did not first know that he was risking it.' (Quoted in Coquillette, Francis Bacon pp.244 and 248, from Aphorism 8 and Aphorism 39–A Treatise on Universal Justice).

The judgment of the Supreme Court of the United States in *Grayned* effectively mirrored Blackstone:

'. . . Law, without equity, though hard and disagreeable, is much more desirable for the public good than equity without law: which would make every judge a legislator, and introduce most infinite confusion; as there would then be almost as many rules of action laid down in our courts, as there are differences of capacity and sentiment in the human mind.' (Commentaries, 3rd ed, 1769, vol.1 p.62.)

33 Recent judicial observations are to the same effect. Lord Diplock commented in *Black-Clawson International Ltd v Papierwerke Waldhof-Aschaffenberg AG* [1975] A.C. 591 at p.638:

'The acceptance of the rule of law as a constitutional principle requires that a citizen, before committing himself to any course of action, should be able to know in advance what are the legal consequences that will flow from it.'

In *Fothergill v Monarch Airlines Ltd* [1981] A.C. 251 at 279 he repeated the same point:

'Elementary justice or, to use the concept often cited by the European court, the need for legal certainty demands that the rules by which the citizen is to be bound should be ascertainable by him (or more realistically by a competent lawyer advising him) by reference to identifiable sources that are publicly accessible.'

More tersely, in *Warner v Metropolitan Police Commissioner* (1968) 52 Cr.App.R. 373, 414 [1969] 2 A.C. 256, 296, Lord Morris of Borth-y-Gest explained in terms that:

'. . . In criminal matters it is important to have clarity and certainty.'

The approach of the common law is perhaps best encapsulated in the statement relating to judicial precedent issued by Lord Gardiner L.C. on behalf of himself and the Lords of Appeal in Ordinary on July 26, 1966 Practice Statement (Judicial Precedent) (1986) 83 Cr.App.R. 191, [1966] 1 W.L.R. 1234.

'Their Lordships regard the use of precedent as an indispensable foundation upon which to decide what is the law and its application to individual cases. It provides at least some degree of certainty upon which individuals can rely in the conduct of their affairs, as well as a basis for orderly development of legal rules.'

In allowing themselves (but not courts at any other level) to depart from the absolute obligation to follow earlier decisions of the House of Lords, their Lordships expressly bore in mind:

'. . . the danger of disturbing retrospectively the basis on which contracts, settlements of property and fiscal arrangements have been
entered into and also the especial need for certainty as to the criminal
law.'

34 No further citation is required. In summary, it is not to be supposed that
prior to the implementation of the Human Rights Act 1998, either this Court,
or the House of Lords, would have been indifferent to or unaware of the need
for the criminal law in particular to be predictable and certain. Vague laws
which purport to create criminal liability are undesirable, and in extreme
cases, where it occurs, their very vagueness may make it impossible to identify the conduct which is prohibited by a criminal sanction. If the court is
forced to guess at the ingredients of a purported crime any conviction for
it would be unsafe. That said, however, the requirement is for sufficient
rather than absolute certainty."

There are two guiding principles: no one should be punished under a law unless it
is sufficiently clear and certain to enable him to know what conduct is forbidden
before he does it; and no one should be punished for any act which was not clearly
and ascertainably punishable when the act was done. If the ambit of a common
law offence is to be enlarged, it "must be done step by step on a case by case
basis and not with one large leap": *R. v Clark (Mark)* [2003] EWCA Crim
991, [2003] 2 Cr.App.R. 28 (p.363), para.[13].

34   These common law principles are entirely consistent with Art.7(1) of the
European Convention, which provides:

"No punishment without law
   (1) No one shall be held guilty of any criminal offence on account of any
       act or omission which did not constitute a criminal offence under
       national or international law at the time when it was committed.
       Nor shall a heavier penalty be imposed than the one that was appli-
       cable at the time the criminal offence was committed."

The European Court has repeatedly considered the effect of this article, as also
the reference in Art.8(2) to "in accordance with the law" and that in Art.10(2)
to "prescribed by law".

35   The effect of the Strasbourg jurisprudence on this topic has been clear and consistent. The starting point is the old rule nullum crimen, nulla poena sine lege
(*Kokkinakis v Greece* (1993) 17 E.H.R.R. 397, para.52; *SW and CR v United
Kingdom* (1995) 21 E.H.R.R. 363, para.35/33): only the law can define a
crime and prescribe a penalty. An offence must be clearly defined in law (*SW
and CR v United Kingdom*), and a norm cannot be regarded as a law unless it
is formulated with sufficient precision to enable the citizen to foresee, if need
be with appropriate advice, the consequences which a given course of conduct
may entail (*Sunday Times v United Kingdom* (1979) 2 E.H.R.R. 245, para.49;
G v Federal Republic of Germany (1989) 60 D.R. 256, 261, para.1; *SW and
CR v United Kingdom*, para.34/32). It is accepted that absolute certainty is unat-
tainable, and might entail excessive rigidity since the law must be able to keep

pace with changing circumstances, some degree of vagueness is inevitable and development of the law is a recognised feature of common law courts (*Sunday Times v United Kingdom*, para.49; *X Ltd and Y v United Kingdom* (1982) 28 D.R. 77, 81, para.9; *SW and CR v United Kingdom*, para.36/34). But the law-making function of the courts must remain within reasonable limits (*X Ltd and Y v United Kingdom*, para.9). Article 7 precludes the punishment of acts not previously punishable, and existing offences may not be extended to cover facts which did not previously constitute a criminal offence (ibid.). The law may be clarified and adapted to new circumstances which can reasonably be brought under the original concept of the offence (*X Ltd and Y v United Kingdom*, para.9; *G v Federal Republic of Germany*, pp.261–262). But any development must be consistent with the essence of the offence and be reasonably foreseeable (*SW and CR v United Kingdom*, para.36/34), and the criminal law must not be extensively construed to the detriment of an accused, for instance by analogy (*Kokkinakis v Greece*, para.52).

36   How, then, does the crime of causing a public nuisance, as currently interpreted and applied, measure up to these standards? Mr Perry, for the Crown, pointed out, quite correctly, that offences such as blasphemous libel (*X Ltd and Y v United Kingdom*), outraging public decency (*S and G v United Kingdom* (App. No.17634/91, September 2, 1991)) and blasphemy (*Wingrove v United Kingdom* (1996) 24 E.H.R.R. 1) had withstood scrutiny at Strasbourg. Only in *Hashman and Harrup v United Kingdom* (1999) 30 E.H.R.R. 241 had a finding that the applicants had acted contra bonos mores been held to lack the quality of being "prescribed by law". It was suggested, as put by Emmerson and Ashworth, Human Rights and Criminal Justice (2001), para.10–23, that

> "the standard of certainty required under the Convention, and under comparable constitutional principles, is not a particularly exacting one."

I would for my part accept that the offence as defined by Stephen, as defined in Archbold (save for the reference to morals), as enacted in the Commonwealth codes quoted above and as applied in the cases (other than *R. v Soul* (1980) 70 Cr.App.R. 295) referred to in paras.[13]–[22] above is clear, precise, adequately defined and based on a discernible rational principle. A legal adviser asked to give his opinion in advance would ascertain whether the act or omission contemplated was likely to inflict significant injury on a substantial section of the public exercising their ordinary rights as such: if so, an obvious risk of causing a public nuisance would be apparent; if not, not.

37   I cannot, however, accept that *R. v Norbury* [1978] Crim. L.R. 435 and *R. v Johnson (Anthony)* [1996] 2 Cr.App.R. 434; [1997] 1 W.L.R. 367 were correctly decided or that the convictions discussed in paras [23]–[27] above were soundly based (which is not, of course, to say that the defendants' conduct was other than highly reprehensible or that there were not other charges to which the defendants would have had no answer). To permit a conviction of causing a public nuisance to rest on an injury caused to separate individuals rather than on an injury suffered by the community or a significant section of it as a whole was to contradict the rationale of the offence and pervert its nature, in Convention terms to change

the essential constituent elements of the offence to the detriment of the accused. The offence was cut adrift from its intellectual moorings. It is in my judgment very significant that when, in 1985, the Law Commission addressed the problem of poison-pen letters, and recommended the creation of a new offence, it did not conceive that the existing offence of public nuisance might be applicable. It is hard to resist the conclusion that the courts have, in effect, re-invented public mischief under another name. It is also hard to resist the conclusion expressed by Spencer at p.77 of his article cited above [1989] C.L.J. 55:

> ". . . almost all the prosecutions for public nuisance in recent years seem to have taken place in one of two situations: first, where the defendant's behaviour amounted to a statutory offence, typically punishable with a small penalty, and the prosecutor wanted a bigger or extra stick to beat him with, and secondly, where the defendant's behaviour was not obviously criminal at all and the prosecutor could think of nothing else to charge him with."

As interpreted and applied in the cases referred to in paras [23]–[27] above, the offence of public nuisance lacked the clarity and precision which both the law and the Convention require, as correctly suggested by the commentators in [1978] Crim. L.R. 435 and [1980] Crim. L.R. 234, Spencer, op. cit., pp 55, 77–79, and Professor Ashworth in his commentary on the present cases at [2004] Crim. L.R. 303, 304–306. See also *McMahon and Binchy, Law of Torts*, 3rd ed (2000), p.676 n.6.

Mr Rimmington's appeal

38   It seems to me clear that the facts alleged against Mr Rimmington, assuming them to be true, did not cause common injury to a section of the public and so lacked the essential ingredient of common nuisance, whatever other offence they may have constituted. The Crown contended that, if persistent and vexatious telephone calls were a public nuisance, it was a small and foreseeable step to embrace persistent and vexatious postal communications within that crime also. I would agree that if the telephone calls were properly covered it would be a small and foreseeable development, involving no change in the essential constituent elements of the offence, to embrace postal communications also. But, for reasons already given, the crime of public nuisance does not extend to separate and individual telephone calls, however persistent and vexatious, and the extension of the crime to cover postal communications would be a further illegitimate extension. The judge and the Court of Appeal, bound by *R. v Johnson (Anthony)* [1996] 2 Cr.App.R. 434; [1997] 1 W.L.R. 367, reached a different conclusion. I am of opinion that for all the reasons given above, and those given by my noble and learned friends, this appeal must be allowed.

Mr Goldstein's appeal

39   The argument in this appeal was very largely directed to the issue of mens rea: what state of mind must be proved against a defendant to convict him of causing a

public nuisance? The Crown contended that the correct test was that laid down by the Court of Appeal in *R. v Shorrock* (1994) 87 Cr.App.R. 67, 75; [1994] Q.B. 279, 289, that the defendant is responsible for a nuisance which he knew, or ought to have known (because the means of knowledge were available to him), would be the consequence of what he did or omitted to do. That was a test clearly satisfied on the facts of that case, where the defendant deliberately permitted use of his field and should have known what the result would be. It is a test satisfied, I think, in all the public nuisance authorities considered above, save those based on vicarious liability (which are hard to reconcile with the modern approach to that subject in cases potentially involving the severest penalties, and may well be explained, as Mellor J. did in *R v Stephens* (1866) LR 1 Q.B. 702, 708–709, by the civil colour of the proceedings). I would accept this as the correct test, but it is a test to be applied to the correct facts.

40   Mr Goldstein deliberately posted an envelope containing a small quantity of salt. He intended it to reach the addressee, Mr Ehrlich. Had it done so there would have been no public nuisance, as the trial judge correctly directed the jury. The public nuisance alleged was the escape of the salt from the envelope, which led to the evacuation of the sorting office by 110 workers for an hour and the cancelling of a second post. I am willing to assume (without deciding) that those events could be a sufficiently substantial injury to a significant section of the public to amount to a public nuisance. But the escape of the salt was not a result which Mr Goldstein intended. Nor, plainly was it a result which he knew would occur, since it would have rendered his intended joke entirely futile. It would seem far-fetched to conclude that he should reasonably have known that the salt would escape, at any rate without detailed consideration of the type of envelope used and the care taken in sealing it. He himself said that he had no idea the salt would leak out (see the Court of Appeal judgment, para.38). But neither at trial nor on appeal was this question squarely addressed. The emphasis was on a foreseeable consequence if there were an escape and not on the foreseeability of an unintended escape. In the event, I conclude that it was not proved against Mr Goldstein that he knew or reasonably should have known (because the means of knowledge were available to him) that the salt would escape in the sorting office or in the course of post. For these reasons, and those given by my noble and learned friends, his appeal must be allowed and his conviction quashed.

41   **Lord Nicholls of Birkenhead**   My Lords, I have had the advantage of reading in draft the speech of my noble and learned friend Lord Bingham of Cornhill. I respectfully agree with his exposition of the common law offence of public nuisance, its boundaries, and the place this offence now occupies in the criminal law. For the reasons he gives I too would allow both appeals.

42   I add just one footnote, concerning hoax messages. Whether a hoax message is capable of constituting the offence of causing a public nuisance depends primarily upon the content of the hoax. In the ordinary course a hoax message which, as intended, inconvenienced only the recipient would lack the necessary public element. Very different would be a hoax message of the existence of a public danger,

such as a hoax telephone call that an explosive device has been placed in a railway station. A hoax message of this character is capable of constituting the offence even though made to one person alone. This is because the message, to whomsoever addressed, was expected and intended to be passed via the police to users and potential users of the railway station. In other words, the message was the means whereby the caller intended to cause public alarm and disruption.

43   **Lord Rodger of Earlsferry**   My Lords, I have had the privilege of considering the speech of my noble and learned friend, Lord Bingham of Cornhill, in draft. I agree with it but add some observations in view of the difficulty and importance of the issues involved.

44   The law of nuisance and of public nuisance can be traced back for centuries, but the answers to the questions confronting the House are not to be found in the details of that history. What may, perhaps, be worth noticing is that in 2 Institutes 406 Coke adopts a threefold classification of nuisance: public or general, common, private or special. Common nuisances are public nuisances which, for some reason, are not prosecutable. See D Ibbetson, A Historical Introduction to the Law of Obligations, 106 nn.62 and 65. So for Coke, while all public nuisances are common, not all common nuisances are public. Later writers tend to elide the distinction between common and public nuisances but, throughout, it has remained an essential characteristic of a public nuisance that it affects the community, members of the public as a whole, rather than merely individuals. For that reason, the appropriate remedy is prosecution in the public interest or, in more recent times, a relator action brought by the Attorney General. A private individual can sue only if he can show that the public nuisance has caused him special injury over and above that suffered by the public in general. These procedural specialties derive from the effect of the public nuisance on the community, rather than the other way round. I therefore doubt whether, in a criminal context at least, it is of much help to follow Denning L.J. in the civil case of *Attorney General v PYA Quarries Ltd* [1957] 2 Q.B. 169, 191 and to seek to identify a public nuisance by asking whether the nuisance is so widespread in its range or so indiscriminate in its effect that it would not be reasonable to expect one person to take proceedings on his own responsibility to put a stop to it.

45   As Lord Bingham has shown, there have been many attempts to define the scope of public nuisance. The concept was applied to a number of disparate situations at a time when there was no perceived need to define its boundaries very precisely. In consequence, it has been aptly described as "a ragbag of odds and ends": J.R. Spencer, "Public Nuisance—a Critical Assessment" [1989] C.L.J. 55, 59. In his Digest of the Criminal Law even the highly rational Sir James Fitzjames Stephen could do little more than reflect this reality. Mr Guthrie Q.C. used this lack of coherence in the definition of the offence as a basis for submitting that its contours were so uncertain as to make it incompatible with Art.7 of the European Convention on Human Rights. While a lack of coherence in defining the scope of an offence may offend modern eyes, it does not follow that there is any violation of Art.7. If the individual elements of the crime are identified clearly enough and the law is applied according to its terms, potential offenders

and their advisers know where they stand: they cannot complain because the law could perhaps have been formulated more elegantly. For present purposes I would be content to adopt the definition in *Archbold*, Criminal Pleading, Evidence and Practice 2005, paras 31–40, under deletion of the reference to morals:

> "A person is guilty of a public nuisance (also known as common nuisance), who (a) does an act not warranted by law, or (b) omits to discharge a legal duty, if the effect of the act or omission is to endanger the life, health, property, morals, or comfort of the public, or to obstruct the public in the exercise or enjoyment of rights common to all Her Majesty's subjects."

46   Mr Rimmington seems to have embarked upon his vile campaign of letter writing in 1992. At all events, the first entry in the schedule relates to a letter received on June 1, 1992. If—most improbably—after sending a number of letters Mr Rimmington had paused to consider whether he was committing the offence of public nuisance, then he would surely have found enough in the books to put him on his guard. While there was apparently no case where the writer of obscene or objectionable letters had been prosecuted for public nuisance, there were several cases, starting with *R. v Norbury* [1978] Crim. L.R. 435, where it had been held or accepted that the making of a large number of obscene or objectionable telephone calls to individuals could constitute public nuisance. It would have been only prudent for Mr Rimmington to assume that the general reasoning behind those decisions would be applicable to the sending of a large number of obscene or objectionable letters. In that situation, superficially at least, the law was sufficiently certain to meet the requirements of Art.7 for Mr Rimmington's purposes.

47   Of course, it does not follow that the law as laid down in the Norbury line of cases was correct: a statement of the law may be definite but wrong. I am indeed satisfied that the law was misstated in those cases. A core element of the crime of public nuisance is that the defendant's act should affect the community, a section of the public, rather than simply individuals. Obvious examples would be the release of smoke or fumes which affect a village or neighbourhood or the emission of loud noises which disturb the neighbourhood. In such cases the release or emission or—where it is repeated—each release or emission affects the public in the area. Of course, if one were to break it down, the general effect on the community might well be seen to be made up of a collection of private nuisances occurring more or less simultaneously. Romer L.J. made this point in *Attorney General v PYA Quarries Ltd* [1957] 2 Q.B. 169, where the court granted an injunction against the defendants carrying on their business in such a manner as to cause splinters to be projected from the confines of their quarry or to occasion a nuisance to Her Majesty's subjects by dust or vibration. In the pleadings as originally framed the Attorney General had included various allegations about the damage caused to occupiers of the adjacent houses and land; that the vibrations were a source of danger to the houses, and that the dust settled on them and made them dirty and uncomfortable to live in. Counsel had later deleted these allegations on the ground that, in a public nuisance action, evidence of individual experiences should not be received, although such evidence would be

highly relevant in cases of alleged private nuisance. Romer L.J. rejected this argument, at p.187:

> "I cannot for myself accept this contention. Some public nuisances (for example, the pollution of rivers) can often be established without the necess-ity of calling a number of individual complainants as witnesses. In general, however, a public nuisance is proved by the cumulative effect which it is shown to have had on the people living within its sphere of influence. In other words, a normal and legitimate way of proving a public nuisance is to prove a sufficiently large collection of private nuisances."

Although the number of houses affected by the flying splinters of stone and by the dust and vibration presumably varied a bit from blast to blast, each blast tended to affect homes in the vicinity of the quarry and a picture of the overall effect of the blasting on the community could be built up from the evidence of individual resi-dents about its effect on them.

48   As my noble and learned friend, Lord Nicholls of Birkenhead, points out, a tel-ephone call or a letter, which is intended to be passed on and broadcast to the public, may be the means of effecting a public nuisance. Suppose, however, that someone makes a series of obscene telephone calls to people living in a vil-lage or neighbourhood. In that situation each call is heard, and is intended to be heard, only by the recipient. Of course, as the calls mount up, more and more resi-dents will be affected and the general peace of the neighbourhood may be disturbed. But each telephone call affects only one individual, not the community in the village or neighbourhood. Therefore, it does not have that quality which is the hallmark of the crime of public nuisance. And no such individual call can become a criminal public nuisance merely by reason of the fact that it is one of a series. Otherwise, acts which were not criminal when originally done would become criminal at some unspecified point when the defendant had made enough calls for it to be said that, taken together, they were affecting the public in the neighbourhood. In my view, therefore, H.H. Judge Beezley set the law off down a wrong course in *R. v Norbury* [1978] Crim. L.R. 435, 435–436, when he ruled that a public nuisance was constituted by

> "a repetition over a long period and on a number of occasions of telephone calls of an obscene nature, intending to cause offence and alarm and result-ing in such offence and alarm to a large number of Her Majesty's subjects, selected from a telephone directory or merely by chance dialling."

In *R. v Johnson (Anthony)* [1996] 2 Cr.App.R. 434, [1997] 1 W.L.R. 367, the defendant was charged on an indictment containing one count of public nuisance, but the particulars referred to telephone calls made on hundreds of occasions to at least 13 women in the South Cumbria area. The defendant was convicted and, on appeal, argued that his conduct did not amount to the crime of public nuisance. The Court of Appeal rejected that argument. Applying the same reasoning as in Norbury, Tucker J. said, at p.438C–D, that it was permissible to have regard to the cumulative effect of the calls in determining whether the appellant's con-duct constituted a public nuisance. In the present case the Court of Appeal were, of course, bound by the decision in Johnson and duly applied it. For the reasons which I have given, I am satisfied that this approach was mistaken and that these decisions should be overruled.

49   Like the defendant in Johnson, Mr Rimmington was charged on an indictment containing one count of public nuisance. In his case the particulars referred to him sending 538 separate postal packages between May 20, 1992 and June 13, 2001. Details about the individual packages were set out in an extensive schedule. The first package in that schedule was received on June 1, 1992 and the next package that could be dated was received in October 1993. The recorded incidents are somewhat sparse until June 1995, after which there are many more packages, often apparently sent in batches posted about the same time but quite often in different areas. The recipients come from a variety of organisations scattered over different parts of London and the South East. Most of them would not know one another. In these circumstances it would be highly problematical, for Mr Rimmington or for a court, to decide at what point, if any, the cumulative effect of the letters meant that his conduct was materially affecting the reasonable comfort and convenience of a class of Her Majesty's subjects—and so, ultimately, to make the initial incident in 1992, retrospectively, one component of a single crime of public nuisance committed over nine years. A crime which was defined so as to apply in such an uncertain way would indeed be objectionable, both in terms of the well-recognised standards of English law and in terms of the Convention jurisprudence. Both are conveniently summarised in the passage from the judgment of Judge L.J. in *R. v Misra and Srivastava* [2005] 1 Cr.App.R. 21 (p.328), paras [29]–[34], which Lord Bingham has quoted. But, as I have explained, I am satisfied that the particulars in the indictment do not disclose a legally relevant charge of public nuisance. I accordingly agree that Mr Rimmington's appeal must be allowed.

50   The course of conduct which Mr Rimmington pursued in sending these letters was so depraved and offensive that it would be a matter of concern if the criminal law could not deal with it. But that is not the case. As his counsel noted, though with understandable diffidence, there are other offences which might cover the kind of conduct with which he was charged. Section 1 of the Malicious Communications Act 1988, as amended, makes it an offence to send another person a letter, electronic communication or article of any description which conveys a message which is indecent or grossly offensive, or which conveys a threat or information which is false and known or believed to be false. The offence is punishable on summary conviction with a maximum of six months' imprisonment and a fine on scale 5. Similarly, by s.85(1) and (4) of the Postal Services Act 2000 it is an offence to send by post a packet enclosing any thing which is likely to injure a postal worker or which is indecent or obscene. The offence is triable either way: on summary conviction it is punishable by a fine, while on conviction on indictment it is punishable by imprisonment for up to 12 months and a fine. Mr Perry accepted, on behalf of the Crown, that some, at least, of the incidents alleged against Mr Rimmington would have fallen within the scope of one or other of the statutory provisions. So any decision by your Lordships that Mr Rimmington's conduct does not amount to public nuisance would leave it open to the

Crown to deal with future offenders by charging them with the appropriate statutory offence.

51   Why then did the Crown not adopt that course in Mr Rimmington's case? Mr Perry gave two reasons. First, by the time that Mr Rimmington was unmasked as the writer of the letters, many of the incidents were so old that there was a bar on any prosecution under statute. Secondly, even where the offences were not time-barred, the sentence available on conviction under statute was regarded as insufficient to mark the seriousness of the appellant's conduct. And, if a number of separate offences were charged together in summary proceedings, the maximum sentence that could be imposed was limited to 12 months. In order to avoid these difficulties, it had been decided to charge Mr Rimmington on indictment with the common law crime of public nuisance.

52   When Parliament enacted the statutory offences, it did not expressly abolish the corresponding aspect of the common law offence of public nuisance. Therefore, if—contrary to my view—Mr Rimmington's conduct in writing the letters had amounted to a public nuisance, it would presumably have continued to do so even after the statutory offences were introduced. So a charge could not have been regarded as bad simply because it was framed in terms of the common law rather than in terms of the statute. To put the matter more generally, where Parliament has not abolished the relevant area of the common law when it enacts a statutory offence, it cannot be said that the Crown can never properly frame a common law charge to cover conduct which is covered by the statutory offence. Where nothing would have prevented the Crown from charging the defendant under the statute and where the sentence imposed would also have been competent in proceedings under the statute, the defendant is not prejudiced by being prosecuted at common law and can have no legitimate complaint.

53   Here, however, according to what Mr Perry told the House, the Crown had deliberately chosen the common law offence in order to avoid the time-bar which Parliament had enacted and to allow the judge, if he thought fit, to impose a heavier sentence than the one permitted under statute. The issue bears some resemblance to the issue in *R. v J* [2004] UKHL 42; [2005] 1 Cr.App.R. 19 (p.277); [2005] 1 A.C. 562. There is no suggestion, of course, that the Crown acted in bad faith. On the contrary, it is easy to understand why they did what they did. In a particular case, such as this, a time-limit which prevents prosecution once a certain time has passed since the act was committed can appear to be arbitrary and to reward an offender for concealing his offences. The sentence available under the statute may also seem inadequate to reflect the gravity of the defendant's conduct. But Parliament has deliberately chosen to intervene and to prescribe a period within which conduct of this kind can be prosecuted summarily under statute. This must be taken to reflect Parliament's judgment that, if the conduct has not been prosecuted within that time, the public interest is now against proceeding. That judgment may be based on various factors. Parliament may, for example, consider that after a certain period everyone should move on and prosecutors should turn their attention to other matters. Police and prosecution resources, it may be thought, are better spent on detecting and prosecuting recent, rather than stale, offences of this kind or recent, rather than

old, incidents in a course of conduct. More serious matters should be given priority. Similarly, in the matter of sentence, Parliament has reached a view that certain conduct is appropriately covered by an offence which can be tried only summarily and which should attract no more than a particular level of sentence. Parliament has also fixed the maximum sentence to be imposed in summary proceedings, even where the defendant is convicted of more than one charge. Again, in any particular case, the sentence available under statute may appear to the prosecutor to be inadequate. But Parliament is entitled to place an offence in what it regards as the appropriate level in the hierarchy of offences and to limit the sentencing power of a court where the accused is not tried by jury.

54   It is not for the Crown to second-guess Parliament's judgment as to any of these matters by deliberately setting out to reject the applicable statutory offences and to charge the conduct in question under common law in order to avoid the time-limits or limits on sentence which Parliament has thought appropriate. It may be that, in the light of experience, Parliament's judgment can be seen to have been flawed or to have been superseded by events. Doubtless, the prosecuting authorities have channels through which they can—and perhaps should—draw any such perceived deficiencies to the attention of the Home Secretary. It is then up to ministers and, ultimately, Parliament to decide whether the law should be changed. But, unless and until it is changed, its provisions should be respected and the Crown should not devise a strategy to avoid them.

55   Lord Bingham has described the circumstances of Mr Goldstein's case. It is plain that he put the salt in the envelope intending it to be a humorous message to his friend, Mr Ehrlich, who would have understood the joke. He posted the letter in a period when, following events in the United States, there were fears about the possibility of anthrax germs being sent through the post. It is therefore not surprising that when, just before 06.00, some of the salt spilled out of the torn envelope on to the hands of a sorter, Mr Owen, he raised the alarm. Indeed, Mr Goldstein accepted that the escape of the salt could have terrified Mr Owen. The Wembley sorting office was cleared and the police were called. They soon saw that the powder was salt but the sorters could not return to work for over an hour. For that reason, the first delivery of letters was somewhat later than usual. The management then decided to cancel the second delivery since, by the time the first delivery had been completed, the postal workers had finished their shift and would have had to be paid overtime to do the second delivery. The judge reminded the jury of evidence that over 35,000 businesses missed the second delivery and that some people had telephoned to complain. He was therefore directing the jury that, in deciding whether Mr Goldstein was guilty of public nuisance, they could take account of the inconvenience to the public caused by the cancellation of the second delivery.

56   In R. v Shorrock (1994) 98 Cr.App.R. 67, 75; [1994] Q.B. 279, 289, the Court of Appeal held that a defendant landowner was responsible for a public nuisance which he knew or ought to have known (in the sense that the means of knowledge were available to him) would be the consequence of activities carried on by him on his land. In the present case the Court of Appeal held that a similar test should be applied to Mr Goldstein. Mr Goldberg argued that the House should disap-

prove the decision in Shorrock and bring the mens rea for public nuisance into line with the approach adopted in *R. v G* [2003] UKHL 50; [2004] 1 Cr.App.R. 21 (p.237); [2004] 1 A.C. 1034. For my part, I was not persuaded by that submission. In *R. v G* the House was considering the proper interpretation of "reckless" in s.1(1) and (2) of the Criminal Damage Act 1971 and, in para.28 of the leading speech, Lord Bingham made it as plain as he could that he was not addressing the meaning of "reckless" in any other statutory or common law context. The decision is therefore not in point. Particularly having regard to the essentially regulatory nature of much of the law of public nuisance, it seems to me that, even if it is unusual, the mens rea described in Shorrock is apt in situations where the offence truly applies. I would accept the reasoning in Shorrock. Applying the test in Shorrock, I am, however, satisfied that Mr Goldstein did not have the necessary mens rea to be convicted of public nuisance.

57   It was not unlawful for Mr Goldstein to put salt into a packet to be sent through the post. Nevertheless, if he had done so with the intention of provoking an anthrax scare and disrupting the post and if those events had come to pass, he might well have been guilty of public nuisance. But, according to the evidence, he had no such intention and, he said, he had never for a moment foreseen that the salt would leak out. Even if he had done so, however, it seems to me impossible to hold that he either knew or had the means of knowing that the events which happened in the Wembley sorting office and in the surrounding district would occur. In the heightened atmosphere of the time, he might have been able to foresee that there would be some disruption in the sorting office, but he had no means of knowing at what time of day his letter would be sorted or that the second delivery of post would be cancelled and cause inconvenience to the businesses in the area. Indeed, as the judge explained to the jury, the manager only decided to cancel it when he realised that they would have to pay overtime to the postal workers to do the work. The disruption to the public, which the jury were invited to consider, was therefore not an immediate consequence of Mr Goldstein's act, but the consequence of an independent commercial decision of the post office management which he had no means of anticipating when he posted the letter. To hold Mr Goldstein guilty of public nuisance on the basis of this (relatively minor) inconvenience to the public would be to stretch the offence beyond its legitimate limits. I accordingly agree that his appeal should be allowed and his conviction quashed.

Baroness Hale of Richmond
My Lords,

58   I agree, for the reasons given by my noble and learned friend, Lord Bingham of Cornhill, that both these appeals should be allowed. It is not open to the courts, however tempted they might be by the history so attractively presented by John Spencer in his valuable article, "Public Nuisance—A Critical Assessment" [1989] C.L.J. 55, to abolish existing offences. Nor it is open to the courts to "widen existing offences so as to make punishable conduct of a type hitherto not subject to punishment" (para 33, above). We are not, therefore, engaged in a law reform exercise. Our task is to define and re-establish the essential ingredients of the crime as they emerged after the publication of Hawkins' Treatise

of the Pleas of the Crown in 1716. The essence of the crime which he and the later institutional writers identified was, as my noble and learned friend has shown, "the suffering of common injury by members of the public by interference with rights enjoyed by them as such" (para [6], above). It is not permissible to multiply separate instances of harm suffered by individual members of the public, however similar the harm or the conduct which produced it, and call them a common injury. Conduct which was not criminal when the first letter was sent would become criminal at some unknown future time when it was thought that enough such letters had been sent to constitute such a common injury. This must be wrong in principle. Nor can it be right to punish someone who had no reason to think that his letter would cause any harm to anyone, because he had no reason to think that the salt would leak out in circumstances where his joke would not be understood.

59   I am pleased to be able to reach both conclusions, because I was a signatory to the Law Commission's Report on Poison-Pen Letters (Law Com No.147, 1985). This resulted in the Malicious Communications Act 1985, which seems tailor-made to identify any culpable conduct in both these situations. This arose from the Commission's examination of the common law offence of criminal libel, as part of its programme of codification of the Criminal Law. Neither in that Report, nor in the preceding Working Paper on Criminal Libel (LCWP No.84, 1982), was it suggested that public nuisance might be available to cover campaigns of multiple malicious communications such as that conducted by Mr Rimmington. This is all the more remarkable, as the Commission had briefly considered public nuisance in the context of its work on public order offences, which eventually resulted in the Public Order Act 1986. The Commission had originally intended to include public nuisance in that work, as it had sometimes been used in public order situations, such as "sit-down" demonstrations in central London: see *R. v Moule* [1964] Crim. L.R. 303; *R. v Adler* [1964] Crim. L.R. 304; cf *R. v Clark (No.2)* (1964) 48 Cr.App.R. 69; [1964] 2 Q.B. 315. In its Working Paper on Offences against Public Order (LCWP 82, 1982, at paras 1.9–1.12), however, the Commission announced that reviewing the offence, either as a whole or insofar as it penalised highway obstructions, would take the project far outside the realms of public order. The "best practicable approach" would be a separate review of the whole offence (para.1.12). Unfortunately, however, this has not been done. The Commission did remark (at para.1.10) that the offence had been used in a wide variety of situations, and referred to the then relatively recent cases of *R. v Norbury* [1978] Crim. L.R. 435 (making a large number of obscene telephone calls) and *R. v Soul* (1980) 70 Cr.App.R. 295 (assisting in effecting the escape of a patient from Broadmoor). So the offence of public nuisance, as recently employed in the courts, was certainly in the minds of the criminal law team at the Commission in 1982 when they were working on poison pen letters. Yet nowhere was it suggested that public nuisance might be the appropriate response to the more serious and prolonged "poison pen" campaigns, although these are by no means uncommon. I am relieved to be able to conclude that the Commission was right to ignore it. It is of interest to note, however, that in its Report on Offences relating to Public Order (Law Com No.123, 1983, at

para.1.8) the Commission did say that if the recommended offences were enacted "it will be preferable for public nuisance not to be charged in situations where there are disturbances to public order", thus foreshadowing the observations of my noble and learned friend at para.30, above.

60   **Lord Brown of Eaton-Under-Heywood**   My Lords, I have had the advantage of reading in draft the speech of my noble and learned friend, Lord Bingham of Cornhill. I respectfully agree with all that he says and for the reasons he gives, I too would allow both these appeals.

61   I also agree with what Lord Nicholls of Birkenhead says in para.42 of his speech and with the speeches of Lord Rodger of Earlsferry and Baroness Hale of Richmond.

Appeal allowed.

R. v TIMMINS

COURT OF APPEAL (Lord Justice Keene, Lady Justice Hallett and Mr
Justice Calvert-Smith): August 4; November 15, 2005

[2005] EWCA Crim 2909; [2006] 1 Cr.App.R. 18

*Alternative verdicts; Indecent assault; Lesser offences; Sexual activity with
children; Time limits*

H1   SEXUAL OFFENCES
      Indecent assault
      *Appellant charged with rape of 14-year-old girl—Consensual sexual inter-
      course admitted—Prosecution for unlawful sexual intercourse time-barred—
      Alternative verdict of indecent assault based on admitted conduct left to jury—
      Whether lawful— Sexual Offences Act 1956 (4 & 5 Eliz. 2, c. 69), ss.6(1), 14,
      Sch.2, para.10(a)— Criminal Law Act 1967 (c.58), s.6(3)*

H2   The appellant was charged with the rape of his former partner's daughter, the
      allegation being that the offence had taken place several years earlier, when the
      girl was 14 years old. The appellant accepted that he had had sexual intercourse
      with the girl but he claimed that it had been with her consent. At the beginning of
      the trial, consideration was given to the possibility of adding to the indictment a
      count of indecent assault, contrary to s.14 of the Sexual Offences Act 1956, to
      cover the appellant's admitted conduct. However, the Crown accepted that
      such a count was not possible since it would be based on the same facts as a
      count of unlawful sexual intercourse under s.6(1), and para.10(a) of Sch.2 to
      the Act provided that a prosecution for unlawful sexual intercourse could not
      be commenced more than 12 months after the offence charged. The judge, how-
      ever, subsequently ruled that indecent assault could be left to the jury as an
      alternative verdict, pursuant to s.6(3) of the Criminal Law Act 1967, on the
      ground that the prosecution was for rape, with the issue being consent, and, there-
      fore, there was no question of the alternative verdict being a procedural device to
      get round a time limit. The appellant was acquitted of rape but convicted of inde-
      cent assault. He appealed against conviction.

H3   **Held,** dismissing the appeal, that the prosecution of the appellant commenced,
      and continued until the verdict, as a prosecution for rape; that Parliament had,
      since the 1956 Act, enacted the Criminal Law Act 1967, which enabled juries
      to return verdicts on lesser charges when the facts they found fell short of
      proof of the greater. The express intention of Parliament in 1967 as to alternative
      verdicts could not be thwarted by an express intention of Parliament in 1956 con-
      cerning the commencement of proceedings for unlawful sexual intercourse,
      which was a different offence from the one which was the subject of the alterna-

tive verdict. Accordingly, the judge was right to rule that indecent assault could be left to the jury as an alternative verdict to rape (post, paras 27–29).

H4   *R. v J* [2004] UKHL 42; [2005] 1 Cr.App.R. 19 (p.277); [2005] 1 A.C. 562, HL, distinguished.

H5   (For sexual offences generally, see *Archbold* 2006, Ch.20, but specifically for ss.6 and 14 of the Sexual Offences Act 1956, see *Archbold* 2004 (and the supplements thereto), paras 20–74 to 20–87 and 20–144 to 20–155).

Appeal against conviction

H6   On April 7, 2005 in the Crown Court at Carlisle (Judge Slinger) the appellant, Mark Timmins, was convicted of an offence of indecent assault as an alternative to the original count of rape. He was acquitted of two further counts of rape and three counts of indecent assault. He was sentenced to six months' imprisonment.

H7   The facts and grounds of appeal appear in the judgment of the court.

H8   *Gregory Hoare* (assigned by the Registrar of Criminal Appeals) for the appellant. *Paul Timothy Evans* (instructed by the Crown Prosecution Service, Workington) for the Crown.

Cur. adv. vult.

November 11   **Calvert Smith J.:** handed down the judgment of the court.

1   On April 7, 2005 at Carlisle Crown Court this appellant was convicted of an offence of indecent assault. The verdict was an alternative verdict, the original count having alleged rape. He was acquitted altogether of two further counts of rape and three of indecent assault. He appeals against conviction with leave of the single judge. The complainant in all six counts was the daughter of the appellant's former partner. Following her parents' separation the appellant had started up a relationship with her mother. The appellant had moved into the family home when the complainant was 12 or 13 years old. The appellant was said to have indecently assaulted her on a number of occasions by forcing her to give him oral sex (counts 4, 5 and 6). This was said to have happened on at least 10 or 11 occasions but the charges formed specimen counts. Four days after the first indecent assault the appellant was said to have raped the complainant (count 1. The appellant was 14 years and six months old at the time. This was said to have happened on a number of other occasions but the other charges formed specimen counts (counts 5 and 6). Several years later, following the appellant's separation from the complainant's mother, the complainant made the allegations to her mother who then informed the police.

2   The appellant did not deny having sexual intercourse per vaginam with the complainant when she was 14 but claimed that it had been with her consent. It is clear from the jury's verdict on this and the other counts that they accepted that his account of this charge and the other charges was or may have been true.

3   The Sexual Offences Act 1956 ("the 1956 Act") under which all the charges in
this case were brought has been repealed and replaced by the Sexual Offences Act
2003 which came into force on April 1, 2004. The 2003 Act is not retrospective.
Sexual offences committed before that date will continue to be dealt with under
the old law. For reasons which are well-known alleged sexual offences often
come before the courts many years after their commission. In this case the conduct alleged had occurred between 1998 and 2001.

4   It is settled law that the act of intercourse is sufficient to amount to an indecent
assault under s.14(1) of the Sexual Offences Act 1956— R. v McCormack (1969)
53 Cr.App.R. 514; [1969] 2 Q.B. 442. By s.14(2) consent is not a defence to such a
charge when the victim is under 16. It is equally clear that an alternative verdict of
indecent assault is available on a charge of rape— R. v Hodgson (1973) 57
Cr.App.R. 502; [1973] Q.B. 565.

5   By s.6(1) of the 1956 Act "it is an offence . . . for a man to have unlawful sexual intercourse with a girl . . . under the age of 16". Paragraph 10(a) of Sch.2 of
the Act, which is given effect by s.37 of the Act provides that, with respect to such
an offence, "a prosecution may not be commenced more than 12 months after the
offence charged." There is no time limit on prosecution of the equivalent offence
in the Sexual Offences Act 2003— s.9(1) and (2)(a).

6   Until recently it had been the practice for many years for prosecutors to prosecute defendants under s.14 in cases in which the time limit for a prosecution
under s.6(1) had been exceeded and in which the prosecutor believed the public
interest would be served by a prosecution. The practice had had at least the
implied approval of this court. In R. v Hinton (1995) 16 Cr.App.R.(S.) 523 the
defendant had pleaded guilty to indecent assault on his 15-year-old stepdaughter.
The reason for the charge being under s.14 was that the time limit for prosecution
under s.6 had expired. The sentence exceeded the maximum for the s.6 offence.
The court reduced the sentence since the maximum sentence for an offence under
s.6 was 2 years whereas the maximum sentence for indecent assault was 10 years.
(The maximum sentence for an offence under the new s.9 Sexual Offences Act
2003 is 14 years.) In that case the defendant had originally been charged with
a s.6 offence. When it was discovered that that offence was time-barred the
charge under s.14 was substituted. In R. v Iles [1998] 2 Cr.App.R.(S.) 63 and
R. v Figg [2004] 1 Cr.App.R.(S.) 68 (p.409) the question of sentence in this
type of case was revisited without any suggestion that the course adopted by
the Crown of charging s.14 offences in suitable cases when the time limit in
respect of the s.6 offence had expired was objectionable either in law or on
grounds of public policy. The point was taken for the first time in R. v Jones
(Micheal) [2003] 2 Cr.App.R. 8 (p.134). It was rejected by the Court of Appeal.

7   However the practice has recently been brought to an end as the result of the
House of Lords decision in R. v J [2005] 1 A.C. 562; [2004] UKHL 42; [2005]
1 Cr.App.R. 19 (p.277) in which the majority clearly ruled that to charge an
offence under s.14 when the facts of the case supported a s.6 offence offended
against the limitation period in Sch.2 para.10(a). In that case a 35–37 year old
man had repeatedly abused a position of trust with a 13–14 year old girl. Unsurprisingly therefore a majority of their Lordships expressed the view either that the

prosecutor had commenced the proceedings in what he believed to be the public interest or (Lord Bingham of Cornhill at para.[14]) that the decision to do so was one "which the general public would applaud".

8   The present case came before the Carlisle Crown Court after the decision in *J* in which the speeches were delivered on October 14, 2004.

9   At the beginning of the trial consideration was given to the possibility of adding a count of indecent assault to cover the admitted conduct of the accused of having vaginal intercourse with the 13-year-old girl. After discussions between counsel it was concluded that the decision in *J* precluded the addition of such a count. (This conclusion has since been confirmed by the decision of this court in *R. v WR* [2005] EWCA Crim 1907 (Judgment July 11, 2005) to which our attention has been drawn by counsel since the hearing.) The trial judge then indicated that at some stage he would wish to hear argument on the possibility of the addition of a separate count or of an alternative verdict at a later stage.

10   On the second day of the trial the judge heard argument and ruled that the alternative verdict of indecent assault could be left on a charge of rape. In his ruling he stated (as transcribed):

> "Historically, when the issue had been one of consent in a rape charge, it had always been accepted that if a girl were under the age of 16, and a jury were to find not guilty of rape on the issue of consent, it was open to a jury—if it accepted that the intercourse had taken place, to find on an alternative verdict a defendant guilty of indecent assault. The issue now is whether that remains still open to the jury. Until the case of *R. v J* [2005] 1 Cr.App.R. 19 (p.277)—until the decision of the House of Lords in the case, no-one had considered that there might be a problem. But, it is submitted by Mr Hoare—to whom I am grateful for his skeleton argument and for his oral submissions—it is submitted that there had been a complete sea change as a result of the case of *J*. Such a sea change, which he submitted, might be thought to have resulted in irrational and incoherent decisions which might bring the law into disrepute, and adopting the view of Baroness Hale in that case the position might well be undeserved, but nonetheless technically correct, and his submission is this.
>
> That when the matters, which are now admitted by the defendant, consist of unlawful sexual intercourse, provided that the case was brought outside the time limit for a proper prosecution for that offence, it is no longer open to the jury on the facts of unlawful sexual intercourse to convict of indecent assault. *J*, he says, now will affect a sea change, both procedurally and substantively, in the time-honoured way in which these matters have been dealt with.
>
> The facts of *J* were effectively these. That there had had been consensual sexual intercourse between a 17-year-old girl. Sorry, a 17-year-old complainant alleged that between the ages of 13 and 15, she had had consensual sexual intercourse with the defendant. He had denied that but was convicted. But [he] submitted—at various stages both before the trial judge and at various stages of appeal—that because the prosecution had

been out of time for bringing the charges of unlawful sexual intercourse, that had deliberately chosen to charge on the basis of indecent assault, it was an abuse of process for the matter to be allowed to continue. The abuse of process argument went before the trial judge and the Court of Appeal, but no doubt at the prodding of the House of Lords, the matter was slightly altered in the sense that what their Lordships really considered was whether the wording of the statute allowed what had in fact happened. So, reflecting again, what had happened was this. The prosecution would have been for unlawful sexual intercourse had it been done timeously. It was too late, and quite openly the prosecution then sought to proceed by way of charges of indecent assault and made it quite clear that that was what they were going to do. And indeed, it followed a line of cases which had come before the Court of Appeal, not on that point, but on the question of the sentencing which was appropriate.

The House of Lords found that where the statutory provision as here, in relation to time limits, was clear and unambiguous, the court could not decline to give effect to it on the grounds that the rationale here of the time limits might have been anachronistic, discredited or unconvincing. That Parliament must have decided there was a reason for a time limit, Parliament had not altered it and that accordingly, when the only evidence of sexual intercourse with a girl under 16 was relied upon, the defendant could not be prosecuted for indecent assault after 12 months had elapsed. And in effect, Mr Hoare now says well that's the situation on the facts. The prosecution on this charge of rape could not have put an alternative matter of unlawful sexual intercourse, and therefore it follows from that indecent assault cannot follow. It is really an attractive argument, but one which I do not accept.

J was concerned with specific facts as to the basis upon which the prosecution was launched. This is a case of rape. It's a case of rape and where the issue—in terms of the time when the girl was under 16—the issue is one of consent in matters where the jury finds that matter occur below the age of 16, the issue is one of consent. It is not a case where a procedural device has been adopted to get round a time limit. There is no time limit in relation to rape and it is my judgment that the Crown is still entitled to ask the jury to consider alternative verdicts of indecent assault."

11   The stark issue for us therefore is whether the decision in *J* means that there are no circumstances in which a defendant who has, before May 1, 2004, had consensual intercourse with a girl under 16, can be convicted of an offence of indecent assault unless proceedings are started within 12 months of the alleged offence. On behalf of the appellant Mr Hoare has submitted that that is the only logical conclusion to be drawn from the speeches of the majority. On behalf of the respondent Mr Evans has submitted:

i) That *J* was dealing with a particular situation and the plain words of the Schedule.

ii) That Lord Bingham in particular left open the question of alternative verdicts albeit in the context of such verdicts as are provided for within the
Act itself rather than those which are the result of the operation of s.6(3)
of the Criminal Law Act 1967 to which no reference was made in any of
the speeches.

12   Does the decision of the judge, at the instance of either prosecution or defence
or on his own initiative, to leave the possibility of an alternative verdict of indecent assault to a jury, or the decision of a defendant to plead guilty to such a lesser
charge which is accepted by the prosecution and the court, infringe the principle
of statutory construction so clearly stated by the majority in *J*? In *R. v McCormack* (1969) 53 Cr.App.R. 514 the court ruled that the decision whether to
leave an alternative verdict is a matter for the trial judge's discretion. In his judgment at p.513 Fenton Atkinson L.J. said this:

> "The view this Court had formed is that the learned Deputy Chairman did
> have a discretion in the matter. Cases vary so infinitely that one can well
> envisage a case where the possibility of conviction of some lesser offence
> had been completely ignored by both prosecution and defence—it may be
> that the defendant has never had occasion to deal with the matter, has lost
> a chance of calling some evidence to cover or guard against the possibility
> of conviction of that lesser offence—and in such case, where there might
> well be prejudice to a defendant, it seems to this Court there must be a dis-
> cretion in the trial judge whether or not to leave the lesser offence to the
> jury."

13   There are two ways in which the question might be answered in the affirmative.
One would be if the words "commence proceedings" are apt to cover the situation in which an alternative verdict is returned on a charge which was not
brought by the prosecution and indeed was a verdict which they had sought to
avoid.

14   Although the House of Lords in *J* was concerned with the institution of proceedings rather than the question of alternative verdicts, there are references in
some of the speeches to this issue.

15   At para.[23] Lord Bingham of Cornhill said:

> "In a case of incest by a man, prohibited by s.10, para.14(a) of Sch.2 pro-
> vided that the jury might, as an alternative verdict, find the accused guilty
> of intercourse with a girl under 13 (contrary to s.5) or intercourse with a
> girl between 13 and 16 (contrary to s.6) . . . I incline to the view that an
> alternative verdict under s.6 in this context was subject to no time limit:
> the s.10 offence itself was not time-limited: nor was the s.5 offence; there
> was no repetition of the s.6 time limit; and the requirement for the Director's
> consent could have been expected to ensure that s.10 would not be used as a
> means of circumventing the time limit applicable to prosecutions under
> s.6."

16   Lord Clyde at para.[43] specifically excluded alternative verdicts from consideration.

> "The present case however is not concerned with problems of alternative
> verdicts."

17   Lord Steyn and Lord Roger of Earlsferry did not specifically mention the issue.
Lord Rodger referred to the submissions of counsel then instructed for the
Crown—para.[65]

> "Deploying his learning and experience, Mr Perry held up the prospect of all
> kinds of difficulties that would, he said, arise if your Lordships were to inter-
> pret the Act in this way. I am prepared to accept that there may indeed be
> some initial difficulties."

18   There is no doubt, though she did not mention it specifically, what the view of
the fifth (dissenting) Law Lord, Baroness Hale of Richmond, would have been
since she saw nothing wrong with the institution of proceedings for the offence
of indecent assault.

19   An authority which was cited to the House and which bears on the current point
is *R. v Cotton* (1896) 60 J.P. 824. In that case the Crown sought to persuade the
trial judge to leave an alternative verdict of unlawful sexual intercourse (then
s.5 of the Criminal Law Amendment Act 1885) to the jury when proceedings
for that offence would have been time-barred. The judge refused the application.
In the course of his judgment he said:

> "The conclusion I have come to is that you cannot go on with the charge
> under s.5, more that three months having elapsed since the last commission
> of the offence. In substance, if this could be done, by shaping your charge as
> a charge of rape, you could always evade the statutory limit of time. In a case
> such as this, it would be the more reasonable construction of the sections to
> hold that the time must be considered as the essence of the charge. In sub-
> stance, an indictment of rape under circumstances such as these must be
> treated as a charge of the lesser offence".

20   Lord Bingham of Cornhill (at para.[19]) in *J* expressed doubts as to the reasoning in that case.

> "The very brief report makes no reference to indecent assault, of which it
> was also open to the jury to convict under s.9. I would hesitate to accept
> all the reasoning of Pollock B."

We share those doubts.

21   In our judgment, whatever the situation which may have applied in the late
19th century the reasoning by today's standards is indeed faulty. It would be a
clear breach of the Code for Crown Prosecutors to bring a charge against a person
against whom there was no evidence whatever of rape (in particular of lack of
consent) in order to circumvent a time limit. It would also amount to a clear
abuse of the process of the court. A dismissal hearing would dispose of the charge
if such a charge was brought.

22   The burden of their Lordships' reasoning is to outlaw the bringing of proceedings because to do so would be to flout the will of Parliament and not because it would amount to an abuse of the court's process. Lord Bingham makes this clear at para.[14].

> "The Court of Appeal was quite right, in my respectful opinion, to hold that the conduct of the prosecution in this case did not fall squarely within the category of abuse of the process of the court stigmatised by Sir Roger Ormrod, delivering the judgment of Lord Lane C.J. and himself, *R. v Derby Crown Court, Ex p. Brooks* (1984) 80 Cr.App.R. 164, 168–169. Nor was it within that considered by the House in *R. v Horseferry Road Magistrates' Court, Ex p. Bennett* (1994) 98 Cr.App.R. 114, [1994] 1 A.C. 42. As Mr Meeke Q.C., for J, roundly acknowledged, the prosecution had not been guilty of any devious, underhand or manipulative conduct. They had not sought to take unfair advantage of a technicality or to prejudice the conduct of the defence in any improper way. The delay in prosecuting *J*, in no way the fault of the prosecution, did not imperil the fairness of the trial. There was no misconduct by the executive. This was a case in which the prosecution, learning of serious criminal conduct when it was too late to prosecute under s.6, sought to discharge its public duty by prosecuting under s.14. It was a decision which the general public would applaud."

Lord Steyn does not rule finally on the point. At para.[38]:

> "Although this conclusion is sufficient to dispose of the appeal I will also consider the position under the common law. The present case is not easily accommodated under any of the traditional categories of abuse of process. It is not profitable to try to analyse it by reference to *dicta* about wholly different categories of abuse of process. On the other hand, it must be borne in mind that the category of cases in which the abuse of process principles can be applied are not closed: *R.v Latif* [1996] 2 Cr.App.R. 92 100–101; [1996] 1 W.L.R. 104, 112–113. In any event, this is pre-eminently a corner of the law which must be considered from the point of view of legal principle."

Nor does Lord Clyde. At para.[49]:

> "The case does not fall readily into the established categories of abuse but the concept of abuse may defy exhaustive definition. What the prosecution did here, albeit with good intention and without malice or dishonesty, was to cut across the intention of Parliament and in particular the provision of a protection for a person against whom a particular offence has been alleged. The substance of the argument on abuse is that the prosecutor should not be entitled to circumvent that protection by resorting to another offence which is less suited to the facts of the case. In my view it can at least be argued that it would be something so wrong as to make it proper for a court to refuse to allow a prosecuter to proceed on such a course. The essence of the wrong is an illegality which in turn is based upon a miscon-

struction of the Act. While the label of abuse may not be appropriate for such a situation the illegality of the course would justify the intervention of the court. At the heart of the matter is the proper understanding of the relationship between the two statutory provisions. The two lines of approach may eventually turn out to be different ways of viewing the same point. But they both lead to the same result."

Lord Rodger of Earlsferry seems to incline to the opposite view. At para.[61]:

"In the court below, and again in this House, Mr Meeke argued that bringing the prosecution under s.14, in order to avoid the time-bar applying to s.6, amounted to an abuse of process on the part of the Crown. The argument was rejected in the courts below. It seems to me that if, on a proper construction of s.14 in the context of the 1956 Act as a whole, it was open to the Crown to prosecute the appellant under s.14, then there can have been no abuse of process. But, equally, if on a proper construction of the legislation, it was not open to the Crown to prosecute the appellant under s.14, the appeal must succeed. The critical question is one of the construction of the Act. It appears that counsel for the appellant veered away from that approach because of the rag-bag nature of the 1956 Act as described by my noble and learned friend Lord Bingham of Cornhill, in *R. v K* [2002] 1 Cr.App.R. 121, [2002] 1 A.C. 462, para.4. Counsel considered that, since the 1956 Act disclosed no single, coherent legislative scheme, one could not argue that s.14 must be construed and applied in a way that respected the time-bar applying to s.6 offences. The fact that the 1956 Act is not by any means entirely coherent is not, however, a reason for the courts to abandon their usual approach to interpretation and to construe its provisions in isolation, as if they had no bearing on one another"

Of course, Baroness Hale of Richmond is clear that it was not an abuse. At para.[81].

"In my view, the countervailing considerations of policy and justice did not require the judge to stay the proceedings as an abuse of process and he was entirely justified in refusing to do so. The public conscience would be more affronted by the prohibition of prosecution for offences which have undoubtedly been committed. Although the categories of abuse of process cannot be closed, it would be a misuse of principle and language to call what happened in this case an abuse."

In our judgment the *ratio decidendi* is clearly based on the words of the statute and the clear parliamentary intention behind them.

23   There are many ways in which the question of lesser verdict may arise. In the context of the statutory prohibition on the commencement of proceedings it may be helpful to describe some of them.

    a. The prosecution may bring a charge for the lesser offence.
    b. The defence may ask for a count alleging the lesser offence to be added to the indictment.

   c. The judge may of his own motion order a count to be added to the indictment.

   d. Without the addition of a further count

      i. The prosecution—at any stage of the case up to the close of all the evidence—may wish to leave the possibility of a verdict of guilty of a lesser offence to the jury.

      ii. The defence may do likewise. On both the above the final decision lies with the judge.

      iii. The judge may decide of his own motion to direct the jury as to a possible verdict on a lesser charge.

   e. Sections 3 and 3a of the Criminal Appeal Act 1968 allow the Court of Appeal to substitute a verdict for a different offence from the one of which the appellant was convicted if it appears that either

      i. The jury must have been satisfied of facts which proved him guilty of the alternative offence (s.3), or

      ii. If he pleaded guilty, that the plea indicated an admission of facts which prove him guilty of the alternative offence (s.3a, which came into force on September 1, 2004).

In all these situations except a. and e. the eventual decision to add a count or to leave an alternative verdict is in the hands of the trial judge. In different situations and for different reasons the request to the judge to leave a lesser offence to the jury may be agreed or objected to by either the defence or the prosecution. Even if both sides agree on a particular course the judge may decide not to follow it. One example of such a situation concerns the question of a possible verdict, on a charge of murder, of manslaughter by reason of provocation. The prosecution may argue that the case is one of murder or nothing. The defence, frequently in such cases relying on self-defence, may argue likewise, believing that there is a danger that if a "compromise verdict" is left to the jury the defendant may be convicted, whereas if no such verdict was left he may well be acquitted altogether. The judge may however decide that there is evidence which could justify a verdict of manslaughter by provocation.

24   Does a decision by the judge to leave a lesser offence to the jury for its consideration amount to "the commencement of proceedings for the particular offence"? Two possibilities arise.

   a) In every case in which an alternative verdict is possible, either because it is provided for in the statute creating the principal offence or because of the provisions of s.6 of the Criminal Law Act 1967, proceedings have commenced in respect of all such offences from the moment the charge for the greater offence is laid. This proposition has only to be stated for its absurdity to become apparent. It would mean that in cases like the present a charge of rape could not be brought in respect of a 14-year-old girl more than twelve months after the alleged offence since any such charge inevitably involves an allegation under s. 6 of the Act.

   b) Proceedings commence in respect of the lesser offence at the moment at which the trial judge makes the decision to leave the lesser offence to the jury for its consideration and the defendant becomes liable to be convicted of it, or on appeal when the Court of Appeal decides to substitute a verdict of the lesser offence. Although in cases in which a count is added to the indictment and a plea is taken it can clearly be said that proceedings have commenced in respect of the offence alleged in the count, it is hard to see how that can apply to the leaving of an alternative verdict. There is no sense in which there have been any "proceedings" in respect of the offence. The proceedings have been brought in respect of a different and more serious offence. No verdict will be taken—or other order made by the court—in respect of the lesser offence if there is a conviction of the more serious one. The acquittal if there is one will be an acquittal on the count in the indictment. It is somewhat fanciful to suggest that the substitution of a verdict by the Court of Appeal (Criminal Division) amounts to the "commencement of proceedings".

25   Even if the taking of an alternative verdict to a lesser charge does not amount to the commencement of proceedings, is the wording of the Schedule such as to give rise to the conclusion that Parliament intended to prevent the conviction under any circumstances of an offender for conduct which amounts to an offence under s.6 of the Act if proceedings are commenced for a more serious offence which is not subject to the limitation period? It was common ground in *R. v J* [2005] 1 Cr.App.R. 19 (p.277) that it is difficult if not impossible to discern a coherent framework within the Act. At para.[48] Lord Clyde:

"It has of course to be accepted that the 1956 Act is a consolidating statute and that a complete coherence is not necessarily to be found among all its provisions. But the two offences detailed in ss.6(1) and 14(1) have in substance co-existed in the legislative history over a long period and should be open to a mutually consistent interpretation."

Lord Bingham of Cornhill at para.[15]:

"The historical derivation of the 1956 Act had been shown to result in much internal inconsistency and lack of coherence (see, for example, *R. v K* [2001] UKHL 41; [2002] 1 Cr.App.R. 121; [2002] 1 A.C. 462, para.4) but the deficiencies of the Act cannot absolve the court from its duty to give effect to clear and unambiguous provisions."

Baroness Hale of Richmond put it more trenchantly at para.[89]:

"In short, the 1956 Act was a mess when it was enacted and became an ever greater mess with later amendments."

Lord Bingham's view, which we have already quoted, though not of course part of the *ratio decidendi*, was that the prohibition did not extend to the possibility of alternative verdicts [Para.23].

26   Their Lordships in *J* were principally concerned with the evasion, circumvention or "side-stepping" of the limitation (freely admitted by the prosecution)

involved in charging the general offence which was not time-barred in preference to the more specific offence which was: see, for example, Lord Steyn at para.[37], Lord Clyde at para.[49], Lord Rodger of Earlsferry at paras [63] and [64].

27   As Mr Evans who appeared for the Crown submitted:

    a)   Schedule 10's words are specific. "A prosecution may not be commenced more than 12 months after the offence charged." Here there was no question of the Crown commencing the prosecution of the defendant with either a s.6 or a s.14 offence. The prosecution commenced, and continued until the jury's verdict, as a prosecution for rape.

    b)   There was strong support from Lord Bingham, para.[14] as well as from Baroness Hale for the public policy public interest considerations of bringing within the criminal justice system those mature men who deliberately groom under-age girls for sex and succeed in having sexual intercourse with them, and guarded support from at least one other of their Lordships (Lord Rodger at para.[57]).

Parliament has, since 1956, enacted the Criminal Law Act 1967, s.6(3) of which enables juries to return verdicts on lesser charges when the facts they find fall short of proof of the greater. In *R. v Fisher* [1969] Q.B. 114, Cusack J. ruled at first instance that a verdict of unlawful sexual intercourse is not available on a charge of rape. This judgment was approved in *R. v Mochan* (1970) 54 Co.App.R. 5; [1969] 1 W.L.R. 1331. The reasoning in those cases had nothing to do with the limitation period but was based upon the age of the victim, crucial in the s.6 offence, but irrelevant in a s.1 offence. Indecent assault, at least since the decision of this court in *R. v Hodgson* (1973) 57 Cr.App.R. 502, as a lesser alternative to rape in cases where the victim is over 13 but under 16, has long been a classic example of the workings of s.6(3).

28   In our judgment to hold that the express intention of Parliament in 1967 as to alternative verdicts should be thwarted by an express intention of Parliament in 1956 concerning the commencement of proceedings for a different offence from the one the subject of the alternative verdict would be quite wrong.

29   We find that the trial judge was right to rule as he did. Neither the speeches in *J* nor the words of Sch.10 compel a conclusion that he was not. This appeal must therefore be dismissed.

Appeal dismissed

R. v WEIR
R. v SOMANATHAN
R. v YAXLEY-LENNON
R. v MANISTER
R. v HONG AND DE

COURT OF APPEAL (Lord Justice Kennedy, Mr Justice Bell and Mrs Justice Dobbs): September 20, 21; November 11, 2005

[2005] EWCA Crim 2866; [2006] 1 Cr.App.R. 19

ⓛ Admissibility; Bad character; Cautions; Credibility; Cross examination; Probative value; Propensity; Similar fact evidence

H1   EVIDENCE
   Bad character
   Admission of defendant's bad character to establish propensity to commit type of offence—Previous offence not in same category as offence charged—Whether evidence of previous offence admissible— Criminal Justice Act 2003 (c.44), ss.101, 103

   Evidence of bad character relevant to important issue between prosecution and defence—Prosecution applying pursuant to statutory provisions to adduce evidence of defendant's bad character—Whether common law rules on similar fact evidence relevant— Criminal Justice Act 2003, s.101(1)

   Defence witness cross-examined as to caution for drug-related offence— Whether caution relevant to witness's credibility— Criminal Justice Act 2003, s.100

   Defendant 39-year-old man charged with sexual offences against 13-year-old girl—Defendant when aged 34 involved in sexual relationship with 16-year-old girl—Prosecution applying to adduce evidence of relationship to show "misconduct"—Whether lawful behaviour capable of constituting "misconduct"— Whether evidence admissible at common law— Criminal Justice Act 2003, ss.98, 101, 103, 112(1)

   Appellants charged with violent disorder—Co-defendant claiming to have

acted in self-defence in response to threat from appellants—Co-defendant apply-
ing to adduce evidence that appellants had propensity to violent conduct—
Whether evidence admissible at common law

H2   In the first case the appellant was charged with sexual assault by touching a girl
under the age of 13 contrary to s.7 of the Sexual Offences Act 2003. The judge
acceded to a prosecution application to adduce evidence that the appellant had
been cautioned for taking an indecent photograph of a child. The appellant
was convicted. On the appeal it was contended that by ss.101 and 103 of the
Criminal Justice Act 2003 (the "2003 Act") [1] evidence of a defendant's bad character was admissible to establish that the appellant had a propensity to commit
offences of the kind with which he was charged. By s.103(2)(b) such a propensity
might be established by evidence that he had been convicted of an offence of the
same category as the one with which he was charged. An offence under s.7 of the
Sexual Offences Act 2003 had been categorised by Order of the Secretary of State
but there was no reference in that category to the offence in respect of which the
appellant had received a caution. Accordingly, the appellant submitted that the
earlier offence was not, for the purposes of s.103(2)(b), an offence of the same
category as the one with which he was charged and the evidence of the caution
should not have been admitted.

H3   In the second case the appellant was charged with raping a woman who
attended a Hindu temple where the appellant was a priest. The prosecution's
case was that over a prolonged period, beginning when she was emotionally vulnerable, the complainant was subjected by the appellant to sexually charged
behaviour which on two occasions culminated in rape. The appellant's response
was one of complete denial. The judge acceded to a prosecution application under
s.101(1)(d) (f) and (g) [2] of the Criminal Justice Act 2003 to call three witnesses of
bad character. Two of those witnesses were women who testified that at a vulnerable time in their lives they were subjected to sexually charged approaches made
by the appellant similar to those made to the complainant. The third witness was
involved in the running of a Hindu temple where the appellant had worked. He
gave evidence that the appellant had been dismissed from his post because he
had lied and because his behaviour towards women had given cause for concern.
This contradicted what the appellant had told the police which was that he had left
the temple of his own accord. The appellant was convicted. He appealed on the
ground that before the implementation of the Criminal Justice Act 2003 evidence
of the bad character witnesses would only have been admitted if it had satisfied
the requirements of similar fact evidence and that the coming into force of the
2003 Act had not significantly altered the test of admissibility of similar fact evidence.

H4   In the third case the appellant was charged with assault occasioning actual
bodily harm and assault with intent to resist arrest. At trial one of the defence witnesses who had been present during the alleged assaults admitted during cross-

---

[1]   Criminal Justice Act 2003, ss.101, 103: see post, para.2.
[2]   Section 101: see post, para.2.

examination that she had been cautioned for the possession of cocaine. The judge ruled that the witness's caution had substantial probative value to her credibility and was therefore admissible under s.100(1) of the Criminal Justice Act 2003 [3]. The appellant was convicted. He appealed on the ground that s.100(1) did not encompass matters of credibility and that, therefore, the witness's caution had not been admissible.

H5   In the fourth case the appellant was charged with rape and two counts of indecent assault against A. At the time of the alleged offences A was 13 and the appellant was 39. When interviewed by the police the appellant said he and A had only had a friendship and that nothing of a sexual nature had occurred between them. At trial the prosecution applied to adduce evidence of a long sexual relationship the appellant had had with B when the appellant was 34 and B was 16. The appellant contended that since the relationship he had had with B had not involved the commission of a criminal offence it could not be regarded in law as amounting to reprehensible behaviour. The judge allowed the prosecution's application ruling that for a man of 34 to have instituted a sexual relationship with a girl of 16 was properly to be described as reprehensible behaviour, and this brought the relationship within the gateway of s.101(1)(d) [4]. It showed a propensity to be attracted to girls of an age which was inappropriate for persons of the appellant's age. The appellant was convicted on the two counts of indecent assault. On the count of rape he was found not guilty but guilty of indecent assault.

H6   In the fifth case the appellants and a co-defendant, C, were accused of having been involved in a running fight between two groups of young men. They were all charged with violent disorder. At trial C said that on the day in question he had armed himself with a knife fearing that he would be attacked. C sought to adduce evidence that the appellants were known to the police from previous incidents. On one occasion they had been the victims of a knife attack but had refused to provide statements. On another occasion they had been arrested on suspicion of committing a serious assault but had been released without charge after the alleged victims refused to provide statements. The judge held that neither previous matter amounted to misconduct as defined by s.112(1) of the Criminal Justice Act 2003. However, the judge went on to hold that evidence of the previous matters was admissible at common law. The appellants were convicted.

H7   **Held,** (1) dismissing the appeal in the first case, that the opening words of s.103(2) revealed that a defendant's propensity to commit offences of the kind with which he was charged could be provided in ways other than by evidence that he had been convicted of an offence of the same description or an offence of the same category. Unless that approach was adopted no proper weight was given to the use of the word "may" followed by the words in brackets. If evidence sought to be adduced was evidence of convictions satisfying the requirements of paragraph (a) or (b) then the task of admissibility was made easier. Accordingly,

---

[3]   Section 100: see post, para.2.
[4]   S.101: see post, para 2.

the categorisation process did have an effect notwithstanding that categorisation was not determinative of admissibility. In the circumstances, the judge had been right to allow the admission of evidence relating to the appellants' caution (post, paras 7, 9).

H8   (2) Dismissing the appeal in the second case, that the 2003 Act had completely reversed the pre-existing general rule; evidence of bad character was admissible, irrespective of whether it had enhanced probative value, if it satisfied certain criteria. If the evidence of a defendant's bad character was relevant to an important issue between the prosecution and the defence for the purposes of s.101(1)(d), then unless there was an application to exclude the evidence, it was admissible. So the pre-existing one-stage test which balanced probative value against prejudicial effect was obsolete. In the circumstances all of the bad character evidence which the prosecution sought to adduce satisfied the requirements of s.101(1)(d). It was plainly relevant to an important matter in issue between the parties, namely the credibility of the complainant on the one hand and the appellant on the other, for the prosecution to show that the behaviour to which the complainant said that she had been subjected (other than the actual offences of rape) followed a pattern used by the appellant in relation to two other women who attended the temple, that his behaviour towards women at his former temple had given cause for concern, and, contrary to his assertion in interview, that he had left his post there because of his behaviour and because he was untruthful. The latter point was relevant to the appellants' propensity to be untruthful for the purposes of s.103(1)(b) of the 2003 Act. The probative force of the bad character evidence was considerable and the admission of it did not have such an adverse effect on the fairness of the proceedings that it should have been excluded (post, paras 36–42, 54).

H9   *O'Brien v Chief Constable of South Wales Police* [2005] UKHL 26; [2005] 2 A.C. 534, HL, considered.

H10   (3) Dismissing the appeal in the third case, that although couched in different terms from the provisions relating to the introduction of the appellant's bad character, s.100(1) did cover matters of credibility. The judge erred in coming to the conclusion that the evidence of the caution had substantial probative value in relation to the witness's credibility but that in the circumstances the conviction was not unsafe (post, paras 72–75).

H11   (4) Allowing the appellant's appeal in the fourth case against his conviction for indecent assault as an alternative to rape, that the verdict of not guilty of rape but guilty of indecent assault meant that the jury was sure of sexual intercourse but not sure as to the issue of consent. The appellant had not been charged with unlawful sexual intercourse and by the time of his trial it was too late to commence such a prosecution as an alternative to rape. Since a prosecution for unlawful sexual intercourse could not be commenced, it was impermissible to commence a prosecution for indecent assault by leaving it to the jury as an alternative to rape. Accordingly, the conviction had to be quashed (post, paras 87–88).

H12   *R. v J* [2004] UKHL 42; [2005] 1 Cr.App.R. 19 (p.277); [2005] 1 A.C. 562, HL, applied.

H13   (5) Dismissing appellant's appeal in the fourth case against the other two counts of indecent assault, that the definition of misconduct in s.112(1) of the 2003 Act was very wide. It made clear that behaviour might be reprehensible, and therefore misconduct, though not amounting to the commission of an offence. However, although the appellant was significantly older than B, there was no evidence of his grooming her before she was 16, or that her parents disapproved and communicated their disapproval to the appellant, or that B was intellectually, emotionally or physically immature for her age, or that there was some other feature of the lawful relationship which might have made it reprehensible. Indeed, it might be inferred that the relationship with B was a serious one, with some real emotional attachment, because it lasted some time. Accordingly, the judge had been wrong to conclude that the sexual relationship between the appellant and B, without more, amounted to "evidence of, or of a disposition towards, misconduct on his part" and therefore evidence of "bad character" for the purposes of s.98 and therefore ss.101, 102 and 103 of the Act. But, although the evidence of the appellant's sexual relationship with B did not amount to evidence of bad character, the evidence was admissible at common law because it was relevant to the issue of whether the appellant had a sexual interest in A. It was capable of demonstrating a sexual interest in early or mid-teenage girls, much younger than the appellant, and therefore bore on the truth of his case of a purely supportive, asexual interest in A. In those circumstances it had not been unfair to admit the evidence (post, paras 94–95).

H14   (6) Allowing the appeals in the fifth case, that there would be cases where previous conduct of a defendant was of probative value and therefore relevant to a matter in issue between him and the prosecution or him and a co-defendant, yet the bad character provisions of the Criminal Justice Act 2003 relating to a defendant's misconduct did not apply. In such cases s.99(1) of the Act, whereby the common law rules governing the admissibility of evidence of bad character in criminal proceedings were excluded, did not exclude the relevant material because it did not amount to "evidence of bad character". But this was not such a case. The evidence of events on November 19, 2002 and June 6, 2004 could only be relevant if it might show that either appellant had a propensity to violent conduct and therefore bear on C's case of self-defence. To show such a propensity it had to amount to "reprehensible behaviour", "misconduct" and, therefore, "bad character". By the same measure as events on November, 19 2002 and June 6, 2004 could not amount to reprehensible behaviour, misconduct or, therefore bad character, they could not bear on C's case. There was no room for taking a more relaxed approach because it was a defendant who sought to introduce the evidence, rather than the prosecution (post, paras120–121).

H15   (For evidence of bad character, see *Archbold* 2006, Ch.13.)

Appeals against conviction

H16   *R. v Weir*

On March 21, 2005 in the Crown Court at Manchester (Judge Lakin) the appellant, Anthony Albert Weir, was convicted of sexual assault by touching a girl under the age of 13, contrary to s.7 of the Sexual Offences Act 2003. He was sentenced to an extended sentence, the custodial part of which was 15 months' imprisonment.

H17   The facts and grounds of appeal appear in the judgment of the court.

H18   *R. v Somanathan*

On January 20, 2005 in the Crown Court at Croydon (Judge Pratt) the appellant, Romanathan Somanathan, was convicted of two offences of rape. He was subsequently sentenced to nine years' imprisonment.

H19   The facts and grounds of appeal appear in the judgment of the court.

H20   *R. v Yaxley-Lennon*

On April 18, 2005 in the Crown Court at Luton (Judge Moss) the appellant, Stephen Yaxley-Lennon, was convicted of assault occasioning actual bodily harm (count 1) and assault with intent to resist arrest (count 2). He was sentenced to concurrent terms of imprisonment of 12 months on count 1 and three months on count 2.

H21   The facts and grounds of appeal appear in the judgment of the court.

H22   *R. v Manister*

On April 15, 2005 in the Crown Court at Bristol (Judge Jack) the appellant, Simon Charles Manister, was convicted of three offences of indecent assault contrary to s.14(1) of the Sexual Offences Act 1956. He was sentenced to a total of five years' imprisonment.

H23   The facts and grounds of appeal appear in the judgment of the court.

H24   *R. v Hong Qiang He and De Qun He*

On March 10, 2005 in the Crown Court at Southwark (Judge Higgins) the appellants, Hong Qiang He and De Qun He, were convicted of violent disorder (count 1), contrary to s.2(1) of the Public Order Act 1986. They were sentenced to 18 months' imprisonment.

H25   The facts and grounds of appeal appear in the judgment of the court.

H26   *Simon James* (assigned by the Registrar of Criminal Appeals) for Weir.
R. Vardon (instructed by the Crown Prosecution Service) for the Crown.
Richard Kovalevsky Q.C. and *Paul Mylvaganam* (instructed by Arora Lodhi Heath) for Somanathan.
Gillian Etherton (instructed by the Crown Prosecution Service) for the Crown.
Andrew Urquhart (assigned by the Registrar of Criminal Appeals) for Yaxley-Lennon.
Nicholas Lobbenberg (instructed by the Crown Prosecution Service) for the Crown.
F. Chamberlain (assigned by the Registrar of Criminal Appeals) for Manister.
Anna Vigars (instructed by the Crown Prosecution Service) for the Crown.
Deepak Kapur (assigned by the Registrar of Criminal Appeals) for Hong Qiang He.
Anthony Dalgleish (assigned by the Registrar of Criminal Appeals) for De Qun He.

L. Mabley (instructed by the Crown Prosecution Service) for the Crown.

Cur. adv. vult.

November 11   Kennedy L.J.: down the judgment of the court.

1   We heard these five appeals consecutively on September 20 and 21, 2005. They were listed together because they raised points in relation to the bad character provisions of the Criminal Justice Act 2003 which have not previously been considered by the Court of Appeal, but the points raised are different in each case. There is no overlap. We therefore deal with the appeals separately in judgments to which all three members of the court have contributed, but it is convenient to begin by setting out those parts of the Act which are relevant in relation to one or more of the appeals.

The 2003 Act

2   **"'Bad character'**
         98 References in this Chapter to evidence of a person's 'bad character' are to evidence of, or of a disposition towards, misconduct on his part, other than evidence which
            (a) has to do with the alleged facts of the offence with which the defendant is charged, or
            (b) is evidence of misconduct in connection with the investigation or prosecution of that offence.

Abolition of common law rules
         99 (1) the common law rules governing the admissibility of evidence of bad character in criminal proceedings are abolished.
            (2) . . .

Non-defendant's bad character
         100 (1) In criminal proceedings evidence of the bad character of a person other than the defendant is admissible if and only if
                (a) it is important explanatory evidence,
                (b) it has substantial probative value in relation to a matter which
                    (i) is a matter in issue in the proceedings, and
                    (ii) is of substantial importance in the context of the case as a whole, ...

Defendant's bad character
         101 (1) In criminal proceedings evidence of the defendant's bad character is admissible if, and only if...
                (c) it is important explanatory evidence,
                (d) it is relevant to an important matter in issue between the defendant and the prosecution,

    (e) it has substantial probative value in relation to an important matter in issue between the defendant and a co-defendant,

    (f) it is evidence to correct a false impression given by the defendant, or

    (g) the defendant has made an attack on another person's character

(3) The court must not admit evidence under subs.(1)(d) or (g) if, on an application by the defendant to exclude it, it appears to the court that the admission of the evidence would have such an adverse effect on the fairness of the proceedings that the court ought not to admit it.

(4) On an application to exclude evidence under subs.(3) the court must have regard, in particular, to the length of time between the matters to which that evidence relates and the matters which form the subject of the offence charged.

'Important explanatory evidence'
102 For the purposes of s.101(1) evidence is important explanatory evidence if

    (a) without it, the court or jury would find it impossible or difficult properly to understand other evidence in the case, and

    (b) its value for understanding the case as a whole is substantial.

'Matter in issue between the defendant and the prosecution'
103 (1) For the purposes of s.101(1)(d) the matters in issue between the defendant and the prosecution include

    (a) the question whether the defendant has a propensity to commit offences of the kind with which he is charged, except where his having such a propensity makes it no more likely that he is guilty of the offence;

    (b) the question whether the defendant has a propensity to be untruthful, except where it is not suggested that the defendant's case is untruthful in any respect.

  (2) Where subs.(1)(a) applies, a defendant's propensity to commit offences of the kind with which he is charged may (without prejudice to any other way of doing so) be established by evidence that he has been convicted of

    (a) an offence of the same description as the one with which he is charged, or

    (b) an offence of the same category as the one with which he is charged.

  (4) For the purposes of subs.(2)—

    (a) two offences are of the same description as each other if the statement of the offence in a written charge or indictment would, in each case, be in the same terms;

(b) two offences are of the same category as each other if they belong to the same category of offences prescribed for the purposes of this section by an order made by the Secretary of State.

'Evidence to correct a false impression'

104 (5) Evidence is admissible under s.101(1)(f) only if it goes no further than is necessary to correct the false impression.

Court's duty to give reasons for rulings

110 (1) Where the court makes a relevant ruling —

(a) it must state in open court (but in the absence of the jury, if there is one) its reasons for the ruling;

(b) If it is a magistrates' court, it must cause the ruling and the reasons for it to be entered in the register of the court's proceedings.

(2) In this section 'relevant ruling' means;

(a) a ruling on whether an item of evidence is evidence of a person's bad character;

(b) a ruling on whether an item of such evidence is admissible under s.100 or 101 (including a ruling on an application under s.101(3);

(c) a ruling under s.107.

Interpretation of Ch.1

112 (1) In this Chapter

'misconduct' means the commission of an offence or other reprehensible behaviour"

Anthony Albert Weir

3   On March 21, 2005 in the Crown Court at Manchester this 44-year-old appellant was convicted of sexual assault by touching a girl under the age of 13, contrary to s.7 of the Sexual Offences Act 2003. He was subsequently sentenced to an extended sentence, the custodial element of which was 15 months' imprisonment. As the sentence was in excess of 30 months he is required to comply with the notification provisions of Pt 2 of the Act for an indefinite period, not, as stated by the judge when sentencing, for 10 years, but that is not a matter with which we have been concerned when considering his appeal.

4   The alleged victim J was a ten-year-old girl living in the same street as the appellant, who lived with his partner and her children C and T. J and C were friends, and sometimes J slept at C's home. J said that when she did so on Saturday July 4, 2004 the appellant assaulted her by touching her vagina over her night clothes. According to J he had exposed himself to her on four or five previous occasions, and on Sunday July 5, he told her that he used to pay girls £5 to watch him masturbate, and asked her if she wanted to watch. She refused,

but on that Sunday when he took the children swimming he peeped into the cubicle when she was naked, and then forced £3 into her hand. J complained to her mother on the following Sunday, and the police were then informed. When interviewed the appellant denied that anything improper took place. He had not exposed himself to the girl, and on Saturday July 4, his partner was away but his friend Dean Allen was with him, and he had only gone into the children's bedroom to check that all was well. On the Sunday when he took the children swimming he had said nothing about masturbation. He had not spied on J, and although he did give her some money it was only to purchase food from the café. His case in relation to the Saturday evening was supported by Dean Allen, who detected no abnormality.

5   On February 16, 2005, at a plea and directions hearing, the prosecution applied to adduce evidence that on August 9, 2000 the appellant was cautioned for taking an indecent photograph of a child, contrary to s.1 of the Protection of Children Act 1978. The application was granted, and it is that decision which is challenged in this appeal. It is common ground that the relevant statutory provisions are those to be found in the ss.101(1)(d), 103(1)(a), 103(2)(b) and 103(4)(b) of the Criminal Justice Act 2003.

6   On December 15, 2004 the Secretary of State exercised his powers under s.103(4)(b) by making the Criminal Justice Act 2003 (Categories of Offences) Order 2004 (SI 2004/3346) which came into force at the same time as ss.98–110 of the 2003 Act. Paragraph 2 of the Order provides:

> (1) The categories of offences set out in Pts 1 and 2 of the Schedule to this Order are hereby prescribed for the purposes of s.103(4)(b) of the 2003 Act.
>
> (2) Two offences are of the same category as each other if they are included in the same Part of the Schedule.Part 1 of the Schedule sets out offences in the theft category. Part 2 is headed "Sexual Offences (Persons under the age of 16) Category". It includes the s.7 offence with which the appellant was charged before the Crown Court, but contains no reference to the offence in respect of which he had received a caution.

7   Mr James, for the appellant, therefore submits that as the offence in respect of which the caution was administered was not, for the purposes of s.103(2)(b) an offence of the same category as the one with which he was charged the evidence of the caution should not have been admitted. The Order, Mr James submits, is plainly selective. It does not include every possible offence, and unless categorisation is determinative of admissibility (where, as in this case, offences are not of the same description and thus within the ambit of s.103(2)(a)) then what is the point of categorisation? That was an argument which appealed to Mitting J. at Preston Crown Court in the unreported case of *R. v O'Neil* February 22, 2005, but that was a case in which no relevant categorisation Order had been made by the Secretary of State, and it is not clear whether the attention of the judge was drawn to para.[131] and [132] of the paper prepared by Professor John Spencer Q.C. for the Judicial Studies Board. As Professor Spencer points out, and as we accept, it is necessary to look carefully at the opening words of s.103(2). They

show that a defendant's propensity to commit offences of the kind with which he is charged can be proved in ways other than by evidence that he has been convicted of an offence of the same description or an offence of the same category. Unless that approach is adopted no proper weight is given to the use of the word "may" followed by the words in brackets, and the conclusion makes good sense because it allows for the admission of, for example, the fact that the defendant has previously asked to have taken into consideration offences of the kind with which he is now charged, despite the fact that an offence taken into consideration, like a caution, is not a conviction (see *R. v Nicholson* (1948) 32 Cr.App.R. 98; [1947] 2 All E.R. 535).

8   Of course if the evidence sought to be adduced is evidence of convictions satisfying the requirements of para.(a) or (b) then the task of deciding admissibility is made easier, so the categorisation process does have an effect, and that seems to us to answer the question which Mr James posed.

9   For those reasons, although we do not agree with the trial judge that "an offence contrary to s.1 of the 1978 Act can properly be regarded (for the purposes of s.103(2)(b) of the Criminal Justice Act 2003) as being within the same category as an offence contrary to s.7 of the 2003 (Sexual Offences) Act" we do agree with the alternative line of reasoning adopted by the judge, and reflected in this judgment. That renders it unnecessary for us to consider the alternative submission put forward by Mr Vardon for the respondent that the evidence of the caution would in any event be admissible pursuant to s.101(1)(g) because the defendant had in effect attacked the character of the complainant. The appeal against conviction therefore fails, and is dismissed.

Romanathan Somanathan.

10   On January 20, 2005 in the Crown Court at Croydon this 42-year-old appellant was convicted of two offences of rape, and he was subsequently sentenced to nine years' imprisonment. In his notice of appeal he seeks an extension of time of approximately four months in which to seek leave to appeal against conviction, and his applications for an extension of time and leave to appeal against conviction were referred to this court by the registrar. During the course of the hearing we granted the necessary extension of time (the delay was attributable to the time required to obtain transcripts) and we granted leave to appeal. We turn now to outline the case.

Outline of the allegations and the Trial

11   W is now 30 years of age. She came to England from Mauritius in 1996 and married, but her marriage broke down and in 2002 she was buying a new flat. At that time she started to attend the Hindu Temple at Thornton Heath where the appellant was the main priest or Aya. It was the prosecution case that after several conversations, on the telephone and at the Temple, the appellant visited her flat on July 11, 2002 to conduct a poojah (or blessing), and that whilst there he raped her. Thereafter he continued to contact her and she continued to attend the Temple. He visited her flat again in September 2002, ostensibly to give her a gift

he had obtained on a religious trip to the Himalayas, and it was the prosecution case that he then raped her for a second time. She became pregnant, she said by him, and an abortion was performed on November 26, 2002. She said that she made efforts to approach people at the Temple about the appellant, but the community appeared closed to her, and it was not until November 2003 that she complained to the police.

12   The appellant was then interviewed on March 11, 2004 and denied any offending. He said that he did visit the complainant's home in July 2002 to conduct a poojah, but there was no impropriety, and in September 2002 he never even went to her home. He also denied having had any previous problems, in particular when he worked at Tooting. The false allegations made against him were, he said, attributable to members of the Mauritian community who wanted to give his Temple a bad name. In his Defence Case Statement served on August 16, 2004 the appellant relied on his answers given during the course of his interview under caution, and added that the complainant "is not a witness of truth and has some ulterior motive in making and indeed pursuing this complaint".

13   At the start of the trial on January 11, 2005 Miss Gillian Etherton for the prosecution applied to call three witnesses as evidence of bad character, pursuant to Ch.1 of Pt II of the Criminal Justice Act 2003. Those witnesses were I, V and Seevaratnam Nagendram. The first two were young women who said that at a vulnerable time in their lives they were subjected to sexually charged approaches made by the appellant similar to those which the complainant would say were made to her. The other two women were not visited by the appellant at home because proposed visits were abandoned when he discovered that they would not be alone, and in neither case was there any allegation of rape. Mr Seevaratnam was the founder and chairman of the Board of Trustees of the Temple at Tooting, and he was able to give evidence as to the appellant's behaviour when employed there, and as to the reasons why his employment was brought to an end.

14   The application to call the three witnesses was resisted by Mr Squirrel, who was then appearing for the appellant, and the main argument put forward was that the relevant provisions of the 2003 Act did not apply to this trial because the investigation and the initial criminal proceedings took place before the relevant provisions came into force. As a result of a subsequent decision of this court it is now clear, and before us it has been common ground, that the defence argument was misconceived, and the judge was right to reject it. During the course of his submissions Mr Squirrel was asked by the judge whether if the new Act applied he could argue against the inclusion of evidence of bad character, and he replied "well, it is going to be difficult, I concede that". A little later, in the transcript, counsel expressly conceded that the applications fell within s.101(1)(f) and (g) of the 2003 Act, but invited the judge to make use of his power to exclude under s.101(3) of the 2003 Act, and possibly also under s.78 of the Police and Criminal Evidence Act 1984.

15   Having regard to the way in which the application was advanced it is not surprising that the judge, after deciding that the 2003 Act did apply, was succinct in dealing with the requirements of that Act. He found that the application was properly made under s.101(1)(f) and (g) if not under (d) as well and continued:

"I have thought hard about my discretionary power under subs.(3) to exclude the evidence, but do not do so. Much of this proposed evidence would have been admissible under the old law in any event."

The trial then began, and on the following day, January 12, 2005, Miss Etherton sought a ruling that the statement of V should be read pursuant to s.23 of the Criminal Justice Act 1988. Evidence was called as to the circumstances under which her statement was obtained, and as to the steps taken to secure her attendance at court. They were conceded to have been appropriate steps, but it was nevertheless submitted, principally by reference to s.26 of the 1988 Act, that the statement should not be read because the evidence was important and could not be challenged. As to that the judge said:

> "There is no doubt that this witness is an important and significant one. She gives evidence of similar fact to the extent of the grooming process that this defendant allegedly employed to wear down the resistance of those that he targeted. However, in my judgment, Mr Squirrel falls into error in saying that the evidence cannot be challenged. The defendant has challenged her account in interview, and, moreover, the defence is as able to controvert the evidence in the statement as ever it was . . . .. And I have come to the conclusion that, having thought about the matter carefully, that the statement ought to be read in the interests of justice, and so doing will not cause an unfairness within the meaning of this section or s.78 of the Police and Criminal Evidence Act, and consequently I allow Miss Etherton's application."

16   The jury then heard the rest of the evidence of the complainant and they heard evidence from two witnesses to whom she complained in June or July and in November 2002. They also heard from I and the statement of V was read. They heard from Mr Seevaratnam (of Tooting Temple) and they heard from Professor Lipner, Professor of Hinduism at Cambridge University, who was able to set in context much of what had been said by others. Most of what the Professor said was not contentious, in the transcript of the Professor's evidence he was asked:

> "Q. If one were a Tamil woman living in England making an allegation of rape by a priest, help us, please, how difficult a thing that would be to do given the community background and the person making the allegation and against who it is made?
> A. Mind-boggling—that would be a mind-boggling thing to do. For a woman to make an allegation of rape or something like that against her priest, given the ethnic circumstances involved, would require—its an extraordinary act and would require a tremendous amount of impulse of one sort or another, either courage or whatever, but it is certainly a very unusual thing to happen."

The prosecution case concluded with evidence in relation to the interview with the appellant on March 11, 2004, and there were also schedules in relation to telephone contacts between the complainant and the appellant.

17   The appellant gave evidence on his own behalf, but the defence which he advanced was not as foreshadowed in his interviews and in his Defence Case Statement. He said that he fell out with Mr Seevaratnam at Tooting because Mr Seevaratnam was running the Temple as a business. He thought Mr Seevaratnam was worried that the appellant was too popular, and he added that by the end he was unhappy and "my contract was not renewed by agreement". As to the complainant he gave details of his dealings with her, maintaining that she attempted to seduce him, and said:

> "W has lied because she was obsessed with me and I rejected her—three times she tried to get me and failed. I accept I didn't mention this in interview; only afterwards did I learn about things."

Referring to I and V as well as the complainant the appellant said:

> "All three women have collaborated and told lies about me."

At this stage it is unnecessary for us to refer to the summing-up. We will deal with specific criticisms made in relation to it later in this judgment.

Issues on appeal

18   Having set the scene we can now summarise the issues raised in this appeal. They are as follows:

(1)   That the judge was wrong to admit the bad character evidence (i.e. the evidence of I, V and Seevaratnam Nagendram) because none of it was admissible under s.101(d), (f) or (g) of the 2003 Act.

(2)   That the judge gave inadequate reasons for admitting the evidence, a point only taken during the course of submissions to us.

(3)   That the judge's directions to the jury in relation to bad character evidence were inadequate.

(4)   That the evidence of Professor Lipner as to the likelihood of a woman making an allegation against a Hindu priest was inadmissible and prejudicial.

(5)   That the judge should not have permitted the statement of V to be read, and failed to give adequate directions in relation to it.

(6)   That each of the convictions is thus rendered unsafe."

For the purposes of this appeal it was common ground that the convictions stand or fall together.

Relevant legislation

19   In this appeal the following sections of the 2003 Act are relevant, and the relevant parts of those sections are to be found set out in our introduction to all five appeals:

Section 99(1)
Section 101(1)(d), (f) and (g)

Section 101(3)
Section 103(1)(a) and (b)
Section 105(6)
Section 110

It will also be necessary to refer in due course to s.23–26 of the Criminal Justice Act 1988, and to s.78 of the Police and Criminal Evidence Act 1984.

Chronology

20   For certain purposes it is important in this case to bear in mind the sequence of events as disclosed by the evidence, so we summarise the chronology.

21   In 1998 the appellant ceased to work at Tooting Temple after being there for two years, and moved to Hendon. In November 2001 he left Hendon to open his own Temple at Thornton Heath.

22   In about June 2002 the appellant was consulted by the complainant. She says that he went to her home to perform a poojah on July 11, 2002 and that was when the first rape took place. The complainant had intended her friend Primeela to be present for the poojah but she was unable to attend. However, according to the complainant, very soon after the rape she spoke to Primeela and to another friend Evelyn Chin-Hom Lap about what had occurred, and Evelyn Lap gave evidence of that conversation at the trial. She said that in about June or July 2002 she was at Manchester University when telephoned by the complainant in distress. She said that her priest had come to her house, didn't want to leave, and had bolted the door. He had pinned her to the floor and she struggled. She couldn't fight him off. He said they should be together. She said no several times, but afterwards she felt weak and dirty. She said he forced her, she didn't want to, and Evelyn Lap understood she meant something sexual.

23   In August/September 2002 the appellant was in India with his family and, according to the complainant, it was in September 2002, soon after his return, that he visited her home with a gift and raped her for the second time. She then became pregnant and consulted a Marie Stopes Clinic with a view to an abortion. She told Danusia Bourden, a nurse at the clinic, that the putative father was the priest at the Temple, and Danusia Bourden gave evidence to that effect. The abortion on November 26, 2002 was preceded by a scan on November 22, 2002, which showed the foetus to be just over seven weeks old, indicating that conception took place early in October.

24   In about February or March 2003 V was planning a fast, and consulted the appellant. According to her, sexual approaches then began which she initially terminated by threatening to tell his wife what he was doing. He then, in about March 2003, offered to do prayers at her house and she agreed because she wanted the house blessed. When he telephoned to say he was on his way she said that her brother was with her and looking forward to meeting him. The appellant then cancelled his visit, saying that he was getting late for the Temple. Later he rang to say that she must be alone for the blessing, which V did not accept, pointing out that her father was a priest. According to her the appellant then became offensive, and she terminated the conversation and changed her telephone number.

25   It was at about the same time, in March 2003, that I, who is the sister-in-law of
V, consulted the appellant, and according to her suggestive conduct of which she
complained continued until July 2003.

26   Meanwhile the complainant was still in contact with the appellant and taking
part in ceremonies at the Temple. In April 2003 she says that she went to Windsor
with her son to visit Legoland, and stayed in a family room at an hotel. According
to the appellant she asked him to perform a poojah at Windsor, and provided him
with a railway ticket. When he got there she took him to her hotel bedroom where
she made advances to him, which he rejected, and he then left. The complainant
accepted that under pressure she told the appellant of her proposed visit to the
hotel and was scared that he might follow her, but he did not do so.

27   On May 6, 2003 the complainant paid £150 to the appellant for a poojah. She
was about to have an operation and, according to her, wanted a poojah in another
Temple with people around, but the appellant found out and insisted that he
would do it.

28   In July 2003 the appellant was to perform a service at the home of I, who
arranged for her sister-in-law V to be present, although the appellant had told
her that she should not have any family member present. About two hours before
the proposed service, at a time when the appellant knew that V was to be present,
the appellant telephoned to cancel the service, saying, according to I, that he had
to have an eye operation. When she saw him a couple of days later there was no
sign of any operation, and he said that his eyes had recovered. According to the
appellant he did not cancel services at the homes of either V or I when he knew
that they would not be alone, nor did he say anything to I about an eye operation.
He was due to meet a priest from India, and simply told her that he had another
appointment.

29   The appellant stated that on September 11, 2003, after a summer visit to India,
he took a gift to the complainant at her home which she rejected. That, he said,
was disrespectful, and although she subsequently visited the Temple he ignored
her because she had been disrespectful.

30   The appellant asserted that in October 2003 he finally rejected the complainant, and the last recorded telephone call between them was in that month.

31   In November 2003 the complainant went to the police. They then obtained
statements from the complainant, V and I, whose name was given to the police
by V, and, as we have already said, on March 11, 2004 the appellant was interviewed by the police.

Issue 1 — Admissibility of bad character evidence

32   We turn now to the first of the issues which arise in this appeal, reminding ourselves that at the outset in the court below it was accepted that the criteria set out
in s.101(1)(d), (f) and (g) were satisfied. Had that not been the case no doubt a
distinction would have been drawn between the evidence of I and V on the one
hand and the evidence of Seevaratnam Nagendram on the other. His evidence
would also have been divided into two parts—the first relating to the reasons

for the appellant's departure from Tooting, and the second relating to what the witness saw or heard relating to the appellant's behaviour whilst at Tooting.

33   Mr Kovalevsky Q.C., for the appellant, submitted to us that none of the bad character evidence (i.e. none of the evidence of I, V or Seevaratnam Nagendram) should have been admitted under s.101(1)(d) because none of it was relevant to any important matter in issue between the defendant and the prosecution. As Miss Etherton, for the respondent, pointed out, s.101(1)(d) does have to be read in the light of s.103(1), which makes it clear that for the purposes of s.101(1)(d) matters in issue include a propensity to commit offences of the kind charged, and a propensity to be untruthful.

34   Mr Kovalevsky submitted, correctly, that the sole issue was whether the complainant's account was true, and he went on to submit, again correctly, that before the implementation of the 2003 Act the evidence of I and V, if not that of Sevaratnam Nagendram, would only have been admitted if it satisfied the requirements of similar fact evidence, as set out in *Director of Public Prosecutions v P* (1991) 93 Cr.App.R. 267, [1991] 2 A.C. 447. Mr Kovalevsky then submitted, contentiously, that the coming into force of the 2003 Act has not significantly altered the test for admissibility of similar fact evidence. In support of that proposition he relied upon certain passages from the speech of Lord Phillips in *O'Brien v Chief Constable of South Wales Police* [2005] UKHL 26; [2005] 2 A.C. 534; [2005] 2 W.L.R. 1038, and upon the reference made to those passages in *R. v Edwards* [2006] 1 Cr.App.R.3 (p.31); [2005] EWCA Crim 1813.

35   As Mr Kovalevsky recognised, *O'Brien* was not a criminal case, and we remind ourselves that s.99(1) of the 2003 Act expressly provides that:

> "The common law rules governing the admissibility of evidence of bad character *in criminal proceedings* are abolished" (our emphasis).

At para.[12] of his speech in *O'Brien* Lord Phillips said:

> "Where a defendant to a criminal charge has a criminal record, his propensity to commit crime will normally have some relevance to the question of whether he committed the offence with which he is charged. As a general rule such evidence has nonetheless been held to be inadmissible on the ground that its prejudicial effect is likely to outweigh its probative value. Exceptions have, however, been made to this general exclusion. The nature and extent of those exceptions have proved a frequent preoccupation of the appellate courts and, on at least four occasions, of your Lordships' House. They are now to be found codified in ss.101–106 of the Criminal Justice Act 2003, which were brought into effect in December last year."

We consider that passage, which is not an essential part of the reasoning in *O'Brien*, to be capable of being misunderstood. The 2003 Act completely reverses the pre-existing general rule. Evidence of bad character is now admissible if it satisfies certain criteria (see s.101(1)), and the approach is no longer one of inadmissibility subject to exceptions (see also the Explanatory Notes to the Act para.358 and the observations of Professor Sir John Spencer Q.C. in his paper for the Judicial Studies Board at para.37 and 143).

36   In para.[33] of his speech Lord Phillips said:

> "The test of admissibility advanced by Lord Mackay in *Director of Public Prosecutions v P* still requires similar fact evidence to have an enhanced relevance or substantial probative value before it is admissible against a defendant in a criminal trial. This is because such evidence usually shows that the defendant is a person of bad character and thus risks prejudicing a jury against the defendant in a manner that English law regards as unfair. Instead of applying Lord Mackay's simple test, the trial judge now has to apply his mind to the matters set out in s.101–106 of the 2003 Act. These preserve, however, by rules of some complexity, the requirement that the similar fact evidence should have an enhanced probative value."

That is also reflected in para.[52] of the speech. The Act does not say anything about "enhanced probative value" or "enhanced relevance" (the words used in *R. v Edwards*). Paragraph 363 of the Explanatory Notes does refer to an "enhanced relevance test" but only in relation to s.100 of the Act. The terms of that section clearly impose a higher test in respect of the introduction of a non-defendant's bad character than the test for the introduction of a defendant's bad character. If the evidence of a defendant's bad character is relevant to an important issue between the prosecution and the defence (s.101(1)(d)), then, unless there is an application to exclude the evidence, it is admissible. Leave is not required. So the pre-existing one stage test which balanced probative value against prejudicial effect is obsolete (see also s.99(1)).

37   In the context of this case we are satisfied that all of the bad character evidence which the prosecution sought to adduce satisfied the requirements of s.101(1)(d). In substance it was the case for the prosecution that over a prolonged period, beginning when she was emotionally vulnerable, the complainant was subjected by the appellant to sexually charged behaviour which on two occasions culminated in rape. The appellant's response was one of complete denial. He did not simply say that there was never any rape. He denied that he had behaved improperly at any time. It was therefore plainly relevant to an important matter in issue between the parties, namely the credibility of the complainant on the one hand and theappellant on the other, for the prosecution to show that the behaviour to which the complainant said that she had been subjected (other than the actual offences of rape) followed a pattern used by the appellant in relation to two other women who attended the Temple at Thornton Heath, that his behaviour towards women at Tooting gave cause for concern, and that, contrary to his assertion in interview that he had no problems at Tooting, he left his post there because of his behaviour and because he was untruthful, thus exhibiting a propensity to be untruthful (see s.103(1)(b).

38   That brings us to the second stage of the procedure required by the statute, namely the application of s.101(3). In this case counsel for the appellant did apply to exclude the evidence, and bearing in mind the provisions of Art.6 of the European Convention, we consider it important that a judge should if necessary encourage the making of such an application whenever it appears that the admission of the evidence may have such a adverse effect on the fairness of

the proceedings that the court ought not to admit it. As Miss Etherton accepts, s.101(3) does require the judge to perform a balancing exercise, and that exercise does require the judge to look carefully at the evidence sought to be adduced.

39   In our judgment the probative force of the evidence of I and V was consider-able because, if accepted, it lent powerful support to what the complainant said about the appellant's technique. Without going into detail the evidence of each woman showed that the appellant sought to strike up a relationship with them when they were at a low ebb in their lives. He belittled their former or intended partners, he admired their clothes, and suggested what colours they should wear, he acquired telephone numbers and addresses and then telephoned regularly, often late at night. He spoke of dreaming of them, of being married to them in a past life, and of the Gods now sending them to him. He offered gifts and did things to their hands and hair in the Temple which were inappropriate because they were only done when a girl became a woman or by her husband. Finally he sought to visit each of them at home when they were alone, and only in the case of the complainant did he succeed. There was no significant indication of collusion although, as we have noted, I and V were related by marriage, and one gave the name of the other to the police. The admission of that highly relevant evidence could not in our judgment, have such an adverse on the fairness of the proceedings that the court ought not to have admitted it, not least because the appellant knew precisely who the witnesses were, and what they would say, so he would be able where appropriate to challenge what they had said, and to adduce evidence to the opposite effect.

40   Turning to the evidence of Seevaratnam Nagendram, we take a similar view of his evidence as to the reasons why the appellant ceased to work at Tooting. The appellant had told the police officers that he had no trouble there, and it was highly probative to show that he had been dismissed because he lied to Seevar-atnam Nagendram and because of behaviour which Seevarartnam Nagendram had witnessed, or put to the appellant. With all of that the appellant could be expected to deal. If Seevaratnam Nagendram had been allowed to give evidence about complaints made in relation to the appellant's behaviour which he received from unidentified third parties and which were not put to the appellant such evi-dence by its nature would have been very difficult for the appellant to meet, and should therefore in fairness to the appellant have been excluded pursuant to s.101(3), but there was no such evidence tendered in this case. Seevaratnam Negendram was quite clear that his concerns, arising from what he saw and heard, were put to the appellant. For example he was asked:

> "Q. Did you speak to him about the concerns that were being raised or coming to your attention about his attitude to some women?
> A. Yes on several occasions I have spoken to him, even spoken about his dress."

41   Similarly in relation to the lies which, according to Seevaratnam Nagendram, the appellant told about his contact with a French family, even to the extent of swearing on God. It is quite clear from the evidence that what mattered to Mr See-

varatnam was the appellant's response to him and the appellant was well able to deal with that.

42   We therefore conclude that the judge was right to admit all of the evidence pursuant to s.101(1)(d) having given consideration to the application made under s.101(3).

43   Our conclusions in relation to s.101(1)(d) make it possible for us to deal more succinctly with the other gateway provisions. We accept that a simple denial of the offence or offences alleged cannot, for the purposes of s.101(1)(f), be treated as a false impression given by the defendant. But that was not the situation in this case. The appellant put himself forward as a man who not only had no previous convictions but also enjoyed a good reputation as a priest, particularly at Tooting, where he had previously been employed, and was the victim of a conspiracy hatched up by members of the Mauritian community at Thornton Heath. That, as Mr Kovalevsky accepted, opened the gateway for the admission of evidence as to what happened at Tooting, but he invited our attention to s.105(6) which states that evidence is admissible under s.101(1)(f) "only if it goes no further than is necessary to correct the false impression". We accept that is a statutory reversal of the previous common law position that character is indivisible (*R. v Winfield* (1940) 27 Cr.App.R. 139), but we do not accept Mr Kovalevsky's submission that all that was required in this case to correct the false impression was for Mr Seevaratnam to state that decisions had been taken not to renew the appellant's contract because of complaints that had been received. The gateway having been opened the prosecution was entitled to adduce a full account of what, according to their witness, brought the Tooting contract to an end. A slightly more difficult question is whether the evidence of I and V would be admissible to correct a false impression given by the appellant. Miss Etherton submitted that it was because of the appellant's allegations in interview about a conspiracy. We prefer to put it slightly differently. In our judgment the evidence of the two women was admissible under s.101(1)(f) because part of the false impression given by the appellant in interview and, as it turned out later by calling seven character witnesses, was that he was a priest who had never behaved inappropriately towards female worshippers at his Temple.

44   We note that the provisions of s.101(3) do not apply to subs.(1)(f), and we see no reason to doubt that s.78 of the 1984 Act should be considered where s.101(1)(f) is relied upon (see the judgment of Lord Woolf C.J. in *R. v Highton* [2005] EWCA Crim 1895 [2006] 1 Cr.App.R. 7 (p.125); [2005] 1 W.L.R. 3472, at para.13, and the views of Professor Spencer at para.21 of the paper to which we have already referred). In this case for the reasons which we have already given when dealing with the application of s.101(3) –101(1)(d) we do not see any way in which, in relation to subs.(1)(f) , s.78 would assist the appellant.

45   We turn now to the final gateway provision relied upon, namely that the appellant at interview and thereafter made an attack on the complainant's character (s.101(1)(g)). Mr Kovalevsky accepts that he did so, but he submitted that the opening of that gateway should not be regarded as rendering all available evidence of bad character admissible. That is a somewhat difficult submission

because in the first place it must be noted that s.105(6) has no application to s.101(1)(g), and, secondly, it is clear from the decision in *Highton* that once this gateway is open the evidence admitted may be used not only in relation to credibility but also in relation to propensity. In our judgment the attack on the character of the complainant clearly opens the door to all of the evidence on which the prosecution sought to rely, subject to the requirements of s.101(3), which we have already considered in relation to s.101(1)(d).

Issue 2— The judge's reasons

46   We accept that the judge's reasons for deciding as he did were brief, but they have to be considered in the light of the argument advanced before him. The principal issue was whether the 2003 Act applied. He was right about that. It was accepted by the defence that the gateway provisions were satisfied, so the only other issue was the application of s.101(3) of the 2003 Act or s.78 of the 1984 Act. The significant difference between those provisions is to be found in the mandatory opening words of s.101(3), but they do not apply until the court reaches its conclusion as to whether the admission of the evidence would have such an adverse effect on the fairness of the proceedings that the court ought not to admit it. In other words the first step is for the judge to perform the balancing act, and it is clear to us that is what the judge did. That is what he was referring to when he spoke of his discretionary power under subs.(3) to exclude evidence. We accept that he could have expressed himself better, but we do not regard infelicity of expression as an effective ground of appeal.

Issue 3— Directions to the jury

47   Mr Kovalevsky submits that the judge failed to direct the jury properly as to the use that could be made of the bad character evidence of I, V and Seevaratnam Nagendram. In particular it is said that the judge failed to refer to the possibility of collusion or innocent contamination as required by *R. v H* [1995] 2 Cr.App.R. 437; [1995] 2 A.C. 596 and, secondly, he did not invite the jury to consider the similarities between the accounts.

48   Collusion was never raised as an issue in this case but the possibility of innocent contamination was put to and rejected by I. During the course of the evidence the judge did caution the jury about the way in which they should approach evidence of bad character, and he returned to the topic in his summing-up, saying in relation to V:

> "Bear in mind the direction I gave you about that, but consider both her account and that of I. In the absence of collaboration and putting minds together and fabricating these allegations that they make, is it likely that these women have separately invented these incidents?

You heard from Mr Seevaratnam, the owner of the Tooting Temple. I referred to his evidence when I gave you a direction about character generally. His evidence is admissible to counter the defendant's assertion in interview that there was never any problem at Tooting, and also the defendant has made an attack on the truthfulness of W."

That, as it seems to us, in the context of this case, satisfied the requirements of *R. v H*, and earlier in his summing-up the judge had referred to the evidence of V and I as evidence capable of supporting the complainant. He said:

"Now, these incidents and aspects of their evidence, if you accept them, are capable of supporting W's account of the defendant's course of conduct or course of behaviour towards her, and the prosecution say that together they show a picture of the targeting of vulnerable women at uncertain times in their lives and a purposeful course of grooming towards a situation from which he could take advantage. Now, that is a matter for your judgment."

The judge went on to deal with the evidence in detail. In our judgment he cannot be criticised for failing to spell out similarities between the accounts, and indeed had he done so he would have been assisting the prosecution rather than the defence.

Issue 4— Professor Lipner

49 Earlier in this judgment we set out one of the questions asked of Professor Lipner and the answer that he gave. Mr Kovalevsky submits that the question should not have been asked, and the answer should not have been given, still less should it have been relied upon by prosecuting counsel in her closing speech and referred to by the judge in his summing-up because "this evidence essentially amounted to an assessment of the likelihood of false allegations of rape being made by a Hindu women against a priest." We disagree. The word false is an interpolation. Miss Etherton did not ask the witness to express a view about the truth or falsehood of the allegation, and he did not purport to do so, but the jury was entitled to know from an expert whether or not within the Hindu community an allegation of this kind was unusual. In our judgment there is no substance whatsoever in this ground of appeal.

Isue 5 — The statement of V

50 V made her statement on March 1, 2004 but later indicated that she did not wish to attend to give evidence, and the judge heard evidence from which he was able to conclude that all reasonable efforts had been made to locate her. That is not disputed. He then had to consider whether her statement could be read, having regard to the factors set out in s.26 of the Criminal Justice Act 1988, namely (1) the contents of the statement; (2) the risk of unfairness to the accused having particular regard to whether it was likely to be possible for the accused to controvert the statement, and (3) any other circumstances that appeared to the court to be relevant. The judge considered those statutory provisions and in a ruling set

out earlier in this judgment decided that the statement could be read. Mr Kovalevsky submitted that his conclusion was wrong because the witness was
important and if she could not be produced and cross-examined her evidence
should not be adduced at all. In our judgment that cannot be accepted, not least
because it would frustrate one important purpose of the statute, which was to prevent a prosecution from being hampered by intimidation of witnesses. The reality
was, as we have already indicated, that the appellant was well able to deal with the
statement of V and, as Miss Etherton points out, his counsel was able to put his
case not only to the complainant but also to I. We consider that the judge's carefully considered decision to allow the statement to be read cannot be faulted.

51   Then it is said that the judge failed properly to direct the jury in relation to the
statement which had been read. When the statement was read the judge warned
the jury to bear in mind that because the witness did not attend they were deprived
of the opportunity to hear her cross-examined, and he repeated that warning in his
summing-up, saying:

> "Remember that Mr Squirrel was deprived of the opportunity to cross-
> examine her and challenge her evidence, and take that into account when
> you assess how much weight to put upon what that witness says, bearing
> in mind that it was a statement made to a police officer in contemplation
> of criminal proceedings. So tread carefully, and bear in mind Mr Squirrel
> was not able to put his case to her in the way that he did, for example, to I."

52   Mr Kovalevsky submitted that the direction was inadequate because the witness was important, and drew our attention to the decision of this court in *R. v
McCoy* December 10, 1999, unreported save in [2000] 6 Archbold News 2. In
that case the statement read was that of the victim of what was alleged to be a
wounding with intent to do grievous bodily harm who identified his attacker.
His evidence was, as this court found, "wholly crucial to the case". It was not
entirely clear why he did not attend, and the judge was precipitate in allowing
his statement to be read before giving sufficient time to exhaust the possibility
of his being brought to court. It was in that context that Laws L.J. said at
para.[25] of the transcript:

> "If a statement of a critical witness is to be read to a jury, perhaps especially
> in an alibi case where identification is the true issue, it must be incumbent on
> the trial judge to ensure that the jury realise the drawbacks which are
> imposed on the defence if the prosecution statement is read to them. It is
> not enough simply to say that counsel has not had the opportunity of
> cross-examining. A lay jury may not appreciate the significance of that
> fact. The judge must at least explain that it means that they may feel quite
> unable to attach anything like as much weight to the evidence in the state-
> ment as they might if it was tested in cross-examination; and where
> appropriate it would be necessary, certainly desirable, for the judge also
> to indicate to the jury by way of illustration the sort of matters that might
> well be put in cross-examination in the particular case."

53   In the present case the evidence of V was important, but it was not crucial, and the judge in his direction drew attention not only to the lack of opportunity to cross-examine but also to the question of how much weight should be put on what the witness said. He also illustrated what might have been put to her had she attended by referring to the cross-examination of I. In those circumstances it seems to us that he did all that was required of him in this case, where the situation was different from that which arose in the case of *McCoy*.

Conclusion

54   Thus we conclude that the appellant has failed to substantiate any of his grounds of appeal, and accordingly this appeal against conviction is dismissed.

Stephen Yaxley-Lennon

The Background

55   On April 18, 2005, in the Luton Crown Court, this appellant was convicted by a majority of 11.1 of assault occasioning actual bodily harm (count 1) and by a majority of 10–2 of assault with intent to resist arrest (count 2). He was sentenced to 12 months' imprisonment on count 1 and three months' imprisonment concurrent on count 2. He appeals by way of leave of the single judge.

The prosecution case

56   The incident in question took place in Luton at around 03.00 on July 4, 2004. The victim was an off-duty police officer called Dalton. He and his neighbours Mr and Mrs Bye were woken by an argument in the street between the appellant and his girlfriend Jenna Vowles. Although living in the same street, Dalton and the Byes did not know each other. Concerned by the screaming and raised voices, the three of them went into the street from their homes.

57   The appellant was described as being "on a short fuse" and that "something had riled him". Miss Vowles was sobbing and hysterical wanting nothing to do with him. Dalton concerned for Miss Vowles, told the appellant that he should let her go home alone. He indicated that he was a police officer and showed the appellant his warrant card. He tried to bring the appellant to the ground. Both men fell to the ground. The appellant managed to get to his feet and kicked Mr Dalton in the head. Dalton had thrown no punches. Dalton then stood up and told the appellant that he was arresting him for assaulting a police officer. It was subsequently decided that such an arrest would not be prudent and that the Byes who had witnessed the whole incident, would ascertain the appellant's address.

The defence case

58   In interview and in evidence, the appellant said that he had been out clubbing. He had drunk one bottle of Smirnoff Vodka. He and Jenna Vowles had an argument. She had dropped her mobile phone and was on her hands and knees trying to pick it up. The eye witnesses must have assumed that he was the aggressor. Dal-

ton came up to him. He asked the appellant what he was doing. His breath smelled of alcohol. Jenna was not sobbing or crying. Dalton told him he was not going home and pushed him around, pushing him in the face and pulled his legs from under him. He did not produce a warrant card or say he was a police officer. The appellant did not kick him. It was only at the end when Dalton was threatening him that he indicated he was a police officer. The appellant did not believe him. He suggested that Mr Bye knew Dalton as he addressed Dalton by his Christian name, telling him to leave it and go home. The appellant and Jenna then ran home.

59   Jenna Vowles gave evidence along the same lines of the appellant, describing the argument as a tiff, but that they were happily going home when the incident broke out.

Background to the judge's ruling

60   During evidence in chief of Jenna Vowles, counsel for the appellant asked her whether she or the appellant had taken any drugs that evening. She replied "No".

61   In cross examination, counsel for the Crown asked her the following questions:

> "Q — You were asked questions by Mr Urquhart about what you had been drinking. Yes?
> A — Yeah.
> Q — And you say you had had four drinks and you were a bit tipsy. Correct?
> A — Yeah.
> Q — And then he asked you about whether you had taken any drugs. Correct?
> A — Yeah.
> Q — Just tell about drugs please for a moment. What do you want to tell us about drugs?
> A — I don't take drugs
> Q — Never taken drugs?
> A — No
> Q — Never possessed drugs?
> A — Yes
> Q — Yes. Tell the jury about that
> A — I was cautioned in November for possession of drugs
> Q — Which drug?
> A — It was cocaine
> Q — Cocaine
> A — It was in my possession. There were two empty bags which I was clearing out my house. I put them in my bag so my parents wouldn't find them"

It was at this point that the judge asked the jury to retire. There then followed discussions between counsel and court.

62   The Crown whilst conceding that they should have made an application to introduce the caution, said that they would not have raised the issue had the wit-

ness not been asked about drugs in evidence in chief. They submitted that the evidence was relevant to the question of credibility.

63   The defence having taken instructions made an application for the discharge of the jury on the basis that the wording of s.100(1)(b) could not include issues relating to credibility and thus the evidence did not relate to a matter in issue in the proceedings. The judge said that it was premature to discharge the jury at that point without more and that he may have to re-visit the decision at a later point.

64   It was agreed between the parties and the court that the witness should be asked further questions about her caution. The witness was then called and questions were put to her in the absence of the jury. Following the voir dire, defence counsel submitted that the evidence could not fall under s.100(1)(a) or (b).

65   The judge ruled that Jenna Vowles' caution for possession of cocaine had substantial probative value to her credibility, which was an important issue in the case. It had been put that she was lying to support her boyfriend's case and there was a stark difference between the Crown and defence accounts. He gave leave for the Crown to ask further questions of the witness in front of the jury, but indicated that he was going to direct the jury that so far as credit is concerned they should ignore the evidence completely, as it could not really help the prosecution prove that she had been lying about what happened in relation to the events of the incident, given that she did not lie in relation to the caution. In the light of the judge's comments, counsel for the Crown did not cross examine further on the matter in the presence of the jury. Counsel for the appellant re-examined the witness on the background facts leading to the caution.

Direction in summing up

66   When summing up to the jury, the learned judge gave a strongly worded direction to the jury, as follows:

> "One exchange between Mr Heimler and her (Vowles) concerned this question of cocaine. I need to deal with it. You have heard about it. Can I ask you to disregard it completely? It has got about as much to do with this case as the price of tomatoes. First of all the caution took place well after this incident itself occurred. . . .. Secondly—and it is important—although her credibility is in issue, clearly just as much as all the witnesses' credibility is in issue, the effect of drugs on that is unknown. It has got really no issue, no bearing on any issue in this case . . . .. I am directing you to disregard her previous caution completely because it cannot help you decide what happened in the street that night . . . .. In fairness please just disregard that completely"

Grounds of Appeal

67   The ground of appeal is that the judge erred in holding that the evidence of the caution was admissible and rejecting the defendant's application to discharge the jury.

68   The appellant's submissions are put on two bases: first, that the evidence did not relate to a matter in issue in the proceedings as the section does not encompass

matters of credibility. Secondly, that even if credibility is encompassed by the section, the evidence did not pass the test of admissibility as it had no substantial probative value in relation to the question of credibility and was not of substantial importance in the context of the case as a whole. It was submitted that the evidence had very little value in relation to credibility and no relevance at all to the offence in question because a) the caution did not relate to an offence of dishonesty or show evidence of untruthfulness; b) it related to an incident after the events in issue; c) the witness by agreeing to be cautioned had accepted her guilt; d) the witness was frank about her caution in evidence; and e) there was no suggestion that she was under the influence of drugs during the incident itself.

69   The appellant also submits that the conviction is unsafe in the light of the majority verdicts on each count on the basis that the evidence could have adversely affected their view of the witness despite the judge's strong warning.

70   On behalf of the respondent, it is submitted that s.100(1) must cover the issue of credibility, for were it not to do so, unfairness would ensue. It was submitted that the evidence of the caution was relevant to credibility, but it was conceded that it was difficult to suggest that the evidence had substantial probative value in relation to credibility in the light of the witnesses' answers.

71   Their primary submission therefore is that the conviction was safe and that the strong warning given by the judge corrected any harm done by the introduction of the evidence.

Judgment

72   We now deal with the submissions and the questions arising therefrom.

Does s.100(1) cover issues of credibility?

73   Although couched in different terms from the provisions relating to the introduction of the defendant's bad character, in our view, s.100(1) does cover matters of credibility. To find otherwise would mean that there was a significant lacuna in the legislation with the potential for unfairness. In any event, it is clear from para.[362] of the explanatory notes that the issue of credibility falls within the section.

Did the judge err in coming to the conclusion that the evidence of the caution had substantial probative value in relation to the witness's credibility?

74   In our view he did err for a number of reasons, including those which were put forward by the judge himself when directing the jury to ignore the evidence of the caution. It follows, therefore, that we find that the evidence of the caution was inadmissible under s.100.

Is the verdict unsafe as a result of the inadmissible evidence being in front of the jury?

75   Mr Urquhart conceded that had the judge found the evidence to be inadmissible but nevertheless declined to discharge the jury, he would have difficulty

persuading the court that the judge had exercised his discretion wrongly. Although the exercise of discretion was not the basis upon which the judge declined to discharge the jury, the practical effect is still the same. We have to take a view therefore whether in the light of the admission of the evidence of the caution, the conviction is unsafe. We have considered the evidence as a whole and in particular the very strong warning given to the jury and come to the conclusion that the verdicts in this case, despite being majority verdicts are not unsafe. This appeal against conviction is therefore dismissed.

Simon Charles Manister

76   On April 15, 2005 in the Crown Court at Bristol, this appellant was convicted of three offences of indecent assault contrary to s.14(1) of the Sexual Offences Act 1956.

77   A, the complainant in each case, was born on March 12, 1990 so she was 13 at the time of the alleged offences; the appellant was 39. He was a friend of the girl's father and he moved into the family home on July 23, 2003 and stayed there until December 2003.

78   A alleged that the appellant touched her sexually on a number of occasions, but the allegations which led to the three counts in the indictment were: count 1, placing his hand between her legs in the region of her vagina, then on her breasts, both over her clothes, in December 2003 soon after he left her family home; count 2 (an allegation of rape of which he was found not guilty but guilty of indecent assault), full sexual intercourse in mid February 2004; and count 3, forcibly kissing her, touching the outside of her leg and her bottom and then between her legs in the area of her vagina, all over her clothes, before putting his hand under her upper clothing and bra and touching her breast, on February 27, 2004. All the offences were alleged to have been committed in his car.

79   A did not make any allegation against the appellant until just over a week after the last, alleged incident, when she was arrested for shoplifting. She was interviewed on three occasions, and the video recordings of the interviews stood as her evidence in chief. In the first interview on March 9, 2004 she spoke of the appellant's relationship with her family and her sympathy for him because he said he had cancer, although it turned out to be a swollen gland in his throat. She spoke of the appellant touching her up on occasions and gave her account of events which led to counts 1 and 3. At the end of the interview she asked what she should do if she later remembered something else. The interviewing officer said A could come back and speak on tape, and asked her if she had told as much as she could. She said, "Yes".

80   The second interview was on May 19, 2004. A spoke slowly and it was difficult for the officer to get much out of her. She said that on an occasion in about mid February the appellant had spoken about paying her for sex, which disgusted her, and he tried to kiss her. She spoke of an earlier occasion just before Christmas when she was in his house and he came down naked after a shower. She spoke of him threatening to kill himself on February 27, 2004. She was asked if there was anything else she wanted to say, and she answered "No".

81   On June 28, 2004 she was interviewed for a third time because she had more to say, and she spoke of the appellant kissing her, pulling her jeans and thong down to her ankles and having sexual intercourse with her in his car on the occasion in mid February 2004. He had ejaculated onto the seat. She had not spoken about it before because she thought people would be mad at her, and she was embarrassed.

82   The appellant had no previous convictions. His case, when interviewed by the police and in his evidence at trial, was that nothing of a sexual nature had occurred between him and A. None of the allegations upon which the indictment was based were true. In interview he said that he and A had a friendship; he gave her a little bit of confidence; he never thought that she thought there was more to their friendship, and he told her "just be mates". In his evidence, he said that his relationship with A was just a friendship where he wanted to help a friend, a teenager. He was someone who was just there, a sounding board, someone to talk to. He accepted that, looking back, it was an emotionally unhealthy relationship, but he had not done any of the improper things that A said he had done.

83   The prosecution relied on various matters in support of the allegations. Semen with the appellant's DNA was found on his car seat. It could not be related to A or any particular woman, and the appellant said it was the result of unprotected sex with other, adult women.

84   There were records of a large number of mobile telephone calls between the appellant and A. He had sent her a card with the message, "Be mine as I miss you lots", which A had hidden under her mattress where it was found by her sisters.

85   The judge ruled that evidence of an earlier sexual relationship with another girl was admissible in evidence, as a result of which the appellant formally admitted, as agreed facts, that from October 1998 to September 2001 he had had a sexual relationship with B, a girl who was 16 at the start of the relationship, when the appellant was 34.

86   The judge also ruled admissible the evidence of C, a sister of A, and 15 at the material time, that after going to the gym with the appellant he had told her, "Why do you think I'm still single? If only you were a bit older and I a bit younger". The appellant denied saying that; it was put to C in cross-examination that she had made it up.

87   The verdict of not guilty of rape but guilty of indecent assault on count 2 must mean that the jury was sure of sexual intercourse, unlawful because of A's age, in mid February 2004, but not sure that A did not consent, or not sure that the appellant was reckless as to whether she consented. In those circumstances, the prosecution does not seek to uphold the appellant's conviction for indecent assault on count 2 in the light of the decisions of the House of Lords in *R. v J* [2004] UKHL 42, [2005] 1 Cr.App.R. 19 (p.277P, [2005] 1 A.C. 562, and of this court in *R. v WR* [2005] EWCA Crim. 1907.

88   The appellant was never charged with unlawful sexual intercourse, and the effect of those decisions is that on April 15, 2005 when count 2 was left to the jury, it was too late to prosecute the appellant under s.6(1) of the Sexual Offences Act 1956 for having unlawful sexual intercourse as an alternative to the alle-

gation of rape, because s.37(2) of, and para.10(a) of Sch.2 to, the 1956 Act provided that no such prosecution could be commenced more than 12 months after the alleged sexual intercourse in mid-February 2004. In accordance with *R. v J* and *R. v WR*, the alternative of indecent assault could not be left to the jury either. A prosecution for unlawful sexual intercourse could not be commenced, so it was also impermissible to commence a prosecution for indecent assault by leaving it to the jury as an alternative to rape. In those circumstances the appeal against conviction on count 2 must succeed and the conviction for indecent assault on that count is quashed.

89   The remaining appeal against the convictions for indecent assault on counts 1 and 3 is based on a number of grounds, but primarily on the contention that the judge was wrong to rule the evidence of B and C admissible.

90   The relevant sections in Pt II, Ch.1, of the Criminal Justice Act 2003 are ss.98, 99(1), 101(1) (3) and (4), 102, 103(1) and 112(1).

91   So far as the potential evidence of an earlier sexual relationship between the appellant and B was concerned, the trial judge concluded that for a man of 34 to institute a sexual relationship with a girl of 16 was properly to be described as reprehensible behaviour, and that this brought the relationship within "gateway" (d) of s.101(1). It showed a propensity to be attracted to girls of an age which was inappropriate for persons of the appellant's age. Since this was the context of the evidence, the passage of five or six years since the earlier relationship was not of significance for the purposes of s.101(4). Having formed a clear view in respect of gateway (d), the judge did not think it necessary to form a view on the additional gateway (f), to correct a false impression, argued by the Crown; he thought it more difficult, but he would not shut it out.

92   The judge ruled that the potential evidence of what the appellant was alleged to have said to A's sister, C, was admissible as "part of the background as to what is going on in this family, involving the defendant, that the jury was entitled to hear and which, if they accept the evidence, may be useful to them."

93   Mr Chamberlain challenged both rulings, as he resisted them at the trial. In respect of the sexual relationship with B, he contended that a perfectly legal relationship could not involve the commission of an offence, which we accept; nor could it, being countenanced by the law, amount to "reprehensible behaviour". There was no exploration of the details of the relationship. What if the appellant had married B? It could not, therefore, amount to misconduct or a disposition towards misconduct. The disputed evidence of what the appellant said to C indicated restraint on his part.

94   In our combined view, the judge was wrong to conclude that the sexual relationship between the appellant and B, without more, amounted to "evidence of, or of a disposition towards, misconduct on his part" and therefore evidence of "bad character" for the purposes of s.98, and therefore ss.101, 102 and 103 of the Act. The definition of "misconduct" in s.112(1) is very wide. It makes it clear that behaviour may be reprehensible, and therefore misconduct, though not amounting to the commission of an offence. The appellant was significantly older than B. But there was no evidence, or none that the Crown put forward and the judge ruled admissible, of grooming of B by the appellant before she

was 16, or that her parents disapproved and communicated their disapproval to the appellant, or that B was intellectually, emotionally or physically immature for her age, or that there was some other feature of the lawful relationship which might make it "reprehensible". Indeed it might be inferred from the simple agreed facts that the relationship with B was a serious one, with some real emotional attachment, because it lasted some time.

95   However, once it is decided that evidence of the appellant's sexual relationship with B did not amount to "evidence of bad character", the abolition of the common law rules governing the admissibility of "evidence of bad character" by s.99(1) did not apply. We have no doubt that evidence of the relationship was admissible at common law, in the particular circumstances of this case, because it was relevant to the issue of whether the appellant had a sexual interest in A. It was capable of demonstrating a sexual interest in early or mid-teenage girls, much younger than the appellant, and therefore bore on the truth of his case of a purely supportive, sexual interest in A. It was not in our judgment unfair to admit the evidence (see s.78 of the Police and Criminal Evidence Act 1984).

96   Although the judge came to his conclusion as to the admissibility of the appellant's relationship with B by a different route, his direction to the jury as to its possible relevance was fair and accurate. He directed them that it was for the jury to decide whether it had any relevance. He reminded them that the age of consent was 16. "It is something that you can take into account in deciding whether he might have been attracted to [A]. It does not mean that he would have behaved as she says that he behaved; that is assaulting her sexually. To state the obvious, you can be attracted to someone without assaulting them".

97   So far as C's evidence was concerned, the judge did not expressly rule on whether it amounted to evidence of "bad character" for the purposes of the Act, or was simply relevant as part of the background as to what was going on in the sister's family, involving the appellant. Unattractive as the alleged conversation was, we do not consider that it could safely be judged to amount to reprehensible conduct on the appellant's part. But his words, with their implied admission of sexual attraction to 15-year-old C, were again, in our view, clearly relevant to the issue of whether the appellant was sexually attracted to A, and therefore admissible for the same reasons which applied to the sexual relationship with B. It was not unfair to admit C's evidence.

98   The judge did not direct the jury as to the potential relevance of C's evidence, but it must have been plain that it fell in the same category as the admission in respect of B, namely something which the jury could take into account in deciding whether the appellant was sexually attracted to A.

99   We therefore reject the challenge to the admissibility of the appellant's conduct in respect of B and C.

100   Mr Chamberlain challenged the judge's direction in respect of the appellant's character. Having indicated in the summing-up that he would give a full "good character direction" he did so in the terms of the standard direction suggested by the Judicial Studies Board which, accordingly, concluded by telling the jury that they were entitled to take into account all that they had heard about the appellant. This, Mr Chamberlain contended, was likely to be understood by the jury to

refer to his earlier relationship with B, and, therefore, to qualify the terms of the good character direction as a whole. We cannot accept this. The relevance of the appellant's lack of convictions, to be taken into account in his favour both as to his credibility and the lesser likelihood of committing the offences of which he was accused, was clearly described to the jury who, nevertheless, had to take account of all they had heard. We see no mischief in that.

101   It was contended that the judge should have given the jury a specific warning to exercise caution in relation to A's evidence in the light of what Mr Chamberlain suggested were weaknesses or implausibilities in her evidence. In particular she told the police in her first two interviews that nothing else had happened, before alleging sexual intercourse, amounting on the face of it to rape, in the third. But the case of *R. v Makanjoula* [1995] 2 Cr.App.R. 469, [1995] 1 W.L.R. 1348, to which we were referred simply says that a judge "may" give a special warning, and we can not fault the judge's decision not to do so in this case. The judge pointed up the possible weaknesses or implausibilities as he reminded the jury of relevant evidence and issues.

102   It was argued that the judge made comments which might have suggested that A's shoplifting was caused by the appellant's behaviour towards her, when he should have directed them that the reprimand for shoplifting was central to her credibility; and that he raised matters which were not canvassed by counsel on either side, including the possibility that A was attracted to the appellant and may have consented to what happened. But the jury was clearly reminded of her shoplifting and the judge's comments all related to questions which would have come to the minds of worldly members of the jury, and were fairly balanced. We reject the final, and associated submission that the summing-up was "overly favourable" to the Crown's case.

103   For all these reasons we reject the challenges to the conduct of the appellant's trial. His convictions on counts 1 and 3 were safe and his appeals against those convictions are dismissed.

104   The success of the appeal against conviction on count 2 removes the sentence of five years. The sentence of 12 months on count 1 was not challenged, but that of three years and six months on count 3 was said to be manifestly excessive in the light of what was contended to be the relatively low level of indecency. But even leaving aside the events of count 2, where the jury must have been satisfied of full sexual intercourse, count 3 was a second occasion of indecency when the appellant had A alone in his car. It was in breach of trust by a friend of her father. It was that friendship which had enabled the appellant to become close to her. Her evidence was that on February 27, 2004 the appellant told her that he felt like killing himself, and that he had a gun in the dashboard (although there was no evidence that that was true); that he smashed her mobile telephone after looking at its images, and then drove at high speed so that she was frightened he would kill them both. Then came the indecent assault. The judge accepted her account, as he was entitled to, for the purposes of sentence. In our judgment the events of that night consisted of indecency after intimidation. The appellant did not have the mitigation of admitting his conduct, and the sentence which the judge imposed on count 3, concurrent to that on count 1, was not excessive.

105   The appeal against the remaining total sentence of three years and six months is
dismissed.

Hong Qiang He and De Qun He

106   On March 10, 2005, in the Crown Court at Southwark, these appellants were
convicted of violent disorder (count 1), contrary to s.2(1) of the Public Order Act,
1986. Each now appeals against his conviction.

107   A co-defendant, Feng He, was convicted of the same count of violent disorder.
A further co-defendant, Pin Shuen Chan was acquitted of the count of violent disorder on the judge's direction, but convicted of wounding with intent to cause
grievous bodily harm (Count 2).

108   The counts arose out of a running fight between two groups of young men in
Chinatown in west central London on the evening of September 9, 2004. Various
weapons including knives and baseball bats were used. Parts of the concluding
events were captured on CCTV in Shaftesbury Avenue.

109   The CCTV film was alleged to show the appellant De Qun He ("De") being
struck on the head after which he ran away up Shaftesbury Avenue. A group
was seen fighting and moving in the direction taken by Hong Qiang He
("Hong"). Hong was said to have used a baseball bat before falling to the ground.
Pin Shuenn Chan ("Chan") was said to have walked towards the group and then
run to where Hong was lying, before bending over and stabbing him twice in the
leg. De was seen to return, pick up an advertising board, and wave it in a threatening manner towards the group fighting over Hong. Hong was helped to his feet
and his friends moved up the street and around the corner. Two of the friends were
carrying baseball bats. De put down the advertising board and went with them.
They turned into Gerrard Place where some got into a car in which some of the
weapons were deposited. Feng He drove the car away. Two got out of the car
in King William IV Street, including Hong who was bleeding badly from leg
wounds. The car was driven off but soon stopped by police. The driver and the
one remaining occupant, De, were arrested. Metal bars wrapped in cellophane,
lawn edge cutters and a hammer were found in the boot.

110   Hong, De and Feng He were alleged to belong to one group, and Chan, who
was arrested in Shaftesbury Avenue, to the other.

111   When interviewed, Hong said he went to the scene to calm the situation. He did
not know if he went to Shaftsbury Avenue. He was hit on the head and stabbed
twice, and taken away in a car.

112   De was not interviewed.

113   Chan said he armed himself with a knife, fearing that he would be attacked. He
was set upon by others who were armed with knives. He denied using the knife to
stab someone, but he was not very clear and did not remember.

114   None of the defendants gave evidence. They put their characters in. Feng He
and Chan had no previous convictions. Hong had a caution and De a conditional
discharge. The judge gave a good character direction in respect of all.

115   The issues in the case of each defendant were his involvement in events and
whether he might have been acting in lawful defence of himself or another.

116   The appeals revolve around the admission of evidence, adduced on behalf of Chan, that the appellants were known to the police from previous incidents. On November 19, 2002 they had been the victims of a knife attack but had refused to provide statements. On June 6, 2004 they had been arrested on suspicion of committing a serious assault but had been released without charge after the alleged victims refused to provide statements.

117   Counsel for Chan submitted that evidence of both incidents was admissible by virtue of s.101(1)(e) of the Act which provides that:

> "In criminal proceedings evidence of the defendant's bad character is admissible if, but only if . . .
>> i. (e) it has substantial probative value in relation to an important matter in issue between the defendant and a co-defendant . . . .''

118   The judge rejected this submission, rightly in our view, because he did not consider that being the subject of the conduct of others on November 19, 2002, and failing to make witness statements, demonstrated "reprehensible behaviour", still less the commission of an offence; nor did the mere fact of arrest on June 6, 2004, without evidence to support a charge against either appellant. So neither previous matter could amount to "misconduct" as defined in s.112(1) or, therefore "bad character", as defined in s.98 for the purpose of s.101(1)(e).

119   However, the judge concluded that the fact that evidence of the previous matters was not admissible as "bad character" did not exclude its relevance. He took the view that

> ii. ". . . it is potentially relevant to Mr Chan's defence, namely that he was attacked. In this regard the position between defendants on the one hand and the prosecution and defendants on the other is quite different. In short a greater latitude is allowed to a defendant and if there is evidence that some defendants are to be found at or about the scene of disturbances such as the one with which we are concerned then it may assist the jury in deciding whom to believe. This is not necessarily one and the same thing as bad character. There is no conduct reprehensible or otherwise necessarily inherent in the circumstances by which someone may be surrounded, but equally the repetition of such circumstances may be relevant . . . in the light of the defence actually advanced by Mr Chan . . . I make this ruling, of course, under the common law".

120   No doubt there are cases where previous conduct of a defendant is of probative value and therefore relevant to a matter in issue between him and the prosecution or him and a co-defendant, yet the "bad character" provisions of Ch.1 of Pt II of the Act relating to the defendant's "misconduct" do not apply. In such cases, s.99(1) of the Act whereby the common law rules governing the admissibility of evidence of "bad character" in criminal proceedings are abolished does not exclude the relevant material because it does not amount to "evidence of bad character". But this was not such a case. The evidence of events on November 19, 2002 and June 6, 2004 could only be relevant if it might show that either appellant had a propensity to violent conduct and therefore bear on Chan's

case of self-defence. To show such a propensity it had to amount to "reprehensible behaviour", "misconduct" and, therefore "bad character". By the same measure as events on November 19, 2002 and June 6, 2004 could not amount to reprehensible behaviour, misconduct or, therefore bad character, they could not bear on Chan's case. There was no room for relaxing this approach simply because it was a defendant, Chan, who sought to introduce the evidence, rather than the prosecution.

121   On the face of the CCTV evidence, interpreted by police officers who knew the appellants, and unchallenged by evidence at trial from the appellants, there was a strong case against each appellant on Count 1, but the admission of the earlier incidents may have poisoned the well so far as their own case of self-defence were concerned, making their convictions unsafe. Their appeals against conviction are accordingly allowed.

122   It is not therefore necessary to consider Hong's second ground of appeal, but we do so for completeness. The prosecution relied on two alleged lies by Hong, in his police interview. Mr Kapur argued that the judge erred when directing the jury: "You must first decide whether the defendant did, in fact, deliberately tell these lies". Those words, Mr Kapur contended, removed from the jury the decision as to whether the statements were lies at all, which was contested. However, that argument depends on a partial reading of the summing-up. The judge had hitherto referred to the "alleged lie", it being "alleged that he lied", and to "the lies alleged" and "the alleged lies". The jury must have understood that it was for them to decide whether either statement by Hong was in fact a deliberate untruth. The remainder of the judge's direction on the topic was fair and accurate. We see no merit in this ground of appeal.

Dismissing appeals against conviction by the first, second, third, fifth and sixth
appellants
Allowing the fourth appellant's appeal against conviction on one count only.

R. v CLAYDON

COURT OF APPEAL (Lady Justice Hallett, Mr Justice Silber and
Judge Patience Q.C.): October 28; November 9, 2005

[2005] EWCA Crim 2827; [2006] 1 Cr.App.R. 20

ᴸᵀ Buggery; Children; Incitement; Mens rea; Presumptions; Sexual offences

H1   INCITEMENT
      Incitement to commit buggery
      Defendant convicted of inciting boy under 14 to commit buggery—Incitement
      occurring prior to abrogation of irrebuttable presumption that boy under 14
      incapable of sexual intercourse—Whether offence committed—Whether mens
      rea of incitee relevant

H2   The defendant was convicted of two counts of inciting a boy under 14 to com-
      mit buggery on various occasions between December 1981 and September 1985.
      The defendant appealed on the ground that the incidents had occurred prior to
      September 20, 1993 when there had been an irrebuttable presumption that a
      boy under 14 was incapable of sexual intercourse. Accordingly, since it would
      not have been a crime for the boy to have engaged in buggery, it had not been
      a crime to incite him to commit such an act.

H3   **Held,** allowing the appeal, that it was a necessary element of the offence of
      incitement that the person incited must be capable of committing the primary
      crime. Accordingly, by virtue of the common law presumption, a person could
      not be convicted of inciting a boy under 14 to commit buggery when the incite-
      ment occurred prior to September 20, 1993 (post, paras [15]–[19], [38]).
          R. v Whitehouse (1977) 65 Cr.App.R. 33; [1977] Q.B. 868, CA, applied.
H4   *Per curiam* A person is guilty of incitement to commit an offence if he incites
      another to do or causes to be done an act or acts which, if done, will involve the
      commission of the offence or offences by the other; and he intends or believes
      that the other, if he acts as incited, shall or will do so with the fault required
      for the offence or offences. The knowledge or *mens rea* of the incitee is irrelevant
      (post, paras [30]–[31]).
          R. v Curr (1967) 51 Cr.App.R. 113; [1968] 2 Q.B. 944, CA, not applied.

H5   (For capacity to commit an offence, see *Archbold* 2006, para.18–12).

      Appeal against conviction

H6   On December 16, 2004 in the Crown Court at Southampton (Judge Leigh Q.C.)
      the appellant, David Alexander Claydon, was convicted of two counts of inde-

cent assault, three counts of committing gross indecency with a child and two counts of incitement to commit buggery. He was sentenced to a total of eight years' imprisonment. He appealed against conviction of the offences of incitement to commit buggery.

H7   The facts and grounds of appeal appear in the judgment of the court.

H8   *Iain Ross* (assigned by the Registrar of Criminal Appeals) for the appellant.
David Jenkins (instructed by the Crown Prosecution Service, Southampton) for the Crown.

Cur. adv. vult.

November 9   Silber J.: handed down the judgment of the court.

I. Introduction

1   This appeal raises the issues of first whether there can be a conviction for inciting if the person incited does not know that what he was being incited to do was illegal, and second whether the appellant could be convicted of inciting before September 20, 1993 a boy under the age of 14 to commit buggery, even when there was no knowledge on the part of the boy that the proposed buggery was unlawful. The significance of the date of September 20, 1993 is that with effect from that date, Parliament abrogated the common law presumption that "a boy under the age of fourteen was incapable of sexual intercourse (whether natural or unnatural)" (ss.1 and 2(2) of the Sexual Offences Act 1993) This provision does not apply, however, to acts done before the commencement of that Act on September 20, 1993 (ibid s.2(3)) and that means that the presumption was in force when the appellant committed the acts of incitement, which are the subject matter of the present appeal.

2   Thus, we will have to consider:

  (a) whether the common law presumption meant that prior to September 20, 1993 the appellant could not be convicted of inciting a boy under the age of 14 to commit buggery because the boy could not commit the offence ("the presumption issue")
  (b) whether the prosecution had to prove that the boy victim knew that the proposed buggery was unlawful ("the mens rea issue"), and if the convictions have to be quashed
  (c) the consequences of quashing the convictions of inciting to commit buggery ("the consequences issue")

II. The background

3   On December 16, 2004 at the Crown Court at Southampton, the appellant, David Alexander Claydon, was convicted after a trial presided over by Judge Leigh Q.C. of a series of sex offences including two counts of inciting to commit buggery, which are the subject of the present appeal. He appeals with leave of the single judge against the decision of the trial judge at the end of the prosecution

case not to withdraw those two counts from the jury on the grounds that the appellant could not be convicted because the complainant, who was born on May 10, 1973, was under the age of 14 years when the offences were committed.

4   The background to these convictions is that in about 1981 the appellant was having a relationship. Shortly after he and his partner started living together, the son of his partner, who is the complainant, came out of foster care to live with his mother and the appellant. About 20 years later, the complainant alleged that on several occasions between December 1981 and September 1, 1985 when the complainant was under 14 years of age, the appellant had sexually abused him. These allegations were denied by the appellant.

5   The two charges, which are the subject of this appeal, are both of incitement to commit buggery, contrary to common law. The material particulars in both counts of the indictment are that between December 31, 1981 and September 1, 1985 the appellant "unlawfully incited [the complainant], a child under the age of 13 years to commit an act of buggery".

6   At the end of the prosecution's case, counsel for the appellant submitted that there was no case to answer but the judge rejected that submission; and it is that ruling which is the subject of the present appeal.

7   The judge rejected the submission that the appellant could not be guilty of inciting the complainant to commit buggery because the complainant was under 14 years of age and there was an irrebutable presumption that he was incapable of sexual intercourse. The judge explained that the presumption would only apply to a boy under 14 years of age, who was charged with an offence and that it could not benefit the appellant, who was an adult perpetrator of a sexual offence against a boy. He also pointed out that it was relevant that the appellant was charged with incitement and not the actual offence of buggery. In all fairness to the judge, we should point out that we have had the benefit of much fuller argument than he did.

8   The appellant appeals with leave of the single judge, contending that the appeal should be allowed because of both the presumption issue and the mens rea issue.

III. The presumption issue

9   Mr Iain Ross for the appellant contends that the irrebuttable common law presumption that a boy under the age of 14 years of age was "incapable of sexual intercourse (whether natural or unnatural)" was of crucial importance on a charge of incitement to commit buggery because one element of the offence of buggery was that of sexual intercourse per anum. He contends that in a case in which this irrefutable presumption applies, a defendant cannot be found guilty of inciting a boy under 14 years of age to commit an offence which involves the boy having sexual intercourse.

10   Mr David Jenkins for the respondent contends that the purpose of the presumption was to protect the complainant, who was the victim, and not to protect an adult defendant with the result that the presumption did not protect the appellant with the result that the judge was correct in rejecting the submission of no case to

answer. This submission entails considering whether the appellant, an adult, can take advantage of the presumption when his victim is a child.

11 Mr Jenkins contends that the presumption goes no further than preventing the conviction of a boy of under 14 of the offence of rape, which both counsel accept would include buggery. It is true that there is much to support that preposition. So in *Hale's Pleas of the Crown* (1 Hale PC 630), it is stated that:

> "an infant under the age of 14 years is presumed by law unable to commit a rape, and therefore it seems cannot be guilty of it."

12 It has also been said by Lord Coleridge C.J., first, that "a boy under 14 is under a physical incapacity to commit the offence. That is a presumptio juris et de jure" (*R. v Waite* [1892] 2 Q.B. 600 at 601); and second that a boy under the age of 14 "could not by law be convicted of rape" (*R. v Williams* [1893] 1 Q.B. 320 at 321).

13 Significantly in none of the authorities to which our attention was drawn is it said or even suggested that the presumption protects an adult rapist when a boy is the victim of the rape but not the perpetrator. The significance of this distinction was recently explained by Laws J. giving the judgment of this court when stating with the original emphasis that:

> "the presumption was not that a boy of under 14 was incapable of the act of intercourse *simpliciter*, it was that he was incapable *himself of committing an offence* whose *actus reus* included sexual intercourse by him. The reasons for the presumption, however they have been articulated in the old cases, cannot begin to justify its application in a case where the boy is not the perpetrator, but its victim" (*R. v Pickford* [1995] 1 Cr.App.R. 420 at 429; [1995] Q.B. 203 at 212–213).

14 We respectfully agree and merely add that it would be very strange if a presumption, which must have been devised and intended to protect boys under the age of 14 years of age, could now be used to protect an adult abuser in cases in which boys of that age were the victims and not the perpetrators. In other words, the presumption cannot assist men like the appellant who commit acts of buggery on boys under the age of 14.

15 Mr Ross' alternative submission is that in a case such as the present where the charge was *incitement* for a child under the age of 14 years of age to commit buggery, the fact that it is not a crime for the boy to engage in buggery because of the irrefutable presumption means that the inciter does not commit a criminal act. In support of that proposition, he relies on the decision of this Court in *R. v Whitehouse* (1977) 65 Cr.App.R. 33; [1977] Q.B. 868 in which a father was charged with inciting his daughter, who was under the age of 16, to have sexual intercourse with him at a time when she was too young to have committed the offence of incest with her father. The conviction was quashed on appeal and Scarman L.J. (who was sitting with Geoffrey Lane L.J. and Donaldson J.) giving the judgment of this Court explained that:

"we have therefore come to the conclusion, with regret, that the indictment does not disclose an offence known to the law because it cannot be a crime on the part of this girl aged 15 to have sexual intercourse with her father, though it is of course a crime and a very serious crime, on the part of the father. There is here incitement to a course of conduct, but that course of conduct cannot be treated as a crime by the girl . . . .. It is regrettable indeed that a man who importunes his daughter under the age of 16 to have sexual intercourse with him but does not go beyond incitement cannot be guilty of a crime."

16   Mr Jenkins contends that this approach does not apply to the charges of incitement against the appellant because in this case the immunity of the complainant is based on an irrebuttable presumption rather than on a statutory rule, as was the position in *Whitehouse's* case. We do not consider that there is any justification for this distinction because this court has held that "it is a necessary element of the element of incitement that the person incited must be capable of committing the primary crime" (per Laws J. in *R. v Pickford* [1995] 1 Cr.App.R. 420, 424). In any event, there is no reason or principle which could possibly explain why it would be an offence for an adult to induce a child to commit a crime which the child could not commit because of an *irrebuttable presumption of law* (such as in the present case) while it would not be an offence if the child could not commit this offence because of a statutory provision, such as in *Whitehouse's* case.

17   Mr. Jenkins then seeks to derive assistance from the statement of Laws J. in *Pickford* that:

"the appellant in the present case would rightly have been found guilty of inciting the mother to have intercourse with her son, even if it were plain beyond argument that he was under 14 at the time." (p.429)

18   This statement is dealing with a different situation from that prevailing in the present case because the mother, who was the person incited in that case, would have been committing an offence if she complied with the incitement as she, unlike the appellant in the present case, was not the beneficiary of a presumption that she could not commit the offence which she was being incited to commit.

19   On the basis of the *Whitehouse* decision, to which Judge Leigh's attention was unfortunately not drawn, this appeal must be allowed and the incitement convictions must be quashed. We stress that like this Court in Whitehouse's case, we reach that decision with "regret" and consider that in Scarman L.J.'s words "plainly a gap or lacuna in the protection of [children] is exposed by this decision" (ibid p.38). We should add that the law has now been changed and inciting a child such as the complainant to commit buggery is now an offence under s.11 of the Sexual Offences Act 2003, but that change does not apply to a case of incitement to commit buggery before, as we have explained in para.1 above, the presumption was abrogated in relation to acts committed after September 20, 1993. In addition we are surprised that the prosecution did not charge or amend the indictment to include a count of the full offence of buggery,

as there was ample evidence to support such a charge by the end of the prosecution case.

IV. The mens rea issue

20   Any decision on this issue is now academic as the convictions for incitement
have to be quashed for the reasons we have sought to explain but we have decided
to give our views on the mens rea issue not merely because we have heard argument about it but also because, in his helpful and full comments in giving leave in
this case, Davis J. explained that the present appeal might be a suitable "opportunity of revisiting the potential application" of the much-criticised case of *R. v
Curr* ((1967) 51 Cr.App.R. 113; [1968] 2 Q.B. 944).

21   Mr Ross contends that the person incited (namely the complainant) must at
least know that the act being incited would be criminal even if he has no intention
of carrying out the act, with the result that the present convictions of inciting must
be quashed as the complainant did not have this knowledge.

22   Mr Jenkins submits that it is not the mens rea or knowledge of the *complainant*
which is relevant on a charge of incitement but what is crucial is the mens rea of
the *perpetrator* (namely in this case the appellant) who must have known that it
was wrong and against the law to incite the complainant who was a boy between
the ages of 8 years and 12 years to bugger him.

23   The riposte of Mr Ross is to rely on the decision of this court in *R. v Curr*
((1967) 51 Cr.App.R. 113; [1968] 2 Q.B. 944) in which the defendant, who traf-
ficked in Family Allowance books, adopted a practice of approaching a woman
with a large family and lending her money on the security of her book. Thus, after
signing some of the vouchers, the woman then would hand the vouchers over to
the defendant as security whereupon the defendant would then use his team of
female agents to cash the vouchers. The defendant then kept the proceeds as
repayment of the loans and interest before returning the cashbooks to each
owner. The defendant was convicted of soliciting the women to commit a summary offence under the provision of Family Allowance Act 1945 on the basis,
first, that he had solicited an unknown woman to obtain on his behalf from Her
Majesty's Postmaster General a sum of money on account of an allowance,
and second and significantly for this appeal, that, he knew that it was not properly
receivable by her. This Court held that the appellant could only be guilty of soliciting the woman agents if they knew that the action, which she was asked to
perform, amounted to an offence.

24   Giving the judgment of the court, Fenton Atkinson J. explained that:

> "In our view, the argument for the prosecution here gives no effect to the
> word 'knowing' in [the relevant statutory provision], and in our view
> could only be guilty. if the woman solicited that, that is, the woman agent
> sent to collect the allowance, knew that the action she was asked to carry
> out amounted to an offence."(pp.121 and 954G)

25   Mr Ross contends by parity of reasoning that in the present case the appellant
could only be guilty of inciting if the person incited, namely the boy victim, knew

that the act being incited of buggery constituted a criminal offence. Mr Jenkins submits that this statement in *Curr* should be approached in the way that it was regarded in *Director of Public Prosecution v Armstrong (Andrew)* (CO/2044/99). In that case Tuckey L.J. with whom Moses J. concurred, said of Fenton Atkinson J.'s statement in *Curr* that

> "it seems to me all the court is saying in that case is that what the appellant was doing was something short of asking the woman concerned to commit a criminal offence. He was not inciting her to commit an offence because the offence required her knowledge that she was committing an offence. There is nothing in the judgment to suggest that the court was making any general pronouncement about whether for the offence of incitement it is necessary to prove that not only the inciter but also the person incited had the mens rea to commit the full offence"

26   In *Armstrong's* case, the defendant had been charged with inciting X to distribute indecent photographs of children contrary to common law. A police informer had been contacted by A asking to be supplied with pornography, but the informer told A that he did not deal in such material but he gave him the mobile telephone number of X, which was a pseudonym for a police officer. Subsequently X, the police officer, received a telephone call on his mobile phone from somebody who asked for pornography. The magistrate found no case to answer on the soliciting charge because before a person can be convicted of inciting it is necessary for "the person to whom the incitement is made [to] have a parity of mens rea to the inciter".

27   The Divisional Court considered that approach to be wrong because in their view, it was not necessary for the prosecutor to show that X intended to supply child pornography to Armstrong because as Tuckey L.J. explained:

> "the offence of incitement was committed when [X] was asked to commit the offence of supplying child pornography with the intention on the part of the respondent that in doing so he would be committing a criminal offence"

28   We respectfully agree because the focus of the offence of inciting is solely on the acts and intentions of the inciter while the intention of the person incited are not relevant when considering whether the offence of incitement has been committed. As *Blackstone on Criminal Practice* (para.A6.7–2005 Edition) explains:

> "In so far as *Curr* [1968] 2 Q.B. 944. appears to require proof that persons incited actually possess such mens rea, it is manifestly erroneous; a person incited need not actually commit the offence at all, so it cannot be necessary to prove his mens rea."

29   Similar views have been expressed by the late Professor Sir John Smith and Professor Hogan, who criticised the decision in *Curr* on the basis that "the real question . . .should have been, whether the women actually had the knowledge, but whether D believed they had" (*Smith and Hogan* on *Criminal Law* 10th Ed. 2002, p.295). Furthermore, Professor Smith has said of a similar decision to *Curr* in *R. v Shaw* [1994] Crim L.R. 365 that "the court has confused the mens rea of

incitement with the mens rea of the offence incited" (ibid p.366). *Russell on Crime* (12th Edition Pt 1 p.200) accepted that the guilt of the inciter cannot depend on the state of mind of the incited because it is the state of mind and intention of the inciter, coupled with the act of incitement, which constitutes the offence.

30   We agree that the mens rea of the person incited is irrelevant and the critical factors are, as Tuckey L.J. explained in *Armstrong's* case, "accurately defined" in the Law Commission's Paper 177 that:

> "A person is guilty of incitement to commit an offence if—
>> (a) he incites another to do or causes to be done an act or acts which, if done, will involve the commission of the offence or offences by the other; and
>> (b) he intends or believes that the other, if he acts as incited, shall or will do so with the fault required for the offence or offences."

31   It follows from the decision in *Armstrong's* case that the offence of incitement in this case would have been committed when the appellant asked the complainant to commit the offence of buggery with the intention on the part of the appellant that in doing so, he would be committing a criminal offence. The knowledge or mens rea of the complainant as the incitee was irrelevant. There was clearly a case to answer on this point but as we have explained the conviction must be quashed and the appeal allowed for the reasons which we have explained in Section III above.

V The consequences issue

32   Mr Ross submits that if the judge had withdrawn the incitement counts from the jury, as he should have done, the appelant would then have applied to discharge the jury because of the prejudicial nature of the incitement counts. So he submits that we should now do likewise and quash all the convictions. We unhesitatingly reject this submission. The evidence on the incitement counts did not amount to the admission of irrelevant or inadmissible material. It was all part of the background of the relationship between the appellant and boy. The evidence showed that the appellant groomed the complainant before indecently assaulting him and before requiring the complainant to perform acts of oral sex on him on five to ten occasions over a period of eighteen months to two years at a time when the complainant was then less than eleven years of age. The appellant was convicted not only of the incitement counts but also of two counts of indecent assault and three counts of committing gross indecency with a child and none of these counts has been the subject of an appeal. So the additional evidence relating to the incitement to commit buggery was not so prejudicial in the light of the other evidence of sexual misconduct by the appellant as to have required the judge to discharge the jury

33   We agree with Mr Ross that the total sentence imposed on the appellant of four years' imprisonment has to be reconsidered, as his conviction on the two counts of incitement has to be quashed. The appellant had been sentenced to two concur-

rent sentences of four years' imprisonment for two counts of indecent assault and four concurrent sentences of 18 months' imprisonment for four counts of indecency with a child as well as two concurrent sentences of eight years' imprisonment for the two convictions of incitement to buggery, which we have quashed for the reasons set out earlier in this judgment.

34   Mr Ross reminded us that the appellant is now aged 61 and is a man of virtually good character having only one relevant matter recorded against him namely a dishonourable discharge from the Royal Navy following a conviction for an offence of gross indecency. He remains convicted of sexually abusing his stepson between the ages of 9 and 11, very many years ago. The two charges of indecent assault with a child related to occasions when the appellant made the boy suck his penis. At the time the offences were committed the maximum sentence permissible by law was only two years. The charges of indecent assault on a male related to acts of masturbation; the maximum sentence for which was 10 years' imprisonment.

35   Thus, it would not be appropriate to consider the level of sentence, which might be passed now for this kind of conduct given the increased powers available to the court. We make it plain that in today's climate we would consider the sentences of 18 months' imprisonment concurrent for three offences of making a nine-year-old boy give his stepfather oral sex unduly lenient. No doubt Judge Leigh Q.C. would too.

36   The judge was faced with offences committed long ago, as are we, and offences for which the maximum was set at a very low level. Bearing that in mind, we remind ourselves that this was a man who groomed the very young complainant, who was in the position of his stepson, to commit sexual acts with him repeatedly. The appellant may not have appreciated the extent of the psychological damage he might cause but he could have been in no doubt that what he was doing was very wrong. The complainant was forced to relive his ordeal in the witness box and gave evidence of the extent to which the abuse had distressed him and led to numerous difficulties in later life. The jury plainly accepted his evidence and rejected that of the appellant. The appellant has shown no signs of remorse.

37   In our judgment this sexual abuse of a very young child over a substantial period of time in breach of trust merited a substantial term of imprisonment even for offences committed so long ago by an appellant of this age and background Accordingly we are not persuaded that a total sentence of four years' imprisonment imposed by the judge was excessive given the appellant's offending overall on the counts that remained. Indeed, in our view, the appellant should consider himself fortunate.

VI Conclusion

38   The appeal has to be allowed and the convictions on counts 6 and 7 of incitement to commit buggery have to be quashed for the reasons we have sought to explain and on the basis of the decision in *Whitehouse's* case (supra) to which

the judge's attention was not drawn. The sentence of the appellant will now be one of four years' imprisonment in total.

Appeal allowed.
Convictions on counts 6 and 7 quashed.

R. v DOOLEY

Court of Appeal (Lord Justice Hooper, Mr Justice Openshaw and
Dame Heather Steel): November 1, 2005

[2005] EWCA Crim 3093; [2006] 1 Cr.App.R. 21

LT Distribution; Indecent photographs of children; Intention; Internet;
Statutory interpretation

H1   CHILD, INDECENT PHOTOGRAPH OF
       Data on computer
       Indecent images of children downloaded from internet file-sharing network—
       Held in folder accessible by other network members—Whether images possessed
       "with a view to" their being distributed or shown—Whether offence committed
       where sole intention was to transfer images to part of computer not accessible
       by others—Protection of Children Act 1978 (c.37), s.1(1)(c) (as amended by
       the Criminal Justice and Public Order Act 1994 (c.33), ss.84(2), 168(3) and
       Sch.11)

H2   The appellant was a member of an internet file-sharing network. He downloa-
       ded from this network onto his computer indecent images of children, a number
       of which, on his computer being seized, were to be found in his "My Shared
       Folder" from which they could be accessed by any other member of the network.
       He was charged with the possession of those images "with a view to their being
       distributed or shown by himself or others" contrary to s.1(1)(c) of the Protection
       of Children Act 1978. It was his case that his sole intention was to move the ima-
       ges from the folder to a part of his computer where it would not be available to be
       accessed by others. In a ruling given prior to a jury being sworn the trial judge
       held that knowledge that an image was likely to be seen by other network mem-
       bers with access to the folder was sufficient to constitute possession "with a view
       to" it being distributed or shown. Following the ruling the appellant changed his
       plea to guilty. He appealed against conviction on the ground that the judge was
       wrong so to rule.

H3   **Held,** allowing the appeal, that a defendant would only be guilty of the pos-
       session of indecent images "with a view to" their being distributed or shown
       if at least one of the reasons or objectives for their being in a folder shared by
       others was to enable the others to have access to them. Knowledge alone that
       the images might be seen by others did not suffice to constitute the offence.
       Accordingly, the judge's ruling was wrong (post, paras [17]–[18]).

       (For s.1 of the Protection of Children Act 1978 (as amended), see *Archbold*
       2006, paras 31-107 and 31-108a)

Appeal against conviction

H4   On March 17, 2005 in the Crown Court at Oxford (Judge McIntyre), the appellant, Michael Dooley, pleaded guilty on re-assignment, after ruling by the trial judge, to six counts of possessing indecent photographs or pseudo-photographs of a child with a view to their being distributed or shown by himself or others, contrary to s.1(1)(c) of the Protection of Children Act 1978 (as amended).

H5   The facts and grounds of appeal appear in the judgment of the court.

H5   *Paul Mitchell* (assigned by the Registrar of Criminal Appeals) for the appellant. *Rachel Drake* (instructed by the Crown Prosecution Service, Thames Valley Branch) for the Crown.

Hooper L.J.: delivered the judgment of the Court.

1   On March 17, 2005 in the Crown Court at Oxford, before Judge McIntyre, the appellant pleaded guilty on re-arraignment to six charges of an offence against s.1(1)(c) of the Protection of Children Act 1978. That makes it an offence to be in possession of indecent photographs or pseudo-photographs of a child with a view to their being distributed or shown by himself or others. By virtue of subs.(2):

> "... a person is to be regarded as distributing an indecent photograph or pseudo-photograph if he parts with possession of it to, or exposes or offers it for acquisition by, another person."

2   Prior to the trial, Judge McIntyre was asked to give a ruling as to the meaning of the words "with a view to" in this section. He gave that ruling. Following the ruling and in the light of it, the appellant pleaded guilty. He now submits that the judge erred in law in his interpretation of the words "with a view to".

3   The phrase "with a view to" can be found in hundreds of different statutory provisions. In so far as the criminal law is concerned, see, for example, s.92 of the Trade Marks Act 1994; s.1(2) of the Theft Act 1968; s.17 of that Act (false accounting); s.20, and s.21, which creates the offence of blackmail. In s.21(1), it is provided:

> "A person is guilty of blackmail if 'with a view to gain for himself or another or with intent to cause loss to another' he makes any unwarranted demand with menaces. . ."

4   The phrase "with a view to" even appears in the Human Rights Act 1998. Section 1(5) provides that a protocol means:

> "... a protocol to the Convention—
> (a) which the United Kingdom has ratified; or
> (b) which the United Kingdom has signed with a view to ratification."

5   The phrase also appears, for example, in the Obscene Publications Act 1964 and in the statutory provisions regarding Drug Treatment and Testing Orders.

6   We turn to the facts of this case. KaZaA is a peer to peer file sharing network that enables Internet users to share any type of computer file. Users become part of a network of other KaZaA members worldwide by downloading the necessary software from the internet. All members have a "My Shared Folder" which contains files which, when the computer is connected to the internet, can be accessed by any KaZaA member. At any one time, there may be in excess of four million KaZaA members connected to the system.

7   KaZaA effectively functions as an enormous "library" with its contents stored on the computers of all its active members at any one time. A member wishing to find a particular type of file will enter a term into a search engine, which is part of the software. KaZaA will then search the "My Shared Folders" of all members currently connected to the Internet and provide a list of matching files. The person searching can then select a file and download to his "My Shared Folder". Unless it is moved from his "My Shared Folder" it becomes part of the "stock" of the "library" and can in turn be accessed by the other members. There is a facility for making the "My Shared Folder" inaccessible to others, but the appellant appears to have been unaware of it.

8   On February 10, 2004, the police searched the appellant's home and seized computer equipment. KaZaA was installed on the computer. There were many thousands of indecent images of children on the appellant's computer, many of which had obtained via KaZaA. Of the thousands of images, only six were found in the appellant's "My Shared Folder".

9   The downloading of images from KaZaA will often take many days, the computer being left on for long periods of time. Rather than just download a few images, the appellant would download a very substantial number of images. The images, so we were told, could not effectively be accessed by others until such time as the "My Shared Folders" had the completed image. Thereafter, on the appellant's case, it was his "specific intention" to remove the photograph or image from the "My Shared Folder" to some other part of his computer, where it could not be seen by others. Because of the large number of images that were downloaded, it took him time to do that. In so far as the six images with which this case is concerned, we were told that they had actually been in the "My Shared Folder" for some 10 days before the police intervened. It thus follows that they were available to be accessed by the many members of this "club" during those ten days.

10   It is perhaps unfortunate, with hindsight, that the judge was not presented with a clear set of facts or assumed facts in order to resolve the legal issue. In his ruling, the judge said:

> "It seems to me that what the prosecution needs to prove is that a participant downloads a particular photograph or image in the knowledge that it is likely to be seen by other participants who have access to [the] same folder into which the image goes."

11   Mr Mitchell, of course, did not have the benefit of the transcript and tells us that, at the time, he did not understand the full impact of that sentence. We return to this passage later.

12 The judge then said:

> "If he downloads the photograph or image with that knowledge he is possessing it during the time it is in the My Shared Folder 'with a view to' its being distributed or shown by him to other members of the club. It may be that the defendant's specific intention is immediately to remove the photograph or image from the My Shared Folder to some other part of his computer where it cannot be seen by others, but whereas that may provide a defendant with a defence if the charge were possession with intent to distribute or show, it does not amount to a defence to possession with a view to its being distributed or shown in the circumstances. I think there is a difference between the meaning of the words 'with the intention of' and the words 'with a view to'. The fact that it may not have been a defendant's specific intention to distribute or show the photograph or image to others merely provides him with mitigation in respect of the charge he faces under s.1(1)(c). The words 'with a view to' have a wider meaning than 'with the intention of'.
>
> It follows that if a person charged with this offence did not know that as a result of using the particular software there was a likelihood of the image or photograph in the My Shared Folder' being accessed by others then he would have a good defence to a charge under s.1(1)(c). And going back to the analogy of the club: it seems to me that if you join a computer club knowing that its purpose is to make material downloaded by you accessible to all members so that there is a likelihood of that material being accessed by other members as a result of your downloading it, then in those circumstances you download it 'with a view to' its being distributed or shown by you to other members.
>
> I hope that ruling is clear. I think at the nub of it is the difference between 'with a view to' and 'with the intention of'."

13 The judge drew a distinction between the words "with a view to" and the words "with the intention of". In our view, he was right to do so.

14 Help for the meaning of the phrase (which has not, it appears, received much judicial attention) can be found in the 11th edition (2005) of *Smith and Hogan's "Criminal Law"*, now edited by Professor Ormerod, p.807. There the meaning of the phrase "with a view to gain" in s.21 of the Theft Act 1968 is briefly examined. It is stated that, whilst it is probably not necessary to show that the defendant's primary purpose in making a demand was to make a gain for himself or another, it must be one of his objectives. We agree that it need only be one of his objectives. In a case like the present, another way of approaching the issue is to ask whether one of the defendant's reasons for leaving the images in the "My Shared Folder" was to enable others to access it.

15 Mr Mitchell submitted that the judge should have adopted this approach and decided that the defendant would only be guilty if one of his reasons for leaving the images in the "My Shared Folder" was to enable others to access the images in the Folder.

16   Ms Drake for the respondent submitted, first of all, that, on the facts of this case, it was sufficient if the defendant had knowledge that the images may be seen by others. She then adopted the judge's approach: "Did the defendant know that the images were likely to be seen by others?" She then changed that to: "Did the defendant know that the images were very likely to be seen by others?" She ended up with: "Did the defendant know that it was inevitable that the images would be seen by others?" before returning to the judge's approach.

17   In our judgment, although it may be very important to examine the defendant's knowledge in the way in which the judge did, nonetheless the question which the jury will have to resolve is: "Was at least one of the reasons why the defendant left the images in the 'My Shared Folder' so that others could have access to the images in it?" If so he would be in possession of indecent photographs of a child with a view to their being distributed or shown by himself. One can envisage circumstances where a person foresees X as a likely consequence of doing Y, but does not do Y with a view to X. To take a far-fetched example, a general may foresee the likelihood of his soldiers being killed in battle, but he surely does not send his troops into battle with a view to their being killed? We should add that it is not necessary in this judgment to refer to the debate about intention and foresight of virtual certainty (*Smith and Hogan*, pp.93 and ff).

18   We have considered carefully whether the conviction is safe. In the light of the judge's ruling about the necessary knowledge, the appellant (we would have expected) must have pleaded guilty on the basis that he knew that the images in the "My Shared Folder" were likely to be seen by other participants. If so, on the facts of this case, it would seem to follow that at least one of the reasons why the defendant left the images in the "My Shared Folder" would be to enable others to have access to them. Mr Mitchell assures us that he understood the ruling to mean that it was not necessary for the prosecution to show that a reason for leaving the images in the folder was to enable others to access them. He tells us that his case was that the appellant did not leave the images there for that reason and he did not assimilate what the judge had said about knowledge. In the light of that assurance, we must quash the conviction. No retrial is sought.

Appeal allowed.
Convictions quashed.

R. v GOODWIN

Court of Appeal (Lord Chief Justice (Lord Phillips of Worth
Matravers), Mrs Justice Rafferty and Mr Justice Mackay):
November 10; December 7, 2005

[2005] EWCA Crim 3184; [2006] 1 Cr.App.R. 22

(LT) Inflicting serious injury; Masters; Navigation; Ships

H1   SHIPPING
       Injury to another
       *Liability for—Defendant's jet ski colliding with another causing serious
       injury—Whether jet ski "vessel"—Whether "used in navigation"—Whether
       defendant "master of ship"—Whether guilty of offence under shipping Act—
       Merchant Shipping Act 1995 (c.21), ss.58(2), 313(3)*

H2   The appellant was riding a jet ski within the port of Weymouth when he colli-
       ded with another jet ski which was stationary in the water. The rider of the other
       jet ski was seriously injured. The appellant was charged with an offence contrary
       to s.58(2)(a) of the Merchant Shipping Act 1995 [1] s.313: (post, para.[5]). By that
       paragraph if the master of a ship, while on board his ship, did an act which caused
       serious injury to another he was guilty of an offence. Section 313(1) of the 1995
       Act provided that "ship" included "every description of vessel used in naviga-
       tion". At trial the judge held that the appellant's jet ski was a "vessel used in
       navigation", whereupon the appellant pleaded guilty. He appealed against con-
       viction on the grounds that the judge's ruling was wrong.

H3   **Held,** allowing the appeal, that it could not be ruled out that a jet ski was
       capable of falling within the first part of the definition of a ship in s.313, namely
       "every description of vessel". For a vessel to be "used in navigation" it was not a
       necessary requirement that it should be used in transporting persons or property
       by water to an intended destination but in the light of the purpose of the Merchant
       Shipping Acts the phrase "vessel used in navigation" was confined to vessels
       which were used to make ordered progression over the water from one place to
       another. Therefore craft that were simply used for having fun on the water with-
       out the object of going anywhere were excluded from the definition of ship or
       vessel. Accordingly, s.58 of the 1995 Act did not apply in the instant case
       (post, paras [27], [33]–[34], [46]).
       Steedman v Scofield [1992] 2 Lloyd's Rep. 163 and *Clark v Perks (No.2)*
       [2001] EWCA Civ 1228; [2001] 2 Lloyds Rep. 431, CA considered.

---

[1]   Merchant Shipping Act 1995, s.58(post, para.[2]).

Per curiam
   (i) Section 58 of the Merchant Shipping Act 1995 only applies to a master
       who is employed as such (post, para.[40]).
   (ii) Failure to comply with the International Regulations for the Prevention
        of Collisions at Sea is made an offence by the Merchant Shipping (Dis-
        tress Signals and Prevention of Collisions) Regulations 1996 (SI 1996/
        75) and that offence carries the same maximum penalty as s.58. Where
        allegations are made of conduct which infringes the Collision Regu-
        lations it would be simpler and more appropriate to charge this
        offence rather than to allege breach of s.58 of the 1995 Act (post,
        para.[45]).

Appeal against conviction

H5   On July 5, 2005 in the Crown Court at Salisbury (Mr Recorder A. Davies Q.C.)
the appellant, Mark Goodwin, pleaded guilty, after a ruling by the trial judge that
a jet ski was a vessel used in navigation, to doing an act which caused or was
likely to cause a serious injury, contrary to s.58(2)(a) of the Merchant Shipping
Act 1995. He was sentenced to six months' imprisonment.

H6   At the hearing of the appeal on October 26 and November 10, 2005 the following additional cases were cited or referred to in the skeleton arguments: *Addison v
Denholm Ship Management (UK) Ltd* [1997] I.C.R. 770, EAT (Sc); *Andalusian,
The* (1877-78) L.R. 3 P.D. 182; *Bankers Insurance Co Ltd v South* [2003] EWHC
380(QB); [2004] Lloyd's I.R. 1; *Butler, The C S* (1874) L.R. 4 A. & E. 238; *Cham-
pion, The* [1934] P. 1, DC; *Chandler v Blogg* [1898] 1 Q.B. 32; *Cook v Dredging
and Construction Co Ltd* [1958] 1 Lloyd's Rep. 334; *Corbett v Pearce* [1904] 2
K.B. 422, DC; *Craighall, The* [1910] P. 207, CA; *Dependable Marine Co Ltd v
Commissioners of Customs & Excise* [1965] 1 Lloyd's Rep. 550; *European &
Australian Royal Mail Co v Peninsular & Oriental Steam Navigation Co*
(1866) 12 Jur. (NS) 909; *Ferguson, Ex p.* (1870-71) L.R. 6 Q.B. 280, DC; *Handy-
side v United Kingdom* (1979-80) 1 E.H.R.R. 737; *Harlow, The* [1922] P. 175;
Hedges & Son v The London & St Katherine Docks Co (1885) 16 Q.B.D. 597,
DC; *Hodge v Higgins* [1980] 2 Lloyd's Rep. 589, DC; *Jenkins v Godwin*
[1983] 1 Lloyd's Rep. 382, DC; *Lighter (No.3), The* (1902) 18 T.L.R. 322;
Mac, The (1882) 7 P.D. 126, CA; *Marine Craft Constructors Ltd v Erland Blom-
quist (Engineers) Ltd* [1953] 1 Lloyd's Rep. 514; *Merchants Marine Insurance
Co Ltd v North of England Protection & Indemnity Association* (1926) Lloyd's
Rep. 201, CA; *Mudlark, The* [1911] P. 116; *Oakes v Monkland Iron Co* (1884)
21 Sc.L.R. 407; *Polpen Shipping Co v Commercial Union Assurance Co Ltd*
[1943] K.B. 161; *R. v Carrick District Council, Ex p. Prankerd* [1999] Q.B.
1119; *R. v King* [2001] EWCA Crim 709; [2001] 2 Cr.App.R.(S.) 114, CA; *R.
v Morling* [1998] 1 Cr.App.R.(S.) 421, CA; *R. v Simmonds* [1999] 2 Cr.App.R.
18, CA; *R. v Taylor* (1840) 9 C. & P. 672; *Raft of Timber, The* (1844) 2 Wm.
Rob. 251; *SW v United Kingdom* (1995) 21 E.H.R.R. 363; *St John Pilot Commissioners v Cumberland Railway and Coal Co* [1910] A.C. 208, PC; *St*

Machar, The (1939) 65 Lloyd's Rep. 119; *Salt Union Ltd v Wood* [1893] 1 Q.B. 370, DC; *Upcerne, The* [1912] P. 160, DC.

H7   The facts and grounds of appeal appear in the judgment of the court.

H8   *Lionel Persey Q.C.* and *Charlotte Lees* (instructed by Mustoe Shorter, Dorset) for the appellant.
      Nigel Teare Q.C. and *Robert Grey* (instructed by the Crown Prosecution Service, Weymouth, Dorset) for the Crown.

Cur. adv. vult.

December 7   Lord Phillips of Worth Matravers, C.J.: handed down the judgment of the court.

1   On July 5, 2005 in the Crown Court at Salisbury the appellant pleaded guilty to a single count of doing an act which caused or was likely to cause serious injury, contrary to s.58(2)(a) of the Merchant Shipping Act 1995. On August 5, 2005, at the same court, he was sentenced to six months' imprisonment. He now appeals against conviction and sentence by leave of the single judge who, on September 22, 2005, granted the appellant unconditional bail pending appeal.

Section 58 of the Merchant Shipping Act 1995 ("Section 58")

2   The following provisions of s.58 are material:

"58 (1) This section applies—
      (a) to the master of, or any seaman employed in, a United Kingdom ship; and
      (b) to the master of, or any seaman employed in, a ship which—
         (i) is registered under the law of any country outside the United Kingdom; and
         (ii) is in a port in the United Kingdom or within United Kingdom waters while proceeding to or from any such port.
      (2) If a person to whom this section applies, while on board his ship or in its immediate vicinity—
      (a) does any act which causes or is likely to cause—
         (i) the loss or destruction of or serious damage to his ship or its machinery, navigational equipment or safety equipment, or
         (ii) the loss or destruction of or serious damage to any other ship or any structure, or
         (iii) the death of or serous injury to any person, or
      (b) omits to do anything required—
         (i) to preserve his ship or its machinery, navigational equipment or safety equipment from being lost, destroyed or seriously damaged, or
         (ii) to preserve any person on board his ship from death or serious injury, or

   (iii) to prevent his ship from causing the loss or destruction of or
          serious damage to any other ship or any structure, or the
          death of or serious injury to any person not on board his
          ship,
          and either of the conditions specified in subsection (3) below
          is satisfied with respect to that act or omission, he shall (sub-
          ject to subsections (6) and (7) below) be guilty of an offence.
   (3) Those conditions are—
       (a) that the act or omission was deliberate or amounted to a breach
           or neglect of duty;
       (b) that the master or seaman in question was under the influence
           of drink or a drug at the time of the act or omission.
   (4) If a person to whom this section applies—
       (a) discharges any of his duties, or performs any other function in
           relation to the operation of his ship or its machinery or equip-
           ment, in such a manner as to cause, or to be likely to cause,
           any such loss, destruction, death or injury as is mentioned in
           subsection (2)(a) above, or
       (b) fails to discharge any of his duties, or to perform any such func-
           tion, properly to such an extent as to cause, or to be likely to
           cause, any of those things,he shall (subject to subsections (6)
           and (7) below) be guilty of an offence.
   (5) A person guilty of an offence under this section shall be liable—
       (a) on summary conviction, to a fine not exceeding the statutory
           maximum;
       (b) on conviction on indictment, to imprisonment for a term not
           exceeding two years or a fine, or both.
       . . .
   (8) In this section—'breach or neglect of duty', except in relation to a
       master, includes any disobedience to a lawful command;
       'duty'—
       (a) in relation to a master or seaman, means any duty falling to be
           discharged by him in his capacity as such; and
       (b) in relation to a master, includes his duty with respect to the good
           management of his ship and his duty with respect to the safety
           of operation of his ship, its machinery and equipment; and
           'structure' means any fixed or movable structure (of whatever
           description) other than a ship."

The facts

3   The circumstances giving rise to the charge under s.58 were as follows. On
May 15, 2004 the appellant was riding a Yamaha Waverunner jet ski ("the
Waverunner") at Bowleaze Cove, Weymouth when he collided with another
jet ski which was stationary in the water. The rider of the other jet ski, Mr Paul
Facer, was injured and thrown into the water. The appellant jumped in and sup-

ported Mr Facer until help came. It proved that Mr Facer had sustained very serious facial injuries. He had to be placed on a life support system and required reconstructive surgery to his cheekbone, eye socket and jaw.

4   The appellant was originally indicted under s.35 of the Offences Against the Person Act 1861. A few days before the trial on that indictment the Crown, without opposition, obtained permission to prefer a fresh indictment under s.58.

5   The appellant applied to Mr Recorder A Davies Q.C. to have the indictment quashed. He argued that the Waverunner was not a "ship" within s.58(1). Section 313(1) of the 1995 Act, the definition section, provides that:

> "(1) 'Ship' includes every description of vessel used in navigation."

The appellant contended that the Waverunner was not a "vessel used in navigation". He relied upon the decision of Sheen J. in *Steedman v Scofield* [1992] 2 Lloyds Rep. 163, which had held that a jet ski was not a "ship" within the essentially identical definition of the Merchant Shipping Act of 1894. The Recorder dismissed the application, holding that the features of the Waverunner differed from the features of the jet ski in *Steedman v Scofield* to an extent that brought the former within the definition of a "ship".

6   Having failed in this application, the appellant pleaded guilty to the charge. He did so on the basis that he was the master of the Waverunner under the definition of "master" in s.313, namely:

> "'master' includes every person (except a pilot) having command or charge of a ship . . ."

and that he had been in breach of duty in failing to keep a good look-out.

7   When the appeal initially came before this court, counsel for the Appellant proposed to take the point relied upon below, namely that the Waverunner did not fall within the definition of a "ship" in the 1995 Act. Counsel for the Crown made it plain that this was being treated as a test case. This caused us some concern for a number of reasons. First, no attention appeared to have been given to the requirement in subs.(1) of s.58 that the ship should be either a United Kingdom ship or a ship registered under the law of a country outside the United Kingdom. Secondly, we were aware of a number of authorities in relation to the meaning of "ship" or "vessel" to which counsel had not referred in their skeleton arguments. Thirdly, we were not satisfied that s.58 had any application to negligent navigation. In these circumstances we adjourned the case so that these points could be considered. When the case came back before us Admiralty leaders had been instructed: in the person of Mr Nigel Teare Q.C. for the Crown and Mr Lionel Persey Q.C. for the appellant. The latter had produced a 38-page skeleton argument and we were referred to some 40 authorities. We are grateful to counsel for the assistance which they have provided in this case, which is one of some general importance.

Registration

8   It is now common ground that the Waverunner was, at the material time, registered neither in the United Kingdom nor in any country outside the United
Kingdom. However, Mr Teare wove his way through a tortuous statutory path
and persuaded both Mr Persey and us that, by reason of s.17(2)(a) and (b) of
the Interpretation Act 1978, Reg.4 of the Merchant Shipping Act 1970 (Unregistered Ships) Regulations 1991 (SI 1991/1366) remains in force and takes effect so
far as relevant, as follows:

> (1) It is hereby directed that s.58 of the Merchant Shipping Act 1995 shall
>   extend to ships (other than fishing vessels) of the following description,
>   that is to say sea-going ships—
>   (i) which are wholly owned by a person resident in . . . the United
>   Kingdom; and
>   (ii) which are entitled to be registered in the United Kingdom under the
>   Merchant Shipping Act 1995 but are not registered whether in the
>   United Kingdom or elsewhere;
> and to masters and seamen employed in them.
> (2) It is hereby directed that the said s.58 shall apply to sea-going ships
>   (other than fishing vessels) which are not registered, whether in the
>   United Kingdom or elsewhere, other than ships falling within para.[1]
>   above, and to masters and seamen employed in them, when such
>   ships are within the seaward limits of the territorial sea of the United
>   Kingdom while proceeding to or from a port in the United Kingdom.

9   The Waverunner was jointly owned by the appellant and a friend of his, also
resident in the United Kingdom. Thus, if the Waverunner was a "sea-going
ship" and the appellant was the "master employed in" her, s.58 applied to him.

The issues

10   The following issues were canvassed before us:

(1) Was the Waverunner a "ship"? If so
(2) Was the Waverunner a "*sea-going* ship"?
(3) Was the appellant the "master . . . employed in" the Waverunner?
(4) Did s.58 apply to negligent navigation?

Was the Waverunner a "ship"?

11   Part 1 of the 1995 Act deals with the registration of British ships. Section 10
requires the Secretary of State to make regulations providing for the registration
of such ships. He has done so. Under these regulations a register of British ships is
maintained. A witness statement from the Operations Manager responsible for
this register informs us that 646 "wet bikes" are registered. (For copyright
reasons jet skis are described as wet bikes on the register). Provided that a British
owner can submit all the appropriate documentation, which includes a survey

certificate for tonnage measurement and a completed "carving and marking note", a wet bike will be registered.

12   Guidance published by the Registry of Shipping and Seamen under the heading "Registering Pleasure Vessels (Part 1)" explains:

> "The main reason for registering a ship has always been to prove its nationality. For merchant/pleasure ships, Part 1 identification is essential for overseas voyages. Another reason for Part 1 registration is to use the ship as security to obtain a marine mortgage which in turn is registered. Ownership details are fully investigated. Purchasers of UK registered ships can obtain a Transcript of Registry which shows the registered owners of the ship and whether there are any outstanding mortgages lodged against that vessel."

We suspect that the reason why so many jet skis have been registered may be because those providing finance for their purchase have required this. We can see the attraction of giving a broad definition to "ship" for the purposes of registration of title. Nonetheless, the fact that such craft are registered does not demonstrate conclusively that they fall within the definition of "ships" under the 1995 Act—see *European and Australian Royal Mail Co Ltd v P & O Steam Navigation Co* (1864) 14 L.T. 704.

13   The Recorder described the characteristics of the Waverunner as follows:

> ". . . it has a length of 3.2m and a beam of 1.2m. It has a boat like deep 'V' planing type hull, and mention is made of a keel. It has seats, not one but three, and inferentially can accommodate a rider (and I use the term loosely) and two passengers. A person can sit in it when it is stopped in the water, as one can in a boat."

We have seen a photograph of the Waverunner. It has handlebars and seats which resemble those of a motor cycle. Thus the seats are in a row one behind the other and one sits astride them. We think that the Recorder's use of the word "rider" was appropriate. We would describe the rider and any passenger as sitting on, rather than in, the Waverunner. The Waverunner has no mast or structure to which a flag could be attached, nor does it appear to have any storage space.

14   Mr Teare accepted that one would not describe the Waverunner as a "ship", giving that word its normal English meaning. He submitted, however, that the normal meaning was extended by the definition in s.313 of the 1995 Act as including "every description of vessel used in navigation". Mr Persey argued that there were two reasons why the Waverunner did not fall within the definition of a "ship". The first was that by reason of the nature of its construction, the Waverunner could not be described as a vessel: the second was that the Waverunner was not "used in navigation".

The construction of the vessel

15   Mr Persey, understandably, put at the forefront of his case the decision of Sheen J., sitting in the Admiralty Court, in *Steedman v Scofield* [1992] 2 Lloyd's Rep.

163. That case involved a collision between a jet ski and a speedboat. The owner of the latter brought a claim in negligence and the defendants sought to have it struck out as time barred under s.8 of the Maritime Conventions Act 1911. The time limit under that section related to any claim against a "vessel". Section 10 of the 1911 Act provided that it was to be construed as one with the Merchant Shipping Acts. Section 742 of the Merchant Shipping Act 1894 provided:

> "'vessel' includes any ship or boat, or any description of vessel used in navigation:
> 'ship' includes every description of vessel used in navigation not propelled by oars . . ."

Sheen J. held that the jet ski did not fall within this definition.

16   Part of the reason for Sheen J.'s conclusion was the nature of the construction of the jet ski. It was very different from that with which we are concerned. When floating in the water it could not be boarded. The rider lay on his stomach on the craft, holding on to the handlebars and squeezed the throttle. Only when the craft attained a sufficient speed to attain stability could the rider pull himself aboard and kneel on the rear deck pad. From that position he could then stand up, operating the jet ski from a standing position. Sheen J. contrasted the jet ski with a boat, which conveyed the concept of a structure with a concave shape providing buoyancy for the carriage of persons or goods. He went on to observe that, in common parlance, a "vessel" was a word used to refer to craft larger than rowing boats, which included every description of watercraft used or capable of being used as a means of transportation on water.

17   The Recorder, understandably, contrasted Sheen J.'s jet ski with the Waverunner which is the subject of this appeal. The latter has a concave hull that gives the craft sufficient buoyancy to enable three riders to sit astride the saddle. The craft bears a much closer resemblance to a boat than that which Sheen J. had to consider. We do not consider that it is possible to conclude, on the basis of its construction alone, that it is incapable of falling within the first part of the definition of a ship in s.313 of the 1995 Act, namely "every description of vessel". Of much more importance is the qualification that the definition adds to that phrase, namely "used in navigation".

"Used in navigation"

18   Before turning to the authorities where this phrase has been considered, it is worth considering the context in which the definition is set. The early Merchant Shipping Acts were concerned with commercial shipping, and this concern remains the predominant theme of the 1995 Act. The primary concern of this legislation is shipping carried on as a business. This is certainly true of Pt III of the Act, in which s.58 appears. Part III deals with "Masters and Seamen". Section 24, with which this Part begins, provides that, subject to certain exceptions, the Part applies "only to sea-going ships and masters and seamen employed in sea-going ships". The excepted sections are not restricted to sea-going ships,

but they are nonetheless directed to ships upon which seamen are serving under contracts of employment.

19   In *Steedman v Scofield* Sheen J. reached the following conclusions in relation to the phrase "used in navigation":

> "Navigation is the nautical art or science of conducting a ship from one place to another. The navigator must be able (1) to determine the ship's position and (2) to determine the future course or courses to be steered to reach the intended destination. The word 'navigation' is also used to describe the action of navigating or ordered movement of ships on water. Hence 'navigable waters' means waters on which ships can be navigated. To my mind the phrase 'used in navigation' conveys the concept of transporting persons or property by water to an intended destination. A fishing vessel may go to sea and return to the harbour from which she sailed, but that vessel will nevertheless be navigated to her fishing grounds and back again.
> 'Navigation' is not synonymous with movement on water. Navigation is planned or ordered movement from one place to another. A jet ski is capable of movement on water at very high speed under its own power, but its purpose is not to go from one place to another. A person purchases a jet ski for the purpose of enjoying 'the thrills of waterskiing without the ties of a boat and towrope' and for the exhilaration of high speed movement over the surface of water. The heading of the craft at any particular moment is usually of no materiality. (I use the word 'heading' because it is more appropriate than the word 'course'. The word 'course' denotes a constant direction on the same heading.) Indeed part of the thrill of driving a jet ski appears to come from frequent alterations of heading at high speed.
> It may be possible to navigate a jet ski but in my judgment it is not 'a vessel used in navigation'."

20   This passage, if correct, is fatal to the prosecution's case. Mr Teare submitted, however, that Sheen J. was in error in *Steedman v Scofield* in stating that "used in navigation" conveyed the "concept of transporting persons or property by water to an intended destination" and in saying that "navigation" was "planned or ordered movement from one place to another". His submission was to the effect that navigation involved no more than controlled travel over water. In so submitting he relied particularly on two authorities.

21   *The "Von Rocks"* [1998] 2 Lloyd's Rep. 198 was a decision of the Irish Supreme Court. At issue in that case was whether a backhoe dredger was a ship or vessel subject to arrest pursuant to the Irish Jurisdiction of Courts (Maritime Convention) Act 1989. That Act provided that "ship" included "every description of vessel" and that "vessel" included "any ship or boat or any other description of vessel used in navigation". The headnote to the report accurately described the dredger as follows:

> "*Von Rocks* was a type of maritime dredger called a backhoe dredger which was primarily used in harbours, channels or estuaries to deepen the waters at such location. When not in operation it was a floating platform comprising

10 individual pontoons bolted together. When in use it was held in position on the sea-bed by three spud legs which were capable of being hydraulically lowered and raised. A backhoe dredger had no bow, no stern, no anchors, no rudder or any means of steering and no keel or skeg. It had no means of self-propulsion mechanical or otherwise and it had no wheelhouse.

On completion of a contract a backhoe dredger could be moored to the site of its next engagement either by being dismantled and transported by road or by being towed by sea. Extensive preparations were required to make the dredger seaworthy for towing for any significant distance. When under tow the dredger was unmanned and played no part in the performance of the operation."

At first instance, Barr J. held that the dredger was not a "ship or vessel" within the Act. In so doing he stated that he accepted the conclusion of Sheen J. in *Steedman v Scofield* that transporting persons or property by water to an intended destination was a concept inherent in navigation.

22   The Supreme Court reversed Barr and Keane JJ., giving the judgment of the court, held at p.207:

"... the fact that the carriage of cargo or passengers is not the exclusive or even the primary object for which the craft is being used is not a decisive consideration. The preponderance of judicial opinion would support the view that, provided the craft was built to do something on water and, for the purpose of carrying out that work, was so designed and constructed as to be capable of traversing significant water surfaces and did in fact regularly so traverse them, it is capable of being classified as a 'ship' despite the absence of any form of self-propulsion or steering mechanism, such as a rudder."

23   Keane J. considered *Steedman v Schofield* [1992] 2 Lloyd's Rep. 163 and observed:

"The finding in that case that a jet ski was not a 'ship' within the meaning of the Merchant Shipping Acts is hardly surprising, but it is questionable, with respect, whether, to come within the category of a 'ship' the purpose of a craft must be 'to go from one place to another'. In the case of non-commercial craft, it seems somewhat unreal to regard their purpose as being a journey from one point to a specific destination. Yachts which take part in the America's Cup are designed and constructed with a view to testing the excellence of their technology and the seamanship of their crews rather than transporting people from one place to another. On a less exalted level, people will for long continue to derive enjoyment from being on the sea, not because they are accomplishing a journey to an intended destination but simply for the pleasure of—in the well worn phrase from The Wind in the Willows—'messing about in boats'."

24   This statement was *obiter*, as Keane J.'s final summary of the court's reasons for finding that the dredger was a ship demonstrated:

"*Von Rocks* undoubtedly lacks some of the characteristics one would normally associate with a 'ship'. It is not self-propelled, it normally is not
manned by a crew and it has no form of rudder or other steering mechanism.
But it is a structure designed and constructed for the purpose of carrying out
specific activities on the water, is capable of movement across the water and
in fact spends significant periods of time moving across the seas from one
contracting site to another. It was indeed in the course of just such a voyage
that it met with the mishap which has given rise to the present proceedings. If
it is to do its normal work, it must be in a seaworthy condition and, it would
seem, the regulatory authorities here and elsewhere treat it as subject to
compliance with the normal requirements as to seagoing vessels."

25   The other decision relied upon by Mr Teare was a decision of the Court of
Appeal in *Clark v Perks (No.2)* [2001] 2 Lloyd's Rep. 431. The issue in that
case was whether jack-up drilling rigs, which were towed from one location to
another to drill for oil, were "ships" for the purposes of the Income and Corporation Taxes Act 1988, which made more generous provisions in relation to
seafarers serving on ships. Reversing the decision of the judge below, and restor-
ing that of the Commissioners, the Court held that such rigs were ships.

26   In the leading judgment, Carnwath J. considered a number of authorities,
including the *Von Rocks* and concluded that:

">. . . so long as 'navigation' is a significant part of the function of the structure in question, the mere fact that it is incidental to some more specialized
function, such as dredging or the provision of accommodation, does not take
it outside the definition. There may be an issue of degree as to the significance of the navigation on the facts of a particular case, but that, as the
observations of Lord Justice Scrutton show, is a question for the fact-finding
tribunal. Those examples also show that 'navigation' does not necessarily
connote anything more than 'movement across water'; the function of con-
veying persons and cargo from place to place (in the judge's words) is not an
essential characteristic."

27   After considering these and other authorities, we have come to the conclusion
that for a vessel to be "used in navigation" under the Merchant Shipping Acts it is
not a necessary requirement that it should be used in transporting persons or property by water to an intended destination, although this may well have been what
navigation usually involved when the early Merchant Shipping Acts were enacted. What is critical in the present case is, however, whether, for the purposes of
the Merchant Shipping Act 1995 definition of ship, navigation is "the planned or
ordered movement from one place to another" or whether it can extend to "messing about in boats" involving no journey at all. As to this question there are a
number of relevant authorities to which we have not yet referred.

28   In *The Mayor of Southport v Morriss* [1893] 1 Q.B. 359 the issue was whether a
launch used for the purpose of carrying passengers on pleasure trips round an arti-
ficial lake half a mile long by 180yds wide was a ship for the purposes of the
Merchant Shipping Act 1854, which defined ship as including "every description

of vessel used in navigation not propelled by oars". In considering a case stated by the magistrates, Lord Coleridge C.J. held that the launch was not a ship. He held at p.361:

> "We are therefore reduced to the question whether this launch was a vessel used in navigation. I think that, having regard to the size of the sheet of water on which it was used, it was not. Navigation is a term which, in common parlance, would never be used in connection with a sheet of water half a mile long. The Attorney-General has asked where we are to draw the line. The answer is that it is not necessary to draw it at any precise point. It is enough for us to say that the present case is on the right side of any reasonable line that could be drawn."

29   Dicta of the House of Lords in *Wells v Owners of the Gas Float Whitton No.2* [1897] A.C. 397 lend further support to the thesis that navigation for the purposes of the Merchant Shipping Acts involves the ordered progression by water from one place to another, usually with cargo or passengers. In that case the relevant issue was whether a gas float, shaped like a boat but moored in tidal waters as an aid to navigation was a ship or vessel that could be the subject of salvage. Holding that it was not Lord Herschell observed at p.343:

> "It was not constructed for the purpose of being navigated or of conveying cargo or passengers."

At p.345, commenting on cases where salvage had been awarded in respect of rafts of timber, he said:

> "But here again it must be remembered that rafts are frequently so constructed as to be in a sense navigated: they are capable of being and are steered. They often have crews resident on board; they are used for the transport, from place to place, by water, of the timber of which they consist and sometimes of timber placed upon them."

30   Lord Watson at p.347 approved the statement that:

> "there are no proper subjects of a maritime claim for salvage other than vessels or ships used for the purpose of being navigated and goods which at one time formed the cargoes of such vessels."

31   Finally we refer to the case of *Curtis v Wild* [1991] 4 All E.R. 172. This was an action by one dinghy sailor against another for personal injuries as a result of being run down after capsizing. The issue was whether the claim was subject to the two-year limitation period imposed in relation to claims against vessels or their owners by s.8 of the Maritime Conventions Act 1911, which fell to be construed as one with the Merchant Shipping Acts. After consideration of *Southport Corporation v Morriss* and a case which distinguished it, *Weeks v Ross* [1913] 2 K.B. 229, Henry J. concluded that navigation involved proceeding from an originating place A to a terminus B and not just the "use of vessels for pleasure purposes by people who were messing about in boats".

32   In considering the effect of these authorities one must not lose sight of the context in which the issue of the meaning of a "ship" arises. This is not easy, as the 1995 Act consolidates a number of statutes dealing with shipping, not least of which is the Merchant Shipping Act 1894, itself a consolidating Act. Whilst, as we have observed, there may be reasons for giving "ship" a wide meaning for the purposes of Pt I which deals with registration, one must not adopt a meaning that makes a nonsense of other provisions which govern the use and operation of ships. Those provisions, as the title "Merchant Shipping" suggests, are primarily aimed at shipping as a trade or business. While it may be possible to extend the meaning of ship to vessels which are not employed in trade or business or which are smaller than those which would normally be so employed, if this is taken too far the reduction can become absurd.

33   The meaning that Mr Teare would give to "used in navigation" adds nothing to the ordinary meaning of vessel. We have concluded that those authorities which confine "vessel used in navigation" to vessels which are used to make ordered progression over the water from one place to another are correctly decided. The words "used in navigation" exclude from the definition of "ship or vessel" craft that are simply used for having fun on the water without the object of going anywhere, into which category jet skis plainly fall. Mr Teare pointed out, by reference to a chart of Weymouth Harbour, that jet skis were required to follow a channel from the shore before reaching more open waters in which they could be driven. He argued that this demonstrated that jet skis are used in navigation. We do not agree. Following the channel was merely the means of getting to the area where the jet skis could be used for racing around in the manner which led to the accident with which this case is concerned.

34   For this reason alone, we have concluded that the Recorder was wrong to hold that s.58 applied to the facts of this case.

"Sea-going"

35   We had little argument as to what was meant by a "*sea-going* ship", perhaps because counsel only realised late in the day that s.58 only applied to the Waverunner if it was a seagoing ship. Mr Teare submitted that the craft was a sea-going ship because it was being used on the sea as opposed to on inland waters. Mr Persey submitted that the craft was not sea-going because it was being used, as the evidence showed, within the limits of the port of Weymouth.

36   Part III of the 1995 Act is headed "Masters and Seamen". Section 24 provides that, with the exception of certain specified sections, Pt III applies only to "ships which are sea-going ships and masters and seamen employed in sea-going ships". Section 58 is one of the excepted sections but, as we have explained in paras [8] and [9] above, only applies to unregistered ships if they are seagoing ships.

37   There is no statutory definition of "sea-going" but a clue to its meaning is given by another excepted section, s.49. This provides:

> "(1) Subject to s.48, if a ship to which this section applies goes to sea or attempts to go to sea without carrying such officers and other seamen

as it is required to carry under s.47, the owner or master shall be liable—

   (a) on summary conviction, to a fine not exceeding the statutory maximum;

   (b) on conviction on indictment, to a fine; and if the ship, if in the United Kingdom, may be detained.

 (2) This section shall, in its application to ships which are not sea-going ships, have effect as if for the words 'goes to sea or attempts to go to sea' there were substituted the words 'goes on a voyage or excursion or attempts to do so' and the words 'if in the United Kingdom' were omitted."

The inference is that a sea-going ship is a ship which "goes to sea" and that a ship which remains within the United Kingdom is not a sea-going ship. What is not clear is whether a ship which remains within coastal waters is or is not a sea-going vessel. We need not resolve this question. Section 49 buttresses our conclusion that a vessel used in navigation is a vessel which is used to make ordered progression from one place to another, though we accept that an excursion arguably extends this concept to embrace a round trip.

38   A sea-going vessel is a vessel which sets out to sea on a voyage. Thus s.42, which applies only to sea-going ships, implies a term into the contract of employment of seamen that the owner and the master will use all reasonable means to ensure the seaworthiness of the ship *"for the voyage."*

39   The suggestion that the Waverunner was a sea-going ship is worthy of A.P.Herbert. By no stretch of the imagination could that craft be so described. While jet-skis are used on the sea in proximity to land, they do not go to sea on voyages nor, we suspect would they be seaworthy in heavy weather. This is a further reason for allowing this appeal.

"Master or seamen employed in the ship"

40   While s.58 states that it applies to "the master of, or any seaman employed in", a United Kingdom ship, Reg.4 of SI 1991/1366 provides that s.58 applies to a "master and crew employed in" an unregistered ship. Mr Persey submitted that the section only applies to a master who is *employed* as such. Not without some hesitation we have concluded that he is correct. Part III deals largely with the terms under which masters and crew serve. Some sections in Pt III expressly apply to a master employed as such. We have concluded that the same must be true of s.58. Were this not so, the owner/master of a yacht registered in the United Kingdom who causes serious damage to its engines or navigational equipment when under the influence of drink will be guilty of a criminal offence punishable, on indictment, with up to two years' imprisonment. We find it hard to believe that Parliament intended to make it a criminal offence to damage ones own property.

41   As the appellant was not employed as master of the Waverunner s.58 did not apply to him. This is a further reason for allowing this appeal.

Does s.58 apply to negligent navigation?

42   Some of the provisions that now form s.58 have a long history. Section 220 of
the Merchant Shipping Act 1894 provided:

> "If a master, seaman, or apprentice belonging to a British ship, by wilful
> breach of duty or by neglect of duty or by reason of drunkenness—
>> (a) does any act tending to the immediate loss, destruction, or serious
>> damage of the ship, or tending immediately to endanger the life or
>> limb of a person belonging to or on board the ship; or
>> (b) refuses or omits to do any lawful act proper and requisite to be done
>> by him for preserving the ship from immediate loss, destruction, or
>> serious damage, or for preserving any person belonging to or on
>> board the ship from immediate danger to life or limb,
> he shall in respect of each offence be guilty of a misdemeanour."

43   In *Deacon v Evans* [1911] 1 K.B. 571 the master of a three-masted barque was
prosecuted under this section for failing to keep a proper look-out when on watch.
His failure resulted in a collision with a steam trawler that sank in consequence
with the loss of 10 hands. The master was convicted before the magistrates, but
successfully appealed by way of case stated. Lord Alverstoke C.J. gave the following short judgment:

> "This section, which has been copied in practically identical terms from
> earlier Acts, is more than 50 years old, and it is no exaggeration to say
> that there have been hundreds and thousands of cases in which, if the con-
> duct of the respondent here is to be regarded as a criminal offence,
> prosecutions might have been maintained. Therefore when we find it
> suggested that the negligent conduct of a man who is purporting to discharge
> his duty of assisting in the navigation of a ship amounts to a criminal
> offence, it is of great importance to determine whether that suggestion is
> well founded. The negligence complained of here was either that the master
> did not keep a proper look-out himself so as to have seen any vessel four or
> five miles away for at least half and hour, or that he did not put a look-out
> man on the forecastle, from which position the man stationed there could
> have seen any vessel right up to the time of the collision; and the question
> is whether such negligence is the kind of neglect of duty which is struck
> at by s.220. In my opinion it is not; that section was not intended to make
> criminally liable a person who has been negligent in the discharge of his
> duty, which he is carrying out or purporting to carry out, in the navigation
> of a ship. If it was intended to make simple negligence a criminal offence
> other language would have been used. The appeal must be dismissed."

44   The provisions of s.220 of the 1894 Act survive as s.58(2) of the 1995 Act,
albeit that the provisions have been extended to cover acts or omissions causing
damage to other vessels and structures, or causing death or serious injury to persons not on board the ship on which the breach of duty occurs. Section 58(4)
extends the description of the conduct which attracts criminal liability.

45   It is clearly arguable that this extension of the ambit of the relevant section embraces breach of duty in relation to the navigation of a vessel, and Mr Teare so submitted. This is not, however, an issue that we have to resolve having regard to our finding that s.58 had no application on the facts of this case. We would simply observe that failure to comply with the International Regulations for the Prevention of Collisions at Sea (1972) is made an offence by the Merchant Shipping (Distress Signals and Prevention of Collisions) Regulations 1996 (SI 1996/75) and that the offence carries the same maximum penalty as s.58. Where allegations are made of conduct which infringes the Collision Regulations it would seem simpler and more appropriate to charge this offence rather than to allege breach of s.58.

Conclusion

46   The prosecution of the appellant under s.58 was, for the reasons that we have given, misconceived. On the advice of his counsel he took one valid objection to the charge. As we have shown, that was not the only ground of objection. This appeal is allowed.

Appeal allowed.
Conviction quashed.

R. v KHELA
R. v SMITH (TINA)

COURT OF APPEAL (Lord Justice Moses, Mr Justice Burton and
Judge Goldsack Q.C.): November 15, 2005

[2005] EWCA Crim 3446; [2006] 1 Cr.App.R. 23

(LT) Alternative verdicts; Discharge; Juries; Jurisdiction; Lesser offences

H1   ALTERNATIVE VERDICTS
       Jurisdiction to return verdicts of guilt on lesser offences
       Trial judge ordering stay of proceedings against one appellant in respect of
       offences charged but allowing jury to consider returning alternative verdict in
       relation to same events—At trial of second appellant jury unable to reach verdict
       on offence charged and discharged by judge from returning verdict on that
       charge but invited to consider alternative charge—Whether jurisdiction to return
       verdicts on lesser alternative charges—Road Traffic Act 1988 (c.52), ss.3A (as
       inserted by Road Traffic Act 1991 (c.40), s.3), 4(1)—Road Traffic Offenders
       Act 1988 (c.53), s.24 (as substituted by the Road Traffic Act 1991 (c.40),
       s.24)—Crime and Disorder Act 1998 (c.37), s.31(1)(a), s.31(6)

H2   The appellant, K, was charged with two counts (1 and 2) of causing the death of
       his children by careless driving while unfit through drink or drugs, contrary to
       s.3A of the Road Traffic Act 1988. Prior to the defence team having the oppor-
       tunity to examine it, the police destroyed the appellant's car. A successful
       application was made on behalf of the appellant to stay the trial on counts 1
       and 2 on the ground that, by virtue of the destruction of the car and the unavail-
       ability of the opportunity for examination by the defence, it would be an abuse of
       process to leave to the jury counts dependent upon causation. After discussion
       with counsel the trial judge directed the jury that they should find the appellant
       not guilty on counts 1 and 2, but he left to the jury the alternative lesser offences
       of driving when unfit through drink or drugs. The appellant was convicted.

H3   The nine-year-old son of the appellant S was in a class run by a trainee teacher.
       S was charged with racially aggravated use of threatening words and behaviour,
       causing fear or provocation of violence, contrary to s.31(1)(a) of the Crime and
       Disorder Act 1998. The evidence for the prosecution was that she had stormed
       into the classroom shouting and swearing, holding her fist directly at the trainee
       teacher's face. The appellant denied making any racist remarks. The Recorder
       directed the jury on the racially aggravated offence, and also on the alternative
       offence available under s.31(6) of the 1998 Act which provided that the offence
       of causing fear or provocation of violence could be without the racial or religious
       aggravation. The jury were unable to reach a verdict on the racially aggravated
       offence and, after receiving a note from them, the Recorder discharged them

from reaching a verdict on that offence. They then returned with a unanimous verdict finding S guilty of the non-racially aggravated offence of using threatening words or behaviour, contrary to s.4 of the Public Order Act 1986.

H4   **Held,** allowing both appeals, that the terms of s.24 of the Road Traffic Offenders Act 1988 (as substituted by s.24 of the Road Traffic Act 1991) and s.31(6) of the Crime and Disorder Act 1998, allowed an alternative charge to be considered only where there had been a finding of not guilty of the offence originally charged. In the Crown Court, even a successful submission of no case to answer should lead to a direction by the trial judge to a jury to enter a verdict of not guilty, and thus to a finding of not guilty. Further, the imposition of a stay of proceedings did not amount to a finding of not guilty. Whenever it was right to consider an alternative charge, the verdict of the jury on the original charge should be obtained. Accordingly, in cases such as these where there had been no finding of not guilty of the offences originally charged, the convictions on the alternative charges could not be upheld (post, paras [11], [26]–[30]).

H5   (For s.24 of the Road Traffic Offenders Act 1988, see *Archbold* 2006, para.32–165. For s.31 of the Crime and Disorder Act 1998, see *ibid.* para.29–38a).

Appeals against conviction

R. v Khela

H6   On April 28, 2005 in the Crown Court at Warwick (Judge Cole) the appellant, Dalbir Singh Khela was convicted of two counts (counts 3 and 4) of driving when unfit through drink or drugs, contrary to s.4(1) of the Road Traffic Act 1988. He was fined £550 on count 3 and no separate penalty was imposed on count 4. Counts 1 and 2 of the indictment, causing death by careless driving when unfit through drink or drugs, contrary to s.3A(1)(b) of the 1988 Act, were stayed as an abuse of process.

H7   The facts and grounds of appeal appear in the judgment of the court.

R. v Smith

H8   On May 3, 2005 in the Crown Court at Snaresbrook (Mr Recorder Riza Q.C.) the appellant, Tina Smith, was convicted of using threatening words and behaviour, contrary to s.4 of the Public Order Act 1986. She was conditionally discharged for 12 months. The jury had been unable to reach a verdict on the original charge of using racially aggravated threatening words and behaviour, contrary to s.31(1)(a) of the Crime and Disorder Act 1998 and the Recorder had discharged them from doing so.

H9   The facts and grounds of appeal appear in the judgment of the court.

H10   *Graham Henson* (assigned by the Registrar of Criminal Appeals) for Khela.
        Adrian Keeling (instructed by the Crown Prosecution Service, Warwick) for the Crown.

Kate Ryle (assigned by the Registrar of Criminal Appeals) for Smith.
Teresa Pritchard (instructed by the Crown Prosecution Service, Snaresbrook) for the Crown.

Burton J.: delivered the judgment of the Court.

1   Two appeals have been taken together before us. The first is *R. v Khela* and the second *R. v Tina Smith*.

2   The facts are of course entirely different in each and we shall deal with them first in order to set the unfortunate cases in context, but there is an issue which straddles the two and which renders it important for them both to be decided together. They were listed together. They have been heard together and, although there is a slight dissimilarity, the submissions of both counsel for the appellants on the one side, and for the prosecution on the other, have co-ordinated.

3   So far as Khela is concerned, there was a dreadful accident on November 19, 2002 in which the appellant was driving. His wife and two children were in the car. He careered off the motorway. His two children were killed and his wife seriously injured. A two-thirds consumed whisky bottle was found in the car and eye witnesses at the time gave evidence that he was strongly smelling of drink when found after the accident.

4   He admitted that he had consumed some whisky before driving and belatedly asserted that he had had more whisky but only, on his case, after the accident, which he said he had not revealed to the police at the time because he was worried that his wife, seriously injured as she was, might have been critical of him for doing so. It is apparent that on those facts his case before the jury was likely to be in some difficulty, at any rate so far as the consumption of alcohol was concerned. He was charged with causing the death of his children by careless driving while unfit through drink or drugs, contrary to s.3A of the Road Traffic Act 1988.

5   Although it was asserted by the Crown that no cause could be located in relation to there being anything wrong with the car, it had in fact been destroyed by the police prior to the defence team having the opportunity to examine it.

6   At the close of the evidence, and prior to closing speeches, an application was made by the defence by Mr Henson, who appeared then on behalf of the appellant as he has appeared before us, on the basis that by virtue of the destruction of the car and the unavailability of the opportunity for examination by the defence, the count charging causing death by careless driving while unfit through drink or drugs should not be left to the jury, because it would be an abuse of the process to leave to the jury counts dependent upon causation in those circumstances.

7   The judge, Judge Cole, reserved judgment overnight after considering that submission. He reached the conclusion that, in the circumstances, albeit he was not going to attribute blame as to who it was who ordered the car to be released for destruction, nevertheless he concluded that it was not the defendant, and that it would be unfair that he should be penalised as a result of what somebody else had done.

8   The judge then giving his ruling, which he gave in the presence of the jury, said this:

> "Be that as it may, what it does do is put a dramatic light on the evidence which you have now to consider. The charges, of course, are causing death by careless driving when unfit through drink.
> Clearly, because I am staying the charge so far as it relates to the careless-ness, the mechanical defect and all that aspect, that will no longer be a matter with which you need be concerned.
> What there is, however, by Act of Parliament is the duty of a jury to consider whether there are alternative verdicts which could be appropriate. In fact, the one alternative verdict which could be appropriate is the last part of the charge that the defendant was unfit to drive through drink or drugs. That is a matter of fact which you will have to continue trying, but you will not be any longer saddled with the anxiety as to whether this man killed his own children by his own [lack of] due care and attention."

At the close of his ruling counsel for both prosecution and defence launched straight into closing speeches.

9   The judge then gave, after closing speeches, his summing-up to the jury. He concluded as follows:

> "What will have to happen—we will help you with regard to the verdict—is, for example, the charge will be put to you [that is the charge in relation to drink and drive, which is what he had left to the jury]; on my direction you will say you find the defendant not guilty if you are satisfied or you believe that it is possible that he may be innocent—you find not guilty. If, on the other hand, you are satisfied so that you are sure that he is guilty of being impaired through drink, unfit to drive, then you would say not guilty to the charge [and that is the causation charge of causing death to which we have referred] but guilty to being unfit through drink."

So at that stage, untutored by counsel, the judge was intending to leave to the jury the alternative count and, if they were minded to convict of the alternative count, he was going to direct them to find the defendant not guilty of the charge depen-dent upon causation. He then concluded his summing-up with some further matters and turned to counsel and said: "Is there anything else?" Counsel for the prosecution, Mr Keeling, who appeared then, and again before us today, said this:

> "Just this. Technically, the jury will not find the defendant not guilty on the count on the indictment because you stayed those."

The judge:

> "No, they cannot, I agree, but they have got to do it in that form or would you suggest merely [saying] guilty or not guilty of unfit to drive through drink."

Mr Keeling replied: "I would suggest that". That is the course that was then taken.

10   The statute in question in the Khela appeal is the Road Traffic Offenders Act
        1988, s.24, which deals with alternative verdicts. There is no doubt at all that the
        offence of driving when unfit to drive through drink or drugs (s.4(1)) of the Road
        Traffic Act 1988 is an alternative verdict to the count of causing death by careless
        driving when under the influence of drink or drugs under s.3A, and a schedule to
        s.24 so specifies.

11   But the circumstances in which a jury is entitled to consider a verdict on to s.4,
        as an alternative verdict on s.3A, s.4 being ordinarily only triable summarily by a
        magistrates' court, are set out in terms in the body of s.24 which reads as follows:

> "Where–
>   (a) a person charged with an offence under a provision of the Road Traf-
>   fic Act 1988 specified in the first column of the Table below . . . is
>   found not guilty of that offence, but
>   (b) the allegations in the indictment or information . . . amount to or
>   include an allegation of an offence under one or more of the pro-
>   visions specified in the corresponding entry in the second column,
>   he may be convicted of that offence or of one or more of those
>   offences."

It is thus quite plain that a condition precedent for the jury to be entitled to convict
on s.4, when faced with an indictment containing s.3A, is that the defendant in
question must have been found not guilty of s.3A.

12   We turn to consider the facts in the Smith case. So far as she is concerned, she
        came before the Crown Court at Snaresbrook in a trial which lasted from April 28
        to May 3, 2005. The charge which she faced was one of racially aggravated fear or
        provocation of violence, contrary to s.31(1)(a) of the Crime and Disorder Act
        1998. The circumstances of the case were that she was the parent of a nine-
        year-old child in a class which was run by the victim, Mr Richard Rogers, a
        trainee teacher.

13   The evidence for the prosecution both by Mr Rogers and by Miss Shaves, who
        was a teacher with 26 years' professional experience who had been training Mr
        Rogers on the day of the incident, and by Miss May, who was a pupil support
        worker with six years' experience in the school and who was also present, was
        that the appellant stormed into the classroom shouting and swearing and said:
        "All you care about is the fucking Pakis and the black children, you black bas-
        tard" and stated she did not care if they called her a racist. She held her fist
        directly at his face as she uttered the words.

14   The appellant's evidence was in effect entirely the reverse. On her evidence,
        she went to pick up her son from school and waited outside the classroom door
        and went inside to talk to Mr Rogers, and she said that he had called her "a stupid
        white bitch" and she denied that she had made any racist remarks.

15   The jury were directed on the racially aggravated offence. They were also
        directed on the basis of the alternative offence, available under s.31 of the
        Crime and Disorder Act 1998, by which Act it was specifically provided that
        an alternative to an offence of causing fear or provocation of violence which

was racially or religiously aggravated could be that offence without the racial or religious aggravation. The Recorder put it in this way in his summing-up:

> ". . . you will first consider whether the racially aggravated version of this offence has been committed; but, if you find that that is not proven, then you go on to consider whether you are sure—and let me remind you of the questions you have to answer. Are you sure that threatening and abusive language was used? Are you sure that the defendant intended to use behaviour that was threatening and abusive, or was she aware that her words were insulting, abusive and threatening? . . .
>
> So, members of the jury, if you are satisfied so that you are sure about those three things, then you can return a verdict of guilty, but not guilty of causing racially aggravated fear of violence. So there you have it, members of the jury. This is the alternative that you can decide if you are so minded."

16   At the close of the summing-up, Miss Oliver, who appeared then for the prosecution, although the prosecution are represented in her absence today by Mrs Pritchard, rose to seek clarification of what the Recorder judge had said. She said as follows:

> "Could I just raise one thing, your Honour, perhaps to make it absolutely clear to the jury because it is a rather complicated scenario you have given them, that, in effect, if they are agreed on their answers to your Honour's questions, they have, in effect, again, three possible verdicts. They either have guilty of the offence on the indictment, not guilty of causing racially aggravated fear of violence, but guilty of causing fear of violence, which is how they would express it in answer to the question, or a straight not guilty. So, in effect, that gives them a form of words they can use for the middle one. So they have not guilty, not guilty of causing racially aggravated fear of violence, but guilty of causing fear of violence, not guilty."

The Recorder accepted what Miss Oliver had said and confirmed that position to the jury in his own slightly different words.

17   The jury passed a note to the Recorder, which he referred to in their absence, having said that he could not pass on the contents, namely that the effect of it was that they had reached a unanimous verdict in relation to the alternative count and they had not in relation to the count on the indictment. He then invited submissions from both counsel, Miss Oliver and Miss Ryle, who appeared on behalf of the appeant then as before us, as to what course should be taken. Miss Ryle did not have anything to add, and left the running to Miss Oliver. Miss Oliver said:

> ". . . they can be given time if there comes a point later on this afternoon when they can be asked if they think there is any realistic prospect of them reaching a verdict which you can take, be it guilty or not guilty. If there is no point in them proceeding, then obviously your Honour would discharge them on that count and take the other verdict."

That in effect is what subsequently occurred, when they later did come back, still unable to reach a verdict. The Recorder asked them whether, if they were given more time on the racially aggravated count, there was any realistic likelihood that they would reach a verdict upon which 10 were agreed and the foreman said "I think not", and the Recorder then discharged them from reaching a verdict on that count in the indictment. There was then a unanimous verdict of guilty given relating to that non-racially aggravated charge, and Miss Oliver then rose to say that the Crown would not seek a retrial on the original racially aggravated charge.

18   Section 31(6) of the Crime and Disorder Act 1998 does contain a similar provision in almost identical words to that in s.24(1) of the Road Traffic Offenders Act 1988. It says:

> "If, on the trial on indictment of a person charged with an offence falling within subs.(1)(a) or (b) above, the jury find him not guilty of the offence charged, they may find him guilty of the basic offence mentioned in that provision."

19   Those then are the facts in the two cases. It is apparent that they each raise the same problem, namely: in what circumstances can a jury proceed to consider and, if appropriate, convict on an alternative count falling within, in one case the 1988 Act, and then in the other case the 1998 Act? The words of the two sections are clear. We are satisfied that no difference between the two can be identified by the reference in the one case to "the jury finding" a defendant not guilty (s.36) and in the other case to the defendant being "found not guilty" (s.24) because in both cases it is a jury at the Crown Court which does the finding of not guilty if anybody does.

20   In the one case before us, in Khela, the reason that there was not a finding of not guilty on the causing death by careless driving charge was the decision of the Recorder that there should be a stay. In the other case of Smith, there was no finding of not guilty because the judge discharged the jury from delivering a verdict. The very unfortunate fact in both cases is that it is quite apparent that the court intended, in each of them, to make use of, or rather allow the jury the opportunity to make use of, the alternative verdict provisions. In each case the relevant section was not drawn specifically to the attention of the learned judge or the learned Recorder. There have been apologies forthcoming from counsel appearing before us, three of whom out of the four were in the court below. Mr Henson puts forward by way of mitigation the fact that he was surprised by the result of the stay application, which he had hoped was going to be entirely successful in discharging any proceedings hanging over his client, although in fact he manfully and speedily rose to his feet and delivered a closing speech immediately after the announcement of the decision. But it can at best be mitigation. It is in effect disastrous in the impact on both these two cases if it turns out that the jury had no jurisdiction simply because of the course that was taken by the court, when by dint of taking a slightly different course, there would have been such jurisdiction.

21   As appears from the passages that we have quoted from the two judgments, it was intended originally by the judge and Recorder to take this course which would have not caused any problem. Judge Cole, in the Khela case, was intend-

ing, until dissuaded by Mr Keeling for the prosecution, to direct a verdict of not guilty on the death by careless driving charge, and then take the verdict on the alternative count at one and the same time. That would plainly have fallen straightforwardly within the words of s.24 of the 1988 Act. The Recorder was, it seems, intending to take a similar course, from which he seems to have been dissuaded by the words of Miss Oliver, for the prosecution, when she said "obviously your Honour would discharge them on that count". It is plain what the intention of the court was and, in our judgment, it would have been simple and straightforward to put that intention into effect. Mr Henson, for Mr Khela, is insistent before us that all he had asked for on his application to the judge was a stay of the indictment, and consequently that is all that he was expecting and all that should have occurred. However it is quite clear to us that, had the precise wording of s.24 been drawn to the attention of the judge, given his purpose, which is clear, then what he would then have said would have been, in the light of the submissions of Mr Henson which might otherwise have led to a stay:

> "I am proposing to leave the alternative verdict to the jury. The way in which to do that is to direct a verdict of not guilty because I shall not allow the death by careless driving to be left to the jury and shall consequently require a finding of not guilty."

22   That is a course which would have been proper and appropriate to give, one which is suggested in similar circumstances by the commentators in relation to the case of *R. v Griffiths* [1998] Crim L.R. 348. Mr Henson has fairly said that, had that course been taken, although it is not one he has espoused, he would not have been in a position to appeal to this court with regard to what occurred. Similarly, so far as the Smith case is concerned, it would, in our judgment, have been open to the Recorder, after a period of time had elapsed whereby it became apparent that the jury was not going to reach a verdict on count 1, to explain to them the consequences which the 1998 Act would have; and no doubt, after hearing submissions, it might well have been appropriate for him to direct a verdict of not guilty, given that he knew, no doubt from the note, what was likely to occur, namely a unanimous verdict on the alternative offence.

23   That is how these cases should have been dealt with. We hope in future that there will be no doubt at all that that is the right course, either in respect of what would otherwise be a stay or in the event of disagreement by the jury which might otherwise lead to a discharge of the jury, if it is intended that either of these two sections, or the equivalent section in the Criminal Law Act 1967, s.6, should be operated.

24   What in fact has happened, however, it is clear to us, notwithstanding the submissions we have heard, and in accordance with the submission of the appellants in both cases, is that the jury had no jurisdiction to give a verdict of guilty, in relation to summary offences which could only be before the Crown Court as a result of an operation of these two sections, both of which are clear in terms. We drew the attention of the prosecution to the case of *Director of Public Prosecutions v Smith* [2002] Crim L.R. 970, which pushed the construction of s.24, per Elias J., as far as it could be taken, in relation to a decision of magistrates

that there was no case to answer, which was concluded to amount to a finding of not guilty. That is how the matter would be dealt with at the magistrates' court. But in the Crown Court, even a successful submission of no case to answer would lead to a direction by the learned judge to a jury to enter a verdict of not guilty and thus to a finding of not guilty within the Act. Without such a finding of not guilty it is clear to us that the court had no jurisdiction to take the course it did.

25   In his able effort to salvage the position on behalf of the prosecution in Khela, Mr Keeling submitted that, although he did not seek to assist his fellow prosecutor in Smith, from which case he differentiated Khela, a stay amounted to a finding of not guilty because there could never be any pursuance of the proceedings, given that there was a stay.

26   We do not accept such submission for two reasons: (i) although Mr Keeling was not able to give any example of a situation in which a stay had ever in fact been lifted, we are certainly not in any position to say, not having had authority put before us, that there could never be a case in which a stay might, in appropriate circumstances, be lifted; (ii) and in any event, an imposition of a stay is not a finding of not guilty.

27   We do not accept Mr Henson's submission that it is the imposition of the stay which assists him. It is quite clear that, if it was simply a matter of there having been a stay, then this matter could still have been thereafter resolved before the judge by one of the courses to which we have earlier referred. What renders the appellants' cases unarguably right is not the existence of a stay, but the non-compliance with the express terms of the two statutory provisions.

28   Given then that there was no jurisdiction for the jury to do what it did, both prosecution counsel, Mr Keeling with rather more verve than Mrs Pritchard, sought to say that nevertheless these convictions should be upheld as safe. It is quite apparent that there is considerable reason for the prosecution to have sought to support both these convictions. The jury in the case of Smith were unanimous in their decision in relation to the lesser offence, and so far as Khela is concerned, through an error by the police, the jury were deprived of the opportunity to decide what would have been an extremely serious offence, and the result of allowing this appeal will be that, notwithstanding the jury's conclusion that he was driving while unfit through drink or drugs, when he was the driver of the car that plummeted off the motorway and killed his children, he will walk out without any conviction albeit of course carrying with him for ever the burden of what he did.

29   But, in our judgment, the arguments put forward by the prosecution simply cannot be right. To suggest that the conviction is safe may be possible where, as was said by the then Lord Chief Justice, Lord Bingham of Cornhill in *R. v Graham* [1997] 1 Cr.App.R. 302 at 309, where the criticism of the conviction is that there has been "some drafting or clerical error or omission or discrepancy or departure from good or prescribed practice". But, where, as Rose L.J. put it in *R. v Mullen* [1999] 2 Cr.App.R. 143 at 161G; [2000] Q.B. 520; [1999] 3 W.L.R. 777, the conviction was not "lawful", it "can hardly be regarded as safe". "Unlawful" of course may mean a large number of things and there may be situations where, with respect, the words of Rose L.J. may be capable of being eaten

away at. In our judgment, where there is no doubt at all is where the action in the Crown Court, and in particular here of the jury, was without jurisdiction. Where the unlawfulness consists of there being no jurisdiction to take the course that was taken, in our judgment such a conviction cannot be safe.

30   In those circumstances, we say with regret, in the light of the clear view of the jury in both cases, that these appeals must be allowed. For a concatenation of reasons, as to which, in the event, both prosecution and defence were agreed, it is not feasible for there to be a retrial in this case, and consequently the result of allowing the appeals, which we do, is that there cannot be any further hearing of these matters. In the one case there is a stay, in the other the prosecution has concluded there will not be a retrial. In those circumstances, the appeals are allowed and there will be no retrials.

Appeals allowed.
Convictions quashed.

R. v RENDA
R. v BALL
R. v AKRAM
R. v OSBOURNE
R. v RAZAQ (AJAZ) AND RAZAQ (ABDUL)

COURT OF APPEAL (President of the Queen's Bench Division (Sir Igor Judge), Mr Justice Bean and Sir Charles Mantell): October 20; November 10, 2005

[2005] EWCA Crim 2826; [2006] 1 Cr.App.R. 24

Admissibility; Bad character; Credibility; Cross examination; False statements; Previous convictions; Probative value

H1   EVIDENCE
       Bad character
       Defendant creating but subsequently withdrawing false impression as to char-
       acter—Reprehensible behaviour other than the commission of an offence—
       Evidence "given" of an imputation made during questioning under caution—
       Bad character of complainant and defendant's witness—Criminal Justice Act
       2003 (c.44), ss.100, 101(1)(c)–(g), 105(1), 105(3), 106(1)(c), 107, 110(1), 112(1)

H2   These six appeals were listed together, and heard consecutively, as each
       required consideration of one or more practical problems arising from the
       "bad character" provisions in Pt II, Ch.1, of the Criminal Justice Act 2003.

       R. v Renda

H3   The appellant was charged with an offence of attempted robbery. At trial the
       appellant sought to enhance his credibility by asserting that he had been a serving
       soldier in the armed forces, who had, while so employed, sustained a serious head
       injury which had resulted in long-term brain damage. He said that at the date of
       his arrest he was in regular employment as a security guard. The Crown had evi-
       dence to show that although it was true that the appellant had served in the armed
       forces, his serious head injury had not been sustained while he was in the course
       of his duties, but while he was on holiday, driving his own vehicle. Although it
       was also true that he had been employed in a security capacity, checking
       "passes", this had been short-term employment only. He was no longer in gainful
       employment. If this evidence was correct, the appellant was seeking to convey a
       misleading impression about his life and history. Additional material available to
       the Crown showed that not only had there been a number of reported crimes of
       violence for which the appellant was alleged to have been responsible, but that

on an earlier occasion, when he had been found unfit to plead to a count of assault occasioning actual bodily harm, the jury were satisfied as a fact that the appellant had approached someone from behind and struck him about the head. The case was disposed of by way of absolute discharge. In cross-examination the appellant was forced to concede the truth. The Crown had sought leave to ask questions about the incident of violence. The judge made a preliminary ruling that the Crown was entitled to ask questions about the appellant's military service, the circumstances of the accident, and his subsequent employment. The judge also ruled that the Crown could ask about the facts of the assault which were relevant to the issue of credibility. The appellant was convicted and appealed against conviction. The grounds of appeal challenged the rulings of the judge, and contended, inter alia, that an absolute discharge following a finding that the appellant was unfit to plead did not constitute a criminal conviction, nor did it constitute "reprehensible behaviour" amounting to misconduct for the purposes of the "bad character" provisions in Pt II of the 2003 Act. It was furthermore submitted that the appellant should be treated as having withdrawn, or dissociated himself from, any false assertion relating to the claim that he had sustained injury while in the course of his duties, so that s.105(3) of the 2003 Act should not apply, and it was therefore no longer appropriate to treat him as having given evidence which was "apt to give the . . . jury a false or misleading impression about" him.

H4   **Held,** dismissing the appeal, that:

(1) For the purposes of s.101(1)(f) of the 2003 Act the question whether the appellant had given a "false impression" about himself, and whether there was evidence which might properly serve to correct such a false impression within s.105(1)(a) and (b) was fact-specific. In the present case the appellant was plainly seeking to convey the impression that he was a man of positive good character (post, para.[19]).

(2) The appellant should not be treated as having withdrawn, or dissociated himself from, any false assertion relating to the claim that he had sustained injury while in the course of his duties, with the proposed effect that s.105(3) of the 2003 Act should not apply. There was a significant difference between a defendant who made a specific and positive decision to correct a false impression for which he was responsible, or to dissociate himself from false impressions conveyed by the assertions of others, and the defendant who in the process of cross-examination was obliged to concede that he had been misleading the jury. A concession extracted in cross-examination that the defendant was not telling the truth in part of his examination in chief would not normally amount to a withdrawal of, or dissociation from, the original assertion for the purposes of s.105(3) (post, para.[21]).

(3) While the appellant was not convicted of a criminal offence, and as a matter of ordinary language the word "reprehensible" carried with it some element of culpability or blameworthiness, the mere fact that the appellant was found unfit to plead, some 18 months after an apparent

incident of gratuitous violence had occurred, of itself did not connote that at the time of the offence his mental acuity was so altered as to extinguish any element of culpability when the table leg in question was used in such a violent fashion; and on the face of it this was reprehensible behaviour and there was no evidence before the judge to suggest otherwise. Therefore, the material was available to help refute the false impression as to positive good character given by the appellant in his evidence-in-chief. If they were sure that he had tried to give a false impression about himself then the jury were entitled to see how it affected the way in which they should approach the evidence about the events subject of the instant count on the indictment (post, paras [24]–[25]).

(4) Although counsel for the appellant had changed her mind after first conceding that the finding by the jury as to the incident of the table leg amounted to a conviction, it was not the case that the judge should have stopped the case because the evidence had thereby become "contaminated" for the purposes of s.107 of the 2003 Act. The latter provision should not be misused. There would of course be occasions when counsel was justified in submitting that a conviction would be unsafe because evidence admitted under s.101(1)(c)–(g) proved to be contaminated. That however did not provide any justification for a submission which was in truth no more than a reiteration of arguments already advanced against admitting the evidence at all. Section 107 dealt with a particular situation where the evidence of "bad character" had been admitted and proved to be false or misleading in the circumstances described in s.107(5). Unless the case fell squarely within that statutory provision the Court of Appeal, Criminal Division, was the appropriate court in which the correctness of the judge's decision should be questioned (post, paras [26]–[28]).

R. v Ball

H5   The appellant was charged with two counts of rape. At trial the appellant alleged consent by the complainant. The complainant, while denying consent, also stated that the appellant after intercourse had said "What are you going to do now, go off and get me done for rape? Look at you, you're nowt but a slag". The appellant, in interview, had stated, inter alia, that the complainant was "easy", "a bag, really, you know what I mean, a slag". On an application by the Crown to adduce evidence of the appellant's bad character arising from his previous convictions and breaches of court orders, the judge concluded that an attack had been made, by the appellant, as recorded in interview, on the complainant's character for the purposes of s.101(1)(g) of the 2003 Act. The judge accordingly permitted the Crown to cross-examine the appellant about his bad character. The appellant was subsequently convicted and appealed against conviction.

H6   **Held,** dismissing the appeal, that the appellant chose to make the observations recorded in interview and if what was said was relevant and served to support the allegation of rape, the evidence was admissible and for the purposes of s.106(1)(c) of the 2003 Act was indeed "given". The appellant's answers in interview purported to be exculpatory, alleging consent, but were said by the Crown with justification to provide evidence which indicated an attitude to the complainant which at least carried with it the implication that the appellant believed that she would have agreed to sexual intercourse with him, and any other man, at any time and in any circumstances, and that if and when she purported to be unwilling to have sexual intercourse, any such refusal should be disregarded as quite meaningless. Therefore, somewhat unusually, answers which might have been treated as exculpatory alone, and possibly not admissible on that basis, formed part of the prosecution case adduced by the Crown. The evidence was properly before the jury as part of the prosecution case. It did not represent any sort of device to enable the Crown to make an application to put the appellant's previous convictions before the jury. Once the evidence was properly "given", within s.106(1)(c), the judge would have been entitled to exclude it as a matter of discretion, but no arguable basis had been shown for interfering with his exercise of such discretion (post, paras [36]–[39]).

R. v Akram

H7   The appellant was charged with dangerous driving. The defence case was that certain witnesses' identification of the appellant as the relevant driver was wrong. The appellant sought to challenge the evidence of those witnesses by reference to four specific areas of evidence, asserting that he wished to demonstrate that one of the two key witnesses, who had been assaulted, had other enemies apart from the appellant. The Recorder approached the issues by reference to s.100 of the 2003 Act and made rulings accordingly. The appellant was subsequently convicted and appealed against conviction and sentence.

H8   **Held,** dismissing the appeals against conviction and sentence, that on the facts there was no justifiable complaint against the Recorder's decision about the proper application of s.100 of the 2003 Act (post, paras [46]–[47]).

R. v Osbourne

H9   The appellant was charged with robbery. At trial he sought to introduce certain evidence as to misconduct by the licensee of the pub at which the robbery was said to have occurred, in particular relating to till shortages and drug usage. As the licensee was not a defendant the admissibility of any evidence of bad character or misconduct or reprehensible behaviour depended on s.100 of the 2003 Act. The judge applied the provision and decided that counsel for the appellant was entitled to deploy all the material, with the exception of a generalised allegation of drug misuse. The appellant was convicted and appealed against conviction.

H10   **Held,** dismissing the appeal, that to be admissible the evidence in issue was
             required to be important explanatory evidence, or evidence with a substantial
             probative value in the context of the case as a whole. However the excluded evi-
             dence did not on the facts help to demonstrate why, or support the conclusion that,
             the licensee was, or might have been, inventing a fictitious crime. Similarly, com-
             plaint as to exclusion of the evidence under s.100 of another witness's evidence
             could not be sustained on the facts (post, paras [55], [57]–[60]).

             R. v Razaq (Ajaz) and Razaq (Abdul)

H11   The first appellant was the son of the second appellant. They were charged with
             assault occasioning actual bodily harm and affray. The jury had to determine
             whether one or both of the appellants might have been acting in what throughout
             the trial was described as "self-defence of another". Analysis of the credibility of
             all the protagonists was required. During the trial an application was made on
             behalf of the first appellant to cross-examine a witness, T, about his previous con-
             victions, and the Recorder had regard to s.100 of the 2003 Act, concluding that
             the application should be rejected on the basis that it failed to establish that T's
             bad character was of substantial probative value in the case against the appellant
             who sought to cross-examine him. After that ruling an application was made on
             behalf of another defendant, SR, to introduce the full story of T's previous history,
             and limited permission was given to do so. Cross-examination took place on
             behalf of all three defendants. The appellants appealed. The principal ground
             of appeal was that the Recorder had erred in rejecting the first appellant's appli-
             cation, and the second appellant complained that the Recorder should have
             permitted broader cross-examination.

H12   **Held,** dismissing the appeals, that the second appellant had no legitimate com-
             plaint. It would only be in exceptional circumstances that a defendant who was
             unprepared to make or expressly associate himself with an application for
             leave to cross-examine a prosecution witness might realistically complain at
             the judge's decision rejecting an application to the same effect by a co-accused.
             The first appellant had a sounder basis for complaint as insufficient weight was
             given to the critical importance of some of the direct evidence implicating him.
             However, the relevant witness was cross-examined about his critical convictions
             and that material, and the character of the complainant making allegations
             against the first appellant, were before the jury. Any prejudice identified was
             cured by the successful application to cross-examine which was made by the
             third defendant (post, paras [76]–[79]).

H13   *Per curiam:* Several of the decisions or rulings questioned in these appeals rep-
             resent either judgments by the trial judge in the specific factual context of the
             individual case, or the exercise of a judicial discretion. The circumstances in
             which this Court would interfere with the exercise of a judicial discretion are lim-
             ited. The principles need no repetition. The same general approach will be
             adopted when the Court is being invited to interfere with what in reality is a
             fact-specific judgment. As explained in one of these decisions, the trial judge's

"feel" for the case is usually the critical ingredient of the decision at first instance which the Court of Appeal lacks. Context therefore is vital. The creation and subsequent citation from a vast body of so-called "authority", in reality representing no more than observations on a fact specific decision of the judge in the Crown Court, is unnecessary and may well be counterproductive. This legislation has now been in force for nearly a year. The principles have been considered by the Court of Appeal on a number of occasions. The responsibility for their application is now for trial judges (post, para.[3]).

H14   (For evidence of bad character, see *Archbold* 2006, Ch.13).

Appeals against conviction

R. v Renda

H15   On May 13, 2005 in the Inner London Crown Court (Judge van der Werff), the appellant, Raymond Renda was convicted of attempted robbery. At the date of the hearing he had not been sentenced. The facts and grounds of appeal appear in the judgment of the court.

R. v Ball

H16   On April 18, 2005 in the Crown Court at Sheffield (Judge Keen Q.C.) the appellant, Nathan Ball, was convicted of two counts of rape. He was sentenced to a total of five years' imprisonment. The facts and grounds of appeal appear in the judgment of the court.

R. v Akram

H17   On March 18, 2005 in the Crown Court at Burnley (Mr Recorder Wright) the appellant, Adil Akram, was convicted of dangerous driving. He was sentenced to 18 months' detention in a young offender institution and disqualified from driving for three years or until an extended driving test had been passed. The facts and grounds of appeal appear in the judgment of the court.

R. v Osbourne

H18   On April 6, 2005, in the Crown Court at Cardiff (Judge Griffith-Williams Q.C., the Recorder of Cardiff) the appellant, Lee Osbourne, was convicted of robbery. He was sentenced to an extended sentence of eight years, under s.85 of the Powers of Criminal Courts (Sentencing) Act 2000, comprising a custodial term of four years and an extension period of four years. The facts and grounds of appeal appear in the judgment of the court.

R v Razaq (Ajaz) and Razaq (Abdul)

H19   On March 18, 2005 in the Crown Court at Isleworth (Ms Recorder Gupta) the appellants, Ajaz Ahmad Razaq and Abdul Razaq, were convicted of assault occasioning actual bodily harm and affray. They were each sentenced to a total of 15 months' imprisonment. The facts and grounds of appeal appear in the judgment of the court.

H20　*Alexandra Felix* (assigned by the Registrar of Criminal Appeals) for Renda.
Grace Ong (instructed by the Crown Prosecution Service) for the Crown in Renda.
J. Hillis (assigned by the Registrar of Criminal Appeals) for Ball.
Richard Newbury (instructed by the Crown Prosecution Service) for the Crown in Ball.
Wayne Goldstein (assigned by the Registrar of Criminal Appeals) for Akram.
Michael Lavery (instructed by the Crown Prosecution Service) for the Crown in Akram.
Laurence Jones (assigned by the Registrar of Criminal Appeals) for Osbourne.
Mary Parry Evans (instructed by the Crown Prosecution Service) for the Crown in Osbourne.
Rossano Cifonelli (assigned by the Registrar of Criminal Appeals) for Ajaz Razaq.
Joseph Stone (assigned by the Registrar of Criminal Appeals) for Abdul Razaq.
Robert Whittaker (instructed by the Crown Prosecution Service) for the Crown in Razaq & Razaq.

Cur. adv. vult.

November 10　Sir Igor Judge P.: handed down the judgment of the court.

General

1　　These six appeals were listed together, and heard consecutively over two days. Each required consideration of one or more practical problems arising from the "bad character" provisions in Pt II, Ch.1, of the Criminal Justice Act 2003.

2　　It will not be necessary or useful for us to set out these provisions in the judgment. In coming to our conclusions, in each case we had an overall view of the structure of this chapter together with the specific legislation said to apply directly to the point in issue. In addition, we shall not spell out all the detailed evidence in support of either sides' case. We only focus attention on those parts of the evidence relevant to our decisions.

3　　We have some general observations. Several of the decisions or rulings questioned in these appeals represent either judgments by the trial judge in the specific factual context of the individual case, or the exercise of a judicial discretion. The circumstances in which this Court would interfere with the exercise of a judicial discretion are limited. The principles need no repetition. However we emphasise that the same general approach will be adopted when the Court is being invited to interfere with what in reality is a fact-specific judgment. As we explain in one of these decisions, the trial judge's "feel" for the case is usually the critical ingredient of the decision at first instance which this Court lacks. Context therefore is vital. The creation and subsequent citation from a vast body of so-called "authority", in reality representing no more than observations on a fact specific decision of the judge in the Crown Court, is unnecessary and may well be counterproductive. This legislation has now been in force for nearly a year. The principles have been considered by this Court on a number of occasions. The responsibility for their application is not for this Court but for trial judges.

4   Finally, even if it is positively established that there has been an incorrect ruling or misdirection by the trial judge, it should be remembered that this Court is required to analyse its impact (if any) on the safety of any subsequent conviction. It does not follow from any proved error that the conviction will be quashed.

5   In the context of these appeals, although other points arose from time to time, it would be useful to set out the provisions which are of direct relevance in each individual appeal.

Renda

6	(a)	Creation of a false impression by a defendant	(s.101(1)(f) and s.105(1))
	(b)	Withdrawal of a false impression	(s.105(3))
	(c)	Reprehensible behaviour other than the commission of an offence	(s.112(1))
	(d)	Discharge of the jury for "contamination"	(s.107)

Ball

| 7 | Evidence "given" of an imputation made during questioning under caution | (s.101(1)(g) and s.106(1)(c)) |

Akram

| 8 | Complainant's bad character | (s.100) |

Osbourne

| 9 | (a) | Bad character of complainant and defendant's witness | (s.100) |
| | (b) | Duty to give reasons | (s.110(1)) |

Razaq and Razaq

| 10 | Complainant's bad character and limits to cross-examination | (s.100) |

Renda

11   This is an appeal by Raymond Renda against a conviction for attempted robbery on May 13, 2005 at the Inner London Crown Court before Judge Van Der Werff and a jury.

12   At the date of the hearing of the appeal he had not been sentenced. He appeals with leave of the single judge.

13   The facts are straightforward. At about 02:00 on November 10, 2003, the complainant, Robert Flint, was walking home along Mile End Road in Stepney Green, London. At about the same time the appellant left a nearby public house, and was walking along Mile End Road in the opposite direction. Their paths crossed, and the appellant stood beside Mr Flint and asked him for money. When Mr Flint responded that he did not have any, and carried on walking, the appellant then fell in to walk beside him, continually pressing him for money. The appellant put his right hand into his jacket pocket saying, "What is this I have got in my pocket?". Hardly surprisingly, Mr Flint began to feel frightened, and the appellant continued to follow him, ordering him to turn into Whitehorse Lane, which, as it happened, was the street in which Mr Flint lived. As Mr Flint walked up the path to his flat the appellant followed him, still asking him for money, and, under an archway, seized hold of him by the neck, swinging him round and pushing him against the gate, saying "Give me your money now". Mr Flint pushed the appellant away, and into a hedge, and ran to his front door, but before he had time to open the door, the appellant returned and pushed him against the wall with his hand on his neck.

14   Two police officers in a passing police car saw what they believed to be a fight, and stopped, and separated the combatants. Mr Flint immediately complained that the appellant had followed him home and tried to rob him. The appellant denied that he had done anything at all, asserting that he was on his way home from the pub and that the allegation must be some sort of joke. When interviewed the appellant declined to answer any questions, but submitted a prepared statement in which he denied that he had attempted to rob the complainant: rather, after making a false accusation, the complainant had attacked him.

15   The issue at trial was therefore straightforward. The jury had to decide whether any offence at all had been committed, and their decision largely depended on their judgment of Mr Flint's veracity, and, if he gave evidence, the veracity of the appellant.

16   The issues in this appeal arise from the appellant's evidence. He sought to enhance his credibility by asserting that he had been a serving soldier in HM Armed Forces, who had, while so employed, sustained a serious head injury, which had resulted in long-term brain damage. He said that at the date of his arrest he was in regular employment as a security guard.

17   The Crown was in possession of evidence to show that although it was true that the appellant had served in the armed forces, his serious head injury had not been sustained while he was in the course of his duties, but while he was on holiday, driving his own vehicle. Although it was also true that he had been employed in a security capacity, checking "passes", this had been short-term employment only. He was no longer in gainful employment. If this evidence was correct, the appellant was seeking to convey a misleading impression about his life and history.

18   The additional material available to the Crown included the appellant's antecedent history and police computer print outs, and a report prepared by a psychiatrist instructed by the Crown. This material showed not only that there had been a number of reported crimes of violence for which the appellant was

alleged to have been responsible, but that on an earlier occasion, in July 2001, when he was found unfit to plead to a count of assault occasioning actual bodily harm, the jury was satisfied as a fact that the appellant had approached someone from behind and struck him about the head with a large wooden table leg. The case had been disposed of by way of an absolute discharge.

19   Our attention was drawn to some earlier authorities, which considered the impact of s.1(3)(ii) of the Criminal Evidence Act 1898. However it is unnecessary to refer to them in this judgment. It is most unlikely to be useful to refer to authorities which were no more than factual examples of occasions when it was decided that an individual defendant had put his character in issue. For the purposes of s.101(1)(f) the question whether the defendant has given a "false impression" about himself, and whether there is evidence which may properly serve to correct such a false impression within s.105(1)(a) and (b) is fact-specific. In the present case the appellant was plainly seeking to convey that he was a man of positive good character.

20   When the appellant was cross-examined he continued to maintain that he had been in regular employment as a security guard, and that he had not been dismissed from that employment. He did however concede that when he described himself as a security guard, his duties amounted to no more than checking passes. He agreed that he had not sustained his head injury during the course of his military duties as a soldier, but while he was on holiday in a car accident. In short, in cross-examination, he was forced to concede the truth.

21   It was submitted that in these circumstances the appellant should be treated as having withdrawn or disassociated himself with any false assertion relating to the claim that he had sustained injury while in the course of his duties. Accordingly s.105(3) should apply, and it was therefore no longer appropriate to treat him as having given evidence which was "apt to give the . . . jury a false or misleading impression about" him. We do not agree. Our reason is simple. There is a significant difference between the defendant who makes a specific and positive decision to correct a false impression for which he is responsible, or to disassociate himself with false impressions conveyed by the assertions of others, and the defendant who in the process of cross-examination is obliged to concede that he has been misleading the jury. A concession extracted in cross-examination that the defendant was not telling the truth in part of his examination-in-chief will not normally amount to a withdrawal or disassociation from the original assertion for the purposes of s.105(3).

22   The Crown sought leave to ask questions about this incident of violence. Judge Van Der Werff decided that it would not be prudent or right for the Crown to explore, through the appellant's own testimony, the details of his psychiatric history, not least because the appellant himself might not be in a position to deal with it properly. He made a preliminary ruling that the Crown was entitled to ask questions about the appellant's military service, the circumstances of the accident, and his subsequent employment. It was appropriate for the jury to understand that the appellant had been charged with assault occasioning actual bodily harm, and that although he was found unfit to plead, he was also found by the

jury to have committed the physical act of assault. The case was disposed of by way of an absolute discharge.

23   The judge was very concerned that the jury should not labour under a false impression about the appellant. He rejected a submission that the Crown should not be allowed to adduce the facts of the assault because proper notice had not been given. Counsel for the Crown submitted that these matters had arisen for consideration during the appellant's evidence, so that it was impractical to have given any notice. The judge ruled that the Crown could ask about the facts of the assault which were relevant to the issue of credibility.

24   Before us it was argued that the judge's rulings were wrong. An absolute discharge following a finding that the defendant was unfit to plead did not constitute a criminal conviction, nor did it constitute "reprehensible behaviour" amounting to misconduct for the purposes of the "bad character" provisions in Pt II of the Criminal Justice Act 2003. We agree that the appellant was not "convicted" of a criminal offence. We also accept that as a matter of ordinary language, the word "reprehensible" carries with it some element of culpability or blameworthiness. What however we are unable to accept is that the mere fact that the appellant was found unfit to plead some 18 months after an apparent incident of gratuitous violence has occurred, of itself, connotes that at the time of the offence his mental acuity was so altered as to extinguish any element of culpability when the table leg was used in such a violent fashion. On the face of it, this was reprehensible behaviour, and there was no evidence before Judge Van Der Werff to suggest otherwise.

25   Accordingly, this material was available to help refute the false impression as of positive good character given by the appellant in his evidence-in-chief. Recognising as the judge did, that this was not an entirely straightforward issue, he was at pains to explain to the jury the precise status of the earlier court proceedings, and in particular, how the process encompassed in the phrase "not fit to plead" works, and what it involves, and that the appellant was not convicted, and indeed had no convictions. He also explained that its relevance in this particular case was confined to helping the jury decide whether the appellant had tried to present himself as a "rather better man" than he actually was, and whether he was in truth, as the jury might consider he was seeking to convey, deserving of sympathy. If they were sure that he had tried to give a false impression about himself, then the jury was entitled to see how it affected the way in which they should approach the evidence about events on November 10, 2003. All that was fairly done.

26   The remaining point arising in this appeal arises from a submission that the judge should have stopped the case because the evidence had become contaminated. The point arose in this way. When the issue of the table leg incident was first raised, counsel for the appellant conceded that the finding by the jury amounted to a conviction. After further research she concluded, rightly, that it was not. Accordingly she sought the discharge of the jury on the basis that the evidence before it was "contaminated" for the purposes of s.107.

27   We can deal briefly with this submission. For the reasons we have given, the evidence was not in fact "contaminated". We are however concerned to ensure

that s.107 should not be misused. There will, of course, be occasions when counsel is justified in submitting that a conviction would be unsafe because evidence admitted under s.101(1)(c)–(g) proved to be contaminated. That however does not provide any justification for a submission which, in truth, is no more than a reiteration of the arguments advanced by counsel against the admission of this evidence. Section 107 deals with a particular situation where the evidence of "bad character" has been admitted and proves to be false or misleading in the circumstances described in s.107(5). Unless the case falls squarely within that statutory provision, the Court of Appeal Criminal Division is the appropriate court in which the correctness of the judge's decision should be questioned.

28   For these reasons, this appeal will be dismissed.

Ball

29   This is an appeal by Nathan Ball against his conviction on two counts of rape on April 18, 2005 in the Crown Court at Sheffield before Judge Keen Q.C. and a jury. The two counts related to incidents of penetration of the mouth and sexual intercourse with the same woman on January 21, 2005.

30   This unpleasant incident needs very little narrative explanation. Prior to January 21, 2005 the complainant and the appellant had been involved in a very casual sexual relationship. Consensual sexual intercourse had taken place after heavy alcohol consumption in circumstances devoid of any hint of affection.

31   On January 21, the pair were drinking in the same public house. There was evidence of some very unpleasant language by the appellant generally and at least in part insulting of the complainant. In any event, they left the premises together. They started to make their way to the rear of a nearby supermarket, and began intimate touching of each other. In the course of this foreplay the complainant fell over and hurt her knee. The appellant was unsympathetic and became aggressive. According to the complainant, she was no longer willing to have sexual intercourse with him, and she made her position absolutely clear. Nevertheless he forced her to take his penis in her mouth, and then proceeded to sexual intercourse. When it was over she reported that the appellant had said to her, "What are you going to do now, go off and get me done for rape? Look at you, you're nowt but a slag".

32   The appellant's case was that this sexual activity took place with the complainant's consent. She appeared to be entirely happy afterwards, but she may have become aggrieved because she thought or understood from what people were saying that the appellant was using her. Perhaps she recollected or heard about the appellant's earlier disparaging remarks about her in the public house, and this provoked her to make a false allegation of rape. In short, the complainant was lying, motivated by a wish for vengeance.

33   No further summary of the conflicting and mutually contradictory accounts of the incident is needed. We must however refer to the contents of the interviews between the appellant and the police. The appellant told the police that most of the men in the local public house had had sexual intercourse with the complainant. He criticised the complainant's sexual promiscuity in very disparaging

terms. She was easy. "She's a bag really, you know what I mean, a slag." This echoed the comment attributed to the appellant by the complainant after sexual intercourse.

34   When the appellant gave evidence, the Crown submitted that his bad character arising from previous convictions and breaches of court orders, should properly be deployed in cross-examination. The judge rejected a number of different bases advanced by the prosecution, including in particular, that he should admit this evidence simply on the basis of the direct attack on the complainant's credibility based on the appellant's instructions that the allegations of rape were fabricated. If we may say so, the judge's approach to this part of the case seems to have been impeccable.

35   However, the judge was troubled by the attack made against the complainant by the defendant in the course of the police interviews. In effect, the appellant asserted that the complainant had behaved or was disposed to behave in a reprehensible way. Accordingly an attack had been made on the complainant's character for the purposes of s.101(1)(g), as explained and expanded in s.106, and in particular s.106(1)(c). Evidence was given "of an imputation about the other person made by the defendant—(i) on being questioned under caution, before charge . . .". The judge considered whether to exclude the evidence under s.101(1)(3) on the basis that its admission would have an adverse effect on the fairness of the proceedings. He concluded that cross-examination about the appellant's bad character should be permitted.

36   Although a number of minor matters were raised in argument, we need only address the complaint directed by Mr Hillis at the judge's ruling that the appellant could be cross-examined about his previous convictions. No criticism is made of the way in which the judge dealt with these issues in his summing up. The complaint is directed at his ruling.

37   Mr Hillis began his argument by submitting that a major difficulty in this case arose from the impact of s.41 of the Youth Justice and Criminal Evidence Act 1999, which although restricting evidence or questions by the defence about a complainant's sexual history, did not extend to the prosecution. We agree that this is a feature of s.41, but it does not advance the argument further. The appellant chose to make the observations reported by the police. If what he said was relevant and served to support the allegation of rape, this evidence was admissible, and for the purposes of s.106(1)(c) was indeed "given". The answers by the appellant in his interview purported to be exculpatory in nature (there was no rape: it was consent) but were said by the Crown, with every justification, to provide evidence which indicated an attitude to the complainant which at least carried with it the implication that the appellant believed that she would have agreed to sexual intercourse with him, and any other man, at any time and in any circumstances, and that if and when she purported to be unwilling to have sexual intercourse, any such refusal should be disregarded as quite meaningless. In reality, therefore, and somewhat unusually, answers which might have been treated as exculpatory alone, and possibly not admissible on that basis, formed part of the prosecution case adduced by the Crown. The highlight, at its most stark, was the epithet, "slag", used by the appellant in the interviews to describe

the complainant which echoed what she claimed he had said to her after sexual intercourse had finished. The Crown also contended that the remark about rape attributed to him by the complainant was inconsistent with a genuine belief that she was consenting to what happened.

38   In our judgment this evidence was properly before the jury as part of the prosecution case. It did not represent (and the judge would have been alert to any such danger) any sort of device to enable the Crown to make an application to put the appellant's previous convictions before the jury. Once the evidence was properly given, within s.106(1)(c) the judge would have been entitled to exclude it as a matter of discretion. He was well aware of the need to exercise that discretion. No arguable basis for interfering with his decision has been shown.

39   Accordingly this appeal is dismissed.

Akram

40   This is an appeal against conviction and sentence by Adil Akram. On March 18, 2005 he was convicted of dangerous driving at Burnley Crown Court before Mr Recorder Wright and a jury. On April 29, 2005 he was sentenced to 18 months' detention in a young offender institution and disqualified from driving for three years and until an extended driving test was passed.

41   The essential facts can be summarised very briefly. On August 1, 2004 Rokab Afzal was driving his car in Nelson, in Lancashire, carrying a passenger, Adnan Khan. They became rather concerned about a potential problem with the steering of the car, so Mr Afzal stopped and got out. While he was there he was approached by a man called Kais Anwar, and they exchanged some unpleasantries. Thereafter a red Peugeot car pulled up on the opposite side of the road, and Kais Anwar went to speak to the driver. After he had done so the red Peugeot revved its engine and drove at the complainant, knocking him over. Fortunately Mr Afzal was not seriously hurt, and he was able to get up and run away into a nearby school. The red Peugeot then drove away from the scene.

42   The prosecution case was that the driver of the red Peugeot was the appellant, recognised both by Mr Afzal and his passenger Mr Khan. The defence case was that the identification was wrong. The appellant had spent the whole of the day, and at the relevant time was at his girlfriend's house. His girlfriend gave evidence to the same effect.

43   The appellant was aware of four specific areas of evidence with which it was proposed to test the evidence of Mr Afzal. The appellant and he had been friends for some time, but eventually a problem arose between them, the precise origins of which depended on which of them was explaining it. From the appellant's point of view he asserted an earlier assault by the complainant in which the complainant counter-asserted that he was the victim. This was described as the "cricket bat incident". There was also a falling out over a car stereo or cassette player which went missing from the appellant's car. According to him, either the complainant, or his associates, stole the car stereo in order to exert a measure of self-help to encourage the appellant to pay a debt: that, too was contentious. It was further suggested on the appellant's behalf that on the day when it was

alleged that he had been driving the red Peugeot car he was assaulted by associates of Mr Afzal, on his instructions. The final area of contention arose from the fact that Mr Afzal had been charged with an offence of kidnap.

44   The applicable statutory provision is to be found in s.100 of the Criminal Justice Act 2003. The Recorder allowed questions to be asked of the complainants about both the cricket bat and car stereo incidents. The allegation of assault on the same day as the offence was not pursued. The Recorder refused the application by the appellant to introduce or cross-examine Mr Afzal about the kidnap charge. This decision forms the basis of complaint before us.

45   It was suggested by the appellant at trial, and before us, that the purpose of this evidence was not to establish that Mr Afzal was a person of "bad character", but in order to demonstrate that others, as well as the appellant himself, might have had a motive for attacking him. The jury knew of the "bad blood" between the two men, and according to the argument by Mr Goldstein, it was essential to the appellant's case to establish that Mr Afzal had other enemies in addition to and beyond the appellant.

46   The problem with this argument is simple. The evidence of "bad blood" between the complainant and the appellant was introduced by the appellant, after permission had been sought and given for it to be raised. Moreover, at the time when the dangerous driving occurred, the alleged kidnap incident remained some four weeks into the future. Mr Afzal made his complaint, and identified the appellant as the driver of the Peugeot car on the day when the incident happened. On any view, therefore, the dangerous driving cannot have been a response to or some sort of revenge for the kidnap incident. Beyond that, however, even if the kidnap incident had occurred before the dangerous driving, it remains difficult for us to see why, even if the kidnap incident had indeed occurred, the victim of dangerous driving should wrongly attribute responsibility for it to Mr Afzal rather than to the individual who, on this analysis, was falsely accusing Mr Afzal of kidnap. In any event, the best that could be said at this stage of the case was that this was a bare allegation, itself wholly unproved.

47   On these facts, there is no justifiable complaint against the Recorder's decision about the proper application of s.100 of the 2003 Act. The appeal against conviction will be dismissed.

Sentence

48   The appeal against sentence focuses exclusively on the length of the custodial term, which Mr Goldstein accepts was inevitable. We have noted the comparative youth of the appellant, 18 years at the time, and his previous good character. On the other hand the incident itself was plainly a culmination of what we have described as bad blood between the two men. This case proceeded as a trial, and the appellant lacked the mitigation of a guilty plea. Taking account of the fact that Mr Afzal was fortunate to escape serious injury, it may very well be that the sentence fell at the top end of the appropriate range. There is however no basis to justify interference with it. Accordingly the appeal against sentence will also be dismissed.

Osbourne

49   This is an appeal by Lee Osbourne against his conviction for robbery at Cardiff Crown Court before Judge Griffith-Williams Q.C., the Recorder of Cardiff, and a jury.

50   The appellant was jointly charged with Alex Jenkins, whose application for leave to appeal against conviction was abandoned.

51   The essential facts can be briefly summarised. In the early hours of September 9, 2004, the police were called to a public house known as the Grasshopper, following a report that the licensee, Russell Cleverley, had been robbed of £200 in cash from the till. The appellant denied any involvement in robbery, and the defence positively called into question whether a robbery had taken place at all. The appellant, a man with a lengthy list of previous convictions suggested that Mr Cleverley fabricated the complaint of robbery in order to cover up his own misconduct as the licensee at the Grasshopper.

52   The precise details of the incident need no repetition. Mr Cleverley knew the appellant personally. At the end of drinking up time that evening very few people were left in the Grasshopper. They included the appellant and Alan Jenkins, who would not leave. After a while Mr Cleverley was threatened by them. Keys to the gaming machines were demanded. The appellant struck him across the left cheek and went with him to the till and demanded money. Mr Cleverley gave him £200 from the till. Jenkins was present at the other side of the bar and told the appellant to take Mr Cleverley upstairs and get the tape. This was a reference to the CCTV tape, which was then removed and destroyed.

53   Mr Cleverley's allegation was supported by a fairly considerable body of additional evidence, but no further narrative of the evidence available to the Crown is required.

54   The material available to the defence extended to four linked areas of alleged misconduct by Mr Cleverley as a licensee. His general conduct and management of the premises produced persistent till shortages. The premises were regularly misused for after hours drinking, free to both staff and late customers, with consequent stock depletion. During these "parties" drug misuse occurred, condoned if not encouraged by Mr Cleverley who participated in the activity. The fourth criticism was directed to Mr Cleverley's personal use of cocaine on the night of the offence itself.

55   As Mr Cleverley was a non-defendant, the admissibility of any evidence of bad character or misconduct or reprehensible behaviour depended on s.100 of the Criminal Justice Act 2003. In brief, to be admissible, such evidence was required to be important explanatory evidence, or evidence with a substantial probative value in the context of the case as a whole. Section 100 was analysed by the Recorder. He decided that counsel for the appellant was entitled to deploy all the material, with the exception of the generalised allegation of drug misuse during after hours drinking sessions. If true, the allegations of general till shortages and the provision of free drink, and so on, lent support to the allegation that any shortage in the till might be attributed to the landlord's misconduct, rather than an alleged robbery. If Mr Cleverley used cocaine on the night of the offence itself,

that might significantly undermine his complaints against the appellant. However, the Recorder was unable to conclude that the drug-taking allegation fell within the rules governing admissibility prescribed by s.100.

56   The complaint is that the Recorder's decision was wrong. The excluded material impacted on Mr Cleverley's general credibility but it went further, and served to demonstrate that he was lying when he claimed that he had been the victim of an offence. Moreover, it was argued, that this material added credibility to the appellant's account to the police in interview.

57   The problem with Mr Jones' fundamental contention can be summarised briefly. The allegation that the premises were misused generally for drug offences did not help to demonstrate why or support the conclusion that Mr Cleverley was or may have been inventing a fictitious crime. In the Recorder's view this allegation therefore lacked the explanatory importance and substantial probative value which was required to be satisfied before evidence of the bad character of a non-defendant could be admitted. These decisions have always to be reached in a particular factual context. We lack what is sometimes described as the trial judge's "feel" for the case. We should therefore hesitate before interfering with his conclusion in a matter of judgment. In our view even if this line of questioning may have had some marginal relevance, given that the Recorder permitted the proper development of lines of questioning which had a direct and significant impact on the issue to be decided by the jury, the prohibition against Mr Jones developing this particular line of cross-examination could have had no bearing on the outcome of the trial. That said, in our judgment the Recorder's decision was right. This particular material did not satisfy the admissibility provisions in s.100.

58   A further complaint arising under s.100 is directed against the judge's decision that a defence witness, Welsh, an employee of Mr Cleverley, described by the complainant as a friend, could be cross-examined about his bad character. His evidence purported directly to undermine Mr Cleverley's allegation that he had been the victim of violence on the night in question. In short, he gave evidence which served to support the assertion that Mr Cleverley had indeed invented the claim that he had been robbed.

59   Welsh had as recently as February 2003 been sentenced to two years' detention for an offence of serious violence. The judge agreed with the Crown that he could be cross-examined about it. The evidence of the conviction fell within s.100, particularly germane to the fundamental question whether or not a robbery had taken place. Without knowing of Welsh's character, the jury would have been deprived of important evidence of substantial probative value in relation to the issue of the credibility of Welsh's evidence on the vital question whether Mr Cleverley had fabricated his complaint, or whether in truth he was rightly to be regarded as a victim.

60   We cannot find any principled basis for interfering with the judge's decision. In agreeing that Welsh could be cross-examined about his previous conviction, the judge observed that the jury was entitled to know about Welsh's character. With respect we would suggest that this was an over-parsimonious compliance with the duty of the court under s.110(1) of the 2003 Act to give reasons for any rulings

made under s.100. However, as the decision itself was correct, the absence of detailed reasons does not impinge on the safety of the conviction. Accordingly this appeal will be dismissed.

Razaq and Razaq

61   Ajaz Razaq is the son of Abdul Razaq. On March 18, 2005 in the Crown Court at Isleworth, before Ms Recorder Gupta and a jury, both were convicted of assault occasioning actual bodily harm and affray. Another son of Abdul Razaq, Shabaz Razaq, was similarly convicted. Each was sentenced to a total of 15 months' imprisonment. Ajaz Razaq and Abdul Razaq appeal against conviction with leave of the single judge.

62   An unpleasant incident occurred at about 18:00 of December 21, 2003. There was an altercation outside a taxi office run by Perwaz Razaq who was later acquitted of witness intimidation. In the result Tarab Raja sustained a superficial laceration to the left side of his face, some 4cms long, abrasions and bruising to the front upper chest, soft tissue swellings to the head, abrasions to the elbow and knee, and cuts to his fingers.

63   For ease of reference, and to avoid misunderstanding, we shall throughout the rest of this judgment refer to Ajaz Razaq as Ajaz, Abdul Razaq as Abdul, Shabaz Razaq as Shabaz, Perwaz Razaq as Perwaz and Tarab Raja as Tarab.

64   The case for the Crown was that as a result of a telephone call from Shabaz indicating that he could now collect £100 he was owed, Tarab was tricked into going into the taxi office. He was there set upon by Shabaz and Abdul, who were later joined by Ajaz. The two brothers were armed with knives: the father was wielding a metal pole.

65   The defence was that Tarab was the aggressor. He attacked Shabaz, whose father Abdul, and subsequently whose brother Ajaz intervened to protect him. Neither of these appellants behaved aggressively or violently save to the extent necessary to protect Shabaz.

66   The precise details of the evidence need no further narrative. Although it was virtually impossible to discover the issues from the defence case statement by Ajaz, in reality the jury had to decide whether one or both of these appellants was or may have been acting in what throughout the trial was described as "self-defence of another". For resolving that question, the credibility of all the protagonists required close analysis.

67   Two further aspects of the evidence require specific mention. Abdul was a man with previous convictions: so was Shabaz. Ajaz was not. He was a man of good character. The first defendant on the indictment was Abdul: Ajaz came next, then Perwaz, and finally Shabaz. This led, as we shall explain, to some tactical manoeuvrings. In the end, each defendant gave evidence.

68   Tarab, too, had previous convictions. The full information about him was that he was cautioned in April 1997, when he was 15 years old, for assault occasioning actual bodily harm, and cautioned again in September 1998 for theft. We were told that the assault was a very serious incident which resulted in the victim being rendered unconscious in the street. Quite apart from cautions, notwith-

standing "not guilty" pleas, he was convicted in July 2000 of violent disorder, grievous bodily harm with intent, and wounding, and sentenced to a total of 30 months' detention at a young offender institution. These convictions represented two distinct and serious incidents of violence. In addition, in April 2004, he was fined £100 for breach of the peace.

69   This leads to the second general aspect of the evidence, arising in the case of Ajaz. Apart from good character, his evidence-in-chief was exceptionally brief. He simply adopted what he had said in his police interviews. This amounted to a denial of any direct involvement. He had seen a fight between his brother and Tarab. He did not see any metal pole, and he had no weapon himself. He pushed the protagonists apart, and in turn was pushed back onto the floor. Apart from accepting Ajaz's presence at the incident, as we have already noted, the defence case statement said absolutely nothing of value. It stated that the defendant denied assaulting Tarab and denied using or threatening unlawful violence by himself or any other person. As to witnesses, he was not accepting the evidence of any prosecution witness which implicated him "as being responsible for any criminal offence". If one bothers to read further on, the statement asserts that it "does not purport to set out every aspect of the defendant's case in detail". In truth it said virtually nothing which was not fully encompassed in the "not guilty" plea.

70   We can now come to the issues raised in the appeal.

71   After Tarab had given his evidence-in-chief, counsel for Ajaz, not we empha- sise, counsel for Abdul, applied under s.100 of the Criminal Justice Act 2003 to cross-examine Tarab about his previous convictions.

72   When the application was made, the Recorder observed that at that stage there was nothing in the defence case statement to suggest that Ajaz was acting in self defence, or indeed that Tarab had initiated the violence. She was concerned that Tarab's conviction for violent disorder had also involved Shabaz when he, too, had been convicted of violent disorder. Thereafter the argument that Tarab's con- victions should be admitted was taken up by counsel for Shabaz, although at this stage he did not adopt the argument on his behalf.

73   The Recorder rejected the application on the basis that the defendant who was making it failed to establish for the purposes of s.100(1)(b) that Tarab's bad char- acter was of substantial probative value in the case against Ajaz. In reaching her conclusion, she was alert to the contents of Ajaz's interview and the defence case statement. This perhaps distracted her from addressing what was said to be Tar- ab's "propensity for violence", and whether, as was inevitably the case, that his credibility, too, was impugned by conviction after not guilty pleas to three differ- ent offences.

74   After this ruling, an application was then specifically made on behalf of Sha- baz to introduce the full story of Tarab's previous history. The end result was that permission was given to counsel to cross-examine in general terms that the wit- ness was a violent man, basing it on the previous convictions for violence, and, according to the transcript of the ruling, but not apparently followed up at trial, the caution for assault.

75   In the result Tarab was cross-examined by Abdul and Ajaz without reference to his previous convictions, and then by Shabaz about the convictions for violence and the overall circumstances of each offence, including his "not guilty" pleas. Neither Abdul nor Ajaz sought leave to further cross-examine, but it is implicit in the arguments that we have heard that the cross-examination on Shabaz's behalf was adopted and later deployed on their behalf. The long-term consequence was that Shabaz's previous convictions also went before the jury. Abdul's did not.

76   The major complaint made by Abdul and Ajaz was that the judge was wrong to reject Ajaz's application to cross-examine Tarab about his previous convictions. We shall assume for present purposes that her ruling limited the cross-examination to the specific incidents of violence represented by the conviction in July 2002. Complaint was made on behalf of Abdul that the full details of both cautions and the subsequent breach of the peace should also have been admitted. Given Tarab's age at the date of the matters which gave rise to the cautions, and assuming that the facts relating to them might also have been admitted, we can see no reason to interfere with the conclusion that this material lacked the substantial probative value required by and did not properly fall within s.100(1).

77   Abdul has no legitimate complaint. He never made an application nor sought in any way to introduce Tarab's previous convictions into evidence. We understand the tactical considerations which may have inhibited his counsel from doing so at trial, but it can only be in exceptional circumstances that a defendant who is unprepared to make or expressly associate himself with an application for leave to cross-examine a prosecution witness may realistically complain at the judge's decision rejecting an application to the same effect by a co-accused. We can see no reason why a defendant has a justifiable complaint if tactical forensic manoeuvres have failed to produce the hoped for result.

78   Ajaz has a sounder basis for complaint. We have some sympathy for the Recorder who was faced with a sparse and deficient defence case statement, and perhaps insufficient focus in argument on the specific allegations made directly against Ajaz by Tarab. Nevertheless, in our judgment insufficient weight was given to the critical importance of Tarab's direct evidence implicating him. In the result, however, Tarab was cross-examined about his critical convictions, and that material, and the character of the complainant making allegations against Ajaz was before the jury.

79   Apart from some generalised unspecific complaint, Mr Cifonelli did not identify any particular prejudice sustained by Ajaz which was not cured by the successful application on behalf of Shabaz. This ground of appeal therefore fails.

80   The Recorder's directions about the use to be made of Tarab's previous convictions are criticised. She had, of course, to exercise a very careful judgment not to direct the jury about Tarab's convictions in such a way to produce an inappropriately adverse reaction to the fact that Shabaz was himself involved in one of those offences.

81   She directed the jury that this material might help them to understand the other evidence in the case, including "the character of the person who brings these charges and the case as a whole". She suggested that the jury might be helped to resolve the issue whether Tarab was lying, and pointed out that a person of

bad character may be less likely to be telling the truth than someone of good character. Later in the summing up she directed that the previous convictions of
Shabaz could be taken into account when deciding whether or not his evidence
was truthful, linking it to the case of Tarab, pointing out that a person bad character may be less likely to tell the truth. She completed her summing up observing
that the jury had to decide to what extent, if at all, Tarab's "character helps you
when judging his evidence". She also gave a full good character direction in
relation to Ajaz covering credit and propensity.

82   There is force in the complaint that the Recorder did not give any detailed
directions about the potential relevance of Tarab's previous convictions for violence to the issue of propensity, and therefore to their possible bearing on the
critical question whether or not he may have been the aggressor rather than the
victim. It is however difficult to imagine that the jury would have failed to consider and given appropriate weight to those convictions when they considered
which of the protagonists was the aggressor. The Recorder had expressly referred
to the assistance this evidence might give to help understand "the case as a
whole", and whether Tarab was lying "about his actions during the incident".
These directions should have been more direct and specific. It needed no more
than perhaps a single clause encompassing words such as ". . . may be taken
into account by you when considering whether Tarab Raja was the victim or
the aggressor". That said, in our judgment, in the context of this case, the
deficiencies we have identified do not undermine the safety of the convictions.

83   We now come to the final, unconnected complaint, that the judge's direction on
"self-defence of another" was inadequate. Properly understood, the defence of
both Abdul and Ajaz was not self defence at all. Neither was responding to a personal threat against his own safety. Each was reacting to protect Shabaz. No-one
addressed s.3(1) of the Criminal Law Act 1967 or, indeed, the common law principle that an individual is entitled to use such force as is reasonably necessary to
protect someone else from a threat of violence. The appeal in *R. v Duffy* (1966) 50
Cr.App.R. 68; [1967] 1 Q.B. 63 was allowed on the basis that the judge had
wrongly withdrawn a defence of rescue in circumstances permitted by the common law. That did not happen here. A very full and complete self defence
direction was given, and it is plain that everyone at trial treated the self defence
direction as if it applied to the situation in which Abdul and Ajaz claimed to have
found themselves. Indeed the Recorder pointed out in express terms, in her brief
summary of the respective contentions, that Abdul said that he was "acting in
defence of another". She subsequently reminded the jury of his case that
Abdul was not fighting with anybody, "only trying to stop them". She also
reminded the jury of Ajaz's case that he stepped between his brother and
Tarab, and pushed them apart.

84   When the summing up was virtually completed, in the presence of the jury,
counsel on behalf of Abdul suggested that the Recorder had dealt with "self
defence of ones' self" but not with what he described as "self defence of
another". She was firmly convinced that she had done so, and recorded that
the jury was nodding. The Recorder went on to recall that she had said that
"they were saying self defence of another" and indicated that the directions

on self defence applied to self defence of another. She then went on to indicate that her directions about self defence applied to Abdul and Ajaz whose only involvement was to defend Shabaz and separate him and Tarab. It is abundantly clear that the jury will have applied the relevant legal principles to each of their cases.

85   Having concluded that none of the individual complaints, taken on its own, impugns the safety of these convictions, we reconsidered whether the convictions were rendered unsafe by the cumulative effect of the problems we have identified. Having done so, we have concluded that these convictions are safe. Accordingly the appeals are dismissed.

Appeals dismissed.

Editor's note: Joseph Stone did not appear on behalf of the appellant Abdul Razaq at his trial in the Crown Court.

R. (TP) v WEST LONDON YOUTH COURT

Queen's Bench (Divisional Court) (Lord Justice Scott Baker and
Mrs Justice Rafferty):   October 7; November 21, 2005

[2005] EWHC 2583 (Admin); [2006] 1 Cr.App.R. 25

(LT) Abuse of process; Learning disabled persons; Right to effective participation; Standard of proof; Young offenders; Young persons; Youth courts

H1   ABUSE OF PROCESS
       Trial in youth court
       *Claimant having low IQ—Judge determining on balance of probabilities fair
       trial possible—Whether youth or limited intellectual capacity leading to breach
       of Convention right to a fair trial—Proper test to be applied—Whether youth
       court able to adapt procedures to enable proper participation by young defend-
       ant with incapacity—European Convention on Human Rights, Art.6*

H2   The claimant, who was 15 years old, faced charges of robbery and attempted
       robbery. The underlying question for the youth court was whether his intellectual
       capacity, which was that of an eight-year-old, was such that he could not effec-
       tively participate in the proceedings. The judge had before him a report from a
       senior clinical psychologist who stated that the claimant knew that there was a
       solicitor there to help him and that he understood the charge, his plea and possible
       sentences. She did, however, think that it was not clear whether he knew that his
       behaviour was wrong and she had some doubt about his ability to give instruc-
       tions. The judge directed himself that the minimum requirements for a fair
       trial for the purposes of Art.6 of the European Convention on Human Rights
       were: (i) that the claimant had to understand what he was said to have done
       wrong; (ii) that the court had to be satisfied that the claimant, when he had
       done wrong by act or omission, had the means of knowing what was wrong;
       (iii) that he had to understand what, if any, defences were available to him; (iv)
       that he had to have a reasonable opportunity to make relevant representations
       if he wished; and (v) that he had to have the opportunity to consider what repre-
       sentations he wished to make once he had understood the issues involved. Thus
       he had to be able to give proper instructions and to participate by way of provid-
       ing answers to questions and suggesting questions to his lawyers in the
       circumstances of the trial as they arose. The judge took account of the fact that
       the claimant was to be tried in a youth court as opposed to a Crown Court and
       that he would be assisted by specialists and experienced youth court representa-
       tives. He concluded that it would not be an abuse of the process of the youth court
       for the case to proceed to trial. The claimant sought judicial review.

H3   **Held,** dismissing the application, that the question to be asked was whether, taking into account the steps that could be taken in the youth court, the claimant would be able effectively to participate in his trial to ensure that it did not involve a breach of the right to a fair trial in Art.6 of the Convention. A fair trial could be achieved since the youth court was a specialist court designed and adapted for hearing cases where young people were charged with criminal offences. Specialist judges with the requisite training sat in them. Moreover, judges, and the advocates who appeared in those courts, had special expertise and experience in dealing with the kind of problems presented by the claimant and other young persons whose intellectual capacity fell at the lower end of the scale. It was also important that the judge who was hearing the trial had a continuing jurisdiction to stay proceedings for abuse of process. Thus, if it became apparent during the course of the hearing that the claimant was unable effectively to participate, the judge could stay the proceedings at that point. That was a better course than staying a prosecution at the outset. Further, having regard to Strasbourg jurisprudence, the attribution of criminal responsibility to, or the trial on criminal charges of, a very young defendant did not of itself give rise to a breach of Art.6 as long as he was able to participate effectively in the proceedings, which the youth court could achieve by adapting its procedures in an appropriate case. In the present case, the judge had concluded correctly that the procedures in the youth court could be adapted so that the claimant could effectively participate and receive a fair trial (post, paras [8], [18], [25], [27]).

SC v United Kingdom (2004) 40 E.H.R.R. 10 considered.

Application for judicial review

H4   The claimant, TP, sought judicial review of a decision of April 22, 2005 of District Judge Simpson sitting in the West London Youth Court, not to stay proceedings against him for abuse of process. The claimant faced two charges, one of robbery and one of attempted robbery. He applied for judicial review on the ground that his intellectual capacity was such that he could not effectively participate in the proceedings and could not, therefore, have a fair trial, so that the proceedings against him should have been stayed.

H5   The facts appear in the judgment of the court.

H6   *Hugh Southey* (instructed by Lawrence & Co) for the claimant.
Mark Heywood (instructed by the Crown Prosecution Service) for the Crown Prosecution as first interested party.
Martin Chamberlain (instructed by the Treasury Solicitor) for the Secretary of State for the Home Department as second interested party.

Cur. adv. vult.

November 21   Scott Baker L.J.: handed down the judgment of the court.

1   At the conclusion of the hearing on the October 7, 2005 we dismissed this application for judicial review. We now give our reasons. This is the judgment of the court.

2   The claimant, who is a 15 year old, sought judicial review of a decision of April 22, 2005 of Simpson D.J. not to stay proceedings against him in the West London Youth Court for abuse of process. The claimant faced two charges, one of robbery and one of attempted robbery, and the underlying question was whether his intellectual capacity was such that he could not effectively participate in the proceedings. If that were so he could not have a fair trial and the proceedings against him should have been stayed. The judge decided he could effectively participate in the proceedings.

The claimant sought judicial review on three grounds.

(1)   The judge applied the wrong standard of proof. He concluded he was not satisfied the claimant would be unable to participate to the extent required for a fair trial; he should have asked himself whether there was a real possibility that the claimant would not be able to participate effectively.

(2)   The judge erred in finding that the claimant's circumstances were not unusual.

(3)   The judge erred in concluding that the claimant's trial would not violate Art.6 of the European Convention on Human Rights ("the ECHR") despite evidence of his limited intellectual capacity.

3   Following the grant of permission to apply for judicial review the two trial dates (which had been set separately for each offence) were vacated pending the outcome of this court's decision.

4   In a clear and careful judgment the judge recorded that the issues raised on behalf of the claimant were whether the court was entitled to find a 15-year-old with an IQ of an eight year old guilty of a criminal offence; whether he was able to understand the proceedings and charges against him and whether he could participate effectively in a trial in accordance with Art.6 of the ECHR. It was not submitted that he was unfit to plead.

5   The judge had before him a report from Dr Marriott, a senior clinical psychologist of five years' experience, who was working in a secure unit for adolescent offenders. She also gave oral evidence. It is to be noted that Dr Marriott did not have experience of youth courts. She also appears to have been under the mistaken impression that the claimant would be tried by jury. The judge recorded that Dr Marriott found the claimant met the criteria for diagnosis for a mild learning disability, with his IQ placing his intellectual functioning within a range of significant mental impairment. However, insufficient assessment had been undertaken to meet the criteria for a formal diagnosis of mental handicap because of mild learning disability. He was aware a solicitor was there to help him and he was confident he would be able to speak to her alone if he needed help. He demonstrated a sufficient level of understanding in terms of his charge, his plea and possible sentences. He would need extra support from his solicitor to improve his awareness of court proceedings and sentences. His low level of cognitive functioning would need to be taken into account and compensated for during the proceedings. Concise and simple language would need to be used. She said in evidence he had difficulty in understanding the difference between robbery and theft

and it was not clear he knew his behaviour was wrong. She had some doubt about his ability to give instructions. Whilst he would be able to point out things in evidence that he disagreed with, he might struggle to generate questions. He would be limited in his participation in a trial as all his levels were below the age of 10 years. Although he was fairly responsive, it was unusual how irritated he became when questioned.

The judge expressed his conclusion in these terms:

> "On the evidence before me I am not satisfied on the balance of probabilities that TP would, in a youth court as opposed to a Crown Court, assisted by specialist and experienced youth court representatives such as Lawrence & Co., and Ms Lambe in particular, be unable to participate to the extent required for a fair trial in accordance with the decision in *SC v United Kingdom* [2005] 1 F.C.R. 347; (2005) 40 E.H.R.R. 10. Many young defendants are intellectually limited and, as evidenced by the number of trials, many have difficulty in appreciating the ingredients of some offences and particularly robbery and joint enterprise. TP's circumstances are, of course, unfortunate and he presents challenges to the court, the prosecution and his legal representatives. His circumstances are, however, not unusual and he is not a stranger to court proceedings. It would not be an abuse of the process of the youth court for his cases to proceed in due course to trial."

6 It was indeed correct that the claimant was no stranger to court proceedings. He had been reprimanded in 2003 for taking a motor vehicle, given a final warning for theft of a motor vehicle in 2004 and allowing himself to be carried and later in 2004 received a referral order for robbery.

7 The judge had earlier correctly directed himself that the minimum requirements for a fair trial for the claimant were:

   i)   he had to understand what he is said to have done wrong;
   ii) the court had to be satisfied that the claimant when he had done wrong by act or omission had the means of knowing that was wrong;
   iii) he had to understand what, if any, defences were available to him;
   iv) he had to have a reasonable opportunity to make relevant representations if he wished;
   v)   he had to have the opportunity to consider what representations he wished to make once he had understood the issues involved.

He had therefore to be able to give proper instructions and to participate by way of providing answers to questions and suggesting questions to his lawyers in the circumstances of the trial as they arose.

8 It was essential to the judge's decision, as is apparent from the passages of the judgment that we have read, that the appellant would be tried in a Youth Court as apposed to a Crown Court and that he would be assisted by specialists and experienced Youth Court representatives. The Youth Court is a specialised court designed and adapted for hearing cases where youngsters are charged with criminal offences. Specialist judges with the requisite training sit in them. Simpson D.J. is one of those judges. Judges, and the advocates who appear in those courts,

have special expertise and experience in dealing with the kind of problems presented by the claimant and other youngsters whose intellectual capacity falls at the lower end of the scale. The Youth Court is the specialist tribunal for criminal cases involving child defendants in England and Wales. The Crown Court, where the more serious cases are tried, has designated court centres and special rules for trying child defendants. But it has never been suggested this case should be tried in the Crown Court.

9   Ever since the European Court of Human Rights decided *V v United Kingdom* (2000) 30 E.H.R.R. 121 (relating to the trial of the boys who murdered Jamie Bulger) there has been an increasing awareness of the need to ensure that young people can effectively participate in the determination of criminal charges against them. V, and his co-defendant T, were of course tried in the Crown Court. The European Court concluded that they were denied a fair hearing and accordingly there was a breach of Art.6(1). The court however observed that in England and Wales children charged with less serious crimes are dealt with in special youth courts from where the public are excluded and there are automatic reporting restrictions on the media. It is to be noted that there was no application in *V* to stay the proceedings as an abuse of process; the European Court was looking at the fairness of the proceedings after the event. In the present case the trial has yet to take place.

10   *SC v United Kingdom* (2004) 40 E.H.R.R. 10 was another case where the European Court of Human Rights had to look back at the fairness of the trial. It held by a majority of 5 to 2 that there had been a breach of Art.6(1) of the ECHR. The applicant, aged 11, and another boy aged 14, approached an 87-year-old woman in the street and tried to take her bag. She fell down and fractured her arm. The applicant's defence to attempted robbery was that he had acted under duress from the other boy. The Youth Court, bearing in mind his significant offending history, committed him for trial to the Crown Court. He was convicted and appealed to the Court of Appeal, contending he had been deprived of a fair trial in the light of his age and impaired intellectual capacity. His appeal was rejected.

11   The European Court observed first that the attribution of criminal responsibility to, or the trial on criminal charges of, an 11-year-old boy did not of itself give rise to a breach of the Convention as long as he was able to participate effectively in the trial. The right to effective participation includes not only the right to be present but also to hear and follow the proceedings. In the case of a child, it is essential that he will be dealt with in a manner which takes full account of his age, level of maturity and intellectual and emotional capacities, and that steps are taken to promote his ability to understand and participate in the proceedings, including conducting the hearing in such a way as to reduce as far as possible his feeling of intimidation and inhibition.

The court went on:

> "29. The Court accepts the Government's argument that Art.6 § 1 does not require that a child on trial for a criminal offence should understand or be capable of understanding every point of law or evidential detail. Given

the sophistication of modern legal systems, many adults of normal intelligence are unable fully to comprehend all the intricacies and exchanges which take place in the courtroom: this is why the Convention, in Art.6 § 3(c), emphasises the importance of the right to legal representation. However, 'effective participation' in this context presupposes that the accused has a broad understanding of the nature of the trial process and of what is at stake for him or her, including the significance of any penalty which may be imposed. It means that he or she, if necessary with the assistance of, for example, an interpreter, lawyer, social worker or friend, should be able to understand the general thrust of what is said in court. The defendant should be able to follow what is said by the prosecution witnesses and, if represented, to explain to his own lawyers his version of events, point out any statements with which he disagrees and make them aware of any facts which should be put forward in his defence (see, for example, the above-mentioned *Stanford* judgment, §30)."

It said it was unable to conclude the applicant was capable of participating effectively in his trial in this sense. The court concluded with these words:

"As noted above, Dr Brennan found that, 'on balance', the applicant probably did have sufficient intelligence to understand that what he had done was wrong, and that he was therefore fit to plead. The Court is not, however, convinced in the circumstances of the present case, that it follows that the applicant was capable of participating effectively in his trial to the extent required by Art.6§1."

12   Mr Hugh Southey, who appeared for the claimant, submitted that the judge applied the wrong standard of proof when considering the application for a stay of the proceedings. He argued that the true test is not whether the claimant has established on the balance of probabilities that he will not be able to participate effectively in the trial, but whether there is a real possibility he will be unable to do so.

13   The first difficulty with this submission, and in our view it is a fundamental one, is that the standard Mr Southey seeks to impose is different from the standard ordinarily imposed by domestic law in abuse of process applications. Mr Southey accepts that, if he is right, there is this distinction but he justifies it by saying that Art.6 is an absolute right and domestic law is insufficient to protect against Art.6 violations.

14   In *R. (Ebrahim) v Feltham Magistrates Court* [2001] 2 Cr.App.R. 23 (p.427), 433 Brooke L.J. observed that the jurisdiction of a court to stay criminal proceedings for abuse of process is "of great constitutional importance and should be . . . preserved:" per Lord Salmon in *Director of Public Prosecutions v Humphrys* (1976) 63 Cr.App.R. 95, p.122; [1977] A.C. 1, 46. But he went on to point out that in most cases any alleged unfairness could be covered in the trial process itself. Staying criminal proceedings for an abuse of process is a power that ought only to be employed in exceptional circumstances, whatever the reasons submitted for invoking it. See *Attorney General's Reference (No.1 of 1990)*

(1992) 95 Cr.App.R. 296, 303; [1992] Q.B. 630, 643G. Apart from cases where the court is seeking to protect its own process from abuse there are, broadly, two categories of case (i) cases where the court concludes that the defendant cannot receive a fair trial, and (ii) cases where it concludes that it would be unfair for the defendant to be tried, see Neill L.J. in *R. v Beckford* [1996] 1 Cr.App.R. 94, 101. Within these categories, which may overlap, abuse of process can come in different forms but in every case, so far as we are aware, abuse has to be established on balance of probabilities. It would be odd in the extreme if one species of abuse, namely that contended for by Mr Southey in the present case, requires proof of a lesser standard.

15   There are other circumstances in the criminal law where a defendant has a burden of proof on balance of probabilities. One example is unfitness to plead and s.4 of the Criminal Procedure (Insanity) Act 1964. As Rose L.J. pointed out in *R. v M, R. v Kerr, R. v H* [2001] EWCA 2024; [2002] 1 Cr.App.R. 25 (p.283); [2002] 1 W.L.R. 824, an application for a stay for abuse of process would be inappropriate on the ground of unfitness to plead alone. If Mr Southey's argument is correct there would be one standard for unfitness to plead and a lesser one for inability effectively to participate in the trial. That, in our view, simply cannot be right.

16   Article 6(1) of the ECHR provides:

> "In the determination of his civil rights and obligations or of any criminal charge against him, everyone is entitled to a fair and public hearing within a reasonable time by an independent and impartial tribunal established by law. Judgment shall be pronounced publicly but the press and public may be excluded from all or part of the trial in the interests of morals, public order or national security in a democratic society, where the interests of juveniles or the protection of the private life of the parties so require, or to the extent strictly necessary in the opinion of the court in special circumstances where publicity would prejudice the interests of justice."

17   Mr Southey's submission is that there is a real possibility in the present case that the claimant will not be able to participate effectively in the trial and that this violates his right to a fair hearing. It seems to me that the concept of a "real possibility" has to be seen in contradistinction to a "fanciful possibility". Be that as it may, Mr Southey's contention opens the door to the prospect that some cases will not proceed to trial because there is a chance that the defendant will not be able effectively to participate albeit he is more likely than not to be able to do so. It is submitted that the Art.6 right to a fair trial is such an important right that it justifies the non-trial of some defendants who could probably, albeit not surely, have a fair trial.

18   Mr Heywood, who has appeared for the Crown Prosecution Service, points out that there is a fundamental public interest in cases and defendants being tried. The Crown Prosecution Service decide, according to well known criteria, which cases should proceed and it is only in exceptional circumstances that the court should descend into the arena and prevent a case from being heard. The first port of call is not to prevent the court from hearing the case but to grapple with the difficulties. A trial should not be abandoned before all practical steps to overcome the diffi-

culties have been exhausted. It is also, we think, an important point that the judge who is hearing the trial has a continuing jurisdiction to stay proceedings for abuse of process. Thus, if it becomes apparent during the course of the hearing that the claimant is unable effectively to participate, the judge can stay the proceedings at that point. This is surely a better course than staying a prosecution at the outset when events would have shown it could fairly have proceeded.

19   Mr Southey submitted that support for his case was to be found in *R. v Secretary of State for the Home Department Ex p. Quinn* [2000] U.K.H.R.R. 386. In that case the applicant was to be held in a prison for the duration of his criminal trial. His defence required him to name a prison officer who was said to have assisted him in a previous escape from the prison. He argued he was at risk of serious harm and so he should be moved to another prison. If he remained in the prison where he was his right to a fair trial would be denied. Richards J., as he then was, said the correct approach was for the court to ask itself whether there was a real danger that the applicant might not be able to put his defence fully and freely. The court had to form its own judgment as to whether the right to a fair trial would be infringed. It had to ascertain the relevant circumstances from the available evidence and determine on the basis of that evidence whether there was a real danger of an infringement of the right to a fair trial. Remote or fanciful risks could sensibly be discounted. On the facts of the case Richards J held that there was no real danger and the application for judicial review of the refusal of the Secretary of State to relocate the applicant failed.

20   Richards J. explained that the case was in many ways an exceptional one and that in the particular circumstances judicial review was a more appropriate route than leaving the matter to be dealt with by the trial judge on an application to stay for abuse of process. One can, with respect, see the obvious good sense in this bearing in mind the decision challenged was, as Richards J said, entirely outwith the trial process. For present purposes the important distinction between *Q* and the present case is that *Q* was not an abuse of process application. We cannot see therefore that the test Richards J. applied in that case has any relevance to the test that should be applied in the present case. He was applying a pragmatic solution to a specific situation. The decision sought to be reviewed could not be revisited during the trial.

21   Apart from *Q*, the "real possibility" test, advocated by Mr Southey, is not to be found in any of the abuse of process cases to which we have been referred. It comes from *Porter v Magill* [2001] UKHL 67; [2002] 2 A.C. 357; [2002] 2 W.L.R. 37, and the cases concerned with apparent bias on the part of a tribunal. Apparent bias on the part of a tribunal is very different from effective participation in the proceedings. A finding of apparent bias does not result in a stay of proceedings; it is not a bar to the issues between the parties being tried, it effects the composition of the tribunal before which those proceedings can be tried.

22   To get his argument on its feet, Mr Southey relies on the concluding passage of the judgment of the European Court in *SC* that we have cited. In particular he refers to the court not being "convinced" that the applicant was capable of participating effectively in his trial to the extent required by Art.6(1). One must,

however, take the passage as a whole. The previous sentence refers to Dr Brennan's finding that "on balance" the applicant probably had sufficient intelligence to understand what he had done was wrong and that he was, therefore, fit to plead. The court then went on to say that: "it is not, however, convinced in all the circumstances of the present case that it follows the applicant was capable of participating in his trial etc". In our view the court was doing no more than saying that it was not convinced of the propriety of drawing an inference as to the ability of the applicant to participate effectively from the fact that he understood that what he had done was wrong.

23   In our judgment Mr Southey is reading too much into the use of the word "convinced". Had the court been intending to lay down any principle about the standard of proof of "effective participation" it is likely that it would have done so in clear and explicit terms. The use of the phrase "not . . . convinced" indicates nothing whatever about the standard of proof or type of evidence required by a judge when considering whether a trial will breach Art.6. There are other contexts in which the European Courts of Human Rights has laid down tests as to the type of evidence required in particular circumstances: see, for example, *Herczegfalvy v Austria* (1993) 15 E.H.R.R. 437, para.[82] (the medical necessity required for compulsory medical treatment of a mental patient must be "convincingly shown to exist"), and *Sunday Times v United Kingdom (No.2)* (1991) 14 E.H.R.R. 229, para.[50] (the need for restrictions on freedom of speech under Art.10(2) must be "convincingly established"). Nothing similar, however, is said in *SC*. Furthermore, as Mr Martin Chamberlain, for the Secretary of State, pointed out, even where such language is used by the court the word "convincingly" refers to the nature and quality of the evidence required to make good the case rather than the standard of proof. See also Munby J. in *R. (DJ) v Mental Health Review Tribunal* [2005] EWHC 587 (Admin) paras [66]–[68].

24   Mr Chamberlain makes the further point that the present claim for judicial review is made before the claimant's trial had taken place. Ordinarily, the fairness of a trial is judged in retrospect, taking into account the trial process as a whole; see *R. (S) v Waltham Forest Youth Court* [2004] EWHC 715; [2004] 2 Cr.App.R. 21 (p.335). In the present case, unusually, permission to apply for judicial review has been granted in advance of the trial. In our judgment it would require the most compelling reasons to set aside the decision of a district judge with special expertise and training in this field. If Mr Southey's argument is correct, the result would be to stay proceedings on the basis of a possibility that the trial would be unfair when, after the event it could well be shown not to have been.

25   The fundamental distinction between *SC* and the present case is that *SC* was tried in the Crown Court; the claimant will be tried in the Youth Court. The question in our view is this. Taking into account the steps that can be taken in the youth court will the claimant be able effectively to participate in his trial? Dr Marriott did not go so far as to say that effective participation would not be possible.

26   It is apparent from the judge's judgment and Dr Marriott's evidence that there are indeed a number of steps that can be taken during the trial. These include:

   i) keeping the claimant's level of cognitive functioning in mind;

   ii) using concise and simple language;

  iii) having regular breaks;

  iv) taking additional time to explain court proceedings;

   v) being proactive in ensuring the claimant has access to support;

  vi) explaining and ensuring the claimant understands the ingredients of the charge;

 vii) explaining the possible outcomes and sentences;

viii) ensuring that cross-examination is carefully controlled so that questions are short and clear and frustration is minimised.

27   In our judgment neither youth nor limited intellectual capacity necessarily leads to a breach of Art.6. It seems to us that a critical conclusion of the court in *SC* is to be found in para.[35] of that decision:

> ". . . when the decision is taken to deal with a child, such as the applicant, who risks not being able to participate effectively because of his young age and limited intellectual capacity, by way of criminal proceedings rather than some other form of disposal directed primarily at determining the child's best interests and those of the community, it is essential that he be tried in a specialist tribunal which is able to give full consideration to and make proper allowance for the handicaps under which he labours, and adapts its procedure accordingly."

That did not happen in *SC*. But the present case is different. The specialist tribunal is the youth court. That is where the claimant will be tried. The judge concluded that, given the steps we have outlined, the claimant could effectively participate in his trial to the extent required by Art.6. He reached this conclusion having applied the right test when he said:

> "I am not satisfied on the balance of probabilities that (the claimant) would in a Youth Court . . . assisted by specialist and experienced . . . representatives . . . be unable to participate to the extent required for a fair trial . . ."

28   Mr Southey's second and third grounds were advanced as very much subsidiary matters. He did not seek to add to his skeleton argument. On the second ground complaint is made of the judge's statement in his conclusion that the claimant's circumstances are not unusual. It is submitted that this is a finding of fact with no evidence to support it; the unchallenged evidence of the claimant's psychologist was that the claimant had an exceptionally low verbal IQ that put him within the bottom 0.3 per cent of the population. Mr Chamberlain seeks to put this point in perspective by reminding us that the claimant has an IQ of 63 and that 23 per cent of young offenders have an IQ of 69 or below and that an additional 36 per cent have borderline learning difficulties—IQ's in the range 70–79 (see Child and Adolescent Mental Health Services Interdepartmental Project Board Report, June 15, 2005, para.8). In our judgment, however, the judge was doing no more than saying that the claimant's circumstances were not markedly different from many young defendants who passed through the youth court.

His incapacity was not beyond the experience of the youth court at West London and, as the judge went on to say in the very same sentence, the claimant was no stranger to court proceedings. We can see no substance in this ground.

29   The third ground contends the judge was wrong to conclude there was no violation of Art.6 in the light of the claimant's limited intellectual capacity. This ground really adds nothing to the first and main ground. The decision in *SC* shows that the trial of a defendant with a mental age of eight does not necessarily involve a breach of Article 6. What is crucial is whether the tribunal hearing the case—in this case the Youth Court—is able to adapt its procedures so that the defendant can effectively participate in the proceedings. The judge concluded that it could.

30   We found that none of the grounds for judicial review was made out and accordingly the claim failed.

Application dismissed.

February 2, 2006. The Queen's Bench Divisional Court certified, pursuant to s.1 of the Administration of Justice Act 1960, that a point of law of general public importance was involved it its decision, namely: "Is it compatible with Art.6 of the European Convention on Human Rights for a defendant to be required to prove, on a balance of probabilities, that he is unable effectively to participate in his trial?"

Leave to appeal to House of Lords refused.

R. v XHABRI

Court of Appeal (Lord Chief Justice (Lord Phillips of Worth Matravers), Mrs Justice Rafferty and Mr Justice Mackay): November 2; December 7, 2005

[2005] EWCA Crim 3135; [2006] 1 Cr.App.R. 26

Ⓛ Admissibility; Cross examination; Hearsay evidence; Witnesses

H1 EVIDENCE

Hearsay

Previous statement of complainant—Appellant allegedly kidnapping, raping and forcing complainant to work as prostitute—Complainant directly or indirectly communicating with third parties during alleged ordeal—Whether third parties able to give evidence as to communications—Whether statutory provisions allowing hearsay evidence infringing right to fair trial—Human Rights Act 1998 (c.42), Sch.1, Pt I, Art.6(3)(d)—Criminal Justice Act 2003 (c.44), ss.114, 120, 121, 126

H2   The complainant, a 17-year-old girl from Latvia, arrived in London in July 2004. In September 2004 she moved into a house where the appellant lived. From the outset, she shared a bedroom with the appellant and on frequent occasions they had sexual intercourse. She started working as a prostitute in brothels described as saunas and either the appellant or an associate of his would drive her to and collect her from work. On one occasion, she left the sauna where she was working and went to York, where she stayed with a friend for five days but she then returned to London and continued working in saunas. In November 2004 the complainant and the appellant moved to another house which, shortly thereafter, was raided by the police. The complainant was found in her bedroom, where she had been locked in by the appellant. The complainant said that she had acted as she did as a result of duress, that the appellant had raped her repeatedly and had forced her to work as a prostitute by threats of physical violence. She said that she had escaped to York but that the appellant had found her and forced her to return to London. The appellant was charged with false imprisonment, rape, threats to kill and control of prostitution for gain. He denied the allegations, claiming that he had had a consensual sexual relationship with the complainant, that she had moved in with him at her instigation and that she was acting as a prostitute by choice and not through any force or influence exerted by him.

H3   At trial, the prosecution proposed to adduce evidence of communications made by the complainant, during her alleged ordeal, to her mother, her father and a friend, to the effect that she was being held against her will by the appellant. The prosecution also wished to adduce evidence from a police officer that, during the relevant time, two people had visited the police station and provided an address where they said that the complainant had told them she was being held against her will. The defence did not seek to prevent the complainant giving evidence of the communications that she had made but they objected to the recipients of those communications giving evidence of what they had been told. The judge ruled that the evidence of the father, mother and friend fell within s.120 of the Criminal Justice Act 2003, which allowed the previous statements of a witness to be admitted to rebut a suggestion that the witness's oral evidence had been fabricated, or that, alternatively, the evidence was admissible in the interests of justice under s.114(d). The judge further ruled that the evidence of the police officer was admissible as multiple hearsay under s.121. The appellant was convicted. He appealed.

H4   **Held,** dismissing the appeal,

(1) that in relation to the evidence of the complainant's father, mother and friend as to the statements made by the complainant during the time when she alleged she was effectively imprisoned by the appellant, the requirements of s.120(7) of the 2003 Act were, or were likely to be, satisfied. The complainant claimed to be a person against whom an offence had been committed, the offence was one to which the proceedings related, the complaint was about conduct which would, if proved, constitute part of the offence, the complaint was made as soon as could reasonably be expected after the alleged conduct (or, in fact, while the alleged conduct was continuing), the complaint was not made as a result of a threat or promise and the complainant was expected to give evidence before the material evidence relating to her previous statements was adduced. Alternatively, the evidence plainly fell within the judge's discretion under s.114(d) and there was no basis upon which it could be suggested that its admission was not in the interests of justice. If the defence case was that the complainant never made the alleged statements then there was every reason why the jury should hear evidence from those to whom the complainant made the statements. Alternatively, if the defence case was that, when making the statements, the complainant was lying, the introduction of the evidence could not unfairly prejudice the appellant. In relation to the police officer's evidence, which was double hearsay, s.121(1)(a) was satisfied since the earlier hearsay statement, the complainant's statement to the two people who visited the police station, was admissible under s.120. Section 121(1)(c) was also satisfied since the evidence was very damaging to the appellant and its value was so high that the interests of justice required it to be admitted. The fact that the two people who had conveyed the information to the police officer were not available for cross-examination was not unfair. Defence counsel would have been in some difficulty in finding any question that it was safe to put to them. Furthermore, all that they were doing was relaying information provided by the complainant, who was available for cross-examination.

Accordingly, the judge was right to rule that all the evidence was admissible (post, paras [35]–[36], [39]–[41], [45]).

(2) There was no question of s.114 being incompatible with Art.6 of the European Convention on Human Rights. The discretion to admit hearsay evidence under s.114 of the 2003 Act was not restricted to situations where the maker of the statement was not available for cross-examination. To the extent that the right to a fair trial under Art.6 would be infringed by admitting such evidence, the court had a power to exclude the evidence under s.126 of the 2003 Act and a duty so to do by virtue of the Human Rights Act 1998. Article 6(3)(d), under which a defendant had the right to examine witnesses against him, was designed to secure "equality of arms". The hearsay provisions of the 2003 Act applied equally to prosecution and defence, so there was no inherent inequality of arms arising out of those provisions. Article 6(3)(d) did not give a defendant an absolute right to examine every witness whose testimony was adduced against him. The touchstone was whether fairness of the trial required that. Almost all the hearsay evidence adduced by the prosecution against the appellant derived directly, or indirectly, from the complainant and she was available for examination. That satisfied the requirements of Art.6(3)(d) (post, paras [42]–[45]).

H5　　　(For s.114 of the Criminal Justice Act 2003, see *Archbold* 2006, para.11-3. For s.120, see para.11-34, for s.121, see para.11–41 and for s.126, see para.11–46).

Appeal against conviction

H6　　　On May 24, 2005 in the Crown Court at Snaresbrook (Judge Reynolds Q.C.) the appellant, Agrol Xhabri, was convicted of false imprisonment (count 1), rape (counts 2 and 3), threats to kill (count 4), and control of prostitution for gain (count 5). He was sentenced to concurrent terms of 12 years' imprisonments on each of counts 1, 2 and 3 and five years' imprisonment each of counts 4 and 5.

H7　　　At the hearing of the appeal on November 2, the following additional cases were cited or referred to in the skeleton arguments: *Asch v Austria* (1991) 15 E.H.R.R. 597; *Kostovski v The Netherlands* (1989) 12 E.H.R.R. 434; *R. v A (No.2)* [2001] UKHL 25; [2001] 2 Cr.App.R. 21 (p.351); [2002] 1 A.C. 45, HL.

H8　　　The facts and grounds of appeal appear in the judgment of the court.

H9　　　*Roger Offenbach* (instructed by Sternberg Reed Taylor & Gill, Barking) for the appellant.
John Livingston (instructed by the Crown Prosecution Service, Snaresbrook) for the Crown.

Cur. adv. vult.

December 7   Lord Phillips of Worth Watravers, C.J.: handed down the judgment of the court.

1   On May 24, 2005 in the Crown Court at Snaresbrook, after a 12 day trial, the appellant was convicted of the following offences: count 1: false imprisonment; counts 2 and 3: rape; count 4: threats to kill; count 5: control of prostitution for gain. On the first count he was sentenced to 12 years' imprisonment. On the second and third counts he was sentenced to 12 years' imprisonment concurrent. On each of the fourth and fifth counts he was sentenced to five years' imprisonment concurrent. His application for permission to appeal against conviction was referred to a full court by the Registrar. This case raises questions as to the application of the novel provisions in relation to hearsay introduced by the Criminal Justice Act 2003. For this reason, we gave permission to appeal at the beginning of the hearing.

The facts

2   The complainant in this case is a young woman from Latvia. At the time to which this appeal relates she was 17 years old. There was little dispute as to what she did in the period covered by the charges. What was critically in issue was why she acted as she did.

3   In May 2004 Mr L, L's father, came to live in England. He found a flat in Newham, East London. On July 25, 2004, L came to England to live with him. Mrs L, L's mother, remained in Latvia. L met and made friends with a young Lithuanian woman called E. E lived at a house in Walton Road, Ilford. Early in September L moved out of her father's flat and went to live in this house. The appellant lived in the same house. From the outset L shared a bedroom with him. On the second day that she was there L and the appellant had sexual intercourse. Thereafter they had sexual intercourse on frequent occasions.

4   While living at Walton Road, L worked as a prostitute in brothels described as saunas. Either the appellant or an associate of his would drive her to and collect her from the sauna.

5   On one occasion L left the sauna where she had been working at King's Cross and took a train to York where she stayed with a Latvian friend for five days. She then returned to Ilford and continued working in saunas as before.

6   Early in November the appellant and L moved from Walton Road, Ilford to Strone Road, Forest Gate.

7   On the night of November 11/12, L was working in the sauna at King's Cross. The appellant collected her by car in the morning and took her back to Strone Road. There they had sexual intercourse. He then left, locking her in the bedroom. The house was then raided by the police who broke down her bedroom door and took her away with them.

8   We now come to contentious areas of facts. Our summary of these is taken from the witness statements, for this was the material before the judge when he made the rulings which are the subject of this appeal. We do not believe that they differ significantly from the evidence subsequently given at the trial.

Duress or consent?

9   It was L's evidence that she acted in the manner we have described as a result of duress. The appellant is an Albanian. There were other Albanians living in the house at Walton Road. On the second night that she was there the appellant raped her. Equally when she and the appellant had sexual intercourse on subsequent occasions, this was because the appellant forced her to submit to him against her will. The appellant forced her to work as a prostitute by threats of physical violence against her and her father. Initially she was too frightened to run away. Another Latvian girl called A was brought to the house at Walton Road and also made to work in the saunas and went to York. She made contact with L and arranged for L to run away to York to join her, which she did, having escaped from the sauna at King's Cross. There was a foreigner called I living in the same house in York as A. He knew the appellant and must have informed the appellant of L's whereabouts, for after five days the appellant appeared in a car and took L, by force, back to London. Thereafter she was forced to continue working in the saunas as before.

10   The appellant made a defence case statement in which he denied that he had detained L against her will, raped her and forced her to act as a prostitute. It was his case that they began a consensual sexual relationship and that she then moved in with him at her instigation due to problems she was experiencing with her father. He knew that she was acting as a prostitute for some, if not all, of the time he knew her but that occupation was of her own choosing and not through any force or influence exerted by him.

The evidence under challenge

11   On May 4, 2005, before the trial began, the defence sought to exclude some of the evidence that the prosecution proposed to put before the jury. We shall refer to that evidence in a little more detail in due course. Suffice it to say that, for the most part, it related to communications alleged to have been made by L, directly or indirectly, with her mother, her father, O, a friend who lived in the same building as her father, and the police. The defence did not seek to prevent L giving evidence of communications that she had made. They objected, however, to the recipients of those communications giving evidence of what they had been told. The prosecution submitted that this evidence was admissible under provisions of the 2003 Act. We shall now set out the relevant provisions.

Hearsay provisions of the Criminal Justice Act 2003

12   Section 118 abolishes the common law rules governing the admissibility of hearsay evidence in criminal proceedings, subject to certain exceptions which are not relevant in this case. Section 114 provides:

"Admissibility of hearsay evidence

(1) In criminal proceedings a statement not made in oral evidence in the proceedings is admissible as evidence of any matter stated if, but only if—

(d) . . . the court is satisfied that it is in the interests of justice for it to be admissible.

(2) In deciding whether a statement not made in oral evidence should be admitted under subsection (1)(d), the court must have regard to the following factors (and to any others it considers relevant):

(a) how much probative value the statement has (assuming it to be true) in relation to a matter in issue in the proceedings, or how valuable it is for the understanding of other evidence in the case;

(b) what other evidence has been, or can be, given on the matter or evidence mentioned in paragraph (a);

(c) how important the matter or evidence mentioned in paragraph (a) is in the context of the case as a whole;

(d) the circumstances in which the statement was made;

(e) how reliable the maker of the statement appears to be;

(f) how reliable the evidence of the making of the statement appears to be;

(g) whether oral evidence of the matter stated can be given and, if not, why it cannot;

(h) the amount of difficulty involved in challenging the statement;

(i) the extent to which that difficulty would be likely to prejudice the party facing it."

13   Section 120 provides:

"Other previous statements of witnesses

(1) This section applies where a person (the witness) is called to give evidence in criminal proceedings.

(2) If a previous statement by the witness is admitted as evidence to rebut a suggestion that his oral evidence has been fabricated, that statement is admissible as evidence of any matter stated of which oral evidence by the witness would be admissible.

. . .

(4) A previous statement by the witness is admissible as evidence of any matter stated of which oral evidence by him would be admissible, if—

(a) any of the following three conditions is satisfied, and

(b) while giving evidence the witness indicates that to the best of his belief he made the statement, and that to the best of his belief it states the truth.

(5) The first condition is that the statement identifies or describes a person, object or place.

(6) The second condition is that the statement was made by the witness when the matters stated were fresh in his memory but he does not

remember them, and cannot reasonably be expected to remember them, well enough to give oral evidence of them in the proceedings.
(7) The third condition is that—
(a) the witness claims to be a person against whom an offence has been committed,
(b) the offence is one to which the proceedings relate,
(c) the statement consists of a complaint made by the witness (whether to a person in authority or not) about conduct which would, if proved, constitute the offence or part of the offence,
(d) the complaint was made as soon as could reasonably be expected after the alleged conduct,
(e) the complaint was not made as a result of a threat or a promise, and
(f) before the statement is adduced the witness gives oral evidence in connection with its subject matter."

14   Section 121 provides:

"Additional requirement for admissibility of multiple hearsay
(1) A hearsay statement is not admissible to prove the fact that an earlier hearsay statement was made unless—
(a) either of the statements is admissible under ss.117, 119 or 120,
(b) all parties to the proceedings so agree, or
(c) the court is satisfied that the value of the evidence in question, taking into account how reliable the statements appear to be, is so high that the interests of justice require the later statement to be admissible for that purpose.
(2) In this section 'hearsay statement' means a statement, not made in oral evidence, that is relied on as evidence of a matter stated in it."

15   Section 126 provides:

"Court's general discretion to exclude evidence
(1) In criminal proceedings the court may refuse to admit a statement as evidence of a matter stated if—
(a) the statement was made otherwise than in oral evidence in the proceedings, and
(b) the court is satisfied that the case for excluding the statement, taking account of the danger that to admit it would result in undue waste of time, substantially outweighs the case for admitting it, taking account of the value of the evidence.
(2) Nothing in this Chapter prejudices—
(a) any power of a court to exclude evidence under s.78 of the Police and Criminal Evidence Act 1984 (c.60)(exclusion of unfair evidence), or
(b) any other power of a court to exclude evidence at its discretion (whether by preventing questions from being put or otherwise)."

L's evidence

16   L stated that initially the appellant dictated a reassuring letter for her to send to her father. She did not have access to a telephone but the appellant twice made her telephone her mother on his mobile phone in order to reassure her, stating that she was working as a cleaner.

17   After she had been working as a prostitute for about three weeks the appellant told her to go and see her father, tell him that she was all right and working in a restaurant and give him £400, which he handed to her. She was driven to her father's home by three associates of the appellant. She was told that if she did not come out after 15 minutes there would be trouble. The door was answered by O. She gave O a bag containing the money. She told O that she was being held by men who would not let her go; that she was scared and that they were watching for her outside. They were Albanians. She did not want to tell her father what was happening because she was frightened as to what might happen to all of them.

18   On a few occasions when working in the sauna at King's Cross she managed to borrow a mobile phone and telephone her mother.

19   She told the security guard, Max, at the King's Cross sauna about her circumstances. He said that he would go to the police and tell them what was happening. She gave him her father's name and address and the address at which she was being held in Walton Road. He told her that he had gone to the police with the sauna's receptionist, a short haired black woman.

20   Between 3am and 4am of November 12, L persuaded a Ukrainian woman who worked at the King's Cross sauna to lend her her mobile. She telephoned her mother and gave her mother the number of this mobile telephone. Her mother said that she would pass this on to her father and that he would phone her. She had been unaware that her father had a mobile telephone. Her father then telephoned her. She gave her father the address in Strone Road where she was living and told her father that she would be at that address between 11am and 4pm on that day. Her father told her not to worry: they were going to release her.

The evidence to which objection was made

Mrs L's evidence

21   Mrs L stated that initially L telephoned her and explained that she had moved out from her father's flat because she wanted to live independently and she was earning well, working in a private hotel. After that there was a long silence. On October 18, 2004 L phoned saying that she was in a lot of trouble, that she had been kidnapped by some Albanians, could not do anything without the help of the police and was being watched and guarded. After this she phoned a few more times. On October 20, her daughter dictated an address which she wrote down: "King kross" "Caledonian Road No1".

22   Towards the evening of November 2, 2004 L phoned again and dictated an address, which she wrote down as "IOFORT 'next to father'" "VV" "Alton Road 173" "7984590605". She said that the telephone connection was unstable

and she could only hear half of what was said. In a subsequent conversation she told L that she had phoned L's father who had gone to the police but the police could not find the address that had been given.

23   On November 11, 2004 during the night L phoned and gave her the number of a mobile phone which L had begged the guard to lend her. She immediately telephoned her husband's mobile phone and gave him that number. The next day, her husband phoned her and informed her that L was with him and everything was fine.

Mr L's evidence

24   Mr L said that between October 4 and 7, his neighbour called O, who rented the room opposite his, brought him a note from L saying that she was working a lot and studying and was passing on money for her mother. The note was accompanied by £400.

25   On October 13, two young men came to his flat. They said that L had disappeared; that L lived with them and that on October 12, she had gone to work but had not come home. They said they were Albanians and asked him where L worked. He said that he did not know. On October 17, the two men came again. They asked if L had come back and he said no.

26   On October 19/20, his wife telephoned him and said L had phoned her saying that armed people were guarding her. If they found she was talking on the telephone they would kill her. They were Albanians. The name of the street was 1 Caledonian Road, King's Cross. He must not contact the police because everything was very dangerous. Despite this he went to the police station at Romford Road on October 23, to report what he had been told. After that he spoke to his wife many times. She said that they had kidnapped L, would not let her sleep or get dressed and they were always threatening that they would kill her. His wife spoke of a subsequent phone call when L said that she was being kept by a gang of Albanians at 173 Alton Road, Ilford. At 05:00 on the morning of November 12, his wife called him and said that L had managed to pass on another address in Strone Road which she gave him. She also gave him a mobile number for L. He telephoned L on this number and she said that from 11am to 4pm she would be at the address in Strone Road. She was very scared and said that the Albanians were very cunning and if they saw people in police uniforms at this address they would kill her straightaway. He passed this information on to the police.

O's Evidence

27   O stated on October 2 or 3, L came to their house. Her father was asleep. L told her that she was living with several Albanians in the house who would not let her go anywhere and accompanied her everywhere. One of them got her job in a massaging salon. They controlled all her telephone calls, beat her and always threatened her that if she didn't listen to them they would kill her father. She stayed with them because she was scared for her father and her own life. She handed over a bag for her father.

The police evidence

28   PC Brandon was based at Islington Police Station. He stated that on October 22, a man and woman came in. The woman was black and the man was eastern European. They said they had information about the sex trafficking trade. In particular they gave L's name and an address in Walton Road. They said that she was kept in a house and prevented from leaving. They said that she was in fear of her life and had made attempts to leave and that she did not want to involve the police because she feared for her life. They gave the address of two saunas where she worked and the address where her father lived.

The judge's juling

29   The prosecution sought to adduce the evidence of Mr and Mrs L and O pursuant to ss.114 and 120 of the 2003 Act. They sought to adduce the evidence of PC Brandon under s.121. The Defence objected that was unfair to admit this evidence, relying on the provisions of s.126.

30   The judge ruled that the evidence of the first three witnesses came "four square within s.120 and that each of the conditions in subs.(5), (6) and (7) clearly applied to it". Alternatively the evidence was admissible under s.114. It was highly probative. It was supported by the evidence of L herself. It was extremely important. The statements containing the hearsay evidence had been made in the normal way to police officers and, in the case of Mrs L, in accordance with normal protocol for statements taken abroad. There was no reason to doubt the reliability of those who had made the statements in question.

31   So far as the evidence of PC Brandon was concerned, this had caused the judge greater concerns. He had no doubt that the officer had recorded what he had been told contemporaneously. The two informants were not identified but they seemed to have given an accurate account of what they had been told. The evidence was admissible under either subs.(1)(a) or subs.(1)(c) to s.121 and should go before the jury.

Submissions made to us

32   Mr Offenbach, who appeared for the appellant, submitted that the evidence challenged did not fall within the provisions of s.120(4). He accepted though that it fell within the discretion afforded to the judge by s.114(d) but submitted that its admission was not in the interests of justice and that it should have been excluded pursuant to s.126. So far as the evidence of the visit of the two unnamed men to Mr L was concerned, these men had not been identified and were not available for cross-examination. The same was true of the two informants whose information formed the subject matter of PC Brandon's statement.

33   Mr Offenbach further submitted that the relevant provisions of the 2003 Act were incompatible with the Human Rights Act 1998. Alternatively he submitted that the judge's ruling was in breach of the requirements of that Act.

Our conclusions

34   As we observed earlier, the defence made no objection to L giving evidence of the various communications that she made to her mother, her father, O and to the security guard, Max, at the King's Cross sauna. Prior to the 2003 Act there might have been some debate as to whether, and on what basis, such evidence could be admitted. Plainly it was in the interests of justice that such evidence should be admitted, not merely as evidence of how L was reacting but as evidence of the truth of the statements that she was making as to her predicament. The jury would obviously wish to know whether she had sought to communicate with the outside world and in what terms.

What of the evidence of those who received L's communications?

35   Mr L's evidence, Mrs L's evidence and O's evidence adduced in the form of hearsay the statements made to them by L during the time when she alleged she was effectively imprisoned by the appellant. The issue is whether these statements by L were properly admitted as evidence. Contrary to the view expressed by the judge, we do not consider that s.120(5) or (6) was applicable. We do, however, consider that the six requirements of s.120(7) were, or were likely to be, satisfied:

  (a) L claimed to be a person against whom an offence had been committed.
  (b) The offence was one to which the proceedings related.
  (c) The complaint was about conduct which would, if proved, constitute part of the offence.
  (d) The complaint was made as soon as could reasonably be expected after the alleged conduct. The complaints were, in fact, made while the alleged conduct was continuing.
  (e) The complaint was not made as a result of a threat or promise.
  (f) L was expected to give evidence before the material evidence relating to her previous statements was adduced.

36   Even if s.120 was not satisfied, the evidence in question plainly fell within the judge's discretion under s.114(d), always provided that admission of the evidence was in the interests of justice. We can see no basis upon which it could be suggested that the admission of this evidence was not in the interests of justice. It was probably not clear at the time that the judge made his ruling whether the Defence case would be that L never made the alleged statements or whether it would be that, when making them, she was lying. If the former, then there was every reason why the jury should hear evidence from those to whom L made the statements. If the latter, the introduction of the evidence could not unfairly prejudice the Defendant.

37   As we understand it the only argument raised by Mr Offenbach against the admission of this evidence was that it was unreliable. We see no merit in this argument. Mrs L's evidence was supported by her husband, to whom she passed on what she had heard. No point was taken that this part of Mr L's evidence was double hearsay. Had such a point been taken, we think that the judge could prop-

erly have held this evidence admissible under s.121(1)(c). The evidence was of substantial value and, according as it did with the evidence of Mrs L and the evidence of L, apparently reliable. For these reasons we reject the contention that this evidence should not have been admitted. We shall deal with the additional arguments advanced before us based on the Human Rights Act 1998 in due course.

38   We turn to the evidence given by Mr L of the two visits by the two Albanian men. In so far as this evidence was to the effect that the two men were trying to ascertain the whereabouts of L, it was evidence of fact rather than hearsay. In so far, however, as it was evidence that the two men had stated that L had disappeared it was hearsay. This was a significant part of the story in that it fitted in with L's evidence of her escape to York. We consider that is was properly admitted under s.114.

The evidence of PC Brandon

39   This was double hearsay because, for the most part, the two witnesses who came to give information to PC Brandon were reporting what L had told them. Section 121 applied to this evidence. The earlier hearsay statement, that is the statement by L, was admissible under s.120(4) for the reasons that we have given when dealing with the other statements that she made. Thus the judge was correct to hold that s.121(1)(a) was satisfied. We think that the judge was also correct to rule that s.121(1)(c) was satisfied. This evidence was, as Mr Offenbach frankly accepted, very damaging to the appellant. The value of the evidence was, in our judgment, so high that the interests of justice required PC Brandon's statement to be admitted.

40   Mr Offenbach argued that admitting this evidence was unfair because the two witnesses who had conveyed the information to PC Brandon were not available for cross-examination. We see nothing in this point. We think that Mr Offenbach would have been in some difficulty in finding any question that it was safe to put to them. Furthermore all that they were doing was relaying information provided by L, who was available for cross-examination.

41   For these reasons we reject the contention that this evidence should not have been admitted.

The Human Rights Act 1998

42   Mr Offenbach's arguments in relation to incompatibility, or non-compliance, with the Human Rights Convention were founded on the following provision of Art.6 of the Convention:

> "3. Everyone charged with a criminal offence has the following minimum rights:
>   (d) . . . to examine or have examined witnesses against him . . ."

Mr Offenbach submitted that because s.114 permitted the court to adduce in evidence a hearsay statement by a witness who was not available for cross-examination, that section was incompatible with Art.6 of the Convention.

There is no merit in that argument. The discretion granted by s.114 is not restricted to the admission of a hearsay statement the maker of which is not available for cross-examination. To the extent that Art.6 would be infringed by admitting such evidence, the court has a power to exclude the evidence under s.126 and a duty so to do by virtue of the Human Rights Act 1998. There can thus be no question of s.114 being incompatible with the Convention.

43   As to the contention that the judge, by admitting the hearsay evidence, infringed Art.6, there is no merit in this either. Article 6(3)(d) is one of the provisions designed to secure "equality of arms". The hearsay provisions of the 2003 Act apply equally to prosecution and defence, so there is no inherent inequality of arms arising out of those provisions.

44   Article 6(3)(d) does not give a defendant an absolute right to examine every witness whose testimony is adduced against him. The touchstone is whether fairness of the trial requires this. In the present case almost all the hearsay evidence derived directly, or indirectly, from L. She was available for examination. This satisfied the requirements of Art.6(3)(d).

45   For all these reasons this appeal is dismissed.

Appeal dismissed.

R. (HASANI) v BLACKFRIARS CROWN COURT

Queen's Bench (Divisional Court) (Lord Justice Hooper and
Mr Justice Gross): December 14, 21, 2005

[2005] EWHC 3016 (Admin); [2006] 1 Cr.App.R. 27

⟨ʟᴛ⟩ Arraignment; Fitness to plead; Hearings; Mental disorder

H1   FITNESS TO PLEAD
      Arraignment
      *Claimant initially found unfit to plead—Jury finding claimant having done
      act—Medical evidence indicating claimant fit to plead at disposal hearing—
      Whether judge having to decide again whether claimant fit to plead—Whether
      jury required again to find claimant having done act—Whether judge required
      to order absolute discharge of claimant—Criminal Procedure (Insanity) Act
      1964 (c.84), ss.4, 4A, 5(2) (as amended by Criminal Procedure (Insanity and
      Unfitness to Plead) Act 1991 (c.25), s.2 and Domestic Violence, Crime and Vic-
      tims Act 2004 (c.28), s.22)*

H2   The judge determined under s.4 of the Criminal Procedure (Insanity) Act 1964
      that the claimant was unfit to be tried for several offences contrary to the Offences
      against the Person Act 1861. Thereafter, a jury found, in accordance with s.4A of
      the 1964 Act, that the claimant had done the acts in question. There was an
      adjournment to enable the defence to obtain up-to-date evidence from the clai-
      mant's treating doctor. At the adjourned hearing, counsel for the claimant
      submitted that, given the view of the claimant's treating doctor that he was fit
      to plead, he should be tried and given an absolute discharge by way of disposal
      under s.5(2) of the 1964 Act. The prosecution argued that, given the claimant's
      apparent recovery, he should be arraigned. The judge agreed with the prosecution
      and made an order for arraignment. The claimant applied for judicial review.

H3   **Held,** allowing the application, that a further s.4 hearing would have be held if
      an accused person who had been found to be unfit to plead, became fit to plead
      before he was dealt with under s.5 of the Act. There was no need to continue
      with the s.4A and s.5 procedures. That would be consistent with the policy behind
      the provisions, which was that a person who was unfit to plead should not have to
      face trial. To require a jury to decide whether an accused person did the act or
      made the omission charged against him when he was fit to plead and play his
      part in criminal proceedings would be a quite absurd waste of time and money.
      Likewise for a judge to make an order for a person's absolute discharge under
      s.5(2) after he had been found to have done the act charged even though he
      was fit to plead would risk bringing the criminal justice system into disrepute.
      That construction also fitted in with s.4, the provisions of which did not preclude

a second hearing. As the judge had fallen into error by not holding a second s.4 procedure his order would be quashed and the case remitted back with a direction to hold a s.4 hearing. (post, paras [14]–[15]).

H3   (For ss.4, 4A and 5 of the Criminal Procedure (Insanity) Act 1964, see *Archbold* 2006, paras 4–167, 4–168 and 4–175a).

Application for judicial review

H4   On July 29, 2005 the claimant, Fluturim Hasani, was found by Judge Samuels Q.C. sitting in the Crown Court at Blackfriars to be unfit to plead to offences of assault; but after his apparent recovery the judge made an order that he should be arraigned and stand trial. He applied for judicial review of that decision.

H5   The facts and grounds of appeal appear in the judgment of the court.

H6   *Rajiv Menon* (instructed by Saunders Solicitors LLP) for the claimant.
Jeffrey Pegden Q.C. and *James Dawes* (instructed by the Crown Prosecution Service) for the prosecution.

Cur. adv. vult.

December 21   **Hooper L.J.:** handed down the judgment of the court.

1   This is the judgment of the court.

2   The question of law which arises in this case is:

> "If an accused person is found to be unfit to plead under s.4 of the Criminal Procedure (Insanity) Act 1964 ('the Act') but becomes fit to plead before he is dealt with under s.5, is the court nevertheless required to follow the procedures in ss.4A and 5?"

3   Judge Samuels Q.C. held that the court was not so required. In his ruling the judge said:

> "This case, as is obvious from the lengthy period during which it has been before this court, has a long and chequered history. I do not propose in my observations today to set that history out with any degree of particularity. Suffice it to say that in one indictment, Mr Hasani is alleged to have wounded a perfect stranger, Drew Laurence Reed, with intent to cause him grievous bodily harm on August 15, 2004, that being an offence contrary to s.18 of the Offences against the Person Act. And similarly, assaulting another stranger contrary to s.47 of the Offences against the Person Act on the same occasion; and having an offensive weapon on that occasion. And in a separate incident which took place on May 11, 2004, Mr Hasani was charged with assaulting another stranger, contrary to s.47 of the Offences against the Person Act.

Following a series of hearings before this court in which a number of psychiatrists were saying that Mr Hasani was incapable of understanding the nature of the proceedings which he faced, it was ultimately decided before me on July 29 this year that Mr Hasani was unfit to plead.

That was in the light of unchallenged medical evidence, and I determined under s.4 of the Criminal Procedure Insanity Act 1964, as amended by s.22 of the Domestic Violence, Crime and Victims Act 2004, that the defendant was unfit to be tried. That welcome modification in the law, which came into force in April of this year, avoided what would otherwise have been the procedural requirement that the issue of unfitness, notwithstanding the unanimity of view at the time held by the doctors who had seen Mr Hasani, had to be tried by a jury.

That left open for determination the issue of whether the defendant did the relevant acts. That issue had to be determined by a jury, and I gave directions on July 29, as to the way ahead. I directed that the defence should by a specific date notify the Crown by letter as I gave directions on the July 29, as to the way ahead. I directed that the defence should by a specific date notify the Crown by letter as to which, if any, of the prosecution witnesses in both indictments were required to give evidence [on] person in the issue of whether the defendant had done the relevant acts.

On August 12, I gave further directions; and on August 19 I authorised joinder of both indictments, there being no opposition to that course on the part of the defendant who was present.

On August 22 counsel then representing the defendant agreed that it would not be appropriate to challenge any of the evidence that the Crown intended to adduce, and the evidence was indeed read from Mr Johnson, Mr Reed and Mr Bailey. The defendant did not give evidence and called no evidence; and the jury, which had been empanelled for the purpose of determining whether the defendant did the acts in question, found unanimously that he did.

At the conclusion of that hearing on August 22, I was asked to adjourn the issue of disposal until September 16, to enable the defence to obtain up-to-date evidence from Mr Hasani's treating doctor.

On September 16 Mr Menon, representing this defendant as he has done today, sought to persuade me that given the view of the treating doctor, Dr Mezey, that Mr Hasani was in her view now fit to plead and to be tried, that the way forward was to grant Mr Hasani an absolute discharge by way of disposal.

That, given the background which I have summarily sought to identify, seemed to me an inappropriate way ahead. And I invited the Crown to consider whether or not either further psychiatric evidence was to be obtained by the Crown to challenge the views expressed by Dr Mezey, or as to the way ahead.

On October 14 Mr Dawes, appearing for the Crown as he does today, submitted that the way ahead—given the defendant's apparent recovery of his ability to be tried and comprehend what was in issue at the trial, and accordingly apparently satisfying all the relevant tests in *R. v Pritchard*

(1836) 7 Car. & P. 303—the right way forward was for the defendant to be arraigned. I accepted those submissions. The defendant was not arraigned; the defendant was ordered to be arraigned at a plea and case management hearing fixed to take place on Friday of this week, November 11."

4   It is the order that the defendant be arraigned which is the subject matter of this challenge by way of judicial review. In the light of the application for permission to apply for judicial review, the case is now listed for January 13, 2006.

5   There is no dispute that if the claimant is fit to plead, he can be tried in the ordinary way (s.5A(4), which we set out below in para.[10], does not, it is agreed, affect this issue). On behalf of the claimant, Mr Menon succinctly submits that the court is nevertheless required to make an order under s.5(2) and he further submits that the appropriate order would have to be an absolute discharge given that the claimant no longer has a mental condition. Given the nature of the offences, it is not surprising that the judge found that result "inappropriate".

6   We turn to the statutory provisions. The preamble to the Act states, in part:

"An act to amend . . . and the procedure for determining whether an accused person is under a disability such as to constitute a bar to his being tried."

7   Section 4 now reads:

"(1) This section applies where on the trial of a person the question arises (at the instance of the defence or otherwise) whether the accused is under a disability, that is to say, under any disability such that apart from this Act it would constitute a bar to his being tried.

(2) If, having regard to the nature of the supposed disability, the court are of opinion that it is expedient to do so and in the interests of the accused, they may postpone consideration of the question of fitness to be tried until any time up to the opening of the case for the defence.

(3) If, before the question of fitness to be tried falls to be determined, the jury return a verdict of acquittal on the count or each of the counts on which the accused is being tried, that question shall not be determined.

(4) Subject to subs.(2) and (3) above, the question of fitness to be tried shall be determined as soon as it arises.

(5) The question of fitness to be tried shall be determined by the court without a jury.

(6) The court shall not make a determination under subs.(5) above except on the written or oral evidence of two or more registered medical practitioners at least one of whom is duly approved."

8   Section 4A now reads:

"(1) This section applies where in accordance with s.4(5) above it is determined by a court that the accused is under a disability.

(2) The trial shall not proceed or further proceed but it shall be determined by a jury
   (a) on the evidence (if any) already given in the trial; and

(b) on such evidence as may be adduced or further adduced by the prosecution, or adduced by a person appointed by the court under this section to put the case for the defence,

whether they are satisfied, as respects the count or each of the counts on which the accused was to be or was being tried, that he did the act or made the omission charged against him as the offence.

(3) If as respects that count or any of those counts the jury are satisfied as mentioned in subs.(2) above, they shall make a finding that the accused did the act or mad either omission charged against him.

(4) If as respects that count or any of those counts the jury are not so satisfied, they shall return a verdict of acquittal as if on the count in question the trial had proceeded to a conclusion.

(5) . . ."

9   Section 5(1) and (2) now read:

"(1) This section applies where

. . .

(b) findings are recorded that the accused is under a disability and that he did the act or made the omission charged against him.

(2) The court shall make in respect of the accused

(a) a hospital order (with or without a restriction order);

(b) a supervision order; or

(c) an order for his absolute discharge."

10   Section 5A(4) reads:

"Where

(a) a person is detained in pursuance of a hospital order which the court had power to make by virtue of s.5(1)(b) above, and

(b) the court also made a restriction order, and that order has not ceased to have effect, the Secretary of State, if satisfied after proper consultation with the responsible medical officer that the person can properly be tried, may remit the person for trial either to the court of trial or to a prison."

11   Section 5A(6) reads:

"In relation to the making of an order under subs.(2)(c) above, s.2(1) of the Powers of Criminal Courts (Sentencing) Act 2000 (absolute and conditional discharge) shall have effect as if

(a) the reference to a person being convicted by or before a court of such an offence as is there mentioned included a reference to the case where s.5 above applies; and

(b) the reference to the court being of opinion that it is inexpedient to inflict punishment included a reference to it thinking that an order for absolute discharge would be most suitable in all the circumstances of the case."

12   Mr Pegden Q.C. rightly points out the practical consequences if Mr Menon is right. In this case the judge would probably have to make an order for absolute discharge albeit given that the claimant is fit to plead such an order would hardly be "most suitable in all the circumstances of the case". Mr Pegden also rightly points out that the s.4A procedure, which sometimes takes some considerable time, would have to be followed even though the accused person is clearly fit to plead. Mr Menon does not disagree but merely insists that the use of the word "shall" in ss.4A(2) and 5(2) shows that the court must continue with the procedures therein laid out even though the accused person is fit to plead.

13   Mr Pegden submitted that we should interpret both subsections as if, after the word shall, were to be found such words as "so long as the accused is unfit to plead". We do not think that it is necessary to adopt this submission quite in that form.

14   We think it is sufficient to say that the ss.4A and 5 procedures are inapplicable if, following a further s.4 hearing, the court has found the accused person fit to plead, a finding which, according to s.4(6) cannot be made "except on the written or oral evidence of two or more registered medical practitioners at least one of whom is duly approved". That second finding obviates the need to continue with the ss.4A or 5 procedures. The solution we have adopted avoids the unfortunate practical consequences to which Mr Pegden adverted and yet is consistent with the policy behind these provisions that a person who is unfit to plead should not have to face trial. To require a jury to decide whether an accused person did the act or made the omission charged against him when he is fit to plead and play his part in criminal proceedings would, in our view, be a quite absurd waste of time and money. Likewise for a judge to make an order for a person's absolute discharge after he had been found to have done the act charged (particularly in a serious case) even though he is fit to plead would be quite absurd and risk bringing the criminal justice system into disrepute. The construction which we have adopted is consistent with the well-known rule of statutory interpretation that, if it is possible, the provisions of an Act must be construed so as to give them a sensible meaning. Furthermore the construction which we have adopted fits in with s.4, the provisions of which do not preclude a second hearing.

15   In the light of our conclusions, we quash the order made by Judge Samuels Q.C. only because he has not held a second s.4 procedure (and indeed was not invited to do so). It is important that the procedure be followed even though the outcome seems clear. Having quashed the order we remit the case back to Judge Samuels Q.C. (or another judge) with a direction to hold a second s.4 hearing (which may only be a formality). If the judge finds the claimant to be fit to plead, then the judge will make the necessary order for the claimant's arraignment. If the judge makes no such finding (which seems unlikely) the first finding continues in force and the judge will then have to continue with the s.5 procedures and make the appropriate order under s.5(2).

Application allowed. Order quashed. Matter remitted back to Crown Court with direction to hold s.4 hearing.

R. v A (PROSECUTOR'S APPEAL)

COURT OF APPEAL (The Vice-President (Lord Justice Rose),
Mr Justice Crane and Mr Justice Beatson): December 15, 2005

[2005] EWCA Crim 3533; [2006] 1 Cr.App.R. 28

(LT) Alternative charges; Date of offence; Sexual offences; Statutory interpretation; Transitional provisions

H1   SEXUAL OFFENCES
       Indecent assault
       Conduct offence under old and new statutes—Uncertain whether occurring
before or after new statute coming into force—Practice to be followed in framing
indictment—Sexual Offences Act 1956 (4 & 5 Eliz. 2, (c.69)), s.14—Sexual
Offences Act 2003 (c.42), s.9(1)—Sexual Offences Act 2003 (Commencement)
Order 2004 (SI 2004/874)

H2   Where Parliament had envisaged but had not provided a transitional regime
covering the repeal of the Sexual Offences Act 1956 and the commencement
of the Sexual Offences Act 2003 the Court of Appeal could not interpret the
2003 Act or the Sexual Offences Act 2003 (Commencement) Order 2004 so as
to provide such a regime.

H3   Accordingly, where a defendant was charged in respect of conduct which
could be an offence under either the Sexual Offences Act 1956 or the Sexual
Offences Act 2003 but the prosecution could not prove beyond reasonable
doubt whether the conduct took place before or after the coming into force of
the 2003 Act on May 1, 2004, the defendant should be charged with alternative
counts on the indictment, one identifying an offence contrary to the 1956 Act, if
the conduct took place before the May 1, 2004 and the other identifying an
offence contrary to the 2003 Act, if the conduct took place on or after that
date. Since the date on which an offence was committed was not generally a
material averment there could be no prejudice to the defendant in this course, providing the conduct relied on was sufficiently clearly identified.

H4   If there was evidence fit for the jury to consider that particular conduct took
place before May 1, 2004 or on or after May 1, or both, an indictment should
be framed incorporating alternative counts. The matter would be reviewable at
the close of the prosecution case as to whether there was sufficient evidence
for the jury's consideration as to the date or dates when the conduct took
place. If, on review, there was such evidence for the jury's consideration, then
the jury would have to be directed in due course to decide, first, whether the conduct complained of occurred and, secondly, whether they were sure that it was
before May 1, or on or after that date. They had, of course, to be sure of both matters before they could convict (post, paras [20]–[23]).

H5   (For s.9 of the Sexual Offences Act 2003, see *Archbold* 2006, para.20–58 and following; for s.14 of the Sexual Offences Act 1956, see *Archbold* 2004 (or earlier editions), para.20–44).

Appeal by Crown

H6   The defendant, A, was charged on an indictment containing nine counts in relation to alleged sexual offences against children, committed between January 1995 and August 2004. In relation to counts 4 to 7, which alleged indecent assault between April 1 and 30, 2004, on a child under 16, contrary to s.14(1) of the Sexual Offences Act 1956, the judge (Judge Jack, sitting at Hull Crown Court) was invited by the prosecution to rule that those counts could, in due course, properly be left to the jury on the basis that they could infer that the offences were committed before May 1, 2004. He declined to do so, and on December 2, 2005 ruled that counts 4 to 7 could not be left to the jury in that form and on that basis. The Crown appealed under s.58 of the Criminal Justice Act 2003 against that ruling

H7   The facts and grounds of appeal appear in the judgment of the Court.

H8   *Caroline Bradley* (instructed by the Crown Prosecution Service, Grimsby) for the Crown.
Catarina Sjolin (assigned by the Registrar of Criminal Appeals) for the defendant.

December 15   Rose L.J. (Vice President): delivered the judgment of the court.
1   If a history of criminal legislation ever comes to be written it is unlikely that 2003 will be identified as a year of exemplary skill in the annals of Parliamentary drafting.
2   In recent months the courts have been taxed with a number of perplexing provisions in the Criminal Justice Act 2003. Today we face, as already have Crown Courts up and down the country, a major problem which arises from the Sexual Offences Act 2003 (Commencement) Order 2004 (SI 2004/874), bringing most of the Sexual Offences Act 2003 into force on May 1, 2004 and thereby simultaneously repealing, by s.140 and Sch.7 of that Act, many provisions of the Sexual Offences Act 1956. This has taken place in the context of the Secretary of State not having exercised his order-making powers under s.141(2)(b) of the 2003 Act to make "supplementary, incidental, saving or transitional provisions".
3   In consequence, there is before the Court today the first appeal to come before this Court under the provisions of s.58 of the Criminal Justice Act 2003, which enables the prosecution to appeal against a judge's ruling in relation to a trial on indictment, in certain circumstances.
4   It is brought by certificate of the trial judge, Judge Jack, sitting at Hull Crown Court. The certificate follows a ruling that he gave on December 2, 2005, in relation to a trial due to begin on January 9, 2006. It is in the following terms:

"This is a matter of law of public importance, in which my ruling may result in a clear injustice. The appeal should be expedited."

5　　　The circumstances are these. The indictment, as presently drafted, contains nine counts in relation to alleged sexual offences against children, committed between January 1995 and August 2004. Counts 1 to 3 make allegations of indecency with a child, contrary to the Indecency with Children Act 1960; counts 8 and 9, allege causing or inciting a child under 13 to engage in sexual activity, contrary to s.8 of the Sexual Offences Act 2003. Counts 4 to 7, to which this appeal relates, allege indecent assault between April 1 and 30, 2004, on a child under 16, contrary to s.14(1) of the Sexual Offences Act 1956.

6　　　The stance of the prosecution before the trial judge and repeated before this Court today, by Miss Bradley, on their behalf, is that the prosecution are not and will not be able to prove, in relation to counts 4 to 7, whether they were committed before or after May 1, 2004. The complainant is a young girl and she is not able to identify the relevant dates.

7　　　The judge was invited by the prosecution to rule that counts 4 to 7 could, in due course, properly be left to the jury on the basis that they could infer that the offences were committed before May 1. He declined to do so, and ruled with regret that, albeit the position was nonsensical, counts 4 to 7 could not be left to the jury in their present form and on that basis.

8　　　Before us, counsel for the prosecution and counsel for the defence have, in essence, repeated the submissions which they made to the trial judge.

9　　　On behalf of the prosecution, Miss Bradley draws attention to the provisions of s.141 of the Sexual Offences Act 2003 which empower the Secretary of State to make orders including, under subs.(2)(b), "supplementary, incidental, saving or transitional provisions". As we have said, the only relevant way in which that power has been exercised is by SI 2004/874, which provides, in para.2, "The Sexual Offences Act 2003 shall come into force on May 1, 2004, in so far it is not already in force."

10　　　Section 140 of the Act repeals the provisions listed in Sch.7, which include the Sexual Offences Act 1956. Miss Bradley referred to *R. v Newbon* [2005] Crim. L.R. 738, where a similar difficulty presented itself to Judge Glen at the Stoke-on-Trent Crown Court, on February 24, 2005. The judge, on that occasion, like the present trial judge, referred to the nonsensical and, as he added, "outrageous" result, which was a consequence of the Secretary of State's failure to exercise his powers under s.141(2), in particular in relation to transitional provisions. Miss Bradley drew attention also to the academic commentary upon Judge Glen's decision. She also referred to the Violent Crime Reduction Bill, which, as brought from the House of Commons has had its first reading in the House of Lords. She accepts that the provisions of that Bill, the date of the second reading of which is not presently known, cannot properly be used as an aid to interpretation of the Sexual Offences Act 1956. But she draws attention to the observations made in the House of Lords by Baroness Clark of Calton, who in para.314 said this:

"It is the Government's view that an offender should not avoid conviction because it cannot be proven beyond reasonable doubt exactly when such an offence took place. The provision made by **cl.48** is intended to make that clear."

Clause 48, which is headed "Continuity of sexual offences law", says this:

"(1) This section applies where, in any proceedings

(a) a person ('the defendant') is charged in respect of the same conduct both with an offence under the Sexual Offences Act 2003 ('the 2003 Act offence') and with an offence specified in subs.(2) ('the pre-commencement offence');

(b) the only thing preventing defendant from being found guilty of the 2003 Act offence is the fact that it has not been proved beyond a reasonable doubt that the time when the conduct took place was after the coming into force of the enactment providing for the offence; and

(c) the only thing preventing the defendant from being found guilty of the pre-commencement offence is the fact that it has not been proved beyond a reasonable doubt that that time was before the coming into force of the repeal of the enactment providing for the offence."

Sub-clause 2 identifies the Sexual Offences Act 1956 as containing offences of the kind referred to in sub-clause 1(a). Sub-clause 3 provides:

"For the purposes of determining the guilt of the defendant it shall be conclusively presumed that the time when the conduct took place was

(a) if the maximum penalty for the pre-commencement offences is less than the maximum penalty for the 2003 Act offence, a time before the coming into force of the repeal of the enactment providing for the pre-commencement offence; and

(b) in any other case, a time after the coming into force of the enactment providing for the 2003 Act offence."

Miss Bradley does not invite us to embark on any construction of those provisions and we do not do so. It suffices for present purposes to say that those are the sort of provisions which, had they presently been in force, might have resolved the difficulties which currently arise.

11	Miss Bradley submits that the courts must have flexibility to adopt a rational and civilised criminal code. The adverse adjectival descriptions of the result of this legislation, adopted by the trial judge in the present case, and Judge Glen in *Newbon*, demonstrate that, if the trial judge's construction in the present case is correct, injustice will result by reason of a nonsensical situation. She prays in aid the undoubted proposition that the Court should strive to acquit the innocent and convict the guilty. Also, she refers to the explanatory note to the Sexual Offences Act 2003 ascribing to Parliament an intention to strengthen the law and protect the public against sexual offences.

12   With that preamble, she advances essentially two principal submissions in support of this appeal. First, she relies on s.17 of the Interpretation Act 1978, subs.(1) of which is in these terms:

> "Where an act repeals a previous enactment and substitutes provisions for the enactment repealed, the repealed enactment remains in force until the substituted provisions come into force."

13   She sought, at one stage in her argument, to draw a distinction between whether legislation was "in force" and whether or not it had been "implemented". But that is a difficult stance to adopt, bearing in mind that SI 2004/874 uses the words, as we have set out, "come into force".

14   Miss Bradley, secondly, invited the Court to adopt a purposive approach and to construe the legislation and/or the statutory instrument in such a manner as to ensure that, in relation to counts 4 to 7, this defendant should not be able to escape justice. She referred first to the speech of Lord Diplock in *Jones v Wrotham Park Settled Estates* [1980] A.C. 74 at 105, where, at letter E, he said:

> "I am not reluctant to adopt a purposive construction where to apply the literal meaning of the legislative language used would lead to results which would clearly defeat the purposes of the Act. But in doing so the task on which a court of justice is engaged remains one of construction; even where this involves reading into the Act words which are not expressly included in it. *Kammins Ballrooms Co Ltd v Zenith Investments (Torquay) Ltd* [1971] A.C. 850 provides an instance of this; but in that case the three conditions that must be fulfilled in order to justify this course were satisfied. First, it was possible to determine from a consideration of the provisions of the Act read as a whole precisely what the mischief was that it was the purpose of the Act to remedy; secondly, it was apparent that the draftsman and Parliament had by inadvertence overlooked, and so omitted to deal with, an eventuality that required to be dealt with if the purpose of the Act was to be achieved; and thirdly, it was possible to state with certainty what were the additional words that would have been inserted by the draftsman and approved by Parliament had their attention been drawn to the omission before the Bill passed into law. Unless this third condition is fulfilled any attempt by a court of justice to repair the omission in the Act cannot be justified as an exercise of its jurisdiction to determine what is the meaning of a written law which Parliament has passed."

15   As to the third of those conditions, Miss Bradley drew attention to the speech of Lord Nicholls of Birkenhead in *Inco Europe Ltd v First Choice Distribution* [2000] 1 W.L.R. 586, at 592F. His Lordship referred to: "the substance of the provision Parliament would have made although not necessarily the precise words Parliament would have used had the error in the Bill been noticed." She relied upon that passage as having a loosening effect on the third of the conditions identified by Lord Diplock.

16   She submitted that the present is a situation in which the precise words which Parliament might have used are not known but, in order to achieve continuity, the

1956 Act should, by construction, be regarded as continuing to operate until the 2003 Act has effect. She submitted that the 2003 Act should be interpreted as being in force provided that it can be proved that the conduct relied on was committed on or after May 1. She posed the question: how can the 2003 Act be in force if one cannot prosecute the man under it? That, if we may say so, is a somewhat novel approach to statutory interpretation, because it would make interpretation of the 2003 Act dependant on the evidence in a particular case. It would also mean that, in some shadowy way, the 1956 Act would be preserved and would continue to be in effect indefinitely, depending on the evidence in the particular case.

17 For the defendant, Miss Sjolin concedes that the submission which she advances is unattractive. But she submits that the conclusion to which the Court is driven is inescapable. Section 140 of the 2003 Act, through Sch.7, repeals the 1956 Act. Section 141 permits and empowers the Secretary of State to make transitional provisions. By those two sections, Parliament has demonstrated its intention and what it envisaged. The Secretary of State has made no relevant transitional provisions. The statutory instrument which has been made, bringing the 2003 Act into force, is short and clear, and it is simply not open to the court to interpret either the 2003 Act, or the statutory instrument, in the way contended for on behalf of the prosecution. It is not open to this Court to cure the inactivity of the Secretary of State by statutory interpretation, purposive or otherwise.

18 Miss Sjolin also invited the Court's attention to a decision of the administrative Court in *R. (Haw) v Secretary of State for the Home Department* [2005] EWCA 2061 (Admin). In particular, she adverted to certain passages in the judgment of Smith L.J. in that case. It is not an authority from which we derive assistance in the present case because the legislation there under consideration, in stark contrast to the legislation here under consideration, was making criminal conduct which had not previously been criminal.

19 As it seems to us, Miss Sjolin's arguments are unanswerable. It is not possible for this Court so to interpret either the 2003 Act, or the Statutory Instrument, in order to provide a transitional regime which Parliament envisaged should be provided by the Secretary of State. It follows that the learned judge was entirely correct to reach the conclusion which he did, and this appeal must be dismissed.

20 However, we add this: by s.14 of the 1956 Act, it was an offence indecently to assault a woman, and a girl under 16 could not give consent preventing an act being an assault. The maximum penalty for that offence was 10 years' imprisonment. By s.9(1) of the 2003 Act, it is an offence for a person aged 18 or over, intentionally to touch another sexually, if the other is under 13, and the maximum penalty for that offence is 14 years' imprisonment.

21 It is apparent that Parliament's purpose was that the deliberate touching of a woman or girl, indecently in the terms of the 1956 Act, or sexually in the terms of the 2003 Act, was and should continue to be a criminal offence. As it seems to us, there can be no prejudice to a defendant if he is charged with alternative counts in the indictment, one identifying an offence contrary to the 1956 Act, if the conduct took place before May 1, 2004 and the other identifying an offence contrary to the 2003 Act, if the conduct took place on or after May 1, 2004.

22   The date on which an offence was committed is not generally a material averment (see for example *R. v Dossi* (1992) 13 Cr.App.R.(S.) 158), and there could
be no prejudice to a defendant, provided the conduct relied upon is sufficiently
clearly identified, in him being charged with alternative offences framed as we
have indicated.

23   The circumstances of the present case, as we have said, are unusual in that the
prosecution are confident that it will not be possible to identify whether the conduct relied on took place before or after May 1. That of itself, we comment in
passing, is sufficient to demonstrate the correctness of the judge's conclusion
that no implication of commission of the offence before May 1, if the offence
were merely charged under the 1956 Act, could properly be made. But there
will perhaps be many cases in which there is evidence fit for the jury to consider
that particular conduct took place before May 1, or on or after May 1, or both. In
such circumstances, we would expect an indictment to be framed incorporating
alternative counts. The matter will, of course, be reviewable, at the close of the
prosecution case, as to whether there is or is not evidence sufficient for the
jury's consideration as to the date or dates when the conduct took place. If, on
review, there is such evidence for the jury's consideration, then the jury will
have to be directed in due course to decide, first, whether the conduct complained
of occurred and, secondly, whether they are sure that it was before May 1, or on or
after that date. They must, of course, all be sure of both matters before they can
convict.

24   For the reasons already given, this appeal is dismissed.

Appeal dismissed.

R. v JAMES
R. v KARIMI

COURT OF APPEAL (The Lord Chief Justice (Lord Phillips of Worth
Matravers), Sir Igor Judge P., Mr Justice Poole, Mr Justice Bean and
Mrs Justice Dobbs): December 19, 2005; January 25, 2006

[2006] EWCA Crim 14; [2006] 1 Cr.App.R. 29

Defences; Precedent; Provocation

H1   HOMICIDE
        Provocation
        *Proper direction to jury in relation to defence of provocation—Conflict of
        authority—Judicial Committee of Privy Council, composed of nine members,
        not applying earlier House of Lords' decision—Whether Privy Council's
        decision to be preferred*

H2   The appellants in both cases appealed against their convictions for murder on
        the grounds that the jury in each case should have been directed, on the question
        of the defence of provocation, in accordance with the decision of the House of
        Lords in *R. v Smith (Morgan James)* [2001] 1 Cr.App.R. 5 (p.31), rather than
        in accordance with the opinion of the Judicial Committee of the Privy Council
        in *Attorney General for Jersey v Holley* [2005] 2 Cr.App.R. 36 (p.588).

H3   **Held,** dismissing the appeals, that where the Judicial Committee of the Privy
        Council, consisting of nine of the 12 Lords of Appeal in Ordinary, had agreed in
        the course of their judgments that the result reached by the majority clarified defi-
        nitively English law in relation to provocation as a partial defence to a charge of
        murder, the Court of Appeal was bound, when hearing subsequent appeals
        against conviction for murder, to prefer the decision of the Privy Council to an
        earlier decision of the House of Lords on the same issue. Accordingly, the jury
        in each case had been correctly directed on the law in relation to provocation
        (post, paras [41]–[43], [45], [51], [65]).
            Attorney General for Jersey v Holley [2005] UKPC 23; [2005] 2 Cr.App.R. 36
        (p.588); [2005] 2 A.C. 580, PC, applied; *R. v Smith (Morgan James)* [2001] 1
        Cr.App.R. 5 (p.31); [2001] 1 A.C. 146, HL, not followed.

H4   (For the defence of provocation, see *Archbold* 2006, paras 19–50 and follow-
        ing.)

Appeals against conviction

R. v James

H5   On February 5, 1980 in the Crown Court at Nottingham (Peter Pain J.), the appellant, Leslie Hall James, was convicted of murder and sentenced to life imprisonment. On March 23, 1982 his appeal against conviction was dismissed by the Court of Appeal. The Criminal Cases Review Commission referred his appeal back to the Court of Appeal under s.9 of the Criminal Appeal Act 1995 on the ground that since the date of his conviction the legal position in relation to the defence of provocation had been changed by the decision in *R. v Smith (Morgan James)* [2001] 1 Cr.App.R. 5 (p.31).

H6   The facts appear in the judgment of the court.

R. v Karimi

H7   On July 29, 1997 in the Crown Court at St Albans (Blofeld J.) the appellant, Jamal Karimi, was convicted of murder and sentenced to life imprisonment. His renewed application for leave to appeal against conviction was refused by the Court of Appeal on May 1, 1998. On June 20, 2003 the Criminal Cases Review Commission referred his conviction back to the Court of Appeal on the ground that the legal position in relation to the defence of provocation had been changed by the decision in *R. v Smith (Morgan James)* [2001] 1 Cr.App.R. 5 (p.31). On February 9, 2005 the Court of Appeal allowed the appeal, quashed the conviction and ordered a retrial. On October 4, 2005 in the Central Criminal Court (Judge Focke Q.C.) the appellant was convicted of murder following a ruling by the judge that on the issue of provocation he should follow the decision in *Attorney General for Jersey v Holley* [2005] 2 Cr.App.R. 36 (p.588) in preference to the decision in *Morgan Smith*. The appellant appealed against conviction on the ground that the judge had erred in directing the jury in accordance with *Holley* rather than *Morgan Smith*.

H8   The facts appear in the judgment of the court.

H9   At the hearing of the appeals on December 19, 2005 the following additional cases were cited or referred to in the skeleton arguments: *Kadhim v Brent LBC Housing Benefit Board* [2000] EWCA Civ 344, [2001] Q.B. 955, CA; *R. v Rowland (Philip)* [2003] EWCA Crim 3636; *R. v Smith (Josephine)* [2002] EWCA Crim 2671; *R. v Weller (David Allen)* [2003] EWCA Crim 815; [2004] 1 Cr.App.R. 1, CA; *Spectrum Plus Ltd (In Liquidation), Re* [2005] UKHL 41; [2005] 2 A.C. 680, HL; *Young v Bristol Aeroplane Co Ltd* [1944] K.B. 718, CA.

H10   *Diana Ellis Q.C.* and *Rudi Fortson* (assigned by the Registrar of Criminal Appeals) for James.
David Bentley and *Sarah Elliott* (assigned by the Registrar of Criminal Appeals) for Karimi.
Sir Allan Green Q.C. and *Christopher Hehir* (instructed by the Crown Prosecution Service, Headquarters) for the Crown.

Cur. adv. vult.

January 25   Lord Phillips C.J.: handed down the judgment of the court.

1   These two appeals have been heard together because each turns on the true interpretation of s.3 of the Homicide Act 1957 ("s.3"). The court has sat five strong because they raise a novel and important question of the law relating to precedent. Should this court accept that the decision of the Privy Council in *Attorney General for Jersey v Holley* [2005] UKPC 23; [2005] 1 Cr.App.R. 36 (p.588); [2005] 2 A.C. 580 has effectively overruled the decision of the House of Lords in *R. v Smith (Morgan)* [2001] 1 Cr.App.R. 5 (p.31); [2001] 1 A.C. 146?

2   Karimi was convicted of murder in the Central Criminal Court, following a retrial, after a reference by the Criminal Cases Review Commission ("CCRC"), on October 4, 2005. He was sentenced to life imprisonment with a minimum term of 11 years. He came before the court on an application for leave to appeal that had been referred by the Registrar. We granted that leave in the course of the hearing.

3   James was convicted of murder in the Crown Court at Nottingham and sentenced to life imprisonment. An appeal was dismissed by the court on March 23, 1982. James has been released on licence. His case has been referred by the CCRC.

4   We shall set out the facts in relation to each appeal in the second part of this judgment. As will appear, the success of each appeal depends upon this court preferring, as the definitive statement of the English law of provocation, the decision of the House of Lords in *Morgan Smith* rather than the subsequent decision of the Privy Council in *Holley*.

Background history

5   The background to these appeals is long and complex. We can and will simplify it. A full account is given in paras [4]–[6] of Lord Hoffmann's speech in *R. v Smith (Morgan)* [2001] 1 Cr.App.R. 5 (p.31); [2001] 1 A.C. 146 and paras [3]–[16] of the Advice of the majority, delivered by Lord Nicholls of Birkenhead, in *Attorney General for Jersey v Holley* [2005] 1 Cr.App.R. 36 (p.588); [2005] 2 A.C. 580.

6   Murder is a common law offence. For well over two hundred years the common law has also recognised a partial defence to a charge of murder in respect of a defendant who killed under provocation. By the end of the 19th century the following elements in this defence were established: (i) the provocation had to consist of conduct, usually physical violence; (ii) its effect had to be to make the defendant lose his self-control; and (iii) the nature of the provocation had to be such as might make a reasonable man react in the same way as the defendant.

7   Section 3 of the 1957 Act, passed in response to recommendations of a Royal Commission on Capital Punishment, did not attempt a complete codification of the common law defence of provocation, but set out a partial definition of some of its elements. It provided:

"Where on a charge of murder there is evidence on which the jury can find that the person charged was provoked (whether by things done or by things said or by both together) to lose his self-control, the question whether the provocation was enough to make a reasonable man do as he did shall be left to be determined by the jury; and in determining that question, the jury shall take into account everything both done and said according to the effect which, in their opinion, it would have on a reasonable man."

8   The test of the reaction of a reasonable man in the context of the law of provocation was never an easy one. On its face the test was objective, but s.3 took the unusual step of preventing the judge from ever withdrawing the issue from the jury. Furthermore, by extending the scope of provocation to things said as well as things done, s.3 made application of the test considerably more complicated. The implications of the change were considered by the House of Lords in *R. v Camplin* (1978) 67 Cr.App.R. 14; [1978] A.C. 705. The leading speech was given by Lord Diplock. He remarked that where provocation consisted of taunts or insults, these might be directed to particular characteristics of the defendant, so that the gravity of the provocation would depend upon those characteristics. Thus, when considering the gravity of the provocation, it was legitimate to have regard to the particular characteristics of the defendant. Neither the effect nor the correctness of this part of Lord Diplock's speech has since been questioned.

9   The part of Lord Diplock's speech that has given rise to controversy related to the implications for the test of the reaction of the reasonable man of the fact that the defendant was only fifteen years of age. Lord Diplock held that, when considering whether the defendant's reaction to provocation had been that of a reasonable man, the jury should have regard to the age of the defendant. At the end of his speech, at p.718, he advanced the following as being a proper direction to the jury:

"The judge should state what the question is using the very terms of the section. He should then explain to them that the reasonable man referred to in the question is a person having the power of self-control, to be expected of an ordinary person of the sex and age of the accused, but in other aspects sharing such of the accused's characteristics as they think would affect the gravity of the provocation to him; and that the question is not merely whether such a person would in like circumstances be provoked to lose his self-control but also whether he would react to the provocation as the accused did."

The controversy

10   The controversy that subsequently developed in respect of Lord Diplock's speech in *Camplin* led ultimately to the extraordinary events that have given rise to this appeal. That controversy extends to the true interpretation of a number of decisions that purported to follow *Camplin* and to the effect of the observations of Lord Goff of Chievely in *R. v Morhall* [1995] 2 Cr.App.R. 502; [1996] A.C. 90;

but we can pick up the story with the decision of the Privy Council in *Luc Thiet Thuan v R.* [1996] 2 Cr.App.R. 178; [1997] A.C. 131. This was an appeal from Hong Kong and the Board proceeded on the basis that the law of Hong Kong was the same as the law of England. The defendant, who had been convicted of murder, suffered from brain damage which reduced his capacity for self-control. The issue was whether this should have been taken into account when considering whether he had reacted as a reasonable man would have done. In giving the advice of the majority (Lord Goff of Chievely, Sir Brian Hutton and Sir Michael Hardie Boys), Lord Goff purported to follow *Camplin*. He held that the standard of self-control to be applied was that of the ordinary person, not that of a brain damaged person. Lord Steyn dissented, expressing the view that Lord Diplock in *Camplin* had held that, when considering the standard of self-control required to satisfy s.3, there must be attributed to the reasonable man any special characteristics of the defendant.

11   Two decisions of this court followed in which the court declined to follow the majority in *Luc Thiet Thuan*, holding that the majority decision was in conflict with decisions of the Court of Appeal and that the law of precedent bound the court to prefer its own decisions: *R. v Campbell* [1997] 1 Cr.App.R. 199; *R. v Parker* [1997] Crim. L.R. 760.

12   The controversy came to a head in *Morgan Smith,* where the Committee consisted of Lord Slynn of Hadley, Lord Hoffmann, Lord Clyde, Lord Hobhouse of Woodborough and Lord Millett. Of these, only Lord Hoffmann remains today a member of the Appellate Committee. The defendant had a mental condition which had the effect of reducing his self-control below that of an ordinary person. The judge directed the jury that they should disregard this mental condition when considering whether a reasonable man would lost his self-control. The Court of Appeal held that this was a misdirection. The judge should have directed the jury that the defendant's mental impairment was a characteristic that should have been attributed to the notional reasonable man when considering the defence of provocation. The Crown appealed.

13   Lord Hoffmann gave the leading speech. After a lengthy and erudite account of the history of the law of provocation he turned to consider the construction of s.3. Approaching the question of construction in what he described as the orthodox way he concluded in para.[6] that "the concept of the reasonable man as a touchstone of the objective element could not have been intended to be the same" under s.3 as it had been before the 1957 Act. This was to be inferred: (i) from the extension of provocation to words; and (ii) from the fact that the issue of provocation had to be left to the jury. The jury "were to determine not merely whether the behaviour of the accused complied with some legal standard but could determine for themselves what the standard in the particular case should be". The jury should find the defence of provocation made out where they thought "that the circumstances were such as to make the loss of self control sufficiently *excusable* to reduce the gravity of the offence from murder to manslaughter".

14   Lord Hoffmann found support for this conclusion in the English authorities that addressed s.3. In particular, he concluded that Lord Diplock in *Camplin*

had held that all the personal characteristics of the defendant should be taken into account by the jury when deciding whether the defendant's loss of self-control satisfied the requirements of s.3. He concluded that the majority in *Luc Thiet Thuan* had been in error and that Lord Steyn had been correct. At para.[11] he described the manner in which a judge should direct a jury in relation to provocation as follows:

> "In my opinion, therefore, judges should not be required to describe the objective element in the provocation defence by reference to a reasonable man, with or without attribution of personal characteristics. They may instead find it more helpful to explain in simple language the principles of the doctrine of provocation. First, it requires that the accused should have killed while he had lost self-control and that something should have caused him to lose self-control. For better or for worse, s.3 left this part of the law untouched. Secondly, the fact that something should have caused him to lose self-control is not enough. The law expects people to exercise control over their emotions. A tendency to violent rages or childish tantrums is a defect in character rather than an excuse. The jury must think that the circumstances were such as to make the loss of self-control sufficiently *excusable* to reduce the gravity of the offence from murder to manslaughter. This is entirely a question for the jury. In deciding what should count as a sufficient excuse they have to apply what they consider to be appropriate standards of behaviour."

15   Lord Slynn and Lord Clyde delivered speeches that concurred with that of Lord Hoffmann. Lord Clyde echoed Lord Hoffmann when he said at p.180:

> "Although the statute expressly refers to a reasonable man it does not follow that in directing a jury on provocation a judge must in every case use that expression. The substance of the section may well be conveyed without necessarily importing the concept of a reasonable man".

16   Lord Hobhouse of Woodborough made a lengthy and vigorous dissent. He differed at almost every point with the analysis of Lord Hoffmann. In particular, he concluded that Lord Diplock in *Camplin* had held that the conduct of the defendant had to be compared with that of a person possessing ordinary powers of self-control. In one respect Lord Hobhouse agreed with Lord Hoffmann. He expressed the view that, when addressing the jury, the phrase "reasonable man" was better avoided. If the jury formed the view that the defendant might have killed as a result of losing his self-control as a result of provocation they should be instructed to ask themselves whether "a person having ordinary powers of self-control would have done what the defendant did". Lord Millett delivered a speech agreeing with Lord Hobhouse.

A novel procedure

17   Up to this point nothing procedurally untoward had occurred. The House of Lords in *Camplin* had interpreted s.3, but there was disagreement as to the effect

of that part of their decision which addressed the test of the reaction of the reasonable man. There were conflicting decisions of the Privy Council and the Court of
Appeal. The House of Lords in *Morgan Smith* had resolved the conflict by a
majority of three to two, declining to follow the majority in the Privy Council,
whose decision was not binding upon them. It was quite clear what the majority
in *Morgan Smith* had decided. That decision became, however, the subject of
considerable academic criticism.

18　　　On rare occasions decisions of the House of Lords are almost immediately
recognised to have been erroneous. Such an occasion occurred when the
House interpreted the Criminal Attempts Act 1981 in *Anderton v Ryan* (1985)
81 Cr.App.R. 166; [1985] A.C. 560 in such a manner as virtually to emasculate
the Act. The error was acknowledged by the House when *Anderton v Ryan* was
overruled by *R. v Shivpuri* (1986) 83 Cr.App.R. 178; [1986] A.C. 1, pursuant to
the *Practice Statement (Judicial Precedent)* [1966] 1 W.L.R. 1234. That Statement reads as follows:

> " *Practice Statement (Judicial Precedent)* [1966] 1 W.L.R. 1234
> Their Lordships regard the use of precedent as an indispensable foundation
> upon which to decide what is the law and its application to individual cases.
> It provides at least some degree of certainty upon which individuals can rely
> in the conduct of their affairs, as well as a basis for orderly development of
> legal rules.
> Their Lordships nevertheless recognise that too rigid adherence to
> precedent may lead to injustice in a particular case and also unduly restrict
> the proper development of the law. They propose therefore to modify their
> present practice and, while treating former decisions of this House as nor-
> mally binding, to depart from a decision when it appears right to do so.
> In this connection they will bear in mind the danger of disturbing retrospec-
> tively the basis on which contracts, settlements of property and fiscal
> arrangements have been entered into and also the especial need for certainty
> as to the criminal law.
> This announcement is not intended to affect the use of precedent elsewhere
> than in this House."

19　　　The decision in *Shivpuri* to depart from such a recent decision, particularly a
decision on statutory interpretation, was very unusual. It would equally have
been unusual had the House, pursuant to the practice direction, decided to depart
from its decision in *Morgan Smith*. In the absence of a suitable appeal, however,
that course was not even available. What did occur was an appeal to the Privy
Council by the Attorney-General for Jersey against a decision of the Court of
Appeal of Jersey that had applied *Morgan Smith* in substituting a conviction
for manslaughter for a conviction for murder. In doing so the Court of Appeal
had to interpret a provision of the Homicide (Jersey) Law 1986 that was in identical terms to s.3. The case was *Attorney General for Jersey v Holley.*

20　　　Normally the result in *Holley* would have been a foregone conclusion. The
majority decision in *Morgan Smith* would have been followed and the appeal
would have been dismissed. The jurisprudence of the Privy Council had estab-

lished that, where an appeal turned on a point of English law, or law identical to English law, the Privy Council should follow a decision of the House of Lords. This was made plain in two appeals from Hong Kong. In *de Lasala v de Lasala* [1980] A.C. 546 at p.558 Lord Diplock dealt with the relationship between the Judicial Committee of the Privy Council and the Appellate Committee of the House of Lords in the following passage:

> "a decision of the House of Lords on a matter which in Hong Kong is governed by the common law by virtue of the Application of English Law Ordinance is not ipso facto binding upon a Hong Kong court although its persuasive authority must be very great, since the Judicial Committee of the Privy Council, whose decisions on appeals from Hong Kong *are* binding on all Hong Kong courts, shares with the Appellate Committee of the House of Lords a common membership. This Board is unlikely to diverge from a decision which its members have reached in their alternative capacity, unless the decision is in a field of law in which the circumstances of the colony or its inhabitants make it inappropriate that the common law in that field should have developed on the same lines in Hong Kong as in England.
>
> Different considerations, in their Lordships' view, apply to decisions of the House of Lords on the interpretation of recent legislation that is common to Hong Kong and England. Here there is no question of divergent development of the law. The legislation in Hong Kong has chosen to develop that branch of the law on the same lines as it has been developed in England, and, for that purpose, to adopt the same legislation as is in force in England and falls to be interpreted according to English canons of construction. What their Lordships have already said about the common membership of the Judicial Committee of the Privy Council and the Appellate Committee of the House of Lords applies a fortiori to decisions of the House of Lords on interpretation of recent English statutes that have been adopted as the law of Hong Kong. Since the House of Lords as such is not a constituent part of the judicial system of Hong Kong it may be that in juristic theory it would be more correct to say that the authority of its decision on any question of law, even the interpretation of recent common legislation can be persuasive only; but looked at realistically its decision on such a question will have the same practical effect as if they were strictly binding, and courts in Hong Kong would be well advised to treat them as being so."

21   Even more pertinent in the present context is the following passage in the advice of a Board of the Privy Council consisting of five Law Lords in *Tai Hing Cotton Mill Ltd v Liu Chong Hing Bank Ltd* [1986] A.C. 80 at p.108:

> "It was suggested, though only faintly, that even if English courts are bound to follow the decision in *Macmillan*'s case the Judicial Committee is not so constrained. This is a misapprehension. Once it is accepted, as in this case it is, that the applicable law is English, their Lordships of the Judicial Committee will follow a House of Lords' decision which covers the point in issue. The Judicial Committee is not the final judicial authority for the deter-

mination of English law. That is the responsibility of the House of Lords in its judicial capacity. Though the Judicial Committee enjoys a greater freedom from the binding effect of precedent than does the House of Lords, it is in no position on a question of English law to invoke the *Practice Statement (Judicial Precedent)* [1966] 1 W.L.R. 1234 of July 1966 pursuant to which the House has assumed the power to depart in certain circumstances from a previous decision of the House. And their Lordships note, in passing, the Statement's warning against the danger from a House of Lords' decision in a case where, by reason of custom, statute, or for other reasons peculiar to the jurisdiction where the matter in dispute arose, the Judicial Committee is required to determine whether English law should or should not apply. Only if it be decided or accepted (as in this case) that English law is the law to be applied will the Judicial Committee consider itself bound to follow a House of Lords' decision."

22   These statements of principle accorded with statements of the House of Lords, such as that of Lord Wilberforce in *Miliangos v George Frank (Textiles) Ltd* [1976] A.C. 443, at 459:

"It has to be reaffirmed that the only judicial means by which decisions of this House can be reviewed is by this House itself, under the declaration of 1996."

23   The procedure adopted and the comments of members of the Board in *Holley* suggest that a decision must have been taken by those responsible for the constitution of the Board in *Holley* to depart from the position stated in the above passages and to use the appeal as a vehicle for reconsidering the decision of the House of Lords in *Morgan Smith*, not just as representing the law of Jersey but as representing the law of England. A decision was taken that the Board hearing the appeal to the Privy Council should consist of nine of the 12 Lords of Appeal in Ordinary. Those sitting were Lord Bingham of Cornhill, the senior Law Lord, Lord Nicholls of Birkenhead, Lord Hoffmann, Lord Hope of Craighead, Lord Scott of Foscote, Lord Rodger of Earlsferry, Lord Walker of Gestingthorpe, Baroness Hale of Richmond and Lord Carswell. Counsel for the respondent is reported at p.585 as submitting that "the Privy Council should not determine whether a decision of the House of Lords is wrongly decided". It seems to us that a decision had already been taken that this was precisely what the Board should do.

24   In the event the Board divided six/three. The majority concluded that *Morgan Smith* had been wrongly decided and that the majority in *Luc Thiet Thuan* had accurately stated the law. The dissentients were Lord Bingham, Lord Hoffmann and Lord Carswell. Lord Nicholls began the advice of the majority as follows:

"1. This appeal from the Court of Appeal of Jersey calls for examination of the law relating to provocation as a defence or, more precisely, as a partial defence to a charge of murder. Jersey law on this subject is the same as English law. In July 2000 the House of Lords considered the ingredients of this defence in the *Morgan Smith* case (*R. v Smith (Morgan)* [2001] 1

A.C. 146). The decision of the House in that case is in direct conflict with the decision of their Lordships' board in *Luc Thiet Thuan v R.* [1997] A.C. 131. And the reasoning of the majority in the *Morgan Smith* case is not easy to reconcile with the reasoning of the House of Lords in *R. v Camplin* [1978] A.C. 705 or *R. v Morhall* [1996] A.C. 90. This appeal, being heard by an enlarged board of nine members, is concerned to resolve this conflict and clarify definitively the present state of English law, and hence Jersey law, on this important subject."

25   At the end of their dissenting opinion, Lord Bingham and Lord Hoffmann added the following comment at para.[68]:

"We must however accept that the effect of the majority decision is as stated in para.[1] of the majority judgment."

26   It seems to us that this can only mean that they accepted that the decision of the majority clarified definitively the present state of English law. Lord Carswell, who gave an individual dissenting opinion, stated at para.[69] that he fully agreed with the reasons given and the conclusions reached in the dissenting opinion of Lord Bingham and Lord Hoffmann. Our understanding is that Lord Carswell's agreement extended to Lord Bingham and Lord Hoffmann's acceptance that the decision of the majority clarified definitively the present state of English law.

27   The majority in *Holley* gave the following explanation for concluding that the majority decision in *Morgan Smith* was erroneous:

"22. . . . The law of homicide is a highly sensitive and highly controversial area of the criminal law. In 1957 Parliament altered the common law relating to provocation and declared what the law on this subject should thenceforth be. In these circumstances it is not open to judges now to change ('develop') the common law and thereby depart from the law as declared by Parliament. However much the contrary is asserted, the majority view does represent a departure from the law as declared in s.3 of the Homicide Act 1957. It involves a significant relaxation of the uniform, objective standard adopted by Parliament. Under the statute the sufficiency of the provocation ('whether the provocation was enough to make a reasonable man do as [the defendant] did') is to be judged by one standard, not a standard which varies from defendant to defendant. Whether the provocative act or words and the defendant's response met the 'ordinary person' standard prescribed by the statute is the question the jury must consider, not the altogether looser question of whether, having regard to all the circumstances, the jury consider the loss of self-control was sufficiently excusable. The statute does not leave each jury free to set whatever standard they consider appropriate in the circumstances by which to judge whether the defendant's conduct is 'excusable'."

While we do not believe that it has any relevance to the resolution of these appeals, we should record that this court finds the reasoning of the majority in *Holley* to be convincing.

Aftermath

28   In 2003 the Judicial Studies Board issued a specimen direction in respect of
provocation that was based on *Morgan Smith*. Directions that followed this specimen direction were unlikely to give rise to appeals. Three judgments relating to
directions on provocation in respect of trials pre-dating *Holley* have, however,
been given in this court since the decision in *Holley*. The first was *R. v van Dongen* [2005] EWCA Crim 1728; [2005] 2 Cr.App.R. 38 (p.632). The appellants had
been convicted of murder. They complained that, although there had been evidence of provocation, the judge had not left that partial defence to the jury.
The court dismissed the appeal on the ground that the jury would inevitably
have been certain that no reasonable man would have reacted to the provocation,
taking that provocation at its highest, in the way that the appellants had reacted.
The appeal was heard before the decision in *Holley* was published, although judgment was delivered after it. The court, presided over by May L.J., observed that
Holley had not affected the decision. It remarked at para.[61]:

> "We assume, but do not decide, because it is not necessary to do so, that *Hol-
> ley*, a decision of the Privy Council, would be taken as binding in England
> and Wales."

29   The second case was *R. v Faqir Mohammed* [2005] EWCA Crim 1880 in
which the court, presided over by Scott Baker L.J., granted permission to appeal
in the course of the hearing on grounds that related to the judge's summing-up in
respect of provocation. The report of *Holley* was published after argument and
the court gave the parties the opportunity of making further written submissions
in respect of this decision. The court recorded at para.[43]:

> "Although *Holley* is a decision of the Privy Council and *Morgan Smith* a
> decision of the House of Lords, neither side has suggested that the law of
> England and Wales is other than as set out in the majority opinion delivered
> by Lord Nicholls in *Holley* and we have no difficulty in proceeding on that
> basis."

30   The third case was an application for permission to appeal, heard by a two-man
court presided over by Hughes J., on July 19, 2005. The applicant had been convicted of murder after a direction on provocation that was found by the court to be
"fully in accord with *Morgan Smith*". The court proceeded, however, on the
basis that "as the law is now understood under *Holley*, a direction somewhat
less favourable to the applicant would have been required".

31   Professor Ashworth, whose comments on this area of the law have assisted the
debate in a number of the decisions to which we have referred, commented on the
decision in *Holley* in [2005] Crim. L.R. 966. He expressed the following view on
its effect:

> "Is *Holley* binding on English courts? There may be a purist strain of argu-
> ment to the effect that it is not, since it concerns another legal system (that of
> Jersey). However, the reality is that nine Lords of Appeal in Ordinary sat in
> this case, and that for practical purposes it was intended to be equivalent of a

sitting of the House of Lords. It is likely that anyone attempting to argue that *Morgan Smith* is still good law in England and Wales would receive short shrift, and the Court of Appeal in *van Dongen* (below, p.931 at para.[61] of the judgment) assumed, without deciding, that *Holley* now represents English law."

32   The Judicial Studies Board has not yet issued an alternative specimen direction to that based on *Morgan Smith* to which we have referred. We understand that it may be awaiting the result of these appeals. We believe, however, that Professor Ashworth's appraisal of the position is realistic and that judges who currently have to sum up on provocation are doing so on the premise that the law is accurately stated in the majority decision in *Holley*.

Precedent and the Criminal Division of the Court of Appeal

33   Before the decision in *Holley* the impact on the Criminal Division of the Court of Appeal of a decision of the Privy Council and a decision of the House of Lords in the light of well established principles of the law of precedent was not in doubt. While there was some doubt as to the circumstances in which the Court of Appeal could depart from one of its own decisions, there was no doubt that it was bound to follow a decision of the House of Lords. If authority is necessary for this proposition one can do no better than refer to this passage from the speech of Lord Wilberforce in *Miliangos v George Frank (Textiles) Ltd* [1976] A.C. 443 at 470–471:

> "It is true that since 1966 your Lordships have power to depart from a previous decision of your Lordships' House; although, in view of the limited resources available to decision-making by a court of law, it is a power which your Lordships have exercised with proper restraint. But the statement of Lord Gardiner L.C. of July 26, 1966 [*Practice Statement: (Judicial Precedent)* [1966] 1 W.L.R. 395], expressly asserted that it was 'not intended to affect the operation of the rule of precedent elsewhere than' in your Lordships' House; and it is clear law that the Court of Appeal is bound by a decision of your Lordships' House and (at least on its civil side) by a previous decision of the Court of Appeal itself: *Young v Bristol Aeroplane Co Ltd* [1944] K.B. 718; [1946] A.C. 163, 160. Any change in this respect would require legislation."

34   The principle that, in civil matters at least and subject to recognised exceptions, the Court of Appeal was bound to follow its own decisions was vigorously emphasised by the House of Lords in *Davis v Johnson* [1979] A.C. 264; the passage of Lord Diplock's speech dealing with this topic runs to five pages of the law report. That principle went so far as to require the Court of Appeal to prefer its own previous decision to a conflicting subsequent decision of the Privy Council, although in practice there have been some notable exceptions to that principle, of which perhaps the most notable is the decision of the Privy Council in *Overseas Tankship (UK) Ltd v Morts Dock & Engineering Co Ltd (The Wagon Mound)* [1961] A.C. 388, which was universally accepted as

having displaced the decision of the Court of Appeal in *In re Polemis* [1921] 3 K.B. 560.

35   In the present context we observe that Lord Clyde commented at pp.70 and 184 of *Morgan Smith* that the Court of Appeal was bound by its own line of authority and thus not required to make any choice between it and *Luc Thiet Thuan*. In *R. v Campbell* [1997] 1 Cr.App.R. 199 Lord Bingham C.J., giving the judgment of this court, referred to a perceived conflict between the decision of the Privy Council in *Luc Thiet Thuan* and a number of decisions of this court. He commented at p.207:

> "We do not, however, conceive that it is open to us to choose between these competing views. The previous decisions of this Court are binding upon us. The decision of the Privy Council is not. It appears to us that unless and until the previous decisions of this Court are authoritatively overruled, our duty and that of trial judges bound by the decisions of this Court is to apply the principles which those cases lay down."

Submissions

36   Counsel on behalf of each appellant understandably invoked the established principles of the law of precedent to which we have referred above. They urged simply that it was not open to this court to prefer the decision in *Holley* to that in *Morgan Smith*. They also urged that the principles in question were designed to ensure certainty of the law and that, if we preferred the decision in *Holley*, we would throw the law into great uncertainty, leaving the lower courts with no clear principle as to when they could follow a decision of the Privy Council rather than a decision of the Court of Appeal or even the House of Lords.

37   For the Crown in each appeal Sir Allan Green Q.C. accepted that there was abundant authority to the effect that decisions of the Privy Council were generally no more than persuasive, but submitted that the position in the present case was exceptional. The Board in *Holley* consisted of nine Lords of Appeal in Ordinary. It was clearly the intention of the Board to declare the law of England. This court should accept that they had done so. Sir Allan referred us to the following statement of Lord Woolf C.J., when giving the judgment of a five member Court of Appeal in *R. v Simpson* [2003] EWCA Crim 1499; [2003] 2 Cr.App.R. 36 (p.545); [2004] Q.B. 118 at para.[27]:

> "The rules as to precedent reflect the practice of the courts and have to be applied bearing in mind that their objective is to assist in the administration of justice. They are of considerable importance because of their role in achieving the appropriate degree of certainty as to the law. This is an important requirement of any system of justice. The principles should not, however, be regarded as so rigid that they cannot develop in order to meet contemporary needs."

38   Sir Allan submitted that, far from creating uncertainty if we followed *Holley* we would create uncertainty if we failed to follow that decision. When we asked him what principles we should identify as justifying departure from the

existing rules of precedent he answered that the less we said the better. We should leave it to the House of Lords to decide whether we had acted correctly and to lay down any change in applicable principles needed to accommodate the procedure adopted in *Holley*.

Practical considerations

39   Thus far the nine Lords of Appeal in Ordinary, who set out in *Holley* to "clarify definitively" this difficult area of English criminal law, appear to have succeeded. The decision of the majority has been taken to be the law on three occasions by this court and, as we understand the position, is being followed in directions to juries in England and Wales. If these appeals, or any other raising the same issue, reach the House of Lords, the result would seem to be a foregone conclusion. Half of the Law Lords were party to the majority decision in *Holley*. Three more in that case accepted that the majority decision represented a definitive statement of English law on the issue in question. The choice of those to sit on the appeal might raise some nice questions, but we cannot conceive that, whatever the precise composition of the Committee, it would do other than rule that the majority decision in *Holley* represented the law of England. In effect, in the long term at least, *Holley* has overruled *Morgan Smith*.

40   If we accept what Professor Ashworth describes as "the purist strain of argument" and allow these appeals, our decision, until reversed by the House of Lords as it surely will be, will have to be followed by judges directing juries in trials around the country. Sir Allan was right to refer to this as reducing the law to a game of ping-pong. We do not wish to produce such a result. If we are not to do so, however, two questions must be faced: (i) how do we justify disregarding very well established rules of precedent; and (ii) what principles do we put in place of those that we are disregarding? The two questions are obviously interrelated.

41   As to the first question, it is not this court, but the Lords of Appeal in Ordinary who have altered the established approach to precedent. There are possible constitutional issues in postulating that a Board of the Privy Council, however numerous or distinguished, is in a position on an appeal from Jersey to displace and replace a decision of the Appellate Committee on an issue of English law. Our principles in relation to precedent are, however, common law principles. Putting on one side the position of the European Court of Justice, the Lords of Appeal in Ordinary have never hitherto accepted that any other tribunal could overrule a decision of the Appellate Committee. Uniquely a majority of the Law Lords have on this occasion decided that they could do so and have done so in their capacity as members of the Judicial Committee of the Privy Council. We do not consider that it is for this court to rule that it was beyond their powers to alter the common law rules of precedent in this way.

42   The rule that this court must always follow a decision of the House of Lords and, indeed, one of its own decisions rather than a decision of the Privy Council is one that was established at a time when no tribunal other than the House of Lords itself could rule that a previous decision of the House of Lords was no

longer good law. Once one postulates that there are circumstances in which a decision of the Judicial Committee of the Privy Council can take precedence over a decision of the House of Lords, it seems to us that this court must be bound *in those circumstances* to prefer the decision of the Privy Council to the prior decision of the House of Lords. That, so it seems to us, is the position that has been reached in the case of these appeals.

43   What are the exceptional features in this case which justify our preferring the decision in *Holley* to that in *Morgan Smith*? We identify the following:

i) All nine of the Lords of Appeal in Ordinary sitting in *Holley* agreed in the course of their judgments that the result reached by the majority clarified definitively English law on the issue in question.

ii) The majority in *Holley* constituted half the Appellate Committee of the House of Lords. We do not know whether there would have been agreement that the result was definitive had the members of the Board divided five/four.

iii) In the circumstances, the result of any appeal on the issue to the House of Lords is a foregone conclusion.

44   We doubt whether this court will often, if ever again, be presented with the circumstances that we have described above. It is those circumstances which we consider justify the course that we have decided to take, and our decision should not be taken as a licence to decline to follow a decision of the House of Lords in any other circumstances.

45   For the reasons that we have given, we approach the individual appeals on the premise that the relevant principle of law is to be found in the majority decision of the Privy Council in *Holley* and not the majority decision of the House of Lords in *Morgan Smith*. We turn now to the individual appeals.

James

46   Leslie Hall James killed his wife Jennifer on May 1, 1979. She was stabbed three times, punched and finally suffocated. It had been an unhappy marriage. The couple had been separated on December 28, 1978, when Mrs James left the matrimonial home. She had formed a relationship with another man, Nigel Dutfield. Between the date of the separation and the offence police were called to disturbances arising between the appellant, Mrs James and Mr Dutfield.

47   On the morning of the killing the appellant left his place of work and travelled to Mrs James's home. He had with him a knife he had previously borrowed from a colleague at work in order to cut a cork template. An argument developed in the course of which the appellant attacked and killed his wife. After establishing that she was no longer breathing he wrapped the body in a counterpane and dragged it to the foot of the stairs. He then returned to work. During his lunch hour he returned to the house and changed the locks. Later that afternoon he collected his daughter from school. The body was discovered that evening by Mr Dutfield, who had to force his way into the house.

48   At the Crown Court at Nottingham on October 26, 1979 prosecuting counsel confirmed that in the light of medical evidence then available a plea of guilty to manslaughter on the basis of diminished responsibility would be acceptable to the Crown. However, the defence were not willing to advance such a plea. Psychiatric reports were obtained from four doctors, but none were placed before the jury. Accordingly when the matter came to trial the judge, Peter Pain J., directed the jury that since the defence had not sought to argue diminished responsibility, they could safely take it that the defendant was a person who had to be regarded as fully responsible for his actions.

49   On re-arraignment on January 29, 1980 the appellant pleaded "not guilty to murder but guilty of manslaughter". The plea was advanced on the basis of provocation, which was not acceptable to the Crown. The trial proceeded, the only issue being provocation. At that time the most recent decision of the House of Lords on the relevant principles was *R. v Camplin* (1978) 67 Cr.App.R. 14; [1978] A.C. 705. The judge directed the jury that they should apply a double test:

> "First of all, was the defendant provoked so as to lose his self-control? Secondly, would a reasonable man have done as the defendant did?"

Dealing with the second limb of the test, the judge directed the jury to apply the standard of self-control to be expected of a reasonable man.

50   The Criminal Cases Review Commission referred this appeal on the ground that the legal position had been changed by the decision in *Morgan Smith*. That decision rendered relevant and admissible psychiatric evidence demonstrating that the appellant's ability to control his behaviour was impaired. The psychiatric evidence that was not adduced at the trial, together with two further psychiatric reports, might result, on the application of the approach laid down by *Morgan Smith*, in the defence of provocation succeeding.

51   The decision in *Holley* has supervened since the reference by the CCRC. It was common ground between counsel that, if we ruled that *Morgan Smith* should be followed, this appeal should be allowed but that, if we ruled that *Holley* should be followed, this appeal should be dismissed. As the latter is the position this appeal must be dismissed.

Karimi

52   The appellant joined the Communist Freedom Fighting Movement in Kurdistan in 1984. He married Mehri Rezai, a member of the same movement, two years later, and they had two children.

53   In 1990, having been injured whilst fighting in Kurdistan, the appellant moved to Sweden. His wife joined him there a year later. Their relationship began to deteriorate. The appellant returned to Kurdistan in about 1992, where he fought for a further short period. His wife came to England in April 1994 and the appellant joined her in October of that year. The relationship did not improve. In February 1996, the appellant moved out of the family home and took a room in a YMCA hostel. He enrolled on a full-time course to learn English and became

friendly with a man called Sirvan Kabadi, whom he was subsequently to kill. He also had been a freedom fighter in Kurdistan.

54   The appellant's wife met Mr Kabadi in August 1996 through the appellant. They became lovers in the autumn of 1996. On December 4, 1996, his wife told the appellant that their relationship was over and he left the house in an emotional state. She was concerned about his welfare and telephoned the YMCA, fearing that he might commit suicide.

55   On December 6, the appellant's wife had arranged to meet with Mr Kabadi in the afternoon, but he contacted her and told her not to come because the appellant was coming then to help him fill in application forms. In consequence, she arranged to see Mr Kabadi later.

56   Earlier during that day, the appellant and Mr Kabadi had been seen to be getting on well without any indication of animosity. At 15:15, as shown by the security video on Mr Kabadi's block of flats, the appellant entered that block. Sixty-five minutes later he left, having killed Mr Kabadi with a knife in a frenzied attack from behind. There were numerous stab wounds; the most severe injury was the cutting of the deceased's throat.

57   When questioned by police the following day the appellant immediately admitted the killing and helped in the search for the knife. He was arrested. In his possession was a Stanley knife, which he said he had just bought to kill himself.

58   The appellant gave an account of the killing to his wife, in part at a meeting immediately prior to his arrest, and in part in telephone conversations with her (covertly taped by the police) from the hospital where he was detained. When he was formally interviewed by the police, he made no comment.

59   It was the prosecution case that the appellant killed Mr Kabadi with the intention to kill or cause grievous bodily harm. The defence case was that the deceased had come at the appellant with a knife and sworn a particularly insulting phrase "Besharef" meaning "You have no honour". The appellant claimed to have disarmed the deceased and then, using the knife, killed him. The defences advanced were: (i) that his responsibility was diminished because of post-traumatic stress disorder; (ii) provocation; and (iii) self-defence. The significant issues for the jury were whether the appellant had been provoked and whether he was suffering from diminished responsibility.

60   The appellant was tried in July 1997 before Blofeld J. and a jury at St Albans Crown Court. At that time the most recent decision of the House of Lords on provocation was *R. v Morhall* [1995] 2 Cr.App.R. 502; [1996] A.C. 90. The judge gave a similar direction to the jury on the law of provocation that included the following passage in respect of the second limb of the test:

> "If, however, your answer to that question is 'yes', then you must go on to consider secondly: may that provoking conduct, whatever you find it to be, have been such as to cause a reasonable and sober person of the defendant's age—40ish, sex: male, and special characteristics: that he is a Kurdish freedom fighter with a background of trauma in Kurdistan, which you look at as a whole—may that provoking conduct have been such as to cause a reason-

able and sober person of the defendant's age, sex and special characteristics to do as this defendant did? A reasonable person is simply a person who has that degree of self-control which is to be expected of an ordinary citizen who is sober, but has, also, this defendant's same age, sex and special characteristics."

61   On July 29, 1997 the appellant was convicted of murder by a majority of 10:2 and sentenced to life imprisonment. The single judge refused leave to appeal to this court and an application to extend time for a renewed application to the full court was refused on May 1, 1998.

62   On July 27, 2000 the House of Lords gave judgment in *R. v Smith (Morgan)* [2001] 1 Cr.App.R. 5 (p.31); [2001] 1 A.C. 146.

63   On June 20, 2003 the Criminal Cases Review Commission referred Mr Karimi's conviction to this court. The appeal was heard on February 9, 2005 before the Vice-President (Rose L.J.), Smith L.J. and Butterfield J. An application to adduce fresh evidence from two psychiatrists was refused. It was common ground, as the judgment records, that "the safety of the appellant's conviction for murder must be judged by reference to the law of provocation as it is now understood and applied". The court concluded that in the light of *Morgan Smith* there had been a material misdirection in respect of the second limb of provocation, in that the judge had limited the relevant characteristics of the appellant to his background in Kurdistan. Accordingly the appeal was allowed and the conviction quashed. As the court considered that on the facts it was inappropriate to substitute a verdict of manslaughter by reason of provocation, a retrial was ordered.

64   On June 15, 2005 the Judicial Committee of the Privy Council delivered its advice in *Attorney General for Jersey v Holley* [2005] 1 Cr.App.R. 35 (p.588); [2005] 2 A.C. 580. The retrial began on September 5, 2005 at the Central Criminal Court before Judge Focke Q.C. and a jury. Following legal argument in the absence of the jury the judge ruled that, on the issue of provocation, he ought to follow *Holley* in preference to *Morgan Smith*. He accompanied his summing-up with written directions on provocation which accurately followed *Holley*. The second limb of the test was stated as follows:

> "(2) In your opinion, having regard to the actual provocation and your views of its gravity for the defendant, decide whether a man of the defendant's age, having ordinary power of self-control, might have done what the defendant did.
> If the answer to that question is 'Yes' then the verdict is not guilty of murder but guilty of manslaughter.
> If the answer to that question is 'No' then the verdict would be guilty of murder."

65   The jury convicted the appellant of murder. Before us the grounds of appeal were simply that the judge had erred in directing the jury in accordance with *Holley* rather than in accordance with *Morgan Smith*. For the reasons that we have

given, we have concluded that the judge was correct to follow *Holley*. For that reason this appeal also must be dismissed.

Appeals dismissed.

The Court of Appeal (Criminal Division) certified, under s.33(2) of the Criminal Appeal Act 1968, that a point of law of general public importance was involved in its decision, namely:

"(i) Can an opinion of the Judicial Board of the Privy Council take precedence over an existing opinion of the Judicial Committee of the House of Lords, and, if so, in what circumstances?

(ii) Is the majority opinion in the *Attorney General for Jersey v Holley* [2005] 1 Cr.App.R. 36 (p.588); [2005] 2 A.C. 58 to be preferred to the majority decision in *R. v Smith (Morgan)* [2001] 1 Cr.App.R. 5 (p.31); [2001] 1 A.C.146?"

Leave to appeal to the House of Lords refused.

R. v MACPHERSON

COURT OF APPEAL (The Vice President (Lord Justice Rose),
Mr Justice Forbes and Mr Justice Calvert-Smith): July 27, 2005

[2005] EWCA Crim 3605; [2006] 1 Cr.App.R. 30

LT Children; Competence; Victims; Witnesses

H1   EVIDENCE
Competence of witness
*Indecent assault—Child complainant—Whether such complainant competent
witness—Proper approach to issue in common law and statute—Youth Justice
and Criminal Evidence Act 1999 (c.23), ss.53(1), (2), (3)(a)(b), 54, 63*

H2   The appellant was charged with having committed indecent assault upon a
child, S, who was about four-and-a-half years old at the time when the offence
was said to have been committed. The trial in the Crown Court took place
about six months later. In the course of the trial the appellant, relying, inter
alia, on the common law having effect before the coming into force of the
Youth Justice and Criminal Evidence Act 1999, and on the legal position after
the Act had come into force, and in particular ss.53(1), (2), (3)(a) and (b), 54
and 63[1] of the Act, submitted that S was not a competent witness. The judge proceeded to watch S's memorandum video and also went to see S himself,
accompanied by counsel for the appellant and the prosecution, and conducted
with S a conversation in the form of questions and answers of a most general
nature. The judge ruled that S was a competent witness, and she gave evidence
at the trial. The appellant was convicted. He appealed against conviction on
the grounds that the judge erred in determining S's competence on the basis of
her memorandum video alone; that he had no or insufficient regard to the requirement that he assess S's ability to understand and answer questions within the
forensic forum as a witness as required by s.53 of the Act; and that, in reaching
his decision, he had no or insufficient regard to S's ability to participate meaningfully in cross-examination.

H3   **Held,** dismissing the appeal, that once the issue was raised as to the competence of a prospective witness, it was for the party calling the witness to
satisfy the court that, on the balance of probabilities, the witness was competent,
and in the ordinary way that issue should be determined before the witness was
sworn, usually as a preliminary issue at the start of the trial. In cases such as the
instant case, the judge should watch the video-taped interview with the child witness and/or ask the child appropriate questions. The test of competence was set

---

[1]   Youth Justice and Criminal Evidence Act 1999, ss.53, 54, 63 (post, para.[17]).

out in s.53(3)(a) and (b) of the Youth Justice and Criminal Evidence Act 1999, and was whether the person appeared to the court to be a person who was able to understand questions put to him as a witness and give answers to them which could be understood. The issue raised by s.53(3)(a) and (b) was one of understanding, namely whether the witness understood what was being asked, and whether the jury could understand the witness's answers. The words "put to him as a witness" within s.53(3)(a) meant the equivalent of "being asked of him in court", so that an infant who could only communicate in baby-language with his mother would not ordinarily be competent, but a young child like S in the instant case, who could speak and understand basic English with strangers, would be competent. Further, there was no requirement in the Act that the witness in question should be aware of his status as a witness: questions of credibility and reliability were not relevant to competence, and such matters went to the weight of the evidence and might be considered, as appropriate, at the end of the prosecution case, by way of a submission of no case to answer, or might be considered at a later stage. In the instant case, the judge had set himself the right test; had not made his decision solely on the basis of the memorandum video; and had come to the right answer, namely that S was a competent witness (post, paras [21], [25]–[31]).

H4   (For the competence of witnesses and the Youth Justice and Criminal Evidence Act1999, ss 53 and 54, see *Archbold* 2006, para.8–36 and following).

Appeal against conviction

H5   On November 14, 2003 in the Crown Court at Snaresbrook (Judge King) the appellant, Ian MacPherson, was convicted of indecent assault. On January 26, 2004 he was sentenced to an extended sentence of eight years made up of a custodial term of four years' imprisonment and an extended licence period of four years.

H6   The facts and grounds of appeal appear in the judgment of the Court.

H7   *Adam Kane* (assigned by the Registrar of Criminal Appeals) for the appellant. *Charles Ward-Jackson* (instructed by the Crown Prosecution Service) for the Crown.

Forbes J.: delivered the judgment of the court.

1   On November 14, 2003 in the Snaresbrook Crown Court, this appellant was convicted of indecent assault. On January 26, 2004 the trial judge imposed an extended sentence of eight years made up of a custodial term of four years' imprisonment and an extended licence period of four years. He now appeals against that conviction by leave of the Full Court.

2   The facts were as follows. The appellant is a 50-year-old Glaswegian, who has been living in London since 1977. Until May 2003 he lived with his partner and their son in North London. They then sold that property to a John L who bought it

as a home for his ex-wife, Mette J, and their daughters, S, who is now aged six-and-a-half and is the complainant in this matter, and her younger sister, Y.

3   The property in question is a four-storey house in multiple occupation with a flat on each storey. It is a two bedroomed basement flat.

4   The allegation giving rise to the charge in this case was to the effect that the appellant committed an opportunistic act of oral sex on S during a visit to his former flat. The defence was a complete denial that any such incident had occurred.

5   Mette J, the mother of S, is Danish. She gave evidence that on June 2, 2003, at about 15.30, she was in the communal garden at the rear of her house, in the company of a neighbour, Mr Christopher Molloy, and her ex-husband. There were also two builders in the house at the time, ripping out the kitchen furniture, preparatory to carrying out work there.

6   At about 16.00 the appellant arrived to speak to his former neighbour and also to collect various garden items that he had left behind. Normal pleasantries were exchanged before the appellant walked into the house with Mr Molloy ostensibly to pass on his new address to Mr Molloy. Ten minutes later Mr L asked Miss J to check on their daughter, S, who had also gone into the house. Walking past the builders in the kitchen, Miss J found S and the appellant both kneeling on the floor of S's bedroom. They were playing with building bricks. Miss J asked the appellant whether he missed his old home and he said that he did. He then followed her out of the bedroom into the hallway. S walked out following them as well. She gave her mother a "sheepish look" which her mother had never seen before. Then S said to her mother in Danish: "this man licked my pussy". The appellant asked what S had just said and S repeated it again in Danish. Miss J took S into the garden and told Mr L what S had told her. He became very angry. He seized the appellant and telephoned the police on his mobile telephone. Miss J took S into the house and asked her again what had occurred. In her bedroom, S lay on her back on the bed, resting on her elbows, and pulled up her skirt. She then pulled her knickers to one side, stuck out her tongue and moved it in a licking motion and said in Danish: "That's what he did to me mum".

7   On arrival, the police found the appellant and Mr L in an angry agitated state. The appellant was arrested and cautioned. He replied: "Okay". One of the officers asked for an account of the events from the parents, which they gave in the presence of S. S agreed with what her parents were saying. She lifted up her skirt, pointed to her knickers and said, this time in English: "He licked me there".

8   At 20.06 on the same day, S was interviewed and the interview was video recorded. During the course of the interview S was asked what had happened. She replied: "Do you know what the naughty man did to me? He did something here. I just lied down on my bed, on my sister's bed then he did do this. He did it with his tongue in here." As she spoke, S laid back on the sofa and pointed at her genitals. At a later stage in the interview, she knelt down on the floor facing the sofa and used a licking motion to demonstrate what she claimed the appellant had done to her. She was asked what the appellant had done with his hands. She replied "nothing."

9   At trial, S was cross-examined. In the course of the cross-examination, she said that she could not remember whether the appellant had put her on his shoulders.

When it was suggested to her that the appellant had not licked her and that she had made up the allegation because she had wet her pants, she replied "yeah".

10   However, in re-examination, she said: "I told her he licked me. I know he was a really naughty man."

11   Detective Sergeant O'Sullivan was the interviewing officer in the video interview and she was referred to the Home Office procedures for obtaining best evidence in such situations. She accepted that there had been no real rapport stage in the course of the interview. Her explanation for that was that S was fidgety and anxious to leave and had immediately gone into an explanation of what had happened herself.

12   The appellant was interviewed at 23.12. He told the officers how he had entered the house to look at the changes taking place. He had seen S in her bedroom, playing with the building blocks, and he had joined in. He said that he only stayed for a few minutes, then both of them had left the room.

13   S's knickers were subjected to DNA analysis. In the crotch area the expert witness, Dr Christopher Mackenzie, discovered staining which indicated the possible presence of saliva and vaginal material which gave a mixed profile on testing. The profile of the male DNA corresponded with that of the appellant. In Dr MacKenzie's opinion it was likely to have been saliva and provided extremely strong scientific evidence to support the view that the appellant had licked S's vagina. It was extremely unlikely, according to Dr Mackenzie, to have come from sweat from the back of the appellant's neck. Secondary transfer was unlikely to have given rise to the quantity of the appellant's DNA which was profiled within the knickers. However, in cross-examination Dr Mackenzie, very fairly, accepted that S's behaviour of putting her hand in her mouth and then onto her knickers could explain the secondary transfer of cellular material.

14   The appellant gave evidence on his own behalf. He said that he had called round to his former address that afternoon in order to collect various garden material. On arrival he had chatted with his former neighbours. He said that he had played with S and he had put her on his shoulders. He was curious about the work that was going on in the house, so he had walked through to have a look. He said that he had seen S sitting on her bedroom floor and that he had then knelt down to help her play with some building bricks. They had chatted for a few minutes, then both of them left the room. He said that he heard her saying something to her mother and was "gob smacked" when S's mother had made the accusation. He emphasised that he had done no such thing. He agreed that he had made no mention in interview of placing S on his shoulders but there was an admission to the effect that whilst the appellant was in the custody suite, he used the word "shoulders" and "wee girl" to his partner during a telephone conversation that took place in the interview suite.

15   Character evidence was called from various witnesses to support the appellant's good character.

16   At trial, counsel for the appellant submitted that S was not a competent witness, applying the criteria set out in case law, largely referable to the common law position prior to the 1999 Act, and also by reference to the provisions of the Youth Justice and Criminal Evidence Act 1999. Counsel maintained that the judge

should satisfy himself as to the child's ability to understand the questions put to her and as to her ability to respond with intelligible answers. Counsel also emphasised the importance of the judge satisfying himself that the prospective witness appreciated the difference between truth and falsehood.

17   The relevant statutory framework is as follows. Section 53 of the Youth Justice and Criminal Evidence Act 1999 ("the 1999 Act") provides, so far as material as follows:

> "(1) At every stage in criminal proceedings all persons are (whatever their age) competent to give evidence.
> (2) Subsection (1) has effect subject to subs.(3) and (4).
> (3) A person is not competent to give evidence in criminal proceedings if it appears to the court that he is not a person who is able to—
> (a) understand questions put to him as a witness, and
> (b) give answers to them which can be understood."

Section 54 provides, so far as material:

> "(1) Any question whether a witness in criminal proceedings is competent to give evidence in the proceedings, whether raised—
> (a) by a party to the proceedings, or
> (b) by the court of its own motion,
> shall be determined by the court in accordance with this section.
> (2) It is for the party calling the witness to satisfy the court that, on a balance of probabilities, the witness is competent to give evidence in the proceedings.
> (3) In determining the question mentioned in subs.(1) the court shall treat the witness as having the benefit of any directions under s.19 which the court has given, or proposes to give in relation to the witness.
> (4) Any proceedings held for the determination of the question shall take place in the absence of the jury (if there is one).
> (5) Expert evidence may be received on the questions.
> (6) Any questioning of the witness (where the court considers that necessary) shall be conducted by the court in the presence of the parties."

Section 19 relates to special measures. Finally, s.63 of the 1999 Act, which deals with general interpretation of the relevant part of the Act, provides that:

> "'. . . witness' in relation to any criminal proceedings, means any person called, or proposed to be called, to give evidence in the proceedings."

18   Having heard detailed submissions from counsel, the judge ruled that S was a competent witness. At the heart of his detailed and careful ruling is the following passage:

> "It seems to me, having regard to [S's] responses in interview, that she is capable of giving answers that can be understood.
> I cite this passage by way of illustration:
>
> > 'Will you tell me what happened today before we go?'

Answer: 'The man do something to me.' Question: 'Well, I wasn't there. Can you tell me everything that happened?' Answer 'Do you know what the naughty man did to me? He did do something here. He is a naughty man.' Question: 'He is naughty, you tell us exactly what went on, right from the start, you can go right back to the start?' Answer: 'No, I just lie down on my bed, on my sister's bed and then he did do this. He did it with his tongue in here.'

I have seen the video disclosure interview and at this point the little girl lay back on the sofa in the interview room, she pulled up her skirt, so as to reveal her knickers, pointed at her genital area and demonstrated with her tongue that she was being licked in that area.

It seems to me that taking that as an illustration of the interview, that it was clear that she was capable of understanding questions put to her and that she was capable of offering answers to those questions in an intelligible way.

The whole essence of the statutory provisions is to seek to prevent the courts from receiving unintelligible evidence, capability, capacity lies at the very heart.

Questions of truthfulness and questions of reliability, I accept, as submitted to me Mr Ward-Jackson, essentially, go to weight to be attached to evidence, rather than to its intelligibility.

Mr Ward-Jackson submits with some force that the words 'as a witness' mean giving answers to the Court, but I accept that there should be no special consciousness, as I have already said, of the status of the individual as a witness, in the forensic process, provided that the individual understands the questions that are put to him or her and is capable of giving intelligible responses, it seems to me that that satisfies the test of competence.

Of course, the law has changed very substantially in the last decade or two. There was a time when I readily accept and even within my own experience, that it was unheard of for a child of five or under to be called as a witness in criminal proceedings, but the law has moved on significantly since ten years ago and now there are available facilities, such as television link equipment, which are designed to put at ease very young witnesses or especially vulnerable witnesses, who some years ago, because that equipment was not available, could not realistically have been expected to give evidence in the intimidating surroundings of the Crown Court and so it seems to me the matter has to be reviewed in the context of legislation and technology and so, in all the circumstances, I do not feel it is necessary for me, personally, to interrogate the witness, having seen the disclosure interview, before ruling upon this submission and in the circumstances, for the reasons that I have adumbrated, it seems to me that my ruling must be that [S] is a competent witness."

19 On behalf of the appellant, Mr Kane puts forward three grounds of appeal. First, that the judge erred in determining the competence of S on the basis of her memorandum video alone. Secondly, that the judge had had no or insufficient regard to the requirement that he should assess S's ability to understand and answer questions within the forensic forum as a witness as required by s.53 of

the 1999 Act. Thirdly, in reaching his decision the judge had no or insufficient regard to S's ability to participate meaningfully in cross-examination.

20   It has to be said immediately that, so far as concerns the first ground of appeal, the judge plainly did not make his decision relating to the competence of S solely on the basis of the memorandum video. He also went to see S himself, accompanied by counsel for both the appellant and the prosecution and conducted a general conversation with her in the form of questions and answers of a most general nature. As we understand it, the conversation was designed to elicit S's ability both to understand what he was saying and to respond suitably.

21   At the heart of Mr Kane's submission and these grounds of appeal, is his contention that it was necessary for the judge to go through some suitable form of enquiry, when satisfying himself as to the competence of S, so as to ensure that he was satisfied that S did appreciate the difference between truth and falsehood. Mr Kane submitted that such an enquiry was a necessity, all the more so because the memorandum of interview had not gone through such an exercise as would normally be the case with a young witness. The reasons for that were dealt with by the interviewing officer in the course of her evidence. As we have already pointed out, the officer had to deal with a child who was fidgety and anxious to get on with the matter, so it was that the normal preliminary questions relating to an ability to understand the difference between truth and falsehood were not carried out in this case.

22   In the course of his submissions, Mr Kane said that the test that the judge had set himself, as expressed in his ruling in the passage to which we have referred, simply did not go far enough. He submitted that the judge had failed to satisfy himself that the prospective witness was capable of answering questions that were put to her "as a witness". He stressed that it was important to establish that the prospective witness in such circumstances was able to understand the difference between truth and falsehood and also appreciate the need to give a truthful answer to the questions put.

23   Furthermore, Mr Kane submitted that the judge's generalised enquiries in the course of his personal interview had singularly failed to provide material which would enable the judge to be satisfied that S was capable of engaging meaningfully in cross-examination.

24   We do not find any of these submissions, reflecting as they do the three grounds of appeal to which we have referred, as persuasive in any way. We accept that once the issue is raised as to the competence of a prospective witness, it is for the party calling the witness to satisfy the court that, on the balance of probabilities, the witness is competent.

25   In the ordinary way that issue should be determined before the witness is sworn, usually as a preliminary issue at the start of the trial. In cases such as this, the judge should watch the videotaped interview of the child witness and/ or ask the child appropriate questions. The test of competence is clearly set out in the Act and it is as follows:

"(a) Can the witness understand questions put to him or her as a witness?
And

(b) give answers which can be understood?"

Those are the plain words of s.53(1)(a) and (b) of the 1999 Act.

26   We agree with the submission put forward on behalf of the Crown by Mr Ward-Jackson in para.7 of his written skeleton that the issue raised by paragraphs (a) and (b) of section 53(1) is one of understanding, that is to say: can the witness understand what is being asked and can the jury understand that witness's answers? That is precisely the test which the judge set himself in this case, and to which we have referred in the passage quoted from his ruling.

27   We also agree with Mr Ward-Jackson's submission that the words "put to him as a witness" mean the equivalent of being "asked of him in court". So, it would be the case that an infant who can only communicate in baby language with its mother would not ordinarily be competent. But a young child like the witness in this case, who can speak and understand basic English with strangers would be competent.

28   We have viewed the video recording of the memorandum interview in this case. It is perfectly clear why the judge reached the conclusion that he did. The little girl plainly understood the questions that were put to her and she gave clear and intelligible answers. Not only that, but she accompanied those answers with careful and graphic demonstrations of what had happened. It was very clear from her account as to what she said had occurred. She had no difficulty in understanding the various question that were put to her. True it is that she did not always answer them, but she plainly understood what was going on.

29   We also accept the submission that there is no requirement in the Act (which is commendably clear in its language) that the witness in question should be aware of his status as a witness. Questions of credibility and reliability are not relevant to competence. Those matters go to the weight of the evidence and might be considered, if appropriate, at the end of the prosecution case, by way of a submission of no case to answer.

30   In our judgment, the judge, in the course of his careful and detailed ruling, set himself the right test and clearly came to the right answer and one with which we entirely agree. It is clear from the video recording of the memorandum of interview that this little girl was a perfectly competent witness.

31   As the Crown submitted, a child should not be found incompetent on the basis of age alone and the question of competence can be kept under review. In this case the judge made it quite clear that he was going to keep the matter under review. However, no questions were actually raised during the course of the trial as to S's competence, after the matter had been dealt with in the way that we have described.

32   Finally, we would simply observe that, in any event, the evidence was strong for the following reasons. S's allegation was consistent through two recent complaints and a lengthy interview. It was supported by the presence of saliva and the appellant's DNA inside her knickers. The appellant was apparently nervous when S made her first allegation in Danish when, if he had nothing to fear, there was no reason for him to be nervous. Finally, the appellant advanced by way of explanation for the DNA, that is to say the fact that he had carried S on his

shoulders at some stage, an explanation that was inherently implausible, not witnessed by anybody and not mentioned in interview. It was also plainly an explanation which the jury, by their verdict, rejected.

33   For all those reasons, we have come to the conclusion that there is nothing in any of the three grounds of appeal that are advanced on behalf of this appellant in this matter. For those reasons this appeal against conviction is dismissed.

Appeal dismissed.

R. v POWELL

COURT OF APPEAL (Lord Justice Scott Baker, Mr Justice Ramsey
and Judge Griffith Williams Q.C.):
November 15, 2005; January 13, 2006

[2006] EWCA Crim 3; [2006] 1 Cr.App.R. 31

⟨LT⟩ Competence; Indecent assault; Sexual activity with children;
Video evidence

H1 EVIDENCE
Competence of witness
*Indecent assault—Child complainant—Interview and trial taking place some
time after alleged incident—Whether prosecution discharging onus of demonstrating competence—Youth Justice and Criminal Evidence Act 1999 (c.23), s.53*

H2   The complainant was a girl aged three-and-a-half. One evening, when there
were several people at her home, she told her mother that the appellant had licked
her "nunny". The family used that word to refer to a girl's private parts. The complainant was interviewed nine weeks after the incident. In due course the
appellant was charged with indecent assault and tried on indictment, although
the trial took place seven months after the complainant had been interviewed.
At the trial, submissions were made in a voir dire and before the complainant
had given evidence that the Crown had failed to prove that the complainant
was a competent witness. The judge ruled that the complainant was indeed a competent witness and the question was not revisited although the judge had said the
decision might need to be reconsidered when the child's evidence was completed. The trial proceeded and the appellant was convicted. He appealed
against conviction on the ground, inter alia, that the judge had erred when she
ruled as to competence.

H3   **Held,** allowing the appeal, that it was clear from s.53 of the Youth Justice and
Criminal Evidence Act 1999 that the age of a witness did not determine whether
he was competent to give evidence. It could not therefore be said that below a certain age a witness was too young to give evidence. The test set out in s.53(3) of the
1999 Act was whether the witness was able to understand the questions put to him
and to give answers that could be understood. On these facts the judge was justified, at the time, in ruling that the complainant was a competent witness when
relying on the material heard and seen prior to the evidence being given. However, it was necessary to go on to look at what happened when the complainant
gave evidence. It was unfortunate that the judge was not requested at the end
of the complainant's evidence to revisit the decision that she was a competent
witness. The judge should have done so and, if she had, she would, or should,

have concluded that the complainant was not a competent witness and then withdrawn the case from the jury, since her answers in cross-examination were not intelligible in the context of the case; and the prosecution had not discharged the onus upon it of establishing competence. It was not possible to know whether the lack of competence resulted from lapse of time and lack of memory, but in any event the judge should have stopped the case at the conclusion of the complainant's evidence, and the conviction was unsafe (post, paras [18], [22], [28], [33]–[34], [40]–[42]).

H4   *Per curiam* Where a case depends on the evidence of a very young child it is absolutely essential that the "achieving best evidence" interview takes place very soon after the event, and also that the trial, at which the child has to be cross-examined, takes place very soon thereafter. As the expert evidence in this case showed, very young children simply do not have the ability to lay down memory in a manner comparable to adults. It was completely unacceptable that the appellant should have been tried for an offence proof of which relied on the evidence of a complainant of three-and-a-half when the trial did not take place until over nine months had passed from the date of the alleged offence. Special efforts have to be made to fast-track such cases, and it is simply not an option to wait weeks, for example, for forensic evidence to become available (post, para.[41]).

H5   (For s.53 of the Youth Justice and Criminal Evidence Act 1999, see *Archbold* 2006, paras 8–36 and following.)

Appeal against conviction

H6   On November 25, 2004 in the Crown Court at Harrow (Judge Tapping) the appellant, Michael John Powell, was convicted of indecent assault and was sentenced to an extended sentence of five years, comprising three years' imprisonment and an extended licence period of two years. He was disqualified from working with children and ordered to register indefinitely with the police.

H7   The facts and grounds of appeal appear in the judgment of the Court.

H8   *David Bentley* (assigned by the Registrar of Criminal Appeals) for the appellant. *Louise Halsall* (instructed by the Crown Prosecution Service, Harrow) for the Crown.

Cur. adv. vult.

January 13   Scott Baker L.J.: handed down the judgment of the Court.

1   This appellant is 43. On November 25, 2004 in the Crown Court at Harrow before Judge Tapping and a jury the appellant was convicted of indecent assault. He was sentenced to an extended sentence of five years' imprisonment comprising a custodial term of three years and an extension period of two years. He was disqualified from working with children and ordered to register indefinitely with the police.

2　　　He appeals by leave of the single judge. On November 15, 2005 we allowed his appeal against conviction. We now give our reasons.

3　　　The complainant in this case is a little girl of three-and-a-half and the first question on the appeal is whether she was a competent witness.

4　　　The facts of the case are as follows. On February 13, 2004 there was a birthday party. A group of 15 to 20 met at a public house to celebrate it. The group included the appellant and his wife and the complainant's parents.

5　　　The complainant and her siblings stayed at home with a babysitter. The complainant was born on August 2, 2000. So she was just three-and-a-half at the time. The trial did not take place until over nine months later, a point to which we shall return in a moment.

6　　　After the pub shut the group went back to the complainant's family home. The complainant's mother had not met the appellant or his wife before that evening. When they arrived back at the house the men congregated around the dining table and the women sat in the living room. As the evening wore on, the women went upstairs and sat on the complainant's mother's bed talking. The appellant came into the room about four or five times, each time to discuss drinks with his wife. On the first occasion he asked if his wife had a drink. The appellant then went downstairs to look for his wife's drink. He came back up the following time to say that he could not find it. The complainant's mother went back downstairs with her friend, J. They had only been sitting there for three to five minutes when the complainant came and sat on the edge of the sofa. The complainant told her, "That man licked my nunny". This was the family's word for a girl's private parts. The mother asked the complainant which man, and the complainant pointed to the appellant. At that point the appellant's wife came over and said they were leaving as the appellant did not feel well.

7　　　The mother asked the complainant where this had happened and she said the kitchen. She said the complainant was confused at first but said that he had stood her on the kitchen worktop, pulled her knickers down, licked her and then pulled her knickers back up. They then went to her bedroom and the complainant tapped the end of her bed. She again said he had put her on there, pulled down her knickers, licked her nunny and then pulled her knickers back up again. The complainant then showed her a one pound coin she was holding and said that the man had given it to her. She then told her husband and the police. She said that when the complainant was examined the following day there were two scratches on the top of each leg that she had not noticed before.

8　　　J, whose husband's birthday party it was, gave evidence that she had known the appellant and his wife for around three years and the complainant's parents for about a year. She said that she was friendly with both couples. She recalled the appellant flitting around that evening. She said that at one point she heard a loud noise, saw the appellant at the foot of the stairs and the complainant standing on the stairs above him. He asked her if the complainant was allowed to come down or whether she should be in bed. Towards the end of the evening he came in and spoke to his wife saying that he felt unwell. At that point she said they all went downstairs. She said the appellant stood in the hallway whilst his wife gave her and the complainant's mother a kiss goodbye. The complainant approached her mother and told her that she did not like the man and pointed to the appellant. When asked why, she said that he had licked her "nunny". She had seen the complainant playing with a pound coin earlier in the evening and assumed initially that her father had given it to her. Then the complainant told her that the man had given the money to her.

9   A forensic scientist gave evidence that analysis had been carried out on the complainant's knickers. DNA matching that of the appellant was found on the inside and the outside of the knickers. It was her opinion that the findings did not assist in addressing whether the appellant had licked the complainant or whether she had touched his beard, which was wet with saliva, and then put her hand in her knickers. She said that there was no obvious vomit staining or smell on the knickers, though she said that vomit that consisted mostly of water would not necessarily have any detectable food particles or odour.

10   In interview the appellant accepted being alone upstairs with the complainant. He said that he was on the landing and picked the child up just after he had been sick in the bathroom. She had touched his beard and then put her hand down her knickers. He put her down and told her off for being naughty. This was the only reason he could think of for her complaint. He said he gave her a one pound coin but that this was motivated by kindness.

11   The complainant was interviewed and a video recording made but not until nine weeks later. The Crown applied for this video recording to be admitted in evidence under s.27(1) of the Youth Justice and Criminal Evidence Act 1999. The defence objected but the judge agreed that it should be admitted.

12   The account in the video recording lacked the detail of the recent complaint to her mother on the night of the incident but did include an allegation of indecent assault by the appellant by licking the complainant's private parts.

13   The appellant gave evidence on the same lines as his answers in interview. He said that he did not want to associate himself with the conversations at the dining room table and that was why he left the table. He said he came across the complainant in the kitchen. She pointed up at the cupboard by the cooker and said "sweets". He lifted her onto the kitchen worktop where she picked up a container designed as a clown and then he lifted her down again. He took her into the living room and asked her parents if she was allowed sweets. The complainant's father accepted that there were two "clown" containers of sweets but could not recall the appellant asking if the complainant could have any. At some point he gave her a pound coin. He said that this was his common practice with children and that his wife had given one of the children 50 pence earlier that night. The complainant had said, "Whoo, pound". He went upstairs to find his wife and there was a brief conversation about her drink. He went up the second time because he could not find it and the third time because he had been told that the drink had already been brought up. He said that later on that night he was sick in the bathroom. When he came out of the bathroom he saw the complainant on the landing. He crouched down and picked her up to take her downstairs but then decided not to carry her downstairs as he had had too much to drink. Before he put her down, she saw spit on his chin and beard and rubbed it with her right hand and said, "Ooh, sticky". She then wiped her hands down her knickers. It appeared to

him that she was rubbing it around her crotch, maybe to clean her hand. He quickly put her down and told her that was naughty and that she was a bad girl. He said he thought it was totally inappropriate for a girl of her age. He told her to come downstairs. He said that what happened next was very strange; she turned around and wiggled her bottom at him. He said it was as if she had been trained. He said he got down the stairs quickly. He was feeling unwell and asked his wife if they could leave. The complainant went to sit with her mother. He said goodbye and left. He later received a threatening telephone call from the complainant's father. Afterwards he rang Peter to find out what had been said.

14   In cross-examination he said that when he was sick there was no food in it only beer. He said that he had not realised that he still had saliva on his beard after he came out of the bathroom. He said he wiped his face with the back of his hand, but had obviously missed a bit. He said that he saw his saliva on her fingers but that there was no colour to it. He said that he had picked the complainant up in the kitchen as he was not sure what she was pointing at. He agreed that she was dressed only in her knickers, but he said that it did not cross his mind that he should not have done it. He ridiculed the suggestion that he had given the complainant "hush" money to keep quiet about what he had done. He said that he had picked her up on the landing because he did not believe a child of that age should use the stairs on her own. He recalled the conversation he had had with J when he asked, "Is she allowed to go up and down stairs"? He said that when he picked her up she did not have the one pound coin in her right hand. He said that when he picked her up he had one hand under her bottom and one hand on her back so that she was sideways onto him so she could get her hand down her knickers. He thought that she was touching herself. He said that when he put her down quickly his hand slipped down her front. He denied that his account in interview and in evidence was made up to explain why his DNA was on the complainant's knickers.

15   The appellant's wife agreed that she had given Peter 50 pence earlier that evening. She gave evidence that when the ladies went downstairs she asked her husband if he was feeling all right. He told her that he was not feeling well and that he had been sick. She could not remember which of them suggested that they left. She said that she did notice some spit on the centre of the front of his chin. She was shocked by the allegation. She described the appellant as an open, honest, loving person and said she had no concerns over his behaviour with children. In cross-examination she said that the spit that she saw was white spit and that she had mentioned it to him at the time and that he rubbed it off.

16   Mr David Bentley, for the appellant, advanced three main grounds of appeal.

(1) The Crown failed to prove competence.
(2) Because of the deficiencies in the video interview the judge should have excluded it either under s.27(2) of the Youth Justice and Criminal Evidence Act 1999 ("the 1999 Act") or s.78 of the Police and Criminal Evidence Act 1984.
(3) The judge should not have left the case to the jury.

We take these points in turn.

Was the complainant a competent witness?

17 Section 53(1) of the 1999 Act provides:

> "At every stage in criminal proceedings, all persons are, whatever their age, competent to give evidence."

But s.53(3) provides:

> "A person is not competent to give evidence in criminal proceedings if it appears to the court that he is not a person who is able to;
> (a) understand questions put to him as a witness
> (b) give answers to them which can be understood."

Section 54(2) provides that the onus of proof of competence is on the party calling the witness on the balance of probabilities.

18 Section 53 makes clear that the age of a witness does not determine whether he or she is competent to give evidence. It cannot therefore be said that below a particular age a witness is too young to give evidence. Rather, the test is as set out in s.53(3) whether the witness is able (a) to understand the questions put to him or her; and (b) give answers that can be understood. It is for the court to make a judgment on this.

19 The judge conducted a voir dire. She heard from two expert witnesses on the question of competency and also the interviewing officer PC Tyldesley. She had also, of course, the video interview.

20 The Crown called Mr David Glasgow, a consultant forensic clinical psychologist; the appellant called Dr Markantonakis, a consultant child psychiatrist. The judge pointed out that neither had met the child in person but both had studied the video. She said Mr Glasgow was critical of the interview. It went on too long; the room was small with adult sized furniture; there were too many distracting and noisy toys with the result that at times the sound was poor. However, the complainant was lively and intelligent with good understanding. She had the normal range of function for her age and a good rapport with the interviewer. The key evidence, such little as there was, did not arise out of leading or inappropriate questions; it came from the child and appeared to be based on recollection. There were no signs of coaching and nothing to suggest she was not competent. The experts were in broad agreement. After two months, the complainant would have lost substantial chunks of information. Dr Markantonakis' concerns were that she would not be able to understand what was being asked of her in court and whether it would be possible to follow what she was trying to explain. As she was frequently distracted and had poor concentration, it would have to be checked frequently that she understood. The judge recorded his concern that she would not be able to deal with the defence proposed line of cross-examination. (Both experts had been provided with a copy of the transcript of the appellant's police interviews.) The judge also recorded that both experts agreed the officer interviewing the complainant was unsuccessful in showing the complainant understood the difference between truth and lies. Neither expert could say how the child had developed since April 2004; nor

could her memory or reactions to questioning be accurately gauged ahead of time.

21   The judge referred to *R. v AS* [2004] EWCA Crim 1294 and *R. v D* [2002] EWCA Crim 990; [2002] 2 Cr.App.R. 36 (p.601); [2003] Q.B. 90 noting that the key word was intelligibility. Ability was required on the part of the witness to understand questions and give answers to them that were understandable, in short intelligibility. She concluded the complainant was a competent witness. She said she was quite capable of understanding questions and giving intelligible answers within the constraints of age appropriate language. But, she added:

> "Ahead of questioning, it is not possible to judge what she remembers of these events now. Both experts agreed time will have eroded her memory but she is likely to have some.
>
> This goes more to her reliability and therefore to the weight to be attached to her evidence. This will be a matter for the jury.
>
> The court, of course, will need to keep the matter under review and the matter may need to be revisited after the child's evidence is complete."

22   In our judgment the judge was justified in ruling, on the material that she had heard and seen prior to the evidence being given, that the complainant was a competent witness. She was right to say that the question might need to be revisited when the child's evidence was complete. By that stage the judge would have a much more complete picture. As the judge pointed out, there were matters the defence needed to ask the complainant about if they were to put their case and obtain her reaction to it. We shall return to the question of competency shortly.

Was the judge right to admit the video evidence?

23   The next issue the judge had to consider was whether the video recording of the complainant's evidence should be admitted in evidence. The power to admit this evidence is to be found in s.27(1) of the 1999 Act. The judge had to consider s.27(2) which provides for the video to be excluded:

> ". . . if the court is of the opinion, having regard to all the circumstances of the case, that it is in the interests of justice the recording . . . should not be admitted."

24   Mr Bentley's submission is that the deficiencies in the interviewing procedure were such that it was not in the interests of justice for it to be admitted in evidence. The deficiencies can be summarised as follows:

- It was poorly planned and conducted, resulting in improvised and incomplete evidence;
- It was undertaken in an environment ill-suited for the purpose;
- There was substantial delay between the incident and the interview with conversation in between relating to the allegations, which meant that what the complainant said had to be treated with caution.

25   It is also pointed out that in his Pro Forma assessment of the interview under the heading "overall utility", Mr Glasgow recorded "little". Mr Bentley complains that not only was there no record of the planning of the interview, there was no record of the conversation between the interviewer and the complainant prior to the interview, although such a conversation plainly took place. Also, there was an inordinate delay before the interview took place and no notes were kept of the complainant leaving the room to see her parents during the interview. Finally, she was eating, playing on a tricycle and playing with toys throughout the interview.

26   All these are valid points but, as Miss Halsall for the Crown points out, the criticisms of the video are not such as to undermine the judge's competence finding. Nor were they such as to make the whole interview process fundamentally unfair. They were all matters which could be brought out at the trial and given such weight as each of them justified. The discretion under s.27(2) is a wide one; it requires the judge to look at the whole of the circumstances of the case and apply an interests of justice test. The interests of justice do not include the interests of the defendant alone. In our view the judge's exercise of discretion under s.27(2) cannot be faulted.

27   The appellant also referred to s.78 of the Police and Criminal Evidence Act 1984, but we do not think on the facts of the present case that adds anything to s.27(2).

Revisiting the competence decision

28   It is necessary to look with some care at what happened when the complainant gave evidence. We do not have a transcript, but the evidence is well covered in the summing up. After the video was played to the jury Miss Halsall for the prosecution asked a few supplementary questions but there was nothing significant to add. She found it difficult to get any words out of the complainant. Her responses were mostly nods (positive) or shakes (negative) of the head.

29   When she was cross-examined, initially she could not remember a clown jar with sweets in it but eventually she did. Nor could she remember anything about "the naughty man".

30   The questioning ran thus:

Q. "Do you remember talking about the naughty man on the film?"
A. She shook her head.
Q. "Do you remember playing with the man"?
A. She shook her head.
Q. "Do you remember touching his beard and finding it sticky?"
A. She shook her head.
Q. "Do you remember the man telling you off? He said you were naughty."
A. She nodded her head.
Q. "Was this because you had wiped your hand on your knickers?"
A. There was an uncertain response to this question.
Q. "Why do you remember that he said you were naughty?"
A. "He did"

Q. "Were you cross with the man, when he said you were naughty?"
A. She nodded her head.
Q. "Did you tell your Mummy a story about the man and he said you were naughty?"
A. She nodded her head.
Q. "Did you think he would tell Mummy you had been naughty?"
A. She shook her head.
Q. "Were you worried he might say you had been naughty?"
A. She nodded her head.
Q. "Do you remember saying in the film that the man licked your nunny?"
A. She shook her head.
Q. "No man licked your nunny, did he?"
A. She shook her head.
The judge then asked the following questions:
Q. "Do you remember telling Mummy a story about the man?"
A. She nodded her head.
Q. "What was the story you told Mummy?"
A. "He hurted me."
Q. "How did he hurt you?"
A. "He punched me."
Q. "Where that happen?"
A. "In the back of the garden."

31   Mr Bentley submits that the complainant had in effect accepted the appellant's case that she had made up the allegation because she was cross that he had told her off and that she thought he might tell her mother. That depends on whether she understood the questions that were being put to her. At face value the evidence might be open to that interpretation, a point that the judge appears to have appreciated in the summing up.

32   Mr Markantonakis had said in his statement that the complainant was unlikely to have a firm enough understanding of the consequences of telling the truth, the importance of telling the truth or whether indeed she understands what telling the truth is. She would be unlikely to understand the questions put to her as a witness and would be unlikely to give answers to them which could be understood. He was, of course, looking forward to how he envisaged the complainant would respond when asked questions at the trial. In our view his concerns are amply borne out by the questions and answers, to which we have referred, that were recited by the judge in her summing up.

33   It is unfortunate that the judge was not requested to revisit her decision on competence at the end of the complainant's evidence. The judge had correctly said that question might need to be reconsidered when the child's evidence was complete. We have no doubt that in this case that would have been the correct course. It is a course that was envisaged by this court in *R. v MacPherson* [2006] 1 Cr.App.R. 30 (p.459), where Forbes J. said it was quite clear the judge was going to keep the matter under review. Had the question of competence been re-examined at this point, it seems to us that while evidence-in-chief through

the pre-recorded video indicated the child just about passed the competence threshold, the position was different when one looked at the whole of her evidence including the largely abortive attempt at cross-examination. What is relevant is the complainant's competence to give evidence at the time of the appellant's trial. It may be it was due to the lapse of time and lack of memory that the complainant was unable to understand the questions or give answers to them which could be understood. One simply does not know. The problem is that her answers simply were not intelligible in the context of the case. She was not, in our view, a sufficiently competent witness for the defence to be able to put its case. The onus of proof was on the Crown to establish competence and they failed to discharge it.

34   In our judgment the judge should have reconsidered the question whether the complainant was a competent witness at the conclusion of the complainant's evidence. Had she done so she would, or should, have concluded that she was not and then withdrawn the case from the jury.

35   There is a further matter that causes us some concern. It is very possibly a consequence of the fact the complainant was not interviewed until nine weeks after the event. The account she gave to her mother on the night of the incident (which was admitted by way of evidence of recent complaint) was in certain respects more detailed than the complainant's account in evidence. The complainant described to her mother two incidents, one in the kitchen and one in the bedroom. The judge gave this direction to the jury.

> "Well the whole investigation was triggered by what [the complainant] said to her mother late that night at home, overheard by J.
>
> How do you treat what the child said that night? The evidence comes from R, the child's mother. It would appear to be relatively shortly after any alleged activity happened and [the complainant] spoke to her mother about it.
>
> Now this is not evidence as to what actually happened between [the complainant] and Mr P, because R was not present and did not see what happened between.
>
> It is evidence that you are entitled to consider, because it may help you to decide whether or not [the complainant] has told you the truth.
>
> The prosecution say that her complaint that night is consistent with what she later said in her video interview and therefore she is more likely to be truthful."

36   This is a classic direction on recent complaint. But Mr Bentley submits that in the particular circumstances of this case the judge should have gone further and told the jury that insofar as the complainant was said to have said things to her mother that were not described by the complainant in her evidence, they did not prove anything. We think there is some force in this submission in the somewhat unusual circumstances of this case. However, the point does not strictly arise, because in our view the judge should have withdrawn the case from the jury at the conclusion of the complainant's evidence.

No case

37   It is unnecessary in the circumstances to deal in any detail with Mr Bentley's
remaining submissions, in particular that the judge should have allowed his submission of no case to answer. The thrust of this point was that the Crown could not
have it both ways. If the complainant was competent then her evidence was so
contradictory as to indicate that she was inherently unreliable. In any event it
could not be properly tested.

38   The judge in rejecting the submission of no case pointed to the final answer in
cross-examination as being the highpoint of the defence submission. That was
when the complainant shook her head in answer to the question, "No man licked
your nunny did he?"

39   The judge said that all of what the child had said should be assessed. Her evidence must be assessed for truthfulness and reliability like any other witness. But
appropriate allowances had to be made for her age and command of language.
The jury could see what she was capable of from the interview in April when
she was obviously more relaxed. It would be wrong to take one question and a
shake of the head in isolation. That of course was on the basis that the complainant was a competent witness which in our judgment she was not.

Delay

40   We return finally to the question of delay. The complainant was not interviewed until nine weeks after the incident. Such delay is strongly discouraged
by the achieving best evidence ("ABE") guidance. Mr Glasgow said there
were two reasons why delay was particularly ill advised with a very young
child. First, cognitive development, including memory, is poorly predicted by
chronological age. So there is a wide variation between different children of a
similar age. Some will cope better than others from the view point of accuracy
and completeness of recollection. Secondly, young children are particularly vulnerable to their recollections being contaminated by information from others. We
were told the reason for the delay was that it was initially felt that the complainant
was too young to give evidence but that this view was later changed when some
thought had been given to s.53(3) of the 1999 Act. Although the videotaped interview took place on April 21, 2004 the appellant's trial did not take place for
another seven months, the trial concluding on November 25, 2004. The trial
was transferred to the Crown Court on June 16, 2004 and a preliminary directions
hearing took place on the July 27, 2004.

41   Explanations can be found for each element of the delay in this case. However
the plain fact is that where a case depends on the evidence of a very young child it
is absolutely essential (a) that the ABE interview takes place very soon after the
event;and (b) that the trial (at which the child has to be cross-examined) takes
place very soon thereafter. As the expert evidence in this case showed, very
young children simply do not have the ability to lay down memory in a manner
comparable to adults. Looking at this case with hindsight, it was completely
unacceptable that the appellant should have been tried for an offence proof of
which relied on the evidence of a three-and-a-half year old when the trial did

not take place until over nine months had passed from the date of the alleged offence. Special efforts must be made to fast-track cases of this kind and it is simply not an option to wait weeks for example for forensic evidence to become available.

Conclusion

42   In our judgment this conviction is not safe. The child was very young, just three-and-a-half. That was not in itself necessarily an insurmountable obstacle for the prosecution. Had she been interviewed appropriately and promptly and had the trial taken place very soon after the event it is possible that when she was cross-examined by the defence she would have given intelligible answers that indicated she was a competent witness. Unfortunately the answers that she gave indicated that she was not. Competency to give evidence relates to the whole of a witness's evidence and not just to part of it. The judge should have stopped the case at the conclusion of the complainant's evidence.

Appeal allowed. Conviction quashed.

R. v ROBINSON (DENNIS)

Court of Appeal (Lord Justice Hooper, Mr Justice Holman and
Mr Justice Fulford): November 11; December 14, 2005

[2005] EWCA Crim 3233; [2006] 1 Cr.App.R. 32

(LT) Bad character; Codefendants; Cut throat defence; Jury directions; Murder

H1   EVIDENCE
Character
*Defendants tried jointly—Cut-throat defence—Second defendant adducing
evidence of first defendant's bad character to support defence of duress—Evidence not admissible at behest of Crown—Judge directing jury to take account
of all evidence when considering cases against each defendant—Whether bad
character evidence relevant only to second defendant's case—Whether misdirection*

H2   The first defendant was charged with murder, the second with perverting the
course of justice. The second defendant adduced evidence of the first defendant's
bad character in support of her defence that she had acted under duress. The evidence was admissible since it was relevant to a fact in issue between the Crown
and the second defendant, but it would not have been admissible had the first
defendant been tried alone. In summing-up the judge directed the jury that all
the evidence could be taken into account when considering the case of each
defendant, including the evidence of the first defendant's bad character. The
first defendant was convicted. He appealed on the ground that the evidence of
bad character adduced by the second defendant had no relevance to his case
and that the jury should have been directed to ignore it when considering the
count against him.

H3   **Held,** dismissing the appeal, that trial judges had to consider the necessity of
giving directions which did not needlessly perplex juries. It would not have been
a misdirection had the judge given the direction sought by the first defendant but,
in the circumstances, it would have required the jury to indulge in the kind of
mental gymnastics which even a judge might find difficult to perform, for very
little, if any, benefit to the first defendant. Accordingly, there had been no misdirection and the first defendant's conviction was safe (post, paras [54], [81], [82],
[87]).

H4   Dicta of Lord Steyn at para.[35] in *R. v Randall (Edward Peter)* [2003] UKHL
69; [2004] 1 Cr.App.R. 26 (p.375); [2004] 1 W.L.R. 56, HL, applied.

H5   *R. v Price (Richard Lyn)* [2004] EWCA Crim 1359; *R. v Mertens (Jan Paul)*
[2004] EWCA Crim 2252, [2005] Crim. L.R. 301 and *R. v Murrell (John
David)* [2005] EWCA Crim 382, [2005] Crim. L.R. 869, considered.

H6   (For evidence of bad character to bolster a particular defence, see *Archbold* 2006, paras 13-21 and 13-72).

Appeal against conviction

H7   On April 28, 2004 at the Central Criminal Court (Judge Moss Q.C.) the appellant, Dennis Robinson, was convicted of murder, count 1 on the indictment. His former girlfriend, Karen Maitland, was also indicted on count 1 but at the conclusion of the prosecution case the judge directed her acquittal on that count. Count 2 charged Maitland alone with perverting the course of justice but the jury were unable to reach a verdict in respect of that count.

H8   The facts and grounds of appeal appear in the judgment of the court.

H9   *Jeremy Dein Q.C.* and *Aisling Byrnes* (assigned by the Registrar of Criminal Appeals) for the appellant.
Sally O'Neill Q.C. and *Michael Holland* (instructed by the Crown Prosecution Service) for the Crown.

Cur. adv. vult.

December 14   Hooper L.J.: handed down the judgment of the court.

1   On April 28, 2004, at the Central Criminal Court (Judge Moss Q.C. and a jury), Dennis Robinson, the appellant, was convicted of the murder of Lyndon Davis. The indictment contained two counts. On count 1 the appellant, together with his former girlfriend, Karen Maitland, faced an allegation of murder. Count 2 charged Maitland alone with perverting the course of justice.

2   At the conclusion of the prosecution case, the trial judge directed the acquittal of Maitland on count 1. The jury were unable to reach a verdict in respect of count 2.

3   In the now sole ground of appeal it is submitted that the trial judge misdirected the jury in relation to the evidence of the appellant's bad character adduced or given by Maitland. Both defendants ran what is conventionally called a cut-throat defence. Both denied murder and both "pointed the finger of blame" at the other. Additionally, Maitland ran the defence of duress on count 2, alleging that she was forced to assist by threats from the appellant.

4   We were particularly assisted by the skeleton argument of Mr Dein Q.C. for the appellant and we are very grateful to him. We have relied on it extensively for the background and facts of the case.

5   At approximately 05.30 on May 3, 2003, the burnt body of Lyndon Davis was discovered in Andrews Road, Hackney. It was the prosecution case that the appellant had murdered Davis at the appellant's home at 215 Dalston Lane, Hackney, and that, together with his friend Everton Husbands, he had deposited the body in Andrews Road before setting fire to it in an attempt to remove evidence. Maitland assisted the appellant by fetching a plastic bag which was put over the deceased's head and by helping to clean the blood from around the flat. Another man, Carey Bent, had also assisted in cleaning the flat.

6 Although no specific motive was ever advanced by the prosecution, it was common ground that the deceased was a dealer in crack cocaine and a former friend of the appellant, who was himself a cannabis dealer. The suggestion was that the appellant murdered Davis in an attempt to gain "respect" or perhaps in order to take over his crack cocaine business.

7 The prosecution case was substantiated in the main by reference to telephone evidence, both of calls made and cell site analysis, local borough CCTV evidence, forensic scientific search evidence, fingerprint evidence and the post-mortem examination. In addition, the prosecution relied upon the testimony of Carey Bent, who, together with Everton Husbands, had pleaded guilty at an early stage to perverting the course of justice for their part in the events of that evening.

8 At approximately 21.00 on March 2, 2003, Lyndon Davis left his home in order to go out. He collected his girlfriend and her friend and drove around the Hackney area delivering crack cocaine. Mobile telephone records show that his phone was in contact with that of the appellant at 21.20 and 22.35. Davis attended 215 Dalston Lane between 22.00 and 23.00 for approximately 10–15 mins.

9 At approximately 01.00, Davis dropped his girlfriend at her sister's house. Thereafter, mobile phone and cell site analysis shows calls between Davis's phone and that of the appellant, with the former travelling towards 215 Dalston Lane, the apparent location of the appellant's phone. It was the prosecution case that the appellant invited Davis to his, the appellant's, flat, where he was to murder him.

10 The last call made by Davis's mobile phone was at 02.09 on May 3, 2003, apparently from the vicinity of 215 Dalston Lane. According to the prosecution, Davis was murdered by the appellant between that time and 02.26. This was because at 02.26 there began a series of calls made from the appellant's phone to that of his friend Everton Husbands. Husbands was living in Enfield and his movements were tracked, by reference to cell site analysis, from his home to 215 Dalston Lane. This, said the prosecution, was in response to a request from the appellant for urgent assistance in removing the evidence of the murder which had taken place.

11 Before Husbands got to the flat, however, Carey Bent, the appellant's lodger, arrived home unexpectedly. The appellant opened the door and Bent saw the motionless body of Lyndon Davis lying on the hall floor. The appellant asked for Bent's assistance and, out of fear of the situation generally and the appellant in particular, Bent helped to roll the deceased in a sheet and load the body into the boot of the newly-arrived Everton Husband's car. Karen Maitland was cleaning the flat.

12 Husbands and the appellant then drove off to Andrews Road where the body was dumped. By reference to local CCTV this was at approximately 03.23. The men then returned to Dalston Lane where an attempt was made to move the deceased's BMW vehicle from where it was parked outside the flat. It would not start and a number of telephone calls were made by the appellant and Husbands in search of jump leads. At approximately 03.39 Husbands purchased a set from a Texaco petrol station. This was, however, to no avail and eventually the appellant, Husbands, Bent and two innocent passers-by pushed

the vehicle into nearby Clapton Square, where it was discovered later on that day. CCTV evidence timed this activity at approximately 04.00.

13   The appellant, Maitland and Husbands then left Dalston Lane in Husbands's vehicle. A series of calls to Bent's mobile from that of the appellant were, according to the prosecution, to ensure that Bent was continuing to clean the flat and not raising the alarm. At approximately 04.21 Husbands filled a canister with petrol at a BP garage and the three returned, still in Husbands's vehicle, to Andrews Road. There the deceased's body was set alight at approximately 04.35. It was the prosecution case that this was all done at the behest of the appellant.

14   Cell site analysis then tracked the movement of the appellant from the area of Andrews Road to Enfield and the home address of Everton Husbands. There, the appellant changed his clothes and disposed of the murder weapon, a hammer, before returning, still accompanied by Husbands and Maitland, to 215 Dalston Lane.

15   The post-mortem examination revealed that Lyndon Davis died as a result of multiple head injuries. There were in the region of 33 separate wounds to his scalp and face, some of which penetrated the skull. The possibility of asphyxiation by means of the plastic bag which had been applied to his head could not be excluded.

16   It was the prosecution case that the injuries were inflicted to the deceased by the appellant, using a claw hammer. Upon being directed there by the appellant in his interview, the police found such a hammer at the work place of Everton Husbands, although no forensic scientific link was established between it and the murder.

17   The prosecution further alleged that the plastic bag was placed on Davis's head either by Maitland, who had admitted as much to Everton Husbands, or by the appellant once Maitland had fetched a bag for that specific purpose. It was in those circumstances that Maitland was originally indicted for murder: the case against her was put on the basis of joint enterprise, although a successful submission of no case to answer on count 1 was made on Maitland's behalf at the close of the prosecution case.

18   The appellant was arrested on June 18, 2003. During the search of his address, traces of the deceased's blood were discovered in the hall and kitchen/living room of the flat. He was taken to Stoke Newington Police Station where he was interviewed in the presence of a solicitor for three days.

19   The appellant said that Lyndon Davis had been a good friend of his and that he had known Davis since the latter's arrival from Jamaica about four years earlier. He also said that he knew Everton Husbands and that he had seen Husbands the previous day.

20   Asked to account for his movements on May 2 and 3, the appellant had no real recollection of where he had been. He thought that he would most probably have been at home or with Husbands in Enfield. He had learned of Davis's death from someone he knew called Gee (Garcia Muir, the deceased's brother's ex-girlfriend and Maitland's cousin) and had seen it confirmed in the Hackney Gazette.

21   He had known that Davis was a crack dealer and had last seen him on either Thursday May 1, or Friday May 2, at about 15.00 or 16.00. He denied having had any part in the death of Davis.

22   The appellant was told that blood had been recovered from the door-frame at 215 Dalston Lane. He suggested that he, the appellant, and Lyndon Davis might once have done some boxing at the flat.

23   The appellant was told that the police had obtained CCTV footage of the deceased's car being pushed in Clapton Square, to which the appellant made no comment. Upon being told later that his fingerprints had been discovered on the vehicle, the appellant said that he had, on an earlier occasion, helped Davis to push his car.

24   The appellant then continued to make no comment to the other questions that were put to him. By way of explanation, he said that he was concerned for the safety of his children.

25   The police then told the appellant that Husbands, who by now had also been arrested, had submitted a prepared statement to the police in which he stated that the appellant had killed Davis and asked Husbands to help him get rid of the body. The appellant continued to make no comment.

26   In a further interview on the evening of June 20, the appellant stated that Husbands had killed Davis in order to take over the latter's crack-dealing business. He said that it was Husbands who had purchased the petrol that was used to set fire to the body and that Husbands had hidden the murder weapon, a hammer, at the school at which he worked.

27   The appellant stated that, with Husbands at the time of the murder was a Yardie, whom the appellant was not prepared to name. He stated that Maitland was not involved and did not mention the presence of Carey Bent.

28   The appellant admitted that he had carried Davis's body to Husbands's car and had driven off with him to Andrews Road. They had later returned and set fire to the body before going to Husbands's address. This was all at the behest of Husbands. The appellant further stated that he had telephoned Davis and invited him to Dalston Lane at the request of Husbands and the Yardie.

29   The accounts of Maitland and Bent were both put to the appellant, who made no comment.

30   The police also found Karen Maitland at 215 Dalston Lane on June 18, 2003. Originally arrested for possessing cannabis, she was taken to Shoreditch Police Station where she was cautioned for that offence. Maitland was then treated as a significant witness by the police. However, the police soon realised that Maitland had been living with the appellant at Dalston Lane at the time of the murder. On June 20, 2003, she was arrested for murder.

31   Maitland was then interviewed under caution in the presence of a solicitor. She initially said that she had not been present when the murder had taken place and that she knew nothing about it. Later that evening she elected to make no comment to questions put to her. Maitland was informed that Husbands had told police that she had told him that she had put a bag over the head of Lyndon Davis.

32   When she was interviewed the following day, Maitland told the police that she had been at home with the appellant at 215 Dalston Lane in the bedroom. The

appellant left the bedroom and she heard "stumbling". When she came out, Davis was on the floor. She stated that the appellant had put the bag over Davis's head.

33   Maitland said that the appellant asked her to clean up the blood and had telephoned Husbands in order to help him to dispose of the body. She stated that the appellant asked her to get a bag from the drawer. This, she knew, was to be put over Davis's head. She later said that this was most probably to stop Davis breathing.

34   Maitland stated that the appellant, Husbands and Bent had carried Davis's body from the flat whilst she remained there, cleaning. She said that throughout she had been under the influence of the appellant, whom she referred to as a "monster". Later she had gone in the car with the appellant and Husbands to Husbands's address in Enfield. On the way, Husbands bought some petrol which he said was to be thrown over Davis's body. This was done out of her sight. Once at Husbands's address, the appellant changed his clothes and the three returned to Dalston Lane, where Bent was still cleaning.

35   Maitland said that she then left Dalston Lane for a period of two weeks, coming home only because the appellant threatened to beat her if she did not. In a later interview, Maitland stated that she had in fact seen the appellant hitting Davis with the hammer.

36   The appellant denied murdering Lyndon Davis but at trial advanced an account different from that set out in his police interviews. It was his case that he and Lyndon Davis had always been friends. Davis had been to the appellant's flat between 22.00 and 23.00 on May 2, 2003 in order to supply him and Maitland with a little crack cocaine: that was the last time the appellant had seen him alive. Just before 02.00 on May 3, 2003, Maitland let two men into the flat. They were Yardie friends from the same part of Jamaica that she came from and they were there to conduct some business involving drugs. One of the men was in possession of a firearm. Their arrival came as no surprise to the appellant as this had happened before. Maitland was an illegal overstayer with a somewhat shadowy past. She was also a user of Class A drugs who mixed in Yardie circles with which the appellant had no involvement. The appellant was given some crack cocaine and he went outside to smoke it.

37   It was whilst the appellant was outside that his mobile phone was used by someone else, possibly Maitland, to telephone Lyndon Davis and, it seems, Everton Husbands. When the appellant returned to his flat, he was horrified to see the body of his friend on the floor. Immediately terrified, and under threat from the still-present, armed Yardies that they knew where his children lived, the appellant did as he was told, namely to telephone Husbands and to get rid of the body.

38   Thereafter, the appellant's account of events is broadly in keeping with that of the prosecution, save that he disputes that he was in charge. On the contrary, it was his case that Maitland and Husbands were controlling the situation.

39   The appellant accepted that the contents of his police interviews were lies: these were told in order to protect his family and in response to the lies being told to the police by Husbands, of which the appellant was informed.

40   He refuted the suggestion made on her behalf that Maitland was dominated by him both physically and emotionally and stated that she was always free to come and go as she pleased. His evidence in this regard was supported by that of Garcia Muir, Maitland's cousin and a prosecution witness, who similarly rejected such suggestions advanced on Maitland's behalf. It was also supported, to a certain extent, by Rudolph Flemmings, a defence witness and boyfriend of Maitland.

41   Maitland, giving evidence, relied upon the defence of duress. On the evening in question she was at home with the appellant in the bedroom at 215 Dalston Lane. At some point the appellant left the room and she heard what she described as "stumbling". She then heard a voice which she recognised as that of the deceased asking the appellant what the problem was. The last thing she heard before she left the room was appellant calling her. When she went out into the hallway she came upon the appellant striking the deceased repeatedly with a hammer. The deceased was lying on the floor. The appellant told her to fetch a plastic bag, which she did. He tied this around the deceased's head. Carey Bent then arrived home and she and Bent were told by the appellant to clean the flat. Everton Husbands, who had been telephoned several times by the appellant, appeared and assisted the appellant to remove the body of the deceased. Thereafter it was the appellant who took charge and whose idea it ultimately was to set fire to the body of the deceased.

42   Maitland asserted that the reason she became involved in cleaning the flat was because she was in fear of her own life were she not to comply with the appellant's requests. The basis of this fear was the nature of the relationship she had with him. Maitland described at considerable length her troubled and violent upbringing in Jamaica. She stated that, when she first met the appellant, the relationship seemed healthy and normal. After a short time, however, the appellant began to abuse her emotionally and physically, often beating her and locking her both in and out of the flat. She lived in fear of him but felt that she had no other place to go. This, combined with the fact that she witnessed the appellant murder a man who had been his friend, led Maitland to do what she did following the murder.

43   She refuted the appellant's case as put to her by his counsel. Although she was cross-examined to some extent by the prosecution in relation to her assertion of duress in relation to count 2, her account of the murder was expressly accepted by the Crown for whom Maitland was, of course, the only eyewitness to the crime.

44   During the course of the prosecution case, the defendants were running defences which were mutually inconsistent. Put simply, each was blaming the other. Following the departure of Maitland from count 1, she continued to elicit evidence of the appellant's bad character in order to bolster her defence to count 2. Mr Dein accepted that the evidence of the appellant's bad character was admissible. He also submits that the evidence would not have been admissible if he had been tried alone. Subject to one caveat, Miss O'Neill Q.C. agrees with that proposition. The ground of appeal relates to the manner in which the trial judge directed the jury about that evidence.

45   During the hearing of the appeal we considered a list of the attacks on the appellant's character adduced, or given in evidence, by Maitland. By the end of the hearing the agreed list read as follows:

    i) The presence of a Stanley knife and holder and a 35cm knife from the appellant's bedroom, coupled with cross-examination about the knife;

    ii) the presence of a club or lump hammer from the appellant's kitchen was similarly elicited;

    iii) the appellant's fingerprints were identified on the magazine of a firearm which was found by the police in Husbands's home;

    iv) when Garcia Muir and Carey Bent were cross-examined by Maitland's counsel, they gave challenged evidence about the appellant's violence towards her;

    v) Maitland gave challenged evidence that the appellant beat her with a belt, slippers and fists;

    vi) Maitland said that he had kicked her whilst she was pregnant and that she had suffered a miscarriage and this was challenged;

    vii) Maitland gave evidence that the appellant had allowed his friend Kevin to use her sexually;

    viii) details of the appellant's rape conviction were adduced in evidence;

    ix) Maitland gave evidence that the appellant told her that he had killed before.

46   We turn to the summing-up. The trial judge summarised the respective cases of the two defendants before him and gave the following direction:

> "How do you approach that conflict? You should examine their evidence with particular care because each, in saying what they do, may be more concerned about protecting themselves than speaking the truth and that is an aspect which you should bear in mind, but you must also remember the following:
>
> > first, that you must, as I directed you, consider the case for and against each defendant quite separately;
> >
> > secondly, that you must decide the case of each defendant on all the evidence, including that of the co-defendant;
> >
> > thirdly, that while bearing in mind when considering the evidence of each defendant that they may have an interest to serve, nevertheless you must assess the evidence of each of them in the same way as any other witness in the case."
>
> (Underlining added)

47   In the words which we have underlined, the judge was telling the jury that all the evidence could be taken into account when considering the case of each defendant. Thus, when considering the case against the appellant, the jury were being told that they could take into account i) to ix) above. The only restriction on the use of the bad character evidence related to the conviction for rape (in contrast to the details). The judge said:

> "What is the relevance of the defendant's previous convictions in this case? The only reason that you have heard them is so that you may have knowledge of the character of the defendant who has made this attack, because it may assist you to judge the truthfulness of his evidence when you come

to consider this matter. What you must not do is automatically assume that he is guilty or that he is not telling the truth, just because he has previous convictions. His convictions are not relevant at all to the likelihood of his having committed the offence and nor are they evidence that he committed the offence [for] which he is now on trial. They are relevant only as to whether you can believe him. You do not have to allow these convictions to affect your judgment at all and it is for you to decide the extent to which, if at all, his previous convictions help you about that."

48   Mr Dein does not criticise this direction.

49   He submits that the jury should have been told that the material summarised in paras i) to ix) had no relevance to the appellant's case and had to be ignored when reaching their verdict in the appellant's case.

50   It is difficult to see how the judge could have done that without carefully identifying the evidence summarised in these paragraphs either as part of a general direction or when going through the evidence in the case. The judge would also have to distinguish that evidence from the evidence given by the co-defendant directly implicating the appellant in the murder. Subject to the third of the three directions we have set out above, the jury were entitled to give what weight they thought appropriate to Maitland's account of the appellant's involvement in the murder. Thus the jury would be told, if Mr Dein is right, to ignore evidence of the appellant's bad character as adduced by, or as given by, Maitland but to take into account her evidence directly implicating him in the murder.

51   The complications do not end there. In assessing the credibility of Maitland's evidence against the appellant that he was the murderer and not her and that she merely helped him out of fear, would the jury be entitled to take into account her evidence of being frightened of him? They must be able to take it into account when reaching their verdict in her case, but would they have to ignore it when considering her credibility as part of their deliberations in the appellant's case? Mr Dein would say "Yes". If Mr Dein is right, the jury would have to ignore Maitland's account of an abusive relationship with the appellant when considering whether to believe her evidence that the appellant was the murderer, but take it into account when considering her defence of duress.

52   If the judge had given the direction for which Mr Dein contends, he would have to have given a corresponding direction for Maitland, identifying the equivalent evidence given or led by the appellant. In this case that might not have been too difficult, but one can easily imagine cases where the complications would multiply, particularly if the jury are considering two or more defendants who remain facing a count of murder.

53   In this case there would be the added complication that the jury would be able to take into account (as Mr Dein concedes) the previous convictions when assessing the credibility of the appellant.

54   Absent any authority, we take the view that the direction sought by Mr Dein would require the jury to indulge in the kind of "mental gymnastics" which even a judge might find difficult to perform, for very little if any benefit to the appellant.

55   Ms O'Neill submits that in a case like the present the jury should be entitled to consider all the evidence, giving it such weight as they think appropriate and bearing in mind that each defendant may have an interest to serve in giving evidence against the other. Subject to being required to reach a different conclusion by reason of authority, we see much force in that argument.

56   Our preliminary view is fortified by what happened after the challenged direction had been given. The judge said:

> "Is there any matter of law which any of learned counsel want to raise with me at this stage, following my directions on the law?"

57   Mr Kay Q.C., who appeared for the appellant at trial, said that there was not. If there was an error in the summing-up on this aspect of the case, it did not strike very experienced leading counsel at the time. If Mr Kay had thought that this direction was unfair to the defendant, one would have thought that he would have intervened and asked for a correction (assuming that the issue had not been considered before the start of the summing-up). The absence of intervention is not decisive but is indicative of the views taken by Mr Kay. We should add that the court made this point when granting leave to appeal.

58   We turn to the authorities. In *R. v Randall* [2003] UKHL 69; [2004] 1 Cr.App.R. 26 (p.375); [2004] 1 W.L.R. 56 Lord Steyn said in para.[35] (which was obiter):

> "For the avoidance of doubt I would further add that in my view where evidence of propensity of a co-accused is relevant to a fact in issue between the Crown and the other accused it is not necessary for a trial judge to direct the jury to ignore that evidence in considering the case against the co-accused. Justice does not require that such a direction be given. Moreover, such a direction would needlessly perplex juries."

59   Their Lordships agreed with the opinion given by Lord Steyn. In the words of Lord Bingham, he "wholly" agreed with the opinion.

60   In *R. v Price* [2004] EWCA Crim 1359, in which I gave the judgment of the court, we followed and applied para.[35]. One of the grounds of appeal in that case was that the trial judge should, as in the instant case, have directed the jury, in effect, to ignore the evidence of the appellant's violence and aggressiveness, evidence relied upon by the co-defendant. The judge had told the jury,

> ". . . the relevance of any previous violence or aggressiveness on other occasions is not to prove: 'Well, he did it or he said it before, so he must have done it on November 12 and 13'; its relevance is to provide you with as complete a picture as possible of what manner of man you are trying."

61   Mr Dein does not seek to distinguish the facts in *Price*. He submits that *Price* is wrong and should not be followed. To support that submission he principally relied on two later cases: *R. v Mertens* [2005] Crim. L.R. 301; [2004] EWCA Crim 2252 and *R. v Murrell* [2005] EWCA Crim 382.

62   Prior to *Price* but unknown to the court another division of the court presided over by Rix L.J. had interpreted para.[35] in the same way: *R. v B (C)* [2004] EWCA Crim 1254; [2004] 2 Cr.App.R. 34 (p.570). We return to that case later.

63   In *Mertens* two defendants each charged with murder sought to blame each other. The appellant called evidence of the previous conviction for manslaughter of his co-accused Billia and appealed upon the basis that the trial judge had wrongly directed the jury that this evidence was not relevant to the co-accused's case. Billia was acquitted. May L.J. said:

> "13. The appeal centres on the fact that Billia had a previous conviction. The appellant relied on his own good character. It was he who introduced into evidence the fact that, as he said, Billia was the more likely perpetrator of this murder given his bad character. In particular he relied on and called evidence about Billia's previous conviction after a murder trial at the Central Criminal Court, when Billia was convicted of manslaughter in 1993 of a man called John Fanning, a homosexual companion of Billia's, in circumstances that in some respects bore some resemblance to the facts of the present case."

64   The trial judge had directed the jury:

> ". . . Mr Billia's previous conviction for the manslaughter of John Fanning. I am going to ask you to be very careful how you will use the evidence about this, and I am going to suggest that you treat it quite differently when you are considering the prosecution's case against Mr Billia himself and when you are considering the prosecution's case against Mr Mertens. <u>When you are considering the prosecution's case against Mr Billia, I suggest you disregard it altogether.</u> It does not form part of the prosecution's case against Mr Billia at all. Mr Ferguson asked yesterday in his final speech, rhetorically, 'Why have the prosecution not called the evidence about the killing of John Fanning? Why was it Mr Mertens's team who did that?' There is a very simple answer to that question. The prosecution could not have called that evidence themselves. It simply is not admissible or relevant evidence to support the prosecution's case."
>
> (Underlining added)

65   Counsel for Mertens submitted that in the light of para.[35] of *Randall*, the judge should have directed the jury that they were entitled to take into account Billia's conviction for manslaughter when considering the case against Billia.

66   Dismissing the appeal, the court held that the main thrust of *Randall* was that where one co-accused has previous convictions which may indicate, or may be regarded as indicating, a propensity relevant to a cut-throat defence, that evidence is relevant in the case of the other co-accused. As far as para.[35] was concerned, May L.J. stated:

> "69. We have been troubled about the extent and relevance of para.[35] of *Randall*. Para.[35] includes this: 'For the avoidance of doubt I would further add that in my view where evidence of propensity of a co-accused is relevant

to a fact in issue between the Crown and the other accused . . .' If one emphasises the word 'relevant', it is to be recalled that Lord Steyn had an extended passage on the subject of relevance and that relevance was discussed in the context of similar fact evidence. As Mr Waters [counsel for the respondent] submits, in the case against a single defendant propensity will never be relevant and admissible unless the facts going to propensity can be elevated to being admissible similar fact evidence. Accordingly, where evidence of propensity of a co-accused is relevant, it may perhaps be read as referring to relevance because the evidence is admissible as similar fact evidence."

67   May L.J. continued:

"70. If, however, we were not sure that that is the correct interpretation in the context of this case of para.[35], we nevertheless have to consider that this judge was faced with having to sum the case up fairly as between both defendants. We accept the submission of Mr Waters that, in the circumstances of this case, he could not have directed the jury that Billia's conviction was relevantly probative in the case against Billia. He could not do that because it was accepted not to be admissible similar fact evidence in his case. So far as the case of Mr Mertens, the appellant, was concerned, this was evidence that Mr Mertens was entitled to rely upon. In substance the judge said as much on p.47 of vol.3 and p.16 of vol.4, where he gave what we read as a clear propensity direction. Judges have to tailor their summing-ups to the circumstances of individual cases. They have to be fair to each or every defendant before the court. In the present case, in our judgment, this judge did just that, and summing up the case against Billia, as we think he had to, in the way that he did, he also in substance we think did what the House of Lords said he should do in *Randall*, at least so far as it was tailored to the present case.
71. For these reasons, in our judgment, there was no misdirection by this judge in this case."

68   Mr Dein submits that the Court in para.[69] interpreted Lord Steyn's dicta as having application only in a case where the bad character of a co-accused was admissible at the behest of the Crown, for example under the similar fact doctrine.

69   We have doubts about this passage, which Mr Dein accepts was obiter. To make the point clearer, para.[35] of *Randall* can be rewritten:

". . . where evidence of propensity of D1 is relevant to a fact in issue between the Crown and D2 it is not necessary for a trial judge to direct the jury to ignore that evidence in considering the case against D1."

70   Similarly rewriting the last part of the cited passage from *Mertens*, it would read:

"Accordingly, where evidence of propensity of D1 is relevant, it may perhaps be read as referring to relevance because the evidence is admissible [against D1] as similar fact evidence."

71   With all respect to May L.J., we do not think that this is right. If the evidence is, in any event, admissible at the behest of the Crown, then there was no need for Lord Steyn to address the issue. The difficulty arises only when the evidence is not admissible at the behest of the Crown.

72   *Price* was not cited to the Court.

73   We turn to *R. v Murrell* [2005] EWCA Crim 382. The appellant and two others were charged with importing cocaine. The co-defendants blamed the appellant and had at trial elicited evidence of his previous conviction for importing cocaine and the finding of firearms and ammunition at his home address. The Recorder admitted the evidence but directed the jury that they should disregard it in considering the appellant's case. Lord Woolf C.J. summarised how the case was summed up:

> "29. When the Recorder came to sum up, no doubt taking his lead from the way the case had been presented on behalf of the Crown, he made it clear that the evidence of the previous conviction and the finding of the gun were relevant to the cases against Flook and Ellis, but not part of the case against the appellant . . ."

74   The appellant unsuccessfully appealed on the basis that the evidence of the items seized was inadmissible.

75   The Court of Appeal, holding that the evidence was properly admitted, also expressly approved the trial judge's direction to the jury. At para.[24], Lord Woolf stated:

> "It is, however, important to have in mind that, subject to Lord Steyn's comments [at para.[35] of *Randall*] that we have cited, the evidence was admissible not as against the appellant. If he had been tried alone, the evidence would not have been admitted; although it is right to point out that the case against him would still have been a very strong case indeed. It was admissible in the case against each of his co-accused."

76   At para.[28], Lord Woolf said:

> "We recognise the difficulty that if what Lord Steyn said in *Randall* is applied too literally, the person against whom evidence is admitted, which would not normally be admitted, would be prejudiced. The trial judge always has to do his best to ensure that justice is done to each defendant before him. This case provides a good example of how justice can be done."

77   In para.[29], Lord Woolf continued:

> "Without causing perplexity to the jury, the judge can indicate the Crown's case against each. It is perfectly possible for a judge to describe the Crown's case against one accused without referring to the evidence which is admissible in support of the case of the co-accused, and then, as this Recorder did, make clear the relevance of the evidence so far as the co-accused are con-

cerned. This may help to minimize the prejudice that may be caused in any joint trial because evidence is admissible as against one accused which is not admissible against another."

78   *Price* was cited to the court. Lord Woolf said:

> "26. The approach of Lord Steyn in *Randall* was endorsed and applied by this court in the case of *R. v Price* [2004] EWCA Crim 1359. *Price* was preceded by *R. v B (C)* [2004] EWCA Crim 1254, in which Rix L.J. analysed in detail not only the decision in *Randall* but also the decision in the other cases and he applied what Lord Steyn had said at para.[35]. Rix L.J. went on to say at para.[56]:
>
> > 'In other words if the propensity of one defendant becomes relevant as between his co-accused and the Crown, no distinction is to be attempted in viewing the position as between the former and the Crown. Thus where propensity is admitted for the sake of a co-defendant's defence, the Crown becomes the beneficiary of that. As Lord Steyn says, that is not unjust and the alternative would be unnecessarily perplexing.'
>
> He added:
>
> > 'A question may, however, be raised as to the ramifications of this position. In the more normal case where previous convictions come to be admitted for reasons other than their relevance to a co-accused's defence, a model direction requires the judge to warn the jury that they are not relevant to 'the likelihood of his having committed this offence'."

79   Lord Woolf noted the difficulty which May L.J. in *Mertens* had had with para.[35] and quoted part of para.[70].

80   In both *Mertens* and *Murrell* the trial judges had directed the jury, in effect, to ignore the evidence of the bad character of D1 adduced by the co-defendant D2 (and inadmissible at the behest of the prosecution) when considering the case against D1. Those directions were approved. In *Mertens* the Court held in effect that D2 could not insist that the trial judge direct the jury to consider the bad character evidence of D1 when considering the case against D1. In this case Mr Dein submits that the appellant (D1 in the example) is entitled as a matter of law to a direction of the kind in *Merten* and *Murrell* and that *Price* is therefore wrong. He relies also on the fact that Lord Woolf, in para.[29], did not think that such a direction would be perplexing. He relies on the reference by May L.J. to trial judges having to be fair to each and every defendant before the court.

81   In our view *Price*, relying on para.[35] of *Randall*, makes it clear that the kind of direction given by the trial judge in this case is not a misdirection. *Price* is binding on us. Whilst accepting that *Mertens* establishes that it would not be a misdirection to give the direction sought by Mr Dein in the present case, that does not mean that *Price* is wrong. The effect of *Mertens* supported by *Murrell* is that trial judges should consider carefully how the interests of justice for all the defendants may properly be met in a joint "cut-throat" trial. But, in accordance with *Randall*, the judge must also consider the necessity to give directions

which will not "needlessly perplex juries". If juries are needlessly perplexed then the defendants in their care will not receive a fair trial.

82   We do not believe that the trial judge in the instant case discussed the matter with counsel before summing-up. If he did not, it would have been better if he had. However, the fact that Mr Kay did not object suggests that he thought the summing up was not unfair to the appellant. If we had taken the view that the appellant did not, as a result of the direction, receive a fair trial, we would have been minded to quash the conviction on the basis that *Price* should be read as being qualified by *Mertens* and *Murrell*. But we do not take that view. The direction given by Judge Moss Q.C. was fair in that a direction of the kind sought by Mr Dein would have needlessly perplexed the jury for the reasons set out in para.[51] and, it follows, with no real benefit to the appellant.

83   We add this before passing on to the next submissions. Unless the evidence of bad character adduced by the co-defendant is in any event admissible at the behest of the prosecution (which it may well be, for example, under Pt 11 of the Criminal Justice Act 2003), it is to be hoped that the prosecution do not seek in closing the case to the jury to rely on it and, should the prosecution be minded to do so, the judge should be informed in the absence of the jury to enable the matter to be discussed. If the evidence is admissible at the behest of the prosecution then the standard directions will normally have to be given: see e.g. *R. v Hanson* [2005] EWCA Crim 824; [2005] 2 Cr.App.R. 21 (p.299); [2005] 1 W.L.R. 3169.

84   In his skeleton argument, Mr Dein submitted that, if the judge was right to direct the jury that they could take into account the matters identified in para.[45] above, then he should have directed the jury that they were relevant to credibility and not propensity. Mr Dein abandoned this submission, accepting during the course of argument that such a direction would make no sense.

85   He further submitted that the jury should have been directed that, before utilising against the appellant any of the disputed matters identified in para.[45], the jury had to be sure that the allegation was true. We do not accept that. It is trite law that a jury only have to be sure that the ingredients of the offence have been proved. The jury do that after considering all the relevant evidence. There is no requirement for the jury to be sure about any particular piece of evidence (unless, without that piece, the ingredients of the offence would not have been proved). In any event such a direction would not assist a defendant. It might well require the judge to examine the evidence in some detail to assist the jury to decide whether they were sure or not. Such an examination would carry the risk that the disputed prejudicial material would be given a status and importance which it did not deserve (it is for a similar reason that counsel for a defendant does not always want a *Lucas* (*R. v Lucas* (1981) 73 Cr.App.R. 159) lies direction, with the risk of overemphasising the importance of a lie).

86   Mr Dein submitted that a *Hanson* type direction was necessary if the judge was right to direct the jury that all the evidence could be taken into account when considering the case of each defendant. We see no merit in that argument for the same reasons as we have set out in the preceding paragraph.

87   For these reasons this appeal is dismissed.

Appeal dismissed

The Court of Appeal (Criminal Division) certified, under s.33(2) of the Criminal Appeal Act 1968, that a point of law of general public importance was involved in its decision, namely: "Where evidence of the propensity of D1 is relevant to a fact in issue between the Crown and D2, is not admissible at the behest of the Crown and is elicited at the behest of D2, (i) should the judge direct the jury that the evidence is inadmissible in the case of D1 and that they should ignore it when considering his case; and (ii) in any event, should the judge give the jury a propensity direction to assist them in making use of the evidence?"

Leave to appeal to the House of Lords refused.

R. v SLOCOMBE

COURT OF APPEAL (President of the Queen's Bench Division
(Sir Igor Judge), Mr Justice Elias and Mr Justice Ouseley):
November 1; November 23, 2005

[2005] EWCA Crim 2997; [2006] 1 Cr.App.R. 33

(LT) Detention and training orders; Indecent assault; Sex Offenders Register

H1 SEXUAL OFFENCES
Notification requirements
Defendant as young person convicted of sexual offence and sentenced to detention and training order—Defendant subject to notification require- ments—Relevant notification period—Whether whole term of detention and training order "equivalent" to sentence of imprisonment—Whether defendant failing to register within period—Sexual Offences Act 2003 (c.42), ss.82, 131(a)

H2 The appellant was born in March 1983. In March 2000 he was convicted of an indecent assault and sentenced in August 2000 to a 12-month detention and train- ing order under which he was required to serve a period of detention followed by a period of supervision, the period of detention being half of the term of the order. The appellant also became subject to the notification requirements contained in the Sex Offenders Act 1997. In November 2004 he completed a term of imprison- ment imposed for theft offences but failed to notify the police of his release or three changes of home address. He was charged with four offences of failure to register as a sex offender, contrary to s.91(1)(a) and (2) of the Sexual Offences Act 2003. By s.82(1)(2) of the 2003 Act where a person under 18 at the date of his conviction was sentenced to the equivalent of imprisonment for a term of more than six months but less than 30 months the notification period was five years; however, for a sentence equivalent to a term of imprisonment of six months or less the notification was three-and-a-half years. By s.131(a) the "equivalent" arrangement applied to a period of detention which a person was "liable to serve" under a detention and training order. The trial judge accepted the Crown's submission that an offender sentenced to a 12-month detention and training order was "liable to serve" the full 12-month term of the order. Accordingly the appel- lant had been sentenced to a term of more than six months but less than 30 months' imprisonment, and in November and December 2004 he was still subject to the notification requirements. The appellant appealed.

H3 **Held,** allowing the appeal, that the period of detention which the offender was "liable to serve" under a detention and training order should be treated not as a reference to the entire term of the order but the period of detention and training itself which is fixed when the offender is sentenced. For the purposes of s.82(1) the appellant was sentenced to the equivalent of a sentence of imprisonment for a term of six months. As he was under 18 at the relevant date, the notification period for him was three-and-a-half years from the date of his conviction on March 18, 2000. Therefore at the time of his release from custody in November 2004 his obligations under the notification requirements had expired. Since the appellant pleaded guilty to the offences following a ruling which was wrong in law the convictions were unsafe (post, para.[19]).

H4   (For s.82 of the Sexual Offences Act 2003, see *Archbold* 2006, para. 20–267.)

Appeal against conviction

H5   On April 11, 2005 in the Crown Court at Exeter (Judge Griggs) the appellant, Nicholas Slocombe, pleaded guilty, following a ruling made by the judge on March 17, 2005, to four counts of failing without reasonable excuse to register as a sex offender, contrary to s.91(1)(a) and (2) of the Sexual Offences Act 2003. He appealed against conviction on the ground that the judge's ruling was wrong in law.

H6   The facts appear in the judgment of the Court.

H7   *Gavin Collett* (assigned by the Registrar of Criminal Appeals) for the appellant. *Gareth Branston* (instructed by the Crown Prosecution Service, Exeter) for the Crown.

Cur. adv. vult.

November 23.   Sir Igor Judge P.: handed down the judgment of the Court.

1   On April 11, 2005 Nicholas Slocombe appeared before Judge Griggs sitting in the Crown Court at Exeter. He faced an indictment which charged four offences of failure to register as a sex offender, contrary to s.91(1)(a) and s.91(2) of the Sexual Offences Act 2003. The particulars alleged that, without reasonable excuse, he had failed to comply with the requirements of notification found in s.83 and s.84 of the 2003 Act. So far as the first three counts were concerned, the relevant dates of non-compliance were November 2004, while the allegation in the fourth count related to December 2004. He had undoubtedly failed to provide the necessary details. The question, however, was whether he was under a legal obligation to do so, and liable to be punished for non-compliance.

2   On March 17, 2005, Judge Griggs heard submissions that as a matter of law Slocombe could not be guilty of these offences. At the dates alleged he was not required to comply with the notification provisions in the 2003 Act. The judge rejected the argument. Accordingly, when Slocombe appeared on April 11, 2005, he pleaded guilty.

3   He now appeals against conviction on the ground that Judge Griggs' conclusion was wrong in law. Any intelligent observer will be baffled to discover that there could be any doubt about whether the appellant was or was not guilty of a criminal offence. There certainly should be none. Yet Counsel, seeking to

assist us to decide this question, made detailed submissions about the legislative provisions in no less than five statutes. Having heard argument, we found it necessary to reserve our judgment. We shall avoid lengthy comment. Such complication and difficulty in achieving a proper understanding of legislative provisions which may result, as this case did, in a criminal conviction and prison sentence, is profoundly unsatisfactory.

4   Nicholas Slocombe was born on March 5, 1983. On March 18, 2000, at Neath and Port Talbot Youth Court, after he pleaded guilty, he was convicted of an indecent assault on a 10-year-old boy, whom he had kissed on the cheek. On May 10, 2000 he was sentenced to a 12-month probation order. On August 15, 2000, he was found to be in breach of the probation order at Caerphilly Youth Court. The probation order was revoked. He was re-sentenced to a 12-month detention and training order.

5   After serving six months, on February 14, 2001, the appellant was released.

6   Between June 2003 and November 2004, the appellant served a custodial sentence for an offence or offences of theft. After his release on November 16, 2004, he failed to notify the police of his release or three changes of his home address. He thought that his notification obligations had expired. He was arrested in December 2004 for unrelated matters, and in due course charged with these offences, contrary to the Sexual Offences Act 2003. The relevant provisions came into force on May 1, 2004.

7   Our attention was drawn first to the Sex Offenders Act 1997, the statutory provision in force at the date when the appellant pleaded guilty on March 18, 2000, when he was sentenced in May 2000, and re-sentenced in August 2000. This included a table relating to notification requirements for young offenders, ascertained by reference to the "equivalent" sentence of imprisonment. For these purposes s.4(1)(a) identified "a period of detention which a person is liable to serve under a secure training order". This provision, and in particular the words "liable to serve" pre-echoed s.82 of the Sexual Offences Act 2003, to which we shall come in due course.

8   On March 1, 1998 the relevant provisions of the Criminal Justice and Public Order Act 1994 came into force, defining the secure training order as an order that the offender "shall be subject to a period of detention in a secure training centre followed by a period of supervision" (s.1(1) of the 1994 Act). With effect from April 1, 2000 this section of the 1994 Act was replaced by ss.73–79 of the Crime and Disorder Act 1998, which produced the detention and training order to which the appellant was resentenced at Caerphilly Youth Court on August 15, 2000.

9   During the course of argument both counsel assumed that there was no specific provision in the 1997 Act which, at the date of the imposition of the detention and training order in August 2000, applied any of the relevant provisions of the 1997 Act to detention and training orders. This led to a certain amount of creative interpretation of the 1997 Act on both sides. In fact the assumptions were incorrect, and overlooked an amendment to s.4(1)(a) of the 1997 Act, contained in para.144 of Sch.8 to the 1998 Act, which covered the introduction of the then new detention and training order. This came into force on April 1, 2000.

10   Section 73(3) of the 1998 Act identified the detention and training order as an
order "that the offender in respect of whom it is made shall be subject, for the
term specified in the order, to a period of detention and training followed by a
period of supervision". Section 75(1) and (2) made clear that the period of detention and training under such an order was to be one half of its term, and by s.76(1)
the period of supervision began immediately on the release of the offender from
detention and training, and ended when the term of the order was complete.

11   Some 10 days after the appellant had been re-sentenced, the relevant parts of
the Powers of Criminal Courts (Sentencing) Act 2000 were introduced, repealing
ss.73–79 of the Crime and Disorder Act 1998, after they had been in force for just
over four months. These are the provisions which now govern the order then
imposed on the appellant. Part V of the 2000 Act deals with the custodial sentences, and includes the detention and training order in the relevant list.
Chapter II is concerned with the custody and detention of young offenders generally, and ss.100–107 apply specifically to detention and training orders. Section
100(3) repeats s.73(3) of the 1998 Act. The distinction between the period of
detention and training and the term of the order in the 1998 Act is maintained.
The period of detention is to be half the term, that is one half of the length of
the order (s.102). Although there are provisions to produce earlier release there
are none to extend the period of detention without an express order of the
court. Similarly, the period of supervision begins with the offender's release
from detention and training, and ends when the term of the order itself comes
to an end (s.103). The term of the order is limited to the periods prescribed in
s.101(1). In short the order expressly envisages two different periods, one
devoted to detention and training, the second to supervision.

12   We must return to the Sexual Offences Act 2003. We are not here concerned
with the objective or indeed the various orders such as the sexual offences prevention orders, found in Pt 2 of the 2003 Act. For present purposes it is
sufficient to notice that by s.81 its provisions apply to the individual who was formerly subject to the notification requirements in the 1997 Act. The notification
requirements on conviction of an offence listed in Sch.3 remain unbroken. The
length of the notification period is determined exclusively by reference to the
sentence imposed by the court. It has no connection with the circumstances in
which or time when release from any period of custody takes place, and the
judge has no discretion to alter the statutory notification period. Section 82(1)
includes a table divided into two halves, one side of which describes the relevant
offender, with an entry opposite under the notification period, specifying the relevant period. Thus, for example, a person who "has been sentenced to
imprisonment for life or for a term of 30 months or more" is subject to an indefinite notification period beginning with the date of conviction. This is the
"relevant date" specified in s.82(6).

13   The first question in the present case is whether the appellant was a person sentenced to the equivalent of "imprisonment for a term of more than six months but
less than 30 months" or a person sentenced to imprisonment "for a term of six
months or less". For an adult the relevant notification periods would be 10
years and seven years respectively. As the appellant was under 18 at the date

of conviction, the periods of 10 years and seven years would be halved (s.82(2)). Accordingly, if the appellant were to be treated as if he had been sentenced to a term of more than six months but less than 30 months' imprisonment, he was, in November and December 2004, subject to the notification requirements. If however the applicable notification period was three-and-a-half years, then he was not. So the ultimate question simply stated is whether the 12 month detention and training order is to be treated as an "equivalent" sentence of imprisonment in excess of six months, or as one of six months or less.

14   Section 82 specifies the relevant notification periods in the context of terms of imprisonment. Imprisonment has no application to young offenders. So, s.131 explains and applies the "equivalent sentence of imprisonment" to the various different orders which apply to young offenders. In particular by s.131(a) the "equivalent" arrangement applies to "a period of detention which a person is *liable to serve* under a detention and training order, or a secure training order . . .".

15   Judge Griggs accepted the submission on behalf of the Crown that an offender sentenced to a 12 month detention and training order was "liable" to serve the full 12 month term of the order. He had in mind that if the offender were in breach of supervision requirements, the youth court might order his detention for the shorter of three months or the remainder of the term of the detention and training order in secure accommodation. He was troubled that if the appellant's submissions were correct, the arrangements by which the offender might be released before the end of the period of detention and training could, in a different case to this one, lead to uncertainty about the notification periods. He noted that if the contrary argument were correct, the notification requirements for those sentenced to detention and training orders would, in effect, be discounted twice, first under s.82(2), because the offender was aged under 18 years, and yet again, if the period of detention and training was confined to the custodial part of the order. He concluded that the relevant period of notification was five years, and subject to an inaccuracy which has no bearing on the substance of the appeal, that in November and December 2004 the appellant was under legal compulsion to comply with the notification provisions.

16   Before us, the Crown supported this ruling, and the reasoning behind it. In a carefully prepared submission, Mr Gareth Branston analysed the relevant statutory provisions. He suggested that the references to "imprisonment" within s.1(4) of the 1997 Act extended to detention and training orders while that Act was in force. The contrary was not argued. He also argued that a re-sentence at least had the potential to extend the notification period, and that a variation in sentence might remove an offender from one category within the notification table into another. Again, the contrary was not argued. He highlighted the circumstances in which a period of detention might be altered without necessarily having any effect on the notification period. These included, for example, the release of the offender on compassionate grounds at any time, or the power of the Secretary of State to release an offender subject to a term of 12-months' detention and training to release after five months (s.75(4) of the 1998 Act and s.102(4) of the 2000 Act). He also pointed out that the period of detention

might be increased, although he accepted that the period of detention and training could not be extended by executive act, without the intervention of the court. In order to achieve certainty, the period of notification pursuant to a sentence should be known at the point of sentence. Mr Branston then suggested that detention and training orders and sentences of imprisonment were, for the purposes of the notification periods, sentences similar in nature. Both sentences involved a "custodial" element, and both involved periods of "supervision", within an appropriate case, conditions attached. It was therefore sensible to treat both sentences in the same way. The equivalent of 12-month detention and training order was a 12-month sentence of imprisonment.

17   We acknowledge the force of these submissions. That said, however, there are significant differences between the regimes which apply to detention and training orders, and what we may describe as the ordinary sentence of imprisonment. (See *R. v B* [2005] EWCA Crim 312; [2005] Crim. L.R. 488). In our view, for practical purposes the period of detention which a person "is liable to serve" under a detention and training order is fixed at the date of sentence. Without a further order of the court, the period may not be extended. The notification provisions are, as we have already explained, directly linked with the sentence of the court. The statutory provisions are not susceptible to judicial alteration. By definition, those made subject to a detention and training order are young offenders who have not been sentenced to detention in a young offender institution. Bearing that in mind we can see no particular reason why the double discount (as it was described) should lead to the wide construction of s.131(a) for which the Crown contends. If Mr Branston were right, it would have been perfectly straightforward for the statutory provision under s.131(a) to have referred simply to "a detention and training order" or "the term of a detention and training order" or "a sentence of detention and training" rather than the "period of detention which a person is liable to serve". Under the detention and training order therefore the offender is not liable to serve a *sentence* of detention and training: he is liable to serve a *period* of detention and training. By contrast with s.131(f)–(j), the detention and training order is one of a group of provisions included in s.131(a)–(e) which focusses specifically on the "period" of detention, or training, or keeping in secure accommodation.

18   We must now consider s.131(f)–(j). Section 131(f) refers to a "sentence of detention" in a young offender institution, paragraph (g) to "sentence under a custodial order", (h) a "sentence of detention" under s.90 or s.91 of the Powers of Criminal Courts (Sentencing) Act 2000, paragraph (i) to "a sentence of custody for life" and finally, paragraph (j) to "a sentence of detention or custody for life". These paragraphs produce equivalents between various "sentences" of detention and the equivalent "sentence" of imprisonment. The distinction between the "sentence" of detention and the "period" of detention must be deliberate. This is consistent with the express distinction already identified between the respective periods of detention and training, and of supervision, and the term of the order which is one of the marked characteristics of the detention and training order.

19   In our judgment, for the purposes of s.131(a) the period of detention which the offender is "liable to serve" is and should be treated not as a reference to the entire term of the detention and training order, but to what it says it is, the period of detention and training itself. By reference to s.131 of the 2003 Act we conclude that for the purposes s.82(1) the appellant was sentenced to the equivalent of a sentence of imprisonment for a term of six months. As he was under 18 at the relevant date, the notification period for him was three-and-a-half years from the date of his conviction, that is March 18, 2000. Therefore at the time of his release from custody in November 2004, his obligations under the notification requirements had expired. He pleaded guilty to these offences following a ruling which was wrong in law. Accordingly these convictions are unsafe. The appeal must be allowed.

Appeal allowed. Convictions quashed.

Index

References in this index take the form of N or N(P) where N is the case number and P is the paragraph number within that case.

Abuse of process
  learning disabled persons, 25
  participation, right to effective, 25
  standard of proof, 25
  young persons, 25
  youth courts, 25
Admissibility
  bad character, 7, 19, 24
  blood tests, 12
  cautions, 19
  credibility, 7, 19, 24
  cross examination, 19, 24, 26
  death by dangerous driving, causing, 12
  death of witnesses, 9
  drugs, establishing the likely or adverse effect on driver of controlled, 12
  examine witnesses, right to, 9
  expert evidence, 10
  false memory syndrome, 10
  false statements, 24
  fresh evidence, 10
  hearsay evidence, 26
  indirect communications with third parties, 26
  medical evidence, 6
  mens rea, 6
  mental disorder, 6
  previous convictions, 24
  probative value, 13, 19, 24
  propensity, 7, 19
  relevance, 12, 13
  similar fact evidence, 19
  voice recognition, 13
  witnesses,
    death of, 9
    examine, right to, 9
    false memory syndrome, 10
    hearsay evidence, 26
    statements, 9
Adverse inferences
  character, 2
  JSB specimen directions, 2
  Lucas directions, 2
  previous convictions, 2
  silence, right to, 2

Alternative charges
  date of offence, 28
  grievous bodily harm, 11
  indictments, 11
  lesser offences, consideration of, 11
  sexual offences, 28
  statutory interpretation, 28
  transitional provisions, 28
  wounding with intent, 11
Alternative verdicts
  indecent assault, 18
  juries, discharge of, 23
  jurisdiction, 23
  lesser offences, 18, 23
  sexual activity with children, 18
  time limits, 18
Arraignment
  fitness to plead, 27
  hearings, 27
  mental disorder, 27
Assault. See Indecent assault

Bad character
  admissibility, 7, 19, 24
  cautions, 19
  credibility, 7, 19, 24
  cross examination, 19, 24
  false statements, 24
  previous convictions, 24
    undue reliance on, 3
  probative value, 19, 24
  propensity, 3, 7, 19
  similar fact evidence, 19
  summing up, 3
Buggery
  children, incitement of, 20
  incitement, 20
  mens rea, 20
  presumptions, 20

Cautions
  admissibility, 19
  bad character, 19
  credibility, 19
  cross examination, 19
  probative value, 19
  propensity, 19

Cautions—*cont.*
similar fact evidence, 19
Certainty
common law offence, existence of, 17
mens rea, 17
no punishment without law, 17
public nuisance, 17
Character *See also* Bad character
adverse inferences, 2
JSB specimen directions, 2
Lucas directions, 2
previous convictions, 2
silence, right to, 2
Charges. *See* Alternative charges
Children. *See also* Sexual activity with
children
buggery, incitement to commit, 20
competence as witnesses, 30
incitement, 20
indecent photographs of, 21
mens rea, 20
presumptions, 20
sexual offences, 20
victims, 30
witnesses, competence of, 30
Codefendants
bad character, 31
cut throat defence, 31
jury directions, 31
murder, 31
Commencement of proceedings. *See*
Institution of proceedings
Common law offences
certainty, 17
existence, of, 17
mens rea, 17
no punishment without law, 17
public nuisance, 17
Competence
children
sexual activity with, 31
witnesses, 30
indecent assault, 31
sexual activity with children, 31
victims, 30
video evidence, 31
witnesses, 30
Conduct. *See* Criminal conduct
Conspiracy
criminal conduct, 8
drug trafficking, 8
jury directions, 8
money laundering, 8
proceeds of crime, 8
proof, 8

Conspiracy—*cont.*
unfair evidence, 8
Construction. *See* Statutory interpretation
Controlled drugs
admissibility, 12
blood tests, 12
death by dangerous driving, causing, 12
likely or adverse effect on driver,
establishing, 12
relevance, 12
Convictions. *See* Previous convictions
Credibility, 7, 19, 24
Criminal conduct
conspiracy, 8
drug trafficking, 8
jury directions, 8
money laundering, 8
proceeds of crime, 8
proof, 8
unfair evidence, 8
Criminal evidence
character, 2, 3, 7
credibility, 7
hearsay evidence, 4
institution of proceedings, time of, 4
preparatory hearings, 4
propensity, 3, 7
statutory provisions, 4
Cross examination
admissibility, 19, 24, 26
bad character, 19, 24
cautions, 19
credibility, 19, 24
false statements, 24
hearsay evidence, 26
indirect communications with third
parties, 26
previous convictions, 24
probative value, 19, 24
propensity, 19
similar fact evidence, 19
witnesses, 26
Crown Prosecution Service
fair and public hearings, right to, 1
jury service, exclusion from, 1
Custody
escaping, from, 15
intention, 15
knowledge, 15
police officers, escaping from, 15
summing up, 15
Cut throat defence, 31

Dangerous driving, causing death by
  admissibility, 12
  blood tests, 12
  drugs, likely or adverse effect on driver
    of controlled, 12
  relevance, 12
Date of offence
  alternative charges, 28
  sexual offences, 28
  statutory interpretation, 28
  transitional provisions, 28
Death
  admissibility
    drugs, establishing the likely or
      adverse effect on driver of
      controlled, 12
    witness statements, of, 9
  blood tests, 12
  dangerous driving, causing, 12
  drugs, establishing the likely or
    adverse effect on driver of con-
    trolled, 12
  examine witnesses, right to, 9
  witness statements, 9
Defences
  cut throat defence, 32
  precedent, 29
  provocation, 29
Defendants *See* Codefendants
Detention and training orders
  indecent assault, 33
  Sex Offenders Register, 33
Directions. *See* Jury directions
Disabled persons. *See* Learning disabled
  persons
Driving. *See* Dangerous driving, causing
  death by
Drug trafficking
  conspiracy, 8
  criminal conduct, 8
  jury directions, 8
  money laundering, 8
  proceeds of crime, 8
  proof, 8
  unfair evidence, 8
Drugs. *See* Controlled drugs, Drug
  trafficking
Drunkenness. *See* Voluntary intoxication

Effective participation, right to. *See*
  Participation, right to effective
Escaping
  custody, from, 15
  intention, 15
  knowledge, 15

Escaping—*cont.*
  police officers, from, 15
  summing up, 15
Evidence. *See* Character, Criminal
  evidence, Cross examination,
  Expert evidence, Fresh evidence,
  Hearsay evidence, Proof, Similar
  face evidence, Standard of proof,
  Unfair evidence, Video evidence
Examine witnesses, right to, 9
Expert evidence
  admissibility, 10
  fresh evidence, 10
  false memory syndrome, 10

Fair trials. *See* Right to fair and public
  hearing
False statements
  admissibility, 24
  bad character, 24
  credibility, 24
  previous convictions, 24
  probative value, 24
Fitness to plead
  arraignment, 27
  hearings, 27
  mental disorder, 27
Fresh evidence
  admissibility, 10
  expert evidence, 10
  false memory syndrome, 10
  grievous bodily harm, 5
  manslaughter, 5
  medical evidence, 5
  murder, 5
  non accidental injury, 5
  shaken baby syndrome, 5

Grievous bodily harm
  alternative charges, 11
  indictments, 11
  lesser offences, consideration of, 11
  manslaughter, 5
  wounding with intent, 11

Hearings. *See* Preparatory hearings, Right
  to fair and public hearing
Hearsay evidence
  admissibility, 26
  criminal evidence, 4
  cross examination, 26
  indirect communications with third
    parties, 26
  institution of proceedings, time of, 4
  preparatory hearings, 4

Hearsay evidence—*cont.*
  statutory provisions, 4
  witnesses, 26

Identification. *See* Voice recognition
Impartiality
  Crown Prosecution Service, jury service and, 1
  fair and public hearings, right to, 1
  jury service, exclusion from, 1
  police officers, jury service and, 1
Incitement
  buggery, 20
  children, 20
  mens rea, 20
  presumptions, 20
  sexual offences, 20
Indecent assault
  alternative verdicts, 18
  competence, 31
  detention and training orders, 33
  lesser offences, 18
  Sex Offenders Register, 33
  sexual activity with children, 18, 31
  time limits, 18
  video evidence, 31
Indecent photographs of children
  distribution, 21
  intention, 21
  Internet, 21
  statutory interpretation, 21
Indictments
  alternative charges, 11
  grievous bodily harm, 11
  lesser offences, consideration of, 11
  wounding with intent, 11
Inflicting serious injury
  jet skis, 22
  masters of ships, 22
  navigation, used in, 22
Institution of proceedings
  criminal evidence, 4
  hearsay evidence, 4
  preparatory hearings, 4
  statutory provisions, 4
  time of, 4
Intention
  custody, escaping from, 15
  escaping, 15
  indecent photographs of children, distribution of, 21
  Internet, 21
  police officers, escaping from, 15
  statutory interpretation, 21
  summing up, 15

Internet
  indecent photographs of children, distribution of, 21
  statutory interpretation, 21
Interpretation. *See* Statutory interpretation
Intoxication. *See* Voluntary intoxication

JSB specimen directions, 2
Juries. *See also* Jury directions, Jury service
  alternative verdicts, 23
  discharge of, 23
  lesser offences, 23
Jury directions *See also* Summing up
  adverse inferences, 2
  bad character, 31
  character, 2, 31
  codefendants, 31
  conspiracy, 8
  drug trafficking, 8
  JSB specimen directions, 2
  jury directions, 31
  Lucas directions, 2
  money laundering, 8
  murder, 31
  previous convictions, 2
  proceeds of crime, 8
  proof, 8
  silence, right to, 2
  unfair evidence, 8
Jury service
  Crown Prosecution Service, 1
  exclusion, 1
  fair and public hearings, right to, 1
  impartiality, 1
  police officers, 1

Knowledge
  custody, escaping from, 15
  escaping, 15
  police officers, escaping from, 15
  summing up, 15

Learning disabled persons
  abuse of process, 25
  participation, right to effective, 25
  standard of proof, 25
  young persons, 25
  youth courts, 25
Lesser offences
  alternative verdicts, 18
  indecent assault, 18
  sexual activity with children, 18
  time limits, 18

Limitation periods. *See* Time limits
Lucas directions, 2

Manslaughter
  fresh evidence, 5
  grievous bodily harm, 5
  medical evidence, 5
  murder, 5
  non accidental injury, 5
  shaken baby syndrome, 5
Masters, 22
Medical evidence
  admissibility, 6
  fresh evidence, 5
  grievous bodily harm, 5
  manslaughter, 5
  mens rea, 6
  mental disorder, 6
  murder, 5
  non accidental injury, 5
  shaken baby syndrome, 5
Mens rea
  admissibility, 6
  buggery, incitement to commit, 20
  certainty, 17
  children, incitement and, 20
  common law offence, existence of, 17
  medical evidence, 6
  mental disorder, 6
  no punishment without law, 17
  presumptions, 20
  public nuisance, 17
  sexual offences, 20
Mental disorder
  admissibility, 6
  arraignment, 27
  fitness to plead, 27
  medical evidence, 6
  mens rea, 6
Money laundering
  conspiracy, 8
  criminal conduct, 8
  drug trafficking, 8
  jury directions, 8
  proceeds of crime, 8
  proof, 8
  unfair evidence, 8
Murder
  bad character, 31
  codefendants, 31
  cut throat defence, 31
  fresh evidence, 5
  grievous bodily harm, 5
  intoxication, 16
  jury directions, 31

Murder—*cont.*
  manslaughter, 5
  medical evidence, 5
  non accidental injury, 5
  self defence, 16
  shaken baby syndrome, 5
  voluntary intoxication, 16

Navigation
  jet skis, 22
  masters, 22
  serious injury, inflicting, 22
  ships used in, 22
No punishment without law
  certainty, 17
  common law offence, existence of, 17
  public nuisance, 17
Non accidental injury, 5
Nuisance. *See* Public nuisance

Offensive behaviour
  racial groups, meaning of, 14
  racially aggravated offences, 14

Participation, right to effective
  abuse of process, 25
  learning disabled persons, 25
  standard of proof, 25
  young persons,
  youth courts, 25
Photographs of children, indecent, 21
Pleas. *See* Fitness to plead
Police officers
  custody, escaping from, 15
  fair and public hearings, right to, 1
  impartiality, 1
  intention, escaping and, 15
  jury service, exclusion from, 1
  knowledge, escaping and, 15
  summing up, 15
Precedent
  defences, 29
  provocation, 29
Presumptions
  buggery, incitement to commit, 20
  children, incitement of, 20
  mens rea, 20
  sexual offences, 20
Previous convictions
  admissibility, 24
  adverse inferences, 2
  bad character, 3, 24
  character, 2, 3
  credibility, 24
  cross examination, 24

Previous convictions—*cont.*
  false statements, 24
  JSB specimen directions, 2
  Lucas directions, 2
  probative value, 24
  propensity, 3
  summing up, 2, 3
  silence, right to, 2
  undue reliance, 3
Probative value
  admissibility, 13, 19, 24
  bad character, 19, 24
  cautions, 19
  credibility, 19, 24
  cross examination, 19, 24
  false statements, 24
  previous convictions, 24
  propensity, 19
  relevance, 13
  similar fact evidence, 19
  voice recognition, 13
Proceeds of crime
  conspiracy, 8
  criminal conduct, 8
  drug trafficking, 8
  jury directions, 8
  money laundering, 8
  proof, 8
  unfair evidence, 8
Proof. *See also* Standard of proof
  conspiracy, 8
  criminal conduct, 8
  drug trafficking, 8
  jury directions, 8
  money laundering, 8
  proceeds of crime, 8
  unfair evidence, 8
Propensity, 3, 7, 19
Provocation
  defences, 29
  precedent, 29
Public hearings. *See* Right to fair and
    public hearing
Public nuisance
  certainty, 17
  common law offence, existence of, 17
  mens rea, 17
  no punishment without law, 17

Racially aggravated offences
  offensive behaviour, 13
  racial groups, meaning of, 13
Relevance
  admissibility, 12, 13
  blood tests, 12

Relevance—*cont.*
  death by dangerous driving, caus-
    ing, 12
  drugs, establishing the likely or
    adverse effect on driver of con-
    trolled, 12
  probative value, 13
  voice recognition, 13
Retrospectivity. *See* No punishment
    without law
Right to effective participation. *See*
    Participation, right to effective
Right to fair and public hearings
  Crown Prosecution Service, jury ser-
    vice and, 1
  impartiality, 1
  jury service, exclusion from, 1
  police officers, jury service and, 1
Right to silence
  adverse inferences, 2
  character, 2
  JSB specimen directions, 2
  Lucas directions, 2
  previous convictions, 2

Self defence
  murder, 16
  voluntary intoxication, 16
Serious injury. *See* Inflicting serious
    injury
Sex Offenders Register
  detention and training orders, 33
  indecent assault, 33
Sexual activity with children
  alternative verdicts, 18
  competence, 31
  indecent assault, 18, 31
  lesser offences, 18
  time limits, 18
  video evidence, 31
Sexual offences. *See also* Indecent
    assault, Sexual activity with
    children
  alternative charges, 28
  buggery, incitement to commit, 20
  children, incitement of, 20
  date of offence, 28
  mens rea, 20
  presumptions, 20
  Sex Offenders Register, 33
  statutory interpretation, 28
  transitional provisions, 28
Ships
  masters, 22
  navigation, used in, 22

Ships—*cont.*
  serious injury, inflicting, 22
Silence, right to. *See* Right to silence
Similar fact evidence
  admissibility, 19
  bad character, 19
  cautions, 19
  credibility, 19
  cross examination, 19
  probative value, 19
  propensity, 19
Standard of proof
  abuse of process, 25
  learning disabled persons, 25
  participation, right to effective, 25
  young persons, 25
  youth courts, 25
Statements. *See* False statements, Witness
    statements
Statutory interpretation
  alternative charges, 28
  date of offence, 28
  indecent photographs of children, dis-
    tribution of, 21
  intention, 21
  Internet, 21
  sexual offences, 28
  transitional provisions, 28
Summing up
  bad character, 3
  custody, escaping from, 15
  escaping from custody, 15
  intention, 15
  knowledge, 15
  police officers, escaping from, 15
  previous convictions, undue reliance
    on, 3
  propensity, 3

Time limits
  alternative verdicts, 18
  indecent assault, 18
  lesser offences, 18
  sexual activity with children, 18
Transitional provisions
  alternative charges, 28
  date of offence, 28
  sexual offences, 28
  statutory interpretation, 28

Unfair evidence
  conspiracy, 8
  criminal conduct, 8
  drug trafficking, 8
  jury directions, 8

Unfair evidence—*cont.*
  money laundering, 8
  proceeds of crime, 8
  proof, 8

Verdicts. *See* Alternative verdicts
Victims
  children, 30
  competence, 30
  witnesses, competence of, 30
Video evidence
  competence, 31
  indecent assault, 31
  sexual activity with children, 31
Voice recognition
  admissibility, 13
  probative value, 13
  relevance, 13
Voluntary intoxication
  murder, 16
  self defence, 16

Witness statements
  admissibility, 9
  death of witnesses, 9
  examine witnesses, right to, 9
Witnesses. *See also* Witness statements
  admissibility, 26
  children, competence of, 30
  competence, 30
  cross examination, 26
  hearsay evidence, 26
  indirect communications with third
    parties, 26
  victims, 30
Wounding with intent
  alternative charges, 11
  grievous bodily harm, 11
  indictments, 11
  lesser offences, consideration of, 11

Young persons. *See also* Children
  abuse of process, 25
  learning disabled persons, 25
  participation, right to effective, 25
  standard of proof, 25
  youth courts, 25